Political Parties in the American Mold

Political Parties
in the
American Mold

Leon D. Epstein

The University of Wisconsin Press

For my colleagues,
past and present,
at the University of Wisconsin–Madison

The University of Wisconsin Press
114 North Murray Street
Madison, Wisconsin 53715

The University of Wisconsin Press, Ltd.
1 Gower Street
London WC1E 6HA, England

Library of Congress Cataloging-in-Publication Data
Epstein, Leon D.
Political parties in the American mold.
Includes bibliographical references and index.
1. Political parties—United States—History.
I. Title.
JK2261.E48   1986   324.273'09   86-40050
IBSN 0-299-10700-0
ISBN 0-299-10704-3 (pbk.)

Contents

Tables   viii

Preface to the Paperback Edition   ix

Preface   xiii

Chapter One   Introduction   3

Chapter Two   The Scholarly Commitment   9

    I. Uncertain Start   10
    II. Intellectual Basis   18
    III. Defenders of Indigenous Institutions   23
    IV. Advocates of Responsible Party Government   30
    V. Common Ground   37

Chapter Three   The Congressional Presence   40

    I. Institutional Context   43
    II. Structural Decentralization   48
    III. Party Organization   54
    IV. Policymaking Cohesion   62
    V. A Less Partisan Electoral Base?   70
    VI. Resilience   77

Chapter Four Presidential Focus 79

    I. Elected Monarch and Party Leader 80
    II. Nominating Process 88
        1. The Convention System: Pure and Mixed 89
        2. The Post-1968 System 95
        3. Prospects 102
    III. Election 108
    IV. Governing 113
    V. Summary 121

Chapter Five State and Local Structure 123

    I. Extension of the National Party Alignment 124
    II. The Old Organizations 134
    III. Postmachine Patterns 144
    IV. Conclusion 153

Chapter Six Parties as Public Utilities 155

    I. Private Power 158
    II. The Impact of the Australian Ballot 162
    III. The Direct Primary 167
    IV. The White-Primary Cases 174
    V. Recent Constitutional Challenges 179
        1. Ballot Access 180
        2. Closed Primaries 184
        3. Intrusions on Associational Rights of Major Parties 189
    VI. Deregulation? 197

Chapter Seven National Organization 200

    I. The Enduring Historical Pattern 202
    II. Recent Developments 208
        1. Democratic Structure 209
        2. Republican Structure 214
        3. Republican Campaign Activity 216
        4. Democratic Campaign Activity 223
    III. Legal Status of National Parties 225
        1. Against Illinois 227
        2. Against Wisconsin 229
    IV. Import 235

Tables

Table 8.1	Party Identification, 1952–84	257
Appendix A	Republicans and Democrats in Congress and the Presidency, 1939–85	349
Appendix B	National Election Results by Party in the Eleven States of the Old Confederacy, 1940–84	350
Appendix C	Party Funds in Federal Elections, 1977–84	351
Appendix D	Federal Contribution Limits	352
Appendix E	Financial Activity of PACs in Federal Elections, 1983–84	353
Appendix F	Disbursements by Parties and PACs in Federal Elections, 1981–84	354
Appendix G	Funds in U.S. House and Senate Campaigns, 1983–84	355
Appendix H	Federal Matching Funds for Presidential Primary Candidates, 1984	356

Chapter Eight   Party Identifiers   239

    I. Party Labels   241
   II. Measurement   250
  III. Recent Decline   256
  IV. Interpreting the Change   263
   V. Summary   271

Chapter Nine   Private Funding of Campaigns   272

    I. The Candidate-Centered Pattern   273
   II. Individual Contributions, Large and Small 275
  III. Political Action Committees   284
  IV. Reacting to Political Action Committees   294
   V. Helping Parties   301
  VI. Another Perspective   308

Chapter Ten   Public Funding of Campaigns   310

    I. The Constitutional Situation   311
   II. Federal Dollars   319
  III. State Dollars   326
  IV. Prospects   334

Chapter Eleven   An Unbreakable Mold?   343

Appendices A–H   349

Notes   357

Index   423

Preface to the Paperback Edition

Except for corrections of simple mistakes, the text of this paperback edition is unchanged from the original edition that went to press in late 1985. I add a few new prefatory pages mainly to note events through mid-1988.

First, however, I want to call attention to an earlier suggestion of the parallel between parties and public utilities that I describe in chapter 6. I now realize, as I did not when I developed my conception of American parties as public utilities, that Alan Ware had already used the term in the concluding chapter of *The Logic of Party Democracy* (London: Macmillan, 1979). His treatment differs significantly from mine, partly because it is briefer and more general, but the conception is similar in many respects. Neither Ware nor I know of any still earlier explicit statement of the parallel, although American parties have often been called quasi-public or quasi-governmental agencies.

Among recent events relevant to the themes of the book, the most important is the U.S. Supreme Court's decision in *Tashjian v. Republican Party of Connecticut* (1986). Anticipated in my discussion of lower federal court rulings in the case, the Supreme Court's opinion provides a partial answer to questions raised in chapter 6 and in note 3 at page 422. The Court held, as had the lower federal courts, that the state of Connecticut could not constitutionally apply its closed-primary law to prevent unaffiliated electoral registrants from voting in a Republican primary election when the Republican party of Connecticut wanted to allow such registrants, along with Republican registrants, to cast ballots in its primary. Thus, the decision follows the Court's tendency of the last decade to require states to respect party rules as expressions of First Amendment rights, specifically freedom of association. But the

Supreme Court decided *Tashjian* by a five-to-four majority in an opinion specifically limited to the kind of rule presented by the Republican party of Connecticut. Though invocable in about 20 other states with closed-primary laws
if a party were to adopt a rule like that of Connecticut Republicans, the Court
opinion went no further. It explicitly reserved judgment as to whether it
would recognize a party's right to have another party's registrants cast ballots
in its primary, and it said nothing about a party's right to nominate in convention instead of in a state-mandated primary. In the absence of such rulings,
which could come case by case, American political parties are still widely
treated as the "public utilities" I describe.

Better-known than the *Tashjian* decision are the elections occurring since
the book's original publication. In 1986, Democrats regained control of the
U.S. Senate, added a few seats to their already substantial House majority,
and lost several governorships while slightly increasing their hold on state
legislatures. The results suggested continued uncertainty about the prospects
for partisan realignment. Whether that uncertainty is reduced by 1988 results
will be apparent by the time this paperback edition is available. So too will
it be known whether the 1988 results confirm, as did the 1986 results, the
House incumbents' high reelection success rate observed in most years since
the 1950s (not merely in the 1970s and 1980s as might be inferred from remarks in chapter 3).

It is already evident from preliminary 1988 reports, as well as from 1985–86
data, that federal campaign finance has not sharply departed from trends discerned in the early 1980s. Republican *party* funds still exceed Democratic *party*
funds, but by a decreased margin at least in 1985–86 as Republican party
money-raising leveled off while Democratic party money-raising increased.
Democratic and Republican congressional *candidates,* obtaining a much larger
share of their money from political action committees and individuals than
from parties, remain more nearly even in aggregate expenditures. An acceler-
ating trend, according to press accounts in 1988, is the solicitation by the national
party committees of large contributions that can be used for general party-
building and that can be directed to state and local parties. Such contributions,
only briefly noted on pages 220 and 305, are not directly for federal campaigns
and thus are not subject to limits imposed by federal law even though they
are plainly helpful in electing a party's candidates—including presidential candidates. The loophole now looks much larger than my text suggests. Useful
though this practice is for enhancing party roles, its violation of the spirit
of campaign finance reform makes it a ready target for proponents of reform.
So far, however, most proposals to toughen the federal campaign finance laws

have concentrated on lowering contributions from political action committees, providing public funds for congressional campaigns, and limiting expenditures on such campaigns when public funds are accepted. These proposals,
debated in Congress several times, are very much alive in 1988. Popular support for public funding is uncertain; federal funds for presidential elections
remain adequate, but in the state (Wisconsin) whose public funding I discuss
at greatest length, in chapter 10, amounts available from taxpayer checkoffs
have recently decreased.

The 1988 presidential nominating contests, concluded as I write, were consistent with post-1968 expectations that primaries and to a lesser extent participatory caucuses determine nominations. Yet early in 1988 it had seemed
possible that the primaries and caucuses would not produce a preconvention
Democratic nominee. And no one can be certain that we shall never have a
brokered convention again. If so, however, it is reasonable to regard the possibility as an exception to the late twentieth-century custom of voters' choice
of presidential nominees.

Were I to attempt revision along with updating, I would take into account
two important new books, one by David R. Mayhew, *Placing Parties in American Politics* (Princeton: Princeton University Press, 1986), and the other by Alan
Ware, *The Breakdown of Democratic Party Organizations, 1940–1980* (New York:
Oxford University Press, 1985), because they call attention to the strength
of traditional state and local party organizations as late as the middle of this
century. I might also say a little more about the variety and complexity of
state primary laws so as to indicate, for example, how requirements for party
enrollment of new registrants may differ from requirements for established
registrants wanting to switch party enrollments. Finally, I would put more
emphasis on the effect of occasional departures from the practice of congressional seniority (page 51).

Madison, Wisconsin   Leon D. Epstein
August 1988

Preface

During almost a decade devoted to this study, my work has been supported from time to time by the Research Committee of the Graduate School of the University of Wisconsin-Madison, the Wisconsin Alumni Research Foundation, the Hilldale Professorship, the John Simon Guggenheim Foundation, and the Woodrow Wilson International Center for Scholars. The last two funding sources enabled me to spend 1979–80 in Washington, D.C., where, besides the advantage of uninterrupted study, I had the opportunity to consult national political practitioners. I am grateful for that year, as I am for the subsequent Wisconsin support that enabled me to complete the research and writing that I projected during my Washington year.

I am indebted also to many scholars. As my citations will indicate, I have drawn heavily on their research findings. Moreover, several scholars served as specialized readers of earlier versions of particular chapters: David Adamany, President of Wayne State University, Professor Ruth S. Jones of Arizona State University, Attorney John G. Kester of Washington, D.C., Professor Gary King of New York University, Professor Warren Miller of Arizona State University, Professor Nelson Polsby of the University of California, Berkeley, Professor Lester Seligman of the University of Illinois-Urbana, Professor Frank Sorauf of the University of Minnesota, and Professors Jack Dennis, Peter Eisinger, David Fellman, Barbara Hinckley, and William Gormley of the University of Wisconsin-Madison. I thank them, as well as two readers of the entire manuscript: Professor John Bibby of the University of Wisconsin-Milwaukee, and Dr. Austin Ranney of the American Enterprise Institute (who had also read earlier drafts of certain chapters). Although I hope that I have corrected and

improved my study as a result of the helpfulness of so many professional colleagues, I remain responsible not merely for the usual reasons but also because
I have adhered to positions with which more than one of my readers disagrees.

Without being asked directly for help, students in my graduate course in
political parties contributed through their responses to my oral presentation
of the themes of the book. In many ways, the written work is the product
of our exchange. The unconventional ordering of topics was first attempted
in teaching the course. I am grateful, too, for the typing of successive drafts
by members of the secretarial staff of the Department of Political Science at
the University of Wisconsin-Madison: Mrs. Norma Lynch, Mrs. Mary Rear-
don, Ms. Suzanne McCann, Ms. Pamela Henderson, and Ms. Christine Wil-
lard. And I appreciate the highly knowledgeable and sensitive copy-editing
by Mrs. Mary Maraniss.

As always, the contributions of Mrs. Shirley G. Epstein have been special.
Not only did she tolerate my protracted absorption in the process of writing,
but she also made editorial suggestions and shared burdensome proofreading
chores.

Two portions of the book were published in other works of mine and appear here by permission of their publishers. A large part of chapter 2 was
published as "The Scholarly Commitment to Parties," in *Political Science: The
State of the Discipline*, edited by Ada W. Finifter (Washington, D.C.: American Political Science Association, 1983), pp. 127–53; and some of chapter 7,
in a different version, was published as "Party Confederations and Political
Nationalization," in *Publius: The Journal of Federalism*, volume 12 (Fall 1982),
pp. 67–102.

Apart from chapter 8, where a table is essential, the tables appear as appendices rather than in the text. Appendix A is most relevant to chapter 3, appendix B to chapter 8, and the remainder to chapters 7, 9, and 10.

Madison, Wisconsin   Leon D. Epstein
November 1985

Political Parties in the American Mold

Chapter One

Introduction

This book presents an extended expository argument about American political parties. It has less in common with a comprehensive introductory text than with interpretive works on the prospects for parties. Some of them call attention, as I do, to the persistence of American parties, but usually with more optimism than I display about the magnitude of revival. Several authors urge far-reaching rejuvenation. Many others, however, stress the decline of parties and see little hope for them in their present form.[1] Almost all assume that parties—continuing entities under whose labels candidates seek and hold elective offices—are organizationally desirable and probably essential in a democratic nation. I share that assumption, but I do not expect as much of parties as do most of their champions. In my perspective, American parties are adapting, as they have adapted throughout this century, to increasingly adverse circumstances. Although they survive not merely as remnants of another era, their roles are more modest than their champions would prefer and certainly more modest than the roles of parties in many other democratic nations.

My theme is hardly dramatic. It does not celebrate the advent of a politics without parties. Nor does it express gloom and doom about the future of a democracy whose parties disintegrate. I have doubts about both the extensiveness of party decline and the earlier glories of American parties. And I do not envision or advocate the transformation of American parties into strikingly new and powerful institutions. While not without certain modest hopes for party revival, I am impressed more than are most revivalists by the limits that American circumstances impose on the growth of party capacities.[2] Much of my book describes those limits, especially their constitutional, historical,

3

and popular roots, and explains how they have made American parties distinctive in the democratic world. For that purpose, American institutions are put in a comparative as well as a historical frame of reference. Having tried in an earlier work to make a similar comparison by discussing American parties in a general study of parties in democratic nations,[3] I concentrate here on the United States and only occasionally cite foreign examples to illuminate the substantially different American phenomena.

The distinctiveness of American parties is old and well established. It is not mainly the product of the last few decades of widely perceived decline. As governing agencies, American parties have nearly always been less cohesive in national policymaking than parties in parliamentary regimes. And as extragovernmental organizations, their strength, where it existed, was traditionally state and local rather than national. Moreover, American parties have ordinarily been without the dues-paying mass memberships characteristic of European parties. First, they were unusual in their dependence on large-scale patronage, and then, since early in this century, they have been unique by virtue of losing control of their own affairs — notably, the selection, or nomination, of candidates, once state-run direct primaries were established. Only the greatly increased use of primaries for presidential nominations is a product of the last 20 years. Certain other customary indicators of party organizational decline, particularly the decreasing power of big-city machines, are also far from being entirely recent. Candidate-centered campaigns, though now more salient and probably more effective because of television, have nevertheless long been familiar in American politics. So have the interest groups whose campaign activities have lately become overt as well as significant through the growth of political action committees (PACs). The fact is that American party organizations have not, at least in this century, dominated election campaigns in the manner of European parties both before and during the television age.

In the past, however, American party voters appeared more loyally partisan than they do today. They cast many more straight-ticket ballots in the nineteenth century and somewhat more earlier in this century, and they identified themselves in larger numbers as Republicans or Democrats even in the 1950s and 1960s than they do now. The party-decline thesis is often stated in terms of the recent drop in major-party identifiers from about three-quarters of the electorate to less than two-thirds. The evidence, accompanied as it is by a wealth of detail about weaker party loyalties even among the remaining identifiers, is formidable. But it relates merely to one conception of party — that of largely unorganized voters counted as a party-in-the-electorate. The significance of party in that sense, and so of its decline, is at least open to question.

From a British standpoint, for example, the old party loyalties of American voters were of little consequence as long as they were not regularly and collectively linked to party policies of elected officials in national government. Accordingly, and with only pardonable exaggeration, a perceptive British scholar, Philip Williams, wondered how in the 1980s American political parties can be said to have lost power when they hardly ever had any.[4] Certainly the "strength" of parties-in-the-electorate did not produce governing strength in the British or European sense. Nor from that standpoint could much have been lost at the national level as a result of the decline in the power of state and local bosses who had been only loosely united to help nominate and elect a president who would add to their patronage. Even the nineteenth century, then, was not truly a "golden age" of American parties.[5] It was the era of parties without relevant principles, Tweedledum against Tweedledee. As the historian Arthur Schlesinger, Jr., has put it; "The nineteenth-century cult of party, in fact, stifled the art of politics."[6]

One need not go so far as to assume that older American parties were entirely powerless or meaningless in order to appreciate their limitations. Once one ceases to idealize the politics of another era, it is easier to accept and even to welcome this century's progressive reforms. Such an acceptance, though without the antipartyism of some reformers, marks my outlook in greater degree than it does that of most political scientists concerned with the health of political parties. I have little nostalgic affection for the old organizations against which progressives reacted, or for the straight-ticket voting that sustained them. The progressive reaction is an understandable American phenomenon, and now so fully institutionalized that, as I shall explain at length, it poses obstacles for even new-style party organizations aspiring to exercise power of the kind wrested from old organizations. The direct primary, the chief institutional monument of progressivism, fits a political culture in which voters choose individuals, not merely parties, to represent them in executive and legislative offices. Party organizations, as I shall emphasize, are surely less effective as a result, but their accommodation to progressivism has not been entirely unsuccessful.

That accommodation is an important part of the more general long-term adaptation that American parties have made to their adverse circumstances. The adaptation takes the form of an institutionalized porousness. Each major party is porous, or permeable, in the sense that it is readily entered by individuals and groups who want its electoral label. Party membership is loosely defined, often by state law that allows access without dues or organizational commitments. Parties so constructed are less meaningful than parties elsewhere, but in my view they fit our circumstances. At the least, they provide labels that candidates seek and that officeholders use for certain collaborative purposes. Remarkably, the labels are the same, Republican and Democratic, in every state as in the nation, and still more remarkably they have been the same, with only minor or transient exceptions, for over 130 years. The longevity and the pervasiveness of Republicans and Democrats, it will be seen, are associated with the porousness of their party structures; each major party is so loosely defined that one or the other absorbs electoral protest that might otherwise find outlets in new parties. Such absorption, after all, is a kind of effectiveness. Even our contemporary candidate-centered campaigns, however personalized by television, are between Republicans and Democrats. And in governmental policymaking these labels have some significance, I shall argue, even though now as almost always they fall short of both British-based expectations and many strictly American aspirations.

In seeking to elaborate and support the case for the survival of distinctive American parties, my focus is chiefly on national politics, where the supposed failure, weakness, or ineffectiveness of parties is of greatest concern. Like almost everyone else, however, I recognize the important linkage of national and state politics. Hence I devote attention to the way in which national party alignments influence state party developments, and a great deal of attention to the relation of state laws and practices to national party arrangements.

Before directly examining the several manifestations of American parties themselves, I review, in chapter 2, the long-standing commitment of political scientists to the need for parties, especially in national politics. For many years, that commitment has been shared by scholars who nevertheless disagreed as to how well or badly traditional American parties fulfilled the need. Its continuity in the academic discipline provides the intellectual context for my subsequent analysis of the subject matter.

The analysis is ordered in an unconventional way. It begins, in chapters 3 and 4, with parties-in-government, specifically with those separately formed in Congress and around the presidency. Textbooks usually treat parties in this sense only after expositions of extragovernmental and electoral parties. I depart from that practice, sensible though it is for undergraduate teaching, because I want to stress that American parties are always constrained by difficulties derived from the constitutional separation of powers. Yet I also want to stress the durable if limited roles that parties have established in our national legislative bodies. With respect to the presidency, my purpose is to indicate the enormous importance of that office as the focus for such national parties as we have had. The importance surely remains although the parties that now nominate and elect a president are of a different nature from those that existed as late as 1968. They are in some sense more national, I shall try to show, as a result of the new more popular and public method of choosing candidates. The post-1968 presidential nominating process thus strikes me as destructive of only one kind of party structure. Unlike many of my colleagues, I do not deplore the change, but accept its general thrust as consistent with twentieth-century American expectations.

Chapter 5 turns to the subnational organization of parties and elections. It includes a discussion of the old party machines, the reaction to them, and the creation of less imposing successors. The impact of the direct primary is more systematically explored here than in earlier chapters, and its historical and legal development also provides much of the substance of chapter 6. There I attempt to explain how, in response to special American experiences and ideas, so distinctive an institution came to be adopted. Along with other state-imposed regulations of political parties, the direct primary belongs to the process by which Americans stopped treating their major parties as private associations and converted them into public utilities, if not actual government agencies. That conversion is now almost as fixed in our laws and political culture as is the constitutional separation of powers, and it similarly limits parties in the United States as they are not limited elsewhere. Although the institutionalization is almost entirely of state parties under state statutes and regulations, it is national in its impact insofar as our national extragovernmental party organizations have remained confederations of state parties.

The extent to which those historical party confederations have lately become more national is the subject of chapter 7. Organizational changes add to the nationalizing tendency of presidential nominations, and in several respects our parties have more national substance than in the past. Although still structural creations of state organizations, they have, thanks to recent Supreme Court opinions, a degree of freedom from governmental regulation that appears at odds with the otherwise established public utility status of American parties. Here, indeed, is a potentially significant constitutional challenge to the regulatory tradition, but for reasons explained in chapter 6, the challenge confronts well-established and for the most part widely accepted practices.

Only as late as chapter 8 do I try to deal directly with the widely noticed decline in party loyalty of voters. Without disputing the statistical evidence, I suggest that less regular party identification and less straight-ticket voting are understandable adjustments of a late-twentieth-century electorate to a very old party alignment. I emphasize the institutionalization of that alignment by state-managed party registration as well as by established custom, and observe that the growth in self-designated independents and in split-ticket voting still results in the election of Republicans and Democrats. Unlike voters in other nations who have become less loyal to old party labels, Americans do not attach themselves to new parties, but rather vote, with few exceptions, for individuals bearing one or another of the old labels. Voters thus respond to increasingly candidate-centered campaigns, it is true, but within a party alignment that remains consequential, I hope to have shown, in government as well as in elections.

So, too, is the American pattern distinctive in campaign finance. Much more than elsewhere, the funding, like the conduct, of American campaigns is candidate centered and not party centered. In chapters 9 and 10, I examine this phenomenon, with special attention to the role of political action committees. American party organizations, it must be emphasized, have long been less than dominant in financing candidates. My reason for devoting considerable space to the subject, however, is primarily to take into account the recent efforts of parties to play larger roles in raising and spending campaign funds, and to consider legislative proposals by pro-party advocates to enhance those roles. Chapter 9 deals with proposals to provide advantages for parties in private fund-raising, and chapter 10 with proposals for the public funding of parties.

Possibilities for thus strengthening parties do exist, but here, as generally, the American political culture imposes limits on what can be done. Those limits, briefly reconsidered in my last chapter, have long confronted the advocates of stronger American parties. How scholars have dealt with the problem is an important element of the intellectual history to which I now turn.

Chapter Two

The Scholarly Commitment

In a century when American parties appear to have lost public support and to have become less effective, it is striking that there should have developed a preponderant scholarly commitment to the desirability, if not the absolute necessity, of parties in a democratic system. The commitment is most clearly discernible among political scientists who study parties as a specialized subject. Treating parties as a large and important segment of politics generally, several of these specialists have been influential members of their academic discipline. And, as will be noted, other leading scholars assert the same commitment to parties within broader studies of American and comparative politics. Remarkably few political scientists dissent. Almost none contemplate happily the possibility of doing without parties altogether.

Historically, however, political scientists have divided over the suitability of existing American parties. Scholars who admired those parties objected only to certain plainly corrupt manifestations. They treated the nonideological and decentralized features of conventional American parties as suited to the constitutional and social order. From that standpoint, the old American parties were successful enough to justify preservation. These defenders of the established parties, while important and prestigious in American political science, have probably attracted less attention than have scholars who emphasized the inadequacies of existing organizational structures and advocated the development of more effective parties. Their advocacy covers a wide range of possibilities from relatively modest suggestions for strengthening established organizations to far-reaching proposals to emulate British or European models. The political scientists embracing such proposals, or strictly American variants approximating the models, belong to a responsible-party or responsible-party-government school of thought. They have engaged in a long debate with the defenders of existing parties.

The debate has been a meaningful one, not yet ended, and its distinct viewpoints will be discussed. But the debate does not preclude an underlying agreement that effective parties are desirable and probably essential in American politics as in democratic politics elsewhere. It is this agreement that I have chosen to stress more than the admittedly significant differences over the kinds of parties that can and should be developed. I believe that the political scientists' commitment to parties of one kind or another cannot be explained away merely as part of the temptation of scholars to believe in the importance of any subject that they have chosen to study.[1] No doubt parties specialists are as likely as any other specialists to yield to that temptation, and I do not entirely disregard it as an explanatory factor. But the case for parties also has a more general intellectual appeal that helps to account for the fact that many political scientists, not merely party specialists, have made positive evaluations of parties in democratic societies.

I

Uncertain Start

The political scientists' commitment to parties is largely a twentieth-century phenomenon. It could not be otherwise insofar as the commitment derives from an academic study of politics that is itself largely a twentieth-century development. Despite important beginnings late in the preceding century, political science hardly existed as a separate discipline before about 1900, and its practitioners tended to have constitutional, legal, and philosophical interests that excluded the study of political behavior and of less formal political institutions than those of the governmental structure itself. Often educated as historians and teaching within history departments, the early academic political scientists might have been expected to treat parties, if they did so at all, as actors in American political history rather than as institutional elements in a democratic system. And those trained in law and especially in jurisprudence plainly had other interests.

Nothing is therefore very surprising about the absence of systematic scholarly inquiry and evaluation of parties during almost all of the nineteenth century. Nevertheless, it seemed to a later generation of political scientists to constitute an unfortunate neglect of organizations that had been important in

American politics and government since the early 1800s. So it was for E. E. Schattschneider when he wrote his major book on parties in the early 1940s. He cited the case of John W. Burgess, a leading figure in nineteenth-century political science, who as late as 1890 "ignored the parties completely" in his two-volume study *Political Science and Comparative Constitutional Law*. Burgess and others struck Schattschneider as excessively formal in their definition of government and politics. Moreover, in Schattschneider's critical judgment, their formalism meant not only a neglect of parties as scholarly subject matter but also a failure to assimilate the role of parties in a general theory or philosophy of democratic government.[2]

The neglect, however, can be overstated, for Burgess is typical of only one significant element in nineteenth-century political science. He had been trained in both American law and German jurisprudence before he founded Columbia University's School of Political Science. Although certainly a leading academic figure in the last decades of the nineteenth century, his influence by the 1890s was largely negative. Burgess's formalism produced something like an intellectual rebellion at Columbia itself.[3]

Even earlier, Burgess may not have been fully representative of nineteenth-century political science. An important academic predecessor, Francis Lieber, had included a chapter on parties in a general political work first published in 1838 and republished in 1875.[4] Although Lieber's chapter contained little information, it accepted the usefulness of parties in the American political system. In this respect, Lieber went a little farther than had Tocqueville in his treatment of the already highly developed parties of the Jacksonian period as more or less unavoidable evils.[5] Admittedly Lieber, like Tocqueville, represented no tide of general intellectual interest in parties. Only after 1870 were there substantial beginnings of scholarly interest, and attention remained limited until the last decade of the century.[6]

Although the slight earlier academic interest in parties can be attributed to the absence of much political science of any kind, it is also possible that nineteenth-century scholars stayed away from the subject because they shared the hostility to parties that had been displayed by the framers of the U.S. Constitution, and by George Washington himself when in his famous farewell address he warned his country of the danger of parties.[7] Undistinguished from factions, parties were regarded as divisive forces disrupting the unity of the political community.[8] At best, they were necessary evils whose effects could, as James Madison suggested, be limited in a large nation where diverse factional interests would offset each other.[9] This federalist approach, though it reflected eighteenth-century attitudes, persisted in the next century. Even after parties became established political forces, they could be perceived as outside the constitutional structure of the founders and thus not entirely legitimate. Not everyone recognized that parties were the means for making that structure work once a mass electorate existed. An older upper class disliked the mass electorate itself as well as the parties that appealed to that electorate. Understandably, the earliest full-scale exposition of the importance of parties was the work of a reflective political practitioner, Martin Van Buren, who had himself been a preeminent founder of the American party system.[10]

If hostility toward parties had anything to do with the absence of scholarly studies about parties during most of the nineteenth century, it certainly did not preclude acclaim for the first important scholar to write substantially about American parties near the end of the century. The scholar was James Bryce, himself experienced in British public affairs. His writing in the late 1880s is widely understood to have led the way for the new scholarly interest in politics, not merely in parties, that marked American scholarship beginning in the 1890s. His interest in studying political phenomena outside of the formal governmental structure was now plainly shared by many American scholars. The success of Bryce's great two-volume work *The American Commonwealth* itself influenced American political science; over 200 pages of the work were explicitly about parties, and other chapters discussed the subject. Although he noted, at the beginning of his section on parties, that there were then no studies describing the actual working of American parties,[11] many such studies appeared in the next few decades.

It should not detract from Bryce's innovative work to say that American scholars could well have been independently interested in parties within the largely new developing discipline of political science during the 1890s and the following decades. Like Bryce, they were likely to be impressed with parties as "the great moving forces" of American government.[12] For Bryce was hardly alone in perceiving American parties of the late nineteenth century as mighty in their capacity to command the loyalty of voters and elected officeholders, and through their organization, the machine, to exercise power from outside the formal governmental structure. Nor was he alone in viewing the American parties of his day as too strong, too self-serving, too corrupt, and too little concerned with principles. Such observations had been characteristic of American political reformers in the decades after the Civil War. Bryce did, however, bring a new comparative perspective to bear on the subject. He found American parties to count for more than British and European parties.[13] In retrospect that comparison, so much the reverse of more recent Euro-American comparisons, tells us something not only about the little-developed European parties of the time but also about the organizational impressiveness of American parties in the nineteenth as compared with the late twentieth century.

Bryce's criticism of the power of American parties, and especially of the way that power was used, did not mean that he thought that American politics could or should operate without parties or with parties of the kind he found elsewhere. He seems, rather, to have accepted much of American party development as inevitable in past American circumstances but to have hoped for reforms within the existing system now that circumstances were becoming more favorable.[14] Bryce thus occupied about the same position as would many other students of American politics at the turn of the century. They too wanted to curb the excesses of American parties, particularly their patronage. Proposals to limit but not eliminate parties often figured prominently in analyses of their activities. Thus the entanglement of political science with reform contributes to what I call "the uncertain start" in the scholarly evaluation of parties.

It is possible, however, to exonerate most of political science, even in early decades of this century, from the advocacy of completely nonparty politics, except perhaps at the municipal level. The point is important for the development of my argument that the study of politics has almost invariably led scholars to believe in the usefulness of parties of some kind. Take first the attack on patronage—the campaign to substitute a merit-based civil service for the spoils system. No doubt, reformers aimed not only to improve the quality of government work but also to deprive party organizations of the services of patronage appointees or prospective patronage appointees. Nor can there be any doubt that insofar as patronage was reduced, the traditional American party organizations, so largely built on spoils rather than ideology, would lose, as they did eventually, much of their strength. Civil service reformers can be assumed to have welcomed that outcome, and in some instances to have happily contemplated the destruction of the old machines without the development of any other kind of party organizations to replace them.[15] But I do not find the latter view characteristic of political science either early or later in the twentieth century. Apart from some scholars principally interested in administration,[16] political scientists, though themselves often supporters of civil service reform, perceived parties as potentially more useful if they could be purified, principled, and nationally meaningful. In that perspective, as will be observed, local bosses and their machines stood in the way of effective parties. Accordingly, a belief in the desirability of strong national parties was far from incompatible with a willingness to destroy the old city machines.

In any event, opposition to city machines did not lead many political scientists, apart from specialists in municipal administration, to provide intellectual support for the nonpartisan ballot that reformers, beginning as early as 1890, succeeded in establishing in many American cities.[17] In fact, as they studied its effects after several decades of operation, scholars became highly critical of the products of the nonpartisan movement.[18] As early as 1917 Charles Beard, the famous historian who soon after served as president of the American Political Science Association, wrote an influential paper expressing what became a typical scholarly skepticism about the efficacy and desirability of trying to eliminate parties from the politics of large cities. Not only did he doubt whether parties could be eliminated, except nominally by keeping them off the ballot, but he also thought that they reflected the economic divisions of modern society and, as such, were related to the same serious urban problems with which parties had to deal at national and state levels.[19] Here Beard rather than progressive reformers, intellectual though many of them were, set the tone soon adopted by political scientists studying nonpartisan municipal politics.

Similarly, it is the skeptical scholarly view of the direct primary that became dominant in political science despite some early academic identification with this popular and widely adopted progressive reform. Early in the century, it is true, many political scientists appreciated the reformers' desire to reduce the power of bosses by transferring control of nominations from party organizations to party voters. They could even have thought of the direct primary, like civil service reform, as a means of purifying rather than destroying parties.[20] In the years near 1900, parties did not appear so fragile that reforms would destroy them. Thus early scholarly doubts were often about whether the direct primary would have any substantial effect in reducing organizational control of nominating results. But more far-reaching doubts came from Henry Jones Ford, one of the earliest scholars to appreciate the contribution of parties to American politics. Even at the start of the direct-primary movement in 1908, Ford thought that the proposed institutional reform would only make things worse.[21]

By the 1920s, another political scientist similarly criticized the direct primary in ways now shared by a number of scholars. Observing the direct primary over its first 15 years in Wisconsin, Professor Arnold Bennett Hall believed that it had broken down "the party system with its accompanying theory of party responsibility. It has done this by taking the functions out of the hands of the organization and placing them in the hands of the people; by diverting public attention from parties to factions and individuals. . . ."[22] Although Hall was not the only political scientist of the 1920s to criticize the primary because of its effects on party responsibility, most of his profes-

sional colleagues still appeared to have at least moderately favorable views of
the new institution. Hall's own teacher, Charles E. Merriam, was probably
typical. Merriam, who wrote the best-known early study of the direct primary, was himself a progressive reformer, but he accepted the primary with
mixed feelings. For him as for most political scientists who followed, the direct primary was an institutional response to American conditions. It had advantages and disadvantages.[23] The disadvantages began to bulk larger after party
organizations actually declined to the point where those political scientists
who appreciated parties began to blame the primary for the decline. But even
before they did so and while they were still entangled with progressive reforms, political scientists did not advance the direct primary as a step toward
the abolition of parties. At most, they were moderate progressives.

Political scientists also resisted the explicitly antiparty arguments that attracted broad intellectual attention early in the century. There is no indica-
tion that they agreed with their contemporary Herbert Croly, the notable editor and publicist, when he argued that we could begin to do without parties
despite their past accomplishments. Croly's emphasis on executive power
was itself appealing, but its link to direct democracy as a replacement for representative government was less compelling for those who believed in the usefulness of intermediaries like parties.[24] Political scientists, as we will observe,
prefer to tie executive power to party leadership—making a president or a
governor responsible through his party. Woodrow Wilson, for example, made
that intellectual connection, although he asserted at times a kind of direct relationship between the American people and himself as chief executive. Significantly, political scientists have usually emphasized the party-responsibility
side of Wilson.[25]

More telling than the response to Croly is the definite and widespread rejection within American political science of the notoriously antiparty opinions
of the great European scholar, Ostrogorski, who wrote the first full-length
study of American and English parties. His two-volume work, published in
the early years of the twentieth century and thus little more than a decade
after Bryce's innovative study, was impressive for its scholarship and systematic
comparative analysis.[26] American political scientists could and did learn a great
deal from Ostrogorski. Many also shared his criticism of many aspects of the
turn-of-the-century American parties that he studied. But never, in any significant numbers, did they accept his conclusion that parties as such were patho-
logical institutions in a democratic society. For, unlike most critics of American parties, Ostrogorski did not point to parties in Britain or elsewhere as
models to emulate. In his view the still-new English parties, while not yet

as bad as the American, were on their way to being so. Ostrogorski thought that any permanent political organization, commanding the loyalty of voters and elected officials from campaign to campaign, interfered with the representation of individuals. Therefore instead of parties Ostrogorski wanted "single-issue organizations," or leagues, which would mobilize in behalf of salient causes and then dissolve when their times had passed.[27] Although thus electing representatives, these ad hoc organizations would not develop the durable extragovernmental structures that regularly controlled nominations and elections, as he thought established parties now did. Such party control, based on a self-perpetuating organizational interest, was objectionable whether the interest was patronage, as in the United States, or something more programmatic, as in England. Parties could not suit Ostrogorski's democratic principles even if they ceased to be corrupt. His principles were so individualistic as simply to make parties inappropriate.

From the beginning Ostrogorski's view, as distinct from his scholarly knowledge, was at odds with the emerging approach of political scientists. Even in Bryce's otherwise favorable preface to Ostrogorski's major work there is disagreement, particularly with his pessimism about English parties but also with his general perspective. Although recognizing here as he had in his own work the excesses of party control, notably in the United States, Bryce clearly states the now-established opinion that "party organization is a logical and inevitable consequence of party government in a large democracy."[28] Bryce still has his own doubts about the value of such organization, as actually developed, but he writes of "their incidental evils," not their inherent evils, and he is skeptical concerning their abolition.[29] So, a few years afterward, was A. Lawrence Lowell, a dominant figure in the first few decades of American political science. Ostrogorski's analysis, Lowell said, had "a slight air of unreality."[30]

Later political scientists were more sharply critical of Ostrogorski. An important example, from the early 1930s, is the biographical sketch in the *Encyclopedia of the Social Sciences*. Written by Arthur W. Macmahon, an eminent scholar of American government and politics, the piece depicts a "vast naiveté" at the core of Ostrogorski's thinking and an assumption of "the existence of atomic citizens at once omniscient and disinterested." Macmahon correctly distinguishes Ostrogorski from "those of his contemporaries in the realistic reorientation of political science who soon proceeded to interpret party abuses as self-corrective adjustments in a defective governmental organism. . . ."[31] The distinction is significant for what it tells us about twentieth-century political science as well as for what it tells us about Ostrogorski. The practitioners of the new discipline did not accept the more or less classical individualism of many nineteenth-century liberals. Instead, they believed in the need for political organization to secure effective popular representation. Hence they did not embrace Ostrogorski's campaign to abolish parties[32] nor the similarly individualistic premises of the indigenously American movement for nonpartisanship.

Ostrogorski was not the only European political sociologist whose criticism of parties became familiar among political scientists without causing them to abandon their emerging commitment to parties. Robert Michels is the other major example. Writing in the second decade of the twentieth century and mainly about German and other continental social democratic parties, Michels argued that even such parties, purporting to be democratic, responded to the "iron law of oligarchy" under which organizational leaders rather than rank-and-file members dominated party policymaking.[33] While thus critical of the democratic quality of parties, as was Ostrogorski, Michels differed in that he advanced no optimistic alternative. He can well be understood to believe in the usefulness of parties in their inevitably oligarchical form — given "the technical indispensability of leadership" in any society.[34] Hence scholars priding themselves on their realism could accept much of Michels, though perhaps disputing how ironlike the law of oligarchy actually was in various parties and nations, and at the same time retain a generally positive if not entirely enthusiastic evaluation of parties.

Among Americans who were influenced at all by Michels, that positive evaluation was likelier than the pessimistic reaction that Michels himself came to have to democratic politics. The totally pessimistic reaction is hard to find among American political scientists. So is the use of Michels's criticism of parties to bolster a scholar's argument for doing without parties as a means of fulfilling democratic politics. As I have noted, that argument — essentially Ostrogorski's — was rejected from the beginning by mainstream political science. The usefulness, even the necessity, of intermediary institutions became a central principle of the new academic discipline.

To be sure, the acceptance of parties by what can be called mainstream political science was not always as enthusiastic as it later became. Unlike recent advocates of stronger parties, writing when the old American parties were already weakened, earlier American scholars were confronted by apparently strong organizations in the form of the objectionable party machines. Thus like Bryce's, their work was often critical of the existing parties not because they were generally weak but because of the nature of their strength and the self-serving purposes for which the strength was used. Reforms were designed to curb certain excesses as well as to make parties more effectively responsible to public purposes. Nevertheless, the early scholars usually treated American parties as more than necessary evils. The tone is evident in the famous works of Wilson, Ford, Lowell, and Goodnow.[35] And it is also to be found in studies by less well known academic figures. For example, in the first decade of the new century Jesse Macy, a Grinnell professor, wrote two sympathetic books about American parties. The first, a history of their crucial emergence before the Civil War, expresses some of the usual criticism of the spoils system, but it contains the flat statement, "I have assumed that the party is a useful agency in the development of democracy."[36] The second book, describing the existing structure of American parties, begins with a declaration that becomes, in effect, the view of the many parties specialists who follow Macy: "The institutional political party furnishes the first clearly definable agency for coordinating and expressing the general will of the subjects of a large and populous state in such a way as to provide a tolerable substitute for despotic government."[37] By the 1920s views of this kind were firmly established. Bryce now wrote, ". . . parties are inevitable. No free large country has been without them. No one has shown how representative government could be worked without them. They bring order out of the chaos of a multitude of voters."[38]

It was probably easier, as I have suggested, for an American scholar happily to accept parties as they lost some of their nineteenth-century organizational features. As Charles Merriam wrote in his 1922 text, patronage was declining, elected officials were superseding nonelected organizational bosses as party leaders, and parties had increasingly adapted themselves to the competition of other political groups. At any rate, Merriam believed that party "is one of the great agencies through which social interests express and execute themselves."[39] Any uncertain start in the political scientists' evaluation of parties was apparently ended. But even the start from about 1890 to 1920 was much more favorable than impressions of nineteenth-century scholarly neglect and of progressive-reform entanglement might imply.

II

Intellectual Basis

So far the commitment of political scientists to parties appears to be based on the simple observable fact that parties have everywhere developed when a large population participates in competitive elections. In other words, where political democracy, Western style, exists in a nation, parties arise in durable organizational form to mobilize voters to elect officeholders collectively bearing a given label. That might have been inferred merely from mid-nineteenth-century American experience. But even before 1900, other nations also had mass electorates along with parties which, in one modern form or another, accompanied democracy. By the turn of the century, American parties, however special their characteristics, were not perceived as unique. Even their stern critic, Ostrogorski, did not so regard them. He saw that parties had developed in other democratic nations, no matter how much he rejected their desirability and their subsequent inevitability. I have emphasized already how exceptional Ostrogorski was among studious observers of politics in responding to the existence of parties by suggesting their abolition. After all, it is characteristic of scholars no less than of anyone else to expect phenomena arising in given circumstances to remain along with the circumstances. And, in the case of parties in a democratic political system, most scholars not only expected them to continue in some form but also wanted them to continue, because they saw no democratic system operating without parties. And the preference at least of American political scientists for a democratic system is clear.

At first, political scientists did not go much farther than to infer—realistically, they thought—the inevitability of parties from their universal existence in democratic nations. What is, they seemed to say, must be and in some sense should be. Since this merely assumes that the existence of something means that it ought to exist, the reasoning could hardly persuade those who disliked parties and wanted to abolish them. Simple inference from empirical studies helps to explain the original commitment of political scientists, but it does not provide a fully satisfying theoretical basis for defending parties against their critics. Such a basis, however, soon developed, and by the middle and late years of the twentieth century it underlay the several and otherwise differing arguments for parties. Hence the theoretical basis should be presented here, although the story of its development carries us a little ahead of the account of the differing schools of pro-party advocacy.

Accepting parties against the strictures of Ostrogorski, we have already seen, was a departure from the individualistic tradition that he championed. Insofar as that tradition, identified with direct popular government and sometimes with Rousseau, was regarded as the classical democratic theory, those who departed from it are said to be revisionists seeking to reconcile popular participation with representative institutions, intermediary groups, and regularized leadership. The word *revisionists* suggests dilution of democratic ideals even when it is not prefaced with the pejorative *elitist*. Naturally, however, those who are called revisionists do not believe that they are diluting democracy. They conceive of collectively organized representation as the only means by which the will of the people can be made effective. A town-meeting style of democracy is impractical in a large national or regional community, and strictly individual representation in legislative bodies is less responsive to popular majorities than party representation. The latter tends to be built around a kind of program or set of policies, but the most severe revisionist might be content with a party competition involving no more than a choice of leadership teams without clearly differentiated principles.[40] In either view, most citizens are assumed to play useful political roles by exercising a choice at periodic elections, as long as their choice is made meaningful by party labels. Many citizens may also participate in party candidate selection and policymaking, as some pro-party writers advocate, but such participation, whatever its advantages or disadvantages, is not required in all versions of the democratic theory justifying parties. The essence of that theory is that voters should be able to choose between recognizable competing leadership groups.

By midcentury, the theory was clearly accepted by the leading students of comparative politics who sought to generalize about democratic experience. Thus Herman Finer, in his well-known text, was at once highly committed to democracy and also to the blunt proposition that most voters lacked the knowledge and capacity to make political decisions without the kind of help that came from parties. In a section titled "Party is King!" Finer described the services that parties so usefully provide as a result of their desire to win elections.[41] He was critical of American parties chiefly because of their weakness in providing those services. Effective democratic government required not only parties but effective parties more like the British than the American models.[42] "Parties," Finer wrote, "are the power behind all thrones." Without party "the electorate would be 'atomized,' as it was intended to be, in the vague speculations of the school of Rousseau."[43] Similarly, Carl Friedrich explicitly puts aside Rousseau's objections to representation, and so to parties, by noting that the belief in the validity only of direct popular participation would "make it impossible to organize responsible popular government in our modern countries with their millions of people."[44] It followed, for Friedrich, that parties, like representative agencies generally, were "indispensable features" of such government.[45] Moreover, Friedrich preferred a democratic order in which parties stood for diverse material interests and principles. He regarded the "absolute democracy" of Rousseau as both impossible in practice and likely as doctrine to lead to the destruction of constitutional government in the name of a falsely claimed majority will that he identified with dictatorship.[46]

A similar belief in representative democracy underlay the case for the parties in the influential work of Robert MacIver. Writing in the tradition of broad

social theory rather than as an empirical political scientist, MacIver emphasized the historical as well as the inherent linkage of party to parliamentary
government. "Party," he said, "is the only means by which the ultimate political sovereign, which we saw to be at most a fluctuating majority, can definitely control government."[47] In a large democracy, the "principle of representation had to be vitalized by the conflict of parties."[48] Public opinion was too
variant and dispersed to be effective unless organized, and parties were essential for that organization. The need for such organization, particularly by
working-class interests, became a major element in the defense of mid-twentieth-
century mass parties. Thus Maurice Duverger, their eminent scholarly champion, treated the scale, centralization, and discipline—even the oligarchic
character—of mass parties as suited to political purposes in contemporary society.[49] His preference for a particular kind and degree of collective representation is not so plainly that of MacIver and other theorists, but the rejection
of individualistic democratic premises is a common element.

Rejecting such premises, it might be argued, does not itself lead to an intellectual commitment to parties. Why haven't political scientists settled on
interest groups as sufficient agencies of representation? Why have they, if not
actually attacking interest groups as too powerful and self-serving, regarded
them as inadequate mobilizers of majority preferences and as incapable of representing broad public purposes? Interest groups retain much of the stigma of
factions in relation to the general interest. On the other hand parties, in political science, are distinguished from factions because of the broader purposes
and roles that they are supposed to fulfill. The point is spelled out most sharply
by Sartori in a recent exposition, but it has been at least implicit in much
of twentieth-century political science. A party, Sartori writes, is "a part of
a whole attempting to serve the purposes of the whole, whereas a faction is
only a part for itself."[50] For Sartori, it is true, faction is by no means synonymous with interest group; he uses the term in an older and more limited sense.
But what he says about party in relation to faction asserts the superiority of
party to any more particularized group. Admittedly, that superiority follows
from Sartori's definition of party as functionally meant to serve the whole
community. It should be added that he believes that party serves that purpose
not so much by representation as by its provision of channels of expression.
Parties, in his view, transmit demands backed by pressure.[51] So, it can be said,
do interest groups. But parties, it is thought, are motivated to relate demands
to public purposes, if only because parties, by their nature, must seek broad
electoral support.

Scholars have not argued that parties are detached from particular interests

—their own or those of various groups. They have often thought of parties as aggregating rather than merely articulating those interests. In any case, as Sigmund Neumann wrote, parties differ from pressure groups in that their interests "must be fitted into the framework of the national collective." When parties fail in this respect, "the modern state is in danger of deteriorating into a neofeudalism of powerful interest groups."[52] Hence, for Neumann as for many other political scientists, parties should be strengthened, particularly but not only in the United States, so as to counter narrower interest groups. Neumann concluded his comparative parties anthology by calling political parties "the peoples' great intermediaries."[53]

The scholars so far cited in this section have all been European in origin although, except for Duverger, they eventually pursued American academic careers. Their importance in American political science is substantial. Whether or not they wrote specifically about American politics, as some of them did, they provided the comparative framework in which American parties could be understood. In conjunction with that framework, they also expounded much of the theoretical basis for a positive evaluation of parties generally and of the somewhat more impressive British and European parties in particular. American political scientists already believed in parties before reading the mid-century comparative literature, but their beliefs could only be strengthened by the new work. Its viewpoint was sharply different from that of Ostrogorski and Michels.

It is well, however, to turn to a primarily American intellectual exposition of the basis for parties. Robert Dahl stands out not as a parties specialist but as an unusually highly regarded analytical theorist with broad interests in American politics. Most political scientists would rank him among their most influential colleagues, perhaps the most influential, in the third quarter of the twentieth century. Two chapters of his sophisticated American government text are devoted to parties. Starting from the now-familiar observation that all modern democracies have political parties, he seeks to explain why it would be difficult for a democracy to operate at a national level without at least two competing parties.[54] Specifically, he thinks that parties are inevitable under the American constitutional system, despite the intentions of the founders.[55] Dahl has no doubt that parties have made substantial contributions to the operation of a democracy like that of the United States. They have facilitated popular control over elected officials, helped voters to make more rational choices, and aided in the peaceful management of conflicts.[56] These contributions are not to be found in the internal affairs of parties but in their external effects—among which have been their assistance for "the many to overcome the otherwise superior resources of the few."[57] The last point is an important one for believers in the democratic virtue of parties. They customarily see the mass of people, and particularly the poor, as underrepresented in interest-group politics, and likely to be underrepresented in an electoral politics conducted exclusively in terms of individual candidacies. Only by collective and organized action, meaning in practice a party capable of mobilizing majority support, can the many obtain governmental policies suiting their interests. That view is most commonly advanced by those who hope for a more coherent majority party than Dahl's own pluralist approach provides.[58] He is far from denying either the legitimacy or the efficacy of the diverse interests that parties seek to combine in winning electoral coalitions. Significantly, however, Dahl shares with more-majoritarian-minded advocates of parties the assumption that parties have a special value for those people whose own individual political power is limited.

There may be some quarrel with the adequacy of the theoretical basis that political scientists have expounded in behalf of parties in a democratic society, but there should be no doubt about its widespread scholarly acceptance. As Samuel Eldersveld wrote in his major study of American party organization, "intellectually, we have become committed to the position in the twentieth century that parties are central to our system. . . ."[59] His page of quotations from eminent scholars makes it clear that the *we* of his sentence means political scientists.

<hr />

III

Defenders of Indigenous Institutions

Constituting one of two loosely defined categories of pro-party political science, the defenders of conventional American parties respect the indigenousness of the very characteristics that believers in more responsible governing parties find objectionable. They appreciate decentralization, limited ideological or programmatic appeals, porousness, relatively noncohesive legislative contingents, and the absence of mass-membership organizations as natural in American political development and often as party qualities especially useful in the social and constitutional circumstances of the United States. Even the patronage on which American parties were originally built has occasionally been defended except in its plainly corrupting forms. Of course, not every defender of American parties admires all of their other characteristics. Some are critical enough to make their inclusion among the defenders questionable.

The categorization is necessarily rough here as it is for the responsible-party-government school, whose ranks include advocates of greatly varying degrees of change in existing party characteristics. And at least one important parties specialist, V. O. Key, is so hard to classify that he may deserve a category of his own. Yet I believe that the twofold division of pro-party scholars captures the dominant tendencies of twentieth-century political science.

In treating the appreciators of American parties, it is well to emphasize at the outset that their favorable opinions are based on the historical roles of parties in the nineteenth century and the first half of the twentieth. The defenders derive no satisfaction from an often-perceived recent decline in party efficacy, nor from the results of old or new progressive reforms designed to weaken parties. These are not the developments regarded as well suited to American circumstances, although they too might strike us as indigenous. No believer in the usefulness of parties applauds their decline and possible demise. Although the defenders of conventional American parties think that we cannot have (and often that we should not have) strong parties on the foreign model, they definitely want parties that perform at least as well as those they have observed in American history.

The political scientists' defense of American parties, like their positive evaluation of parties generally, coincides with the emergence of the scholarly study near the turn of the century. Admiration of British parties, though established early among intellectuals, did not lead every scholar to follow Woodrow Wilson in urging that something like those parties be substituted for the American model. Even A. Lawrence Lowell, who shared Wilson's belief in the superiority of Britain's more responsible parties, thought the less-cohesive American parties better suited to the American constitutional preference for a government in which no majority, acting through a cohesive party, could gain complete control.[60] Fuller praise of American parties came from Henry Jones Ford. Publishing his first book in 1898, Ford can well be regarded as the founder of the twentieth-century defense of American parties. Contemporary political scientists often acknowledge his insightfulness—brought, incidentally, to a Princeton professorship from journalism and after his first book had begun to command attention. Although Ford, like Wilson and Lowell, was critical of the limited degree to which American parties assumed policymaking responsibility, his hopes for developing that responsibility did not preclude an emphasis on the considerable accomplishments of the country's historic parties. Sharing the view, also held by Lowell and Wilson, that American parties owed much of their special character to the separation of executive and legislative powers established by the Constitution, Ford argued that parties in fact made the difficult system work. To a useful extent they bridged the separation. The extensive extragovernmental apparatus of the nineteenth-century boss-run machines impressed Ford as understandable in the circumstances in which parties had had to develop in the United States.[61] Even more than Bryce or Ostrogorski, Ford saw the American parties of his day as more elaborately organized, outside of government, than those of Britain or other nations. And Ford thought that the organizations were necessary if not entirely desirable. Accordingly, he had doubts about progressive reforms and especially, as noted earlier, about the direct primary. Depriving bosses of power in the absence of other leaders who could exert such power would, he thought, only make parties less responsible than they already were.

Ford's emphasis on the usefulness of traditional party organizations became a familiar theme for many political scientists as those organizations slowly declined in the early twentieth century. This was notably so for a relatively conservative defender of American parties like E. M. Sait. Writing the first edition of his important text in the 1920s, Sait quoted Ford approvingly with respect to the success of American parties and, in a section labelled the "Peculiar Importance of American Parties," praised their accomplishments in harmonizing organs of government, enabling the electorate to function, advancing national unity, checking religious intolerance, assimilating foreign elements, softening the clash of economic interests, and adopting similar consensual platforms.[62] Like Ford, Sait was skeptical about the claims for the direct primary, but observing only its first two decades of operation, he did not think it as destructive of party responsibility as later political scientists would find it to have become.[63] Nevertheless, Sait was already concerned about the apparent decline of the old organizational loyalties, whatever the cause. The decay of partisanship, he said, "cannot be viewed without disquiet. The democratic regime can no more function satisfactorily without strong parties than parties can function without strong organization."[64]

By the 1920s, it was not only the formerly much-criticized organizational strength of traditional American parties that nonreformist political scientists appreciated. The absence of well-defined distinguishing principles between the major parties now also became a kind of virtue in the American system. For example, Sait included the moderating and unifying contributions of American parties among the praiseworthy accomplishments already cited. Similarly Arthur Holcombe, author of a standard exposition of American parties in the 1920s, responded directly to the "empty bottles" criticism that went back at least to Bryce. To have any chance of winning elections in the diverse American nation, parties needed to make broad rather than particularized appeals, such as those of an exclusively capitalist or socialist party. By their broad appeals in the United States, Holcombe said, parties tended to conciliate social strife. "The wide extent and diversified interests of the major parties," he added, "are the best guarantee which the people possess that power will be used with moderation."[65]

Familiar in the political science literature of the next several decades, Holcombe's line of defense also appeared in the midcentury work of Herbert Agar, an historian and editor widely read by students of American politics. Compromising, office-seeking American parties are very much the heroes of Agar's political history. To such parties he attributes the successful working of the constitutional system; only when they were sharply divided by principles, just before the Civil War, did the system fail. American parties, Agar said, "are unique. They cannot be compared to the parties of other nations. They serve a new purpose in a new way. . . . It is through the parties that clashing interests of a continent find grounds for compromise. . . ."[66] They do not stand for opposed philosophies or represent opposed classes. Rather than seeking divisive principles, an American party "is intended to bring men and women of all beliefs, occupations, sections, racial backgrounds, into a combination for the pursuit of power. The combination is too various to possess firm convictions. The members may have nothing in common except a desire for office."[67] Thus Agar accepted Bryce's description of American parties but rather than deploring such parties extolled them.

To be sure, Agar's rhetoric is more enthusiastic than that of most academic defenders of American parties. And his specifically regional concerns, southern in origin, are unusually marked. Agar likes traditional American parties especially because they have conciliated sectional interests and so helped, during most of our history, to preserve the federal union. By no means, however, is he unique in appreciating the loose and compromising qualities associated with our decentralized federative parties. It is common among defenders of the traditional American parties to regard these parties as better suited to a pluralist society and to pluralist values than a more cohesive national party could be.[68]

The general point is fully argued by Ranney and Kendall in their textbook's extended effort to present a theoretical basis for understanding midcentury American parties. Although the authors are attracted by the logic of absolute majority rule, which would in principle support a cohesive national party, they are "convinced that our present parties *are* appropriate to the governing system the American people really want."[69] Not only does our decentralized governmental system lead to decentralized parties, but so does the nature of the Amer-

ican community and its belief system. Hence a major American party is a bundle of compromises, a cross section not a segment of the community, and
even with majority voting support it has policies that are the product of plural-
istic bargaining.[70] Somehow, in the Ranney-Kendall view, parties thus enable
Americans in practice to reconcile majority rule with cherished minority rights,
logically incompatible though these principles have seemed in the authors'
presentation. Government does respond to popular majorities, rallied by a
party, but the majorities are themselves loose and negotiated combinations.
Parties as they exist are useful in the United States, and the price to be paid
for more centralized and disciplined American parties would be too high.[71]

The more highly centralized and disciplined parties to which Ranney and
Kendall refer are for them, as for others, *the* alternatives to the defended American parties. There is, by midcentury, an awareness both of the existence of
such parties in Europe and of their advocacy by other American political scientists. No alternatives by way of nonpartisanship are seriously considered. The
belief that parties are useful, and almost certainly necessary, in any democratic
nation remains as firmly held in recent years among defenders of the traditional parties as it is among the champions of European models. For example
William Keefe, writing a parties text in the 1970s, treats coalitional parties
as natural in the heterogeneous American society and hopes that they can be
revitalized. "It is inconceivable," Keefe writes, "that democracy could exist
in the absence of a viable party system."[72]

With good reason, many defenders of traditional American parties have
found their case most fully and persuasively stated in midcentury form by
Pendleton Herring. Particularly in *The Politics of Democracy: American Parties
in Action*, first published in 1940 and reprinted in the 1960s, Herring wrote
a highly sophisticated defense of American institutions. It came to be regarded
by his fellow political scientists as a classical statement of the pluralist position. Herring was in the mainstream of twentieth-century political science,
particularly in the decades after World War II, and his defense of American
parties could appeal to many political liberals as well as conservatives. He
treated the New Deal legislation of the 1930s as an accomplishment of existing institutions—evidence of their workability. It is true that Herring could
not thus satisfy those liberals who, as we shall see, looked for continued and
greater policymaking accomplishment through more highly disciplined legislative parties, particularly of the British type that Herring rejected as models
for the United States.[73] But Herring's argument attracted moderates of various persuasions. Because his argument was so influential and fully presented,
it is worth close attention here.

Herring certainly regards parties as essential elements in a democratic politi-cal system. He quotes approvingly from Graham Wallas, the famous British political scientist who, earlier in the century, had treated party as a critically important institutional response to citizens' needs for objects of durable elec-toral loyalty.[74] For Herring, American parties served such needs well not by "framing issues and drawing up distinctive programs" but by "trying to dis-cover some way of bringing together into a reasonably harmonious relation-ship as large a proportion of the voters as possible."[75] Irrational party loyalty, he believes, was normally essential in this process. "The meaning of a national party," Herring contends, "is not to be measured solely in terms of its ideol-ogy. . . . At best all a party can hope to maintain is an attitude, a temper, or an approach."[76] To have instead two distinctive parties, each determined to carry out its program for which it claims a majority mandate, "would necessi-tate a change in our form of government."[77] And Herring is far from advocat-ing such a change. Apart from its unlikely political feasibility, abolishing the separation of executive and legislative powers, along with other constitutional checks, appears to have no attraction for Herring. Rather, he writes favorably about the American constitutional system, and unlike many American politi-cal scientists, he expresses no preference for British parliamentary government or for the cohesive parties in that system. Herring looks instead to presidential leadership, within the existing structure, as an effective means of obtaining positive action when required. "The New Deal," he said, "demonstrated that rapidity of action was possible within the limits of present institutions."[78]

Rather than deploring the fact that neither major party was a unified na-tional entity, Herring found advantages in having only "a loose confederation of state and local organizations."[79] He treated these organizations as meaning-ful, the professional politicians at their center as usefully in control, and their regular followers and supporters as significant despite, or because of, their di-verse interests and principles. "Our parties," he said, "seek to be as inclusive as possible without actually crumbling because of the very incongruity of the constituent elements. Those working toward this inclusiveness are the profes-sional politicians; those most repelled by such a tendency are intellectuals, ideal-ists, and others"[80] preferring a greater policymaking consistency. "Increased discipline," Herring recognizes, "is the price for more 'meaningful parties.'" And he doubts the feasibility of disciplined parties in our diverse society. In any event, Herring contends, "the very fluidity of our national party organiza-tion offers an opportunity for intelligence to compete freely for a hearing."[81] Elsewhere, he adds that "adjustment and compromise are the primary prod-uct if not the primary objective of our party system."[82]

Herring's analysis in 1940 may represent a high point in the defense of American parties, because of its intellectual quality and because later defenders were less certain that American parties performed as well as Herring had argued. It might well have been easier to be enthusiastic about the performance of parties and the rest of the American political system immediately after the New Deal period than in either earlier or later years. For the 1930s, the American performance could even be compared favorably, as it was, with Britain's.[83] In dealing with economic depression or foreign threats during the pre-World War II years, the British responsible-party model showed no evident superiority. Although the model always retained its American champions among those who were dissatisfied with their own country's less disciplined parties, it could now more persuasively be put aside by defenders of our parties. American parties were seen to suit us not only because they were indigenous but also because they might be superior in a general comparative sense.

So highly favorable a view of the performance of American parties was not characteristic of most of their defenders after World War II. Even scholars who shared Herring's evaluation of the usefulness of parties in earlier American experience, including the 1930s, often found contemporary parties inadequate as a result either of their decline or their failure to change sufficiently to meet new demands. With the latter emphasis, political scientists might well belong to the responsible-party-government school in the sense of advocating much different and stronger national organizations than any we had had traditionally. The line between defenders of indigenous institutions and more-responsible-party advocates becomes harder to draw. I do so only roughly when I consider V. O. Key among the defenders. Admittedly he is rightly well known for his belief in strengthening and making more effective the American parties that he studied so intensively and insightfully in the two decades after World War II. But he suggested no foreign models for American parties to emulate. Insofar as he had models, they appeared to be modernized variations of successful American parties of the fairly recent past. In fact, Key often deplored the twentieth-century decline in the organizational strength of parties and most emphatically the absence of strength in particular places. The sense in which he wanted parties to be responsible, or at least responsive to voters, was very much within the limits imposed by the constitutional structure. He did not advocate the full-fledged responsible party government that he thought unachievable in American circumstances.[84] Nor did he advocate a mass-membership party of a type largely unfamiliar in the United States. Rather, like most defenders of American parties, Key looked to the self-interest of party leaders to produce a responsiveness to the electorate.

Indeed, it was crucial in Key's approach that there should be party leaders and specifically more than one set of leaders — that is, competing teams. In the American context, that meant two parties rather than only one. His most famous study, *Southern Politics*, is an extended criticism of the shortcomings of traditional one-party politics in which voters lack the clear-cut alternatives posed by competing teams bearing different party labels. Factional conflicts within parties, though fought out in direct-primary elections, do not provide a satisfactory continuity for voters or a sufficient association between gubernatorial and legislative candidates. One-party politics is issueless and also, most significantly, without a plain electoral choice between well-defined groups of politicians, the ins and the outs. In the long run, Key believed, the have-nots in a society are the losers from a politics so disorganized as to preclude their effective influence.[85]

Similar themes are stressed in Key's more general study of state politics. For the North as well as the South, he believes that party competition is the best means of enforcing accountability. Key associates its absence in certain northern states with the decay of party organization. The vigor of two-party competition has declined, he finds, during the first half of the twentieth century. One cause is the direct primary, which has often, he believes, transferred competition from an interparty basis to a less meaningful level of personalities.[86] Here as in his other works Key reflects a good deal more dissatisfaction with existing American parties than is customary among their defenders.[87] And while he regards them as having been more effective in the past, his praise for their historical record is unenthusiastic. On the whole, Key is best understood as defending traditional American parties only in the sense that, when organized and competitive, they were the best that we were likely to have. Accordingly, he found advantages in two-party competitive states and in such national two-party electoral competition as occurred despite the disadvantages of decentralized confederative organizations.[88] But Key did not proclaim virtue for the limits in strength and coherence that flowed from the indigenous development of American parties. He merely accepted these limits, or most of them, as painful necessities.

IV

Advocates of Responsible Party Government

Political scientists whom I categorize as advocates of responsible party government are chiefly distinguishable by their desire for American parties to transcend the limits within which traditional parties have operated. Whereas defenders of indigenous institutional developments accept those limits either enthusiastically or resignedly, members of the party-government school argue for parties that would assume collective responsibility for governmental policy-making in a manner that has so far been uncharacteristic of American experience. Although they might praise American parties of the past as much better than no parties at all, the advocates of party government do not regard them as satisfactory models. They seldom suggest entirely new parties, but they want to transform the existing Republican and Democratic parties into essentially different political institutions. In their minds, a democratic society requires not merely parties of one kind or another but two strong and cohesive parties, each offering the electorate policy commitments which it could fulfill after winning government offices.

Party responsibility thus has a special import here that differentiates it from the ordinary meaning of the phrase. After all, the defenders of traditional parties, indeed all believers in the usefulness of parties, prefer responsibility in some sense. But the advocates of party government want parties to be so much more responsible as to make for a difference in kind and not merely in degree. They sharpen this difference through a trenchant criticism of existing parties and through arguments for basic changes. These arguments are often cast as moral imperatives for overcoming the American institutional and social obstacles in the way of effective parties. The ablest advocates of change have understood those obstacles, but they believe that they can and should be surmounted. Thus the tone, at least, is different from Key's. He too wanted more responsible parties, but his hopes and suggestions were more modest and dispassionate than those of political scientists who would transform American parties.

The transformation that party government advocates have in mind is principally at the national level. Although they also deplore the frequent absence of party responsibility in state and local politics, their emphasis is on the weakness and incoherence of national parties. Attention is fixed on the inability of either Republicans or Democrats to promise and deliver policies through party control of Congress as well as of the presidency. They want *national* party government.

With its emphasis on national politics, the party-government school has existed for as long as American scholars have studied parties. Woodrow Wilson early in his academic career propounded a version of the doctrine specifically drawn from the British model, and others near the turn of the century were attracted by it.[89] It has more recently been heavily identified with E. E.

Schattschneider, a champion of stronger parties from the 1930s through the 1960s. As he said of himself, "I suppose the most important thing I have done in my field is that I have talked longer and harder and more persistently and enthusiastically about political parties than anyone else alive."[90] If during his career parties declined rather than becoming stronger, as he had hoped, Schatt- schneider did not lack academic followers or influence. On the contrary, his views are representative of a substantial number of other scholars, many of them younger and still actively propagating the faith. For a time these views had less prestige among political scientists than those of pluralist defenders of existing parties, but they were never disregarded and their popularity re- vived in the late 1960s and 1970s.

That popularity may be partly attributed to the sharpness with which Schatt- schneider stated the majoritarian premise of the party-government position. Unlike his pluralist opponents, he was not satisfied with direct interest-group representation and with parties that sought only to accommodate diverse in- terests in coalitional representation. Schattschneider assumed that there was a legitimate and definable majority interest that a party should mobilize and represent. Hence in 1942 he put into the conclusions of his best-known book, ". . . party government is good democratic doctrine because the parties are the special form of political organization adapted to the mobilization of ma- jorities. How else can the majority get organized? If democracy means any- thing at all it means that the majority has the right to organize for the purpose of taking over the government. Party government is strong because it has be- hind it the great moral authority of the majority and the force of a strong traditional belief in majority rule."[91] The majority, in Schattschneider's writ- ing, has a more public purpose than do minority interest groups, and its su- periority in this respect derives from its inclusion of the great mass of people whom he believes to be unorganized and unrepresented by pressure groups.[92] Egalitarianism thus underlies Schattschneider's majoritarianism. He saw a strong party as capable of representing less prosperous and otherwise less powerful people. Because our parties are not strong enough, he thought, particularized business interests too often dominate American politics and especially con- gressional policymaking.[93]

Interestingly, Schattschneider did not seek to strengthen American parties by participatory reforms. He favored neither the direct primary nor any other large-scale democratizing of party organizations. Instead he accepted, much as did Key, the sufficiency of the competing-teams concept of party. "Democ- racy is not to be found *in* the parties but *between* the parties."[94] Voters need not be burdened with party affairs. Nominations could be settled by organizational activists and by the leaders themselves. So could party policies and issue-positions. Voters would be well served jf given a choice between sets of leaders, each united in its commitment to a party and its program. The trouble was that such a choice did not really exist in American politics. Neither the Republicans nor the Democrats presented coherent leadership teams. Thus the two-party system did not fulfill its advantage by way of a real majority winner. Neither party's majority was cohesive enough. The apparent success of major American parties in electing candidates was not followed by their effective mobilization to govern as a united force.[95] It was not enough to simplify alternatives, limiting the voters' choice to two instead of many parties or many separate individual candidates. The choice had to be made meaningful by the capacity of a party in office to act cohesively in behalf of electoral promises.

Schattschneider had no doubt that the weakness of American parties as governing agencies flowed from constitutional circumstances, notably the separation of powers, but also federalism.[96] But unlike the early Woodrow Wilson and other admirers of British parliamentary government, Schattschneider did not propose constitutional changes as a precondition for more responsible parties. He sought to strengthen American parties so that they could themselves bring together, more fully than they had so far, the constitutionally separated legislative and executive branches. Difficult though the task was, it might well seem less remote than rewriting the fundamental principles of the U.S. Constitution. The American people could have party government if they wanted it. And Schattschneider thought they could be persuaded to want it.

Schattschneider, in his own writing, provides little blueprint for change, but there is one prominent theme: build a national party leadership that would not be dependent on state and local politicians. Decentralization of party authority was the enemy of responsible party government at the national level. The major American party, as "a loose confederation of state and local bosses," meant agreement for but limited purposes, chiefly patronage.[97] A party built around state and local bosses lacked policy coherence. Most emphatically, Schattschneider preferred a national leadership strong enough not only to control congressional party majorities but also to cut off patronage to local bosses.[98] Before and after elections, presidential and congressional candidates would share genuinely public purposes. When Schattschneider spoke of party government, he meant party centralization.[99]

Considerably more specific proposals for achieving party government appear in the famous 1950 report of the American Political Science Association's Committee on Political Parties. Schattschneider chaired the committee, and its report reflected his intense belief in the democratic need for two competing

national parties to present alternative governmental programs. Although the
report's proposals for intraparty democracy are at odds with Schattschneider's
earlier acceptance of a policymaking leadership, many of its other detailed
suggestions are consistent with his approach. So too is the report's basic and
explicit assumption that parties can be made responsible without formally
changing the U.S. Constitution.[100] In that respect, the APSA committee spoke
for much of the responsible-party-government school during the postwar years.
This is not to say that it spoke for most political scientists or even for most
parties specialists. Despite the committee's unusual status as an agency of the
professional association, its report, published as a supplement to the APSA's
journal, evoked immediate dissent from the defenders of conventional American parties. And the report was subsequently criticized because its advocacy
lacked the kind of empirical support that political scientists had come to expect in later decades.[101] Many of its proposals, however, continued to appeal
to responsible-party advocates even in the 1970s. Interest in the report remained
high.[102] Virtually all students of American politics agreed at least that effective
parties of some kind were necessary, and many may well have preferred the
committee's kind of effective parties, although they did not always share the
committee's belief that they could be established in the United States.

The APSA committee report included specific proposals for more active roles
for national party conventions and committees, a new national party council
to help make the party's platform a binding statement, the strengthening of
congressional party organization and leadership at the expense of congressional
committee autonomy, and a new type of participating membership related to
national party policymaking.[103] The committee accepted the direct primary
as the now-established American method of candidate selection, but expressed
a strong preference for the closed form of primary in which only publicly identified partisans could help choose party candidates. That form, the committee
believed, was more compatible with a responsible-party system that was the
open primary. Moreover, the committee also welcomed efforts of various party
committees and councils to propose candidates, as organizational choices, before primaries took place.[104]

Here and elsewhere the APSA report links the responsible-party doctrine
to the participation of issue-oriented organized activists both in selecting candidates and in party policymaking. Activists could be expected to endorse and
help to nominate candidates willing to carry out party policies that their organizations had developed. The participatory membership would be a means
for achieving coherently responsible party government despite the direct primary and other institutional obstacles. Accordingly, Schattschneider's acqui-

escence in the committee's organizational recommendation is not incompatible with his principal purpose. It is true that he had said, in his previously published work, that his purpose could be accomplished without intraparty democracy—that large-scale citizen participation in a party's internal affairs was not a democratic essential as long as citizens had a clear interparty choice. But he might well have viewed participatory activists as genuinely committed party organizational members, not so far removed from smaller leadership groups. Party activists were very different from mere party voters, whose membership Schattschneider had treated as a fiction created by primary registration laws. At any rate, the committee's preference for organizational activism remained an important element in the advocacy of responsible party government. Also, in the 1960s and 1970s, similar broad citizen participation in party affairs was advocated, even by scholars who otherwise dissociated their arguments for more effective parties from certain other aspects of the APSA report.[105]

Another persistent theme in responsible-party advocacy has been presidential leadership. For some scholars, a national party is essentially the president's, or the presidential candidate's. Congressional members and candidates are perceived as members of his team. The nature of the presidential-party relationship, however, is not the same for all believers in responsible party government. Woodrow Wilson, for example, came to put so much emphasis on a president's own popular mandate, received directly and individually from the electorate, that he can be charged with a departure from party government altogether.[106] After all, party government implies collective rather than strictly personal leadership. Thus stronger parties are often specifically advanced as a means to secure effective government without a too-powerful president governing independently of party or other intermediaries between himself and the people. For the responsible-party school, the president is important as the leader of a team, but he is responsible to others on that leadership team as well as to the voters.

Among recent responsible-party advocates emphasizing presidential leadership, James MacGregor Burns is preeminent. In his several widely read books, he seems equally concerned with a strong party and a strong leader, each complementing the other.[107] Burns seeks a leader capable of mobilizing a party majority rather than a personal, independent, or bipartisan majority. And he conceives of such a party majority as effective only if headed by a strong president. Specifically, Burns wants a presidential party able to lead a congressional majority: ". . . each presidential party must convert its congressional party into a party wing exerting a proper, but not controlling or crippling hold on party policy."[108] He would also have his presidentially led national party

build a mass-membership organization, but undoubtedly most of his hopes
for party policymaking rest on innovative leadership to which party members
would actively respond by way of campaign efforts to elect congressional candidates committed to the program of the president's party.[109] Writing as an
activist liberal Democrat himself, Burns has in mind a particular kind of programmatic party and often a particular leader devoted to that kind of party.

Like many other proposals for responsible party government, Burns's
presidential-leadership version looks like an attempt to achieve the results of
British parliamentary government by American constitutional means. Even
without citing the British model, it is plain that Burns is trying to establish
a national party whose elected legislators would regularly unite more or less
in the manner of a British parliamentary party under its prime ministerial and
cabinet leadership. Occasionally the British model is specifically cited by advocates of responsible party government. Schattschneider refers to it favorably
in a few instances, and the APSA committee, while mentioning British practices only briefly, does so admiringly. Moreover, one committee member recol-
lects that "the British model was significant" for a number of his colleagues.[110]

Undoubtedly, the British model was also significant for many other American political scientists in the early postwar years when the British Labour government enacted its 1945 election program of social welfare legislation and
nationalization of key industries. Among liberals, frustrated by the inability
of congressional Democrats to unite sufficiently to enact President Truman's
domestic program, the cohesive British parliamentary party then appeared most
attractive.[111] Party-line voting in the House of Commons, long understood
to be much more nearly uniform than in the U.S. Congress, was at a high
point in the early postwar years. It thus reflected a distinctive period of British
history when the two-party division was particularly sharp and meaningful.
Even more than in earlier or later years, there was great pressure, inherent
in parliamentary government, for a party's members of the legislative body
to vote so as to provide the solid majority thought necessary to maintain their
leaders in executive office. American admirers often understood the distinctiveness of these conditions and the unlikelihood of duplicating them in the United
States. Neither Schattschneider, the APSA committee, nor Burns proposed the
requisite American constitutional changes. Working, therefore, with the separation of powers, they could not and did not explicitly follow the British model
even though they admired it. Yet they did want American parties to be more
like British parties. Organizationally this meant, for the APSA committee and
for Burns, a nationally organized membership of issue-oriented activists. And
in government it meant a congressional party that at least resembled a parlia-

mentary party in its programmatic unity, although that unity was to be achieved under a strong presidential leadership that was decidedly unBritish.

Not all advocates of responsible party government made such limited use of the British model as did the best-known proponents whom I have discussed. One can find American political scientists who believed, long after Woodrow Wilson, in the need to adopt a version of parliamentary government in order to have responsible parties. One of the most recent and able scholars to argue for the British-style constitutional changes is Charles Hardin. Writing in 1974, when the American presidency had been darkened by Watergate and Vietnam, Hardin saw in the British system a means to achieve coherent policymaking without having to depend so heavily as did Americans on an individually strong president. In that perspective, Burns's emphasis on presidential leadership as a principal means to achieve responsible party government would take us in the wrong direction. Hardin wanted collective policymaking and a leader, like a British prime minister, who would be subject to the control of his legislative supporters. Executive authority could thus be strong and yet effectively limited.[112] The strength is party strength, and the way to achieve it is to adopt the constitutional system under which it develops.

Unrealistic though it seems to change the U.S. Constitution so drastically and fundamentally, Hardin's proposal may be analytically more attractive than the advocacy of responsible party government without a parliamentary system. The latter advocacy is based on no working model, but mainly on the hope that American parties can themselves be transformed, while operating in the same constitutional circumstances that helped, in the first place, to make them unsuitable to the purposes of responsible party government. The hope often seems a fallback position for those who might prefer constitutional change but think it politically impossible. No less than Hardin, they want American parties to be strong in ways not so far characteristic of American experience.

V

Common Ground

The differences between the two broad categories of pro-party scholars remain significant, but they are now less salient than the dissatisfaction in both schools with the recent state of American parties. Sharing a belief in the usefulness of parties, neither the defenders of indigenous institutions nor the advocates of responsible party government welcome an increasingly candidate-centered politics. As always, political scientists doubt that elections can be meaningful or government satisfactorily responsive unless parties play a major role, especially at the national level. They still disagree, it is true, about the adequacy of conventional American parties to fulfill that role. But given the widely perceived decline of those conventional parties, their defenders have less to defend and their critics less to criticize. In the 1970s and 1980s, those who admired the old confederations of state and local leaders look to their revival, and the advocates of responsible party government now seek to fill a gap rather than to replace substantial working organizations.

Far from abandoning the cause in adverse circumstances, party specialists of different persuasions united in a Committee for Party Renewal during the late 1970s.[113] In addition to some political activists, the committee included scholars who (like Austin Ranney) looked primarily to a restoration of the traditionally competing leadership coalitions, others (like James MacGregor Burns) long identified with the advocacy of responsible party government under presidential leadership, and still others who were convinced of the need for large-scale participatory organizations. The committee made its case both in and out of the profession. For example, it appeared before a congressional committee considering proposals for government financing of House election campaigns, and urged that at least a substantial share of any such financing be provided to parties rather than to the candidates alone (as the representatives' own bills specified).[114] In this as in other respects (like presidential nominating conventions), the Committee for Party Renewal sought to rebuild parties as a counterforce to the now-established candidate-centered politics. A leading member of the committee, Gerald Pomper, edited a book devoted both to arguments for party renewal and to useful studies of actual renewal efforts. The tone is clear in Pomper's introductory chapter: ". . . we must either acknowledge the mutual reliance of our parties and our democracy— or lose both."[115]

Pomper's language is more typical of responsible-party advocates than it is of defenders of the old institutions, but the two schools of thought surely stand together as embattled champions of institutions that appear decreasingly popular among many other Americans. Seldom do political scientists accept with equanimity the decomposition of parties; a continued decomposition leads at least one major parties specialist, Walter Dean Burnham, to reflect something close to despair about the future of democracy.[116] It is rare, now as always, to find a scholar who rejects parties altogether, along with representative government, in the manner of Rousseau;[117] it is nearly as rare for political scientists to express anything like satisfaction with relatively weak parties. Only a few writers are even willing to contemplate democratic politics without parties or with much weaker parties than we now have.[118] Among political scientists there is no antiparty school or even nonparty school. At most, a few scholars now have more sharply limited expectations with respect to party activities and accomplishments, particularly in policymaking spheres, than they once had.[119]

The continued scholarly commitment to parties resembles the profession's treatment of our actual governmental institutions — Congress, presidency, courts — whose strengthening is frequently advocated by specialized scholars. But strengthening in the case of parties now often involves a reaction against the results of progressivism as well as of various other twentieth-century American developments. Certainly political scientists, like everyone else, are aware of those developments even as they want stronger parties as counterforces. My own awareness, as I have already indicated, differs in that it leads me to suggest more accommodation than reaction to what I see as largely unalterable circumstances. Yet that theme of my discourse does not place it outside the broad and well-established scholarly commitment to the usefulness of parties in a democratic society. Indeed, I think of my work as belonging, in its own way, to the intellectual tradition that I have expounded. Its spirit, if not its substance, will be observed to resemble that of the defenders of indigenous American parties. What is now indigenous, however, differs from what was once defended. And what is now possible by way of change also differs.

Chapter Three

The Congressional
Presence

Nowhere has the political scientists' commitment to the usefulness of parties been more clearly reflected than in a concern with their performance in Congress. The concern was evident in the early work of Woodrow Wilson, and the responsible-parties school has been especially interested in strengthening congressional parties under executive leadership. But members of that school have never been alone in their quest. Lately, in particular, they have had a good deal of intellectual company.

The intensity of academic concern with the subject is but one reason to start an analysis of American parties with a description of their presence in Congress. Another reason is chronological. Parties began in parliamentary bodies almost everywhere. In Britain, for example, Whigs and Tories had an eighteenth-century existence as parliamentary "parties"—loose factional groups of like-minded legislative representatives—long before they developed national electoral organizations. Similar alignments formed in several continental countries whose parliamentary bodies possessed significant powers before the enfranchisement of large and nationally mobilizable electorates. Even in the United States, where mass electoral participation followed closely the establishment of government under the Constitution, national parties first appeared in Congress when one set of members supported the executive leadership of Washington and Hamilton while another set opposed it. This is not to say that all parties originated in legislative bodies; several European labor and socialist parties, for example, first organized as external movements designed to elect representatives to parliamentary bodies in which they had previously had no members. But because they were thus seeking to add a new parliamentary party to compete with previously established parties, their success is not at odds with the view that parties as general political phenomena first emerge in legislative chambers.

More important for my purpose, parties have always emerged in legislative bodies exercising meaningful authority at a national level (and ordinarily at a regional level too). The historical association tends to confirm the common-sense observation that parties, or something very like them, are essential in the operation of legislative bodies competitively elected to represent large geographic areas. These bodies tend to have numerous members who must somehow organize to produce legislative results. That they should organize in groups according to different policy positions, or in favorable or unfavorable response to policy positions of executive leadership, seems as natural as it has been usual. That these groups should be relatively stable, and not merely ad hoc coalitions, has also been customary if not inevitable. Whether parliamentary groups should be called parties before they developed electoral organizations outside of their legislative chambers is a nice terminological question that I prefer to settle affirmatively by following historical usage. Eighteenth-century British parliamentary groups were and are called parties despite their electoral limitations.

So fully have parties been associated with the development of national legislative powers that it is peculiarly hard to envision a body like the U.S. Congress working without parties. Even among those who accept, however reluctantly, a continued decline in American parties as useful electoral agencies, there is a belief, as Crotty and Jacobson put it, that parties remain "essential to effect collective action by Congress. They provide the machinery through which members cooperate to make national policy."[1] The parties in Congress, now as in the past, are indispensable elements in a national party system. With them and nothing else by way of party organization, we might well have a limited and ineffective system. But without congressional parties, we might have no national party system at all (or at least none between presidential elections).

In fact, among the several manifestations of *national* parties in American experience, the congressional parties are the most continuously organized, the most regularly important, and the most nearly similar to their counterparts in other Western democratic nations. European politicians visiting Washington and asking to see our parties would have no difficulty recognizing House and Senate Democrats or Republicans as roughly comparable to their own parliamentary parties. American congressional parties, though less impressively cohesive than most European counterparts, would look more substantial and so more familiar than either our historically weak and still federative national party committees or the candidate-centered presidential followings that we sometimes call "presidential parties."

Neither discontinuous nor transient, congressional parties, majority and minority, are always with us. Their durability is truly remarkable. Not only have parties of some kind operated since the earliest congresses of U.S. history, but the same two parties, Democrats and Republicans, have held overwhelmingly dominant shares of the seats in both the House and the Senate for over a century. One or another of these two parties has commanded a majority of members in each house since 1861. And the other party has included almost all minority members.[2] In other words, very few senators or representatives have been anything but Democrats or Republicans. Independents are always scarce, and so usually are third-party or minor-party members. The latter, while slightly more numerous in the late nineteenth and early twentieth centuries than in the last few decades, were never so many as to preclude majority party control or to challenge the preeminence of the second party as *the* minority and often as the conceivable alternative majority after a subsequent election. Nor have any recent developments, including the apparent weakening of traditional extragovernmental party organizations and of voter-identification with parties, diminished the established two-party preponderance in Congress.[3] Even less often now than in the past do significant numbers of senators or representatives get elected except as Democrats or Republicans, and no more than in the past do they, once elected, cease to be Republicans or Democrats. The pattern, it will be observed, is repeated in our state legislatures.

Unmistakably continuous though they are, the Republican and Democratic congressional parties do not, as I have suggested, impress many professional observers as consequential enough. By the standards of certain parliamentary parties, American congressional parties have never appeared very cohesive in legislative policymaking. And in recent decades they often seemed even less effective in this respect than they had in several earlier periods of American history. The relative weakness that thus emerges from either cross-national or chronological comparisons cannot be ignored. Yet the durability of the major congressional parties is itself a strength. To be sure, it would not be so if there were merely persistent Republican and Democratic labels without meaningful organizational structures. But such structures, as I shall stress, do indeed exist. Their limitations — a term I prefer to weakness — may be necessary if virtually all legislative representatives from many disparate constituencies are to be continuously organized by only two parties. Moreover, certain limitations surely derive from the language and development of the U.S. Constitution. The American institutional context is sufficiently distinctive for us to expect congressional parties to differ from parliamentary parties in other Western democratic systems. Accordingly I shall first pay attention to the general context and next to the decentralization that has increasingly characterized Congress's exercise of its great powers within the American system. Congressional parties will then be discussed under the headings of their centripetal organizational efforts, policymaking roles, and changing electoral bases.

I

Institutional Context

My main thesis here is simple. The American separation-of-powers doctrine, firmly embedded in constitutional letter and practice, makes the Congress capable of operating apart from or against executive leadership in a manner unlike that of any other national legislature. To be sure, Congress constitutionally shares powers with the president—obviously so, for example, in enacting legislation subject to presidential influence and presidential veto. Hence one can describe the system more exactly, as does Neustadt, by speaking of "separated institutions *sharing* powers."[4] Powers, in the sense of governmental tasks and responsibilities, are in fact not so much separated as they are shared. It is because "powers" also mean the institutional authorities themselves, Congress and the president as well as the judiciary, that we use the language of separation. In that sense, they are significantly independent of each other. Not only can Congress and the president act separately in certain areas, but each institution has its own electoral base and its own tenure of office. Congress is thus sharply different from a conventional British or European parliament whose electoral mandate is also the executive's.

The difference has two vital aspects. First, the Congress does not produce executive authority in the shape of its majority leadership, as in parliamentary systems, or by its choice of anyone else. The constitutional prohibition against holding both executive and legislative offices precludes a parliamentary system, and political customs have effectively excluded congressional control of the presidential succession by other means. Only in the early days of the Republic did a congressional caucus of the dominant party select a presidential candidate and thus, de facto, determine the election outcome. That procedure, successful during the Virginia presidential dynasty of the early nineteenth century, ceased to work in the Jacksonian era of popular election of presidential electors, and it was soon superseded by national party nominating conventions. In fact as in law, Congress has long since had no role in selecting the president, apart of course from its latent constitutional role when there is no electoral college majority or when the vice-presidency is vacant.

Congress's undoubted capacity to remove a president through impeachment is hardly political in the usual sense; the two serious uses of the constitutional power, against Andrew Johnson in 1868 and against Richard Nixon in 1974, tend to establish its constraints. The failure to convict Johnson, despite the narrowness of the margin, has been accepted as a justified rebuff to a partisan effort to remove a president because of disagreement with his policies. Only with criminal behavior genuinely at issue, as in Nixon's case, did impeachment finally look legitimate. Its likelihood, along with the likelihood of conviction, did then force a president to resign. But that result does not run counter to the view that it is inappropriate for Congress to invoke its power of impeachment merely because of presidential policies.

The second vital aspect of the difference between Congress and other national parliaments is a positive accompaniment of its separation from the executive. Lacking the power to put the president in office, or politically to remove the president, no congressional majority is bound in the same degree as is a parliamentary system's majority to support an executive leadership's program. The executive leadership is not necessarily Congress's leadership. A congressional majority, whether or not of the same party as a president, can defeat a president's legislative program without driving him from office or forcing him to abandon advocacy of his program. Nor, of course, does Congress subject itself to the risk of an early election, as does a European parliament, by rejecting an executive's policies. In short, the U.S. Congress is a much more independent law-making body than is a parliamentary body whose majority ordinarily feels politically compelled to follow its own executive leadership. In Nelson Polsby's words, "The analogies to parliaments which predominate in intelligent conversation about Congress do the powers of our national legislature less than justice. For unlike parliaments the world around, the American Congress dissolves neither itself nor the government when it has serious disagreement with its Executive."[5]

Other scholars too, often sensitive to the comparative perspective, understand that Congress is a special kind of legislative body. For example, David Truman asserts; "The Congress today is more nearly a legislature in the strict sense than is the national assembly in any other major country in the world."[6] And David Olson, using a highly developed comparative approach, treats the U.S. Congress as "a unique institution" among the world's legislative bodies.[7] Usually the uniqueness is linked to the separation-of-powers doctrine, although not always with as much emphasis as I put on the relationship. That emphasis derives from a perception of the separation of powers as the central and apparently immutable feature of the institutional context in which congressional parties operate.

This is not to say that the separation of legislative and executive powers is the only apparently immutable feature of the relevant American institutional context. A less central and less sharply distinctive feature is bicameralism, a sturdy fixture nationally as it is in almost all American states. The United States is not unique in having two national legislative bodies, but it is nearly so in making them practically equal in power. More precisely, the United States is unusual in giving a less popularly based body about the same authority as that of a body whose members come from districts of roughly equal populations.[8] Neither the House nor the Senate dominates the other, and to a large degree each operates as a separate institution. To be sure, cross-chamber consultation and collaboration occur, notably in jointly arranged conference committees to settle differences between House and Senate bills on the same subject, but the two bodies are thus associated, sharing powers, much as the Congress generally shares powers with the president. Structurally as well as in their electoral bases, House and Senate are distinct bodies.

Each chamber separately provides a setting for party organization. Hence we do not find a single Republican or Democratic structure and leadership covering both houses, but instead, separately established Republican and Democratic organizations in each house. And just as neither Senate nor House dominates the other, so neither is a Senate party or a House party in a position to dominate the other. Senate leaders and House leaders may well consult and collaborate as fellow-Democratic or fellow-Republican partisans, but the relationship is as plainly equal as is that of senators and representatives of both parties working together in a conference committee. In other words, Senate and House parties, like the two chambers in which they are based, have separate though not isolated power structures. The institutional imprint is apparent.

One other aspect of the setting for congressional parties is consequential as well as distinctive and sufficiently fixed to be treated as of the institutional context. It is the strongly constituency-oriented nomination and election of members of Congress. The cause is not merely that electoral constituencies are states and districts. Several other national legislatures resemble the U.S. Congress in using single-member districts rather than the multimember districts required by proportional representation. For example, the British House of Commons, the Canadian House of Commons, and the Australian House of Representatives are all like the U.S. Congress in using single-member districts. Yet the British, Canadian, and Australian houses, despite regional conflicts, especially in Canada, have members whose nomination and election usually involve more heavily national party considerations than do the nomination and election of members of Congress.

The contrast is sharpest in the British case, because the constituency parties that select (or as we would say, nominate) their candidates do so as branches of national parties and in response mainly to their perceptions of the national party cause. And subsequently, the election is between party choices much more than between individual candidates seeking nonparty constituency interest followings. But in other countries also, including those (like Canada and Australia) where constituency parties are branches of provincial or state parties rather than directly of national parties, the national party cause looms larger in nominations and elections than it does in the United States. Or, put the other way around so as to stress again the American distinctiveness, why are congressional nominations and elections so strongly, though of course not wholly, constituency oriented?

No doubt the separation-of-powers doctrine again provides some of the explanation, if only because under it there is not the same degree of pressure for national party unity that arises in a parliamentary system where a majority is expected to maintain executive authority. Thus American senators and representatives, observed already as relatively independent of executive responsibility and authority, have that status reinforced by the processes of their nomination and election. Since they can and do represent constituency interests when in conflict with party programs, they can and do seek nomination and election at least partly on the basis of those interests and of their personal ability to champion the interests effectively. No doubt members of other national legislative bodies also seek some votes on the basis of their constituency service and individual merits. But American senators and representatives act in an institutional framework that provides greater opportunity and incentive to conduct candidate-centered campaigns.

Near the end of this chapter, I shall explore the possibility that the opportunity and incentive have increased significantly in the last several decades. Here it need only be noted that that possibility is often attributed in part to a twentieth-century institutional change—specifically, to the adoption of direct-primary laws that remove party nominations for Congress, as for other offices in almost all American states, from party organizations and put them into the hands of loosely defined or identified party voters. No one doubts that a contested direct primary ordinarily requires an ad hoc candidate organization, and that such organization tends to be carried into a subsequent general election campaign. Accordingly, it is reasonable to view the now firmly established direct-primary laws and practices as elements of the institutional context in which representatives and senators are encouraged to act independently of party. Only in America, as I shall say many times in this book, is there anything like the opportunity that the direct primary provides for individual success in capturing a party label without (and even against) organizational efforts.

At this point, the American institutional context is so presented as to stress the limitations imposed on congressional parties seeking unity and effectiveness. Indeed, the context thus understood has struck some proponents of stronger parties as so unfavorable to their cause that they have wanted to transform it by fundamental constitutional and statutory changes. Accordingly, Charles Hardin's relatively recent proposals, noted in the previous chapter, are worth a closer look. Among other reforms, Hardin argued that legislative power be concentrated in the House (with the Senate having power only to delay passage of a bill), that House members and the president be elected simultaneously for four-year terms, that enough candidates for Congress be elected at large and as a result of a victory for their party's presidential candidate to ensure their party's majority, that a party's congressional candidates should nominate their party's presidential candidate, and that party officeholders should nominate at-large congressional candidates and also have the power to reject candidates nominated for district seats.[9] Note that Hardin's proposals strike at all three elements of the American institutional context that I have described: separation of powers, bicameralism, and constituency-oriented nomination and election. His institutional framework would be national as well as decidedly parliamentary—the president, like the British prime minister, becoming the choice of a legislative majority party composed of many members whose election would be linked to their leader's rather than to state and district constituencies or to their direct primaries.

For those of us who doubt the feasibility of Hardin's proposed transformation, the spelling out of what he would change may again only emphasize the limitations on congressional parties that American institutions impose. I do not, however, want to leave the subject on so entirely negative a note. Although our firmly settled institutions strike me as precluding British-style parties in the Congress, I do not assume that they preclude parties of considerable effectiveness. Within the constraints of the American system of government, such parties have certainly functioned over considerable periods of time. Their accommodation to the system need not be regarded as weakness but can even be look on as a kind of strength in adapting to a special environment conducive to the representation of diverse constituencies.

II
Structural Decentralization

Not only must parties in Congress accommodate to the general institutional context, notably that imposed by the U.S. Constitution, but they must also work within a decentralized structure that Congress has itself developed in the exercise of its substantial autonomous power. The structure is so firmly established that it too may be seen as an element of the institutional context. In both the House and the Senate, standing subject-matter committees and subcommittees are the familiar elements of that structure. Having such committees, each specialized and thus influential in a given area of legislative policymaking, seems essential if Congress is to discharge its constitutional responsibilities effectively and intelligently. The need for a similarly strong and elaborate legislative committee structure is not so plain in parliamentary systems where executive and legislative authority are effectively concentrated in a cabinet serving as the single great "committee." The British House of Commons, where standing committees have a much less independent role than the American, is the leading case in point.[10] Not all parliamentary bodies resemble the British in this respect, but when, as in West Germany, committees have developed as independent policymakers, their power ordinarily remains short of that regularly exercised by American congressional standing committees.[11]

Much of my concern later in the chapter focuses on the ways that congressional parties have coped with the distinctively decentralized institutional structure in which they operate, and particularly on party efforts to organize and influence standing committees. The starting point for that analysis is the firmly established custom, in House and Senate, that the majority party hold a majority of the seats and the chair on each committee and subcommittee. But, as we know, the dominance thus suggested may not mean that the majority party collectively controls, through its caucus or elected leadership, the actions of committees and subcommittees. Difficulties in the way of any such decisive central influence have been increasingly evident in the late twentieth century, as committees and now their subcommittees develop more substantial lives of their own. Yet the need to cope with inherently centrifugal forces is an old one.

Standing committees, first established in the House of Representatives, have been important centers of power in both houses since the first decade of the nineteenth century, despite the fact that their structure was not firmly settled in the Senate until 1861.[12] Congress, as Samuel Patterson has said, is "an extraordinarily stable institution" in which Henry Clay, who served in both houses during their formative years, would still find much that was familiar.[13] Even more clearly is there continuity from the 1880s, when Woodrow Wilson wrote that "Congressional government is Committee government" and that our government is "by the chairmen of the Standing Committees of Congress."[14] By no means, however, have the power relationships remained static. They were changing even as Wilson wrote, and in a decentralizing direction. Notably, in the House during the 1880s the once-dominant authority of the Appropriations Committee, and so of its chairman, was curtailed by the transfer of several kinds of supply bills from its jurisdiction to that of particular subject-matter committees.[15] Subsequently there would be more numerous policymaking centers and particularly more policymaking chairmen. Not all committees have been equally important, but their number in the first half of this century indicates the fragmentation of authority. Before the Reorganization Act of 1946 dropped and merged enough committees to cut the total by more than half, there were 48 standing committees in the House and 33 in the Senate.[16] Standing committees since have been limited to about 22 in the House and about 15 in the Senate (plus a few joint committees and a few select and special committees in each chamber).[17] But their subcommittees have become more potent centers of authority, especially in the House after its reforms of the early 1970s.[18]

With certain exceptions, each congressional standing committee has several specialized subject-matter subcommittees. Their numbers vary considerably from session to session, but the 1983–84 totals of 130 House subcommittees and 103 Senate subcommittees appear fairly typical.[19] Each subcommittee has a chairman from the majority party in the given house, and because of limits on how many chairs a given member can occupy, a relatively large number of members of a majority party will hold chairs of subcommittees if not of full committees. In the Senate it is possible for every majority party member to hold at least one chair. And even in the larger House, about one-half of the members of the majority party occupy chairs of one kind or another.[20] Accordingly, with subcommittees now foci of policymaking authority, there are many more congressional barons than in Woodrow Wilson's day or even in John F. Kennedy's. Leadership has come to be broadly dispersed in the House as it may ordinarily have been, to a greater extent, in the smaller and traditionally individualistic Senate.

The evidently increased dispersion of authority among members of Congress is an understandable response to the greater and more specialized legislative tasks accompanying the growth of governmental policymaking in the twentieth century. Representatives and senators have themselves responded by more often becoming full-time professional legislators with long-term congressional careers focused on the subject matter of their committees and subcommittees. The development is part of what Nelson Polsby perceptively described, for the House of Representatives, as "institutionalization."[21] Polsby measured it partly by the increase, from the nineteenth century to the mid-twentieth, in length of House service, and by the accompanying decrease in first-term representatives. Specifically, mean two-year terms of service of representatives rose from about two in the middle years of the nineteenth century to about three at the turn of the century, then to about four by 1929–47, and to over five by the early 1960s.[22] The mean even went as high as six in 1971 before it dropped back to about four and one-half or five in the late 1970s and early 1980s, mainly as a result of an evidently short-term rise in voluntary retirements.[23] But even in the 1970s and early 1980s, first-term representatives were never more than 20 percent of the House, and as low as 10 percent in 1985, in contrast to characteristic nineteenth-century figures in the 30 to 50 percent range. Thus, despite the moderate and perhaps only temporary reversal in the 1970s, the historical shift is unmistakable. It occurred gradually over about a century, but with an acceleration, as Polsby notes, between 1890 and 1910.[24]

The dates are meaningful because of the association of the increase in average years of House service with the procedural changes produced especially in 1910. This was the year of a successful revolt of members against a centralizing leadership, chiefly the Speaker's, that had for a time asserted itself effectively against the centrifugal forces of the committee structure. Only after 1910 was seniority regularly observed in selecting House committee chairs, and only after World War II was it so firmly established as to allow virtually no exceptions for over a quarter-century.[25] In the 1970s, it is true, seniority became a little less sacrosanct under rules adopted by the House Democratic majority.[26] Instead of routine caucus acceptance of the nomination of the full slate of committee chairmen, each of whom was the majority member with the longest continuous service on the particular committee, a separate caucus vote was now required for each nomination by a party leadership committee (which might itself violate seniority in making its nomination). The result in 1975 was the rejection of three committee chairmen and the election instead of slightly less senior Democratic members of the committees. These cases seemed, however, nearly unique events explicable by then special congressional circumstances.[27] Over the next ten years, neither the Democratic leadership nor the Democratic caucus violated seniority in bestowing committee chairs, and seniority was seldom violated even with respect to subcommittee chairs. Not until 1985 was another full committee chairman rejected. On that occasion, the Democratic caucus first voted down the leadership's nomination of the 80-year-old chairman of the Armed Services Committee and then elected the seventh-ranking Democrat over the second-ranking Democrat, who was the leadership's next nominee.[28] This significant double revolt reflected policy preferences as well as objections to age and lack of vigor. And it showed that there could again be special circumstances, as there were in 1975, when seniority would be overridden. The threat to override, present since the 1970s, was thus made more meaningful though still rarely invoked.

Yet it must be stressed that seniority prevails as the working principle in both houses almost as regularly as it did when Polsby described its development into the 1960s. In fact, it has not been violated at all in the U.S. Senate either by the Democratic majority of the 1970s or the Republican majority of the early 1980s. Although the means by which those majorities could override seniority are in place, they have not been used for that purpose. Accordingly, the violations of seniority by House Democrats, in 1975 and 1985, appear even more exceptional in the total congressional picture than they do in the experience of the House alone. The point is important, because seniority both recognizes and fosters the working autonomy of committees and their individual members. It is thus linked to the dispersal of authority that, in Polsby's language, Congress has institutionalized instead of hierarchy or centralization.[29]

The pattern of dispersal was surely followed in the 1970s when the House Democratic majority strengthened subcommittees and their chairmen in relation to full committees and their chairmen. Admittedly the seniority custom was not itself thereby strengthened (or necessarily weakened). The new rules, in addition to their more general provisions for subcommittee operational autonomy, took from the committee's chairman the power to select subcommittee chairs, and gave that power to the majority party members of the full committee. Seniority, prevalent anyway in bestowing subcommittee chairs, might well be observed almost as regularly by vote of a full committee's majority members as it had been by a committee's chairman. And with a few exceptions that has apparently been the case since 1975.[30] Significantly, only the especially powerful House Appropriations subcommittee chairmen, along with full committee chairmen, are subject to approval by the Democratic caucus.[31] Otherwise, Democratic subcommittee chairmen hold their positions solely by decision of their Democratic fellow committee members.

Even if these fellow members ceased so regularly to make their decision in accord with seniority, they would be likely to employ criteria of specialization and professionalism that derive from their work as committee members rather

than to rely solely on general party policy considerations. In other words, decentralization of authority could be preserved without the strict observation
of seniority in awarding subcommittee chairs. Only if a chamber's majority,
through its leadership or its whole membership in caucus, were to impose
its choices on the committees and the subcommittees would there be an effective reversal of the decentralization now associated with seniority. And the
exercise of that kind of centralizing authority, despite its occasional use in the
House in 1975 and especially in 1985, remains uncharacteristic of late-twentieth-
century congressional behavior. Its greater use in the future cannot be completely ruled out, but anything like a central domination of committees and
subcommittees through appointment of their chairs is so antithetical to the
practices as well as the interests of most members that it looks improbable.

The relatively autonomous status of committees and subcommittees is but
the most familiar of Congress's signposts of decentralization. Another, increasingly evident in recent decades, is the congressional resource base of the individual member. Not only have more members of each house acquired authority as subcommittee chairmen, but even without such positions both the
junior members of the majority party and all minority party members have
professional staffs and substantial services of various sorts. In these respects,
representatives are almost as well fixed as senators. Ranking minority members of committees and subcommittees are especially well provided with staff
assistance, but even the most junior member of each party has an office whose
budget compares with that of a small bureaucracy or business enterprise. In
fact, a representative's office has been called a not-so-small business, in a study
of the behavior of new members in the mid-1970s. At that time, each House
member was allowed 18 personal staff employees and a maximum payroll of
a quarter of a million dollars.[32]

Like the additional staff serving committees, subcommittees, and the House
and Congress more generally, personal staff became much more numerous,
professional, and expensive over the two decades before the mid-1970s. The
upward trends have continued, though a little less sharply, into the 1980s.
By 1983 there were over 7,600 personal staff employees in the House, and over
4,000 in the Senate. In each case, the number was a little more than three
times greater than it had been in 1957. And the contrast with the past is much
sharper when it is realized that as late as 1900 representatives had no personal
staffs, and all senators together had only 39 personal assistants.[33] The significance of the change is hardly diminished by the fact that slightly more than
one-third of the House's personal staff and about one-quarter of the Senate's
are in district or state offices rather than in Washington. Employees thus con-

tribute to their member's continued electoral success while helping to perform congressional services. Other congressional employees, particularly those appointed by the chairmen and the ranking minority members of committees and subcommittees, also enhance the status of representatives and senators. To a considerable extent, these Washington employees are personal too. And they are numerous as well as professional. In 1983, House standing committee staff totaled almost 2,000 (more than double the number of a decade earlier), and Senate standing committee staff totaled over 1,000 (200 more than a decade earlier).[34]

Impressive though the numbers are, they still exclude many employees who serve each house as a whole or Congress generally (as do a few thousand employees of the General Accounting Office and the Library of Congress), and so should not be counted even indirectly as working for particular Representatives or Senators. Altogether, however, Congress has a big bureaucracy; its 1984 appropriation was almost $1.5 billion. About $107 million of this total was for mailing costs—a five-fold increase in 12 years and thus another measure of the sharply increased provision of service for members of Congress.[35]

No doubt individual members, even if without committee or subcommittee chairs or analogous senior minority party positions, are now well equipped to operate independently—to be in business, politically, for themselves. Congressional authority, in this sense, is more widely dispersed than the strengthening of subcommittees itself suggests. Decentralization of this kind with 535 individual power centers might be much harder for congressional party leaders, as well as for presidents, to cope with than anything encountered in earlier days when there were fewer congressional barons. Fragmentation may now be a better descriptive term than decentralization.

This is not to say that ordinary members of the U.S. Congress were ever as readily led as the disciplined backbenchers who characterized the House of Commons especially in the first seven decades of this century. U.S. senators, we well know, have traditionally been independently powerful figures in national politics, and members of the House of Representatives have also, at least in the twentieth century, often been able and willing to assert legislative policy preferences at odds with those of their leaders. For many decades, more U.S. representatives than British M.P.s have been full-time professional legislators whose interests, information, or preferences might well run contrary to the policies of their leaders.[36] And, as always, members of the U.S. Congress could vote against their party leaders without incurring the political costs for themselves or their party that often accompany defections in a parliamentary system.

III
Party Organization

It is hardly novel to treat party as a centralizing or integrative force in contrast to the centrifugal tendencies linked to the specialized concerns of committees and individual members. Such treatment should not, however, imply that party is potentially an organizational substitute for the specialized and decentralized committee structure that each legislative body has developed for discharging its responsibilities. In this institutional context, the congressional party may be perceived as a means for working with and through a decentralized structure rather than as a replacement for that structure. The centripetal force of party may thus be complementary to the centrifugal force of the committee system. Just as Congress decentralizes its great authority to ensure specialized consideration, so it also, at some point in the legislative process, has a mechanism sufficiently integrative to facilitate majority decision-making. In the U.S. Congress as in other national legislatures, party is the familiar mechanism for that purpose.

The fact that the decentralized congressional structure, as well as the representational demands of American constituencies, imposes special difficulties on parties—and probably thus limits their effectiveness—does not make parties in Congress any less necessary than they are elsewhere. They may even be peculiarly necessary in the United States *because* of the nature of its institutions.

The party alignment that appeared in Congress even before 1800 took at least an embryonic organizational form, with recognizable leaders, before the Civil War.[37] During the last 125 years, representatives and senators have not merely been elected under Republican or Democratic party labels; they also belong, in each house, to a collegial entity bearing one of those labels. Generally, that entity is called a caucus, although officially only House Democrats use the term for their organization. House Republicans, as well as Senate Republicans and Senate Democrats, prefer to call their organization a conference. Under either name, party authority can be exercised directly by its membership or through its elected leaders. However limited the exercise of that authority may look to critics seeking more highly disciplined congressional parties, it is meaningful for many purposes.

The congressional party in this century has come to have a substantial organizational apparatus despite fluctuation or decline in policymaking influence. Earlier, apart from the Speaker of the House of Representatives, congressional party leadership tended to be mainly informal. But between the 1880s and World War I, majority and minority party leadership positions, along with party whips, were established on a continuous basis in each house. Similarly continuous party committees, one set for policy and another for assigning standing committee members, were created a little earlier in the Senate and a little later in the House.[38] Different practices prevail between Senate and House as well as between the two parties in each chamber. But generally, an institutionalization of congressional party leadership has developed in this century, as has an institutionalization of standing committees.

The most elaborate and probably the most important party organizational apparatus belongs to House Democrats. Constituting a majority for three decades, the House Democratic party has been not only regularly larger than any other congressional party but also so diverse, geographically and ideologically, as to indicate the need for internal communication devices even to attempt to achieve coherence. Accordingly, House Democrats have now established an imposingly large organization of whips to assist their elected Speaker and majority leader. By 1985, they had a majority whip, a chief deputy whip, seven deputy whips, and 31 at-large whips.[39] In addition to these agents of their leadership, the Democrats had 23 other whips chosen by and for 19 zones to which members belong on the basis of the states they represent. Altogether, leaders and whips, totaling 65, were thus about one-fourth of all House Democrats in 1985.

Large numbers of whips, though hardly a measure of the effectiveness of party leadership, surely suggest concerted and systematic effort. At the very least, the House Democratic leadership has the means for learning, through the zonal whips, how party members intend to vote on a given roll call. Once waverers or potential opposition to party policy are thus identified, they may be subject to persuasion from the appointed whips or even, in tough cases, from the leaders themselves. In this process, it should be noted that the zonal whips, elected by their state or regional delegations, serve as reporters rather than as persuaders. Nevertheless they are an important link in the intraparty communication process. So, too, is the House Democratic leadership assisted by eleven salaried staff persons in the majority whip's office. On this score as in other ways, the House Democratic organization appears larger and more elaborate than that of House Republicans or that of either Senate party. But apart from its greater size, it is not untypical. In any case, because of the persistent Democratic majority in the House, the example is significant even if not entirely representative of the other three congressional parties.

Top congressional party leaders are elected by their caucuses or conferences without the nearly automatic observance of seniority that has characterized the bestowal of standing committee chairs. Besides electing the Speaker of the

House of Representatives (technically the choice of the whole House but actually that of the majority party) and majority and minority party leaders, each of the four congressional parties chooses certain other party committee leaders and party committee members — sometimes through separate state or regional delegations rather than by the whole caucus or conference. House Republicans and both Senate parties also elect their principal whips, instead of having them appointed by other leaders as House Democrats have done through 1985. By either method, however, the choice of party leaders involves more than long service in Congress.[40]

Although party leaders in recent decades have almost always been chosen from among relatively senior members, they need not be and seldom are the very most senior members. Speaker O'Neill's career provides a fair example; entering the House in 1953, he became Democratic whip in 1971, majority leader in 1972, and Speaker in 1977. But even in the early 1980s, Speaker O'Neill was not quite *the* most senior Democrat in the House. Similarly, long though not necessarily the longest service characterizes Republican leaders in the House and both Republican and Democratic leaders in the Senate. Furthermore, without the same strict observance of seniority that marks standing committee procedure, it is even possible, particularly in the Senate, for a relatively junior member to enter the leadership. Thus Lyndon Johnson, after only three years of Senate service, became the Democratic whip in 1951 and the Democratic leader in 1953. Once chosen, party leaders tend to be rechosen. Yet they are less certain of holding their positions, from Congress to Congress, than are standing committee chairmen. And while there is ordinarily a progression (like O'Neill's) up the party leadership ladder, it too is not a sure thing. Republican leaders in both the House and Senate have been especially vulnerable to successful revolts during the last few decades.

In short, congressional party leaders, chosen in the first place because of their colleagues' personal or factional support (as well as their own experience) need to retain that support. Yet their somewhat less secure position than that of standing committee chairmen should not obscure the substantially common ground occupied by party leaders and standing committee chairmen. They share relatively long congressional service, similar institutional stakes in the system, and the same basis for authority — the acquiescence of party colleagues.

It may be suspected that the elaborateness of congressional party organizations is a response to the formidable obstacles in the way of party power and influence in a highly decentralized legislative body. If, for example, the House Democratic leadership found it easy to mobilize almost all of its party members in support of its legislative policy preferences or those of the majority of the Democratic caucus, it might not need as many whips to communicate with Democratic representatives. More effort is needed to persuade than to summon representatives on the basis of either a widely shared ideology or a set of disciplinary weapons. Leaders do call on party loyalty, but except on certain organizational matters they can rarely demand it. On questions of legislative policymaking, party influence is "important, but not crucial."[41] The well-known consequence is the limited party cohesion in congressional roll-call voting, a record that will be examined in the next section of this chapter.

A very different record of congressional party solidarity exists with respect to organizing each house. Here each House and Senate party, and crucially the majority party in each case, has historically as well as recently acted monolithically. Not only does a cohesive majority party effectively choose the Speaker of the House of Representatives, but in the Senate as in the House the majority party votes together in fixing the size of its majority on each standing committee. Moreover, each congressional party, minority as well as majority, assigns its own members to serve on each standing committee. Here, it would seem, party power might counter the decentralizing force of the standing committee system. So it does, customarily, but within rather narrow limits. Just as the caucus's power to select standing committee chairmen is usually constrained by seniority norms, so too are the party's collective powers over committee memberships exercised with considerable deference to the established expectations of members. Even in the original assignment of new representatives or senators to standing committees, the relevant party committee on committees (under one name or another) finds it expedient to honor member requests for particular committees that are of special interest to members' constituents (often historically) or to members themselves. And once the assignment has been made, it almost invariably continues from session to session unless the member requests a change or unless the member's party has lost so many seats that it is forced to surrender a committee position or positions—in which case the first to go is the most junior member.

Only very rarely is a representative or senator removed from a standing committee for any other reason, and such reason almost certainly goes beyond mere disagreement over legislative policy. Accordingly, in 1983, when the House Democratic party dropped Representative Phil Gramm from its contingent on the Budget Committee, it did so not only because Gramm had voted with Republicans, on and off the particular committee, but also because he had worked actively with Republicans against the Democratic leadership, when he was thought to have agreed not to violate that organizational norm. Moreover, the Budget Committee was not an ordinary standing committee; assignment to it was not for an indefinite period but for no more than three congressional terms, each of which required caucus election at the start of a new Congress. Accordingly, Gramm's assignment to the Budget Committee could be treated as a more readily withdrawn award than could any other committee membership. At any rate, it was so treated by the party leaders, who recommended successfully that Gramm be dropped after only one term on the Budget Committee.[42] The case is too novel and its circumstances too special to suggest any trend toward greater party control of continuing committee assignments. To be sure, there is a mechanism for such control. Each congressional party's committee on committees includes the party's principal elected leaders and some of their appointees, along with elected or appointed representatives from regional and other groups within the congressional party. For House Democrats in particular that arrangement, adopted only in the 1970s, involves a deliberate attempt to strengthen the party leadership.[43] Previously, their committee on committees consisted of the Democratic members of the House Ways and Means Committee, whose seniority-based power and status could have insulated them from leadership influence in making committee assignments.

So far, however, the House Democratic leadership has used its new role in the committee on committees in ways that suggest considerable circumspection. Rather than trying, except rarely, to remove conservative Democrats from standing committee assignments, the party's committee on committees has merely followed a time-honored practice and added loyal Democratic representatives to certain important standing committees. It did so even in 1981, after the loss of Democratic seats in the 1980 election, by using the party's continuing though lessened majority to fix the ratio of Democrats to Republicans on Ways and Means, Appropriations, and Rules at a considerably more favorable level than the ratio of Democrats to Republicans in the whole House.[44] And in 1983, following the 26-seat Democratic gain in the 1982 election, the House majority leadership used the same means to counter the tendency of conservative Democrats to vote with Republicans on standing committees. In fact, nonconservative Democrats also overloaded certain subcommittees to give themselves real working majorities. The leading example is provided by the subcommittees of the powerful House Committee on Energy and Commerce. With 27 Democrats and 15 Republicans on the full committee—itself a slight Democratic disproportion relative to the ratio of Democrats to Republicans in the whole House—each of the six Energy and Commerce subcommittees had in 1983 just over twice as many Democrats as Republicans (9 to 4, 13 to 6, 11 to 5, or 7 to 3).[45] Relatively circumspect as such arrangements may be, in that they require no removal of a Democratic committee member and so no violation of seniority, they are nevertheless an exercise of collective power along party lines. The opportunity for party thus to influence policymaking, though indirectly, may be at least as significant as the more overt but exceptional use of power, by leadership or caucus, to depose a committee chairman.

Similarly, an opportunity for such influence flows from another set of legislative arrangements that are the business of congressional parties and particularly of majority congressional parties. Their leadership, in each house, customarily proposes the calendar for legislation to be taken up on the floor — what will be considered, how long it will be considered, and at what point in a session it will be considered. Although leadership proposals in these procedural matters are subject to majority acquiescence and to the counterpressure of certain strategically placed individual representatives or senators, they are nevertheless decisive often enough to command attention as prime examples of the centripetal force of party. Particularly is this the case in the House of Representatives, whose size does not permit the virtually unlimited debate accorded individual senators.

Unlike the Senate, where party leaders must depend most heavily on informal means for mobilizing consent to their arrangements for the conduct of legislative business, the House vests a formal control in its Rules Committee. This committee decides which bills will come to the floor, the time each will have there, and whether or not amendments can be proposed on the floor. Because it is a standing committee, observant of seniority customs, the House Rules Committee may not always be an instrument of the majority party's leadership. Indeed, it functioned with some independence for a few decades from the late 1930s, when its conservative Democratic chairman, supported by his Republican committee colleagues and some fellow Democrats, kept from the floor certain measures preferred by an apparent majority of Democratic representatives in the whole House. But the Democratic leadership asserted its influence in the early 1960s by loading the Rules Committee with new and less conservative Democratic members.[46] Since that time, the party leadership has further strengthened its hold on the committee by providing that its Democratic members should be appointed by the Speaker himself rather than through the usual committee-on-committees procedure.[47] Even without that provision, however, the Speaker's influence was usually great enough to make the Rules Committee an instrument of party leadership during most of the last 100 years. The decades between the late 1930s and the early 1960s now appear exceptional.

Moreover, in certain earlier years the Speaker was not merely influential but was almost completely dominant in determining the flow of House business. The high point was evidently just before and after the turn of the century, when in the House as well as the Senate majority-party control was more fully established than it was before or has been since.[48] Between 1890 and 1910, the Speaker exercised that control in the House. Called the czar, he appointed committee members and chairmen (often without respecting seniority), chaired and dominated the Rules Committee, and generally decided what could be done on the floor of the House. Overthrown by the already noted revolt of a majority of House members in 1910, the Speaker's czardom was briefly succeeded by party caucus control over House policymaking. Like the Speaker's dominance, such control depended on an unusually strong party spirit that soon ceased to characterize either house of Congress as it had between 1890 and 1915. In that quarter-century, congressional-party voting had reached levels higher than those of the earlier nineteenth century and considerably higher than those in most middle and later years of the twentieth century.[49]

Unusual as the period 1890–1915 seems in congressional history, it provides a substantial example of effective party roles in the American legislative system. No doubt these roles were then possible because of favorable electoral circumstances. Evidently each major party's elected members represented sufficiently similar constituency interests and opinions to facilitate relatively high cohesion in roll-call voting. Since 1915, such circumstances have recurred only for brief periods, notably in the mid-1930s, but their subsequent development is not inconceivable.

Even without the constituency bases of 1890–1915, the members of each congressional party have a substantial common interest in electoral success for themselves and for candidates seeking initial election under the same party label. Enough must win if members of their party are to enjoy the substantial advantages of majority status and enhanced opportunities to advance any shared policy preferences. The common interest of each party's congressional candidates is reflected in distinctive Republican and Democratic campaign models that may well develop from informal intraparty communication rather than from organizational efforts.[50] But significantly, each of the four congressional parties maintains its own campaign committee. Like other party committees with which they often collaborate, the congressional campaign committees are by no means dominant in the financing or the conduct of the candidate-centered efforts of representatives and senators. Their role is increasing, however, and each committee—National Republican Senatorial Committee, Democratic Senatorial Campaign Committee, National Republican Congressional Committee, and Democratic Congressional Campaign Committee—is a firmly established means for collecting and distributing funds to help elect and re-elect party members to a given chamber.[51]

Enjoying financial access to various Washington-based interest groups, the congressional and Senate campaign committees, especially the Republican Congressional Committee, have also succeeded since the mid-1970s in tapping many modest contributions by direct-mail solicitation. At the same time, they are less exclusively incumbent-protection clubs; more often lately they have also tried to help selected challengers as well as holders of marginal seats. And, in conformity with the post-Watergate ethics of campaign finance, their operations have been moved from government offices to private quarters. But each of the four campaign committees remains an arm of the particular House or Senate party. Committee members are themselves representatives or senators, chosen in one way or another by a party's several state delegations. Their chairmen are also representatives or senators who, while exercising considerable authority over staff and funds, are chosen by their party colleagues, either by all of them in full caucus or by those elected to the campaign committee. Each of the four campaign committee chairmen becomes effectively part of a congressional party's elected leadership. Like the rest of that leadership, the campaign committee chairmen may collaborate with the national party committee or with a particular president. But each House and Senate campaign committee retains the kind of autonomy that corresponds with that of a congressional party generally and with the independent authority of each house of Congress.

Along with the rest of the considerable party organizational apparatus in Congress, the House and Senate campaign committees suggest that party is a meaningful reference group for representatives and senators. No matter how much a member may find it useful electorally to play an independent or nonpartisan role in presenting himself or herself to constituents, he or she is a Republican or Democrat for many purposes in Washington. Even a good deal of social intercourse, a casual observer will notice, follows party lines. No doubt, the meaningfulness of party as a reference group varies among individuals. And it certainly varies from period to period as the strength of the organizational apparatus itself rises and falls in changing political circumstances. This is clearly the case with respect to the party caucus, whose occasional revival by junior House Democrats in the 1970s and 1980s encouraged intraparty discussions along with exceptional revolts against seniority.

IV
Policymaking Cohesion

Contrasting with my portrayal of a substantial congressional party organization continuing to exercise a meaningful though fluctuating authority in structural and procedural affairs, there is the now widely held perception that parties in Congress have declined as legislative policymakers. Put more precisely, it is thought that House and Senate parties are less cohesive on roll-call votes than they once were. Usually the decline is treated as a long-run phenomenon, interrupted only briefly here and there since early in this century, and more marked than ever by the 1970s. Hence our congressional parties, understood throughout this century as much less regularly cohesive policymakers than their British parliamentary counterparts,[52] strike many observers as even less likely at present to play the effective law-making roles they occasionally played in earlier periods. Even if one is more impressed (as I am) with the similarities of past and present congressional parties in this respect, and also with their ups and downs in response to changing issues and alignments, the evidence of long-run as well as recent decline cannot be ignored.

Most striking in terms of an historical trend is Burnham's tabulation of an "index of party dissimilarity" for the 100 years from 1873 to 1973. Using all nonunanimous House roll-call votes, the index simply measures the extent to which Democratic and Republican representatives are voting in opposition to each other. Clustering the century's Congresses into periods, Burnham finds the indices generally lower for the three decades after 1940 and sharply lower for the post-1965 Congresses. And he finds the 1969–70 Congress to have the lowest global difference between the two parties since the creation of the Republican party in the 1850s. On the other hand, Burnham's table shows that during his eight periods the high point of party dissimilarity was in the years 1895–1911 rather than earlier and that the index was higher in 1933–39 than it had been in 1883–93.[53] Thus the trend is not consistently one of decline, although the general direction is plain. Admittedly, as Burnham himself suggests, the measure is gross, in that it counts all nonunanimous roll calls without taking their relative importance into account. Other more familiar measures of congressional party voting are, however, similarly gross.

Most of these other measures, unlike Burnham's, relate only to the twentieth century.[54] For example, Keefe cites a study in which House "party votes" —votes in which 90 percent of the voting membership of one party opposed 90 percent of the voting members of the other party—declined from 17 percent in 1921–48 to about 6 or 7 percent between 1950 and 1967.[55] And Hinckley, relying on data based on the less severe and more usual definition of House party votes — in which a majority of one party opposes a majority of the other — notes that two-thirds of all roll calls were thus party votes early in the century, about one-half in the years after World War II, and under 40 percent for much of the 1970s. Although Hinckley's tabulation for individual Congresses displays a less steady decline, again the direction is unmistakable.[56] So it is even into the early 1980s. But does this decline indicate as great a drop in meaningful party policymaking as the numbers suggest? Fewer party votes, whether defined by the majority or the 90 percent criterion, may merely reflect an enlarged area of congressional business that, because of its consensual character or its low salience, is unlikely to produce partisan voting. In other words, the decline in party voting on all roll calls, or all nonunanimous roll calls, may be measuring a change in the nature of those roll calls rather than a change in the influence of party on matters of importance. Support for this suspicion is found in an analysis of "key votes" — about a dozen roll calls a year that *Congressional Quarterly* had judged to be most significant according to its published criteria. Over 39 years, 1945–83, party voting on these selected roll calls did not decline by any of three measures that the analyst employed. It even appeared to increase moderately in recent years, according to one measure, but generally to fluctuate considerably rather than to show a decided trend one way or the other.[57]

Even without concentrating on key votes, it is possible to point out another measure that demonstrates at least a less striking recent decline in party loyalty than the one previously cited. The measure is of the average percentage of party members voting with their congressional party on party roll calls (defined here as votes in which a majority of one party opposes a majority of the other party). Whereas about 80 percent of representatives (and senators too) voted with their parties on these party roll calls in most years during the late 1950s and early 1960s, the figure was closer to 75 percent in the late 1970s. But then it rose to 80 percent for Republicans in the House (in 1981 and 1983), to 85 percent for Republicans in the Senate (in 1981), and to 82 percent for House Democrats (in 1983).[58] Even if the 1981–83 increases are put aside, only a small decline appears over nearly three preceding decades in the tendency of party members to vote together in the still considerable (though diminished) percentage of roll calls classifiable as party votes. As scholarly observers of congressional behavior have often said, party remains the most important single cue for roll-call voting of representatives and senators. Never completely or invariably determining, as we know, congressional party membership is still meaningfully related to legislative policymaking, even though by some measures it appears less often operative than in times past. Similarity over time is more striking than change.

Congressional party voting is not now, and probably never was, explicable merely as a product of the authority of party leaders over other party members. The elaborate whip apparatus in the House is a means for persuasion but not control, and it may not always be used even to persuade. Accordingly, it is not surprising to learn from Kingdon's congressional interviews, in 1969–70, that only 10 percent of his sample spontaneously mentioned party leadership when asked about influences on roll-call voting. Many, of course, needed no persuasion to vote in agreement with party leaders. The influence of leadership, Kingdon also discovered, was hard to separate from the influence of ranking committee members, because party leaders tended to go along with the views of such members. Kingdon was impressed, as are most close observers of congressional behavior, with the persistence of party voting by most members most of the time.[59] He discerns an "intraparty compatriot feeling" that rests on constituency bases, distinguishing many members of each party from the opposition, and on considerable interaction among members of a given party.[60] For example, the large number of Democratic representatives from urban industrial districts occupy common ground vis-à-vis the large number of Republican representatives from middle-class suburban and relatively rural districts.

Such a difference can help to account for a considerable degree of party regularity on congressional roll calls, particularly on those involving labor and welfare issues. But not all Democrats, or all Republicans, are in fact from districts that fit the general characteristics. And even some of those from such districts may be responsive to diverse regional variations on issues like conservation and agriculture.[61] Hence the constituency bases for each party's total congressional membership can produce higher degrees of party voting on certain policies than on others.

The difference in party solidarity as between policy areas has been well documented. In studies of voting in the House and Senate first for 1953–64 and then for 1963–72, Clausen (and a co-author in the second study) finds substantially greater cohesion among both Democrats and Republicans on domestic economic policies than on issues concerning civil liberties or international involvement. Specifically, he first reports the greatest cohesion in the policy area labelled "government management," in which he includes issues of government ownership, regulation, spending for public works, distribution of tax burdens, and budget balancing. Particularly in the first decade of his analysis, voting on such issues reflected considerably greater solidarity of Democrats against Republicans than did voting in any of the other policy areas. By the second decade, party cohesion on government management votes had declined sufficiently so that it was not much above the fairly high cohesion also exhibited on social welfare policies.

Significantly, however, on both government management and social welfare, cohesion was still high — as it was on agricultural policy — compared with voting on civil liberties and international involvement.[62] Together, the domestic economic policy areas provided grounds for discerning a substantial ideological division between the two congressional parties. It overshadowed their internal differences in these areas. A similar division between Democrats and Republicans, particularly on government management questions, has been found in the Congresses of the 1930s.[63]

A majority party can thus be programmatically effective in at least some policy areas. It can be so although its cohesion is well short of unanimity — as indeed it has been even on government management issues. The usual and understandable test of effectiveness is the degree of success achieved by a majority party in enacting its policies. Obviously, success is possible despite defections of party members; a party majority may well be large enough so that 10 to 20 percent of its members are not needed for roll-call victories. A majority of that magnitude is by no means unknown in American congressional experience. When it exists in both houses for the same party and when that party also holds the presidency, the record shows substantial legislative success for policies identified with party.

The identification, it is true, ordinarily stems in this century from presidential initiative, approved and fostered by majority party leaders in the Congress. Accordingly, congressional majority parties scored their clearest successes when responding to President Wilson's leadership in 1913–15, to President Roosevelt's in 1933–35, and to President Johnson's in 1965–67.[64] These three periods have other common characteristics besides substantial Democratic party majorities in both houses along with a Democratic president. They followed resounding presidential election victories associated with sweeping congressional election victories that produced either a new majority or a newly enlarged majority for the president's party. On the Republican side, the elections of 1894 and 1896 produced similar conditions conducive to congressional party success.

A close study of the House of Representatives after the 1896 election and after the 1932 election shows a rise in party voting sufficient to support the view that critical realigning elections like those two "created the conditions for party government." Policy changes were then enacted by "cohesive, unified majority parties."[65] The same generalization may be applied to the Congresses that met after the elections of 1912 and 1964. In the House at least, the election results enabled a majority party to overcome the obstacles that diverse constituencies ordinarily place in the way of effective policymaking cohesion. The fact that congressional party success here is linked to presidential success as well as presidential initiative hardly diminishes its significance. On the contrary, the link is usually perceived as a vital component of effective party government.

In that perspective, a high level of congressional support for presidential recommendations is often a rough measure of party success. Thus from 1953 to 1984, the highest proportion of presidential victories on House and Senate roll-call votes, where presidents took clear-cut positions, was 93 percent in 1965 — the congressional session immediately after the landslide election of Lyndon Johnson and the election of large Democratic majorities in both houses. After 1965, the presidential success rate was below 80 percent (well below in several Nixon and Ford years) except for 1981, the first year of the Reagan presidency and a Republican Senate, when the figure was 82 percent.[66] The Reagan record, although achieved with a Democratic majority in the House, nevertheless reflected mainly his own party's support for the Administration's tax and spending program. Not only did members of the Senate's Republican majority (augmented, to be sure, by some Democrats) usually vote for the President's proposals, but so, on key roll calls, did almost all members of the large Republican minority in the House. The solidarity of House Republicans was as essential to Reagan's success in 1981 as were the votes of a few dozen conservative, mainly southern, Democrats on crucial roll calls. President Reagan's success rate declined to 72 percent in 1982 and to 66–67 percent in 1983 and 1984.[67] By 1983, no matter how solidly House Republicans might vote, they were not numerous enough, though joined by a few dozen conservative Democrats, to constitute a roll-call majority now that more liberal Democrats had won seats in the 1982 congressional election.

Obviously, a cohesive congressional party is not enough for actual enactment of presidentially sponsored or supported policies when the party bearing the same label as the president's is a minority in at least one house. It was strikingly insufficient for Republicans during all eight years under Nixon and Ford, when Democrats held majorities in both houses. Common though such divided government has become in recent decades, it has not led many critics to prize a noncohesive congressional majority party as a means for a president to secure sufficient support for his legislative program. Instead, as in earlier years, attention is focused on the effects of a noncohesive congressional majority when it shares a president's party label—as did the Democratic majority in each house during the Carter presidency.

For example, Everson has treated President Carter's major domestic proposal of 1977–78, the omnibus energy program, as a test case in the working of party government. House Democrats passed the test. Thanks to Speaker O'Neill's effective leadership, especially in using an Ad Hoc Select Energy Committee to coordinate aspects of the legislation and in obtaining party support for expeditious procedures, the energy bill that soon won House approval contained much though not all of what Carter had proposed. But Senate Democrats did not similarly operate as a cohesive majority under a well-defined leadership. The result, after Senate changes and an interhouse conference committee report, was finally, in 1978, a much less comprehensive enactment than Carter had proposed and than the House had originally passed.[68]

In retrospect, the energy program looks like a harsh test for party government. Although the Democratic majorities were substantial in both houses, they owed little or nothing to Carter's presidential victory. The majorities had been similarly substantial since the 1974 election, and few Democrats had any reason to think that they owed their congressional offices to presidential coattails, especially since Carter's victory was so narrow. Moreover, the energy program was not a conventional party issue, as New Deal issues had been in dividing Democrats from Republicans. Rather, the energy issue tended to produce regional cleavages cutting across party lines. Therefore, the Democratic party success in the House is more notable than the failure in the Senate. The latter would seem the more predictable event, given the general difficulties posed for party government in the American system and given also the historically more individualistic, less party-organized upper house.

At any rate, neither the energy bill nor any other legislative experience during the Carter presidency should inevitably lead to broad generalizations about a continuing decline of party policymaking in Congress. There is not even firm evidence that the Carter presidency, despite its reputation for increasingly poor relations with Congress, represented a peculiarly low point in majority party solidarity. Carter's own success rate, while well below the best years of Eisenhower, Kennedy, and Johnson, was about the same as that of Johnson's last three years, and it was better than that of Nixon, Ford, and later Eisenhower years, as well as that of Reagan in 1982, 1983, and 1984.[69] Furthermore, Democrats in the House and Senate voted with their party a little more often in the last year of Carter's presidency than they had in the last year of Johnson's.[70]

Consequently, congressional party cohesion in the Carter years looks much like that of the last several decades—limited but still very much in evidence. So too do the first few years of the Reagan Administration reflect roughly similar patterns, despite the upward thrust of Republican cohesion in 1981. After all, occasionally higher rates of cohesion have characteristically accompanied changes in party control of the White House and of congressional majorities. What happened following the 1980 election was but a modest and evidently short-lived version of larger party electoral victories in certain earlier years.

Although congressional roll-call behavior in the Carter and Reagan years is not sharply distinguishable from behavior in the preceding two decades, it may be that all of the last three or four decades of congressional history are special relative to earlier times. In this perspective, each congressional party has, since the late 1930s, appeared so divided between liberals and conservatives as to have made cohesive party policymaking even harder to achieve than it had been historically. The Republican division, between a larger number of conservatives and a smaller number of liberals, has received less attention than the Democratic division, between a larger number of liberals and a smaller number of conservatives, perhaps because the Republicans have been the minority party in both houses during much of the last half-century and so ordinarily less directly consequential in any effort to achieve party government. Yet it is worth noticing that in recent decades Republican representatives and senators have not voted with their party much more often than Democrats have with theirs.[71] Whether the shift to conservatism discernible in Republican ranks in the early 1980s will reduce that intraparty ideological division remains uncertain.

Regardless of the significance of the Republican division, there is no doubt about the long-term difference between liberals and conservatives in Democratic congressional parties. The difference is largely though not entirely between northern and southern Democrats, and it is crucial in understanding the frequent inability of Democratic majorities to enact party programs. The Democratic party, while almost always a majority for purposes of organizing each house, has often lacked a party majority willing to vote for many liberal domestic policies. Only after an unusual Democratic landslide, as in 1964, have northern liberal Democrats been numerous enough to constitute a congressional majority without southern conservative support. Accordingly, for over 40 years it has been well understood that on many issues there is a dominant conservative coalition of most Republicans and most southern Democrats.[72] The coalition thus defined has waxed and waned in the last few decades, but in the years between 1957 and 1983, it appeared—that is, a majority of Republicans voted with a majority of southern Democrats—on from 11 to 30 percent of all roll calls in the House and on 11 to 32 percent of all roll calls in the Senate. So, too, have coalition *victories* varied by particular Congresses. In the House, the coalition won 32 percent of the times that it appeared in 1966 but 91 percent in 1959; and in the Senate it won 39 percent of the times that it appeared in 1965 but 100 percent in 1957. In a more nearly typical year, the coalition in each house appeared about a quarter of the time and won about two-thirds of the times that it appeared.[73]

Since conservative coalition appearances and victories occur on some of the most important domestic policy questions in Congress, a weakening of the coalition must occur if party cohesion, notably Democratic party cohesion, is to increase. Its weakening has been suggested whenever liberal Democrats are elected in increased numbers, mainly from the North but occasionally from the South too, and especially whenever conservative Democrats are replaced by conservative Republicans in southern seats. Already the results are evident in diminished southern influence in the House Democratic caucus. Simultaneously, southerners have become more important to the Republican party in Congress, reflecting the fact that by the early 1980s half of the southern senators and about one-third of the southern representatives were Republican.[74] The numbers contrast sharply with those of 1960, when no southern Republicans were elected to the Senate and only seven were elected to the House. It is hazardous to project the 25-year shift into the future; it would suggest a continuing party realignment in which each major party in Congress becomes, more than at almost any time in its history, an ideologically defined body of elected officials.[75] If that should soon occur, in even a nonrigid fashion, we might well look back on the last several decades as a kind of transition period between the fairly cohesive parties of the earlier twentieth century and a newly established cohesiveness at the end of the century. There might then be a much greater likelihood of an effective Democratic congressional majority, even without overwhelming numbers, and also a greater likelihood of an effective Republican congressional party, if only because its chances for majority status would have increased as it won more southern conservative Democratic seats.

Of course, to be meaningful for legislative policymaking, congressional party majorities would have to appear in both houses and also coincide with the election of a president bearing the congressional majority's party label. Realignment theory rests on that expectation—explicitly on a restoration of a close tie between presidential and congressional elections that would be both a cause and effect of greater policymaking cohesion of congressional parties.

V
A Less Partisan Electoral Base?

A diametrically different future for the congressional party is suggested by studies of congressional elections that stress their increasingly candidate-centered character. The now-familiar thesis of many of these studies is that representatives as well as senators have come to depend more heavily on their own individual efforts, not on the party's or even so much as formerly on the party label, for election and reelection. Their congressional behavior then reflects this change by becoming less responsive to party cues than to personal and constituency-related interests, and perhaps to special interest groups that help to finance campaigns. Associated with such behavior is the depiction of Congress as more decentralized, even fragmented, by the greater power of subcommittees and of more fully staffed, well-informed members. But the essence of the argument is that members of Congress have become, and are further becoming, more independent of party because their electoral base is less partisan than it once was. They are all still Republicans or Democrats, belonging for certain important purposes to the substantial congressional party organizations described earlier, but their party membership is thought to be of diminishing consequence. Even the congressional party campaign committee, so plainly designed to help members gain and hold office, is perceived as but one of several sources of electoral support and by no means the greatest, despite its recent growth.

The thesis of increasingly candidate-centered congressional elections does not exclude the likelihood that the party label still accounts for many, perhaps for most, of each congressional candidate's votes in a general election. But, as I stressed earlier, the label is seldom bestowed by a party organization of any kind. It was, of course, so bestowed before the direct primary, but by a state, district, or other local organization in the absence historically of national party control of the congressional nominating process. The non-national party organizations did not necessarily lose all of their influence or control over nominations as soon as the direct primary was adopted early in this century. Their roles in many places (though not in all) appear to have diminished most sharply only during the last few decades.

Lately, at any rate, most successful congressional candidates, like candidates for almost all other offices in the United States, secure party nominations by running candidate-centered campaigns in direct primaries.[76] For that purpose they have their own staffs, their own campaign funds, their own volunteers, and their own advertising. Then in general elections, while materially benefiting from a party label (particularly the majority party's label), candidates tend to conduct a similarly candidate-centered campaign in order to attract a crucial number of voters who do not cast ballots strictly by party label. In short, representatives and senators, never merely party candidates, have become less fully partisan. It is therefore thought that representatives and senators may less often act in Congress as party members. They are expected to find it useful as well as personally satisfying to establish records appealing to their constituents, although that might mean voting, in legislative roll calls, against most of their congressional party colleagues and leaders.

To be sure, limited cohesion is a characteristic long familiar in our history and readily attributable, as noted earlier, to various distinctively American institutional arrangements. But lately, it has also been observed, cohesion may have become still more limited. Insofar as that has been the case — and some measures, I grant, do support the declining cohesion thesis — it is often connected to the development of a less partisan electoral base for congressional elections. Such a development, suggesting long-term and perhaps permanent effects of candidate-centered politics on congressional parties, deserves close examination.

An analytical difficulty arises, however. We cannot assume that a decline in partisan voting for Congress is a decline in *national* partisan voting. The latter, as noted earlier in this chapter, has never been regarded as characteristic of American congressional elections relative to parliamentary elections elsewhere. In the past, many voters could well have been casting party ballots for essentially state and local reasons that were not any more clearly conducive to congressional party unity than the individual preferences thought to be now at work. Historically, American congressional elections have been heavily affected by constituency forces; the point is persuasively made in a sophisticated quantitative comparison with British parliamentary elections. National forces in the United States are shown to have long accounted for a considerably smaller share of the variance in party success from election to election than in Britain. The author of the study, Donald Stokes, also shows that American constituency forces, while declining relative to national forces over almost a century, remained considerably stronger than the British when the study was made in the 1960s.[77]

Stokes's statistical demonstration confirms certain conventional impressions. For example, Herring wrote in 1940 that most members of Congress were "not beholden to a national party machine" and that their "political lives depend upon the loyalty of one Congressional district or, in the case of senators, upon a single state."[78] And Ripley, a contemporary authority on Congress, summarizes the nature of House and Senate elections in terms at least as applicable to the past as to the 1970s and 1980s that he is writing about. These elections, Ripley states, *"are local events with national consequences and (sometimes) are influenced by national events."*[79]

The traditional nature of congressional elections may not have been made much more local by the advent of the direct primary. The candidate-centered nature of a primary nomination contest does not mean that local, rather than national, considerations play any larger part in determining the result. The old state, county, and city organizations, particularly those party machines thought to have bestowed congressional nominations, were hardly branches of a national party or necessarily responsive to it in selecting candidates. Local party organizations had, in their way, constituency-oriented interests as strong as those of today's individual candidates. It is no wonder that 40 years ago the leading champion of more cohesive congressional parties wanted to *reduce* the power of the local bosses.[80]

By no means, however, has the reduction of the power led to more nationally partisan voting in recent congressional elections. Most familiar is the fact that the House of Representatives, in particular, did not become Republican in 1972, 1980, or 1984 despite Republican presidential victories—indeed, despite landslide presidential victories in 1972 and 1984. On the other hand, even the moderate Republican presidential victory of 1980 was accompanied by fairly large Republican gains in the House as well as by an actual Republican majority in the Senate. And the Reagan reelection of 1984 coincided with modest Republican gains in the House (and larger gains in *votes* for Republican candidates). Moreover, as recently as 1964 a Democratic presidential victory coincided with a substantial increase in an already large Democratic House majority.[81] Yet there can be no doubt that greater resistance to party turnover of House seats has appeared in the last few decades than at certain earlier times.[82]

The continuous Democratic majority in the House for three decades since 1954 is itself a new phenomenon. So too is the frequency of divided government —a president of one party and at least one house of Congress held by the other party.[83] Not only is such divided government itself incompatible with party government, but the related absence of large-scale partisan turnover of congressional seats may also make party government more difficult to achieve. It has been shown that newly elected representatives, replacing members of the other party, provide the strongest support for policy changes and for congressional party positions.[84] Hence if congressional election landslides, even moderate landslides, have become less likely, the chances for effective party government may also have receded. And a case for the diminished likelihood of such landslides appears in the record of the last three decades. Never in the congressional election years from 1954 through 1984 did either the Republicans or Democrats score a net gain of as many as 50 House seats. And there was a net gain over 40 only three times. By contrast, one party or the other scored net gains of 56 in 1910; 63 in 1912; 69 in 1914; 61 in 1920; 74 in 1922; 53 in 1930; 90 in 1932; 75 in 1938; and 75 in 1948.[85]

A greater resistance to partisan election turnover in House membership is evident,[86] and it is widely treated as a result of a recently enhanced will and capacity of incumbents to win reelection. From the 1950s through 1984, the success rate for incumbent representatives seeking reelection has never dropped below 86 percent; it was below 90 percent in only four of 18 elections (1950–84), and it was over 95 percent on three occasions. These calculations take primaries as well as general elections into account; since some incumbents (though a lesser number) lose primary elections, the success rate for incumbents standing in general elections is slightly higher than the percentages cited. Either way, the record of incumbents is imposing. It is still more so when one realizes that between 1950 and 1984 the overwhelming majority of the 435 House members did stand for reelection in any given year—no fewer than 382 (in 1978) and as many as 411 (in 1956, 1966, and 1984).[87] The 25 to 50 voluntarily leaving the House each year would over a few decades bring about a nearly complete turnover of members, but that number does not at any one election provide many of the open seats often assumed to be relatively advantageous for opposition party candidates.[88]

The recent remarkable reelection rate of House incumbents is not so regularly paralleled in the Senate. It is true that in 1984 only three senators lost, among 29 seeking reelection, only two among 30 in 1982, and only one among 29 in 1960. But otherwise, between 1950 and 1984, the senatorial success rate was never as high as 90 percent. It was often in the 70 to 85 percent range, and it was at 64 percent, 60 percent, and 55 percent in the successive elections of 1976, 1978, and 1980.[89] Accordingly, it is only for the House that incumbency advantages might materially account for the absence of a once-greater partisan turnover. This is not to say that Senate elections are less candidate centered than House elections. They may even be more candidate centered, now as well as historically, but less advantageous for incumbents, because Senate challengers are more likely than House challengers to mount effective personal as well as partisan campaigns.

Distinctive though the House electoral situation may be, it is plainly important that incumbents in the designedly more popular chamber have become increasingly likely to be reelected. The likelihood is established not merely by high incumbency success rates but also by an increase in the number of seats won by large margins. The increase was especially sharp between 1956 and 1972, but a slower rise had occurred for over a century.[90] Resulting in what were called the "vanishing marginals" in the 1970s, the development is readily measured in terms of the proportion of House incumbents winning by at least 60 percent of the vote. That proportion, about three-fifths in 1956, 1958, and 1960, rose to the range of two-thirds to three-quarters in elections from 1968 to 1982.[91]

It may be observed that even a 60 percent margin in a given election, or a series of previous elections, will not always assure a representative of subsequent reelection. Apart from vicissitudes of redistricting, an incumbent may have good reason to fear a subsequent challenge from a new, younger, more vigorous, and better financed candidate bearing the label of the opposition party. Conceivably, too, that opponent might, in a given year, benefit from a more than usually favorable perception of the opposition party label. But it is not expected that a strictly partisan electoral swing would alone be enough to defeat a House incumbent who at the last previous election had a 60 percent margin. A strong candidate-centered campaign, as well as a partisan campaign, appears essential.[92]

Tempting though it is to think of the increased safety of incumbent representatives as a permanent condition, we cannot be certain that the recent success rates, fortified by large margins of victory, should be projected for subsequent decades. Caution is suggested by the different Senate experience and by the greater (if not entirely successful) Republican *party* effort in House elections beginning in 1978. But insofar as there is a case for a continuing and perhaps increasingly high incumbent-success rate in House elections, it would rest on a belief that certain now firmly established political conditions are responsible for the high success rate of the last few decades. One of these conditions is a less fully partisan electorate. The percentage of voters identifying themselves as Republicans or Democrats has declined, and the percentage of party identifiers who are so intensely partisan as to vote straight Republican or Democratic tickets has also declined. These declines, whose measurement and meaning are more fully and skeptically examined in a later chapter, are broadly relevant here, insofar as they indicate that a larger portion of the electorate is open to individual candidate appeals. Admittedly, such openness may itself be but a temporary circumstance preceding a period of party realignment, but it unquestionably increased after the mid-1960s. It thus coincides with the growth of House incumbents' reelection success so as to suggest a connection.

The nature of the connection is the subject of considerable scholarly inquiry. For example, Mann and Wolfinger analyze 1978 congressional election data and show not only that Independent voters cast ballots much more heavily for House incumbents than for challengers, but more significantly (because of larger numbers), that voters identifying with the challenger's party cast ballots slightly more often for the House candidate of the *opposition* party than for their own party's candidate when the opposition party's candidate was the incumbent. The study also shows that the frequency of all defections by party identifiers, in House elections, rose steadily from only 9 percent of all voters in 1956 to 22 percent in 1978. This demonstrated rise in non-party-line voting reflects, Mann and Wolfinger state, "the greater ability of incumbents to attract votes from people who identify with the other party."[93] That more such voters are thus attracted across party lines might look merely like a diminished intensity of partisan identification. But because identifiers with the incumbent's party show no clear defection like that of identifiers with the challenger's party, it is reasonable to follow Hinckley in attributing defections in House elections to the influence of incumbency.[94]

In contrast to most challengers for House seats, incumbents are shown, from sample survey data, to be both well known and highly regarded by voters. The advantage is a familiar one in congressional studies of the last decade, and it is often linked to the greater opportunity that members of Congress have—and their greater eagerness to use such opportunity—to advertise themselves, to take credit for popular policies, and to perform constituency services.[95] Senators too, it is acknowledged, have this opportunity, similarly increased by the growth of governmental programs and by larger congressional office staffs, but they are thought not to have benefited electorally because of their longer terms, their larger constituencies, or the greater likelihood of a well-known and well-regarded opponent in a statewide contest.[96]

The last of these explanations of the Senate-House difference in recent re-election successes is consistent with the view that the House incumbents' advantage is not invariable despite its prevalence in the last decade or two. The advantage can be linked to weak opposition, and especially to underfunded opposition. Indeed, Mann and Wolfinger believe that "House incumbents benefit more from the scarcity of serious challenges than from the perquisites of office."[97] And support for their belief is found in the occasional victories won by strenuous campaigns in behalf of well-publicized, popular challengers for House seats. It is at least possible that more such strong challengers and so more victories over incumbents will appear, especially as the Republican party devotes more resources to winning enough Democratic seats to end its long

minority status in the House. The large-scale development of the National
Republican Congressional Committee for this purpose is conspicuous.

By no means, however, should the House incumbent's advantages be treated
as of little consequence now or for the future. Because those advantages are
unlikely to erode through diminution of officeholding perquisites, challengers
need greatly enhanced resources to win, even when there is some partisan
swing in favor of their party. They must overcome not only partisan voting
for incumbents but also the government-provided staff, budget, computer services, and franking privileges that enable members, in the words of one practitioner, "to create their own personal political parties able to manage every-
thing from precinct canvassing to ward heeling."[98] Such personal "parties"
are organizations designed primarily for reelection campaigns. They often involve highly developed "district outreach" programs in which incumbents and
their home-office staffs maintain regular relations with as many constituents
as possible. Although these intensive efforts may not always be sufficient to
enable a representative to hold a closely contested district, they have been successfully adopted particularly in districts originally won by small margins.

Even in nonmarginal districts, much congressional time and energy are devoted to constituency relations. "Home style" has been carefully described by
Fenno for 18 representatives whose activities he observed in the early 1970s.
His account of the volume of constituency activity is itself impressive, and
so is his emphasis on the candidate-centered nature of the activity. Only a
minority of the 18 maintained an integrated working relationship with a local
party organization or campaigned loyally for a party ticket, and even they,
like the others, were also "in business for themselves."[99]

An increasingly intense constituency cultivation, while designed, with evident success, to make for incumbent safety, may also be perceived as an indica-
tion that without such personal cultivation an incumbent would be unsafe.
The intense cultivation may even have become a virtual necessity in many districts where strong partisan challenges could be mounted against an incumbent who spends too much time in Washington. The need to pursue time-
consuming, year-round individual campaign-style activities, it has been suggested, causes some members to retire altogether—leaving congressional politics more fully to those willing and able to maintain close constituency relations (which, after all, consume the time of representatives as well as of their
staffs) and to pursue biennially the now-large campaign funds often required.[100]

None of this discussion means that it is an entirely new phenomenon for
members of Congress to be in political business for themselves. Although in
the past the party label could automatically have produced more votes than
it does now, many candidates have long had only limited party organizational

links. State and local parties have not in this century played important roles everywhere, and national party organizations were in earlier years of less importance in congressional campaigns than they have lately become. What has changed is the scale of candidate-centered campaign activity. No doubt even that kind of change makes congressional elections less fully partisan contests. But it is hardly certain that the electoral base is thus transformed so as to reduce substantially the traditionally limited but still meaningful response of members to their congressional party ties.

VI
Resilience

As my skepticism over the long-run impact of candidate-centered congressional campaigns suggests, parties still impress me as durable means for organizing and conducting congressional business. Their presence seems nearly as consequential — which is to say important, but limited — as it has usually been over the course of U.S. history, and their decline less clear than their fluctuation in power from period to period. Thus I reiterate the durability theme with which I began the chapter, and add to it an emphasis on the resilience that congressional parties have displayed in the changed and in some respects more difficult circumstances of the late twentieth century. Operating as always within institutions that are less conducive to legislative party unity than is a parliamentary system like Britain's, American congressional parties have in recent decades faced an evidently less partisan electorate, an increased decentralization of congressional authority (following from greater and more specialized legislative business), the growing professionalism of individual members in both legislative and constituency services, and complex issues on which cleavages do not readily correspond with established partisan divisions.

At times, it is true, congressional parties have not responded to these new circumstances effectively to counter tendencies to fragmentation of legislative authority. But, as Ripley wisely observes in his scholarly text, "fragmentation within the institution is a more 'natural' state of affairs in Congress than integration, although it is not inevitable." Parties remain, as he points out, "major potential integrating forces."[101] Without them, I would stress, it is hard to see how fragmentation could be effectively countered in the United States or elsewhere. It is worth repeating that neither in the Congress nor in the national legislature of any other democratic nation is there any substantial experience without parties.

The need for parties, I realize, does not ensure their meaningful existence.

American circumstances might conceivably become so unpropitious that congressional parties, unable to cope with them, would wither away. So far, however, the experience of the last few decades does not suggest a withering away. On the contrary, congressional parties enlarged and strengthened their organizational apparatus and leadership in the 1970s. House Democrats did so most notably, even as they simultaneously decentralized authority by increasing the power of subcommittees and their chairmen. One might even view the Democratic party effort as a response to the House's greater decentralization—that is, as an integrating step made all the more desirable because of the increased number of power centers that the new Congress now established. Similarly, one might perceive the expanding activity of congressional party campaign committees as a response to a more candidate-centered campaigning that threatens to erode further the partisan electoral base for congressional election. At the least, these are significant vital signs of congressional party life. So too is the revival in the late 1970s and early 1980s of the Republican party as a genuinely competitive force in the House and Senate. Congressional parties may have looked especially limited in the 1970s because of the long Democratic ascendancy.

Yet nothing about the very recent organizational responses of congressional parties points toward an early or even an eventual transformation of the conventionally limited governing capacity of these parties. Just as one should not overstate their decline, so one should not readily infer the beginning of a much more cohesive party policymaking than has characterized the U.S. Congress during most of its history. It is realistic to expect in the near future as in the past that congressional parties, while employing new organizational means, will as a rule exert power for but limited purposes and only occasionally, in favorable political circumstances, to accomplish broad policymaking results. No more is likely, given the fixed institutional context and the kind of Congress that has developed within that context. As always, each congressional party is bound to tolerate considerable diversity in its ranks if it is to remain one of only two dominant parties. Democrats and Republicans in Congress have good reason, as well as the institutionally based opportunity, to maintain a doctrinal and disciplinary looseness not often found in parliamentary parties elsewhere. By thus reflecting the porousness or permeability of American parties generally, the two congressional parties are able still to play their customary roles.

Chapter Four
Presidential Focus

The constitutional provision for a separately elected, politically powerful chief executive has led to a party development even more distinctly American than our congressional parties. The latter, while differing significantly from more cohesive legislative parties under executive leadership in less independently strong parliaments, nevertheless have familiar counterparts in those systems. By contrast, the presidential (and gubernatorial) focus for party has no counterpart in a parliamentary system whose chief working executive is the product of legislative elections.

Among European democracies, few deviate from the parliamentary tradition to provide anything like the American presidency's focus for electoral mobilization around a separately powerful office. The French Fifth Republic has a popularly elected, politically powerful president, and Finland has a popularly based president who exercises power in foreign affairs despite an otherwise dominant parliamentary leadership. Certain aspects of French experience in the last two decades can be compared with the American presidency, but neither it nor the Finnish experience is a firmly established product of a constitutional separation of powers. Indeed, the French president appears, in the first quarter-century of the Fifth Republic, to have dominated the legislative majority to a degree largely unfamiliar in the United States. Elsewhere, though constitutional provisions exist for the separation of powers (as in Latin America), experience with the arrangement is seldom continuous and substantial enough to make for ready comparison with the United States. It is therefore reasonable as well as customary to treat the American presidency as distinctive in contrast to the more widely established parliamentary based executive.

I want, however, to make most explicit a particular feature of the presidency that may not always be apparent in the usual contrast with parliamentary regimes. It is the ambiguity of an office whose conception was originally nonpartisan and whose development retained its nonpartisan attributes even after the emergence of partisan election and partisan leadership. *Nonpartisan* refers not merely to ceremonial roles, like those of a twentieth-century British monarch. The American president does have those ceremonial roles, thus combining, it is often said, the two British positions of monarch and prime minister. But the president is also expected to be nonpartisan even in the exercise of certain powers, or of powers in certain areas (notably but not only defense and foreign affairs). No doubt a British prime minister responds to similar expectations, but compared with the partisan role, they do not bulk as large as they do for an American president. And of course a British monarch, while surely meant to be nonpartisan, is not expected to wield much power of any kind.

The ambiguity of the president's position is so important for party development that I concentrate on it in the historical review that follows. Nonpartisan attributes of the office have always, it will be seen, complicated but hardly prevented the use of the presidency as a focus for party. Hence the first section of this chapter is an essential prelude to analyses of nomination, election, and governing, each of which considers the significance of recent changes, mostly in the nominating process. My theme is that these changes, along with other twentieth-century influences, have reduced certain conventional party linkages, but that their reduction is neither entirely novel in American experience nor devastating in long-run consequence. New linkages may be emerging, and these may be as compatible with the nature of the presidential office as were the older party ties.

I

Elected Monarch and Party Leader

Seeking an alternative to hereditary executive authority, the late-eighteenth-century statesmen who wrote the U.S. Constitution invented a president who would be a powerful elected monarch.[1] As the rejected British king was supposed to have done, the American president would represent national and nonpartisan interests rather than more particular and factional interests inevitably appearing in legislative bodies. A public-spirited president could thus be an important element in a constitutional system meant to limit the influence of factions. To that end, the founders gave the president substantial powers, alongside those of Congress, and stipulated that neither the president nor others in the executive branch could also be members of Congress.

Providing the president with a separate electoral base from that of Congress was more difficult. Direct popular election, which now seems the straightforward method, was in fact seriously proposed at the constitutional convention of 1787. Understandably, however, it was put aside at least partly because of the practical difficulty of conducting such an election when suffrage requirements differed from state to state, and perhaps also because of aristocratic objections to the direct popular election of so powerful an officer.[2] Not all of the founders, as we know, had unlimited faith in the judgment of the masses. Even those who favored direct popular election, it is reasonable to believe, were not thinking of vote-seeking campaigns in behalf of popular leadership.[3] Nor of course were they thinking of partisan candidates, the very phenomena they sought to avoid in their elective monarchy.

The presidential-election method actually adopted at the constitutional convention did serve, though imperfectly, a principal intention of the founders. The electoral college, consisting of electors appointed by each state in a manner determined by its own legislators, represented the nation, however indirectly, and its base was thus distinct from that of Congress. The Constitution explicitly excludes members of Congress, along with other national officeholders, from service as electors. Only if the electoral college produces no majority winner is Congress called upon to decide among leading presidential candidates. That troubling deviation from the separation-of-powers doctrine had originally seemed likely to arise, but it has not occurred since 1824.[4] We readily recognize that an electoral college majority is a nearly certain product of the two-candidate competition that our major parties ordinarily, if not quite uniformly, provided after 1840. It is therefore ironic that the conversion of presidential elections into partisan contests, surely unwanted as well as unintended by the founders, turned out to help maintain the separation-of-powers doctrine to which the founders were committed.

Before looking more closely at the role of parties in presidential elections, the democratization of those elections should be stressed. For it is in connection with the democratization that parties developed. By the early decades of the nineteenth century, the president was for practical purposes elected by popular vote. In 1800 prospective electors were already committed to particular presidential candidates, and by 1832 the electors in all but one state were chosen by the state's enfranchised voters.[5] In effect, then, citizens voted for president while voting for electors. To be sure, their votes, then as now, took formal effect with less than full arithmetic equality in the electoral college, but the idea that the electors, as a small, experienced, and knowledgeable group, should exercise their own judgment in selecting a president had not prevailed for long. Perhaps that idea had not been firmly fixed even when the electoral college was established. Many of the founders preferred direct popular election, and others apparently assumed that electors would include in their judgments an awareness of the public acceptability of presidential possibilities. The widely expected first presidential choice, George Washington, appealed as much to ordinary citizens as to leading citizens likely to be electors. Washington, in fact, was so fully the model elected monarch that one suspects that the founders developed the office with him in mind. He was respected as well as famous, and his great reputation rested on neither partisan identification nor demagogically suspect popularity.

Only Washington, and perhaps only at the start of his presidency, may have clearly fulfilled the elected monarch model, but the nonpartisan intention of the founders retained a residual force during almost two centuries of apparently partisan presidential elections. Although bearing a party label, the president has increasingly in this century championed domestic as well as foreign policies by appealing generally to citizens rather than merely to partisans. Through most of American history, the nonpartisan potential of the office has been used to mobilize support in elections, particularly in wartime as it was by Lincoln and his Union ticket of 1864. It has been used in governing to seek approval for emergency domestic programs, and more than ever in the last few decades, for foreign policies and defense expenditures. Thus the elected monarchy of the founders endures and prospers.

De facto popular election of the president, it should be evident, is not in itself incompatible with the nonpartisan elected monarchy conception of the founders. Whatever their reasons for rejecting such election in the first place, they could well understand how, in a democratic age, only popular election confers sufficient legitimacy for the exercise of executive power. But to suit the founders, a president would have to be popularly elected as Washington could have been, without party as well as without personal demagogy (or even personal campaigning). In practice, our presidential elections have not met those standards. Historically, parties have played major if not completely dominant roles in the election of most American presidents. I have suggested that at most, the founders' nonpartisan ideal has significantly coexisted with long-standing partisan elections.

Perhaps as early as the contests between Adams and Jefferson in 1796 and 1800 but more clearly by 1840, presidential candidates and their electoral slates were identified with parties under whose labels they sought office.[6] Moreover, these parties were to a large extent mobilized nationally in order to compete for the presidency. Paradoxically, then, the very office meant to be nonpartisan is primarily responsible for the existence of national parties as well as for their special nature. This is not to say that we would have had no national parties without an elected presidency. They might well have developed, as have national parties in parliamentary systems, to compete for the executive power that would, in the absence of a separately elected chief executive, be based on congressional majorities. In that highly imaginary circumstance, congressional parties could have linked their campaign committees to state party organizations, under a common label, and then built federated organizations designed to bring their leaders to national power. Perhaps the results would have been an extracongressional party organization as continuous and durable as the actual congressional parties have been, and accordingly, more like extraparliamentary parties in Britain. Whatever the results, however, they would almost certainly differ markedly from the national parties that have in fact developed to seek the presidency.

The way in which national parties were established around the presidential office is clearly and convincingly presented in Richard McCormick's analysis of the Whig-Democratic competition that had established itself by 1840.[7] Unlike the first party system in which Jeffersonians won the presidency from Federalists, that which developed between 1824 and 1840 was not closely tied to congressional divisions. Neither did it disintegrate into a one-party or no-party pattern, as had the first system, when one of its parties virtually disappeared. Rather, the Whig-Democratic competition was replaced, after a brief transition, by the familiar Republican-Democratic alignment. Moreover, the system of 1840 is more relevantly modern than that of 1800 in the crucial sense that popular election of presidential electors had become the standard practice by 1840 whereas only a small minority of states were using this system in 1800.

In short, the development of national parties between 1824 and 1840 was the kind of response to the democratized American constitutional structure that would remain characteristic after the Republicans replaced the Whigs. The nature of that response is well stated in McCormick's summary of the theme of his book: ". . . the second American party system had its origins in the successive contests for the presidency between 1824 and 1840. It did not emerge from cleavages within Congress, nor from any polarization of attitudes on specific public issues, nor did it represent merely the revival in new form of preexisting party alignments. The second party system did not spring into existence at any one time. Rather, new party alignments appeared at different times from region to region."[8] Significantly, as McCormick explains, these new party alignments tended at first to be national—that is, largely presidential. Especially in the then new states, there were for a time no clear counterparts in state politics. State elections often remained nonpartisan for some years after the presidential contests had become partisan.[9] Although by the 1840s Whigs and Democrats competed for state as well as national offices almost everywhere, the fact that the national party alignment preceded the state party alignment tells us a good deal about the special significance of presidential politics.

That an American national electoral party should have developed primarily around the presidency rather than Congress is understandable even in a comparative context. Not only is the presidency (with the vice-presidency) our only elected national office, but it is also the rough equivalent of the kind of executive power that parties in a parliamentary system organize to seek when they focus around legislative elections. Thus it is not the purpose of our principal national parties that distinguishes them from parties in parliamentary nations. Executive power is sought as clearly in the one case as in the other. It is the kind of party that results from the presidential focus that is necessarily distinctive, if only because it is separable from legislative party success or failure. To call the following produced by the presidential focus a presidential party can be confusing. The term tends now to mean more than merely the national party committee originally created as a confederation of state party organizations to contest presidential elections. The presidential following that looks like a party is at least partly personal—attracted by an individual candidate (and president) or perhaps by a succession of individuals of a similar character, ideological or otherwise. As such, it is by no means an entirely new phenomenon in American politics; the party of Jefferson and the party of Lincoln are familiar landmarks. But the relative importance of a personal presidential following has lately increased as parties in certain other senses have apparently diminished.

It may be granted that *presidential party*, apart from the national party committee, is more nearly a figure of speech than is *congressional party*. When referring only to the following of a particular president, or of a particular presidential candidate during an election campaign, it applies to a transitory organization lasting no longer than eight years or often no longer than several months. Yet however unlike the remarkably durable congressional parties, at least one recognizable presidential following always exists. It is readily distinguishable from parties bearing the same label in Congress or elsewhere.

Most individuals in the president's following also belong to a party in a non-presidential sense, as does the president himself, but the overlapping membership does not reduce the salience of the presidential entity. For the president's adherents, it is the significant "party" — as long as it lasts. To be sure, it does not last long, except amorphously, for a losing candidate or a retiring president. Ordinarily, for about three of every four years no single or clear-cut presidential opposition party exists to face the incumbent president's party.

Despite the absence, especially on the opposition side, of a well-defined presidential following, one might perceive a kind of continuous presidential "party" among the adherents of previous candidates — be they FDR Democrats after 1945, Stevenson Democrats throughout the 1950s, or Reagan Republicans after 1976.[10] Accordingly, from a study of campaign organizations in 1972, John Kessel concluded that "a presidential party at any time is a residue of its past campaigns."[11] He reports that very large percentages of activist workers for McGovern as well as for Nixon had begun their presidential campaign involvement in previous elections by supporting other candidates of roughly similar ideological persuasion. For example, Democrats first attracted by John F. Kennedy often remained to rally behind McGovern, and Republicans first attracted by Eisenhower later supported Nixon. To be sure, they were also Republicans or Democrats in the more conventional party sense. But they had become active, and perhaps also more fully identified as Republicans or Democrats, by enlisting in a particular presidential candidate's campaign. Partly because Kessel sees these adherents as attracted by issue advocacies,[12] he unabashedly uses the term *presidential party* without the quotation marks that qualify it. And he thus treats the phenomenon as something more enduring than an ad hoc candidate-centered coalition. With a little hesitation, I am inclined to do likewise, even though *party* here refers to a following of activists rather than to larger numbers of voters.

At any rate, the presidential party is a more coherent *national* phenomenon than is any other kind of American party. Congressional parties are national too, but each is so diverse, given the considerable independence of its members in relating to their separate constituencies, that it unites only for limited purposes. Even a transient presidential party, on the other hand, exists to elect or reelect an individual to our one elected national office, and if electorally successful, to help carry out that individual's policies. The following may sometimes be more highly personal than ideological or programmatic, but it is focused on national purposes, electorally and governmentally.

What of presidential relations with the well-known national party organizations, the Republican and the Democratic national committees? Although often loosely structured, they have had a continuity, like that of the congressional parties, that no particular presidential party can match. Long established, they were until recently the principal structures through which presidential candidates conducted their general election campaigns and through which incumbent presidents maintained their partisan followings. But even when they exercised their traditional roles in presidential campaigns, the national committees acted primarily as agencies for presidential nominees (or incumbent presidents) rather than as independently powerful organizations. In between campaigns, it is true that the national committee of the losing presidential candidate tended to be independent of him and of any prospective candidate. But that did not make the national committee very powerful. Mainly the committee awaited a takeover by the next party nominee while providing general services, including preparation for the national convention.[13]

With or without the national committee, the presidential party has long been organizationally separate from the congressional party that bears the same Republican or Democratic label. In the past, the political impact of that separation might have been less than it has been in the last few decades, but never after the very early 1800s have congressional and presidential parties been anything like a single political force. Neustadt shrewdly observes, "What the Constitution separates our political parties do not combine. The parties are themselves composed of separated organizations sharing public authority. The authority consists of nominating powers."[14] Yet the very idea of a party label common to a president and members of Congress suggests the possibility of a bridge over the separation of powers. Certainly the common party affiliation served in that way during much of American history, occasionally with striking success and more often with some success. The bridge, rather like a drawbridge, has not always been usable, and it has been difficult to maintain. But its existence has been significant.

It is true that in the early days of the Republic, before the development of the second-party system, the constitutional separation was diminished by means subsequently unavailable to parties. In addition to the need for the House of Representatives to choose the president as a result of inconclusive electoral college results in 1800 and 1824, congressional caucuses nominated presidential candidates for each election between those years and in effect elected their nominees, except in 1824. As yet, there was no separated presidential party or any national party organization distinct from the congressional caucus. But in 1832, after Andrew Jackson's successful use of an aggregation of state-based nominations in 1828, that aggregation became sufficiently national to have a convention, as did the newly organized supporters of his principal opponent.[15] The subsequent presidential nomination by national party convention, along with the popularization of the election process, as Lowi has aptly said, "totally split Congress off from the presidential succession and established, for the first time, an institutionalized, *real* separation of powers."[16] Moreover, the separation has certainly persisted, despite the great changes in the national party organization since 1832 and especially since 1968. Conventions now register a preceding semipopular choice rather than the preferences of state and local party leaders, but their nominations are probably even farther removed from congressional party control than they were in the first century or so after 1832.

Put more positively, presidential candidates as well as presidents possess their own political constituencies and power bases apart from those of Congress. The separate status is recognized not only by the absence of efforts to revive the long-dead congressional caucus method of presidential nomination but also by Congress's reluctance to use its impeachment power to end a president's tenure on partisan or even general political grounds. Certainly during the twentieth century, presidents, like presidential candidates, have been in little danger of becoming instruments of congressional power, even though they have often been frustrated by it.

On the other hand, presidents have tried to assert a leadership of congressional parties whose Republican or Democratic label they share. As the last chapter indicated, their frequent efforts to bridge the separation of powers have had their successes as well as rebuffs. So too has the much less frequent attempt of presidents to intervene in congressional nominations and elections. At most, presidents have been able to influence, not control, congressional parties. Yet occasionally their successes have been impressive enough to encourage the gap-bridgers to hope for more and stronger presidential leadership. The twentieth-century models have been Woodrow Wilson, Franklin Roosevelt, and briefly, Lyndon Johnson, all of whom led large congressional majorities elected under the same party label as the president's and enacting domestic programs identified as their party's. The countermodel is Jimmy Carter, widely perceived as unable to lead his party's large congressional majorities.

Partisan leadership of Congress, it is often suggested, has become more difficult for contemporary presidents. Some of the reasons for that view emerged in the discussion of Congress. Other reasons remain to be explored in the rest of this chapter. But it must also be stressed, in light of the constitutional and historical background, that party leadership is but one of the president's roles.[17] It is possible, and probably necessary, for a president also to be effective as something like the nonpartisan figure that the founders intended when they

created the chief executive office. Moreover, the president's election as an individual, not by virtue of legislative party leadership, fosters the development
of a personal political following which, whether or not it is called a presidential party, may transcend the more conventional party appeal.

II

Nominating Process

Limiting the public's effective choice of presidents to nominees of party organizations does not, we readily recognize, serve the nonpartisanship suggested
by the institutional context of the American presidency. Yet at least from 1840
through 1968 major parties in practice thus limited the electoral choice; specifically, for over 100 years Republican and Democratic delegates at national
conventions selected the only nominees subsequently elected. To regard so long-
established a system as odd, no matter how far removed from the preference
of the founders, would itself be odd, even perverse. After all, the party nominating process worked for so much of our history that it looks like a "natural" development in American politics. On the other hand, convention nomination is not the only conceivable means for narrowing the public's election
choices. That much is evident from the replacement of the old method, in
substance if not in form, by the arrangement used after 1968 to register popular preferences in a series of curiously scheduled primary-election contests.
And, of course, it would be possible to rationalize the registration of popular
choices by adopting a single national primary.

As against the more directly popular method, in either the post-1968 mold
or a more straightforward form, many political scientists and practitioners
believe that the traditional system provided a better means for nominating
presidential candidates. Reflecting as it did the influence of leaders, the old
convention is supposed to have produced nominees more likely to unite their
parties both for the campaign and for effective government after a successful
campaign. In that perspective, much though not all of the difficulty in the
way of party government in this last decade or so is attributed to the changed
nominating process. A president whose nomination rests on popular support
in primaries and the news media appears more decisively separated than his
predecessors from party organizations and party officeholders.[18]

One need not accept all of the argument against the popularization of the
nominating process to appreciate the importance of the change in that process.
Much is at stake in adopting a new method to determine the presidential

nominees from whom the general electorate will choose. The importance of a change in the process was evident earlier in contemplating the political institutionalization of the separation of powers that accompanied the abandonment of nomination by congressional caucus. Although not all changes increased popular participation in the nominating process, control generally has tended to shift, unsteadily, from small groups of leading political figures to larger numbers of citizens mobilized by presidential candidates themselves. The direction has been from peer review of prospective nominees toward more popular decision making.

1. The Convention System: Pure and Mixed

The popular direction is clear as early as the pre-1840 change from congressional caucus to the national party convention. It ended more than an embryonic parliamentary system that would have closely linked president and congressional party. The change also ended the sharply focused peer review by which small numbers of political participants in the national capital chose a nominee whose previous experience, in Congress or the executive branch, they would almost certainly have had the opportunity to observe and evaluate as most non-Washingtonians could not. Whatever the advantages of such true peer review, they did not prevail against the criticism in the Jacksonian age that nomination by so small an establishment was undemocratic.[19] Hence the new national party convention not only took the presidential nomination out of Congress and out of Washington but, as significantly, also gave power to a somewhat larger and supposedly more broadly representative group in which members of Congress were outnumbered. The larger group might still provide peer review, especially insofar as state party delegates at national conventions knew about candidate qualities from their own experience or from that of their delegation leaders. Nevertheless, the peer review of conventions was almost inevitably less intimate than it had been in the congressional caucus. And it did not always operate as admirers of its principles would have liked.

Within the 1832–1968 era of presidential nomination by national convention, it is useful to distinguish at least two periods — one until about 1908 and the other from 1912 to 1968.[20] The first is the purer party organizational variant, because all or virtually all delegates were chosen within each state by party caucus, district convention, state convention, executive committee, leadership, or some combination of such organizational agencies. Not yet were delegates chosen in state-run primary elections as they would be, in varying but significant numbers, after 1908.[21]

In trying to understand the party organizations that chose national convention delegates, we start with the fact that the *organizations* were not national although their electoral followings probably were; insofar as individuals "belonged" to a party structure, it was to a state or local apparatus that was but loosely confederated in a national entity. Then as now, "members" of parties were almost always defined simply as eligible voters openly professing to be Republican or Democratic. In principle, these very large numbers of "members" could participate in the local party caucuses (precinct and county) which were long used in most places (and still used in some states) to choose delegates who at their subsequent district and state conventions would elect delegates to the national convention. In contrast to other old practices in which leaders or executive committees chose delegates, the more commonly used caucus-convention procedure appeared to allow popular participation. Although such participation was at a stage well removed from the final choice of national delegates, it could have led in the nineteenth century, as it may now, to substantial representation of rank-and-file sentiment.[22] When a nominating contest evoked fairly wide public interest, truly open caucuses were vulnerable to takeovers by new groups outside the established party leadership. Yet public interest was often limited and readily discouraged by the scheduling of caucuses at inconvenient times and places. Thus party leaders, with patronage-holding or patronage-seeking allies, tended to control poorly attended caucuses (in ways that I describe in chapter 6 when discussing the use of caucuses for other nominations besides the presidential).

Not all caucuses were effectively closed, nor were all state and national conventions so clearly boss-controlled. Nevertheless, the old system looks like one in which state and local party leaders influenced the choice of delegates, led the delegations themselves, and largely determined their state's votes in the national conventions.[23] The state and local leaders might also have been state or national public officeholders, and in any case they were chiefly professional politicians pursuing careers durably tied to their party cause. They had the interest and usually, it is thought, the capacity to dominate the party-determined method of choosing national convention delegates, especially at a state convention itself composed of delegates previously chosen at precinct, county, or district caucuses.

Not only from 1832 to 1908 but also in the next 60 years of the national convention, regular party leaders seemed to be the decisive actors, for in that second period most delegates were still selected by the caucus-convention method. Presidential primaries, although significant in numbers and influence after 1908, did not in their first 60 years regularly determine nominations. Few states had meaningful presidential primaries during the first few decades of the century, even when they used direct primaries to nominate candidates for other partisan offices. Until the 1970s, presidential nominations thus remained the great exceptions to the twentieth-century American norm for partisan nominations.

Nevertheless, from 1912 to 1968 enough presidential primaries were held to warrant calling the system mixed. No longer was the process exclusively that of a private organization, once laws in certain states required delegates to be chosen by party voters in state-conducted primary elections. The mixture of delegate-selection methods, of primaries and chiefly caucus-convention devices, varied considerably between 1912 and 1968. The high point for primaries was in 1916, when 26 states had some kind of presidential primary and when over half of each party's national convention delegates were elected in some kind of primary.[24] "Some kind of primary" is a term of art here because a particular state's version did not necessarily constitute a meaningful contest between presidential candidates. No state's presidential primary was, or could be, a direct primary. In one way or another, the most that it could give voters was an opportunity to elect delegates pledged to a presidential candidate, or an opportunity to express a preference for a presidential candidate to whom delegates might be pledged. And either opportunity was often frustrated, intentionally or otherwise, by the ways presidential primary laws were written and administered. In many states it was relatively easy for state party leaders, under such laws, to control delegations by having them elected as either uncommitted to any candidate or committed to favorite-son candidates. It would then be possible for the leaders to bargain at national conventions much as did leaders still heading delegations chosen by the caucus-convention method.

Even if all presidential primaries had been meaningful, however, they could not have been decisive under the mixed system as they would be after 1968. Only between 1912 and 1920 did they seem likely to dominate — as President Woodrow Wilson apparently thought they would when he urged Congress in 1913 to enact a national primary law.[25] The number of presidential primaries declined, especially after 1920, and many of those that remained seldom played meaningful roles in the nominating process.[26] In 1968, presidential primaries were held in 17 states, choosing only about one-third of each national convention's delegates. And not all of that third consisted of delegates effectively committed to candidates for whom voters had expressed preferences.[27]

Granting that under the mixed system party leaders retained most of their customary power over presidential nominations, certain primaries in certain years nevertheless affected results. For example, in 1960, when primaries were too few to permit a candidate to get close to nomination *only* by winning all of them, John F. Kennedy needed certain salient primary victories to demonstrate electability to various party leaders who doubted his capacity to overcome objections to his religion and his youthful inexperience. Perceiving Kennedy's successful nominating campaign in this way is not to treat it as an exception to the generalization that party leaders remained the crucial decision makers in the mixed system. At most, it could be argued that the favorable response of some party leaders to the demonstration of Kennedy's popular support, in national polling surveys as in primaries, was so reluctant as to cast doubt on the reality of their power. That kind of doubt, however, seldom arose before 1960. When winners of presidential primaries were actually nominated, they were also the evident choices of most though not all party leaders. Often, as in the nomination of Woodrow Wilson in 1912, the candidate's electability may have accounted for the support of regulars whose own preferences were for someone else. But electability in Wilson's case was calculable apart from the primaries he had won. In fact, electability had always been an obviously important factor. Before primaries or public opinion polls, it surely operated when the Republican convention of 1868 nominated Ulysses S. Grant.

Apparently still more to the point of the limited role of presidential primaries during most of the twentieth century is the fact that on more than half of the nominating occasions under the mixed system, the winners of the largest number of primaries were not nominated. Specifically, from 1912 through 1968, in the 21 seriously contested Republican and Democratic nominating contests (when incumbent presidents were not almost automatically renominated), on 12 occasions the winners of the largest number of primaries failed to secure the nomination.[28] The import of that count is a little less telling than it first seems. In a few of the 12 instances, the rejected candidate had not won many more primaries than had a principal opponent, and had lost a particularly salient late primary (as Harold Stassen did in 1948 and Estes Kefauver in 1956). In at least one other case, Robert Taft's loss of the 1952 nomination to Dwight Eisenhower, his more numerous primary victories were less convincing demonstrations of popularity than write-in campaigns and other signs of the electability of an opponent who entered too late for an extended series of primary campaigns. It must also be noted that only one of the 12 rejections of a primary winner—the rejection of Eugene McCarthy in 1968 —occurred after 1956, and it was in extraordinary and politically disastrous circumstances.

One might thus suspect, despite the numerical record, that primaries had become more influential under the mixed system during its last decade or two. They did not determine results, as they would after 1968, but by the late 1950s, perhaps even in the 1940s, they were a significant part of almost every serious campaign for a major party nomination. Even Adlai Stevenson, who had been nominated in 1952 without having participated in any primaries, secured the 1956 nomination only after defeating Kefauver in California's Democratic primary.

Stevenson's 1952 nomination, however, is more often cited because it illustrates how the convention system could work to select a party candidate different from the primary-winning candidate — and also, it is argued, to select a better candidate than the primary winner. "It is generally conceded," Polsby and Wildavsky write in their standard work, "that Adlai Stevenson would have made a rather better president than Estes Kefauver, who ran and won in most of the primaries in 1952."[29] At any rate, the party leaders, whose delegations dominated the Democratic convention, preferred Stevenson as their nominee for a combination of personal and political coalitional reasons ordinarily respected by admirers of the convention system and its peer review. More than Kefauver, whose campaign had won a popular following largely outside of regular party channels but who had offended important fellow Democrats, Stevenson was thought likely to unite party supporters even if neither he nor any other Democratic nominee had a good chance to defeat Eisenhower. Therefore, despite Stevenson's loss in the general election of 1952 and again in 1956, his nomination remains a favorite among defenders of the convention system. If that system were still in force, its defenders imply if they do not actually say, neither George McGovern nor Jimmy Carter would have been nominated. (Presumably, however, Walter Mondale might well have been.)

The old system did not always work in a way that would draw the praise that it seems to have drawn with respect to the Stevenson nomination. Both before and after 1912, the evidently dominant professional politicians occasionally found it difficult to agree on a highly consensual choice. Their interests as state and local leaders were often highly sectional, and they were bound to reflect the differing electoral support anticipated for each candidate in a given part of the country. It was not unusual for a nomination to be won by only a bare majority after a sharp conflict like that between Eisenhower and Taft forces in 1952. And a prolonged deadlock could produce, as it did most notoriously in the Democratic convention of 1924, a compromise candidate without popular appeal in a general election.[30] Or a convention with several important contenders, none near a majority, could be brokered and nominate a dark-horse candidate acceptable to party regulars and capable of winning the general election. So it was when the Republican convention of 1920 agreed on Warren G. Harding.[31] But despite his landslide election, Harding's subsequently disastrous presidential years hardly make the Republican nomination of 1920 look like a triumph for the convention system.

Nor is Harding's the only presidency that might cause one to question the peer judgment of professional politicians. Alongside the historically admired choices, most notably Abraham Lincoln and Franklin Roosevelt, there are failures to contemplate. The Republican choice of Richard Nixon in 1960 and 1968 is a case in point. Although bolstered by primary victories and poll standing in both years, Nixon was first of all a favorite of most state and local party leaders, partly because he had campaigned with these leaders and partly because, in Republican terms, he was a centrist most likely to unite the party. Admittedly, Nixon might well have been nominated originally even in a plebiscitary contest like that of the 1970s, but the fact remains that his first two nominations were mainly intraparty affairs.

Not only could the old system, or any other system, produce retrospectively mistaken choices like Harding and Nixon when it was operating as it was supposed to operate—that is, when it nominated consensual party figures; it also was not always able to preclude a decisively destructive ideological nomination. The Democratic party, during its convention and not as a result of preconvention preferences, nominated William Jennings Bryan in 1896 and so fixed its minority status as an agrarian party of the South and West for most of the next 16 years (during which it nominated Bryan two more times). Barry Goldwater, himself a candidate in 1964 before primaries had superseded the old system, was not the first ideological choice of a national convention. More generally, too, the old system was open to the nomination of "outsiders," although by a different process from that of the plebiscitary system. State and local party leaders, even when free to exercise their own preferences, occasionally chose to nominate candidates because of their nonpartisan and even nonpolitical reputations. So within the 100 years after the Civil War, the system put General U.S. Grant and General Dwight D. Eisenhower in the White House for a total of 16 years. It also nominated and elected Herbert Hoover when his reputation rested much more heavily on his career as a businessman and a nonpartisan organizer of World War I relief than on his entirely nonelective political career as a Republican cabinet officer. And the Republican convention of 1940 nominated Wendell Willkie despite his lack of any prior party involvement or governmental officeholding.

Enough of the old system's nominations, including several of those mentioned, may have been so wise that one could conclude that the system served us well despite a few mistakes conceivable under any system. So much can be said without conceding all of the advantages that critics of the new post-

1968 system tend to attribute to the old. Nor should the contrast between the two systems be exaggerated. Before the recent changes in delegate-selection practices, party leaders (despite their decision-making powers) were always unsure whether they could afford to reject a candidate enjoying the broad popular support needed to win a general election, for a more regular party candidate or a more experienced officeholder. By the middle of this century that popular support could be demonstrated, often amply though less than decisively, in several primaries and in the newer public opinion polls. Party leaders were thus subject to increased pressure to make commitments before conventions began. Brokered conventions went out of style well before the 1970s. First-ballot nominations occurred in all Republican conventions after 1948 and in all Democratic conventions after 1952, even though party leaders still influenced the results decisively. And beginning in 1956, each successful candidate displayed at least a crucial primary victory if not a string of successes or, as Hubert Humphrey did in 1968, high standing in public opinion polls.

2. The Post-1968 System

Despite the several indications of more or less popularly influenced nominations before 1968, especially in the 1950s and 1960s, voter preferences in the 1970s came so evidently to control, rather than only to influence, presidential nominations that it is reasonable to write of a distinct post-1968 system based principally on primary results. It is true that preferences are not aggregated in a straightforward national count; voters still do not nominate presidential candidates as they do candidates for other offices. Without national presidential primaries, conventions retain their nominal authority, although by the end of the 1970s they did little more than register, perhaps in distorted form, the public's choice, not the party organization's. The "plebiscitary" system, as a critic labeled it, was now established as the means for nominating presidential candidates.[32] Most directly a product of post-1968 reforms, its development may also be attributed to the campaign finance legislation of the 1970s, the power of mass media of communication, and the weakness (for various reasons) of the old state and local party organizations. However it happened, the development loomed large, especially to admirers of the old system. Thus for Jeane Kirkpatrick, by 1976 the single most important fact about contemporary party politics was "the inability of either major American party to control the nominating process for the nation's most important political office."[33]

The "party" that Kirkpatrick means, it is well to recall, was the old confederative gathering of state and local party leaders, along with some national officeholders, who had previously controlled the nominating process. Their representational base, I have stressed, was ill defined in terms of party membership. Their domination of delegations and so of nominations depended most often on delegate selection procedures in which the participants were mainly leaders themselves, with a handful of faithful followers. Leadership methods in maintaining that domination, most conspicuously through "closed caucuses," became the targets for the post-1968 Democratic party reformers who began the process of change leading directly or indirectly to the plebiscitary system for both parties.

Responding to complaints about the traditional ways in which many delegates had been selected for its unhappy 1968 convention, the Democratic party's McGovern-Fraser Commission tried to develop rules that would, among other things, require open caucuses. Most members of that commission, in the words of a scholar-member, "believed that if we made the party's nonprimary delegate selection processes more open and fair, participation in them would increase greatly and consequently the demand for more primaries would fade away."[34] To this end, the commission recommended and the national Democratic party adopted requirements (among others) that caucuses be held at publicized times and places encouraging Democratic voters to attend, and that subsequent delegate selection, through county, district, and state conventions, fairly reflect caucus preferences.[35] The new rules were enforceable, and they ensured opportunities for nonregulars, especially candidate enthusiasts, to determine caucus results against the readily outnumbered regulars. Only in the absence of local activist supporters of contesting presidential candidates could party leaders expect to maintain their former control of the process. Incidentally, Republican practices, without quite the same national rules, resembled those of the new Democratic open caucuses.

Open-caucus attendance has no doubt varied greatly from place to place since 1968, as it did before wherever similar opportunities existed, but the number of participants now has often made the caucus look more like a presidential primary than the old closed caucus. Especially in a state whose caucuses attract great media attention, as have Iowa's because of their placement at the start of the delegate selection season, turnout figures are impressive, although well below those in contested presidential primaries. In 1980, over 100,000 persons participated in the caucuses of each of Iowa's major parties. Thus Everett Ladd may not overstate so greatly when he declares that "Party caucuses in the modern sense *are nothing more than restrictive primaries*."[36] They have been found to produce the same types of delegates, reflecting similar candidate commitments as do primaries.[37] And relative to primaries, caucuses are "restrictive" only in that their participants devote a few hours to attend a meet-

ing rather than merely a few minutes to cast a primary ballot. More significant, however, is the special representational opportunity that caucuses provide not only for candidate enthusiasts but also for interest groups. Their role
in Iowa's Democratic caucuses has been well documented, and it may be growing in other states.[38] Such groups, like candidate enthusiasts, can also mobilize
to influence primaries, as labor unions did for Walter Mondale in his campaign
for the 1984 Democratic nomination, but interest groups appear more directly
effective in caucuses when their own participating members are numerous enough
to determine results without the mobilization of other voters needed to win
primaries. Hence in helping Mondale win caucus delegates in 1984, unions
could more readily be accused of achieving nonpopular victories.

Although open caucuses are decidedly relevant in the plebiscitary system,
they have not, so far at any rate, been the chief means by which popular preferences have been recorded in that system. Instead, despite the intentions of
McGovern-Fraser reformers, presidential primaries became much more consequential in the 1970s. Numbers alone tell some of the story. From only 17
Democratic and 16 Republican presidential primaries in 1968, there were by
1980 31 Democratic and 33 Republican primaries selecting nearly three-quarters
of each convention's delegates (compared with fewer than half in 1968). Even
in 1984, when for the first time since 1968 more states dropped than added
primaries, there were still 24 Democratic and Republican primaries among
the 50 states and the District of Columbia. And these primaries determined
the choice of substantially more than half of each convention's delegates. Moreover, in the contested Democratic case, Mondale needed to win certain crucial
primaries and probably to emerge first in overall primary voting (which he
barely did), though not in a majority of state primaries. The support — greater
than that of his opponents — that he obtained from delegates selected by nonprimary processes was also essential, but it seems unlikely that it would have
sufficed if Mondale had failed in a few more primaries.[39]

Accompanying the enhanced importance of primaries has been the tendency
for many more delegates, in practice if not by binding party rule, to be committed to national presidential candidates well before the convention. The change
is apparent in caucus-convention states as in primary states; indeed, with some
form of open participation almost everywhere, uncommitted delegates as well
as favorite-son delegates became scarce. Hence each national convention was
effectively transformed into a mechanism for recording earlier choices by primary voters and caucus-convention attenders. In 1980 only 3.5 percent of the
3,331 Democratic delegates and only 5 percent of the 1,994 Republican delegates were uncommitted.[40] Even at the 1984 Democratic convention, when

14 percent of the delegates were party leaders and public officeholders who under a new rule could have remained uncommitted, only 5 percent of all 3,933 Democratic delegates were listed as uncommitted just before the convention.[41] To be sure, more than 5 percent — presumably the full 14 percent — were free from the kind of commitment that other delegates owed to primary voters or even caucus participants whose presidential preferences they represented. Most of the party leaders and public officeholders (including a large congressional contingent) composing the ex officio 14 percent merely declared their own candidate preferences.[42] In some instances they did so early and in others only after the last primaries. More of them favored Mondale than favored other candidates, and they may well have provided a significant increment, just before the convention, enabling Mondale to claim a majority of all delegates. Even so, they appear only to have helped ensure the nomination of the candidate who had won the largest share of delegates chosen by primaries and caucuses. The theoretically uncommitted delegates surely did not broker the convention in anything like the old style that would have violated the now-established public expectation that the presidential nominee should be the choice of the popularly determined preferences of most delegates.[43] That expectation is the essence of the post-1968 system — the means by which party leaders are deprived of the power to determine nominations.

As the principal recorder of popular preferences for presidential candidates, the primaries deserve a little more attention. They became dominant when enough states, or state parties, adopted them for presidential delegate selection. Usually in both parties, six states shifted to primaries between 1968 and 1972, eight more between 1972 and 1976 (while one shifted in the opposite direction), and seven more between 1976 and 1980 (while three shifted in the opposite direction).[44] Although in 1984 seven states shifted from primaries back to caucuses on the Democratic side (and a few more on the Republican side), they did not, as already observed, materially reduce the attention given to primaries, which still elected most of the delegates. None of the seven new Democratic caucus states, except Texas, was large, and two of them had shifted only because the national party forced them to abandon their wide-open form of primary as part of the process of delegate selection.[45] Whether these states will retain caucuses is doubtful; their 1984 procedure was subject to considerable criticism especially but not exclusively from losing candidates.

With some exceptions, states adopting presidential primaries (or caucus-convention methods) have applied the same system to both parties. Hence Republican presidential primaries became about as numerous as Democratic, even though most legislatures that changed their systems in the 1970s (and the early 1980s) had Democratic majorities that were probably responding to their national party rules. Those rules may well have made caucuses less attractive to state Democratic politicians in the 1970s. But it is likely also that both Democratic and Republican legislators reflected the general post-1968 reform ethos that supported a more participatory democracy, and what nomination method could be more broadly participatory than a primary? After all, it was already used in its more direct form in virtually every state to nominate candidates for other partisan offices. Why not for the presidency too?

We cannot know, without a full, careful state-by-state study, how large a part the general reform preference for primaries played in determining the presidential primary legislation of the 1970s. Nor can we be sure how to weigh other factors. For example, candidates and their supporters might have fostered a primary in a given state in order to win more delegates than they could have expected under a caucus-convention system. Or state and local Democratic party leaders might have persuaded their legislature to adopt a presidential primary because they thought it provided an easier route than caucuses to comply with the new national rules. Or such leaders elsewhere might have thought that they could obtain less unhappy political results in a primary than in the now necessarily open caucuses so readily flooded by issue-oriented candidate enthusiasts. After 1972 the latter calculation was likely because of McGovern's success in certain open caucuses.[46]

Whatever the explanation for the shift to primaries, their number and salience mean that a successful nominating campaign needs a large and well-funded candidate-centered organization. It cannot depend mainly on a coalition of state and local party leaders and public officials. As Neustadt puts it, "We have left the age of barons and entered the age of candidates. Its hallmarks are management by private firms, exposure through the tube, funding by direct-mail drives as well as fat-cats, and canvassing by zealous volunteers."[47] Correctly, I believe, he sees signs of the new age developing in the Republican party as early as Goldwater's campaign of 1964, before the massive reform in delegate selection practices, and he regards the system of the 1970s as the product of about twenty years of change in national parties. One might also trace its beginnings to the 1940s and 1950s when, as I suggested earlier, presidential primaries were occasionally significant public events. But no one doubts that the change was fulfilled after 1968 as it had not been before.

Ideological or issue-oriented candidates like George McGovern, George Wallace, or Ronald Reagan may have advantages in building the kind of organization now needed in nominating campaigns. But, as Jimmy Carter showed in 1976, it is possible to attract the requisite strength on a more personal basis

and without well-defined policy positions. The common ingredient for success under the new plebiscitary system has been prolonged, extensive, and intensive campaigning that capitalizes on early primary or caucus victories to
capture national media attention. Such attention, as we learned from McGovern's experience in 1972 and Carter's in 1976, enables a candidate to rise rapidly in the public opinion polls that had originally reflected his obscurity or
at least low name-recognition compared to the established national figures who
started as front-runners. Those who begin as front-runners, however, can maintain their status by early victories of their own, like Reagan's in 1980, or even
by slightly later victories, like Mondale's in 1984, provided that national journalists perceive them as sufficiently newsworthy. The political writers' definition of victory is the operative one, and they may understandably treat a less
established candidate's stronger-than-expected vote, though good only for a
respectable second place, as more interesting than a clear-cut majority for a
leading contender. So it was that McCarthy in 1968 and McGovern in 1972
benefited from their strong second-place showings in New Hampshire's primary, and Carter in 1976 from his surprising capture of more of Iowa's precinct caucus delegates than any other candidate, though he had well below
a majority and fewer than the number of uncommitted delegates.

Undoubtedly, the national publicity suggests that the journalists covering
the nominating campaigns are important political actors. One of the most
thoughtful and respected of these national journalists, David Broder, admits
as much by saying that he and his colleagues "are uncomfortably aware of
the fact that we are an increasingly influential part of the process we are reporting." Correctly, I believe, he sees journalists inheriting some of the influence that the old party power-brokers used to exercise in decisive fashion.
"What we write, or fail to write, becomes a major determinant of the outcome."[48]

So, more conspicuously, do television and radio producers, talk-show hosts,
and reporters help to determine the outcome by their choice of candidates
to interview or otherwise present. Such decisions have become especially critical in those campaigns, beginning in 1976, in which financial resources were
limited by the expenditure ceilings that accompanied the granting of federal
matching funds and by the prohibition of really large individual contributions. Being thus limited in buying advertising, particularly expensive television advertising, presidential primary candidates needed more than ever to
obtain free news coverage from the media.[49] Performing in a newsworthy way,
with or without primary "victories," is thus increasingly important. The results have been called "medialities," meaning "media-based situations that al-

ter the shape or direction of a campaign." The scholar who thus defined medialities thinks that they were less crucial in 1980 than they had been in 1976,
as journalists worried about their influence, but he nonetheless believes that
the media, especially television, remain, as they have been since 1972, the key
concern of campaign strategy for candidates seeking presidential nomination.[50]
Television suits the plebiscitary nominating system. This is not to claim that
television is principally responsible for the system. A different and stronger
kind of party organization might not have yielded its candidate-selection powers, now even for the presidency, to primary voters, nor its intermediary functions to the media. European parties have not thus yielded their powers, despite the nearly universal impact of television.

It ought to be pointed out, however, that an apparently great and special
influence of the news media in presidential nominating campaigns is a result
of a peculiar aspect of those campaigns rather than of American politics more
generally. By accident, not because of anything inherent in a popularly based
selection process here or elsewhere, the campaigns are conducted in a way that
focuses attention on states that schedule their election events early in the
nominating season. New Hampshire, by its own legislation, has long insisted
on holding the first presidential primary, and Iowa, more recently, has scheduled its local caucuses still earlier. Under the post-1968 system, such early participatory events loom larger than they did when popular results, early and
late, did not determine nominations so clearly. By the 1970s, they served to
give outsiders and previously disregarded candidates like McGovern and Carter
a chance to become well-known contenders by concentrating their efforts at
a crucial time in states where only relatively modest expenditures are required
and where, notably in New Hampshire, a candidate who has the time can
personally reach a large share of a party's primary electorate. And for front-
runners, like Reagan in 1980, winning at least one early event seemed necessary to confirm their lead and to maintain "momentum."

The influence of the news media in such cases is related not only to their
role in determining who really "won," by measuring votes against expectations in complex multicandidate contests, but also to the extent of their coverage. In 1980, a leading national television network gave 14 percent of its total
coverage of *all caucuses and primaries* to Iowa's caucuses and another 14 percent
to New Hampshire's primaries. The comparable figures for a major wire service were 13 percent and 15 percent.[51] Plainly, from a national standpoint,
no one would design a system in which a relatively small state like Iowa and
a very small state like New Hampshire receive such grossly disproportionate
news coverage. But that coverage is an understandable media response to a

political schedule over which journalists themselves have no control. Iowa and
New Hampshire provide interesting news because their events come first. They
could be made less newsworthy if national parties (or Congress) insisted on
a different timetable. The Democratic national party has tried, with limited
success in 1984, to reduce the impact of the two states by establishing a 13-week
season for all other states and by specifying that New Hampshire's primary
should be no earlier than seven days and Iowa's caucuses no earlier than 15
days before that regular season.[52]

If not by that modest national party measure surely by something subsequently stronger, the disproportionate influence of certain state events could
be reduced within the confines of the post-1968 system. Indeed, the heart of
that system—broad participation in the nominating process—would be bolstered if participants in the 50 states became more nearly equal in their impact
on the nominating results. The number of participants, particularly in primaries, is impressive: in 1980 over 19 million voted in the various Democratic
presidential primaries and almost 13 million in the Republican, and in 1984
over 17.8 million voted in the reduced number of Democratic primaries and
nearly 6.5 million even in the uncontested Republican primaries.[53] Increasing
the significance of more of these votes would be another step away from the
old system in which state and local party leaders retained power to determine
presidential nominations.

3. Prospects

As I write, the post-1968 system has prevailed, with incremental modification
and modest Democratic retreat in 1984, during only four nominating years.
That is a short time, compared with the life of the old system in either its
pure or mixed form. Might not the tide of popular participation in presidential nominations be yet rolled back in the 1980s, as it was in the 1920s after
its initial surge in 1912 and 1916? Without doubt, many political scientists
and political practitioners now want to roll back that tide. Counterreformation advocacy, weighty if not widely popular, mounted in the late 1970s and
became a substantial opinion-making force in the early 1980s. Academics, journalists, and politicians gathered at conferences and in commissions to express
dissatisfaction with the consequences of changes in methods of presidential
nomination. The study of how to revise those methods became a growth industry in the study of American politics.[54] It even commanded a measure of
public attention when at least a large minority of American citizens were dissatisfied with the 1980 results of the new nominating system. Many Democrats,
unhappy with Carter, blamed the new system for his original 1976 nomina-

tion as well as for his presidency and 1980 renomination. Nor did all Republicans at the time regard Reagan as an alternative as capable as another nominating system might have provided.

Criticism of the post-1968 system, implicit in the preceding discussion of the system's development, has several closely related bases. One is the absence of the kind of peer-group judgment that was possible, though not uniformly successful, at a deliberative nominating convention of mainly uninstructed delegates responding to experienced leaders. Now, it is thought, "nationally inexperienced" candidates are more readily nominated.[55] At the same time, candidates win nomination without having to form coalitions of party leaders and interests; they win by depending almost entirely on their own vote-seeking campaign organizations.[56] Hence the nomination ceases to be a genuine party affair from which the successful candidate emerges as the leader of a coalition united organizationally for the general election campaign and for governing after winning the election. Instead, it is argued, the new system produces — in the sense of making more likely — a candidate like Jimmy Carter, whose general election campaigns and presidency, especially, were so much less successful than his nominating campaigns.

The argument, advanced with skill and sophistication by Nelson Polsby, is necessarily limited because it rests almost entirely on the single case of Jimmy Carter. Only two other nominees before 1984 were clearly products of the new system.[57] The first, George McGovern, illustrates no more than the failure of a general election campaign (which, in any event, one major-party nominee always loses). The other nonincumbent nominee in the 1972–80 period, Ronald Reagan, conducted a winning general election campaign as well as a presidency that might well be judged favorably in terms of party leadership. Certainly Reagan succeeded in uniting his party after winning its nomination by the plebiscitary method. Not only did he use the old coalition-building device of giving the vice-presidential nomination to a principal opponent, but he also acted in various other conventional ways to close party ranks. Furthermore, Reagan was able to prepare the way for his unifying Republican party campaign in the 1980 general election even while still competing in presidential primaries. For him, at least, the new system of winning nomination mainly by attracting party voters rather than party leaders did not preclude the subsequent formation of effective coalitional support of the old party type.[58] And, it must be stressed, the nominating system was essentially the same for Republicans as it was for Democrats, despite the fact that the Republican national party had not itself adopted the same detailed rules imposed by Democratic reformers and that therefore certain Republican procedures varied from

state to state more than did Democratic procedures. The crucial practice—
popular election of candidate-committed delegates—now prevailed generally
in determining Republican nominations, as it did Democratic.

If it has nonetheless been easier for a Republican than a Democratic nominee to unite his party, and not merely easier for Reagan personally than for
Carter (or Mondale), the explanation would have to rest on differences between the two parties other than those having to do with nominating methods. The Republican party has a smaller and perhaps also a more homogeneous electoral base that can facilitate post-convention unity. That explanation
may help to account for the concentration of opposition to the post-1968 system among Democrats, academic and nonacademic. Not only do they regard
their party, through its reform commissions, as largely responsible for the new
system and so as the agency for any counterreformation, but they often see
themselves as the chief losers in the system of plebiscitary nomination. Their
nominees, though of a party holding an electoral majority, lost three of the
first four post-1968 elections and barely won the fourth in 1976. Republicans
have no similar party-linked grievance against the workings of the new system. Little effort has been evident within the Republican party to introduce
counterreforms. And two Republican-oriented political scientists—a fairly rare
professional breed—are among the few scholars of American politics to accept the new presidential nominating system with considerable equanimity
if not with reform-minded enthusiasm.[59]

To some extent, however, counterreformation sentiment crosses party lines
and also includes unaffiliated minders of the public good. The latter, while
probably having less concern than partisans for coalition-building potentials
of one system as against another, are at least as likely as Democrats or Republicans to be dissatisfied with the qualifications for the presidency of those
nominees lately selected. They also share the fairly common adverse reaction
to the need, under the new system, for first President Ford and then President
Carter to campaign actively for renomination and thus be distracted from governing responsibilities for about a year rather than for only a few months of
a general election campaign.

It is clear that a president can no longer count on the old ties to state and
local leaders to virtually ensure renomination. Before 1968 only William Howard Taft had to fight for renomination during this century, and his case seems
to have been genuinely exceptional because he faced, in the brief early heyday
of presidential primaries, a highly successful and still young expresident. Otherwise, under the old system, even a president as unpopular as Herbert Hoover
in 1932 readily secured convention support. But lately, we know, neither Ger-

ald Ford in 1976 nor Jimmy Carter in 1980 found renomination easy, even though their presidencies were less unpopular than Hoover's. On the other hand, neither Richard Nixon in 1972 nor Ronald Reagan in 1984 had to campaign for renomination in the primaries dominating the selection process. Nixon was popular enough and Reagan plainly so very popular that their appeal within the party's primary electorate precluded serious challenge. Nevertheless, Ford's experience and especially Carter's with time-consuming and politically distracting presidential renominating campaigns have led, along with more party-oriented criticisms of the post-1968 system, to proposals for restoring at least some of the power of leadership groups to bestow nominations. Broadly speaking, these proposals are of two kinds, but because they are complementary they may be advanced together. The first is to increase the number of delegates selected by the caucus-convention method, at the expense of the now-dominant presidential-primary method. The second kind of proposal is to have a substantial number of delegates chosen by virtue of their party or public office and not as a result of any process, caucus or primary, that would fix their commitment to presidential candidates.

To achieve the objective of the first proposal, a national party might require states and state parties to produce more caucus-convention delegates either by specifying that only a certain percentage of delegates from a given state could be chosen in primaries or by limiting the number of states allowed to use primaries in any given year. Or a national party might merely encourage states and state parties to use the caucus-convention method. With or without national inducement, some states do respond to local arguments for abandoning their presidential primaries. A few did so even in the 1970s when the trend was in the opposite direction, and more responded, as already observed, in the early 1980s. It is too soon to perceive a trend back to caucuses like that of the 1920s, just as it is too soon to conclude that presidential primaries will remain as dominant as they have recently been or give way to a national primary.

Tentatively, however, prospects for something closer to the dominance of presidential primaries look likelier than a massive shift away from them. Unlike the situation in the 1920s, the public in the 1980s is accustomed to popular participation in the nominating process. Direct primaries for other offices are now long-standing institutional fixtures, and meaningful presidential primaries themselves have been around almost as long in many states. The news media have made these primaries highly salient national events. Even if politicians wanted to abolish a state's presidential primary, they would often suspect that legislative votes for abolition would be unpopular. After all, primaries have much larger turnouts than caucuses. Even Iowa's famous 1980 caucuses, attended by over 200,000 Republicans and Democrats, meant a turnout of only about 10 percent of the state's voting-age population, whereas the highest 1980 presidential-primary turnout, in Wisconsin, was 45 percent, and the turnout in all 1980 presidential primaries considered together was 25 percent.[60]

Moreover, it is by no means clear that politicians in many states see advantages for themselves in returning to the caucus-convention system when caucuses are now, by rule or custom, open to nonregulars and so to takeovers by candidate enthusiasts and interest groups who can hardly be counted on to follow the preferences of professional party leaders and officeholders. No longer able to exclude nonregulars by the old organizational tactics, party leaders cannot count on controlling the caucus outcome when a nomination is seriously contested. Even without a popular antiorganizational protest movement like McGovern's and without the kind of media attention that built attendance at Iowa's caucuses, at least modest numbers of nonregulars can be mobilized by candidate organizations and interest groups. It is true that leadership influence in such situations is possible in at least some of a state's many caucuses and perhaps in enough for politicians to try the caucus method instead of a primary.[61] But in other situations, organized interests can appear to pack a caucus, as unions did most conspicuously for Mondale in 1984, and create a public relations problem.

Despite such difficulties, the caucus may tempt party leaders because of its party-building potential. Much more than primary voters, caucus-attenders are potential organizational helpers. Once they attend a party meeting, which in a sense the caucus is, they look like citizens who might profitably be asked to participate in subsequent party campaigns or at least to contribute funds to such campaigns. Nonregulars might thus become regulars. So far, however, party leaders in most states have not found in the party-building potential of caucuses a sufficient incentive to abandon presidential primaries. They may well prefer to avoid caucuses in their open form for the very reason that a champion of liberal activism like James M. Burns believes that they are useful —because they can foster ideological causes and candidates.[62]

The second kind of counterreformation proposal reasserts more directly the influence of party leaders in the nominating process. By making enough of these leaders ex officio and uncommitted delegates at national conventions, it is theoretically possible to have presidential nominations determined once again by politicians rather than by primary voters and open-caucus participants. At an extreme, a national party could even provide that its whole convention, or an overwhelmingly large share of it, consist of ex officio and uncommitted delegates. A little less unrealistically, a party could stipulate that perhaps half of its convention seats be reserved for such delegates; they would then presumably be numerous enough to be decisive in determining contested nominations under most foreseeable circumstances. So far, no such drastic counterreform has been seriously considered. The Democratic party, in revising its rules for 1984, only discussed moves in that direction before adopting the requirement that 14 percent of its convention delegates be both ex officio and uncommitted.[63] Well short of enough to be almost surely decisive, the percentage was nonetheless substantial. It allowed about three-fifths of the Democrats in Congress, plus specified Democratic state and city officeholders and state party officeholders, to attend the convention without having to contend for election in primaries or caucuses and without being pledged to particular presidential candidates.

In a way, the 1984 Democratic provision can be viewed not as counterreformational but merely as a device to reinvolve party officeholders, and especially members of Congress, in conventions which the post-1968 party practices had discouraged them from attending.[64] As but 14 percent in a sea of almost 4,000 Democratic delegates, mainly committed by voter preferences to presidential candidates, the uncommitted officeholders did not so much change the plebiscitary system as complement it. Although arithmetically conceivable that only 14 percent could determine a result in a close nominating contest or at least help determine a result, as probably happened in 1984, it is hard to envision such a determination being made in behalf of a candidate who had not also won more voter-committed delegates than anyone else. Only a most astonishingly bold group of politicians would in our time nominate someone other than the already acclaimed popular preconvention choice. Apart from media-induced national pressure, the states and districts of the technically uncommitted officeholders record voter preferences for presidential candidates, and many officeholders have political reasons to respect such preferences.

In other words, it is not solely because 14 percent is a small proportion that the change left the nominating process much as it had been since 1968. Rather, my belief is that there cannot be so direct a turn away from the plebiscitary system as would be implied by having ex officio and uncommitted delegates determine presidential nominations. The very political reality that kept the Democratic party from going to 30, 40, or 50 percent ex officio uncommitted is what makes it unlikely that 14 percent would assert its own choice against a popular winner. Even without playing that role, the help that most of the ex officio 14 percent gave Mondale in 1984 produced a reaction against their presence. In establishing a new Fairness Commission to review delegate-selection rules for its 1988 convention, the Democratic convention's rules committee recommended that the commission sharply reduce the percentage of ex officio uncommitted delegates and at the same time recommended the elimination of certain exceptions to proportional representation that had, in several primaries and caucuses, helped Mondale win delegates in 1984.[65] The convention did not mandate these recommendations, and during 1985 the Fairness Commission responded to different interests by suggesting that the Democratic National Committee retain most of the 1984 rules and actually increase the number of ex officio delegates by a few percentage points. In any event, presidential nominations, like nominations for virtually all other offices, appear fixed as large-scale public rather than private organizational affairs. They would be even more clearly so if the post-1968 system yielded to a national primary or a set of nationally imposed regional primaries. And, of course, presidential nominations would be no less public if the system were rationalized by reducing the peculiar impact of particular state events.

My reasons for regarding at least the essence of the post-1968 system as a fairly well established fact of contemporary American political life are readily summarized. Nonorganizational means of nomination fit not only the now usual American practice with respect to nonpresidential offices but also the traditional nonpartisan side of the American presidency. In this light, the post-1968 changes, while triggered by a specific reform movement, are also the products of long-standing and distinctively American developments fostering candidate-centered politics. It is true that for a century those developments were subject to the constraints of presidential nominating conventions ordinarily dominated by party leaders and party interests. But the constraints had visibly loosened even before 1968, as the nonpartisan demands of the presidential office became more salient and as the conventional power of state and local party organizations withered. Accordingly, the candidate-centered politics of the new plebiscitary nominating system have deeper historical roots than the decade or so of that system's operation would itself indicate.

III

Election

A look at presidential elections reveals a large measure of candidate-centered politics in the years before the new nominating system compelled candidates to build their own extensive campaign organizations in order to become general election nominees of major parties. Granted, that compulsion virtually ensures a candidate-centered organization for the general election as the old system did not; now a nominee has such an organization in place as the election campaign begins and thus is most unlikely to abandon it. But even without an organization originally built for presidential primaries and even without primaries, there were major-party nominees who conducted candidate-centered campaigns alongside if not in place of party-conducted campaigns.

As far back as 1896, before any primaries existed to produce the kind of nominating campaign with which we have become familiar, William Jennings Bryan depended heavily on an extraparty organization in the general election contest that followed his Democratic convention nomination. He did so in part because many traditional and conservative Democrats deserted him, and because party professionals were thought to distrust him enough so that he could not count on their help. As Richard Jensen adds in his explanation of the nature of the 1896 campaign in the Midwest, "Like all crusaders, Bryan and his cohorts avoided established party leaders and organizations." Jensen cites networks of "silver clubs" consisting of newcomers to politics, operating outside the party hierarchy and appealing in behalf of Bryan's populist monetary philosophy to "citizens regardless of party loyalties."[66] Bryan's experience remains exceptional in significant respects, but it displays the capacity of American presidential politics to break out of traditional party channels even in the past.

For different reasons from Bryan's, it became common for twentieth-century nominees to seek votes outside as well as inside the ranks of their own party and to use personal organizations for the purpose. For example, a Citizens for Eisenhower organization played a significant role in the 1952 campaign along with the Republican National Committee. If the loyalty of a party organization was not suspect, its effectiveness was doubted, especially in appealing to those voters for whom party label might be indecisive. Hence even when candidate-centered organizations did not supersede party organizations in presidential campaigns, they were often crucially important. As Koenig, in his standard work on the presidency, wrote in 1964, "Many a Presidential nominee views the available party organization as an enterprise of limited dependability and feels it the better part of wisdom to build a personal organization to conduct much of the post-convention campaign."[67]

One nominee whom Koenig had in mind was John F. Kennedy, whose 1960 general election campaign depended heavily on a candidate-centered organization. In this instance, the organization had been created originally to campaign for the Democratic nomination and especially in the minority of states then holding primaries. Like later successful candidates, Kennedy not only used his organization in the general election following his initial nomination but he maintained and even further developed it during his years in office, with the intention of using it for the 1964 reelection campaign. Although Kennedy worked with many state and local party leaders, his own organization in the large northern industrial states was, as Koenig remarks, "in some ways more powerful than the regular Democratic organization."[68]

However substantial the candidate-centered organization that Kennedy and others developed before the 1970s, the phenomenon did not become an object of widespread concern until 1972 and the Watergate-inquiry years that followed. Richard Nixon's Committee to Re-elect the President (CREEP) was a creation of the 1970s, but it did not develop principally to conduct a nominating campaign in the now-numerous presidential primaries. Nixon faced no serious challenge for renomination. The purpose of CREEP, though organized well before the Republican nominating convention, was for it to conduct Nixon's general election campaign, despite the fact that Nixon was also in a position to control the National Committee. This suggests again that various circumstances, in addition to the new kind of nominating competition, encourage the use of candidate-centered organizations in presidential campaigns. Their use in general elections survived the scandalous fund-raising methods of CREEP. Although the methods tended at first to give presidential candidate-centered organizations a bad name generally, efforts to abandon these organizations in favor of greater reliance on party machinery did not persist. Instead the organizations, along with other campaign vehicles, were subject to new regulatory and public-financing legislation meant to eliminate the vices associated with CREEP. Candidate-centered organizations operating under this legislation remained dominant in presidential campaigns of 1976, 1980, and 1984.

The campaign finance legislation of the 1970s is often treated as encouraging candidate-centered campaigns for the presidency. One provision gave each major-party nominee a large sum of public money (over $40 million in 1984) on condition that expenditures over that sum be severely restricted.[69] The result was to free candidates from a dependence on party or on anyone else for raising general election campaign funds and to limit the expenditures of parties for presidential candidates. Another provision partially funded nominating campaigns by matching private contributions up to $250, thus adding incentives for candidates contesting the primaries to build campaign organizations based on direct-mail solicitation of funds rather than on party ties. Nevertheless, these provisions of the campaign finance legislation may be seen as acknowledging as much as encouraging the already dominant candidate-centered organizations in contemporary American elections and nominations.

We know that such organizations were becoming increasingly significant before the reforms in nominating procedure as well as in campaign funding. Now, given the increased importance of direct personal appeals, it is hard to believe that even a party nominee who had not had to campaign for delegates would fail to perceive the usefulness of building his own organization to contest the general election. So it was that President Nixon in 1972 used CREEP as the major component of a campaign aimed, from the start, at the public whose votes determined November results. And so it was also that Reagan in 1984 had an organization collecting private funds and federal matching dollars during the preconvention period, despite the absence of a nominating contest. Candidates assured of renomination, as were Nixon and Reagan, may have the luxury of starting a little later than candidates who have to fight for nomination or renomination. But no matter when they develop their organizations, they will have been able from the beginning to appeal beyond the partisan electorate that votes in primaries and participates in open caucuses.

Neither the tactics nor the personnel chosen to help win nomination are necessarily the best for winning the voters outside one's own party who may be crucial in general elections. Despite a candidate's natural reliance on those who have already helped him win a nomination, he could find it useful to be without some of the commitments of a strenuous nominating campaign. Thus, for example, George McGovern's candidate-centered organization that served him so well in securing the Democratic nomination in 1972 was less helpful in reaching the constituency he needed in the general election. It was almost irretrievably linked, as was McGovern himself, to the issues, the interests, and the groups that constituted a majority in the convention but not in the country. Of course the limitation of this linkage was but one of McGovern's handicaps in the general election, and like some others it may have been peculiar to the ideological character of McGovern's preconvention support. A more personal, less ideological preconvention organization like Jimmy Carter's was probably more readily adapted to a general election campaign, although in his case that campaign was only marginally successful, even in 1976.

On the other hand, Ronald Reagan in 1980 succeeded handsomely in using an ideologically based organization that had won him the nomination to help also in winning the general election. As noted earlier, Reagan satisfactorily united the Republican party after winning its nomination. He also adapted his candidate-centered effort to the general election task of securing enough non-Republican votes (to defeat, it should be granted, an unpopular opponent).[70] Reagan's success in 1980 shows that primary and general election efforts can at least be compatible. It ought therefore to be weighed carefully before concluding from a few other instances, including Mondale's in 1984, that joint successes are inherently contradictory.

At any rate, with a nominating campaign (as for Reagan in 1980) or without one (as for Nixon in 1972 and Reagan in 1984), presidential nominees have come to make the most of their appeal in general elections by strongly personal campaigns conducted mainly by themselves and their closest associates rather than by the old party organizations. They thus exploit in a new organizational way the nonparty element that American presidential politics have always contained. The nominee's own organization now does for him what a national party committee and its network of state and local party organization did for U.S. Grant or any other nominee whose personal popularity exceeded his party's. National committees and state and local parties remain important helpers in the presidential election cause, but no longer the prime movers.

The distinction between the two organizational efforts—the candidate's and the traditional party's—should not be so sharply drawn as to suggest two completely different sets of active campaigners. Kessel's "presidential party," discussed in the first section of this chapter, includes many regular state and local party officers. He reports "a progressively greater overlap between the presidential campaign committees and the regular party organizations as one moves from the national to the county levels."[71] The officers of the party organizations are often activists who were originally attracted to party politics as supporters of a particular presidential candidate. They remained not only to work again for the same candidate or a similarly attractive candidate but also to sustain the party effort locally as well as nationally. In this light, the separate candidate-centered presidential campaign organization appears, in a general election, to be less than novel in its import. State and local party organizations have always recruited at least some of their troops on the basis of the appeal of presidential candidates. Insofar as more party workers might now be thus recruited, and fewer because of strictly local concerns, the organizations would be more nearly national. The very conception of a presidential party implies such nationalization, as well as an effectiveness by no means less impressive (though differently structured) than that of the old loosely confederated state and local party leaders.[72]

Whatever the organizational impact of the fuller development of candidate-centered presidential politics in the last few decades, the development itself needs a little more exposition. Apart from boosts in the 1970s because of new nominating rules and public funding, why should the candidate-centered potential have been so much more fully exploited in our time? One ready answer is that the presidency has become a more salient and consequential responsibility as the powers of the national government and especially of its chief executive have grown prodigiously. Thus the personal attributes of the individual holding or seeking the office seem even more significant than in times past, and strictly party connections much less so. The consequent individualization of the electoral contest is not exclusively an American phenomenon. It has been found, for similar cause, to characterize elections of independently powerful presidents in other nations.[73] The French Fifth Republic provides the most telling examples.[74]

A second still-more-familiar explanation for the recently increased candidate-centered presidential campaigns rests on the suitability of modern electronic communications media for projecting personal appeals. The use of television in particular is so striking, especially since mid-century, that it may appear an almost sufficient explanation for candidate-centered politics. But in light of the difficulty of disentangling the effects of television from the impact of the new presidential responsibilities, the decline of old party organizational strength, and other changes in American circumstances, one should be cautious about treating television as the only important reason for the change that has taken place. Also, it must be conceded that television has not sufficed to produce candidate-centered organizations in parliamentary systems, although television is associated with more highly personal appeals of party leaders seeking to become prime ministers. This suggests that either the nature of the American presidency or other characteristics distinguishing the United States from nations with parliamentary systems (or perhaps both) help to account for the candidate-centered campaigns in which television, by its emphasis on personalities, is so useful. Possibly without television we would not have such highly developed candidate-centered campaigns, but that does not mean that television itself is principally responsible for reducing the role of conventional party organizations in general election campaigns any more than it was principally responsible for new kinds of nominating campaigns.[75] Those organizations were giving way to candidate-centered campaigns as the television age began, and they were thus not able, as were European parties, to dominate the political use of the new medium.

IV
Governing

Because presidents are nominated and elected by increasingly candidate-centered efforts, they are thought to be more inclined now than earlier to govern through

personal helpers and broad public appeals rather than conventional party organizations and their coalitions of interests. The new pattern, notably President Carter's, has appeared less effective than an older kind of presidential
leadership. Thus Nelson Polsby, treating the post-1968 nominating system as
a major element in facilitating the change, stresses the increased tendency of
a president, owing little to party leaders, to conduct an Administration without their active involvement.[76] But even if one regards the nominating system as less important in this respect, the possibility of a new and less effective
kind of presidential government needs to be examined.

Generalizing from the Carter experience is risky not only because it is but
a single case. Insofar as the Carter presidency failed, it did so in public leadership as well as in party leadership. Successful presidents tend to play both roles
effectively, though with varying emphases. Now as in the past, the presidency
has nonpartisan or supraparty expectations to be fulfilled along with those
of party. In seeking to fulfill these expectations, contemporary presidents have
less reason to rely on the old confederations of state and local party leaders.
One response is to make more use of their own adherents — presidential parties
— and another is to depend more heavily on a nonpartisan base of support.

Cabinet appointments provide a convenient though rough means for measuring changes in presidential styles of governing. In times past, when presidents were presumably the choices of party leaders and of certain institutionalized party interest groups (labor or farm organizations, for example),
presidents were, also presumably, induced or even compelled to choose department heads many of whom who were more or less representative of that diverse party coalition which had done the nominating and electing. No one
suggests, however, that the practice was as fixed as it is in the British parliamentary system, where prime ministers almost invariably find it expedient and
often necessary to appoint their party's several major leaders to major ministerial positions. Apart from other differences, the American cabinet, unlike
the British, has never been consistently important as a collective decision
maker. Presidents may take the advice of their cabinet members, collectively
or individually, but they may also override such advice. Presidents, not their
cabinets, are politically responsible. Nevertheless, American cabinet positions
are consequential enough so that the backgrounds of persons appointed to
them can tell us something about the way in which presidents intend to govern. To take a famous historical example, President Abraham Lincoln was concerned enough about party unity to name, among the Republican leaders in
his cabinet, two principal rivals for the presidency; he appointed one secretary
of state and the other secretary of the treasury.

We know, too, that presidents have sought to build party support in Congress by choosing influential members of Congress to serve in their cabinets. So it was when President Franklin Roosevelt appointed Senator Cordell Hull as his secretary of state. But even in Roosevelt's time and maybe earlier, there were not many appointees like Hull, despite the then still-prevalent party organizational influence in nominations and elections. Roosevelt's cabinet, for example, had only one other member who was apparently chosen mainly to represent a party interest, and that was James Farley, the patronage-distributing postmaster general who was simultaneously chairman of the Democratic National Committee.[77] But Farley had also been, before his DNC chairmanship, the manager of Roosevelt's successful nominating campaign. He might then have been regarded as one of the president's own adherents. Apart from Hull and Farley, Roosevelt's cabinet, while including other Democratic politicians, was not primarily a vehicle for representing diverse party leaders. At the start it included two members, Secretary of Interior Harold Ickes and Secretary of Agriculture Henry Wallace, who had not been party Democrats but progressive independent supporters of Roosevelt. And in 1940, during World War II but before U.S. entry, Roosevelt named Republicans to both the Army and Navy secretaryships. The Departments of Agriculture, Labor, and usually Commerce were headed by individuals oriented to the interest-group clientele of those departments, but Frances Perkins, the secretary of labor throughout Roosevelt's long presidency, was not herself from the ranks of organized labor nor the choice of its leadership. Like the almost equally long-serving secretary of the treasury, Henry Morgenthau, Perkins is best categorized as a long-time associate of the president himself.

From the Roosevelt example, it is evident that a president could succeed politically, as FDR surely did by winning four elections, with a cabinet appointed primarily for reasons having little to do with party building and maintenance. In that light, let us look at more recent cabinet making. Polsby's analysis, while directed also to Nixon's later appointments and less sharply to Eisenhower's and Kennedy's, concentrates on Jimmy Carter's appointments as the products of a system in which a president feels free from the old constraints that party connections once imposed on cabinet selection. That freedom, Polsby suggests, allowed Carter to weight his cabinet with "can-do technocrats" who commended themselves to the president for essentially nonpolitical reasons.[78] Characterized variously as generalist executives, subject specialists academically or otherwise, or Washington careerists, these appointees occupied over half of the seats in Carter's original cabinet. Although nominally Democrats in most instances and in only one case an identifiable Republican,

the technocrats had not been important party leaders, nor had they been leading members of Carter's own campaign organization. A few had played some
part in the Carter campaign, but like the other technocrats, they seem to have
been chosen primarily because the president respected their reputations for
management and for knowledge of governmental policy in a given area. The
number that Carter thus chose may well be unusually high compared to the
record of his predecessors and of his immediate successor, but it is not generally out of line with cabinet-making tendencies in recent decades, before as
well as after the new nominating system could have provided presidents with
the freedom that Polsby emphasizes. "Can-do technocrats" would suit any
modern president who in his elected monarch role seeks competency, efficiency, and ability.

Even with Carter's larger-than-usual number of technocrats, his 1977 cabinet had room for several other kinds of appointees. Three were Democrats
from the House of Representatives and one was a former Democratic governor. Two of those four, ex-Representative Bob Bergland at Agriculture and
Idaho's ex-governor Cecil Andrus at Interior, came from the constituencies
with which their departments dealt. Nevertheless Polsby contends that "the
constituencies suggested by the old New Deal voting coalition" — representatives
of European ethnic groups, cities, labor unions, and long-time active party
members — were hard to find. "The Carter cabinet," he states, "was far stronger
in symbolic than in traditional interest group representation."[79] At least three
cabinet members (a black man and two women, one black and one white)
could have provided the symbolic representation that Polsby writes about. But
should they be treated as only symbolic, or as more symbolic than the traditional representation of other groups, ethnic or whatever? Blacks especially
might simply be regarded as now so large a part of the Democratic coalition
as to require representation, and women important enough to have two places
rather than the one position usual after 1933. In other words, interest groups
were represented in Carter's cabinet, but not entirely in accord with a highly
regarded traditional formula.

A more meaningful characteristic of Carter's cabinet, it seems to me, is the
limited number of its members named from the president's own campaign
organization. Only two, Griffin Bell as attorney general and Bert Lance as
director of the office of management and budget, were close early associates
of Carter; Lance especially was close to Carter after his governorship. Perhaps their fellow Georgian, Andrew Young, ambassador to the United Nations, should also be classified as a Carter associate because of his early campaign help. Otherwise, none of Carter's cabinet members had been important

leaders of a "presidential party" organized to win the nomination and election. Thus Carter did not, as one might expect under the new system, use in a large way his own adherents to replace the conventional party as a source of cabinet members. And insofar as he did draw most crucially on his own political associates at this level, notably in appointing Lance, the effort ended early with Lance's forced resignation.

By comparison, President Reagan did choose cabinet members more substantially from his previous staffs, one built for the campaign and another overlapping one that dated from his California governorship. He named associates from these staffs to at least three of his initial cabinet positions — Caspar Weinberger as secretary of defense, William Smith as attorney general, and William Casey as director of the Central Intelligence Agency — and later a fourth, William Clark, as secretary of interior. Two or three other Reagan cabinet members, active but less prominent among his campaign supporters, might marginally be counted among early presidential adherents.[80] Although some of the earlier associates like Weinberger qualify also as "can-do technocrats," they differ from Carter's technocrats in their previously established ideological and often personal loyalty to the president. In this respect Reagan's cabinet, more than Carter's, looks like the result of a system in which a presidential party is the source for major executive appointments.[81]

Significantly, Reagan's choice of his own adherents is consistent with a trend discerned in other recent presidencies. A decade ago, John Kessel noted that insofar as presidents still chose a few cabinet officers from among active and heavily identified party politicians, these appointees were not representative of the whole party under whose label the president had won election. Kessel found, instead, that almost all of the president's partisan appointments, not only to the cabinet but also to the sub-cabinet and White House staff, were "drawn from the nomination and electoral coalitions that supported the successful candidate."[82] Confirmation of this trend is provided by a later study in which Roger Brown emphasizes that presidents since Kennedy, while still giving most major appointments to persons bearing their party label, have relied increasingly on their staffs rather than on the national party committee to identify those to be appointed. Reagan may differ, as Brown suggests, only because of a greater ideological concern in selecting appointees. In that case, as Brown also notes, ideology may be providing the basis for a new and effective kind of presidential party.[83]

Whether or not other contemporary presidents seek ideologically compatible appointees so assiduously as the conservative Reagan is supposed to have done, they are readily perceived as trying to direct the now-massive executive branch through able and loyal lieutenants of their own choosing. For this purpose, one close observer of presidential management, Stephen Hess, sees administrative advantages in the diminution of old-party constraints. He treats the increased presidential freedom to appoint cabinet officers more fully on the basis of ability as especially useful, because he wants the government to be managed by department heads on whom a president can rely rather than trying, futilely, to manage the whole executive branch through the White House staff.[84]

So far, however, the White House staff rather than the cabinet has been the conspicuous means for recent presidents to attempt to manage their administrations. That staff, whose rapid growth in the last few decades is a principal mark of the contemporary presidency, is the heart of the "president's party" in government. By the 1970s, the White House had over 600 employees, including about 120 with professional titles, compared with the total in 1933 of 37, only nine of whom were professionals. The White House staff, it should be understood, is separate from the less closely related presidential help in the larger Executive Office, whose several agencies, mainly post-1933 creations, now have thousands of employes.[85] Almost all of the latter are plainly recruited on a more or less regularized bureaucratic basis to facilitate the management of government and its policies. The White House staff, while its members are most closely tied to the president in office, includes members — those serving the national security adviser, for example — who are not directly related to the president's campaign organization. Hence their presence or influence cannot be attributed to the new candidate-centered presidential politics. Nor can we be sure that even many of the White House staffers who play domestic political roles — those who seek to influence Congress, for example — would not be needed by any contemporary president, no matter what kind of campaign he had to wage to get elected or would have to wage to get reelected.

Although the growth and complexity of the national government, and with it the growth of presidential responsibilities, can largely account for the members and the influence of the White House staff, the development is accelerated when a president suspects that the permanent bureaucracy cannot be trusted to carry out his policies.[86] Nixon was notoriously suspicious, as we know, and he did try at one stage to manage government departments through his White House staff and at another time to place persons loyal to that staff in key departmental positions.[87] Some presidential distrust of the bureaucracy may have become endemic to the system. As Heclo points out, even many of the political appointments that the president is able to make at the top of the bureaucracy are drawn, inevitably, from the ranks of relatively permanent bureaucrats. They are neither party nor personal presidential choices; their experience is technical and not political.[88] Presidents, then, must depend on their own staffs to press their own policies.

Allowing for an enlarged presidential staff regardless of the method of nomination and election, it can still be said that candidate-centered politics have added to the personal nature of the staff. Conceivably, an old-style party president might have felt constrained, as he did in making cabinet appointments, to represent leading party factions on his staff, or at least to appoint staff members most able and willing to conciliate those factions. But in a way such appointments, insofar as they would mean choosing persons whose loyalty was not primarily to him, run counter to the very purpose of a White House staff. A president would be unlikely to want a staff unless it was his own. And it is surely too much to claim that a stronger party system would have precluded an enlarged White House staff altogether. It might merely have made it more difficult to operate. The personal character of the White House staff, although explicable independently of changes in nominating and election processes, is consonant with candidate-centered presidential politics. Certainly it serves such politics.

The way in which the White House staff serves contemporary presidential politics may be observed in the president's relations with Congress. These are the relations that one would expect to see affected most clearly by candidate-centered politics; presidents long used their party ties to congressional leaders as a means of attempting to exert influence, just as members of Congress used those ties to try to influence the president. Franklin Roosevelt's use of staff members to influence legislation was evident though informally organized.[89] In 1953, Eisenhower institutionalized the relationship when he established the White House Office of Congressional Relations. It remains in 1985 with a staff of ten—five full-time lobbyists for the House and four for the Senate, serving under an assistant for legislative affairs.[90]

In the Democratic Administrations of Kennedy and Johnson, the OCR was often able to work effectively with the Democratic majority party leaders in Congress, although it was not uniformly successful in attaining its legislative objectives.[91] For Nixon and Ford, its work was complicated but hardly precluded by the continuous congressional Democratic majorities serving with Republican presidents. Carter's use of the OCR, along with his personal relations with members of Congress, was widely regarded as inept, but Reagan's OCR and Reagan himself, especially in 1981, won much better reputations for effectiveness.[92] Significantly, the effectiveness relates to dealings with many individual senators and representatives as well as with party leaders. In the new Congress, with its many foci of power in subcommittees and independent-minded members, more votes than before must be won directly by the White House rather than merely through party leaders and committee chairmen. To do so requires a substantial staff to at least target members whom the president must persuade. The president alone might, as earlier, be able to work with a few congressional party leaders, but so much more is now required that the OCR is a fitting institutional feature of this century's effort to bridge the separation of powers. Even a president chosen by a revived convention of party leaders would need the OCR or something very like it to deal with a present-day Congress.[93]

Much more than a well-staffed OCR is obviously needed if presidents are to win congressional support for their policies. It is but one of the means by which a president must seek support among senators and representatives of the opposition party, as well as among senators and representatives who share his label but feel even less bound than did members in earlier years to follow his party leadership. Of greater significance is a president's capacity to mobilize broad public support for himself and his programs by playing his nonpartisan role. Seeking such support has been encouraged in recent decades both by the absence of assured majority party support and by the changing nature of executive responsibilities, notably in foreign affairs.[94] A modern president seeking to influence policy must, as Neustadt says, "make the most he can out of his popular connection."[95]

Television and radio provide the opportunity for presidents to reach the public even more fully than they do for presidential candidates, and it is commonly believed that a skilled mass communicator like Reagan makes good use of these opportunities and so scores legislative successes that eluded Carter. But it ought also to be pointed out that the presidency itself, not only radio and television, is well suited to the mobilization of broad public support. Its use antedates radio and television. Though less direct and instantaneous than they, the printed word could in the past also draw on the appeal inherent in the elected monarchical side of the presidency. That appeal is now simply readier at hand and probably more essential than ever for effective government.

Dwight Eisenhower, very much a modern president before the post-1968 nominating system, provides an example of how the nonpartisan role may be skillfully used. Unusually well cast for the role because of his military background and lack of previous partisan activity, President Eisenhower, as Fred Greenstein writes in *The Hidden-Hand Presidency*, played "the part of nonpolitical chief of state so convincingly" that the political or "prime ministerial" side of his presidency was largely concealed. Eisenhower left "a public impression that he was not a political strategist, but rather a head of state who was above politics."[96] The clear implication is that his emphasis on the nonpolitical head-of-state role, or on what I have called the elected monarch role, made Eisenhower more, not less, effective as a Republican party leader at the same time that it enabled him to achieve the broader non-Republican support that a successful presidency required.[97]

V
Summary

I do not mean to end this chapter by suggesting that we look for another Eisenhower as the modern fulfillment of the Washingtonian figure whom the founders sought for the presidency. Few if any presidents are now likely to come to office with Eisenhower's (or George Washington's) background. Only an approximation of Eisenhower's broad public appeal would ordinarily be feasible. But as Reagan demonstrated in his first term as in his landslide re-election, it is possible for a president to attract support well beyond party ranks without the special advantages of military stature and reputation. More-over, Reagan was able to do so even as he also fulfilled a strongly ideological role as party leader more openly and probably more substantially than had Eisenhower.

Significantly, too, Reagan's party leadership included working arrangements with Republican leaders in Congress who had by no means been responsible for his nomination. Like Carter before him, Reagan owed his original nomination mainly to voters in primaries and to his own organized adherents who helped to mobilize those voters. Unlike Carter, however, Reagan became the effective head of a working coalition of congressional partisans as well as of his narrower though more cohesive prenomination organization. Thus while the new nominating system may have produced one president unable or un-willing to work successfully with his party's congressional leaders, it produced another president whose first-term record appears relatively impressive. Never-theless, one might still agree with Polsby that the new nominating system is more likely to choose an ineffective coalition builder than did the old convention method of nomination. If so, we may have to live with the disadvantage. For reasons that I have gone into, the essence of the new system seems here to stay for presidential as for other nominations.

In any event, the new nominating system is but one of several changes that might be held responsible for increasing candidate-centered politics and thus for greater difficulties in presidential-congressional governing relations. Presidential elections themselves, like congressional elections, have become even more individualized affairs than they used to be, and certainly Congress itself has so dispersed its power that it is harder than ever for presidents, as for congressional party leaders, to achieve their purposes. It is by no means clear that the president's own highly organized adherents, though more national and policy oriented than conventional parties, can play as important a role in government as they do in nominations and elections. They constitute a party in only a limited sense. A president, now even more than before, is thus compelled to draw on general public support along with what he can muster from his own party. As always, his office has some of the character of an elected monarchy, of a national leadership beyond partisanship, despite its continuing preeminence as the focus for partisan electoral alignment.

Chapter Five

State and Local Structure

Historically, neither Republicans nor Democrats built truly national extra-governmental organizations comparable to their congressional or presidential parties-in-government. Congressional campaign committees have become useful fund raisers but not mobilizers of numerous party activists. Presidents and presidential nominees, while always the focus for national electoral alignments, have only lately been perceived as organizers of their own parties of issue activists. Such parties still look suspiciously ad hoc, even if more coherent than older party organizations at the national level. The established Republican and Democratic national committees, though they have become more significant in ways to be explored in chapter 7, have long had confederative structures resting on parties organized at the state and local level. Accordingly one must look to that level, even in a work about parties in national politics, for the traditionally substantial extragovernmental organizations. And that requires a discussion of the general characteristics of state and local party politics.

It is understandable that parties in the United States, as in other federal systems, should be organized as state units. They are products of a constitutional and social order in which important foci of governmental power exist below the national level. Indeed, during much of American history, state rather than national legislation clearly dominated governmental domestic policymaking. Even with the growth of national government programs in this century, state governments have so increased their activities in absolute terms that they remain major legislative policymakers over large areas of economic and social affairs. They are durable units of government, and so are *their* cities and counties.[1]

I

Extension of the National Party Alignment

Less predictable than the development of state and local party organizations competing for the substantial power available in the subnational units of the American federal system is that such organizations should, when effective, almost always and almost everywhere bear the labels of the two major national parties. Since the 1860s, partisan electoral competition has been mainly between Republicans and Democrats for state offices as it has for Congress and the presidency. And as far back as the second-party system of Whigs against Democrats, the national labels were used in state elections; then too, as observed in the last chapter, state electoral alignments followed from the national and most particularly the presidential alignment. No matter how much more concerned state and local organizations may have been with state and local offices than with national offices, they and their candidates have nonetheless made good use of their national party's electoral following in their own constituencies. To be sure, in many places one party is often electorally so much stronger than the other that interparty competition is only nominal or even nonexistent. But this is only to say that the national alignment extends in different ways to different states, making for Republican or Democratic dominance in some situations and for serious Republican-Democratic competition in others. The striking fact remains that the pattern is entirely unlike that of Canada, with its persistence of regionally strong third parties that are able to win power in the provincial governments of that federal system.[2]

In the United States, seriously contending parties under other labels, always exceptional throughout the long Republican and Democratic era, have in recent decades virtually disappeared in state as in congressional elections. Nothing similar to the substantial minority showing of third-party presidential candidates, notably George Wallace's in 1968, has lately developed in statewide elections. The closest to exceptions are the votes for Conservative party and Liberal party candidates in New York State, but those who win or run strong races are almost always candidates simultaneously carrying the Republican or Democratic label.[3] New York's distinctive election law permits multiple nomination as well as multiple ballot placement, and in various other ways enhances the status and opportunity of minor parties so that they are effectively institutionalized as they are not in other states.[4] But neither in New York nor in any other state has a third party, since the 1940s, captured a governorship or enough seats in a state legislature to become potent even as a minority.[5] In fact, no third-party members occupied any of the over 7,400 state legislative seats in 1983 (and only seven were Independents, apart from Nebraska's 49-member nonpartisan and unicameral legislature).[6]

Exceptions were more numerous and substantial during earlier decades. Not only did Socialist and various other protest parties occasionally elect minority contingents in certain states, but there were two twentieth-century instances in which third parties, Minnesota's Farmer-Labor party and Wisconsin's Progressives, actually won gubernatorial elections and legislative majorities. In the 1930s, each of these parties effectively displaced a Democratic party as one of two major parties in state politics. Interesting though these successes were in the otherwise virtually universal dominance of Republicans and Democrats, their brevity is of greater long-run significance. Neither the Farmer-Labor party nor the Progressive party survived as a separate entity after the mid-1940s. Minnesota's third party, after losses in several successive elections, merged in 1944 with the Democratic party under the Democratic–Farmer-Labor label. The Wisconsin Progressives, also after sharply declining electoral fortunes, abandoned their separate party label in order to compete again in Republican primaries or, below the top leadership level, to become Democrats. In both instances, the experience neatly illustrates the triumph of national electoral forces over those elements of a state's own political culture that had been hospitable to a third party.[7]

From the Wisconsin experience, I can readily amplify the illustration.[8] Like most of the upper Great Lakes region after the Civil War and more pronouncedly in the early twentieth century, Wisconsin was mainly Republican in both national and state voting; for a quarter-century before the 1930s, the most meaningful electoral competition was ordinarily between progressives (notably the members and followers of the La Follette family) and their stalwart (conservative) opponents in Republican primaries. Only in most unusual circumstances did Democrats win statewide contests. Those circumstances were present in 1932 in the depth of the Great Depression. Then Wisconsin not only voted overwhelmingly for Franklin Roosevelt but also elected Democrats to statewide offices, including governor and U.S. senator, and installed a Democratic legislative majority as well. Suddenly the Republican label, whether worn by a progressive or a stalwart, was discredited. It still seemed so in 1934 when progressives, principally Robert La Follette, Jr., seeking to retain his U.S. Senate seat, and his brother Philip, seeking to regain the governorship, decided to launch their third party. Because progressives had been virtually a party within the Republican party ever since Robert La Follette, Sr., had been governor in the first decade of the century, both an apparatus and a following were available. But why did they not go into the Democratic party if the Republican party had to be deserted as a sinking ship?

Given Wisconsin's open primary, many progressives might have been able to win Democratic primaries, as they had won Republican primaries, even though in 1934 they would often have been running against incumbent Democrats. The likelier impediment was that the Democratic label, even if won in primaries, had for so long been unattractive to most Wisconsin voters that its value after 1932 and possibly 1934 was dubious. Moreover, most of the state's Democratic leaders, and specifically many elected to office in 1932, were conservative and, at the same time, associated with a kind of old-time patronage politics decidedly at odds with Wisconsin's moralistic political culture. In other words, the Democratic party had a bad name in the state. Although it was now the party of Franklin Roosevelt, it was not yet so firmly the party of liberalism that it became after 12 years of Roosevelt and eight years of Truman.

At any rate, the third-party option worked in 1934 and 1936 when Progressives won state and congressional elections but failed, apart from a few special cases, after Republicans (with conservative Democratic help) reestablished their majority in 1938. When Wisconsin Republicans were effectively challenged again after World War II, it was by a new state Democratic party whose leaders were very much in line with the northern liberalism of the national party, specifically with its presidential campaigns. The third-party Progressives had not been able to retain the loyalty of voters, who now, particularly in urban areas, identified with the Democratic party of FDR and Truman in national politics. The national electoral alignment was simply too strong a force to counter, and Wisconsin reemerged as an arena for competition between Republicans and Democrats. More precisely, it became in the late 1950s more clearly two-party competitive than it had been in the years of Republican dominance preceding the three-party period.

A much more persistent and widespread exception to Republican and Democratic competition in the twentieth century is the elimination of party labels altogether. I am not writing here of Independents who win state or even congressional offices by defeating Republicans and Democrats; such instances are about as few as are recent third-party successes, and no more significant. Rather, I have in mind the vast number of elective offices that are filled under state laws prescribing nonpartisan ballots. Two states — Nebraska since 1935 and Minnesota from 1913 to 1974 — have even elected their state legislators without party labels. More commonly, though not universally, states prescribe nonpartisan ballots to elect their judges and various administrative officers (apart from the governor and a few others), and also require such ballots for many local offices. In the 1960s, it was estimated that at least 85 percent of all school elections and 65 percent of all municipal elections used nonpartisan ballots; the latter number was up to 76 percent in 1976.[9] Variations among the states are numerous. For example, Illinois law allows Chicago's mayor to be elected on a partisan ballot while the city council is not. Other states, though specifying nonpartisan ballots for all city offices, retain partisan ballots for many county positions. Hence the offices of sheriff, district attorney, and other elected courthouse occupants often survive as bastions of local partisanship.

The widespread use of the nonpartisan ballot in American cities is chiefly the product of municipal reform in the late nineteenth and early twentieth centuries. Reformers, interested in efficient and honest administration of services, sought to separate city government from party voting in accord with national alignments, and thus liberate city government from what were regarded as baneful machines that depended on the loyalty of impoverished and immigrant populations. While the machines ordinarily worked with particularly important business interests, the municipal reformers tended to be upper- and middle-class citizens whose idea of good government suited the more general purposes of the business and professional community. A similar coincidence of purposes probably occurred when the nonpartisan ballot was aimed not at Republican or Democratic organizations but rather at the new Socialist parties that had begun to elect mayors in various cities during the first two decades of the twentieth century. For example, in 1912 the Wisconsin legislature was persuaded to impose the nonpartisan municipal ballot partly because of its supposed usefulness in defeating a Socialist candidate for mayor of Milwaukee.[10] But even without Socialists in the picture, rural and small-town legislators in many states could well have been attracted by a measure aimed at any big-city machine. At any rate, the banning of party labels was more widely adopted than most of the other means — use of city managers, commission governments, and at-large council elections — that reformers of municipal politics proposed in the same period.

Nevertheless, not all states imposed the nonpartisan ballot on their cities. New York and other northeastern states, where party organizations were strongest, retained party labels on municipal ballots. And in some places, even when labels were removed, as in Chicago for its council elections, most successful candidates remained de facto party choices. The ethos of nonpartisanship has not always accompanied the legal effort to provide it. Only when that ethos is strong, as it is in Wisconsin, are party organizations deterred from open involvement in municipal campaigns. And when parties can and do become involved, officially or unofficially, they are almost invariably Republican and Democrat. The alternative, frequent to be sure, is candidate-centered politics, occasionally including roles for ad hoc organizations or local good-government associations but rarely for a new or third party that might, from a municipal base, challenge Republicans or Democrats in state and national politics.

Without significant third-party challenges to the Republican-Democratic alignment, it is the competition, however imperfect, between the two major parties that commands attention in the states. One-party domination over long periods is familiar at both local and state levels and even regionally. I have already suggested, however, that such domination is not properly an exception to the extension of the national alignment but is one of the products of that extension. The point is effectively made in a leading recent work on state parties and elections: "National party alignments determine the approximate proportion of Democrats and Republicans in a state and establish the bases for (or virtually prohibit) two-party competition in a state."[11] The parenthetical phrase is loaded with meaning. It refers to states whose voters have been so heavily attracted by one national party, and so repelled by the other, that one-party domination rather than competition prevails.

How great one-party dominance must be and how long it must last before interparty competition becomes meaningless is not always clear. One party's candidates might win all statewide offices and legislative majorities over several decades, but if their margins were occasionally close it would be hard to say that interparty competition was meaningless. The second major party could well remain a plausible electoral alternative. And so it could be if one or more of its statewide candidates won now and then although its other candidates lost by large margins almost always. Uneven competition is not the same as one-partyism. In fact, it would be surprising if interparty competition were not highly uneven in the states to which the national electoral alignment extends. Whatever the social and economic basis for that alignment, each major party cannot be expected to have roughly equal numbers of followers everywhere, or even to have enough followers in a particular state or locality to preclude victory by the other party over several decades. Nevertheless, slightly more than half of the states have been classified "competitive two-party" as measured by gubernatorial and legislative election results between 1961 and 1982, and all others except seven southern states as either "Democratic majority" or "Republican majority" — meaning at least an occasional minority-party victory in a gubernatorial election.[12] Admittedly, the virtually complete

Democratic domination in most southern states for over a century represents no ordinary unevenness in distribution of partisan voters. We treat it as an aberration produced by peculiarly traumatic historical circumstances. Otherwise, the uneven spread of party competition in the United States does not itself appear unusual. In other nations too, with or without governmental units resembling American states, one party or another tends to dominate many constituencies and often whole geographic clusters of constituencies.

The United States is unusual, however, in its provision for a special kind of electoral competition in one-party situations. The direct primary, while also widely used in competitive interparty situations, is most important when a given party label, once obtained, virtually ensures subsequent general election success. Then, the primary election may give voters a meaningful choice that they would not otherwise have. Moreover, it can be argued that the direct primary was adopted early in this century at least partly to escape the consequences of post-Civil War one-partyism, especially in southern Democratic states and some northern Republican states, where without popular participation in nominating candidates there could be no effective popular participation at all. The argument is supported by evidence of earlier adoption of the direct primary in one-party states than in two-party competitive states.[13] But more distinctively American reasons, which I describe in the next chapter, must also have been responsible for the direct primary. After all, other nations, despite numerous one-party dominated constituencies and regions, have left party candidate-selection or nomination to party organizations. Nowhere outside of the United States are there government-run elections in which ordinary voters choose party nominees.

Whether or not the direct primary was itself a response to one-partyism, it appears likely to maintain or even strengthen an existing one-party pattern, especially but not only when a primary is open to voters without the requirement of prior party registration or declaration. Those who seek office against incumbents or against the dominant party's organizational leaders may perceive the primary of the dominant party as a more advantageous vehicle for success than entry, however easy, as candidates of a minority party. Protests, along with ambition, talent, and interest, are thus attracted to a single party. The tendency is marked in whole states and still more often in smaller constituencies—legislative districts, cities, and counties. Of course, a dominant party would almost certainly have a somewhat similar attraction for many aspiring candidates even if its nominations were conferred by an organizational convention rather than by a direct primary. But protest movements with greater potential strength among voters than among organizational delegates might not be so readily tempted to seek nominations in a dominant party whose convention had the authority to confer the label. Without the direct primary, it is reasonable to speculate that such movements and their candidates would be likelier to try to win the more readily obtainable label of a nondominant party and thus increase the possibility for interparty competition.

However reasonable, the speculation is hard to support empirically. What can be shown, as it was strikingly by V. O. Key, is that voting tends to concentrate in the dominant party's primary more heavily than in the dominant party's column at the general election.[14] It follows, Key said, that "as states deviate from equality of strength between parties, the frequency of sharp competition within the stronger party increases."[15] But we still do not know that any specific state has thus substituted primary competition for interparty competition in a way that makes the latter less likely. Perhaps the state would have lacked significant interparty competition in any event, even if it had not adopted the direct primary. Inferences from the record are inconclusive. In southern one-party states, for example, not only did extreme one-partyism develop before the direct primary, but the social basis for that one-partyism long continued to be so tenacious that the primary seems less than crucial, though surely useful, for Democratic dominance. And when that social basis changed, as it did most significantly after 1960, one-partyism finally began to diminish despite the direct primary. At most, it could still be contended, the primary helped to delay the growth of a Republican opposition. An analogously uncertain generalization can be made about the experience of a once dominantly Republican northern state like Wisconsin. Having adopted the direct primary when it meant electoral competition for Republican nominations that were tantamount to election, Wisconsin surely used the arrangement for that purpose for most of the first three decades of this century. But if the primary helped in those years to maintain one-partyism, with only a brief Democratic revival in the early Wilson years, it was insufficient to maintain it under the impact of the Rooseveltian New Deal and the national politics that followed. Two-party competition came to Wisconsin in response to the force of the same national alignment that affected other states in the upper midwest. Here too, however, it can still be argued that the direct primary tended to delay the development of two-party competition. The fact that such competition did finally become established by the 1950s — and then much more fully than it is even now in most of the South — does not mean that the direct primary was an unlikely deterrent in the upper Midwest as well as in the South. On the contrary, because one-partyism in the North was never as overwhelming nor its social basis as tenacious as in the South, it might have been expected to yield still earlier to two-party competition if the direct primary had not provided alternative opportunities for popularly based opposition. That is to say, the primary could be more influential in delaying two-party competition in the less extreme one-party states of the North.

So far I have followed the custom of discussing the direct primary's relation to one-partyism as opposed to two-party competition. That fits the context of American state politics, especially during the last half-century, and it is usual for American political scientists to put aside the alternative of multiparty competition that concerns students of European and comparative politics generally. Hence Americans give less attention to the possibility that the direct primary may deter third-party development than to its apparent tendency to limit the use of a second party. Yet in a comparative perspective, the speculative argument for the effect on third parties seems more plausible.[16] The weakness of third parties, or at least of persistent third parties, in American elections is a more distinctive phenomenon than the one-party domination of many constituencies. The latter characterizes politics elsewhere, but the weakness of third parties does not. Even Britain, though smaller and less diverse than the United States, has now, and has had during much of this century, a much more nearly multiparty pattern than the United States.

It is arguable, therefore, that the also distinctively American institution, the direct primary, is a cause of the distinctively American weakness of third parties. The reasoning is that third-party efforts are discouraged by the opportunity to capture the label of one or the other major party in a primary. At the start of any analysis, however, we must recognize that American two-partyism had been firmly established in the nineteenth century, and that in 1896, before the adoption of direct primaries, the Democratic party effectively absorbed most of the followers of the relatively new but substantial Populist party. The two-party alignment, though then highly sectionalized, seemed about as pervasive as it was to be after the institutionalization of the direct primary. Thus, to attribute to the direct primary an influence in deterring third-party development, it is necessary to argue that the twentieth century, more than the late nineteenth, would have provided other favorable political conditions for the growth of a new party if the direct primary had not existed. One such condition is the aging of a two-party alignment that rested so heavily on Civil War issues. Another is the rise of progressivism, socialism, and trade unionism in response to the newly overwhelming industrial and urban character of the country. In most other nations such forces, particularly a unionized working-class, led to a new and large socialist or labor party that soon became one of two, three, or four major parties. The American Socialist party might have seemed to possess that kind of future when it grew substantially in the second decade of the twentieth century, but it requires a wild imaginative leap to conclude that its subsequent failure to realize that future can be attributed to the direct primary. It is possible to find more impressive explanations for the failure of socialism in the United States.[17]

Other twentieth-century American third parties, while occasionally attracting more votes in presidential elections, are not in most respects as much like important European counterparts as was the Socialist party. Not only was the latter a national party, nominating presidential candidates over several decades, but it also had enduring pockets of organizational and electoral strength (even some electoral success) in certain states and cities. Only on a much smaller scale do the still new Libertarian party and a few older ideological or single-issue parties parallel the Socialist effort. The better-known American third parties in this century have characteristically been either short-lived presidential election phenomena—Theodore Roosevelt in 1912, Robert La Follette in 1924, Henry Wallace and Strom Thurmond in 1948, George Wallace in 1968, and John Anderson in 1980[18]—or single-state phenomena—Minnesota's Farmer-Labor party and Wisconsin's Progressive party of the 1930s, and New York's Conservative and Liberal parties of recent decades. The presidential election vehicles, despite initially large popular votes, seldom developed electoral strength in campaigns for congressional or state offices, and they did not always nominate candidates for these offices even in their best years. Their leaders have ordinarily soon returned to one or the other of the old major parties from which they came. And single-state third parties declined or completely disappeared, as in Minnesota and Wisconsin, without achieving a successful national or even regional presence.[19]

For state as for national third-party leaders, the direct primary no doubt made it easier to reenter Republican or Democratic ranks than would an older organizational control of nominations. Thus early abandonment of evidently failing third parties may be encouraged by the same intraparty electoral opportunity that appears to make third parties less useful in the first place. The evidence is only circumstantial, as it was for the direct primary's encouragement of one-partyism, but it adds plausibility to the speculation that the distinctively American nominating method helps to account for the otherwise puzzling preservation in the states, as in the nation, of only two electorally useful party labels.

The significance of that preservation would, however, be limited if the direct primary has destroyed party organizational influence as well as control of the nominating process. There might then be a kind of no-party politics conducted under the Republican and Democratic labels. In fact, we know that campaigns to win party nominations are sometimes so candidate centered, even in two-party competitive states, as to have great impact in the general election contest as well. Yet because general election opponents do carry party labels their contest is not purely candidate centered. In state legislative and gubernatorial elections as in congressional and presidential elections, each party label, Republican or Democratic, has a collective meaning, though secured initially by individual rather than party organizational effort. Even in the absence of organized party help in the general election campaign, the label produces many and probably most of the votes for a candidate. Still more significantly, the winning candidate becomes a member of an officeholding party bearing the same label as that used in the general election.

Among state officeholders and also among local officeholders in some places, governing parties of Republicans and Democrats exist as they do in the national capital. Gubernatorial parties and especially legislative parties resemble the parties of officeholders in Washington. With only Nebraska now as the exception, state legislatures have Republican or Democratic majorities that almost always organize their houses and otherwise function collectively to try to manage legislative business. As in Congress so in state legislative chambers, the "normal pattern," a recent survey confirms, is for presiding officers to be the choice of a majority-party caucus. The relatively few exceptions tend to occur in overwhelmingly one-party states or in most unusual situations encouraging individual or factional defections. No trend toward bipartisanship is discerned.[20]

In other respects, too, most state legislatures remain highly partisan in their organization. Standing committee memberships almost invariably reflect the majority party's strength, sometimes even disproportionately in order to ensure control. Furthermore, control of committees by party leaders is in one vital respect likelier in state legislatures than in Congress. State legislatures are not nearly as firmly bound as Congress by seniority norms in awarding committee chairs or in continuing committee assignments. Average legislative service is shorter than it is in Congress, and accordingly, long-time legislative professionalism is less characteristic of state legislators, although now developing as certain urban states "modernize" by increasing legislative salaries and staff assistance.[21] Altogether, state legislative circumstances are still relatively conducive to majority-party effectiveness in public policymaking as well as in strictly procedural and organizational matters. Studies of legislative roll-call votes in New York and some other urban two-party states show more party cohesion than has been found in congressional parties.[22]

This is not to say that party government is in other ways easier to achieve at the state than at the national level. The separation-of-powers doctrine operates in each state, as it does nationally, in a way that frequently splits control of the elected branches between the two parties,[23] and that in any event elects an executive and legislators who, even though of the same party, are not mutually dependent in the manner of executive and legislators in a parliamentary system. Governors may not succeed much more often than presidents in persuading legislative majorities to follow what they define as party positions. Nevertheless governors, like presidents, are party leaders among other things, and again like presidents, they do on many occasions seek to use the party tie to achieve policy results. For that purpose, extragovernmental party organizations, supposedly stronger in states than nationally, might well be relevant.

II

The Old Organizations

However much the traditionally strong state and local extragovernmental party organizations have declined, as almost everyone believes they have in adverse twentieth-century circumstances, they deserve attention as the most substantial party organizations ever to exist in the United States. Not all of them have entirely disappeared, and in any event, their historical strength indelibly marks American politics. Despite their primarily state and local concerns, the old party organizations not only derived electoral advantage from the Republican and Democratic labels of the national alignment, as state and local parties still do, but they could also benefit from the addition of national patronage to state and local sources. To seek such patronage from Washington, the old organizations were indeed willing to join forces to choose their party's presidential nominees and then to help elect them. By no means is this fact at odds with the observation that the bastions of the old successful party organizations were their relatively durable state and local centers of power.

The patronage that distinguishes the old organizations, dating from the nineteenth century but persisting well into the twentieth, meant enough government jobs to provide, at taxpayers' expense, party workers at and between elections for the successful mobilization of voters. Government jobs are only one kind of patronage or spoils of office, to be sure, but other kinds — business contracts, licenses, and favors of all sorts — have often remained available when government jobs in large numbers ceased to be subject to patronage. It is reasonable, therefore, to regard old-style organizations as existing only when civil service laws have inadequately protected rank-and-file employees from being hired and fired because of the effectiveness or ineffectiveness of their vote-getting efforts. In the nineteenth century and the early decades of the twentieth century, when such protection was unusual, old-style organizations could thrive almost everywhere in the United States. Even in the middle and later decades of this century, civil service protection remained nonexistent or unenforced in significant jurisdictions. Thus Chicago, at least into the 1970s, had an organization whose numerous ward and precinct workers could be and were rewarded with government jobs. There and elsewhere, the number of such jobs was crucial. Nothing like an effective vote-getting organization could be created from control of appointments to policymaking positions and judgeships alone. But with 30,000 local jobs available in Chicago, or more properly to the Cook County Democratic party, there was indeed a patronage basis for organizational vote-mobilization.[24]

Similarly large numbers of jobs were characteristically at the disposal of many party organizations during their heyday. There were jobs in police, fire, and sanitation services, in street departments, in city offices of all kinds, and in city construction (even by private contractors).[25] The many patronage jobholders were ordinarily expected to help produce votes on election day, and they were often financially assessed, in well-understood percentages of salary, to support party campaigns.[26]

The familiar American term for the large patronage-dispensing organization is *machine*, and I shall use the term interchangeably with *old* or *old-style organization*, despite its implication of an efficiency that might not have often existed and despite its connotation of fraud and corruption that might not have been applicable to all of the older organizations.[27] The machine and its boss are best known as urban phenomena. They flourished at one time or another in every large American city,[28] but also in many smaller cities and rural counties.[29] And there have been statewide machines whose power often meshed with that of local organizations, notably city machines in the Northeast and Midwest.[30] Although not uniformly prominent nor continuously powerful everywhere, the old machines dominated politics in so many of the most visible governmental arenas that they seemed for over a century the typical American extragovernmental party organizations. They were, as I shall stress in the next chapter, the organizations against which reformers reacted when they sought to regulate and restrict parties. And even where they no longer exist, they are still the symbolic targets for a good deal of the antiparty sentiment that has become so characteristically American.

A general antiparty sentiment, it may be granted, goes back to the constitutional founders and thus antedates the machines and the reaction to them. But that sentiment did not prevent the large-scale development, in the middle decades of the nineteenth century, of extragovernmental party organizations. They were then highly innovative institutions. Unlike congressional caucuses, which served as parties-in-government analogous to British parliamentary parties, the new American extragovernmental party organizations had no real parallels in other nations. Nowhere else at the time were vote-getting organizations developed on as large a scale, and nowhere else were they so relevant; because even when meaningful elections were held in other nations, the franchise was very limited. In the United States, however, as early as 1824, almost 50 years before mass male suffrage began to be regularly established in most of Europe, all but three American states extended the right to vote to almost all adult white males.[31]

In retrospect, some extragovernmental party organization appears to have been nearly inevitable in response to the mass franchise. The inevitability is suggested by the subsequent development in other nations of such organization when those nations did extend the franchise to large numbers. But because American party organizations arose in earlier and different circumstances, they developed significant characteristics of their own. Their reliance on the control of the many government jobs had developed to a degree virtually impossible in nations like Britain that did not have modern mass parties until after a merit-based civil service was established. Also, American parties, unlike many European parties, were not originally organized by or for an already large industrial working class seeking, in addition to the franchise, a radical transformation of capitalist society. The United States in the first half of the nineteenth century was too rural and too expansive a society to provide a basis for a major socialist party, with its distinctive organizational features, or for the kind of party, capitalist or religious, that Europeans built to resist socialists.

This does not mean that there were no ideological, economic class, or other divisions to provide a basis for the early American party alignment and so for the recruitment of organizational activists. But they were either insufficient to maintain durable party strength or less useful for the purpose than was the distribution of government jobs to faithful party workers. "To the victor belong the spoils" was legitimated in the age of Andrew Jackson and Martin Van Buren, at the national as well as the state and local levels, and that legitimation seems itself strongly American in that it was based on the popular democratic belief that ordinary citizens could perform most government tasks that might elsewhere be reserved for an elite of some sort. The jobs, dispensed to those who had helped the victorious party, were numerous enough and good enough, even in the absence of modern big government, to sustain a large organization. Well before the Civil War, American parties were based on the spoils system. As their organizational scale developed later in the nineteenth century, they became more controversial.

In contrast to the years during and near the Civil War, when the major parties were in unusually sharp ideological disagreement on slavery and reconstruction issues, the last two or three decades of the century were marked by a devotion to office for its own sake. The spoils of office, especially the material rewards associated with government contracts and subsidies along with the government jobs themselves, were now much greater as business and industry grew rapidly.[32] It was then, in the late nineteenth century, that James Bryce observed the power of the political machines and emphasized how much larger and more elaborately organized American parties were than British parties of the same period.[33] American parties of the 1880s and 1890s, while not always admired, were the organizational wonders of the democratic world.

Eventually the powerful post–Civil War party organizations became the prime targets for regulatory reform that treated them and parties generally no longer as strictly private associations. First, however, their opponents undertook the still-continuing effort to deprive the machines of their workers through the establishment of a merit system for government employees.[34] That effort, when it began in the late nineteenth century, challenged an arrangement that for two generations had been fixed in national as well as state and local politics. As Leonard White perceptively remarked, "patronage must have seemed the natural order for a republic."[35] Politicians could well have regarded their distribution of many government jobs as essential for parties in a democratic society.[36] Understandably, then, civil service reform was only slowly achieved. The landmark enactment in 1883 of the Pendleton Act's provision for a federal Civil Service Commission was at first of limited effectiveness.[37] Even when it was extended during the next century to most employees of the national government, similar reform was for many years very unevenly achieved in state and local governments. Although often advanced primarily to improve administrative efficiency and honesty, civil service reform was always also an attack on the organizational basis and thus on the effectiveness if not the very existence of the traditional party machine.

Civil service reform may finally succeed everywhere in destroying the machine's organizational base, but the survival of the old organizations in many places during this century suggests that they have often suited American conditions. Several studies of big-city machines emphasize how usefully they served the needs of large populations in urban settings. Precinct captains, one for each neighborhood of about one thousand people, are depicted not merely as vote mobilizers but also as providers of social service to their constituents.[38] The service went well beyond the organizational gift of the famous Christmas turkey. It included mediating help for citizens in their dealings with governmental authority of all kinds. Precinct captains were found to have worked harder in providing such unofficial service to their constituents than they did in their salaried government jobs.[39] Recent immigrants may have had a special need for party intermediaries, or at least have been most readily induced to become dependent on precinct captains. And it is true that the machines thrived most notably in cities that attracted masses of immigrants during the great movement of population from Europe to the United States in the late nineteenth and early twentieth centuries.

Similarly, the organizations that continued to thrive later in the twentieth century were often able to add to their old European ethnic blocs the new intra-American migrants, including blacks moving from the rural South to northern cities. The efficient machine extended friendship and recognition along with material help to disadvantaged newcomers generally, and found room in the organization for representatives of many new groups. Yet the machines were not solely the product of large-scale immigration. From the start, before the Civil War, they showed a capacity to mobilize masses of people, nonimmigrant as well as immigrant, and they often retained the loyalty of ethnic groups long after the members of those groups had ceased to be immigrants or even children of immigrants. Thus we cannot conclude from the large numbers of immigrants among the urban poor that they were crucial to the development of the American machine, although they were historically identified with it in most large cities.

Another apparently distinctive American need, in addition to that of immigrants, is relevant in explaining the usefulness of the city machine. The formal structure of government, it is argued, was itself too fragmented and decentralized to provide sufficient authority to deal with the problems of urban growth. In that light, the machine, with its boss and hierarchical structure, provided the means to establish informally the authority to govern.[40] Or, as Robert Merton put it in a well-known sociological exposition, the machine's centralization and maintenance of constitutionally scattered fragments of power was a prime example of its latent as well as its manifest functions in the social order.[41] Operating either as a public official himself or solely as the head of the party organization, the boss was in a position to deliver commitments and favors of all kinds. It is well to add, as Merton does, that among these functions was material service to business interests and not just to impoverished citizens. The machine bestowed substantial privileges on building contractors, electrical utilities, traction companies, and many other economic organizations that either did business with the city or required city licenses and possibly official toleration of suspect operations. The price might occasionally have been high, in terms of expected campaign contributions or even personal kickbacks, but substantial business interests found the arrangement workable even when other business interests, perhaps less directly dependent on city government, supported the reform movement of middle and upper income citizens alarmed by the graft and corruption accompanying machine control.[42] Not all bosses were corrupt, but when they were not, many of their lieutenants were. The grossest corruption could and did destroy some bosses.

A characteristic of an effective machine was its capacity to control party nominations.[43] Doing so was plainly crucial. And it was customarily managed without difficulty as long as the nominating authority remained in caucuses and conventions whose participants were mainly organizational leaders and their party workers. But many of the old machines continued, de facto, to exercise the power to nominate their candidates even when and where the direct primary formally gave voters the opportunity to bestow party labels. With precinct captains at work, the machines often brought enough of their own loyal voters to the polls to ensure, in usually low-turnout primaries, the nomination of slates of endorsed candidates. So it was for most offices most of the time in Richard Daley's Chicago through the 1960s and into the 1970s.[44] The control occasionally faltered, especially for the more highly visible offices based on larger-than-local constituencies, but it generally meant in an overwhelmingly one-party city, as Chicago was Democratic after 1930, that the machine determined the eventual winner merely through its ability to determine the outcome of the primary. Chicago is the extreme case, it may be granted, but only because the nearly pervasive machine control of nominations lasted so very long. In most other cities the old machines remained effectively masters of direct primaries only into the 1940s and 1950s. In preceding decades, when the primary was new, the control had been still more widespread—occasionally, as in Philadelphia, that of a dominant Republican rather than Democratic party.

Hence for the machines, unless or until their strength was sapped by other reforms and social changes, the direct primary was a surmountable obstacle. It complicated their political life, but by itself it does not appear to have destroyed machines that existed in otherwise congenial environments. At most, the direct primary looks like one of several forces working against the long-run survival of machines in twentieth-century America. Its effects, as we shall observe, may be more clearly adverse to efforts of nonmachine organizations to control or influence nominations.

Power, office, and material gain of one kind or another are ordinarily treated as the main incentives of both the machine bosses and their workers.[45] Even scholars who view their latent functions, particularly service to the urban poor, as benignly useful do not suggest that machines were primarily concerned with political issues or policy questions. In fact, it is now often thought that the old machines were organizationally effective because their workers had been recruited on the basis of economic incentives rather than principle or ideology.[46] Needing their government jobs, the old precinct captains could be counted on to perform party chores much more steadily than amateur volunteers and to do so without proposing any of the possibly unpopular policy commitments of the ideologically committed.

This is not to say that machine politics were issueless in every sense. Electorally, if not organizationally, the old machines no doubt secured support not only because of issues associated with their national party labels but also from the machines' own loose or general identification with the ethnic and class perceptions of their constituents. No matter how much the bosses and their assistants might have enriched themselves, they maintained popular images as representatives of the great urban masses. Doing so often meant acceptance of much of the twentieth-century liberal agenda, despite the tendency in some places for machines to support business hostility to labor unions.[47] Beginning especially in the New Deal years of the 1930s, big-city Democratic machines, whether old or newly successful, surely benefited electorally from the popularity among their constituents of New Deal governmental welfare programs. Moreover, local bosses benefited materially insofar as they themselves were able to distribute the money and jobs flowing from federal and state programs.

Nevertheless, national issues remained of secondary interest to the old organizations. "Machine politicians," it has been aptly said, "had learned their trade in their neighborhoods and wards, and theirs was a politics of ethnicity and trade-off, not of issues. The machines were peculiarly local organizations, a product of the segregation of ethnic voters from the rest of society."[48] Even Mayor Richard Daley of Chicago, long a power in the state and national Democratic party, is reported to have regarded state and national policies as of secondary or tertiary concern. His well-established interest in presidential politics, for example, is not ascribed to an overriding concern for national public policy or for the national Democratic party. Rather, it is usual to declare, as did Rakove in his study of the Chicago organization, that Daley's presidential interest was "more closely tied to the sheer mechanics of politics and elections, and to a recognition of benefits to be derived for the local Democratic organization from a relationship with a Democratic president who would owe a debt of gratitude to that organization for its help in electing him to office."[49] Whether liberal or not, a Democratic president could thus usefully contribute to the strength of the local organization. By no means, however, did that mean presidential intervention in local party affairs. No boss wanted to share his local power with the president or any other national or state leader. He wanted only to augment it from national and state sources of patronage. Significantly too the old local bosses, in contrast to more recent mayors, were not, as far as we know, customarily interested in holding national or state offices themselves.

The fundamentally local orientation of the old machines makes it clear that they provided no basis for a truly national party organization. They were nearly autonomous participants in the loosest of periodic coalitions designed to elect a president. Analogously, the local organizations also participated in congressional politics by nominating and electing representatives and senators who would then almost necessarily respond to the needs of those same local organizations. Accordingly, machine-supported members of Congress tended to become agents for obtaining federal patronage for their local machines. The patronage often seemed a kind of presidential payment to local organizations for the support of their members of Congress. Presidents might thus use a party means to secure approval for their policies, but the price they paid was to subject their administrative appointments to the control of local machines as well as to individual members of Congress. It was hard to say that there was a national party administration in the heyday of the old machines.[50]

That heyday, everyone agrees, is long since gone except perhaps in Chicago and a few less conspicuous places.[51] Elsewhere in the United States, organizations called machines still survive, but they are without the large, regularized corps of precinct workers who, thanks to numerous government jobs, made the old organizations so distinctive. It is true, however, that as recently as the late 1960s and early 1970s, close observers could discern enough government jobs, along with other forms of patronage, in certain eastern cities and states to sustain organizations at least approximating the old type.[52] Their death may occasionally have been prematurely proclaimed. Yet their withering away, though uneven as well as slow, looks inexorable.

There is more room for argument about the causes. One controversial but popular explanation is that the New Deal killed the old machines by substituting government welfare programs and professional social workers for the services of precinct captains. The argument is hard to sustain in the face of the actual growth of some city machines during the New Deal era. Pittsburgh's Democratic machine is a leading case in point; powerless in 1930, it consolidated its strength by 1940, partly by controlling the local distribution of New Deal jobs, and persisted for another quarter-century.[53] Other examples of Democratic organizations that gained patronage from the new federal programs can be found in Boston, Memphis, New York, Kansas City, Jersey City, and of course Chicago.[54] But because most of these machines did not survive the 1940s and 1950s, the New Deal might be thought to have killed them in the long-run. If so, however, why wasn't the Chicago organization killed off or at least seriously weakened before the 1970s? The fact is that the Daley machine was evidently stronger than ever in the 1960s, when surely the impact of the New Deal should have finally been felt. In Chicago, the old machine thrived along with long-established federal and state programs of economic and social assistance. No doubt these programs and their professional employees did displace some of the old more-or-less-charitable roles of precinct captains, but the latter could still be useful not only in rounding up votes but also in helping citizens deal with the now more numerous and complex governmental bureaucracies. Furthermore, expanded governmental services meant that there were, along with necessarily professional positions, more jobs of all kinds that might be controlled by the organization.

Because the Chicago organization did in fact control the now still more numerous jobs, it survived handsomely. That continued control, it seems to me, is crucial to the survival of the old machines generally. Without it there can, virtually by definition, be no effective organization of the old type. With it, I grant, an organization might nevertheless be ineffective. Nongovernmental employment may be so plentiful that few citizens want government jobs requiring diligent party service. Or party leaders may be reluctant to hire and especially to fire government workers on the basis of campaign activities, even when they have the legal opportunity to do so.[55] The point remains that the opportunity itself must be available. It was available in Chicago at least into the 1970s (and perhaps later); civil service laws were so lax or so laxly interpreted that an old-style machine could be maintained with the 30,000 local government jobs and often additional state government jobs at the disposal of party leaders who were not reluctant to use them for patronage. Some of the jobs were formally excluded from civil service protection, and many others were effectively removed from their de jure protection by the postponement of examinations for long periods or scheduling of them at obscure times and places.[56] Provisional appointments could thus be of indefinite duration, or more precisely of a duration that the machine wanted. Such practices may well continue in Chicago and elsewhere, but their usefulness has become more dubious since the mid-1970s as a result of U.S. Supreme Court rulings invalidating partisan criteria for most appointive governmental offices.

Appropriately, the leading legal case in this matter is from Chicago, specifically Cook County, whose newly elected Democratic sheriff sought to replace Republicans who were among the employees (about half of the sheriff's 3,000) outside the merit-based civil service. Discharging such employees solely because of their partisanship, the Court said, was a violation of First Amendment rights. "In summary," it declared, "patronage dismissals severely restrict political belief and association."[57] They could not here or in similar situations be justified by considerations of efficiency or policymaking in response to electoral results, as partisan replacements might be for limited numbers of higher-level positions. Nor could the dismissals be justified by the importance of patronage to the existence of parties and thus to the maintenance of the democratic process. Parties, the Court found, could and did exist without the kind of patronage at issue. Although the Court opinion here was that of only three justices, supported on narrower grounds by two others, while three justices dissented and one did not participate, the declared unconstitutionality of the essence of the old patronage system has since become prevailing judicial doctrine. It was confirmed and apparently extended in 1980 when the U.S. Supreme Court, by a vote of six to three, decided that assistant public defenders in a New York county could not be discharged because they were Republicans rather than Democrats. The policymaking of these legal officers, along with their access to confidential information, seemed to the Court to be linked to their roles as lawyers serving individual clients and to have no bearing on any party concern with policies.[58] Hence the patronage basis of traditional American party organization is further undermined, as the dissenting justices emphasized and deplored.

It may still be too soon to conclude that no old-style organization can survive the U.S. Supreme Court's new-found application of the First Amendment. But we know that even Chicago's has fallen on relatively hard times and partly because of enforceable court decrees that severely restrict, in accord with the Supreme Court opinions, the number of government jobs that can be used as awards for partisanship.[59] If, then, I am correct in regarding numerous government jobs below policymaking levels as the sine qua non of the old machine, the withering-away will finally be accomplished.[60] Other kinds of organizations, perhaps using other kinds of patronage, might remain or arise, but they are surely different phenomena from the once characteristically American machine.

III
Postmachine Patterns

In the absence of machines and their many patronage workers, American party organizations have most often been skeletal in character. Like an army of officers without privates to fill its ranks, the parties have typically had only a few leaders and close associates in their organizational structures. However elaborate those structures, with layers of local, district, and state committees, they have seldom been based on the regularized, dues-paying membership commonly found among parties in other nations and among almost all nonparty organizations in the United States. Called cadre parties, in contrast to European mass-membership parties, skeletal organizations have been a prevalent American form both before and since the heyday of the old machines, and in many places even during that heyday.[61] The machines themselves may look like variants of cadre parties because their bosses operate through the same familiar committee structure. But they were significantly different, it seems to me, as long as they had large numbers of regularly organized party workers, thanks to bountiful patronage jobs, and thus an organizational substance that cadre parties by definition do not have.[62]

There are times when American cadre parties attract broad participation. Not only do they mobilize ad hoc campaign workers from time to time, but they also occasionally involve numbers of activists in their caucuses and conventions as well as in primary elections.[63] It is unusual, however, for many of these participants to be regularly organized. They are party members in the limited sense of being declared party voters and thus, by custom and often by law, entitled to participate in their party's organizational affairs. The American principle allowing such open access to parties, in contrast to organizations maintaining dues-paying qualifications, is a curious one that I shall explore in the next chapter. Here it is enough to note that while under it there is sporadic participation by more than a small established leadership group, the principle is also plainly compatible with the maintenance of merely skeletal organization in many places over long periods.

Not everyone agrees that having a cadre party of officers without organized rank-and-file members is a deficiency of American politics. When numerous party voters nonetheless exist, the absence of an ideologically based membership may even be seen as an advantage. Pragmatic party leaders and party candidates are thus unencumbered by possibly unpopular doctrinaire policies that such a membership might impose. They can concentrate on winning elections through the use of what has been called a "rational-efficient" model for vote mobilization.[64] Certainly the cadre party fits that model less fully than did the old machine with its numerous campaign workers, maintained at no ideological cost. Conceivably, a cadre party might raise and spend campaign funds to compensate for the absence of the old government jobholders. And in some places it might also have enough volunteer activists as precinct leaders to mobilize votes effectively.[65] Nevertheless, since the decline of the old machines, American extragovernmental party organizations seem peculiarly underdeveloped compared to other political organizations (notably interest groups) and compared to political parties in most other nations.[66]

There have been exceptions to this trend. In certain states and cities, efforts have been made in the last several decades to change the pattern of underdeveloped party organizations by building and maintaining regular, dues-paying memberships. Those memberships tend to be in clubs or similarly voluntary extralegal organizations rather than in the statutorily established parties that are, by law, usually open to all party voters and subject to many restrictions on their campaign activities. Thus the club form of membership differs from the occasional large-scale participation in a cadre party's caucuses, committees, and conventions.[67] Of course, club members themselves may also participate in and even take over the structure of the cadre party. Incentives have been heavily though not entirely ideological, and often nationally oriented despite state and local membership structures. Especially in the 1950s and 1960s, both Democratic and Republican dues-paying organizations appeared to thrive in Wisconsin and California.[68] But they have not spread much more widely and their presence even in Wisconsin and California became less substantial in the 1970s.[69] They seem to have been no more durably successful in several cities where they attracted attention over twenty years ago.

It would be a mistake, however, to believe that the absence of regularized dues-paying membership parties always means the absence of effective party organizations in the late twentieth century. In fact, such membership parties are no longer as completely characteristic of European politics as they were taken to be about 30 years ago; in several instances, direct individual memberships have declined along with the relative importance of their typical campaign activities.[70] Mass-membership organizations are not now so clearly the wave of the future in Western democratic nations, and the United States may be less peculiarly different in this respect than it was in the 1950s. American cadre parties, with limited numbers of leaders who are joined though irregularly by more numerous activists, are at least an informal organizational substitute for a dues-paying membership. Moreover, the activists now attracted to participate in cadre parties tend, like the more exceptional dues-paying party members, to be concerned with national political issues and often specifically with presidential nominations and elections.[71] They give any state or local organization in which they participate a more national orientation than was usual in the old machines. In this respect, the result may more nearly resemble the European pattern.

In one vital respect, however, American party organizations surely remain sharply different from party organizations elsewhere as well as from their earlier forms. Deprived by direct primary laws of the power officially to bestow their labels, party organizations in most states cannot offer active members the same opportunity to engage in the selection of candidates that exists in parties in every other democratic nation. Ordinarily they provide only one of several channels of influence in fostering candidates who seek nomination in primary elections. Hence a most meaningful incentive for regular party participation, dues-paying or otherwise, is missing in the United States. That may help explain why so few Americans actually join party organizations, although many more join other political organizations.

Organizational influence on direct-primary nominations, resembling that of the old machines that routinely won primaries for their slated candidates, survives in certain jurisdictions, particularly for less visible offices, but widely if not uniformly the direct primary seems to have operated to deprive party organizations of the power to control nominations. As Key wrote, the direct primary "created circumstances that made difficult the maintenance and operation of statewide party organization. The new channels to power placed a premium on individualistic politics rather than on the collaborative politics of party."[72]

The results were soon apparent in one-party states where the primary of the dominant party provided the only seriously contested election, but one without the benefit of different ballot labels or even, in many instances, without recognizable policy-oriented factions. When Key wrote in the 1950s, however, there were still large northeastern states, mainly two-party competitive states like New York, in which primaries were either unused or unimportant and where party organizations effectively controlled nominations.[73] But beginning in the 1970s, even New York's primary began to be effective in law and in fact, especially for statewide offices where convention choices had previously prevailed.[74] Indiana and Connecticut, which had long continued to nominate in conventions, now adopted or extended primary laws. Connecticut, it is true, made its primary only a means to challenge a convention choice under specified circumstances, as a few other states had done earlier.[75] That arrangement, however, hardly ensures organizational control of nominations. In New York a somewhat similar law worked so that statewide nominations came to be regularly decided in primaries after strongly candidate-centered campaigns; organizational influence, if not actual control, continued to be decisive in legislative and local-office primaries.[76]

The lingering organizational influence on nominations in several states is linked directly to the strength of the old machines and their residual heirs, but also to the laws regulating nominations. These laws, dating from early in the century, often continued to favor organizational roles where the old machines had been especially strong in the first place. Obviously they did so in the few states that did not enact statewide primary laws until after midcentury.[77] But primary laws themselves vary in the opportunity they provide for organizational influence. As of the early 1980s, reflecting long-established patterns, 24 states (including California and the largest northeastern states) registered or enrolled voters by party before primary elections and made such registration or enrollment a condition for primary voting (except that five of the 24 states allowed nonenrolled voters to declare their party affiliation on the day of the primary, and one, Louisiana, now ran a kind of open primary in which party registration was irrelevant). Four other states, apart from the 24, recorded the voter's choice of party at the primary election, and three of the four required notification, before the primary, by voters wanting to change party. Eleven more states provided for a declaration of party preference or a request for a particular party's ballot by a voter wanting to participate in a given primary, but made no notation of party preference on voter registration lists.[78] Altogether, then, almost four-fifths of the states specified some kind of public statement of party preference as a ticket of admission to primary elections; and that specification would seem likely to limit participation where, as in many of those states, the statement had to be made in advance and could not be changed in the period just before the primary. That period varied from 15 days to almost a year (in New York), and in several states it was long enough to prohibit changes in party affiliation after the close of the candidate-declaration period for the coming primary election.[79]

The more firmly closed the primary, and thus the smaller and more regular the electorate, the greater the opportunity for a party organization to nominate its slate of endorsed candidates. Indeed, it was partly because of restricted electorates that after the first few decades of the direct primary it appeared that prophecies of party destruction were unfulfilled. Surveying the workings of the direct primary in the late 1920s, Merriam and Overacker found that most party organizations still functioned to win nominations through their use of preprimary slates and preprimary conventions.[80] No doubt the organizations then were often the old machines that have now mainly ceased to exist, and therefore no one would argue that what Merriam and Overacker perceived in the 1920s holds in the 1980s. Nevertheless certain vestiges of the old organizational influence on nominations do survive.

Postmachine party organizations in several states have also tried to determine primary results. Sometimes these organizations are the extralegal membership parties, but more often they are the statutory parties whose cadre structures accommodate participating activists. In either case, caucuses, committees, or conventions endorse candidates and commit their organizations to campaign for those candidates in primary elections. When large numbers of locally selected delegates do the endorsing at a statewide convention, the process looks like the old nominating method. But endorsement is really quite different from nomination in that the convention itself is not empowered to award the party label for the general election. Only six states give an endorsed candidate a legal advantage by way of a place on the primary ballot for which other candidates can qualify only by meeting specified conditions.[81] That advantage may reduce the likelihood of a primary contest, but nowhere is it certain to preclude such a contest.[82]

With or without a legally conferred advantage, recent party organizational endorsements have a mixed record of success and failure. The record most readily studied is that of public endorsements by party agencies (ordinarily conventions), and not the often-private endorsement of candidates by party leaders who may extend meaningful organizational help in local as well as in statewide primary campaigns. Publicly declared party endorsements have been numerous enough to be worth systematic attention. Twenty-one states have had preprimary gubernatorial endorsements by party organizations at one time or another during recent decades.[83] McNutt's study of eleven of these states, where parties also endorsed U.S. Senate candidates in at least some election years between 1954 and 1974, concluded that organizational choices usually won primaries, with one significant exception, New York. The vehicle for endorsement in all eleven states was the statutory party, not an extralegal party, and the eleven included the six states providing a legal advantage of some kind to the endorsed candidate.[84]

Jewell's still more recent study of five states included four of McNutt's eleven (New York, Connecticut, New Mexico, and Massachusetts—each, though marginally in Massachusetts, giving a legal advantage to the endorsed candidate), plus Minnesota, where party endorsement is not officially recognized. Concentrating on 1982 gubernatorial contests, Jewell found that four of the ten endorsed Republican and Democratic candidates in his five states lost their primary elections.[85] That count shows a less impressive organizational success than McNutt had found a little earlier. Moreover, at least one of Jewell's six primary winners (the Republican Lewis Lehrman in New York) had become the convention choice not as the organization's favorite but because he plainly had the personal resources to conduct a formidable campaign in the primary and in the general election.[86] Of the four losers, one was the New York Democrat (Mayor Edward Koch, defeated by Mario Cuomo), one was the Massachusetts Republican, and the other two were the choices of each of Minnesota's major parties.

The Minnesota losses are interesting because they occurred in a state where the principle of endorsement had been well established in both the Democratic–Farmer-Labor party (DFL) and the Independent Republican (IR) party —to use the strictly Minnesota names for the major parties. Apart from a few conspicuous DFL exceptions, endorsement had been successfully used in the years before 1982.[87] Remarkably, that pre-1982 organizational success had been achieved without a legally conferred advantage for the endorsed candidate and under an open-primary law plainly helpful to an antiorganizational challenger. Significantly, too, it had been achieved by organizations sharply different from the old machines. Both the DFL and the IR have been issue oriented and ideological; their precinct caucuses are often well attended by policy activists as well as by candidate enthusiasts,[88] and their conventions are large, heavily publicized events.

In contrast to Connecticut, whose selection of delegates to state endorsement conventions appears heavily influenced by established cadre organizations,[89] Minnesota's process is highly participatory—much as it is when party caucuses engage in presidential delegate selection. Thus party endorsements of candidates in Minnesota are not so much those of a well-defined organization of leaders and their lieutenants as they are the choices of fairly large numbers of activists who choose to attend the caucuses that elect the state convention delegates. It is in this form that the Minnesota organizations have been able to foster, if not firmly establish, political norms against primary challenges. These norms are less uniformly effective than those of Connecticut, where a convention-chosen candidate has a recognized status, not only legally but customarily, as *the* party candidate.[90] The Connecticut political environment now seems unusual in its preservation of various elements of tra-

ditional party strength. Primaries elsewhere, as in Minnesota, are more formidable obstacles for party organizations seeking to nominate their endorsed
choices. And it is realistic to regard these obstacles as relatively permanent.[91]

In only a few states have the obstacles appeared so formidable as to make
it nearly impossible for party organizations to exert influence over nominations. California is most often cited because its laws have explicitly prohibited statutory parties from endorsing or otherwise helping specific candidates.
And the voluntary extralegal organizations of club members, the California
Democratic Council and the California Republican Assembly, did not regularly
succeed in winning primaries for their candidates and thus declined in importance after their growth in the 1950s. More recently, party leaders and activists have tried to change the legal status of California's statutory parties so
that they might become vehicles for organizational effort.[92] Wisconsin's experience is also relevant. There by the 1950s both Republicans and Democrats
had well-established extralegal, dues-paying membership organizations whose
local branches and statewide conventions were free to endorse and engage in
various campaign activities without the restrictions imposed on the statutory
organizations.

Although Wisconsin's extralegal parties were themselves eventually given
a kind of statutory recognition for certain purposes, they remain sufficiently
private not to be legally prohibited from endorsing candidates in primaries.
Nevertheless the post-1949 Democratic party has always, by its own constitutional rule, barred itself from endorsing. And the Republican party, whose
rules before the 1980s had required conventions to make statewide endorsements, reacted against the primary defeat of its endorsed choices for governor and other offices in 1978 by making endorsement only permissive and
then by choosing not to endorse statewide candidates in either 1980 or 1982.[93]
Earlier, the Wisconsin Republican party had a long record of endorsing candidates who usually won their primaries, thanks partly to organizational resources; the exceptions were mainly understandable failures to win nomination for challengers against incumbent officeholders. The once-considerable
success of Republican endorsement in Wisconsin, like that of either party in
Minnesota, was achieved in the unfavorable legal environment of the open
primary and its ethos.

Even without endorsement, as well as without uniformly successful endorsement, postmachine party organizations may not be entirely without influence on the nominating process. Cadre party leaders themselves, as I suggested earlier, have resources that they are willing to use to foster candidates
in primaries. Financial resources, in particular, may thus be available even if

numerous campaign workers are not. And whenever the caucuses and conventions of cadre parties attract activists, though only sporadically, they provide opportunities for candidates to mobilize supporters within an organizational framework. Hence despite the absence of regularized endorsement, campaigns to win primary nomination are not always as purely candidate-centered as they appear. But admittedly they are heavily so, especially in one-party states where a kind of no-party politics often prevails in seeking the party label.

In addition to observing postmachine party organizations in nominating campaigns, political scientists have tried to measure their strength by studying the development of state party headquarters. It appears that such development is often largely independent of any large-scale participatory membership or activism in party organization. A regularized dues-paying base may be a useful source of financial support, but it is not necessary. Contributions without memberships are usual, and they have been sought both in large sums from big givers and in small sums from more numerous small givers (reached by mail solicitation). The financial support has been sufficient in many states to establish and maintain professionally staffed, bureaucratic party services. As a modernization of state party organization, the development parallels the widespread modernization of state government itself during the last few decades. Parties, like governors and legislatures, have become more highly professional. More obviously, the development resembles the larger growth in national party headquarters.[94]

In an early study of the new type of state party organization, Huckshorn (in the mid-1970s) stressed its nonideological character. He noted that over 90 of 100 state parties then had a headquarters office and that over half of these had developed since 1960. More often than in the past, state party chairpersons were salaried, and two-thirds of the state parties now had full-time executive directors.[95] State governors might well remain the de facto leaders of parties in certain instances, and not merely heads of their own candidate-centered factions as they had become in many states, but in any event there was now a party headquarters capable of providing a continuity of campaign help to candidates for various state offices.

Huckshorn and three other able political scientists (Cotter, Gibson, and Bibby) systematically surveyed a substantial sample of state party organizations in 1979–80 and confirmed the organizational development discerned in the early and mid-1970s. They found that state party budgets had grown since the early 1960s (though not so impressively when inflation was taken into account), that over 90 percent of the parties had either full-time state chairs or executive directors, that over two-thirds operated get-out-the-vote campaigns linked to voter identification or registration by party, and that many parties were increasingly active in providing various campaign services to candidates.[96] Regional variations existed, but the study shows considerably more Republican than Democratic organizational strength regardless of region.[97] The authors' general point remains: state party organizations, rather than declining along with electoral-party identification during the last two decades, have gained strength according to certain measures.[98] The measures may be challenged, and one critic has already argued that party budgets, when adjusted for inflation, have diminished rather than increased over the 20-year period. The same critic contends that the study's reliance on interviews with state party chairpersons and executive directors could have produced a too-glowing picture of organizational activities in which the interviewees had pride and a vested interest.[99]

Although the finding of increased state organizational party strength is thus not universally accepted, it is supported by other scholarly work. Most directly applicable is the report of a 1983–84 survey (by mail questionnaire) of state parties, through their chairs or executive directors. Conducted under the auspices of the Advisory Commission on Intergovernmental Relations, the survey discloses not only substantial budgets but also in many instances large staffs and considerable party activity by elected officials. Again, Republican organizations are more impressive than Democratic.[100] Also showing recent organizational activity, though not at state party headquarters, is Eldersveld's compilation of data on local parties in Connecticut, Michigan, Houston, Chicago, Pittsburgh, Los Angeles, and Detroit.[101] The record in these places is consonant with the national survey of county organizations that Cotter, Bibby, Gibson, and Huckshorn included in their work and that revealed continued (though not increased) local party activity.[102]

It should be stressed that none of these studies suggests a massive upsurge of party organization in the states. With good reason, scholars are cautious about going much beyond the finding that state parties have developed new and more professional roles. That they should be doing so can be understood as a response to present-day needs of party candidates. Especially in races below the statewide level and notably for state legislative seats, there is an economy of scale in centralized maintenance of expensive and technical campaign assistance by way of polling, computerized mailing lists, public relations, and facilities for using the mass media of communication. Hence a party's candidates, despite the capacity of many of them to raise their own funds and to run their own campaigns, have good reason to use the services of a party headquarters as well as to seek its direct financial help.[103] The result may well be an institutionalization of a kind of party organizational activity that is entirely compatible with the shape of contemporary American politics and yet is by no means neglible in its import. It can be expected that a party's professional bureaucratic staff, like the staff of any other organization, would not be without influence.

IV
Conclusion

From my limited survey of state and local politics a few themes clearly emerge. As always but now even more fully than earlier, the national electoral alignment of Republicans and Democrats extends to the states. Party competition is almost entirely conducted under the two major-party labels. The always exceptional state third-party strength has diminished in the last several decades, and so has the once much more extensive one-partyism. Organizationally, however, the situation has changed more significantly. The structure of most state and local parties, Republican and Democratic, differs sharply from the old machines that dominated so much of American politics in times past. Without patronage by way of numerous government jobs, state and local parties have often become mere cadres of leaders without many regular organizational members or helpers. When parties occasionally do attract participating activists, through dues-paying clubs or ad hoc caucus attendance, their incentives appear ideological or programmatic in accord with national party orientations. The organizations thus developed, while still concerned with winning state and local offices and with state and local policymaking, tend to have stronger national programmatic commitments than did the old machines for whom the national label was mainly a useful means for mobilizing voters and obtaining federal patronage. The same may well be true of the less formally organized but numerous financial contributors to the newly developed state party headquarters operations. To be sure, neither Republican nor Democratic state parties have become branches of national organizations, even though Republican state parties receive substantial financial help from their national organization.[104]

More readily apparent than any growing national orientation of state and local organizations is their inability, in comparison with the old machines and with membership parties in other nations, to determine which candidates shall carry their party label in general elections. Deprived by this century's direct-primary laws of the legal power to nominate candidates, most American party organizations now also lack the strength that the old machines retained for so long to influence the primary electorate's choice of candidates. Party endorsement, even when attempted, is by no means tantamount to nomination in a political environment often hostile to party organizational influences but hospitable to candidate-centered campaigns. Hence newly strengthened state party headquarters, with substantial funds, professional staff, and technical capacity, may in general elections merely be helping candidates who have won nominations without endorsements from an organized membership or even from a party leadership managing the headquarters.

The very fact that party membership or activism does not automatically carry with it a determining role in the candidate-selection process helps to explain why postpatronage parties in most states should be less highly developed than their European counterparts. This is to say that American party organizations in this century function under distinctive legal and conventional restraints produced by our political culture. Comprehending those restraints is therefore an essential step in an attempt to appreciate the situation of American parties. I turn to it in the next chapter.

Chapter Six

Parties as
Public Utilities

The distinctive restraints imposed on American parties are elements of their treatment as quasi-governmental agencies or, in my terminology, public utilities. While that treatment includes certain legally conferred privileges, it is often heavily regulatory, and most significantly, it ordinarily includes a state-established direct primary in which voters select party nominees. The direct primary's form and use vary among the states, as the previous chapter indicated, but its pervasiveness, like that of other similarly varying regulations, is a fact of American political life. After almost 80 years of state legislation on nominating procedure, we may well take for granted the treatment of parties as state agencies rather than as private political associations. Yet the treatment, it should be remembered, differs from our own nineteenth-century practice as well as from contemporary practice elsewhere. To explain how and why American states, and only American states, have thus restrained parties is the principal task of this chapter. Little has to be said about national laws, since apart from campaign finance legislation (especially in the 1970s), the U.S. Congress has so far left parties, along with elections, mainly to state regulation.

The purpose here is not to stress the already explored impact of the direct primary, but to explain the political culture that produced and now sustains the direct primary along with other party regulations. It ought, therefore, to be clear at the outset that I regard the twentieth-century regulatory treatment of American parties, distinctive though it is in the democratic universe, as a response to durable historical circumstances. In this light, the direct primary itself is not so much a cause of candidate-centered politics as it is an institutionalized means for pursuing such politics in a civic culture that is broadly hostile to party organizational control. The means, to be sure, are consequential. Without the direct primary and the related presidential preference primary, candidate-centered campaigns might not have flourished so handsomely in the United States although they would probably have existed in greater degree than elsewhere.

As I shall argue, the unique legal status of twentieth-century American parties is linked to, but only partly explained by, the presence of their labels on government-provided general election ballots.[1] Without that privilege, no obvious legal basis exists to regulate or control the way in which parties bestow their labels on candidates. For example, Australia, which kept party labels off its ballots until 1984, simply treats parties much as it does other private associations, subject to general rather than specially directed regulation of organizational activities.[2] British practice is similar, although party labels, banned entirely from pre-1970 parliamentary ballots, are now added to the ballot almost uniformly by individual candidates.[3] Many other nations, however, also avoid American-style regulation even though, more clearly than Britain, they provide official ballot recognition for party labels. Such recognition is actually essential in the party-list proportional representation elections that prevail in most of continental Europe. Yet only in West Germany, Turkey, and Norway are there any legal regulations of party candidate selection, and these regulations do no more than stipulate participation of a party's dues-paying members in a process itself run by an essentially private association.[4] Generally, in other words, parties outside of the United States do not purchase the privilege of ballot access by surrendering control of their label bestowal to a government-conducted election or even to an election or other process closely supervised by governmental authority. Nor are these parties ordinarily subject to most of the other legal regulations imposed on the internal affairs of American parties.

The question of why "only in America" parties should have so special a legal status is especially intriguing given our constitutional principles and conventional preferences for limited government. The First Amendment, now if not in the past, might well seem to stand in the way of such control, and the general American commitment to private enterprise might be expected to lead to lighter rather than heavier regulatory burdens than those imposed by more collectivist-minded European nations. On the other side, however, is an old American practice with respect to economic activities that at least resembles state regulations of parties. It is the statutory treatment of certain business enterprises as public utilities.

I have gone so far as to adopt the phrase *"public utilities"* to describe the treatment of parties under state laws. Even as metaphor it is not a perfect fit. But it better serves my conceptual frame of reference than does *quasi-governmental, state agency, governmentalized,* or *quasi-public.* Although those terms accurately describe the party electoral activities that our states now control, they cannot be extended to all other party activities. By constitutional right and well-established custom, American parties, like parties elsewhere, engage in many organizational and campaign activities that are subject to little more regulation than are similar activities conducted by private associations generally. The parties thus engaged, it is true, may appear to be different entities from the regulated electoral parties; they may even, though using the same Republican or Democratic name, occasionally be organizationally separated from the legally recognized parties. Nevertheless, the private associational party and the publicly controlled electoral party are so evidently intertwined that it is seldom useful to treat them as distinct.

When instead the concept of party is broadened enough to include non-electoral as well as electoral roles, the designation *public utility* is more fully descriptive. It suggests an agency performing a service in which the public has a special interest sufficient to justify governmental regulatory control, along with the extension of legal privileges, but not governmental ownership or management of all the agency's activities. In this sense of the term, certain "private enterprises engaged in the provision of transport, communication, electricity, gas, and other utility services" have in the United States historically been regulated with respect to their services and rates. Originally, at least, they were thought to be peculiarly "affected with a public interest," often but not always because of monopolistic positions.[5] Although that distinction was not sustained beyond the early 1930s, as regulations were extended to other industries, it long helped to support governmental intervention in a nation ideologically committed to private enterprise. It may still do so despite recent deregulatory pressures in several areas. The form of governmental intervention has remained characteristically American. In most other nations, industries "affected with a public interest" have commonly become government owned and managed enterprises. The United States, rather than converting such industries into completely public enterprises, has usually chosen to regulate them under formal laws and rules but as privately owned and managed businesses.[6]

The analogy to our treatment of parties is illuminating though inexact. Significantly, as I shall stress, American states began to regulate parties—without regulatory commissions, to be sure—at about the same time and in more or less the same progressive reform spirit that they, and in some areas the national government too, began to regulate business enterprises performing special public services. Like many of these enterprises, political parties were perceived in monopolistic terms; only two parties, so technically duopolies, or in many places only one party, actually elected public officeholders and exerted control over governmental policymaking. Moreover, the state's legal recognition of such duopolies or de facto monopolies might in at least limited respects solidify and perpetuate advantages for existing parties. Established parties, it is true, could not be so fully protected against competition as were regulated electrical companies, but guaranteed ballot access was a privilege ordinarily denied minor or new parties. And though there is nothing in the history of party regulation like the industry-minded utility commission,[7] state legislatures have not always been entirely unresponsive to the major parties they were regulating. Legislators themselves have been Republicans and Democrats whose interests, even if antiorganizational, were not such as to cause them to legislate in favor of other parties. One might thus account for certain apparently benign aspects of party regulation of the major parties.

In calling attention to the American custom of public utilities regulation, I begin explaining the distinctive legal status of American parties by suggesting that it is roughly analogous to other regulatory practices of the previous 100 years. The suggestion, I admit, does not carry us very far. The hard question remains, Why has the United States alone among democratic nations subjected *parties* to so much legal regulation and control? In most of the remainder of the chapter, I look to special historical circumstances for an answer. It is these circumstances, chiefly our post-Civil War parties (and the reaction to them), that sets the United States apart. Hence I shall first look again at our preregulated parties of the late nineteenth century, the old machines of the last chapter, before considering the impact of government-provided ballots and the regulatory efforts leading to direct-primary elections. In the process, I hope to explain why government-provided ballots led to state regulations in America but not elsewhere. Finally, I deal with recent constitutional challenges to the exercise of state powers, and their deregulatory implications.

I

Private Power

Even more clearly than in other nations, parties in the United States began as private political associations without any special legal status. As we know, they were neither provided for nor wanted by the founders of the American republic. George Washington was not alone in fearing their effects, nor James Madison in considering parties as at best necessary evils. The curse of the constitutional founders no doubt lingered especially among upper-class citizens disdainful of the mass participation encouraged by parties, and the antiparty spirit was later revived in a larger portion of the public. Nevertheless, parties rapidly developed early in the nineteenth century and they were widely accepted by custom if not by law. Their organizations, the first in the world to mobilize mass electorates, were built on so bountiful a spoils system as to be set apart from parties that developed in Britain and elsewhere *after* merit-based civil service had been established.

Perceived as machines run by bosses, the American organizations became targets for reform not only through civil service laws, to curtail patronage, but also through regulation of parties themselves. Local party bosses seemed to select and elect candidates and then influence heavily, if not fully control, the governmental decisions and appointments of those whom they helped win public office. In that perspective, bosses exercised public power without always being elected to public office themselves and, during most of the nineteenth century, without statutory recognition of their party organizations.[8] Their roles may have been exaggerated, but they were effectively portrayed as the holders of governing authority outside the formal governmental structure. Thus reformers, who also tried without much success to launch intraparty revolts against bosses, had an argumentative basis for turning to statutory regulation. As Ranney has aptly said, the idea is that parties "will not voluntarily mend their ways and so must legally be forced to behave."[9] That attitude, developing soon after the Civil War and still assuredly alive in the United States, derives its force from the reaction to organizations regarded as corrupt and powerful. Nowhere else in the western democratic world did parties look so evil, at least to middle-class citizens, as they did in the United States. However useful the old machine might have been to its beneficiaries, including many of the poor in large cities, it lacked legitimacy in the eyes of the public-spirited partly because its "members" worked for the spoils of office instead of for programmatic causes. And such a party organization hardly seemed legitimate at all when it assumed, as a private association, evidently public and even governmental roles.

The problem of legitimacy arose most sharply with respect to party nominating procedure, or party candidate selection, as it is called elsewhere. Significantly, party nominations became a matter of public concern even before the American version of the Australian ballot gave those nominations a new legal recognition in the late 1880s. While parties themselves, rather than state and local governments, still provided the general election ballots (the party tickets) in the first two post-Civil War decades, the overwhelming electoral importance of being put on those ballots made major party nominations as crucial in fact as they later became in law. Republican and Democratic domination of elections and of election results was well established in the 1870s and 1880s. Hence those who were able to select Republican and Democratic candidates for public offices effectively limited the voters' choices for those offices to two candidates, or where two-party competition did not exist, Republican or Democratic selectors effectively chose the winning candidate. The American way of democratically legitimizing this selection process during the nineteenth century was to open it in principle to party members rather than to leave it in the hands of legislative or congressional caucuses that had exercised the nominating power in the early days of the Republic.

Party members, however, were loosely defined or hardly defined at all. Major American parties, then as now, seldom had dues-paying memberships in the manner of most other private associations or of many later European parties, and the tendency was to count as members all those who claimed to be party voters. Hence large numbers were at least entitled to attend the local meetings, or caucuses, that nominated candidates for local office and selected delegates to the conventions that nominated candidates for state or other higher office. The participatory principle gave the nominating process not only a democratic appearance but also a more or less public character: caucuses open to unorganized party voters looked like public elections although still conducted by private associations. Indeed, the caucuses came to be called "primary elections," or primaries, in many parts of the United States by the early 1880s.[10] Today, of course, we reserve those terms as shorthand ways of referring to the state-conducted direct primaries, which we juxtapose with the caucus-convention method of nomination. But it is well to remember that originally a primary election was a means by which a caucus of party voters nominated its local candidates or selected convention delegates to do the nominating at district or statewide levels.

The same kind of caucus of self-defined party voters is still familiar to many Americans because of its use as the first stage in selecting delegates to national party conventions. As observed in chapter 4's discussion of the presidential nominating process, the caucus was part of the most usual method of selecting national convention delegates in the nineteenth century and during most of this century. Its persistence even recently is remarkable given its inherent difficulties. Without a dues-paying or otherwise regularized membership, a party caucus could achieve democratic legitimacy only by opening itself to self-selected voters whose organizational loyalty might well be dubious. It must have been tempting, especially when parties were more strictly private associations, for leaders to pack caucuses with their own followers and to attempt by one means or another to exclude potential dissidents. The temptation, given the opportunities in the loosely constructed caucus, was bound to give rise to suspicions even in the absence of evidence of wrongdoing. And in the late nineteenth century, considerable evidence did exist.

As early as the 1860s, parties in New York reported primary votes of 4,000 to 7,000 in wards where the party never received more than 2,500 general election votes and where only 500 attended the primaries.[11] As yet without state control over the process, the primary elections were traditionally "held in a ward's worst 'dive' with swarms of drunk 'repeaters' overexercising their franchise rights."[12] Another kind of abuse was noted in New York during the early 1880s: the practical exclusion of the great majority of party voters and thus the control of nominations by those who controlled the spoils organization.[13] Even bribery, while punishable at general elections, was not generally a legal offense at a primary or caucus. "Voters," as Merriam and Overacker wrote when describing the post-Civil War party nominations, "might be bought and sold with no pretence of concealment, for there was no remedy or penalty at law."[14] With or without written ballots, caucus results could readily be falsified in case all other manipulations of voting arrangements had failed to produce organizational choices. "In short," Merriam and Overacker concluded, "the primary election, having become one of the most important steps in the process of government, was open to every abuse that unscrupulous men, dazzled by prospects of almost incredible wealth and dictatorial power, could devise and execute. Not all of these evils appeared in one place and at one time; but they were likely to occur at any time when factional rivalry became sufficiently intense. Especially were these abuses felt in the great cities where opportunities were largest and rewards most alluring, and where the shifting population rendered personal acquaintance among all the voters impossible."[15]

Early reform-minded responses to these abuses were limited in number and effectiveness, partly because, before the late 1880s, parties were still regarded as private associations largely immune from mandatory legal regulation. They could, of course, reform themselves, as both Republicans and Democrats tried to do in New York City during the early 1880s,[16] but there was little confidence that new party rules could prevent the established abuses. Several states tried to develop statutory remedies even while treating parties as private associations. Dallinger reports a weak and ineffective New York statute as early

as 1866, and a more stringent act of 1882 regulating the duties of inspectors
at primaries and imposing penalties for illegal voting and for bribery of primary voters and delegates.[17] Ohio and Pennsylvania enacted regulatory legislation in 1871, Missouri in 1875, and California in 1872 and 1874. Similar
legislation seeking to prevent bribery and corruption in party primaries was
enacted elsewhere in the 1870s. At the same time, a few states — Ohio, Pennsylvania, Missouri, and California — went a little further in trying to provide
for such matters as adequate public notice of caucuses. Regulatory provisions,
however, were either local, rather than statewide, or optional for parties, and
sometimes they were both local and optional.[18] Even with the slightly greater
reform efforts of the mid-1880s, states tended to help parties regularize their
nominating procedures only if they were willing to be thus helped. Michigan's
law of 1887, for example, provided for optional voter registration in connection with ward primaries and conventions.[19] Such legislation, while still limited, displays the beginning of the governmental regulation that was soon to
be widely established. The still-prevalent legal view of parties as private associations was already being qualified with respect to their most public responsibility, nominating candidates.

II
The Impact of the Australian Ballot

It is tempting and perhaps usual to emphasize the adoption of the Australian
ballot, in its Americanized form, in explaining the conversion of political parties from private associations to what I have called public utilities. When the
states decided, mainly in 1888–90, to provide government ballots for general
elections *and* to put party labels on those ballots, they gave parties a legal status that they had not had as long as they themselves provided the ballots to
be cast at general elections. However modest the change may seem, access
to the official government ballot became part of the legal basis for a great
deal of the subsequent legislation regulating parties and especially their nominating procedures. Before 1888 there had, as indicated, been little legislation
of that kind. Though part of a broad concern with finding a means to end
well-known abuses, the early legislation indicates only an undeveloped reform
impetus. Its capacity for further development without the Australian ballot
cannot be demonstrated. Substantial regulation of parties, apart from the effects of civil service provisions, did not occur until the Australian ballot was
adopted. The adoption itself was a major goal of reformers.

Although we cannot disentangle the greatly increased regulation of American parties from the impact of the Australian ballot, the entanglement need not be assumed to establish causation. We cannot be absolutely sure that the Australian ballot was a crucial requisite for subsequent American regulations, and we know from the experience of other nations that government-printed ballots, with or without party labels, have not elsewhere produced our kind of regulation. As suggested earlier, we must also look to what was most distinctive about the United States when the Australian ballot was adopted: a hostile reaction to the old machine. In short, the Australian ballot may well have been a necessary condition, at least legally, but not a sufficient condition for treating our parties as public utilities.

Some of the reasons for adopting the Australian ballot in the United States were the ones that moved other countries in the same direction at nearly the same time. Privately printed party ballots, while superior to the older oral voting used only in Kentucky by 1885, had several defects. One of these was their nonsecret nature.[20] Certainly the desire for secrecy in voting was a universal motivation for adopting the Australian ballot; *secret ballot* and *Australian ballot* became virtually synonymous. But in many nations, secrecy was prized mainly to prevent intimidation, often subtle, of working-class voters by their employers or their social superiors; such intimidation seemed possible especially in Britain, where before the Australian ballot the conventional method of voting was still oral. In the United States, where voters already cast party-provided tickets, the secrecy of the Australian ballot was aimed more sharply at the prevention of bribery and fraud as well as at other defects of the party-provided tickets. Ballot-box stuffing, in particular, was a target, and since the stuffing was done by party organizations, the adoption of the Australian ballot was related to the party reform movement.

Nevertheless, the form given the Australian ballot in the United States was not entirely hostile to parties. State legislation, instead of adhering to the Australian practice of omitting party designations on general election ballots, officially recognized political party nominations for elective public office. Not only did states usually list nominees by party on their ballots, but they also institutionalized by law the procedures that party delegate conventions or other party agencies used in nominating their candidates.[21] We now see such legislation as regulatory precedent for the state-imposed direct-primary laws of the twentieth century, and we have reason to believe that party leaders would have preferred no legislation at all.[22] But the legislation of the 1880s and 1890s did not reflect the fuller antiorganizational spirit that characterized the later campaign for the direct primary.

More hostile to parties in the 1890s was the beginning of the campaign for nonpartisan ballots in municipal elections. That campaign's considerable success in the first half of the twentieth century contrasts sharply with the nearly universal and continuous use of party labels on state and national ballots.[23] Once that use was established in the late 1880s it was seldom abandoned. Hence the original legislation appears critical, and so does the fact that American parties were then important enough, despite their reputation for corruption, to Americanize the Australian ballot, when they had to accept it, in a way that would satisfactorily institutionalize their status. After all, in most states they secured, through party-column ballots, government printing of the party ticket that they had previously produced and distributed at their own expense. Admittedly, these new government-provided ballots facilitated split-ticket voting in a way that the old separately provided party tickets had not, and such voting increased even in states that adopted party-column ballots. But it rose more sharply in states that listed candidates under the office for which they were running so that one could not vote a straight party ticket by checking the party label at the head of the column.[24] Significantly, in the latter cases, too, candidates bore party labels beside their names.[25]

No doubt it would have been difficult in the 1880s to conceive of American elections, at least at the state level, conducted without party labels to guide voters. Not only were Americans accustomed to casting party ballots, but the fact that they were asked to vote to fill so many offices, executive as well as legislative, made it almost impossible to expect them to pick and choose among individual candidates from outside their own local communities. In other words the long ballot, already characterizing American elections, provided a weighty argument for party labels. Organizational interests were surely served by the official recognition of those labels, but those interests did not provide the sole justification for party access to the ballot. Voters could well have needed the cues — perhaps more so in the late nineteenth century than in our own time.

Although the parties, either through their own power or because of the long ballot, successfully institutionalized their status when the Australian ballot was adopted, the ballot reforms of 1888–90 sought to limit parties in certain respects. Massachusetts' office-column ballot was meant to discourage but not preclude strictly party voting, and the case for the Massachusetts form was made on that basis.[26] Moreover, early agitation for the Australian ballot came from outside the Republican and Democratic party organizations or from dissidents in those organizations. The first specific proposal was made by Henry George in 1871, and it was taken up by Populists before its acceptance by the major parties.[27] Given these origins, the Australian ballot cannot fairly be re-

garded as intended to disfranchise working-class citizens by making it harder
to vote effectively. Many later successful advocates of the Australian ballot were
upper-middle-class reformers hostile to party machines based on working-class
voters, but their legislation did not make elections less meaningful to anyone
as long as party labels appeared in one way or another on the governmental
ballots. The Americanized Australian ballot might have made it harder for
illiterates to vote,[28] but more direct ways of limiting their franchise were available. So too were these direct ways, voter registration requirements, for example, available to lower the turnout of even literate citizens. The Australian ballot, at least by intention, would have helped to block only those wanting to
vote more than once.

Less disputable than the effects of the Australian ballot on voting turnouts
is the impact of the Americanized version of that ballot on the legal status
of parties. Although American parties *might* eventually have been subject to
considerable regulation without the new ballot form, the official ballot recognition of parties in 1888–90 provided the legal argument for the most important regulation that followed. From its inception, official ballot recognition
required that a party's nominations be certified by party officers to government officials, and that only officers of certain parties—usually those polling
a certain percentage of votes at a previous election—could thus certify. Accordingly, Republicans and Democrats were privileged, while new or minor
parties could qualify for ballot listing only by submitting petitions containing
substantial numbers of signatures. As Merriam and Overacker wrote, "It was
an easy step from permitting the two great parties to have their candidates
placed upon the ballot, when certified by the party officials, to requiring that
these nominations should have been made only in accordance with such rules
and regulations as might be deemed necessary; in short, to prescribing in detail regulations governing the entire procedure of party primaries."[29] They had
in mind the 1890s, when most states began to regulate the caucus-convention
procedures that then constituted party "primaries." But the same principle,
they well understood, later supported the fuller state intervention by way of
the mandated direct primary.

Merriam and Overacker quote Justice Holmes's famous dictum of 1902 on
the import of official ballot listing: "The legislature has a right to attach reasonable conditions to that advantage, if it has a right to grant the advantage."[30]
Holmes's opinion, issued for the Massachusetts Supreme Judicial Court when
he was its chief justice, upheld the constitutionality of the state's 1898 statutes
regulating the party caucuses whose nominees were legally entitled to general
election ballot positions. These statutes provided, among other stipulated cau-

cus procedures, that no person who had voted in the caucus of one political party could take part in another party's caucus within the ensuing twelve months, that check lists of eligible party voters could be closed twenty days before a caucus took place, and that tax funds could be used to pay for caucuses.

As these provisions indicate, the statutory regulation of nominating procedure that immediately followed adoption of the Australian ballot tended mainly to regularize the methods that the major parties had previously established. During the first 15 or 20 years of government-provided ballots, the states did not fundamentally alter the nineteenth-century procedure. Instead, they usually tried to prevent fraud in the use of that procedure. The Massachusetts case illustrates the point; what Holmes upheld was the application of the statute to an alleged conspiracy for illegal voting at a caucus. In this light, the years from 1888 until at least 1904 constitute an interim or transitional period between the era of largely unregulated private associations and the era of state-imposed direct primary elections. The interim is characterized by considerable detailed legal regulation of the caucus-convention procedure and of party organizational arrangements more generally. Parties are already treated as public utilities, particularly with respect to their nominating procedures, but these procedures remain essentially intact, even though they must now conform to state-imposed rules in certain respects. By 1896 all states but one had statutory regulations for nominating candidates for elective office. These regulations always required that voters in a caucus or primary be legal voters in the given district where the caucus or primary was held, and occasionally that such voters be registered by party.[31] Nevertheless, a good deal of the defining of eligibility for party caucus voting in the 1890s was left to party rules.

We have a good description of the Michigan system as it existed from 1890 to 1904. Five times between 1887 and 1901, the Michigan legislature enacted statutes designed to remedy abuses in the party primaries that now selected candidates entitled to access to the state's official ballot. The abuses were familiar from earlier decades. For example, caucuses were held in saloons until Michigan law prohibited that location in 1893, and they were held at hours suited to party leaders despite laws attempting to set reasonable times.[32] The general picture is of ineffective statutory regulation. Other states varied considerably in what they attempted and in what they accomplished. New York followed its earlier, pre-Australian-ballot attempt to curb nominating abuses by the enactment of a law in 1898 establishing a state-run *indirect* primary. Under this law, government officials enrolled party voters and subsequently operated, as they did the general election, the election of delegates to the party's nominating convention. Although New York did not thus provide enrolled party voters the opportunity to choose their nominees for public office directly, the state had surely converted a formerly private process into a partially state-operated activity. It represented a bigger step than most states had yet made toward a state-run direct primary (which New York itself did not adopt until 1911).[33]

Hard though it is to generalize about state regulations of the caucus-convention system during the first two decades after 1888, they seldom satisfied the critics of the long-standing abuses in that system. Effective regulation might not have been realizable without the direct primary that most states imposed beginning in the middle of the first decade of the twentieth century. It was, and still is, peculiarly difficult to regulate caucuses or primaries run by parties that do not have regularized dues-paying memberships. The very fact that each American party was supposed to count all its general-election voters as members meant that the party itself could not maintain a satisfactory list of those eligible, as members, to participate in its caucuses or primaries. How, especially in a large city, were party officials supposed to identify their party voters and be held to legal account for the way in which they did so? Even if the state were to register voters by party, as Massachusetts as well as New York was willing to do, it would still have to monitor or otherwise manage party caucuses in order to be sure that persons properly registered, and only those properly registered, were in fact able to participate. That is so large a step toward state control of the nominating process that a state-run direct primary would look only somewhat more radical. It might even be argued that the special nature and status of American parties led almost inevitably to the state-provided direct primary once the Americanized form of the Australian ballot was adopted. In American circumstances, nothing less seemed likely to legitimize the special access of major party nominees to the general election ballot. Party organizations were simultaneously too bossed and too loosely defined to be allowed to nominate on their own while subject merely to regulations applied generally to private associations.

———————

III

The Direct Primary

The mandatory state-administered direct primary clearly transforms party nominations from the private to the public sphere. Party action thus becomes state action. Or, for the purpose of nominating its candidates, a party is made into an agency of the state. The transformation, as I have suggested, had its origins in the regulatory efforts of the late nineteenth century, and these included a conversion, like New York's, of the party primary to a partially public activity. But the halfway houses of the transitional decades should not obscure the significance of the change from established party practice of nineteenth-century United States and from the continuing party practice in other countries. In particular, the direct primary of most of twentieth-century America differs sharply from a nominating contest that a party runs itself. A regularized dues-paying party in another nation—Australia, for example—sometimes arranges for all of its members to vote by paper ballot to select a party candidate, instead of leaving the selection to an elected body of representatives or delegates.[34] But still, only an organized membership participates. And it does so in a party-run process, not a state-run election.

Similarly, nineteenth-century American parties, even without regularized dues-paying memberships, had their own participatory mechanisms for caucus-attending party voters. As early as 1842, local parties in Crawford County, Pennsylvania, adopted secret ballots for party "members" to use in selecting candidates.[35] Here and elsewhere, the Crawford County system was a voluntary internal party practice, dependent on the honesty and efficiency of party officers. Insofar as it was used directly to nominate, and not merely to choose delegates to do the nominating at a higher level, it was limited by practical considerations to local offices—county and city levels in areas of limited population but ward levels in large cities. For statewide party nominations, any direct primary would almost certainly be best administered by the state in the manner of a general election. Of course states could merely authorize direct primaries to be used if parties so desired. The earliest laws on the subject, in southern states, were thus optional, and several such laws remain. But most American states, when adopting direct-primary legislation in the twentieth century, followed the mandatory pattern established by Wisconsin in 1903. At any rate, the direct primary usually means that major parties, granted labelled access to general election ballots, will nominate their candidates in state-established elections. No longer does the direct primary refer to a solely internal organizational arrangement. Even in the several southern states that give party officials important roles in running their primary elections (and in collecting filing fees to finance them), the primaries are not really private affairs. Like all primaries authorized by statute, they are understood to involve direct nomination by party voters, unorganized as well as organized.

Although the direct primary may have been an almost inevitable means of dealing with party nominations in turn-of-the-century American circumstances, it was crucial in establishing our parties as public utilities and in subjecting them to a kind of regulation virtually unknown in other Western democracies. The reasons for such special treatment of American parties emerge from the preceding discussion. Unlike their counterparts elsewhere when the Australian ballot was adopted, American parties were already unable on their own to meet public expectations with respect to candidate selection. Their failure was most flagrantly but not solely a result of fraud, corruption, and other organizational abuses. It was also a result of the special quality of American public expectations.

Long dominating the electoral process, the two major parties were supposed to open their nominating processes to all their identifiable voters rather than only to fixed memberships of activists or dues-payers. In other words, Americans expected their parties to be open to participation like no other private associations in the United States or parties in other nations. Naturally, American party practices often failed to live up to these participatory principles. The failures became more glaring in the increasingly urban circumstances of 1890–1910, and more objectionable legally after the Australian ballot had been adopted. In this light, the direct primary was a feasible method for American voters to participate in nominations as they were supposed to have been able to do under the theoretically open caucus-convention system. The direct primary sought to institutionalize by state action an otherwise unfulfilled American expectation. Radical innovation though it was in many ways, including its legal ramifications, the direct primary is nonetheless explicable as an extension of American historical experience.

In any event, the direct primary quickly became as American as apple pie. By 1912 a majority of states had adopted mandatory primary laws, and by 1917, all but four states had direct-primary laws for at least some state offices.[36] A few states held back, maintaining conventions to nominate especially for certain statewide offices, but these states finally gave way in the last few decades, and now direct primaries prevail almost everywhere, although occasionally only as a means to challenge prior convention nominations.[37] Even certain states that continued to recognize convention nominations for certain statewide offices nevertheless established direct primaries to nominate candidates for the U.S. Congress, their own legislatures, and many local offices. A more significant exception to the direct primary's pervasiveness has been presidential nominating procedure. Only Congress could enact national presidential primary legislation, and at least until recently it might not have been able to do so without a constitutional amendment.

In the absence of national legislation, the states could seek only indirectly to transform the presidential nominating conventions by developing preferen-

tial primaries in which voters, in effect, selected convention delegates committed to particular presidential candidates. We have observed the rapid growth
of these presidential preference primaries before 1916, their decline in numbers
and importance during the next half century, and their proliferation and new
dominance in the 1970s and early 1980s. The most recent of these developments, described in chapter 4, can be understood as a long-delayed substitution for caucus-convention arrangements that had remained in use for national
party delegate selection long after such arrangements for other nominations
had been superseded by the direct primary. After all, the reasons for changing
to presidential primaries in the 1970s were often similar to those for changing
to direct primaries for other offices earlier in the century. The caucuses that
were supposed to be open were often effectively closed by party leaders, and
when reform became inevitable it was usually popular or expedient, even for
many party leaders, to adopt the primary rather than to try to run open caucuses.

Despite the dramatic revival of presidential primaries in the 1970s, it is still
fair to regard the general movement for primaries as very much a part of the
progressive spirit that arose in the first few decades of the century. The reforms of the 1970s reflect the same spirit, in particular the desire to transfer
power from organizational leaders to unorganized voters and so finally to extend to presidential candidate selection the practices that progressives had long
since established for most nonpresidential nominations. The progressivism that
had succeeded in 1900–1914 is aptly described by Hofstadter: "Its general theme
was the effort to restore a type of economic individualism and political democracy that was widely believed to have existed earlier in America and to
have been destroyed by the great corporation and the corrupt political machine. . . ."[38] Against the corporation and the political machine, progressives
were willing to apply the power of the state as their regulatory instrument.
Antitrust legislation and less drastic though more continuous rules administered by governmental commissions were developed to deal with corporate
businesses. Political party organizations, the machines, were also to be curbed
but more drastically, through the legal removal of their most important function, the nomination of party candidates. Progressive antiparty machine legislation, Hofstadter believes, was itself really aimed at big business. "Unless the
machine and its leader, the boss, could be broken, unless the corrupt alliance
between special interests and the machine could be smashed, it seemed that
no lasting reform could be accomplished."[39]

No doubt La Follette in Wisconsin and many progressives in other states
did regard big business corporations, often railroads in particular, as their principal enemies, and they believed that institutional reforms like the direct pri-

mary were likely to limit the political power of big business much as public service and trade regulatory commissions would limit its economic power. Yet progressives were also independently hostile to established party organizations; they preferred a more direct connection between voters and candidates for public office than that which would be encouraged by powerful party organizations with or without big business connections.

I write here of the progressivism that prevailed in most of the Midwest and West and in parts of the Northeast. In the South, the early twentieth-century reforms, including the direct primary, were associated with a rather different spirit, although it too was often called progressive. Southern states that adopted the direct primary did so after already effectively disenfranchising blacks, who had voted during the Reconstruction years, and many poor whites as well, and after Republican competition had been virtually eliminated.[40] Thus southern primaries were solely Democratic primaries for some whites only. To be sure, they provided more electoral competition than there could have been with caucus-convention nomination in a one-party system. To that extent, southern primaries had a little in common with the spirit of northern progressive reform, but not its antiorganizational impulse or its animus against big-business domination.

In whatever spirit the several states acted when they established direct primaries, they tended to provide a governmental process where there had been private associational power. Most often state laws, not party rules alone, authoritatively defined eligibility for voting in party primaries, even though the laws might only incorporate what had been party rules or customs. Usually states specified public registration or other public declaration of party identification as a condition for voting in Republican and Democratic primaries. At the same time, party officers and committees, themselves often elected by party voters at primary elections,[41] were legally recognized to discharge various public responsibilities including poll watching and any necessary replacement of nominees who could not run (because of death, for example) after being nominated in primaries. Several southern states, as already noted, even authorized party officers to administer their primary elections. Altogether, state governments became accustomed to mingling public and private actions.[42]

The trade-off implied by the mingling of private and public actions raises the possibility that parties, like many regulated business enterprises, succeeded in using the power of the state to protect their own interests. If parties were thus advantaged, their situation would be like that of many corporate utilities, railroad corporations for example, that secured benefits from the body originally established in response to public hostility towards them. The resemblance, however, is limited. Not only have parties been without regulatory commissions that could be captured, but unlike most utilities (notably electric utilities), parties as organizations have had little if anything to *gain* by their special legal treatment. Understandably, then, party organizations were not in the vanguard of the reform movement that led to the direct primary. Electric utilities, in contrast, often wanted regulation by state commissions in order to be protected against municipal ownership or corrupt administration of municipal franchises.[43] Moreover, they needed to operate as legalized monopolies in order to remain solvent; for electric companies, therefore, there was indeed a material gain in return for state regulation. But for parties, virtually no gain appeared beyond the intangible one of a new legitimacy for their nominating process—at the price of surrendering authority over that process. The organizational loss here would seem to outweigh heavily the gain unless party leaders and their supporters could still control or regularly and decisively influence the outcome of direct primaries. As described in the last chapter, such control or influence was achieved by many old organizations for several decades. And it was facilitated by direct-primary laws that more often than not had been designed in ways that strong party organizations could have been expected to favor when, under progressive reform pressure, they and their legislative representatives had to accept some form of direct primary.

The clearest case in point is the closed form of primary in which voters must officially register or otherwise publicly declare themselves party adherents in order to vote in a state-run nominating contest. Though hardly representing a gain for parties over preprimary days, the closed primary did at least preserve under state auspices some of the old caucus definition of eligibility of participants for the nominating process. Just as parties had been able to get their labelled tickets put on the Australian ballots adopted in 1888–90, so they often salvaged something from even the more clearly antiorganizational thrust of direct-primary legislation. For the first three or four decades of the twentieth century, they may have salvaged a good deal. As Berdahl wrote authoritatively as late as 1942, "the general tendency throughout the development of party regulation has been toward greater strictness in this respect, toward more effective protection of the party organization against the independent voter with a careless party conscience." The closed primary, he added, "has become more and more tightly closed."[44] Berdahl was writing during the period when the old machines were in many places still able, almost routinely, to win primaries for their slated candidates. No doubt their power and interest helped to keep primaries closed. Many primaries, however, remain similarly closed even into the 1980s without any longer being dominated by old organizations or any similarly effective successors. Now we observe the inability of most contemporary party organizations regularly to determine the outcome of nominations. Issue-oriented activists, whether in extralegal clubs or within statutory party frameworks, do not exercise the power once wielded by the old machines.

Yet in a strictly nonorganizational and electoral sense, major parties can be said to have gained something from the establishment of direct primaries. The dominance of their labels in elections, now that their nominees possess the democratic legitimacy of success in state-established primaries, has been institutionalized by statute even more completely than it was earlier by the adoption of the Americanized version of the Australian ballot. The advantage is no less real for being intangible. I have already described, in the last chapter, how the direct primary allowed new interests and new groups to compete openly for nominations within each major party and especially within the dominant party in the several virtually one-party states, and how it thus, in effect, discouraged such interests and groups from seeking power by establishing new parties or by persisting in efforts to build up existing minor parties. The latter course was also made more difficult by legal burdens that states imposed on new and minor parties as well as on independents. For them to gain the ballot access automatically granted Republicans and Democrats on the basis of prior votes, they were required to submit petitions signed by large numbers of registered voters.[45] In most states, to be sure, the third-party route was never so difficult as to be virtually impossible, and in the last few decades, largely because of newly applied constitutional standards, it has become less difficult for new parties to obtain ballot access. Nonetheless the institutionalized electoral duopoly remains.

I have treated the direct primary as the heart of this institutionalization. Although it is ordinarily accompanied by the legislative establishment of elected party committees charged with state-mandated electoral functions, state authority may not ever have clearly extended to certain other spheres of party activity. No law prevents, and constitutionally none is likely to prevent, citizens from organizing an association, calling it a Democratic or Republican party, and conducting a primary or general election campaign on its behalf. At most a state might try, as some have, to limit a statutory party's campaign activities, but constitutionally that too is now dubious. At any rate, despite pages of statutory provisions for party nomination and party structure, states commonly leave a large share of party organizational work to be conducted under rules the parties themselves adopt. For example, a recent study of leadership of state party organizations found that state election laws provided only 5 percent of the controlling provisions with respect to powers of party chairpersons.[46]

Again the legal status of parties is strikingly similar to that of public utilities. Regulated, even officially taken over, by the state with respect to their nominations, as are electric companies with respect to their equally vital rates, parties are nevertheless able to manage many of their activities in the manner of private associations. In this perspective, party organizational efforts to control nominations are analogous to the attempts of electric companies to influence the rates that regulatory commissions will approve. This is not to say that American party organizations, statutory or voluntary, actually determine nominations as a rule. We know that they have often failed recently, even when trying to mobilize primary voters. But the law does not make failure inevitable. Moreover, when a party organization succeeds in a primary, its victorious nominees are then democratically legitimized by the state-run primary process. Unofficial party choices can thus become official, state-blessed party choices entitled to privileged ballot positions at the general election.

IV

The White-Primary Cases

The constitutional distinction between state-established primaries on the one hand and party activities to influence their outcome on the other hand was blurred in the 1940s and 1950s by Supreme Court rulings in the famous white-primary cases. Court opinions then came close to suggesting that party actions generally were to be treated as state actions and, by inference, that states might constitutionally manage or regulate even more party activities than they had. I must therefore detour slightly to discuss the white-primary cases before taking up recent constitutional challenges to state regulation of parties.

In my detour, I adopt an interpretation of the white-primary rulings that limits state actions to those party actions officially recognized in state elections. The interpretation is based on a forceful and persuasive analysis by John Kester, from whose work I draw extensively. Kester argues that the white-primary decisions rested on the nature of state elections, and that the exclusion of blacks from primaries violated the Fifteenth Amendment's protection of the right to vote against its denial by state action. Even when parties were allowed to set the primary's voting rules, the Supreme Court had found the primary to be part of the state's election process because it led to privileged access to its general election ballot. For Kester, the crucial point is that *elec-*

tions were state actions and hence the right to vote was constitutionally protected against what appeared to be only party actions. By no means does he believe that many other party actions are thereby also state actions, or so involved with state actions as to be subject to the same judicial control. Kester's distinction rests in part on another distinction that he made between the requirements of the Fourteenth Amendment and those of the Fifteenth Amendment, which with the Nineteenth Amendment could be applied only to voting in elections.[47]

The white-primary cases did not raise the question directly of how far states could go in regulating parties. They did, however, concern the extent to which party actions are state actions and thus subject to control by the courts and, at least inferentially, by state or national governments. Kester's conclusion is that the white-primary decisions left political parties largely outside such control. They remain "free, absent state involvement, to go about their ordinary business — setting membership standards, choosing officers, organizing, holding caucuses and conventions, drawing up rules — free from federal constitutional restraint."[48]

Nevertheless, it is important to understand how the white-primary cases could have seemed to make party actions so generally state actions that Kester saw the need to argue the contrary. The U.S. Supreme Court, in disposing of these cases, had followed a long and tangled path. At first, it treated all primaries, white or other, as though they were not elections in the constitutional sense of the term; the circumstances were then special and the Court's meaning not entirely clear.[49] Soon afterward, however, the Supreme Court in 1927 found unconstitutional Texas's first legislative effort to bar blacks from the state's Democratic party primary (while not legally barring them from voting in general elections).[50] The judicial opinion in this case was a straightforward application of the Fourteenth Amendment's requirement that states not deny equal treatment, on grounds of race, to their citizens. Texas's denial by statute was plain: blacks were barred from voting. Following the 1927 decision, Texas tried to accomplish its purpose by slight indirection; it enacted a new statute that gave each political party's executive committee the power to prescribe its own qualifications for membership and voting. Promptly and predictably, the Texas Democratic Party's State Executive Committee adopted a resolution barring blacks from its primaries, and promptly and predictably, a black citizen was barred and did appeal. The U.S. Supreme Court held that the new procedure was also unconstitutional because the party committee had acted as the agent of the state.[51] But on Texas's third try, after the state's Democratic convention had restricted membership to whites and a black citizen had been denied a primary ballot, the Court upheld the white primary on the ground that the discrimination was the party's and not the state's. The Democratic primary in Texas, while regulated by the state, was paid for and in large enough measure run by the party so that the Supreme Court did not regard it as a state election.[52]

That opinion of 1935 was sharply reversed in less than a decade. The way to do so was paved by a 1941 Louisiana case that concerned not the voting rights of blacks but the alleged fraud committed by election officials running a primary election. Now, in contrast to some of its earlier opinions, the Supreme Court declared that a primary, where legally an integral part of the election machinery, is itself an election subject to constitutional protection. Louisiana's primary was in fact conducted by the state at public expense.[53] Subsequently, in 1944, despite the different manner in which Texas's primary was run and paid for, the Court found it too a part of the state's election machinery. In the landmark case *Smith v. Allwright* the Court, observing that Texas law stipulated procedures for selecting the party officers who would conduct the primary elections, found that "primary elections are conducted by the party under state statutory authority." With respect to these elections, it added, significantly: "We think that this statutory system for the selection of party nominees for inclusion on the general election ballot makes the party which is required to follow these legislative directions an agency of the State in so far as it determines the participants in a primary election."[54] The "in so far as" clause might well be stressed. Without it, the Court's opinion could lead one to think that party was much more generally regarded as an agency of the state than it was. The Court also stopped well short of that when it said that the privilege of party membership may be no concern of the state, but when, as in Texas, "that privilege is also the essential qualification for voting in a primary to select nominees for a general election, the State makes the action of the party the action of the State."[55] Explicitly, then, Texas violated the Fifteenth Amendment's guarantee of the right to vote rather than the Fourteenth Amendment's broader guarantees.

Following *Smith v. Allwright*, the federal courts found that they had to impute state action to still more party actions in order to protect the voting rights of blacks. Southern states did not surrender their white primaries without ingenious efforts to circumvent the Supreme Court rulings. For example, Georgia's law did not require a party to hold a primary, it used no state funds to pay for a primary, and it allowed persons not chosen in a primary to appear readily on the general election ballot. Nevertheless, a federal circuit court decided that the state's involvement was extensive enough to amount to the state's adoption of the Georgia Democratic party's racially discriminatory membership rules.[56] South Carolina's method met a similar judicial fate after the state had responded to *Smith v. Allwright* by repealing its laws regulating primaries. But when the South Carolina Democratic party adopted almost all of the former statutory provisions and barred blacks from primary voting, a federal circuit court found that the party officials managing the election machinery were "election officers of the state de facto if not de jure, and as such must observe the limitations of the Constitution." The court also declared that "political parties have become in effect state institutions, governmental agencies through which sovereign power is exercised by the people."[57]

Not until a U.S. Supreme Court ruling of 1953, however, did the federal judiciary touch its high-water mark in *seeming* to treat a party as though it were a state agency even when the party acted on its own in the candidate-selection process. Again a white primary was at issue, but it was of a rather different kind from any previously considered in protecting the voting rights of black citizens. The case, *Terry v. Adams*,[58] concerned the Jaybird Democratic Association, or Jaybird party, that had existed in a Texas county since 1889. Whites, but no blacks, were automatically association members if their names appeared on the official lists of county voters. In May of each election year, after candidates for county offices had submitted their names to the association's elected committee, the Jaybirds conducted a straw ballot (a "preprimary" primary) to determine which candidates to endorse in the official Democratic primary in July. With few exceptions in 60 years, association winners subsequently won, without opposition, the Democratic nomination and then the noncompetitive general election. Accordingly, Justice Black found that the Jaybird party, however unofficial, had been "the dominant political group in the county since organization, having endorsed every county-wide official elected since 1889."[59]

The dominance, however, did not rest on the use of a ballot label; *Jaybird* was not on the July primary ballot as *Democratic* was on general election ballots after official party primaries, white or otherwise, in Texas or elsewhere. The state of Texas, in other words, did not recognize the Jaybird Association by conferring legal status upon it. Nevertheless, for the Court the distinction was one only of form, not of substance. So was the general absence of state control of the Jaybird Association. "It is immaterial," Justice Black said, "that the state does not control that part of this elective process which it leaves for the Jaybirds to manage. The Jaybird primary has become an integral part, indeed the only effective part, of the elective process that determines who shall rule and govern in the county."[60]

Black's opinion, while representing the views of only two of his colleagues, was roughly similar to Justice Clark's concurring opinion, joined by three other justices. Clark declared that the record disclosed that the Jaybird Association operated as part and parcel of the Democratic party, an organization existing under the auspices of Texas law, and that the association's activities fell "within the Fifteenth Amendment's self-executing ban."[61] The record to which he referred included data from three elections in the 1940s that showed larger turnouts in the Jaybirds' own primary in May than in the Democratic party's primary in July. These results mattered less in a third concurring opinion, Justice Frankfurter's, that stressed the participation and acquiescence of state officials in the Jaybirds' denial of black voting rights.[62] Only Justice Minton dissented, on the ground that the Jaybird Democratic Association was a pressure group not involved in state action in the manner of a party conducting a state-recognized primary.[63]

Therefore, despite differences among the other eight justices, the Supreme Court emerges from *Terry v. Adams* as heavily committed to the view that even a private political association may be prohibited from selecting candidates according to its own rules. Here, as in the earlier white-primary cases, the prohibition was by no means the state's; Texas was as far from seeking to ban the Jaybirds' discrimination as it had been from seeking to ban the Democratic party's discrimination in *Smith v. Allwright*. Instead, the state obviously tolerated and effectively encouraged the offensive party policies. Nevertheless, *Terry v. Adams* may well have been perceived as going so far in imputing state action to a private political association that few limits were likely to be imposed on state, or national, regulation of parties. Unquestionably, *Terry v. Adams* must be interpreted more narrowly by those who believe in limited governmental intervention in party affairs. It is a special problem for Kester, whose analysis, as I have noted, generally seeks to interpret the white-primary cases as justifying intervention only with respect to party roles in elections.

Terry v. Adams, Kester argues, "stands for no general principle that a political party's action is state action—certainly not under the Fourteenth Amendment, which no opinion relied on, or even under the Fifteenth Amendment, except in the extreme and unusual circumstances *Terry* presented."[64] The circumstances were not merely the de facto power of Jaybird endorsements but also the racial exclusion which, while that of a private association, was effectively the same exclusion that Texas and its officially recognized Democratic party had practiced until the U.S. Supreme Court held it unconstitutional. By 1953, the Court was so committed to the protection of the right of blacks to vote that it had only to find an election meaningful in the eventual choice of public officeholders, as the Jaybird primary certainly was, in order to treat that election as something other than a private affair. Hence no matter how far the Court went in treating a political association as though it were performing a state function, it did so only with respect to activity affecting the right to vote.

V

Recent Constitutional Challenges

Observing the U.S. Supreme Court's zeal during the last two decades to protect First and Fourteenth Amendment freedoms, we should surely expect new constitutional challenges to the states' treatment of parties as regulated public utilities. And we should also expect the challenges to raise issues seldom explicitly discussed during the preceding century of regulation. To be sure, there was for a long time an implicit recognition of constitutional limits to state control of party activities, resting on the distinction between the constitutionally valid state conduct of party primary elections and the presumably protected rights of parties to undertake private associational activities. But that distinction, as the white-primary cases illustrate, was unclear and uncertain. It remains an elusive legal doctrine, but it is now more often defined in a way that suggests substantial areas of freedom for political parties.

The absence earlier in the century of effective U.S. constitutional challenges to state regulation of parties is explicable as a matter of legal history. Although the First and Fourteenth amendments have long been parts of the U.S. Constitution, only in the last several decades have they been interpreted by the U.S. Supreme Court so as to suggest the possibility of fundamental attack on the authority of state governments to limit political parties. Most significantly, the First and Fourteenth amendments had not been understood to suggest that possibility during the years from 1890 to 1920, when most of the progressive regulatory legislation was enacted. In that period, the Fourteenth Amendment's provisions against state action that violated due process of law or equal protection of the laws were mainly used to challenge economic regulations. Before the 1920s and 1930s, the U.S. Supreme Court did not incorporate the First Amendment's guarantees of freedom into the Fourteenth Amendment so that such freedom could be protected by the federal courts against state as well as against federal government actions. And before the 1950s, the Court did not explicitly extend constitutional protection to freedom of political association.

Understandably, then, the great twentieth-century wave of state regulation of parties stood for years virtually unchallenged in the federal courts. It was challenged occasionally in state courts, under common law doctrines or state constitutional provisions, but with a rare early exception, the party regulatory legislation survived.[65] Like most other state regulatory legislation, it was constitutional as long as it was not "arbitrary, discriminatory, or unreasonable."[66] Only when a legislature reached out broadly to forbid campaign activities by individuals, groups, or the party type of committee was a state court likely to find the very purpose of the law invalid under a state constitution.[67]

Recent challenges under the U.S. Constitution have been more far reaching in their potential for overturning state regulation of parties. They raise significant questions about barriers to ballot access for minor parties, about closed primaries, and most fundamentally, about the validity of state regulations in light of associational rights of party organizations. I shall discuss separately each of the three subjects of challenge, but it should be clear at the outset that the first two subjects, ballot access and closed primaries, concern laws customarily thought to be advantageous to major established parties at the expense of other parties, independent candidates, and independent voters. Challenges to such laws have not usually been made by major parties seeking to escape regulation. The challengers have often been anti-party, or at least anti-established party, and thus similar to the successful judicial challengers of patronage practices who invoke the First and Fourteenth amendments to oppose the interests of established parties.[68] Yet the challenges concerning ballot access and closed primaries strike at the legislative structure of presumed privileges of regulated parties; they relate to the status of regulation as the patronage cases do not. Moreover, one challenge to a closed primary was actually raised by a major party.

1. Ballot Access

Constitutional challenges in ballot-access cases have scored some recent successes without substantially changing the state-recognized party duopoly. States still require independent candidates, new parties, and continuing minor parties (unless they polled in the preceding election a substantial percentage of the popular vote) to submit numerous supporting signatures in order to obtain a place on the general election ballot that each major party obtains by virtue of its prior electoral percentage.[69] Similarly, states ordinarily run primary elections only for parties thus previously qualified and accordingly provide their democratic legitimacy only for successful nominees of those parties. Since 1968, however, the U.S. Supreme Court has imposed new limits on how far states may go in protecting major-party duopoly. Barriers to ballot access have always varied greatly from state to state, and certain states had by mid-century if not earlier imposed such heavy burdens on independents, new parties, and small continuing parties that access was prohibitively difficult. The burdens seemed greater than could be justified by a state's understandable desire to provide an uncluttered ballot at reasonable cost.

The first important recent challenge came from George Wallace's American Independent party when it sought ballot access in Ohio in 1968. The Ohio law provided in the usual way for parties, meaning Republicans and Democrats, to put their labels on ballots because of their previous vote. Also in the usual way, the law required other parties not thus qualified to present petitions signed by specified numbers of voters in order to gain ballot access. But the rigor of Ohio's requirement was not entirely usual: to get on the presidential general election ballot, the AIP had to present signatures totaling 15 percent of the ballots cast in the last gubernatorial election and to do so by early February of the presidential election year. Having failed to meet the February deadline although it eventually gathered the required number of signatures, the AIP persuaded the U.S. Supreme Court, in *Williams v. Rhodes*,[70] that the Ohio law, by making it virtually impossible for a new party to get on the ballot, violated the equal protection clause of the Fourteenth Amendment. The Court found that while a state interest in preserving the two-party system was not illegitimate, Ohio had gone too far in protecting the Republican and Democratic parties. It therefore put the AIP on Ohio's 1968 ballot, but not another party, the Socialist Labor party, that had challenged Ohio's law without having collected the required number of signatures.

By no means, then, did the Ohio case effectively destroy the favored status enjoyed by the two major parties under state laws. A few years afterwards, the Supreme Court confirmed that status by upholding a Georgia statute that granted legal advantages to established major parties but did not exclude other parties as rigorously as had Ohio. Georgia specified that any political organization receiving at least 20 percent of the votes at the most recent gubernatorial or presidential election is a "political party" able to conduct a primary whose winner goes on the general election ballot. Nominees of other groups, or independents, need signatures of at least 5 percent of the eligible voters in order to appear on the general election ballot. Unlike Ohio, Georgia imposed no unreasonably early deadline, allowed write-in votes, and recognized independent candidates. So it did not unconstitutionally freeze the status quo, as had Ohio, although it provided substantial advantages for established parties.[71]

The 5 percent requirement, while higher than that imposed by some other states, did not apparently demand more signatures than would be constitutional. Accordingly, in the words of a leading legal authority, the Supreme Court will allow states, "in order to keep ballots manageable and protect the integrity of the electoral process," to require significant support but not so much that minority parties or independent candidates would have "no real chance of obtaining ballot positions."[72]

Several cases beyond the two already noted illustrate the moderate degree to which judicial rulings impinge on the legal duopoly. Illinois statutes have twice been ruled discriminatory. Once the Supreme Court invalidated a provision requiring independent candidates for presidential elector positions to obtain the specified 25,000 signatures, with at least 200 from each of at least 50 of the states's 102 counties. Plainly burdensome for a party whose strength was concentrated in the state's most populous counties, the law was found in 1969 to discriminate against the residents of such counties and thus to violate rights under the Fourteenth Amendment.[73] Again, ten years later, the Supreme Court ruled against an Illinois statute that required, in an election for local office, an independent candidate or a new party to obtain signatures from 5 percent of those who had voted in the previous election for local office.[74] The trouble was not the 5 percent as such[75] but rather the fact that it came to 35,947 signatures in Chicago, whereas only 25,000 signatures were then required to run for statewide office. Thus the provision violated the equal protection clause of the Fourteenth Amendment, since there was no rational basis for requiring more signatures for Chicago local office than for statewide office.

In contrast to the Illinois laws, in which the state had gone too far in protecting major parties against other contestants, less restrictive California and Texas laws were upheld by the Supreme Court in 1974. California prohibited an individual from obtaining general election ballot position as an independent if he or she had had a registered affiliation with a qualified party in the year before the immediately preceding primary election. In *Storer v. Brown*,[76] the Supreme Court held that California's prohibition was aimed at maintaining the integrity of the various routes to the ballot and involved no discrimination. The Texas case, decided the same day, involved a larger part of the process by which a state provides for major parties, minor parties, and independents.[77] Texas statutes specified four methods for nominating candidates in a general election—that is, four methods for getting on the general election ballot. The first was by primary election for candidates of parties whose gubernatorial choice polled more than 200,000 votes in the last general election. The second was by primary or convention, and it was available for candidates whose parties polled fewer than 200,000 but more than 1 percent of the vote cast in the preceding gubernatorial election. The third and fourth methods required signatures of 1 to 5 percent, depending on the office sought, but with no more than 500 signatures required in any district election. Other provisions prohibited a voter from signing a party's ballot-seeking petition after having participated in another party's primary or nominating contest, and from signing an independent candidate's petition after having participated in another party's nominating process or having signed a nominating petition for the same office. The Court granted that as a consequence "the pool of possible supporters" for those seeking signatures between a primary and a general election was restricted, but the Court in upholding the restriction called it "nothing more than a prohibition against any elector's casting more than one vote in the process of nominating candidates for a particular office."[78] Also, given the modest number of signatures required, the Court may well have thought that the restricted pool of possible supporters was large enough. The point remains that the Supreme Court was upholding a law that protected major parties by preventing their participants from helping rivals obtain ballot access in a given general election.

In light of the Court's acceptance of the California and Texas statutes as well as that of Georgia, the legal disadvantages of minor parties and independents might appear firmly fixed despite the invalidation of the unusually onerous Ohio and Illinois provisions. But a still later case from Ohio suggests a more critical judicial attitude. In *Anderson v. Celebrezze*,[79] the Supreme Court in 1983 again invalidated an Ohio statute pertaining to presidential candidacy, this time on the basis of an independent rather than a third-party attempt. Ohio law as of 1980 required an independent candidate for president to file a statement of candidacy by March 20 in order to qualify for the general election ballot in November. John Anderson did not file until May 16. Thanks to a federal district court order, Anderson actually appeared on the Ohio general election ballot. But almost three years later the case reached the U.S. Supreme Court after a Circuit Court of Appeals had upheld Ohio's law. Judicial validation might well have seemed consistent with the Supreme Court's acceptance in *Storer v. Brown* of the California statute that prevented one from becoming an independent congressional candidate if one had a party affiliation within the preceding year. Not only was Anderson still a Republican member of Congress in 1980, but he had run in several Republican presidential primaries in the early spring before he switched to independent candidacy in April (before Ohio's June presidential primary). It could not be doubted that Anderson's decision to run as an independent, in Ohio as elsewhere, was made in

light of the probable outcome of the national Republican nominating contest
(and perhaps the Democratic one too). But in this instance that very fact seemed
crucial in the Supreme Court's rejection of the statute. The effect of the March
deadline, as the Court saw it, was to preclude independent candidacy when
such candidacy might well have become relevant only after apparent major
party results.

Accordingly, in a five-to-four decision, the Court held that the Ohio law
"places a particular burden on an identifiable segment of Ohio's independent-
minded voters." The Court added: "A burden that falls unequally on new or
small political parties or on independent candidates impinges, by its very nature, on associational choices protected by the First Amendment."[80] In the
opinion of the Court majority, but not of the dissenting minority, the case
was distinguishable from *Storer v. Brown* in that Ohio, unlike California, discriminated against independents as such rather than against sore losers. Furthermore, Ohio did so in a presidential election. Significantly, in *Anderson v.
Celebrezze*, the Court also said that "Ohio's asserted interest in political stability amounts to a desire to protect existing political parties from competition. . . ."[81] That kind of statement poses the possibility of a more drastic
attack on the legal structure of party duopoly. After all, do not ballot-access
provisions generally serve to protect major parties from competition, even if
they do so but modestly and more or less reasonably? Yet the Court has tolerated a great deal of such protection, in effect if not in intent, on the ground
that the state has an interest in an uncluttered ballot and the integrity of the
election process. The toleration has diminished only slightly in response to
recent challenges, and it is therefore fairly safe to assume, despite an occasional
question, the continuation of at least moderately privileged ballot access for
major parties.

2. Closed Primaries

Like ballot access, closed primaries represent elements in the legal institutionalization of major parties. In challenging such primaries, independent individuals and groups question the constitutionality of a state-run election that
excludes voters who are not publicly professing party identifiers. However
benign the exclusion may strike most party organizations, individuals have
claimed that their right to participate should prevail against the statutory effort to protect parties against interlopers. The argument, it should be stressed,
is advanced consistently with the doctrine that underlay the white primary
cases — that primaries are state elections rather than private associational affairs
and that individual rights to participate are therefore constitutionally pro-

tected. The point is significant because it is precisely that doctrine of state action that must be put aside or narrowly interpreted when, in my third category of cases, challenges are made in the name of private associational rights.

Individual challenges to closed primaries have met with only limited success, despite the continued acceptance by the Supreme Court of the state action doctrine that is invoked by individuals claiming the right to participate. Two cases that reached the U.S. Supreme Court in 1973 suggest difficulty and uncertainty in deciding how fully states may close their primaries. In *Rosario v. Rockefeller*,[82] the Court upheld a New York law that required party registration (called enrollment in New York) 30 days before a general election in the year preceding the primary in which one wanted to vote—meaning ordinarily an October registration for a primary between the next June and September. The 8 to 11 months' period did not seem too long to the majority of the Court, although it did to four dissenters. The majority thought that New York, which had had a closed primary for over 60 years, justified its restrictions by its interest in protecting a party against the raiding of its primary by opposition-party voters. On the other hand, later the same year, the Supreme Court in *Kusper v. Pontikes*[83] ruled an Illinois law unconstitutional, apparently because, unlike New York, Illinois locked voters into a party from one primary to the next. Specifically, Illinois (which used party-primary voting declaration rather than New York's separate party registration) prohibited a person from voting in the primary election of a political party if he had voted in the primary of any other party during the preceding 23 months. Seven members of the Court decided that Illinois thus infringed on rights of free political association as protected by the First and Fourteenth amendments. While still recognizing, as it had in the New York case, that the state had a legitimate interest in the prevention of raiding, the Court suggested that Illinois attain that result by "less drastic means."[84]

A more interesting and radical challenge to a state's closed primary was the subject not of a Supreme Court opinion but of that Court's affirmation of a U.S. District Court decision in 1976. Nonetheless the case, *Nader v. Schaffer*,[85] deserves attention. Objecting to Connecticut's statute, Nathra Nader and Albert Snyder, the plaintiffs, were represented by the Public Citizen Litigation Group, associated with Nathra Nader's famous son Ralph. Both plaintiffs were registered voters who by conviction were not members of any political party; Nader had never been a party member during his half-century of voting, and Snyder had ceased to be a party member about two years before the suit. Because the plaintiffs were not therefore enrolled on a party list with the official voting registrar, Connecticut law denied them the right to vote in the state-conducted party primaries. Nader and Snyder challenged the denial in principle and not in terms of any claimed burdensome time period.

Actually Connecticut's statute made it easier for voters to change their party preference than did the New York statute that the Court had upheld, and in one way easier than had the Illinois statute that the Court invalidated. A Connecticut voter switching from one party enrollment to another could vote in his newly chosen party primary if only six months had passed from his application to transfer party enrollment. This six months' waiting period, plainly valid as a barrier to party switchers under the terms of *Rosario v. Rockefeller*, was not itself challenged by Nader and Snyder. For them, it was irrelevant. Enrolled in neither party, Nader and Snyder would have been allowed by Connecticut law, then in force, to qualify as party voters by so registering as late as the third Saturday before the primary in which they wanted to vote. By refusing that option and insisting that they should have been allowed to cast party primary votes without party registration, Nader and Snyder squarely raised the question of the constitutionality of any legislation excluding independent voters from party primaries. The question, as counsel later argued, had never been considered by the U.S. Supreme Court.[86]

Nor did the Supreme Court consider the question in this case except insofar as it affirmed, without opinion, the decision of the U.S. District Court upholding the Connecticut statute. The District Court's decision, in behalf of a three-judge panel, must have looked consistent with *Rosario v. Rockefeller* and other cases in which the judiciary held that a state could establish party enrollment as a condition for voting in primary elections. As in the Connecticut case, the prevailing view was, and is, that the establishment of such a condition served a legitimate state interest. Only when the condition appeared unnecessarily onerous, as in the Illinois case, had the Court invalidated it. Therefore it could be said that Nader and Snyder asked for a reversal of accepted doctrine despite their argument that the doctrine had been developed to exclude untimely party switchers and not independent voters. They claimed that the state's denial of the primary vote to independents deprived them of their Fourteenth Amendment right to equal protection of the law, that the state's requirement that they choose between party enrollment and the right to vote in a primary election forced them to choose between their voting right and their right freely to associate for the advancement of political ideas, and that the state infringed on their right to vote as guaranteed under the Constitution's Article I as well as the Fourteenth and Seventeenth amendments. They could not participate in the primaries that were, they said, an integral part of the process by which their U.S. senators and representatives are chosen.

In making their claims, the plaintiffs emphasized the involvement of the state in managing and financing primary elections—much as had those who complained about the white primaries. Nader and Snyder sought only to participate in what they perceived as state elections; they did not argue that they had a right to participate in the party caucuses and conventions that preceded the state's primaries and that might, under Connecticut's "challenge primary" law, obviate the use of primaries. Moreover, they argued that 36 percent of the state's electorate, independent voters who like themselves were unenrolled as party members, were excluded from primary participation unless they let themselves be coerced into "joining" a political party through the enrollment process.[87] They also cited a recent growth in the percentage of independent voters—to 38 percent nationally and over 45 percent among voters under 30 years of age—to support their contention that the Court should now face the constitutional problem posed by statutory exclusion of independents from state primary elections.[88]

Novel though the Nader challenge was, the data just noted suggest real and substantial interests underlying the case. Significantly, U.S. Senator Lowell Weicker, a possible beneficiary if independents were allowed to vote in a Connecticut Republican primary, filed a brief supporting the plaintiffs. Others too, though not similarly motivated, could be troubled about a law that works so that over one-third of a state's registered voters choose—voluntarily to be sure—a status that precludes participation in a primary election. Even Connecticut, traditionally such a strong party state that it adopted a statewide direct primary only in 1955 and in a form that limited its use, does not have the same overwhelming majority of party identifiers that would once have made a closed primary more natural and acceptable. Now, in barring independents from its primaries, Connecticut excludes a group as numerous as were the blacks excluded from the old white primaries. The reason for exclusion is hardly as offensive as the color bar; independents, unlike blacks, have determined their own status and can change it. Plainly they cannot invoke the Fifteenth Amendment, which had finally been applied to invalidate white primaries, because it forbids the denial of voting rights only on account of race, color, or previous condition of servitude. Independent voters like Nader and Snyder must rest their case on the Fourteenth Amendment's more ambiguous equal protection clause and on other general constitutional guarantees.

New and successful challenges on those grounds may yet be made,[89] but so far *individual* objections to closed primaries have prevailed in federal courts only when a state has imposed a barrier as troubling as that of Illinois. The Illinois ruling had a significant consequence because Illinois, after its 23-month

barrier was invalidated, was more clearly a state that simply permitted all voters to declare a new or an old party preference at each primary election. Hence
while not technically open in the same sense as a primary like Wisconsin's,
where no public declaration is ever required, the Illinois primary, like similar primaries in a dozen other states, is occasionally classified as an open or
a crossover primary. The good practical reason for that classification is that
many independents and party switchers do use their opportunities. The Illinois kind of arrangement, however, might not provide voting opportunities
for Nader and Snyder; announcing a party identification might well be as objectionable to them on a primary polling day as it was three weeks before
that day.

State legislatures could of course modify their closed-primary laws in either
the Illinois or Wisconsin direction even though those laws remain constitutionally valid. In 1984 Connecticut Republicans, responding to U.S. Senator
Lowell Weicker's urging, proposed such modification, specifically that unaffiliated voters (but not registered Democrats) be allowed to cast ballots in certain
Republican primaries. When the Connecticut legislature, then dominated by
Democrats, did not respond favorably, the state Republican party filed suit
in the U.S. District Court against the constitutionality of the Connecticut
law that kept unaffiliated voters from voting in a primary of a party whose
convention wanted such voters to participate. The purpose of the suit resembled that of Nader and Snyder in that it would open the state's primary, or
at least one party's primary, to voters unregistered by party, but the grounds
differed not only from those of Nader and Snyder but also from other earlier
challenges to closed primaries. Now instead of claims of individual rights to
vote in a state-run election, it was argued that the associational rights of a
party were violated when the state imposed a more restrictive qualification
than the party wanted. Hence the case properly belongs in my next category
of challenges, where attention is given to the U.S. District judge's ruling in
favor of the Republican party and to its affirmation by the Court of Appeals.[90]

Here it is enough to observe that the Connecticut Republican challenge,
as well as its success, was novel among suits against closed primaries. Now
a major party organization, historically thought to benefit from the closed
primary, wanted to enlarge its potential primary electorate. It is true that it
did so as the smaller and less often victorious of the state's two major parties
in elections during the two decades before 1984. Connecticut Democrats had
not wanted to open their primary or that of the Republicans to unaffiliated
voters. But conceivably any Republican or Democratic party in a state where
it was the second of the two major parties might see advantages in opening

its primary to unaffiliated voters. Thus a constitutional challenge like that of Connecticut Republicans is possible elsewhere unless the Connecticut result should be reversed by the U.S. Supreme Court. Success will depend on the recently developed judicial respect for the associational rights of major parties. And that respect, as the following pages indicate, has been the product of cases where state regulations were plainly antiorganizational and so different from, even diametrically opposed to, the purpose of Connecticut's closed-primary law.

3. Intrusions on Associational Rights of Major Parties

I come at last to the direct attack that major parties themselves have made against statutory restrictions that they, and their scholarly champions too, regard as limiting organizational effectiveness. Invoking constitutional rights under the First and Fourteenth amendments as have anti-party challengers, pro-party advocates rely heavily on associational claims that do not follow from the doctrine used by those who assert individual rights to participate in state-run primary elections. Indeed, that doctrine, converting party action to state action insofar as nominations and elections are concerned, must be limited in its reach if parties are to win greater constitutional freedom for their activities. Ultimately, for something like full associational freedom, the state-action doctrine would have to be substantially reversed by the invalidation of the state-run direct primary and the restoration of the party's power, as a private association, to determine its own nominations. So drastic a change in American practice seems inconceivable even at the hands of an alleged imperial judiciary, and the recent challenges to state laws go only as far as to object to particular features of direct-primary laws and other related regulatory legislation intruding on claimed associational rights of party organizations. The challenges do, however, ask courts to narrow the scope of state action by treating certain party activities as private. In contrast, individuals seeking to participate in closed primaries base their claims on the assumption that nominating contests are state elections in which barriers to voting are unconstitutional.

Put a little differently, insofar as a court responds to individual claims against a state's closed-primary law or even a ballot-access law, it treats a party matter as state action. But insofar as a court responds to a party's complaint against state regulation of party activity, it treats a party matter as private rather than state action. Moreover, the second response is pro-major party in its impact while the first is anti-major party. The second removes burdens, and the first removes privileges. In their impact, however, a common element is a tendency toward legal de-institutionalization of the public utilities status of major parties. And in judicial terms the evidently different responses are more or less reconciled by distinguishing between two kinds of party activities, those that the state can constitutionally control as elements in its election process and those that it cannot so control because they are private associational affairs.

The distinction, while always implicit if not explicit in the constitutional history of a century of regulation, has become more salient now that the U.S. Supreme Court treats freedom of political association as a right to be protected against state regulation. Judicial doctrine in this respect emerged in 1957 and 1958 in cases involving the Communist party and the National Association for the Advancement of Colored People (NAACP).[91] But the Supreme Court's broad language upholding associational rights in these cases did not cause parties to rush into the federal courts to challenge existing statutes. Instead, in the first 16 years following the 1958 opinion concerning the NAACP, the most relevant federal cases were ones in which courts were asked to rule state laws invalid not because parties objected to them but because individuals claimed that parties were permitted, by state law, to choose certain of their officials in ways that violated the rights of voters. The significance for associational freedom was indirect in that the cases provided the federal courts with an opportunity to limit the state-action doctrine. For example, the U.S. Court of Appeals for the Third Circuit upheld a Pennsylvania Democratic practice of electing county party leaders by a voting method that would have violated equal protection of the law if used in a state-run primary election to nominate candidates.[92] Consistent with that case, a U.S. District Court in 1970 upheld a Washington State Republican practice of electing state party committee members on other than a one-person, one-vote formula, because such election was not part of the state-created election process; but it ruled invalid a Washington State Democratic practice of electing state and county party convention delegates partly by geographic area rather than solely by population, on the ground that such delegates, who would choose national convention delegates, were part of the presidential nominating process.[93] In other words, state-authorized procedures had to conform to strict constitutional requirements when nomination or election to public office was involved, but not when party officials were chosen to manage other party business. The difference in standards reflected the old distinction between state and private action that underlay earlier judicial views of regulation.

In 1975, however, it became evident that much more direct challenges to state regulatory authority were feasible. Early in that year, the U.S. Supreme Court dramatically proclaimed the private associational rights of a political party to manage its own affairs. The case, *Cousins v. Wigoda*,[94] is vitally important here, and also with respect to the relation of national and state parties. I shall discuss the latter aspect at length, along with the equally important *Democratic Party v. La Follette* (1981),[95] in the next chapter on party nationalization. Yet a brief summary is in order now. In both *Cousins* and *La Follette*, the U.S. Supreme Court held that a state could not require a national party to seat convention delegates selected in primaries according to state law but in violation of national party rules. The cases, it is true, involved a national party and its presidential nominating conventions; they might thus be understood only to preclude state regulation of a national party. But the Court in each instance, and especially in *La Follette*, was so emphatic in proclaiming broad associational rights that opponents of state regulation of state parties were understandably encouraged to challenge such regulation as they had not done before. If national parties were now freed from state control, as they were also in practice from national governmental control, why should not state parties assert the same right to be constitutionally protected from statutory restrictions? The language of the First Amendment would seem as applicable in the one situation as in the other.[96]

So it was in the eyes of the U.S. District Court that, before the end of 1975, invalidated a Rhode Island statute requiring a chairman of a city party committee to add members to that committee. The committee had functions almost wholly of internal party management, and thus the court held that the state's requirement imposed an unconstitutional burden on party associational rights. In so holding, the court relied most directly on the recently decided *Cousins* case, citing it along with *NAACP v. Alabama* and other similar precedents. Indeed, the district court was explicit in declaring that the associational rights in *Cousins* were not solely invokable against a national party. They were also relevant to the Democratic party of the city of Providence and specifically to two of its "members" who as registered Democratic voters had brought suit against implementation of the state requirement.[97] The fact that the suit was thus in behalf of individual members rather than of a party organization or its leadership should not conceal the triumph of associational rights. Its significance, however, was limited by both the narrow statutory particulars and the district court level at which the case was decided.

In a broader context, the U.S. Supreme Court itself had a post-*Cousins* opportunity in 1979 to rule on the validity of state regulation of state parties. The case, *Marchioro v. Chaney*,[98] concerned a Washington state law stipulating, in fairly usual fashion, how party committees are to be chosen and how these committees are to discharge certain legally imposed responsibilities connected to state-run elections. Washington requires each major party to have a state committee consisting of two persons from each county, and it gives this committee the power to call conventions, to provide for the election of delegates to national conventions and for the nomination of presidential electors, and to fill vacancies on the party ticket. In the Democratic party, with which the case deals, the committee's numerous other activities, including campaign activities, are authorized by the charter of the state Democratic party—that is, by the rules of an apparently private association meeting in a state convention recognized by both the charter and Washington statute as the governing body of the party.

Only the provision for the Washington State party committee's membership was challenged before the Court. The challenge was based on the committee's refusal to seat additional delegates chosen in accord with a new Democratic charter amendment for a committee membership larger than the two-per-county provided by statute. It was argued that the state, by restricting committee membership, violated the rights of party members to freedom of association under the First and Fourteenth amendments. The U.S. Supreme Court rejected the challenge, as had the Washington State Supreme Court, on interesting grounds that reveal a good deal about the special legal status of political parties. The state, the Court said, entrusted the committee with authority to perform limited functions directly related to the "orderly participation of the political party in the electoral process."[99] To the performance of these functions no objections were being raised.

Specifically, certain Democratic party members and officers challenged the statute in relation to the committee's other, nonelectoral activities—those concerned with internal party affairs authorized by the Democratic charter. The challengers thought that the state unconstitutionally imposed on their private political association by stipulating membership on a committee undertaking those activities. The Court's answer to this complaint was that the state did not require its statutory committee to undertake any activities beyond the specified electoral functions. The Democratic party convention had given the other tasks to the committee, and the convention could, if it liked, create a new or an enlarged committee of its own for the purpose. In short, the state did not interfere with internal party affairs when it restricted its statutory committee membership, because it did not require that the committee perform except in well-established electoral roles. The specificity of the *Marchioro* holding is striking. State regulatory power is upheld *because* it applied to parties only in fairly direct relation to elections. In other respects, state power is clearly limited by First Amendment rights to freedom of political association.

Since *Marchioro*, the judicial battle ground is chiefly over which state regulations of parties can be justified even by the states' power to conduct elections. An especially interesting test again arose in the state of Washington when Democratic state party leaders, in *Heavey v. Chapman*,[100] challenged Washington's blanket primary law. The ground for the challenge was that the law, allowing any voter to participate in the nomination of Democratic candidates, deprived members of the Democratic party of their associational rights, under the party charter, to choose their own nominees. The argument was thus far-reaching, in that it could be used not only against Washington's (and Alaska's) blanket primary but also against the open primaries of nine other states and probably against any others that made it relatively easy for independents or opposing party identifiers to enter a party's primary.[101] Note well that the attack here is at odds with that made against Connecticut's closed primary, first by independent voters in *Nader v. Schaffer* and then by the Connecticut Republican party. Now, in *Heavey v. Chapman*, the objection was to an open primary like that which Nader and the Connecticut Republicans had wanted. The objection did not prevail. Washington's blanket primary was upheld as a valid exercise of state power.

The ruling in *Heavey v. Chapman* was the state supreme court's, and it was not reviewed by the U.S. Supreme Court as *Marchiori* had been. *Heavey*, however, concerns the same constitutional issue as *Marchiori*, in which the Washington court was upheld, and it is worth noting because of the context in which the court discussed the conflict between state powers and associational rights. Its opinion began by acknowledging that it had to face the question in light of the federal constitutional doctrine that had evolved since an earlier Washington Supreme Court had, in 1936, upheld the state's then new blanket-primary law. Now, in reaching the same conclusion, the court observed that no substantial burden on associational activity was shown, or even claimed to be shown, by the Democrats who objected to the blanket primary, and that the state had a sufficiently compelling interest in open electoral participation. Nevertheless, the court dealt seriously with the question.[102] And it did so in June 1980 and thus before the U.S. Supreme Court ruled, in *Democratic Party v. La Follette* (1981), that Wisconsin could not force the national Democratic convention to seat delegates chosen as a result of the state's open primary. This is not to say that *Heavey* would have been decided differently a year or two later. It might well have remained crucial that Washington Democrats could show no substantial burden on their associational activity. Moreover, *La Follette* might have been put aside because it involved a national party.

Most decidedly, however, *La Follette* was not put aside in 1984 when the

U.S. District Court in Connecticut held that the state's *closed* primary law abridged the right of association of a Republican party that wanted unaffiliated voters to participate in its primaries. In my earlier reference to the case, *Republican Party of Connecticut v. Tashjian*,[103] I suggested that its main significance lay in its successful associational claims, even though these claims were against rather than in defense of the traditionally pro-party closed primary. The same associational right that the national Democratic party had established in *La Follette*, justifying rejection of delegates elected in Wisconsin's open primary, was now invoked in behalf of the Connecticut Republican party's challenge to a state law preventing the party from opening its primary. The result must seem pro-party from the standpoint of Connecticut Republicans, but it might not be so for Connecticut Democrats who could be forced politically to drop their preferred closed primary in order to compete for the unaffiliated voters the Republicans had chosen to welcome.

The federal district court's decision in the Connecticut case, affirmed by a U.S. Court of Appeals (see n. 90), is, as I write, subject to possible Supreme Court review, but its potential import is so great that it requires a closer look. Like the Court of Appeals, the district judge was well aware of the case's novel implications when he said that it was the first "to present the situation in which a political party challenges a closed primary law on First Amendment grounds."[104] He distinguished it from *Nader v. Schaffer* in which the same Connecticut statute had been challenged but by individual unaffiliated voters. After referring to the earlier ruling "that Connecticut was justified in preventing these unwanted intruders from disrupting party primaries," the district judge observed that "the Connecticut Republican Party is no longer a willing beneficiary of the protections afforded by the state's closed primary law. The party now seeks to open its candidate selection process to unaffiliated voters. Accordingly, the concern with barring unwelcome 'outsiders' that motivated the result in *Nader* is not present here."[105] And still more pointedly: "if the Connecticut Republican Party opts to invite 'outsiders' to vote in its primaries, these 'outsiders,' by definition, are not intruders."[106] Consequently the "state interests"—prevention of raiding, avoidance of voter confusion, preservation of the two-party system—used to justify closed primaries are not so "compelling" as to be applied against a party's own preference. The court clearly held "that a party's decision to permit unaffiliated voters to participate in its primaries is constitutionally protected."[107] Unlike unaffiliated voters who had unsuccessfully challenged closed primaries but who could have voted in them if willing to comply with the statutory requirement that they declare a party affiliation, the Republican party could do nothing under the law, the judge declared, to include unaffiliated voters in its primary. No doubt that distinction is relevant, but alone it may not be weighty enough to explain the greater judicial deference to associational claims than to voter claims. Whatever the explanation, the deference drawn from U.S. Supreme Court opinions, chiefly in *Cousins* and *La Follette*, would afford parties new opportunities to challenge state regulations. Constitutionally, the newly developed doctrine would allow parties to try to *close* primaries in states with open-primary laws if they ever found it politically expedient to do so.

Associational rights have already been successfully invoked against other state provisions relating to parties. Illustrative is a Florida case first decided by a federal district court in 1978 and affirmed by a federal appeals court in 1981. The court invalidated a Florida statute prohibiting a state executive committee or a county executive committee of any political party from endorsing or opposing any candidate of its party seeking nomination in any primary election. The statute had actually been enacted in 1978 to prevent a particular county executive committee from endorsing candidates at its "grass roots" convention in that year.[108] No doubt the imposition on party freedom was egregious, but it was not so different in kind from longer-standing laws that elsewhere restricted the campaign activity of party committees. Restrictions have tended to accompany the legal recognition of party committees as state agencies responsible for electoral functions.

California statutes provide the best-known and perhaps most extreme example. They have forbidden the state-established party conventions and committees from endorsing, supporting, or opposing any candidate in the party's direct primary elections (or in certain nonpartisan elections). Recently, instead of working outside these statutorily restricted parties through voluntary or extralegal party organizations, California leaders and activists have sought to revitalize the official party committees.[109] To that end, both Democratic and Republican committees, joined by the heavily academic Committee for Party Renewal, brought suit in U.S. district court against the enforcement of the statutory restrictions on the relevant party campaign activity as well as against restrictions pertaining to the method of selecting committee members and the terms of committee chairpersons. The result, at least in the district court in 1984, was a major victory for the party cause. The U.S. district judge found that California was far from showing any compelling interest in prohibiting preprimary endorsements, and that in the absence of such showing the prohibition was an unconstitutionally imposed burden on freedom of political association.[110] So too, the judge held, was the statutory dictation of the manner of selecting state central committee members and the fixing of the chairperson's term of office. While subject to appeal at this writing, the district court decision appears consistent enough with the Florida ruling as well as with broad Supreme Court doctrine probably to be upheld, at least with respect to the matter of preprimary endorsements. States, it seems likely, will now be more firmly limited than earlier when they try to prevent their statutorily established parties from influencing nominations. The fact that those party organizations simultaneously perform official electoral functions does not mean that their private associational activities can be banned.

The recent trend toward greater freedom of parties from state regulatory control appears in a different and more surprising form in a Massachusetts case that also arose in the early 1980s. Here the issue goes beyond the old one, in the Florida and California challenges, of how far a state could restrict the campaign roles of its officially established parties. And the case, *Langone v. Commonwealth*,[111] may well have significance beyond Massachusetts even though resolved by that state's own Supreme Judicial Court. At issue was a Massachusetts law stipulating that candidates seeking party nomination for statewide office could qualify for the state's primary ballot by being enrolled members of the relevant party and by filing nomination papers containing at least 10,000 certified voter signatures. The requirements themselves were neither so unusual nor so onerous as to be challenged. Rather, they fell short of what the charter of the state's Democratic party specified for a candidate's participation in a statewide Democratic primary: at least 15 percent of the vote on any ballot at the party's convention. That charter provision resembled statutory specifications in certain other states, and the Massachusetts authors of the Democratic charter had earlier tried and failed to obtain legislative adoption of the provision along with the charter itself.[112] Hence in 1982 and 1983, when *Langone* was being decided, the 15 percent rule was merely that of a private political association. Yet the secretary of the Commonwealth, acting in accord with an advisory judicial opinion, applied it to deny ballot access to persons who had met the statutory requirements for candidacy in the Democratic primary. Subsequently, in 1983, the Supreme Judicial Court upheld the secretary's denial. It did so consistently with its advice in 1982 to the governor on the unconstitutionality of a bill that explicitly excluded party charter requirements for primary candidacy.[113] In its 1983 opinion, the Supreme Judicial Court made it clear that the existing statute's requirements would also be unconstitutional if they were interpreted in a way that would preclude additional requirements imposed by party rule. Accordingly the court, like the secretary, interpreted the statute so as to allow the imposition of the party's own requirement. Indeed, the statute had to allow a party to impose its requirement, or, in the court's opinion, it would violate the freedom of association of party members. That freedom, it was argued, had now been firmly established by U.S. Supreme Court opinions in a line of cases among which the *La Follette* decision of 1981, against the application of Wisconsin's open-primary law, was most extensively cited.[114]

Subsequently, in an appeal to the U.S. Supreme Court, the application of *La Follette* to the Massachusetts primary was challenged on the ground that an absolute right of parties to set minimum ballot access qualifications threatened the state's capacity to ensure open and fair selection of primary candidates. The Supreme Court, without opinion, dismissed the appeal for want of jurisdiction, although there was a fairly long written dissent in behalf of three justices who believed that a substantial federal question was present.[115] Thus it is uncertain whether the Massachusetts court's constitutional reasoning in *Langone* will eventually be persuasive. Its thrust is surely to reverse almost a century of regulatory practice. If a party, acting as a private political association, has the constitutional right to determine the eligibility of candidates in a state-run primary, would it not also have the right to determine the eligibility of voters? And would it not then be able, contrary to the Washington state decision in *Heavey*, to override a statute prescribing an open primary — as Connecticut Republicans sought to override their state's prescribing a closed primary? Or, to turn the question around, would states still be constitutionally empowered to operate party nominating contests as public rather than private associational affairs? Even to raise such a question is a dramatic challenge to the established American political order. Ironically, the challenge is suggested by the very state court that had in 1902, under Holmes, issued a famous statement upholding the legitimacy of the state's interest in the nominating process.

VI
Deregulation?

Suggestive as are *Langone* and several other recently successful constitutional challenges to state authority, they are not yet landmarks on a fully deregulatory path. No doubt the far-reaching judicial proclamation of the rights of the Republican party of Connecticut could, if sustained, provide the constitutional basis for challenging not merely a particular kind of primary but any primary when a party preferred caucus-convention nominations. But such a challenge would be at odds with deeply institutionalized American political patterns. Almost everywhere in the United States, the direct primary is the democratically legitimate way to nominate party candidates. And the state's role in conducting the primary is a principal element of that legitimacy. It will remain so even though a state may now be forced to alter its rules to suit a party's preference as to who should participate in its primary. Moreover, when the alteration means opening a closed primary, as Connecticut Republicans have sought to do, the result is not what most pro-party advocates of deregulation have had in mind. They have wanted to strengthen parties by restoring some of their nineteenth-century status as private associations rather than to make them more public and open to unaffiliated voters. Now they may find that, as in Connecticut itself, the newly established rights of a political party will be invoked to broaden participation in candidate selection. Given increasing numbers of independent voters unwilling to declare party affiliation, opening a primary seems a more popular cause for a party than an effort to close a primary or return to caucus-convention procedures.

Looking back on the several kinds of recent constitutional challenges, one might well be impressed by their failure *so far* to do more than modify the twentieth-century status of parties under state law. Parties are still treated as public utilities. Thus some of their activities are legally controlled and others are not. The balance has shifted only moderately in favor of the latter. Something similar can be said for the more or less legally privileged positions of major parties. Republican and Democratic parties retain their ready ballot access, but the accruing advantages are lessened by a judicially enforced liberalization of access for minor parties and independent candidates. The development is significant but not revolutionary. Moreover, it is offset somewhat by new privileges accorded major parties in public funding legislation enacted in the 1970s by several states as well as by the U.S. Congress. When challenged, as was the national government's funding of major-party conventions and major-party presidential candidacies, the legislation was upheld by the U.S. Supreme Court in an important decision that I shall discuss in later chapters devoted to campaign finance.[116] Conceivably, the national public funding of parties, as well as of candidates, might be used to justify a national regulation of parties that has not existed during the era of state regulatory control. National regulation, however, would be not only novel, but counter to the freedom of the national parties that the Supreme Court has already so amply recognized in *Cousins* and *La Follette*.

At any rate, public funding is hardly crucial as a cause for governmental regulation. In European nations, public funding has been adopted on a large scale and for parties rather than for candidates, and it has not led to anything like the pattern of governmental control established by American states long before public funding. That pattern, as I argued early in the chapter, developed only in the United States and evidently in response to various special circumstances. One of these circumstances was the adoption of the government-provided Australian ballot, but European nations, when they adopted the same kind of ballot, did not thereby convert their parties to public utilities in the American style. Plainly the Australian ballot, like public funding, did not itself lead to regulatory control, even though it provided a legal argument for it. The other circumstances that I rely upon to explain the twentieth-century status of American parties have been more distinctively American.[117] Surely this is true of the party machines that Americans long reacted against, and it also seems to hold for the progressive principles of voter participation in affairs that elsewhere belonged to party members who paid dues or were otherwise actually involved in an organization. These are the very principles, especially since they have been institutionalized for most of a century, that sustain the treatment of American parties as public utilities rather than merely private associations. Americans now expect major parties to be so regulated that their affairs, particularly their nominations, can be settled by masses of voters.

Chapter Seven

National Organization

National organization of major American parties was long embryonic and only lately substantial. It was limited despite the national nature of the presidential following in the electorate and despite the national character of our long-established parties in Congress. Outside the national government itself, state and local party organizations joined only in quadrennial presidential nominating conventions and in Republican or Democratic national committees. The very word *committee* suggests limited national structure. Each national committee's members represented essentially independent state party organizations loosely united by their common label and by a common interest in presidential elections. Accordingly the committees, far from being national, were not even federal. As Key explained in 1964, "Federalism in our formal governmental machinery includes a national element independent of the states, but in our party organization the independent national element is missing. Party structure is more nearly confederative than federal in nature."[1]

Key's perception was widely shared by observers of American politics. It could be qualified by recognizing that a president, through domination of a national party committee, periodically introduced a strongly national element. And it could also be qualified by an appreciation of the large role that each national committee headquarters played for a few months every four years in presidential campaigns. But no one equated the Republican or Democratic national committees with the national organizations of parties in most other democratic nations. Unlike British parties, for example, neither Republicans nor Democrats had a national organization in whose branches individuals became party members. American party structure more nearly resembled that in other federal governmental systems, like Australia's and Canada's, where state or provincial parties are of considerable importance. But Australian and Canadian parties have nevertheless appeared organizationally more national than those of the United States, perhaps because their most salient membership branches correspond to national parliamentary constituencies.[2] More tellingly national, relative to the United States, have been the long-standing Australian and Canadian party leadership-selection practices. Each major Australian party chooses its leader—in effect, its prime ministerial nominee—by vote of its elected members of the national parliament. And each major Canadian party, departing more than 60 years ago from the British and Australian practice, chooses its leader in a national convention dominated by representatives of constituency parties who vote as individuals.[3] In contrast, the still-established U.S. method of balloting by state delegations was well adapted to the dominant role of state and local party organizations. The American national party convention, like the national party committee, was in fact as in structure truly confederative.

The confederative character of American parties contributes to the view that our parties are generally less centralized than parties elsewhere. That view was strikingly confirmed in a systematic comparative study of Western democratic nations in 1957–62. "American parties," Janda found, "are clearly less centralized than the European norm, and they are certainly among the most decentralized parties in the world." The finding is impressive partly because the study did not in all other respects confirm conventional scholarly wisdom. American parties, it turned out, do have about as much formal structure as parties elsewhere. The distinctive element is the decentralization of power in that structure. Hence, Janda concluded by suggesting that the way to strengthen the role of American parties is "through an increase in the centralization of power at the national level. . . ."[4]

Janda's suggestion is broadly in line with one of the two main traditions of the parties scholarship that I reviewed in chapter 2: our conventional parties have been too weak, especially as national entities. In that tradition the often strong state and local organizations were treated as unfortunate obstacles in the way of a truly national party program. But even in the other scholarly tradition, where strong state and local organizations were accepted as useful elements in the confederative arrangement, there was agreement with the critics on the facts of decentralization and even on their significance for the representation of state and local interests as against any overriding national program.[5] Now also the two schools of thought might well agree that state and local party organizations have ceased to be strong enough to represent those interests. In that perspective, defenders of the old order often look to other means for preserving a diversity of interests. And the critics of the confederative party can now see a strengthened national party as needed not so much to overcome the influence of state and local organizations as to fill a gap created by their atrophy.

Given the confederative nature of our conventional American parties, the recent effort to strengthen national party authority could be said to federalize rather than nationalize the party structure.[6] That is to say, somewhat more powerful national party organizations, unlikely to supersede or take over state parties, would only establish a new and differently balanced relationship with those units. Confederation would thus give way to federalism, or federation, in party affairs as it did long ago in American government. Something like this, we shall see, has now occurred. Yet it is part of a nationalizing process that may yet go further. Therefore, with reservations, I use the term nationalizing to describe recent organizational developments. Before taking up those developments, some Democratic and some Republican, and then the legal status of national parties, I want to say a little more about the historical pattern and its slow and less striking changes earlier in this century.

I

The Enduring Historical Pattern

Given the amply demonstrated early development of national *electoral* followings for presidential candidates, it is not immediately understandable why the party organizations devoted to the nomination and election of those candidates should have persisted in their predominantly confederative form. A long period elapsed from the early 1830s, when national party conventions began, until the early 1970s, when one may discern the start of a possibly radical transformation. For over a century and a half the pattern changed little, and never so strikingly as to alter the basically confederative party organizations. Even before the convention era their character was apparent. The congressional caucus that nominated presidential candidates between 1800 and 1824 was itself a "capital faction"—Jeffersonian Republican against Federalist—and thus in a sense more national than the later convention. But like its convention successor, it sought to mobilize an electoral following through state and local structures.[7] Then, as later, presidential electors had to be won state by state, even though issues and alignments were national in large degree. Perhaps the electoral college, along with state government, thus helps to explain why state parties were not merely branches of a national organization, even though they were often first established in response to presidential politics and almost always adopted a national party label.

At any rate, the national convention that replaced the congressional caucus produced a more decentralized presidential nominating process. Of course, it was not more decentralized than the nominating practices that prevailed in the transitional years of the late 1820s, between the collapse of the caucus method and the institutionalization of the convention. Then, presidential nominations were left to state legislatures and their party caucuses, and no single national party nominee emerged. The national convention was the means for providing such a nominee — the choice, in effect, of an assembly of state and local parties. Hence, unlike the congressional caucus's choice, the convention's could claim to be compatible not only with the separation-of-powers doctrine but also with a grass-roots kind of participation broader than that provided by members of Congress meeting in the national capital. The decentralization thus established was at first an evident virtue in an increasingly democratic age.

Like so much else in American political history, the national convention bears the mark of its early origins. First used by the minor Anti-Masonic party in 1830, the convention was adopted by the National Republicans (later Whigs) in 1831 and by the Democratic Republicans (later Democrats) in 1832.[8] At a time when governmental power itself was decentralized in a large and diverse nation of states, it was natural enough to have only the minimum of national party rules. Accordingly, while the convention itself had to determine a state party's allotment of delegates, it could and did leave the method of delegate selection, as it did many other matters, to each state party. Once arranged in this way, the pattern remained until very recent decades. For the Democratic party, this meant a continuous history of conventions from 1832. And for the Republican party, succeeding the Whigs as the second major party, it covered the years from its first presidential nominating convention of 1856.[9] Significantly, the Republican party, despite its early identification with a national cause against a states' rights party, did not deviate greatly from the older Democratic and Whig structures. Many Republicans were not only former Whigs or Democrats, and therefore experienced in working through established forms, but also already in Republican state organizations and even in state or congressional offices as Republicans, before their first national convention was called to nominate a presidential candidate.[10] It is hardly surprising, then, that the Republicans should also have established a confederative party in 1856.

In one conspicuous organizational respect, the Republican party convention did for a long time differ from the Democratic convention. Republicans nominated presidential and vice-presidential candidates by simple majority vote of all delegates, but Democrats, from the 1830s to 1936, required a two-thirds majority for nomination. The two-thirds rule looks like a hyperconfederative feature because it allowed a minority, concentrated among states' rights southerners, to block a majority nomination. Moreover, the two-thirds rule was accompanied by another distinctive Democratic practice, the unit rule, that also appeared to have a states' rights flavor. The Democratic unit rule, abolished only in 1968, permitted a state party to instruct its national convention delegation to cast its entire vote in accord with the wishes of a majority of the delegation. Whatever the intention, the unit rule, along with the two-thirds rule, tended to magnify the importance of state delegations.[11] But even without these old and now discarded rules, state delegations have remained salient at the Democratic convention as well as at the Republican. Individual delegates, though committed to various presidential candidates, cast their ballots within a state delegation, whose chairperson reports the numbers in response to the tedious and time-consuming roll of the states. Radio listeners and television viewers have been amused, though often eventually bored, by this quaint custom derived from another era.

National party committees, like party conventions, were established before the Civil War. The Democratic committee dates from 1848 and the Republican from 1854.[12] In each case, the purpose was to have a body to issue the call for the convention and to act in limited areas between quadrennial nominations and elections. Unlike the convention, whose delegates were allocated in accord with a state's electoral vote and thus largely by population, the committee's membership was rigorously confederative. Every state, regardless of population or voting record, was entitled to the same number of committee members. Only in 1952 did the Republicans modify the formula, for a period of several years, to reward a state party for its electoral success by giving an extra committee position to its chairperson.[13] And the Democrats did not change to take either population or voting into account until they did so much more drastically in the 1970s. Hence it is fair to say that for well over a century each national committee was grossly unrepresentative; it was like the U.S. Senate without the U.S. House of Representatives and the president. Being unrepresentative meant that each national committee lacked a legitimate and politically realistic claim to policymaking authority. A body in which, for example, North Dakota Democrats had as many votes as New York Democrats was not likely to exercise much power, nor did anyone expect it to do so. The national committee did not even, in effect, choose its own chairman during the obviously important periods when a presidential candidate or a president was available to impose his choice.

It is remarkable that both parties resisted organizational centralization at the national level for so long. It seems especially remarkable in the Republican case because of the great though temporary national campaign effort under Mark Hanna in 1896. Yet, as an historian of the late nineteenth-century Republican party has written, ". . . no organizational mechanism held together national parties except for the common need to come together every four years to choose and then to electioneer for a presidential candidate."[14] The electioneering was surely national, especially in national committee fund raising under Hanna and less spectacularly at least as early as 1876. But the committee's fund raising, like its campaigning, was quadrennial and thus limited in its continuity as in its purpose. Hanna's committee chairmanship, though certainly significant in presidential elections near the turn of the century, did not yet lead to the establishment of a substantial year-round national organization in Washington or elsewhere. Financial contributors were distinguished more by the size of their donations than by their numbers. Neither they nor any other individuals were members of a national party organization. Campaign workers, while then often highly organized patronage seekers, were in state and local parties that responded, as their interests dictated, to presidential nominees. State and local parties were by no means ineffective in national campaigns, but they were surely autonomous units within a confederation rather than branches of a national party. Fittingly, as substantial, established parties, the state organizations were, as we have seen, legally institutionalized early in the twentieth century in a way that national parties have never been. Insofar as national conventions and national committees were subject at all to governmental regulation, it was through state laws determining the nature of the activity of the state party components of each confederative structure. For example, state legislative action, not merely state party action, often specified the means — presidential primary or caucus-convention — that could be used in choosing national convention delegates. Insofar as state law thus reached the national party, it did so by treating that party as an agency of its several state components rather than as an independent entity. Such treatment was in accord with the political reality of the confederative arrangement.

Nevertheless, national party organizations did become modestly more substantial even before the developments of the last few decades. They were not entirely immune to the nationalizing political forces so familiar in other respects in the middle years of the twentieth century. Although the tenacious resistance of our parties to those forces is more impressive than any pre-1968 organizational changes, the changes themselves should be noted. They take the form of an increasingly substantial national party presence, particularly after 1932 when the national government became newly important in domestic policymaking. That development, in headquarters staff, was not precluded by the continued confederative character of the national committee, nor by its continued powerlessness as a collective body in relation to state parties as well as to presidential leadership.

Cotter and Hennessy, writing authoritatively about national parties in the early 1960s, observed tendencies for headquarters activities to increase but at the same time stressed the weakness and even the feudal nature of the committee structure. The national committees might well be regarded as "nonthings"[15] but not the chairmen and their staffs. Their financing was sometimes generous; the Republicans had a national finance committee that in 1960 raised over $8 million (for the RNC and the senatorial and congressional campaign committees). They had begun to use a state financial quota system in the late 1930s, and the Democrats started the same system in 1953. National dinners were established fund-raising devices, and the Republicans began to use direct-mail solicitation in the 1960s.[16] Such national party efforts between as well as during campaigns, along with other signs of headquarters activity under organizational-minded chairmen, persuaded Cotter and Hennessy to project a greater development than their emphasis on committee powerlessness would itself have then suggested. "The trend," they wrote, "clearly is toward greater national party organization and activity. Reflecting general sociopolitical forces in America and to some degree characterized by a conscious drive toward greater party centralization and responsibility, the national committees seem fated to play an increasingly important role in American politics."[17]

More strikingly active nationally than party committees, however, were many nonparty political groups that by midcentury also undertook fund raising and campaign expenditures as well as congressional lobbying. In addition to long-established business associations and labor unions, certain completely and explicitly political associations collected money nationally and distributed it to congressional candidates who shared their policy positions. These nonparty groups, lately so much more numerous and prominent under the name of political action committees (PACs), were already beginning to perform political functions that elsewhere belonged to national parties. One of them, the National Committee for an Effective Congress, was the subject of full-length study of its activities from 1948 to the mid-1960s.[18] It was plain from this study that nationalizing forces were affecting American politics whether or not parties responded with more highly national efforts of their own.

A simple way to measure the limited response of national parties is to look at headquarters staffing, itself a strictly twentieth-century phenomenon. Insofar as it meant year-round operations and regular rather than ad hoc campaign employment, such staffing was a Republican innovation in 1918 under Chairman Will Hays, but it was not yet substantial. The Democrats began their continuously operating national headquarters only after their defeat in 1928. The Republicans went a step farther in 1936 when they made John D. M. Hamilton the first full-time salaried national chairman—subsequently the norm in each party.[19] Hamilton's four-year regime involved a major modernization through the use of paid professional employees; the change was based to some extent on an admiration for the national headquarters of the British Conservative party.[20] Despite these interwar beginnings, which indicate a general twentieth-century trend toward a more effective national party headquarters, regular staff members became numerous only after World War II. By the late 1950s, each national party maintained staffs of 75 to 100 in nonpresidential years (and over 200 in presidential years). The numbers rose in the 1960s particularly for the Republicans, who began even then to employ well over 100 in nonpresidential years.[21]

It is useful to recognize that these expansions of national party headquarters preceded not only any major changes in committee composition or power but also the major changes in presidential nominating rules and procedures that affected Republicans along with Democrats after 1968. To a large extent, then, the increase in staff numbers and activities occurred independently of the recent nationalization of the nominating process. Certainly this holds for the Republicans. For them as for the Democrats, however, the headquarters development of the 1950s and 1960s may well be connected to a more general nationalization of American presidential politics. Television even more than radio had already made presidential campaigns more fully national than they had been. Other factors also served to make presidential elections less sectional in character; Republican candidates had a reasonable chance to win southern electoral votes, which apart from 1928 had been impossible since Reconstruction, and Democratic candidates were competitive in certain northern states where they had seldom been serious contenders before.[22]

Perhaps the old committees and conventions had become anomalies even before the 1970s. Especially might this have been the case with respect to the federative decision making of national conventions. David Truman suggested as much as early as 1962 when he contrasted the decentralized character of nonincumbent presidential nominations with an increasingly centralized electioneering function; local considerations, he said, played a large part in dele-

gate selection and in convention negotiations.[23] The process that Truman had
in mind was still dominated by the old baronial coalition that did not give
way until the post-1968 plebiscitary transformation of presidential nominations. No doubt the old process was already shaky and subject to considerable
popular influence by the 1960s, but its passing could not yet be observed. The
nominating convention remained a confederative decision-making body.

II

Recent Developments

What happened to national party organizations in the 1970s and early 1980s
is not entirely separable from the post-1968 transformation of the presidential
nominating process. As we shall see, a newly asserted national party authority
had something to do with the transformation, even though its accomplishment may owe more to a broad public preference for presidential primaries.
Significantly too, the new presidential nominating system is in itself national
as well as popular or plebiscitary. Therefore, despite having already written
about it in chapter 4, I would like briefly to recall how, under the new system, presidential candidates seek delegates through large organizations of their
own and by direct personal appeal to masses of voters. While delegates must
still be won state by state, candidates are able to bypass state and local party
organizations and their leaders. Presidential nominations are no longer made
in a party convention of state and local leaders, nor are they made by representatives of a regularized national party membership in anything like a European
sense. Rather, the nominations are based on an electoral mobilization well
beyond the ranks of an organized party. Arguably, that candidate-centered following can be called a presidential party.[24] In any event, it is national as the
old confederative nominating authority was not.

At the same time that the presidential nominating system has become more
national, the long-established national party organizations have been strengthened not as nominating authorities but in other roles where they had traditionally been weak. Their conventions may now merely register a more or
less popular nominating verdict, but the organizations have become more substantial in two other ways. The first is structural, and it has been an almost
entirely Democratic party development. The second involves campaign activity, and it is much more heavily but not entirely Republican. I shall discuss
each in turn.

1. Democratic Structure

The most striking structural change is the assertion of national Democratic party authority over the selection of convention delegates. Although Democrats have modified their organizational arrangements in other important ways as well, the new delegate-selection rules rightly command prime attention because of their political impact. They also represent a major departure from a cardinal principle of confederative party practice—that state parties, first as private associations and in this century as state-regulated agencies, were largely free from national direction in choosing their delegates. The national party always had the authority, through its convention and its credentials committee, to decide whether to seat a state's delegates, and that authority was exercised to settle disputes when rival factions claimed seats and accused each other of fraud or chicanery. But the authority was not exercised to standardize or otherwise prescribe methods of delegate selection. To do so in this century, it must be understood, would assert national party supremacy not only over state parties but also over state laws under which state parties operated in delegate selection as in many other matters.

In light of the historical and legal traditions of American parties generally, the Democrats' newly asserted national authority after 1968 was less predictable than the continued deference of Republicans to state parties and state laws with respect to delegate selection. The Democratic party, with its states' rights background, had been the more conspicuously confederative of the two major parties in its toleration of the unit rule (until 1968) and in its use of the two-thirds rule until 1936. More relevant for the present discussion, the Democratic party, in the decade before 1968, had intruded on states' rights by adopting two new rules for seating convention delegates. In 1956, reacting against southern state parties that had in 1948 given the Democratic label to the Dixiecrat presidential ticket rather than to the national convention's nominees, the convention imposed as a condition for seating a state's delegates that the state party ensure that the party's national nominees appear on the state ballot as the regular Democratic nominees. And the 1964 convention adopted a rule requiring a state party to guarantee the absence of racial discrimination preventing full participation in its affairs. As a result of the latter, the 1968 convention denied seats to Mississippi's delegation and half of Georgia's.[25] In retrospect these steps, in particular the 1964 rule, appear to begin the Democratic nationalizing process, but they were small steps to meet presumably special circumstances. Precedents they may be, but they were hardly sufficient to prepare anyone for the sharp departure, after 1968, from the traditional hegemony of state parties.

The post-1968 national authority in delegate selection was a product of a reform movement whose main objective was to open the presidential nominating process to new participants who believed that their presidential candidates had been handicapped by the dominance of party regulars in the 1968 nominating contest. Representing the "new participants"—often peace activists, feminists, university students, leftist liberals, and assorted middle-class intellectuals—the reformers sought and in fact secured new rules allowing them to wrest control of the next national convention from party regulars. For the reformers, greater national party authority, though not an end in itself, was a welcome means to achieve ascendancy along with a more open and presumed fairer nominating process.

Not only were the new delegate-selection rules to be imposed and enforced by the national party, but they were also developed by an essentially national commission and staff only weakly linked to the old confederative party. The commission was formally called the Commission on Party Structure and Delegate Selection and informally known as the McGovern-Fraser Commission; its creation was authorized by the 1968 convention as a concession to their new-politics opponents by the otherwise victorious regulars, who were then nominating Hubert Humphrey. Byron Shafer has fully described how this happened and how it led to a major transformation in the nature of presidential nominations. From his detailed account, it is plain that the commission, appointed by national chairman Fred Harris in 1969, was dominated by reformers rather than regulars, and that its staff, which became the effective policymaker, was completely dominated by reformers.[26] The Democratic National Committee did approve the commission's product before it went into full effect, but with surprising inattentiveness and possibly with an unawareness of the consequences.[27] Thus a Washington-based staff acting in behalf of a nationally oriented political movement was triumphant.

The new delegate-selection rules were so demanding and detailed that their enforcement was bound to increase the authority of a centralized agency. Official guidelines were established for the timing and openness of delegate-selection procedures, for the eligibility of voters who would help select delegates, for the intrastate distribution of delegates in proportion to candidate preferences of primary voters or caucus-convention participants (eventually prohibiting statewide winner-take-all primaries), for the representation of women, minorities, and youth in state delegations, and for various other procedures previously determined by state party regulations or state laws.[28] In the words of William Crotty, a proponent of Democratic party reforms, "The McGovern-Fraser guidelines constituted a totally new departure, an active, persistent national party agency *demanding* change and, most significantly, getting it."[29] There may be dispute about the value and even the nature of the change, but none concerning the reality of the new centralized authority. It can readily be appreciated by observing the submission, in advance, of elaborate state party delegate-selection plans for approval by the national party, or by recollecting the rejection in 1972 of delegates not selected in accord with the guidelines.[30]

Ultimately, it is true, the centralized power rests on the national committee and national convention, which established the reform commission and adopted its guidelines, and these national agencies might still be regarded as confederations of state parties. So they undoubtedly were before 1972 when they accepted the guidelines. Once they did that, however, they—or the state parties represented on the national committee and at the national convention—effectively established a new kind of power not entirely compatible with the old structure. This suggests an abdication that we would not expect of any power holders. Possibly some state parties were already too weak to resist any aspect of the post-1968 reform wave. Others might have thought themselves beneficiaries if not actually part of the reform. Still others, as Crotty believes, may not have realized until too late that the reforms were going to be enforced as well as adopted.[31]

However the change was accomplished, it unquestionably shifted the distribution of power within the Democratic party. On this point, the party's reform enthusiast, Crotty, and the party's reform critic, Austin Ranney, fully agree. "The historic relationship between the national party and its local and state units was altered," Crotty has written, "and before reform had run its course, dramatically reversed."[32] Furthermore, he concludes that the new power of the national party, relative to state parties, "would have to rank as the most significant and far-reaching outcome of the entire reform era."[33] Ranney, himself a McGovern-Fraser Commission member who came to doubt the usefulness of many of the results of the commission's labors, is just as impressed with the nationalization as Crotty. The new rules, in his view, "constitute the first increase in the power of a party's *national* organs since the heyday of presidential nominations by congressional caucuses from 1800 to 1824."[34] Hence by the end of the 1970s, with party enforcement of new rules upheld by the courts, Ranney thought that the power of the national party organs over the presidential nominating process was "at its highest peak by far since the early 1820s."[35] Insofar as he faulted the new rules, it was not because they were national but because their destruction of the power of the old state and local party leaders meant that no effective party organization could now control or decisively influence the presidential nominating process. Obviously, nothing like the old congressional caucus or any other recognized national party leadership was put in charge. Candidate-centered organizations, winning nominations by means of victories in primaries and open caucuses, were not national parties in the view of critics of the new order.[36]

In that perspective, the greater Democratic national power over delegate selection may seem to add little by way of positive organizational consequences. The increased headquarters staff needed to police the guidelines does not itself make for party effectiveness in any electoral sense, and it requires funds that might otherwise be available for campaign purposes. Checking on state parties is not as useful as helping them win elections. On the other hand, it can certainly be argued that, once established, the national authority over delegate selection can be used in ways that many critics of the new nominating system would recognize as party strengthening. For example, successive Democratic commissions in the 1970s succeeded, in ways that I shall describe, in enforcing a rule against the use in delegate selection of open primaries—those which allowed voters to participate without either registering or publicly declaring their party preference. And in principle, though against formidable political obstacles, the national party now has the authority to insist on other changes further limiting participation in the delegate-selection process—perhaps to voters willing to register or declare their Democratic commitment *in advance* of polling day rather than merely at the polls. In fact, too, the authority can be used, as it was by the Hunt Commission for the 1984 convention, to develop rules explicitly designed for counterreform purpose; the addition of unpledged ex officio delegates is the leading case in point. Admittedly, such use of national Democratic rule making for counterreform may turn out to be exceptional and even reversible in a predominantly progressive political culture. But it is at least possible.

Whatever the particular use of the party's national authority over the nominating process, that authority must still contend with effective resistance from state parties and state legislatures on many matters. The remarkable success in establishing and enforcing the new demanding delegate-selection guidelines in 1972 did not mean that Democratic party power was fully centralized. A good deal of bargaining takes place between national and state parties, and exceptions to rules have been made in response to particular state parties. A well-known example is the national party's deference to Iowa and New Hampshire when those states insisted in 1984, as they had before, on scheduling their delegate-selection events earlier than the beginning of a 13-week nominating season that was being prescribed for every other state. First, the na-

tional party specified in its rules that Iowa's caucuses could occur 15 days before the season's opening and New Hampshire's primary seven days before the
opening; then when Iowa and New Hampshire insisted on dates one week
earlier still, they were not effectively challenged.[37] Here, as in certain other
cases, the national party recognized the difficulty of forcing compliance against
a popular state custom often entrenched in state law.

National party rules have allowed exemptions for state parties that made
a good faith effort but failed to change state laws at odds with national party
guidelines. In 1976, the DNC's Compliance Review Commission granted such
exemptions to allow three states (Wisconsin most controversially) to use the
open primary then otherwise prohibited in the delegate-selection process. By
1980, when national rules had been toughened so that a good-faith effort exemption could not be granted to a violator of the ban on the use of an open
primary, exceptions were still made for three states, but only because political
pressure was effectively brought to bear while the national party's power to
enforce its open-primary ban was being tested in the courts. With the subsequent judicial victory of the national party, no exceptions to the open-primary
ban were allowed in 1984 (though they may well be in 1988).

Even the 1976–80 experience preceding the triumph for national party authority in 1984 illustrates the working of a party structure that is more federal
than purely national. This is the point of Gary Wekkin's excellent analysis
of the open-primary controversy along with other disputes between the DNC
and state parties after 1968. Most perceptively, Wekkin calls attention to the
way in which conflicting political interests influence party rule making much
as they affect policy outcomes as between national and state governments.[38]
Thus presidential candidates and their supporters foster national rules or state
exemptions in accord with calculations of what is useful for their own purposes.

Beyond the salient national delegate-selection rules, the Democratic party
has made its structure less confederative in other respects too. The changes
appear modest only in relation to the ambitions of some responsible-party reformers who, in the early 1970s, hoped to establish a national card-carrying
organization of dues paying or at least enrolled members. The party's charter,
adopted at its first midterm conference in 1974, proclaims a national party
supremacy even though the organization is built on state party representation.
In the event of conflict between the charter or national party action under
it, on the one hand, and state laws (as well as state party rules), on the other,
"state parties shall be required to take provable positive steps to bring such
laws into conformity and to carry out such other measures as may be required
by the National Convention or the Democratic National Committee."[39] The

charter provides not only for the convention, the Democratic National Committee, an executive committee, and a national chairperson, but also for a judicial council to settle disputes, and a national education and training council. It authorizes subsequent midterm conferences — mini-conventions — and these were held in 1978 and 1982. For 1986, however, the midterm convention was abandoned by the DNC at the suggestion of its chairperson, although by 1982 it was dominated by party-building leaders rather than by policymaking activists.[40]

The charter's most explicit step away from party confederation was to change the DNC's composition. Instead of state parties having equal numbers of members, they were now to be represented to some extent as they were in the national convention. Two hundred members were added to the DNC for this purpose. Thus each state party, besides its chairperson and highest ranking officer of the opposite sex, was allotted members on the basis of its state's population and Democratic presidential voting record, but in no instance fewer than two more members.[41] The formula still overrepresented small states, but not nearly so grossly as had been the case. For example, California now had 18 members and Nevada four on a DNC of 377 members (a few of whom were ex officio and several others from the District of Columbia, Puerto Rico, and five territories). Over three times as large as the DNC used to be, the new body surely looks more representative and more like a legislative authority than did the old confederative structure. But whether it is in fact much of an independent policymaker in between conventions remains doubtful. Like national committees of the past, the new DNC is overshadowed by its party's presidential candidate during campaigns and by its party's president when one is in office. Only in the absence of either of those does the DNC have much chance to exercise authority on its own. It then does so in choosing its chairperson, as it chose Charles Manatt in 1981,[42] but the chairperson, a full-time official in charge of a full-time Washington staff, subsequently exercises a de facto authority that would be impractical for a committee of 377 members that is far from being in continuous session. Still, it might be argued, the relatively representative character of the new DNC provides a firmer foundation for the authority of the chairperson and headquarters staff.

2. Republican Structure

On the Republican side, no comparable structural change has taken place. The confederative principle remains in force. The Republican National Committee has three members from each state, and neither it nor the Republican convention or any other national party agency has asserted new authority over delegate-selection rules. The Republicans already had codified national rules precluding many of the practices that the Democrats sought to ban after 1968. Non-use of the unit rule was only the best-known case in point. Nevertheless, in the early 1970s, without the turmoil that afflicted the Democratic convention of 1968, the Republican party did have two committees review its rules. The party adopted recommendations for open delegate-selection meetings and for various other practices, but nothing stronger than proposals to encourage but not require greater representation for young persons, women, and minorities. Most tellingly, the RNC in 1975 and the Republican convention in 1976 rejected a proposal, from the second of the two committees, that would have had state parties file reports on positive, or affirmative, action plans. Despite the absence from the proposal of national party enforcement power, it represented more central control over delegate-selection procedure than Republicans would accept.

Generally, as Bibby has reported, the Republican party "explicitly adopted rules that protect state delegate selection procedures."[43] Accordingly, Republicans, unlike Democrats, permit statewide winner-take-all presidential primaries and open primaries when stipulated by state law. Nor has the national Republican party sought to force states to schedule their delegate-selection events within a newly shortened nominating season. On this matter as on others, however, state Republican parties have been indirectly affected by national *Democratic* rules that cause states, often dominated by Democrats, to change their laws. For a state to schedule Republican and Democratic presidential primaries on the same day, and run them according to the same rules with respect to voter eligibility, is plainly economical and convenient. Moreover, states that responded in the 1970s to the new Democratic rules by switching from caucus-convention procedures to primaries usually applied the new statutory arrangement to both parties. The consequence, as I have emphasized, is as plebiscitary for Republican as for Democratic nominating procedure, and therefore also national in each case. But insofar as the confederative power of Republican state and local leaders in presidential nominating contests has thus been reduced, it has not occurred as a result of new national Republican party rules.

Rather than doing anything deliberate to modify the confederative character of their party structure, Republicans have seemed intent on preserving it, even while dramatically increasing their national campaign activities in ways that I shall soon describe. Readily observed in the expanded RNC headquarters in Washington is a reluctance to speak of a national Republican *party*; one is told that there is only a national *committee* representing state parties.[44] The

greater success of the RNC than of the DNC in soliciting financial contributions from numerous supporters has not meant that Republicans have tried
to build a mass party of rank-and-file activists after the style occasionally envisioned under the Democratic charter. Indeed, the Republican structure in
this respect strikes at least one scholarly observer as sharply different from the
Democratic party development. Longley sees the post-1968 Democratic national party model as based on popular participation and elite accountability,
even if not yet fully realized, while the Republican party remains "a confederation of state parties." Partly this is a matter of the continued geographical
basis of representation on the RNC and on convention-related committees,
while the Democrats have shifted to a more "popular" basis that takes into
account population and votes. But it is also, in Longley's view, a result of
the decision of Republicans "to become a contemporary derivative of the classical cadre party model." Unlike the Democratic mass-party model, the new
Republican party is "keyed to contesting elections above all else." For this purpose, it has "generally well-insulated party elites."[45]

3. Republican Campaign Activity

One need not draw any invidious inferences from Longley's comparison to
appreciate that he is indeed describing a Republican party organization of a
kind conventionally effective in winning American elections. The novelty lies
in the fact that it is a *national* agency whose campaign activity is much greater
in size and scope than anything that either national committee previously maintained. Its success in the late 1970s and in 1980 led the DNC to try to emulate
the Republican effort, but so far the RNC, along with Republican campaign
committees for House and Senate elections, represents by far the more impressive development. Fortunately, political scientists have given us good, insightful accounts of the strengthening of the RNC, and I shall draw on several
of these.

Almost always better able to raise funds than the DNC, the RNC tended
even earlier in the century to pioneer by having a full-time chairman and continuous headquarters staffing. In the 1960s, under Chairman Ray Bliss, the
development was fairly substantial. But it diminished sharply during Nixon's
presidency. As late as 1975, the RNC raised only $300,000 of its $2.3 million
budget, and it was near bankruptcy.[46] Rejuvenation was evident in 1977, when,
not so coincidentally, the Republicans were out of the White House for the
first time in eight years. They were also unusually weak in Congress and state
houses, having failed in 1976 to regain much of what was lost in the disastrous election of 1974. Party building became the order of the day, and the
new party chairman, William Brock, was a devoted and skillful builder.

Other circumstances were also propitious. The new federal campaign finance laws, first effective in 1976, provided special opportunities for parties even though the laws appear, on balance, to bolster candidate-centered politics. Parties may obtain somewhat larger contributions than can congressional candidates or even political action committees, and parties may contribute more to candidates, in one way or another, than can individuals or political action committees.[47] The legal advantages are not so great as pro-party advocates would like, but they are not insignificant when candidates are legally deprived of large individual contributions. Moreover, a party is subject to no legal limit on expenditures for its general cause (as distinct from expenditures to help particular candidates). Indirectly, too, national party committees may have been encouraged to develop in new areas by their lessened responsibility in presidential general elections. Once the occasion for virtually their only campaign activity, the presidential election had in the decade or so before 1976 come to be dominated by the presidential nominee's own candidate-centered organization. The new legislation confirmed the arrangement by appropriating public funds to the nominee, not the national committee, and by stipulating that a national committee could spend only a limited amount, from privately raised funds, to help elect its presidential nominee. The committee remained in charge of the nominating convention, but convention costs were paid by federal funds. Financially, then, the national committees were free to raise and spend money mainly for more general purposes than those focused on the presidential election. Raising large amounts of money did in one respect become harder than it had been before the new laws restricted the size of individual contributions. Now no party or candidate could legally collect a large total from only a few very rich and generous donors. Instead, the route to successful major fund raising was through the recently available computerized methods of direct-mail solicitation of small contributions.

Although parties had previously been slow to adopt the large-scale direct-mail solicitation which various other political groups and a few candidates had already used successfully, the RNC now began vigorously and regularly to solicit potential contributors. For the 1978 campaign, the RNC made over a half-million solicitations, for 1980 1.2 million, for 1982 1.7 million, and for 1984 perhaps as many as 2 million. Among these were some contributors of large amounts; for example, 865 individuals each gave $10,000 to the Republicans' Eagles Program in 1980. But the overwhelming majority, who provided most of the total, gave in small amounts. Eighty-seven percent of the contributors in 1978 gave less than $50, and the average gift from contributors in 1980 was less than $30. The numbers of contributors, not the size of most of their contributions, provide impressive total receipts: in 1983–84 the RNC reported net receipts of almost $106 million, the National Republican Senatorial Committee (NRSC) over $81 million, and the National Republican Congressional Committee (NRCC) over $58 million.[48] The NRSC and the NRCC also use direct-mail solicitation, although they, especially the NRSC, may be less dependent on it than the NRC. Their receipts, separately gathered and distributed, are important elements in the new pattern of national Republican fund raising. Increasingly, too, the NRSC and especially the NRCC work with the RNC, even though they remain agencies of their House and Senate members.

Altogether, the three Republican committees have raised enough money over successive years to support a kind and level of organizational activity never before sustained by an American party. It is fairly said that finally a party organization has made the transition to "the cash economy of the new campaign politics"—a transition that candidates themselves had made earlier in different ways.[49] Significantly, the transition is most emphatically at the national level, although more or less simultaneously, state parties have also begun to adopt direct-mail fund raising and to operate headquarters staffs on that basis. The strikingly national Republican effort is readily apparent from the fact that the RNC has been able from its directly raised funds to help finance state parties instead of depending heavily on those parties, as the RNC once did, to raise money for the national party. By effectively reversing the flow of money as well as by greatly increasing it, the RNC neatly illustrates a highly consequential aspect of the nationalization process. Nothing was more clearly confederative than a national committee's dependence on money from state parties, and nothing is more clearly federal, if not national, than the committee's ability, like that of the national government under the U.S. Constitution, regularly to raise its own funds and to use them for its purposes in the states.

Symbolically, the Republican national presence has been evident in the Eisenhower Center, occupied by the RNC since 1970 and owned by the party since the late 1970s. Located near the Capitol, the building is an imposing and convenient home for the RNC as well as the NRCC. Ownership of the national party headquarters is itself an important departure from the old custom, followed by the Democrats until 1984, of moving from one set of rented offices to another for successive elections. The Eisenhower Center lends an air of permanence to national Republican activities. Permanence is also represented by the size and professionalism of the RNC staff. Already at 220 in the late 1970s, compared with fewer than half that number a decade before, the RNC's paid staff totaled about 350 in 1982.[50] The great majority of staff members are professionals in that they have expertise in media use, polling, public relations, or computerized mailing. They are also professionals in that, apart from certain top political operatives, they have fairly long-run career commitments to their jobs. They thus resemble civil servants, although they are in fact the modern successors of the old political professionals who, with less technical expertise, manned state and local party organizations.[51]

Still another way to stress the new character of the RNC is to recognize the changed status of its chairman. Although still a politician rather than a technician and still likely to recruit top aides from political ranks, the Republican chairman has had to be, since 1976, a paid, full-time official. And at least when the party does not hold the presidency, the chairman may well develop a substantial political constituency of his own because of the scale of his organization's activities. Thus William Brock, highly successful as chairman for almost four years from 1977, was able to retain his position during the 1980 presidential campaign, although the previously established practice was for the new presidential nominee to replace the chairman with his own choice. Reagan, despite pressure from his own supporters, decided to retain Chairman Brock.[52] Only after the election, when Brock joined the Reagan Administration, was he replaced. Subsequently, Reagan further strengthened his own party leadership by securing the appointment of his friend, Senator Paul Laxalt, to a new part-time post of general chairman, partly to coordinate RNC, NRCC, and NRSC activities. At the same time, a Laxalt protégé, Frank Fahrenkopf, became the full-time RNC chairman.[53] Although these changes display the traditional presidential command of a national committee, they constitute no reversal of the increasingly significant role of the RNC. On the contrary, President Reagan was notable for the use he made of the RNC during the early 1980s. The RNC became an even larger fund raiser and organizational spender than it had been before the 1980 election.

Recently ample national Republican funds have made it possible to spend effectively in at least three broadly different ways: general national party activity; contributions in cash and in kind to party candidates; and help, financial and organizational, to state parties. The expenditures are plainly related, and it is not always possible to separate one kind from another since their purpose — to elect more Republicans — is the same. But it will help analytically to take each of the three in turn to illustrate the nature of the new national campaign effort.

The first category, which I call general party activity, is by far the largest in dollar terms, especially for the RNC. It is so partly because of the absence of federal legal limits on how much parties can spend as long as the expenditure is not in behalf of particular federal candidates or in the form of contributions to those candidates. The law also makes it easier to raise money for general party activity, because some kinds of contributions to the party for that purpose are not subject to the limits imposed on size and source of contributions for use in federal candidate campaigns.[54] In any event, the RNC raises and spends a large portion of its funds to maintain salaries, facilities, and year-round services of the headquarters staff as well as of field staff. The RNC produces a continuous flow of both polemical and informational literature, mainly distributed by mail, and it publishes a serious political magazine. More publicly visible is its institutional advertising of the Republican cause in various national media. The best known are $9 million worth of television spots that from February to November 1980 attacked Democratic policies and concluded with "Vote Republican, For a Change." But the RNC also ran other advertisements in 1980 and afterward. In 1981 there was a $2.3 million campaign, and in 1982, for the midterm election, the RNC mounted advertising at a cost of nearly $15 million.[55] Still another general RNC expenditure became important in 1980 and again in 1984: a nationally organized voter registration and get-out-the-vote campaign.

The second category, contributions to candidates, is one in which the RNC's share is much smaller than that of the NRCC and the NRSC. Moreover, the contributions of all three party committees, considered together, are considerably smaller than the amounts that candidates raise from individuals and from political action committees. Party money, however, may be more useful dollar for dollar, because it is often invested in an early stage of a congressional candidate's campaign as a kind of seed money to publicize and help a challenger raise money from other sources. Early investment may be part of the process by which the national party encourages a likely prospect to become a candidate. Contributions from the national Republican committees have markedly increased since the late 1970s.

A more substantial increase is apparent when we include what the law terms "expenditures on behalf of candidates"—amounts that one national committee and one state committee of each party can spend in general elections over and above their direct contributions to candidates, but in coordination with candidates. Although these "on behalf of" expenditures are themselves legally limited in size, they are substantial, particularly for U.S. Senate seats in large states. Republican committees together spent $14.3 million in 1981–82 and $20.1 million in 1983–84 on behalf of federal candidates, in addition to the $5.6 million in 1981–82 and $4.9 million in 1983–84 that they contributed directly to federal candidates.[56] Republicans have used a provision, described in chapter 9, permitting a national party committee not only to spend up to its own legal maximum on behalf of a Senate or House candidate but also, by acting as agent for a less prosperous state party, to provide up to that state party's legal maximum for the same candidate — thus effectively doubling the national party's contribution. In 1982, for example, Republican party committees could and did spend over $1.3 million on the California Senate race. No one will regard that amount as insignificant, although it was hardly the major share of the nearly $7 million that Pete Wilson spent to win the California Senate seat.[57]

Similarly, in 1981–82, the total that Republican party committees contributed to all federal candidates and spent on their behalf — $19.9 million — was a healthy but not overwhelming 13.7 percent of the $145 million spent by the Republican candidates.[58] Note also that a good deal of general party activity, especially the RNC's, is intended at least indirectly to help federal candidates. In that light, the $19.9 million (9.3 percent of all Republican party expenditures of $214 million in 1981–82)[59] was merely the most clearly designated assistance to Republican candidates.

Whether or not they are legally counted among contributions to federal candidates, expensive services are provided candidates and their staffs. Services include campaign-management colleges offering a week's training in campaign techniques, separate schools for campaign secretaries, facilities for producing and distributing media advertising, and extensive computerized information drawn from polls and other research sources. Certain RNC services have been extended to Republican candidates in state gubernatorial and legislative elections. The RNC has also contributed funds directly to those campaigns — over $2 million in 1978 and about half that in 1980.[60] Furthermore, the RNC sought to recruit candidates for state and local offices as it did occasionally for congressional office, and it has furnished its own staff members to help particular odd-year gubernatorial campaigns.

The third category of national Republican expenditure assists state party organizations and not merely individual candidates in state or congressional races. The two kinds of activity are complementary in that the obvious long-run purpose of strengthening state organizations is to enable them to help elect party candidates. But in assisting state organizations, the RNC may be perceived as less directly national in its intervention than when itself recruiting, training, financing, and otherwise directly servicing candidates. In this light, the RNC's recent relations with state parties represent an interesting and important development in the old confederative structure. From 1977 to 1979 the RNC even paid the salaries of state party organizational directors in an expensive attempt to encourage staff professionalization at the state level.

More regularly, the RNC has provided regional political directors and finance directors to work with state organizations, a data processing network for computer services at minimal cost to state parties, and a local elections campaign division to assist in state legislative campaigns. The regional political directors, each responsible for two to six states, have provided RNC services and access while also coordinating the work of the Republican senatorial and congressional campaign committees in their regions.[61]

Such organizational activity is newly national no matter how cautious it must be in respecting the traditional autonomy of congressional as well as state campaigns. The same can be said for the RNC's attempt to get each state party to develop a campaign plan in 1978; its inducement was the lure of national funds and staff to help state parties whose plans met the RNC's expectations. The national influence could be exercised without mandatory directives. So was it also in the program of the RNC's Local Elections Campaign Division (LECD), which Bibby understandably regards as "unprecedented in the history of American political parties."[62] In trying to gain Republican state legislative seats in 1978, the LECD had over 20 staff members and spent $1.7 million. It collected and analyzed data to help state organizations target districts and at the same time assisted candidates more directly by sponsoring political education seminars, by allocating about $1 million in cash grants, and by survey research in selected races. The RNC also played an important role in gubernatorial elections by its financial contributions to the Republican Governors Association that sought primarily to help challengers, as had the LECD in legislative contests.

Generally, in Bibby's account, the RNC activities under Chairman Brock appear to have been achieved without national-state party conflict. State party Republicans, however, did react against occasional RNC intervention in their primaries, and the reaction led the 1980 national Republican convention to adopt a party rule sharply limiting RNC intervention. Specifically, the rule forbids the RNC, without prior approval of a state's three RNC members, from contributing to any candidate except the Republican party nominee or an unopposed Republican primary candidate.[63] Thus, with respect to the sensitive area of intraparty nominations for various state and national offices, state party power is staunchly reaffirmed in truly confederative form. Nevertheless, the new rule does not so much reduce the RNC role as require that it be exercised collaboratively with state party leaders. State parties may now even more happily accommodate themselves to RNC attention. After all, state party headquarters, not merely candidates, have received financial and other help from the RNC. The two sets of recipients, not always sharply distinguishable, have both been beneficiaries of the "process of party nationalization" that Bibby found underway in the late 1970s.[64] In fact, the Republican development may be a more substantial organizational part of this process than the better-known and more coercive Democratic nationalization through delegate-selection rules. It certainly continued into the 1980s when the Republican National Committee was found to give "far more assistance," in direct financial aid as well as most categories of service, than the less affluent Democratic National Committee. Significantly, the assistance provided especially large shares of Republican state party budgets in the South where Republicans had been weakest.[65]

While not openly rejecting the confederative aspects of party structure, the Republicans have nonetheless nationalized their campaign effort by a method analogous to the federal government's grant-in-aid system. Like categorical grants allocated to states and cities that agree to carry out federal programs in accord with federal standards, national party funds and other assistance went to parties and candidates willing and able to maintain organizations or conduct campaigns serving general Republican purposes, including most definitely the improvement of the party's position in state governments that would legislate post-1980 congressional redistricting. Also like the nationalizing influence of federal government grants-in-aid, that of the RNC in 1978 and 1980 depended on superior financial resources, in this case new in scale and type for an American party. The results, like those in intergovernmental relations, may not be entirely happy for state and local party organizations. As Margaret Conway has pointed out, they seem to be helped less than individual candidates, and the national party, through its control of resources, may itself exercise a new influence over who will successfully compete for office.[66] The impact would then be decisively national, in terms of party loyalty of elected officials, no matter how confederative the RNC structure. A more direct national influence than the RNC's might be expected from the NRCC and NRSC. Their financial contributions to House and Senate candidates are much greater than the RNC's, and their early intervention in campaigns is not subject to the party rule that restrains the RNC.

4. Democratic Campaign Activity

The DNC began later than the RNC to develop a mass fund-raising capacity, and, despite gains in the early 1980s, it has so far been so much less successful that it is sometimes suggested that it will never come close to matching Republican receipts and expenditures. Perhaps considerably fewer potential Democratic donors respond to direct-mail appeals because the party's following is less middle class and also less ideologically homogeneous. Most Democratic supporters may prefer to give, if they do at all, through nonparty agencies, notably labor unions, or only to individual candidates. Before as well as after federal legislation severely restricted the size of individual contributions, the DNC even more than the RNC depended on a relatively small number of large donations to maintain its relatively modest operation. Occasionally it sought larger numbers of small donations to help liquidate debts from a previous presidential campaign. For 1976 and 1980, however, it did not raise large sums to help presidential nominees who were now financed from federal funds. At the same time, congressional Democrats, holding majorities and running as incumbents, often with the support of labor unions, had less need for party organizational help than did Republicans who more often were challengers. To some extent, the difference in party activity may be attributed to temporary political circumstances that encouraged Republican party committees to make an early and large start. But the difference remains impressive.

Even in 1983–84, when the DNC reported net receipts of $46.6 million, it was well below the $105.9 million reported by the RNC. And the Democratic Senate and House committees, despite their increased activity, reported a total of $19.3 million compared to nearly $140 million raised by their two Republican counterparts. It is true that earlier the ratio of Republican to Democratic national party committee receipts was still more uneven. In 1980 and 1982, the RNC raised about five times as much as the DNC, and the two Republican congressional committees about nine or ten times as much as the two Democratic congressional committees. Catching up has been difficult for the Democrats. The DNC's contributor list had only 25,000 names in 1980 and 200,000 in 1982 (compared to the RNC's 1.7 million). Even its planned 500,000 for 1984 left the DNC well short of the 2 million the RNC counts for the same year. DNC staffing reflects its smaller financial base: only about 80 in 1980 and 1982 compared to the RNC's 350.[67] Nevertheless, it may be more significant for the long run that national Democratic party activities have increased substantially since 1980 even though they remain so far behind the Republican pace. In 1982 these activities, under the sponsorship of the DNC as well as by Democratic Senate and House campaign committees, included media assistance for candidates, campaign training programs, and institutional advertising that was like the party-cause advertising that the Republicans had pioneered in 1980.[68] In 1984 the DNC raised money in order to conduct a voter-registration drive parallel to that of the RNC. And finally, in 1985 the Democratic party occupied a Washington building of its own, as had the Republican party since the 1970s.

As a product of a party's out-of-the-White House years, the post-1980 de-

velopment of the DNC parallels, though on a smaller scale, the RNC development of the late 1970s. In many respects, DNC chairman Charles Manatt's
role was like the earlier role of RNC chairman William Brock. And, like Brock
in 1980, Manatt remained as chairman during the presidential campaign at
the end of his four years in office, despite an evident desire of the party's presidential nominee to follow the older custom of immediately replacing him.
At least a degree of institutionalization is thereby suggested in the Democratic
as in the Republican case. The national committee, in each instance, had become a sufficiently important campaign force between presidential elections
to give its successful chairman a recognizable claim on the loyalties of many
of the party candidates and activists with whom he had worked. Like the RNC
after 1980, the DNC might follow the pattern of substantial subordination
to a president of the same party—when one is again in office—but that need
not mean, any more than it has for the RNC, a diminished level of fund-
raising and campaign activity.

III
Legal Status of National Parties

A changed legal status is closely related to the structural development of the
Democratic national party and at least coincident with the increased campaign
activity of both national organizations. Only since 1975 has a national party
been clearly recognized as a political association enjoying a legal position superior in certain respects to state parties and state laws. Previously, Democrats
and Republicans at the national level were as confederative in the eyes of the
law as they were in their organizational structure. Leaving the regulation of
parties along with elections to the states, Congress never treated parties as
national public utilities. Indeed, national parties, though long visible through
their conventions and national committees, remained almost entirely unknown
in national law during virtually all of their history. Even now they are not
subject to anything like the regulatory control that is common for state parties
under state laws. Their presidential nominating process is still free from national control in the form of a congressionally mandated primary or any other
congressionally prescribed method. And their organizational structures, in
particular the national committees, are not prescribed or generally regulated
by statute.[69]
    Lately, it is true, national parties have been recognized significantly in na-
tional law as they, along with other political groups and individual candidates

for federal office, are subject to the federal campaign finance legislation of the 1970s. The recognition is substantial in a number of ways already indicated in my discussion of the RNC's response to the legislation. More detail will be found in chapters 9 and 10. Here it is necessary only to recall that the legislation includes both limitations and benefits for parties. Like other groups and individuals engaged in campaigns for federal office, parties must file periodic reports with the Federal Election Commission. They must also conform to various contribution limits, but these advantage parties in some degree. So do certain expenditure provisions and postal rate concessions. Moreover, the major national parties are explicitly beneficiaries in that their nominating conventions and the campaigns of their presidential nominees are subsidized by federal funds. Nevertheless such recognition, it must be stressed, has not so far produced a *national* regulatory treatment of parties distinctively different from that applied to other political groups and individual candidates.

Insofar as a national party is subject to distinctive governmental regulation, it is now as before the result of state regulation of the state parties on which the national entity is built. Lately, as I shall emphasize, a national party has legally overridden state regulation in important respects, but state laws, even with the post-1968 Democratic party rules, still determine a large part of the presidential nomination process. Thereby, the national nominating convention, the party's highest authority, has consisted of delegates selected mainly by primaries or caucus-convention methods prescribed by state laws. Legally, the convention and the national committee operating under its authority have looked like artifacts of state-regulated state parties and, in a sense, of state governments. As late as 1971, the Court of Appeals for the District of Columbia Circuit, faced with questions about the constitutionality of national convention allocation formulas, said in one case that the relevant national party decisions were "in reality, the decisions of the states acting in concert,"[70] and in another, that the decision made by a political party at the national level was "tantamount to a decision of the states acting in concert. . . ."[71] The fact that the Court of Appeals in these cases nevertheless upheld the validity of the allocation formulas does not detract from the import of this prestigious court's view, at the time, of the somewhat artificial character of our national parties.[72] Yet the substance and continuity that we observed in their national headquarters by midcentury suggest a little more. Even in the eyes of the law, the national parties, through these headquarters, must surely have existed and performed certain activities — collecting money, renting space, hiring employees, and contracting for services. The parties were real though anomalous.

Their reality came to be asserted in a surprisingly forceful way by the U.S.

Supreme Court in the decade after 1971. It appeared, undefinitively, in 1972 when the Court barred last-minute judicial intervention in the Democratic party's preconvention credentials disputes. A new judicial doctrine did not emerge from the Court's refusal in this case to decide the merits of disputes that had not yet been taken from the credentials committee to the party convention and that the Court had little time to hear argued before the convention met. Leaving the initial decision to the party in these circumstances reflected a well-understood, though nonunanimous, judicial preference to avoid intervention in a matter (delegate seating) that parties, however constituted, ordinarily decided. At the same time, one might find a hint of a new departure in the Court's reference to "our national political parties" as having come into being "as voluntary associations of individuals. . . ."[73] Perhaps such language was not entirely novel in or out of judicial circles during the history of our parties. Yet to use it, as the Court would soon do in opinions upholding national Democratic rules, had novel consequences.

1. Against Illinois

The first of the two leading cases in which the Supreme Court upheld national party rules against the states was *Cousins v. Wigoda*.[74] Familiar by now as precedent-setting doctrine, this Illinois case had its origins in one of the credentials disputes that the Court had refused to decide in 1972;[75] three years later it returned in different form. Wigoda and others associated with Mayor Daley's local party organization had been elected as delegates in an Illinois primary in 1972. They had obtained an Illinois state court injunction enjoining the rival Cousins delegates from taking the seats that the Democratic national credentials committee, eventually supported by the convention, had given them when unseating the Wigoda group. In refusing to obey the injunction — that is, by serving as delegates — the Cousins group challenged the legal power of Illinois to determine the state's representation at the national party convention.

With the national Democratic party championing the Cousins challenge, the issue was now sharply drawn between state power and the rules of a national political association. The Illinois law in question stipulated the election of national party convention delegates in a primary election, which the Wigoda group had won. The relevant national party rules were those that the Democrats had adopted as part of the McGovern-Fraser reforms specifying certain procedures as well as strong affirmative-action guidelines for selecting delegates. These party rules, it appeared, had been violated by the Daley organization when it chose, at its party meetings, the slate of delegates (Wigoda and others) that it would successfully support in the state's presidential primary. Hence the Wigoda delegates, although elected in that primary, were unseated because of the practices used in their original preprimary selection. Not only were the state primary election results thus rejected by the national Democratic party; they were also effectively reversed by seating the rival Cousins group, who had not been elected by Illinois voters but who nevertheless met party guidelines to the satisfaction of the credentials committee and the convention majority.

These were the national party acts that the U.S. Supreme Court upheld when it rejected the Illinois court injunction and the contempt charges against the Cousins group for having disobeyed the injunction. In so doing, Justice Brennan, speaking for the Court, used remarkably broad language about the freedom of a national party from state regulation. "The National Democratic Party and its adherents," he said, "enjoy a constitutionally protected right of political association."[76] The word *adherents* implies something less well defined than *National Democratic Party*. They are apparently assumed to be individuals and not merely state organizations, composing a party confederation, and yet they are a narrower category than all usual Democratic party voters. Perhaps Justice Brennan was thinking of active participants who attend meetings, campaign, or contribute money, even though they, if organized at all, belong to state and local parties. Whoever they are, these adherents and the party to which they adhere had, in the eyes of the Court, a right superior to the state's asserted interest in protecting the integrity of its electoral processes and the right of its citizens to effective suffrage. The significant fact, for Justice Brennan, was that the suffrage "was exercised at the primary election to elect delegates to a National Party Convention."[77] He added: "The Convention serves the pervasive national interest in the selection of candidates for national office, and this national interest is greater than any interest of an individual State."[78]

Despite the breadth of its language, *Cousins v. Wigoda* left open certain questions. It did not involve the constitutionality of state regulation of state parties in nonpresidential primary elections or the constitutionality of any future national government regulation of national parties. Although one might infer that the right of political association could be used to question the validity of all such regulations, especially as they determine the means by which party nominations are made, it was also possible to interpret Justice Brennan's opinion so that it clearly invalidated only the kind of interference with a political association that included "an extraterritorial extension of the state's jurisdiction."[79] Even that interpretation, however, meant a great deal.

2. Against Wisconsin

Having become constitutionally protected in its refusal to seat delegates chosen under state law but against party rules, the national Democratic party began in 1976 to impose a different kind of delegate-selection standard from any involved in *Cousins*. As observed in the discussion of Democratic structure, the national party wanted to enforce its preference for allowing only those willing publicly to identify themselves as Democrats to vote in presidential primaries or caucuses. Unlike its already enforced affirmative-action and open-procedure requirements, whose intention was to expand participation, the rule against nonparty identifiers would restrict participation. It was aimed, we have seen, at the few open-primary states, particularly Wisconsin, that also held presidential primaries and accordingly allowed any eligible voter to cast a ballot in either party's presidential primary. After reluctantly tolerating exceptions in 1976 for state Democratic parties that had tried unsuccessfully to persuade state legislatures to close their primaries, the DNC insisted in 1980 that delegates selected through an open primary should not be seated at the nominating convention. Now a state Democratic party that wanted seatable delegates, but was unable to secure a change in the open primary under which it had operated, was supposed to develop its own party-run caucus-convention system for identifying Democrats. In Michigan, also a state with an open presidential primary, Democrats willingly responded by choosing their 1980 national convention delegates through caucus procedures, although Michigan Republicans continued in the same year to use the state-established open primary to select their delegates. By no means, however, were Michigan Democrats forsaking a well-established state tradition; while Michigan had long used an open primary in state elections, it had had no presidential primary of any kind in the years from 1932 through 1968.[80]

Wisconsin Democrats, and to some extent Idaho and Montana Democrats, have stronger attachments to the open presidential primary. Wisconsin's experience with it was continuous over almost three-quarters of a century. As a result, even when Wisconsin Democrats controlled both state legislative houses and the governorship in the mid-1970s and again in 1983, they would not change the state's popular and traditional open-primary law. Efforts to do so by some of their nationally oriented leaders were abortive, although they proposed to modify the law only for a presidential primary and only to require a voter to declare a party preference orally when receiving a ballot. Sufficient then and later to satisfy the DNC, that relatively modest change, well short of a primary really closed by prior party registration, was nonetheless too much for Wisconsin. Not enough Democratic legislators could be persuaded to adopt any restriction of the freedom of the state's voters to cast primary ballots without publicly declaring their party identification. Not only did many of these legislators themselves prefer the open primary; they also believed, with good reason, that it was popular among their constituents and that their Republican adversaries, already criticizing the proposed changes, would benefit from the likely reaction of voters to a Democratic-imposed closure. In 1979 and 1980, Wisconsin Democrats could not on their own have changed the open-primary law even if they had been willing to do so; the governor was a Republican while the Democrats still had legislative majorities. But after 1982, when they again held the governorship as well as both legislative houses, they still did not modify the law, and having by then lost their legal challenge, Wisconsin Democrats were forced in 1984 to use the caucus method for selecting national convention delegates.[81]

In 1980, however, Wisconsin Democrats turned to the courts in an effort to avoid the charges of boss rule in smoke-filled rooms that would inevitably accompany the use of caucuses. Appreciating the strength of Wisconsin's devotion to its open primary is crucial to understanding the court case that was eventually decided. Since its early adoption of the direct primary as a mandatory governmentally managed means for nominating candidates for various offices, Wisconsin had always used the open form. And, also in the first decade of the century, it applied the same form when it extended the primary to the election of national convention delegates. Therefore, voters in Wisconsin have had no experience with a system in which they must publicly disclose their party preferences in order to cast primary ballots. Incomprehensible as it may be for advocates of responsible party government or simply for persons accustomed to closed primaries in other states, a requirement of public disclosure of party preference, as a condition for primary voting, would for many Wisconsin citizens violate the secrecy of the ballot much as would a forced disclosure of party preference in a general election.

In other respects, too, Wisconsin could find democratic virtue in its challenged system. Certainly the state associated the open primary with its pride in and reputation for good government by way of either honest and efficient administration or progressive social policies. Wisconsin citizens had been accustomed to thinking of their state as a model for the nation ever since the beginning of the century when Governor Robert M. La Follette, Sr., made Wisconsin an "experimental laboratory" within the federal system and, among other innovations, secured the adoption of the direct primary.[82]

They could also have regarded their particular use of that primary for selecting national convention delegates as a virtuous model. Indeed, after several

changes over a half-century, Wisconsin had, before the McGovern-Fraser reforms, provided a presidential primary ballot that allowed voters to cast their
ballots directly for presidential candidates who would then be awarded delegates in accord with their popular support. Readily adapted to the national
party's new proportional representation formulas and to its provisions for
candidate-approved and candidate-committed delegates, the Wisconsin presidential primary by the 1970s surely registered popular preferences in a more
clear-cut and meaningful way than did those primaries in states where presidential candidate preferences could not be directly expressed at all or where
such preferences were expressed separately from the election of delegates who
might or might not be identified by their candidate preferences.

In particular, Wisconsin differed from Illinois, where, as was evident from
the *Cousins* case, the voters elected delegates whose names were on the ballot
(and where voters separately cast ballots for presidential candidates running
in a nonbinding poll—a beauty contest). Unlike Illinois Democrats, Wisconsin Democrats in the 1970s held their caucuses of declared party supporters
to select delegates *after* the primary. The delegate selection itself was not a
violation of national party rules. In fact, Wisconsin's Democratic caucus procedures for selecting delegates were immaculately proper and devotedly observant of affirmative-action guidelines. Rather, Wisconsin's violation lay in the
fact that the delegates so selected were allotted in accord with votes cast for
presidential candidates in an open primary. Hence in challenging Wisconsin
practices, the national Democratic party was rejecting a more broadly participatory procedure than its reforms had specified and not one that was so
tightly controlled as to be found defective, as was Daley's slate making in Illinois. More significantly, the national party was now claiming that a state's
primary law was itself in conflict with the freedom of association of national
Democrats. In *Cousins*, it was really the local party procedures that were objectionable; the Illinois primary entered the case only because it had been successfully used by the offending delegation.

The latter distinction provided a basis for arguing that *Cousins v. Wigoda*
should not lead to the same judicial declaration of national party supremacy
over Wisconsin as it had over Illinois. However promising or unpromising
this or other legal arguments might be, the state of Wisconsin in 1979 took
the initiative against the national Democratic party. The state's Democratic
attorney general, Bronson La Follette (grandson of the sponsor of the state's
primary law), petitioned the Wisconsin Supreme Court—an elected body of
seven members—for declaratory and injunctive relief against the national Democratic party's threatened exclusion of delegates chosen according to Wisconsin

law. Without undertaking the difficult step of clearly enjoining the national party, the state supreme court did unanimously hold, in January 1980, that the relevant election statute was constitutional and binding, that Wisconsin delegates to the Democratic national convention should be apportioned as required by the statute, and that they should not be disqualified as a result of such apportionment.[83] Among the state court's interesting explanations for its decision, in light of the apparently contrary *Cousins* precedent, was the view that Wisconsin, unlike Illinois, was not merely trying to protect the result of its primary. "Wisconsin," the state court said, "has a compelling state interest in maintaining the special feature of its electoral law—a primary which permits private declaration of party preference."[84] This special feature, the court thought, imposed no substantial burden on the national party's associational rights. In the absence of such a burden,[85] the constitutionality of the Wisconsin primary law was upheld. Posed in this way, it is hard to conceive of a different result, especially in a state court. How could a long-established open-primary law be held unconstitutional when its alleged offense was to encourage rather than limit voting?

The majority of the U.S. Supreme Court, however, did not pose the question in the same way when early in 1981 it reversed the Wisconsin decision and ruled, as in *Cousins*, in favor of the national party. Speaking for himself and five colleagues in *Democratic Party of the U.S. v. La Follette,*[86] Justice Stewart refused to consider, as had the Wisconsin court, whether the open feature of the state's primary law was constitutional. On that issue, he thought that the state court might well have been correct. "In any event," he went on, "there is no need to question its conclusion here. For the rules of the National Party do not challenge the authority of a State to conduct an open primary, so long as it is not binding on the National Party Convention. The issue is whether the State may compel the National Party to seat a delegation chosen in a way that violates the rules of the Party."[87] Justice Stewart's negative answer on this issue was supported by his observation that Wisconsin sought, also by law, to require that at the national convention members of its delegation vote for presidential candidates in accord with the state's open-primary results.

In other words, Wisconsin could not enforce the results of its open primary in Democratic presidential nominating contests. Its Democratic presidential primary might continue as merely a beauty contest so long as the national party persisted in rejecting delegations reflecting its election results. Hence the practical consequence for the state, and the state Democratic party, is the same as would have been produced by an opinion that had specifically ruled the open-primary law itself to be unconstitutional in its application to national Democratic nominations. The supremacy of national party rules over state law is as evident in the one instance as in the other.

Although the *La Follette* case was explicitly decided in accord with the *Cousins* precedent, Justice Stewart's opinion differed in at least one significant way from Justice Brennan's in the earlier case. Now the Court did not appear to rest its objection to the exercise of state authority even partially on the grounds of the state's attempted "extraterritorial extension" of its authority. Unlike Justice Brennan in *Cousins*, Justice Stewart based his opinion on the national party's constitutionally protected right of political association, without suggesting that the judicial maintenance of this right might be limited to a situation in which a state sought to impose its will outside its territorial jurisdiction. It is true that the First Amendment right here asserted was applied, by the Court, as one of the freedoms that the Fourteenth Amendment protected against state action. But Justice Stewart's opinion does not foreclose the possibility that the same right of political association could also be asserted against any prospective national government regulation of a national party. Nor does the opinion discourage any future claims that the long-established state government regulation of state parties might be unconstitutional. Consequently, the *La Follette* opinion looks broader than the more ambiguous *Cousins* opinion in opening up possibilities for a more general challenge of the governmental regulation of parties. Those possibilities, revolutionary in their import, have already been noticed at the end of the previous chapter. But so far, while state parties have been successful in asserting greater freedom in some respects from state regulation, they have by no means won the right to nominate candidates in the manner of private associations.

From *La Follette* as from *Cousins*, what is clear is that state regulation of national parties is not enforceable when in conflict with national party rules.[88] Hence national parties, as long as they are also unregulated by the national government, enjoy a freedom from control that state parties, traditionally the critical organizational units, do not have. To cite the prime example, a national party is now able to nominate a presidential candidate according to its own rules, while a state party's nominees for various offices are ordinarily choices of voters in state-run direct primaries. True enough, the national party does not now use its rule-making authority to preclude the influence of state-run presidential primaries on its nominations, or to keep states from adopting many other delegate-selection methods of their own choosing. But legally, the national party could put an end to such state roles by requiring, let us say, that all convention delegates be chosen in caucuses of a certain kind, or in primaries held on a given day. Of course, Congress could preempt the rule making of the national parties as well as of states by enacting legislation establishing a national direct primary to nominate presidential candidates. Possibly the Democrats had some such threat in mind when they passed a resolution at their 1976 convention urging Congress not to "legislate in any manner which is in derogation of the right of a National Party to mandate its own affairs."[89]

The process by which the national parties have been judicially strengthened deserves a little more attention. In now treating a national party as more than a confederation of state parties, Justice Stewart in *La Follette* not only cited Justice Brennan's language from *Cousins* concerning national party "adherents" but also spoke of "the members of the National Party" much as though there were individual members of a national party as of state parties. Thus, "the associational freedom of members of the National Party"[90] was the subject of Wisconsin's substantial intrusion. The point, I grant, was not further discussed by the Court, so that one cannot be sure in what sense Justice Brennan or Justice Stewart conceived of party adherents or members; perhaps they meant only membership through state parties. If so, they could have been thinking of the national party as a collective decision-making body expressing the will of a majority of individuals adhering or belonging to its several state components rather than directly to the national party itself. Even in that perspective, however, it is evident that the Supreme Court did not regard the national party as merely an artifact of the several state parties and so of the several state laws recognizing those parties.

Interestingly, the dissenting opinion in *La Follette* came closer to discussing the membership problem. Justice Powell, joined by Justices Blackmun and Rehnquist, noted that the national Democratic party is "not organized around the achievement of defined ideological goals."[91] He also quoted approvingly from another Court opinion that our major parties "have been characterized by a fluidity and overlap of philosophy and membership."[92] Few would dispute the historical description, but many of the post-1968 Democratic reformers, concerned with both the charter movement and the enforcement of closed-primary rules, certainly want to organize a national party "around the achievement of defined ideological goals." Whether they have yet done so in any individual membership sense is unclear, but they now have a better opportunity to accomplish their purpose, thanks in part to the judicial ruling from which Justice Powell dissented. Justice Powell spoke for the older confederative order in which national parties had been less independently meaningful entities than they now seemed in process of becoming. He was even explicit in deploring, at the end of his dissent, the Court's departure from the long-established process of accommodation under which states regulated the major political parties in federal and state elections.[93]

IV
Import

In describing the new legal status of national parties as well as the nationalization of Democratic party structure and of Republican (and to a lesser degree, Democratic) organizational campaign activity, I have stressed the extent, the novelty, and the unidirectional nature of change from the old confederative order. Though undoubtedly important, the change and its consequences should not be exaggerated. Even as elements of a more national kind of American politics, the structure, campaign activity, and legal status of national party organizations may be less consequential than the development of national presidential followings, or presidential parties, that thrive partly because of the post-1968 plebiscitary nominating process. It is these issue-oriented, candidate-centered followings that have largely displaced the old state and local parties which, through the confederative structure, used to control the vital business of nominating presidential candidates. And that development, it seems to me, occurred only partly because of one of the changes emphasized in this chapter; it owed something to the post-1968 national Democratic rule-making authority, but a good deal more to the revived progressivism that led states to adopt presidential primaries.

It is particularly useful to recognize the so far limited political effect of changes in party structure despite their now legally bolstered status. Significantly, those changes, all by Democrats, have not been emulated by Republicans. Instead, the RNC has built its much more impressive campaign activities without modifying its confederative structure. Even when the RNC aided state or congressional candidates directly, the aid was, with exceptions, offered circumspectly enough to give no offense to state and local Republican organizations. And, of course, in providing national party funds to state parties with conditions, the RNC followed the conventional grant-in-aid formula of the federal system. Democrats, too, did not substitute anything like a fully national organization when they altered their confederative structure. Their charter did not establish national party membership for individuals; rather, it retained state party representation on the national committee although now partly in accord with population and voting.

Even the national Democratic party's dramatically new rule-making authority, after its initial imposition in 1972, has been exercised in a relationship that while no longer confederative is more federal than exclusively national. Every four years, as successive Democratic commissions have produced new delegate-selection rules, the results reflect considerable bargaining with state parties and the interests that they represent. Not only have a few states been allowed to conduct their selection processes outside of a proclaimed national season, but several states have been able to elect their delegates by methods substantially deviating from the proportional representation that was supposed to have been a national Democratic goal. When the DNC did successfully persist in pursuing another of its goals, banning the open primary in presidential delegate selection, its victory came only after it had allowed exceptions in 1976 and 1980. Moreover, the victory, though judicially supported, may have been politically short-lived. Wisconsin Democrats, unhappy with their forced use of caucuses in 1984, succeeded in 1985 in persuading the national party's Fairness Commission to recommend that the DNC allow the Wisconsin-style open primary to be used in the 1988 delegate-selection process.[94]

More substantial in political consequences are the campaign activities developed by the RNC and the closely related Republican House and Senate campaign committees. Here, I believe, is the principal evidence of meaningful nationalization of American politics through a party organization. Its mark, certainly in the Republican case, is genuinely national, mass-based funding resembling that of previously established and still-thriving nonparty organizations also operating on a national scale. Like many of them, the RNC has only a special kind of national "membership." Its "contributing members" may have Republican party cards, as grateful acknowledgments of their financial support, but no entitlement to roles in organizational policymaking except insofar as decisions to send or not to send checks could exert a kind of influence. Interestingly, the DNC also called its check-writing givers "contributing members" when it expanded its direct-mail solicitation in the 1980s. Apparently these donors have the same limited role as the RNC's more numerous contributors. Though they are tapped directly by a national organization rather than through state party channels, they do not constitute a mass party as do organized activists in many European parties and in even a few American state parties. Rather, the RNC is a distinctively American party organization.

The Republican contributors seem only to support, not control, a professionalized staff still responsible in principle to the federative national committee. In practice, the staff under a capable and strong-minded chairperson may itself be a substantial policymaking influence in the manner of other established professional bureaucracies. The staff members can thus be important elements of the "generally well-insulated party elites" which, in Longley's words (cited earlier), characterize the new Republican national model in contrast to a projected Democratic model for mass participation. The fact that the Republican model is like that of most durably successful nonparty political organizations suggests to me, as it has to Kayden, a close scholarly observer of the RNC, that it "appears to be representative of the party system of the future."[95] She has in mind, and so do I, both the centralization of party activity and the technical professionalization of that activity.

Kayden is understandably uncertain whether the new model will always be controlled by professionals interested first and foremost in winning office, or by activists interested in advancing issue positions.[96] In other words, can the professionals be well insulated? The question of insulation from national committee influence is not so likely to arise, because most committee members, as established party professionals of another type, are assumed to be as primarily interested in winning elections as are the professionals in party headquarters. But the many regular party contributors may be so issue oriented as to condition their responses to direct-mail solicitation on ideological grounds. Perhaps many of the RNC's numerous contributors send their checks because of the party's apparently conservative commitments of one kind or another. If so, the Republican party would have to adhere to, even fulfill, such commitments to be certain of continued financial support, especially in competition with the direct-mail solicitation by unabashedly conservative PACs. Though formally powerless in the Republican organizational structure, the contributors could still vote with their checkbooks. The truth, however, is that we do not yet know whether any such indirect influence will be exerted. Nor for that matter do we know to what extent the Republican contributors have really been ideological. We do know, however, that their numbers grew rather than diminished after the Republicans won the White House in 1980 and no longer solicited funds as the party of opposition to a Democratic Administration as well as to a Democratic Congress. Money, it turned out, could be obtained without the solely negative appeals thought mainly responsible for the direct-mail successes of 1977–80. To be sure, the appeals of 1981–84 were as ideological as those of the preceding years; the Reagan Administration was conservative enough for the purpose. The RNC may well have had to work harder to collect money, but its total receipts indicate success into the mid-1980s. We cannot be absolutely certain that such success will continue, but there is much less reason for doubt than there is with respect to the DNC's ability to match the Republican record.

The disparity between Republicans and Democrats in national party funding is significant, although it hardly means that Republican candidates for Congress receive more money from all sources than do Democratic candidates. In 1983–84 the latter actually reported larger total receipts, reflecting in part the greater amounts that Democratic incumbents received from PACs. But Republican candidates are the beneficiaries of much more national party help of an indirect kind that does not appear in their own total receipts. It is the help that comes from the Republican party's massive general spending in the party cause and also from its substantial expenditures in behalf of candidates (in addition to its contributions to candidates). The greater party activity on the Republican side might lead one to expect Republican senators and representatives, more than their Democratic counterparts, to be responsive to party policy.

Nevertheless, a knowledgeable observer has already said, after the 1982 congressional elections, that "The new directions in which both major parties are moving appear to be changing the relationship between party and candidate in a fundamental way."[97] The trend at least is clear over the last several years. And it is a trend not only toward a greater party role, in what admittedly remains a largely candidate-centered politics, but specifically toward a greater *national* party role. Therein lies the novelty of the developments described in this chapter. We used to have strong state and local party organizations, and we may still have some. Strong national party organizations, however, are new American phenomena. Now that they have finally begun to be substantial, it is easy to believe that they are here to stay and that their previous absence was an anomaly in a political and social system already predominantly national in so many other respects.

Chapter Eight

Party Identifiers

Most students of American politics will recognize the subject of this chapter as party-in-the-electorate—the mass of potential voters who regularly identify themselves as Republicans or Democrats and who, therefore, respond positively to a party label. Only limited numbers of these identifiers belong to party organizations in either a dues-paying or an activist sense, and still fewer are public officeholders elected under party labels. Party-in-the-electorate, or the electoral party, is a third and rather special conception of party that political scientists put alongside the two more tangible entities, party-in-government and party organized outside government to conduct campaigns.

Although party-in-the-electorate could apply to the many regularly partisan voters in any nation, it has been a very American conception since the 1950s and 1960s when V. O. Key, adapting Ralph M. Goldman's coinage, gave it an analytical place in his influential textbook. Key wrote of "persons who regard themselves as party members" and are mobilized as Republican and Democratic groups only on election day, but who often also react in characteristic ways to public issues between elections. This kind of party, he granted, "is an amorphous group, yet it has a social reality."[1] As such, it has remained a fixture in American political studies. For example, the conception is prominent in Frank Sorauf's parties text, which by the 1970s had succeeded to the leading place that Key's book had occupied. Sorauf considers party-in-the-electorate largely a "categorical group" within which there is no interaction, no structured set of relationships, no organizational or group life. It is characterized by "feelings of loyalty to or identification with the party."[2] He writes of a "cognitive party," and of "the party *within the elector*," employing a psy-

chological definition already familiar in the thriving academic study of voting behavior.[3] Sorauf, like Key and other scholars, thus carefully distinguishes
party-in-the-electorate from any organized following. Nevertheless a reader
might infer the existence of a more tangible entity, thereby hypostatizing
party-in-the-electorate. Partly because of that possibility, I prefer the more
matter-of-fact *party identifiers*. The term is less imposing, but it refers to the
same "social reality" as does party-in-the-electorate.

Party identifiers have seemed so great a social reality in the United States
that they command more scholarly attention than party organizations. The
Republican and Democratic loyalties of the electorate long provided much of
the material for American political history. And since the advent in the late
1930s of sample surveys, political scientists have fastened on the self-identification
of party voters as a central element in their analysis of voting behavior and
election outcomes. Especially in the middle of the twentieth century, when
party organizations outside as well as inside government had apparently declined, the continuing party identification of about three-quarters of the electorate was a striking feature of American politics. Each major party appeared
to consist mainly of loyal identifiers who would ordinarily vote for candidates
bearing their particular party label. In numbers and stability, these American
party identifiers compared favorably with European counterparts.[4] Understandably, terms like party-in-the-electorate and electoral party were invented to
describe the phenomenon. It was thought that the United States had developed a special kind of party that was effective, at least electorally, without
strong organizational ties. The Republican or Democratic label sufficed to unite
voters and candidates. In light of the great importance attributed to party identifiers, any decrease in their numbers during the last few decades suggested
that American parties were declining in their one most impressive sense. If
many more voters were ceasing to identify as partisans, how relevant could
party labels be in government or election campaigns? Might not a diminution
of party identifiers threaten the significance of party altogether, and so of the
governmental parties and the campaign organizations that I have portrayed
as substantial, even increasingly substantial, national entities?

Before confronting these questions and even before presenting the historical
background with which I approach them, it is useful to be explicit about a
point readily taken for granted but which I have in mind in preferring to write
of party identifiers rather than of party-in-the-electorate. Party identifiers are
primarily responders to candidates, officeholders, programs, issues, policies, and
organizational efforts. Like voters generally, party identifiers do not themselves produce parties. Rather, they are mobilized by leaders. Once mobilized,

or brought into being as electoral followings, they may well be influential in many respects. Obviously they are the basis for enduring partisan alignments. The long-standing existence of great numbers of Republican and Democratic identifiers constitutes a kind of political power. But their existence in the first place came about because of something that the party label represented. While identification as a Republican or a Democrat outlives the original cause, its continuation or its modification within a given generation as well as between generations involves responses to new leaders, interests, and circumstances. In particular, as I stressed earlier, our national electoral alignment has focused around the presidency and hence around the personalities and policies of party nominees for that office. That alignment is surely subject to change, if only as a result of new political stimuli that come with the passage of time. Indeed, change more than stability among party identifiers seems predictable, given the great transformation of American society in the century after the Republican-Democratic alignment was established. But because considerable stability has nonetheless long characterized the American electorate, it first requires explanation.

I
Party Labels

What has to be explained is not only that the Republican and Democratic labels have lasted longer than those of major parties in any other nation, but that they are the symbols of a duopoly in voter identification that is distinctively American. Almost everywhere else there is an established multiparty pattern, or a changing two-party pattern in which a new party occasionally attracts enough voters to be a major force and perhaps supersede one of the two previously dominant parties. Only a few nations have had electoral alignments that resemble the American duopoly, and they fall well short of the 130 years during which American voters have almost exclusively used the Republican and Democratic labels. Britain is a case in point. Its electorate can be said to have been almost fully aligned under Conservative and Labour party labels for no longer than the half-century from the 1930s through the 1970s, and even in those decades a persistent third party often intruded substantially. In contrast, the two familiar American party labels survived from their preindustrial origins through the industrial age and into a postindustrial society. Considered almost natural in the United States, the continuity of these labels, still carried by almost all elected national and state officeholders as well as by voters professing any party identification, is a most unusual phenomenon in comparative politics.

The phenomenon has three closely related aspects: the historical emphasis on party labels as such in American elections, the early dominance of only two party labels, and the long-standing dominance specifically of the Republican and Democratic labels. The first aspect followed from the usefulness of labels for voters asked to fill the numerous executive and legislative offices subject to simultaneous election in the United States. As far back as the 1790s, the "party ticket" became the means for voters, without having to make individual choices, to cast ballots for presidential electors, members of Congress, and state officials.[5] Throughout most of the nineteenth century, when the ticket was a party document representing the choices of a nominating convention, the voter had only to deposit it at a polling place. The United States was not the only nation to use such a party ticket, but it was the only nation that had so many executive as well as legislative offices to be filled by voters and thus so great a need for the ticket. Especially in the last century, when educational levels were lower, mass communication decidedly limited, and nonparty political information generally sparse, voters would have had few cues more helpful and meaningful than the party label. It was even hard to vote according to any other cues as long as candidate names appeared only on party tickets.

The long ballot, helpful though it is in accounting for the usefulness of party tickets, cannot contribute similarly to an explanation of the other two aspects of the American attachment to party labels. Three or four important party tickets could have served voters as well as only two. Yet, as we well know, the American electorate followed a two-party pattern at the start of national competition between Jeffersonians and Federalists, again when the Whigs faced the Democrats, and finally during the prolonged era of Republican-Democratic competition. Only briefly and transitionally was there anything resembling national multiparty politics.

The persistent two-party division has been explained many times as the product of special American social and institutional circumstances. Among these the favorite is the winner-take-all nature of the presidential election. The need for a majority in order to win this one powerful national executive office provides a strong incentive for candidates and their supporters to combine forces in large and broad combinations capable of mobilizing such a majority. In the earlier discussion of presidential politics, I stressed the manner in which national combinations imposed their pattern on state politics so that, after the 1830s, a nearly universal electoral competition occurred under the labels also used nationally. In many places over long periods, it is true, only one of the two major-party labels has been popular enough to be used to win elections. But one-party states or regions were merely geographic units whose voters had become overwhelmingly attached to a given national party label. They did not thereby break the major-party dominance. Instead, as described in chapter 5 successful third parties have been about as infrequent and transient in state as in national politics. Their short lives may be related to the fact that their noninvolvement in presidential elections left them without national labels like those of the established major parties.[6] Also, to be taken seriously as a national force, a third party would have to compete not only for the presidency but also for Senate and House seats over a large part of the country. Developing the state and district strength for that purpose is a formidable task in a diverse nation. Even the largest third-party presidential campaigns—Theodore Roosevelt's in 1912, Robert La Follette's in 1924, and George Wallace's in 1968—did not compete effectively, if at all, for other offices.

A much disputed explanation of American bipartyism relates to the single-member, simple-plurality system long employed in congressional elections (though not always or exclusively by every state during much of our history). It is thought to discourage third-party candidacies as they would not be discouraged by proportional representation in multimember districts. Or it can be argued that Americans simply like to limit their choices to two competing teams, in politics as in sports, or that divisions over issues and interests, while numerous, have almost always been moderate enough to permit the luxury of a bipartite alignment. Whatever the likely explanation, the historical tendency to such an alignment became an important feature of American politics even before the ascendancy of Republicans and Democrats.

Nevertheless, the Republican and Democratic labels are the ones that were institutionalized in the distinctive American style when, in the late 1880s and 1890s, state governments provided official ballots for voters to use instead of the party-printed tickets.[7] Although it was thus made easier for voters to cast ballots for candidates of different parties—to split their tickets—it was also easy, as before, to use the label to simplify choice. Most American states retained not only the old party labels but also a party column that allowed voters, often by a single check mark, to cast their ballots for a long list of party candidates. The same American practice—to elect many officeholders and thus to have a long ballot—prevailed, as it does today, and so the party label remained a helpful cue as it had been earlier. While some voters may now have thought party labels less essential than had earlier generations, they nevertheless had ballots that officially presented the traditional sets of choices. The

Republican and Democratic parties were thus privileged, even as their organizational powers were limited in ways that I stressed earlier. On the basis of the substantial number of votes that had been cast for their parties' candidates in previous elections, Republican and Democratic nominees were listed as such on government-provided ballots. We have seen in chapter 6 that the privilege was consequential relative to the ballot access of new and minor parties.

However high a price in terms of governmental regulation the major parties paid when they secured privileged ballot access, their labels surely remained crucial for the electoral success of candidates if not for organizations or common programs. The Republican and Democratic labels hardly lost their value because they were won in state-managed primaries rather than in party conventions. Almost everywhere and almost all of the time, candidates continued to compete seriously for national and state offices only under one or the other of the two major-party labels.

Privileged major-party ballot access, however, is by itself far from a sufficient explanation for the absence of persistently successful third parties in twentieth-century American politics. Various third and minor parties have often won ballot access, and, as already observed, since 1968 the U.S. Supreme Court has reduced the highest obstacles imposed by certain states.[8] Now even a presidential candidate who decides only during an election year to run outside major-party channels, as John Anderson did in 1980, can secure a place on every state's ballot after a few months (admittedly of strenuous effort). Yet, as in the past, parties gaining such access have not endured as serious competitors against Republicans and Democrats.

More important than ballot access, in accounting for the continued electoral dominance of the Republican and Democratic labels, is the manner in which the direct primary institutionalized those labels. States do much more than merely impose legal burdens on the use of third-party labels by insurgents. As already observed, the direct-primary laws of the several states provide unusual opportunities for insurgents to win major-party nominations and thereby the valuable state-conferred labels accompanying those nominations. Challengers outside the ranks of an established party leadership and organization are thus encouraged to seek intraparty electoral routes to power, and voters become accustomed to choosing among groups and individuals competing, especially for the party label that probably ensures general-election success in a given constituency.[9] No doubt this use of primaries by voters as well as by aspiring officeholders can be understood as yet another manifestation of the looseness of American party structure and of the tendency of each major party to accommodate considerable diversity.[10] These characteristics antedate the direct primary. Hence the primary may be viewed as the twentieth-century means for confirming the traditional porousness or ready permeability of American parties. I would add, however, that the primary contributes to the porousness as well as confirming it in statutory form. Nothing quite like the American pattern of intraparty electoral competition exists in other nations, and it is not unreasonable to suggest that its absence may help explain why parties in those nations have been less successful than the major American parties in pre-empting incipient third-party territory.

I am aware of a paradox in my argument. The very element that weakened American major parties organizationally and perhaps governmentally is proposed as a factor strengthening them electorally. In a special sense, that is what I am arguing. My view is that the electoral looseness of the established major parties, especially as it is legally institutionalized, acts as a preservative. But like a preservative in food processing, or perhaps like an embalming fluid, it also changes the nature and quality of what is being preserved. In the case of parties, the end product may be little more than an electoral label whose value or meaningfulness beyond election day is often questioned.

The preservative element in the legal institutionalization of major-party labels is readily observed in state requirements that voters register or declare their party preference in order to vote in party primaries. However obtained—in written form and in advance or merely by public declaration at the polls—the preference is a forced choice that the state imposes on voters who want to participate in what is often the decisive electoral contest. Even in the minority of states that require no public registration or declaration of party before entering a primary election booth, a voter usually has to decide, though within the privacy of the voting booth, whether to choose a Republican or Democratic party ballot. At least a little temporary party identification is thus at work. The identification that accompanies public registration or declaration is much clearer. Here is a legal inducement to express traditional electoral attachments.

Such inducement to identify publicly, while hardly uniform, is widespread. The 24 states which, with the District of Columbia, provide party registration (or party enrollment, as it is often called) have just over half of the nation's population (as of 1980). The four other states that record public declarations have an additional 9.5 percent, and the 11 states that make use of an announced party preference at the primary polls but do not maintain a record of it have another 28 percent.[11] Thus almost 88 percent of the U.S. population live where a form of public choice of party is necessary for voting in a primary. The requirement does not make all of these primaries truly closed, as observed in chapter 5, but it must encourage voters to think of themselves as Republicans or Democrats. Some states evidently do more encouraging than others. Even among party-registration states, those that prevent unaffiliated voters from changing temporarily to a party affiliation on primary day tend to have higher percentages of party registrants than do states that tolerate such shifts. And a state can produce more party registrations when it omits instructions for registering as an unaffiliated voter or when it posts notices warning voters that nonparty registrants cannot vote in a subsequent primary. Accordingly, substantial variations exist in percentages of party registrants from state to state, and even from time to time within a state as it modifies its registration rules.[12]

Despite variations, however, total Republican and Democratic party registrations, as percentages of all voter registrations, ordinarily run well above percentages of party identifiers counted in sample surveys. In 18 party-registration states for which in 1982 there were also exit-poll data from the midterm congressional elections, the difference was more than 10 points in all but four states. Not untypical were California, where 88 percent of its registrants listed themselves as Republicans or Democrats but only 73 percent of its surveyed voters identified with the major parties, and New York, where the comparable percentages were 80 and 67. The difference, though less in some states, was over 20 points in seven of the 18 states. Such a result is not surprising in light of the fact that more than 90 percent of the voters were recorded as Republicans or Democrats in nine states, two of which were near the 97 percent level.[13] No figures even approaching that number appear in response to samplesurvey questions asking voters whether they consider themselves Republican, Democrat, Independent or something else.[14]

Because party registration is higher than survey-produced party identification, it is reasonable to suppose that some voters officially record a party preference that they do not really hold. Social pressure and even job holding or job seeking may be factors. So might the desire to vote in the primary of the locally dominant party although one might think of oneself as an independent or even as an identifier with the other major party in national politics. We might thus account for very high Democratic registrations in certain states that often produce Republican majorities in statewide elections, and for overwhelmingly high Democratic, or Republican, registrations in particular counties whose elections are less lopsided.[15]

Acknowledging the existence of some false identification-by-registration does no more than marginally qualify the role that I assign to party registration (or declaration) in preserving the traditional electoral alignment. Even voters who register a party preference for pragmatic reasons could nonetheless be influenced by it. Others may simply be influenced by the apparent need to make a choice not otherwise presented. Still others may find in registration a kind of confirmation of a preference already arrived at. The relation between registration and survey data revealed in the 1982 study is consonant with these possibilities. Even as party registrations tend to be higher than survey-reported party identifications, both tend to be relatively high in some states and relatively low in others. In particular, the states that most strongly encourage party registration, by firmly closing their primaries to unaffiliated voters, record not only higher party-registration percentages but also higher percentages of party identifiers in surveys than do states with more permissive registration procedures. Can we then infer that party registration inflates the numbers of party responses to survey questions? Do some voters say Republican or Democratic when asked for party identification in a sample survey *because* they believe that they are supposed to give their party registration even if it is not always their real preference? The only effort I know to answer these intriguing questions suggests tentativeley affirmative answers.[16]

Insofar as party registrations add to the number of party identifiers in sample surveys, it would be natural to expect any decline in party registrations to be reflected in a decline in party identifications. Without data directly pertaining to that phenomenon, I can only suggest the possibility. It rests on two previously noted matters: the smaller number of both party identifiers and party registrants in states whose registration rules are most permissive, and the decrease in party registrants that follows when a given state makes it easier to register as an unaffiliated voter. The second matter can be amplified from the New York experience. When New York introduced mail registration in 1976, it also provided a new form with a box marked with the notation "I do not wish to enroll in any political party." Voters registering in person, now as in the past (when it had been the only way to register), had no such box but only the option of leaving all party boxes blank when wanting no enrollment in a party. It was found in the first year that mail registrants checked the box much more frequently than in-person registrants were willing to leave all boxes blank. Accordingly, the percentage of nonparty registrants rose significantly along with mail registration in the years after 1976.[17] But the percentage had risen a little even before the new 1976 procedure; from less than 8 percent in 1960, it was near 10 percent in 1975, before going to 13.5 percent in 1976 and 14.2 percent in 1979.[18]

California shows a somewhat similar trend. Its category of nonparty registrant, called "Declined to State," rose from about 3 percent in the mid-1960s to between 6 and 8 percent in the late 1970s and to about 10 percent in 1982.[19] Changes of that magnitude are not apparent in all party-registration states; for example, Pennsylvania has continued to record as Republicans or Democrats about 94 to 95 percent of all registrants.[20] And among the few other states whose data I checked, Connecticut even shows an increase in party-registration percentages during the quarter-century since it first adopted the direct primary.[21] Connecticut's experience is almost certainly untypical, because the state adopted its direct primary as late as 1955 and then in a special form that minimized its use.[22] Even by the early 1980s, its Republican and Democratic registrants were only about two-thirds of all registrants. And they may diminish again if, as now seems likely, Connecticut's unaffiliated voters will be able to enter a party primary.[23] It is, of course, that kind of permissiveness, not merely the ease of recording unaffiliated status, that can reduce party registrations. Without having to register by party in order to obtain an admission ticket to a party primary, fewer voters would be likely to record weak or almost nonexistent preferences with election officials. And, more speculatively, fewer would then think of themselves as Republicans or Democrats when surveyed by pollsters.

That speculation implies that the relation between registrations and surveyed identifications is one in which the former influence the latter. Within limits, I believe such influence does exist, but only as one side of a complex relationship flowing from the American institutionalization of party labels. Plainly, party registrations, along with party primaries, did not originally create party identifiers. Rather, party registrations and party primaries were established when most voters—probably more than now—already identified themselves as Republicans or Democrats in response to leaders and their programs. What our states did in running party primaries, as well as in recording voters by party as a condition for participating in those primaries, was to recognize an existing alignment of the electorate. Doing so, it is also clear, helped to perpetuate that alignment during almost all of this century. And it still does. Yet institutionalized help in this respect depends on a measure of public acquiescence. Enough insistent independent voters could undoubtedly reduce party-registration requirements and produce more open primaries, as may indeed be about to happen, or even, much less probably, force a new party alignment altogether. Or as the previous chapter suggested, our courts, with or without public acquiescence, could put an end to the treatment of American parties as public utilities.

Turning again, however, to what has actually happened in this century, the institutionalization of the major party labels can be seen to support the electoral continuity of those labels. Otherwise, I would find it hard to account for the truly extraordinary maintenance of nineteenth-century party labels through most of the twentieth century. Without their institutionalization in the early decades of this century, might not one or both of the old labels have been replaced? Something like that change occurred in most European nations during the twentieth century, and it happened earlier in American history.

It is conceivable, however, that the Republican and Democratic labels had come to mean so much socially before 1900 that they could have been preserved without legal institutionalization. Americans of the late nineteenth century were deeply attached to these labels, and often to particular leaders who made them meaningful. Links with economic class divisions always existed, though less clearly than elsewhere. Moreover, each major-party label had strong, recently embittered sectional associations and also considerable reinforcement from ethnic and religious divisions. On the latter, one historian of the late nineteenth century's intense partisanship goes so far as to say that "major-party identifications were rooted primarily in ethnoreligious group conflicts." Thus, he adds, "For most social groups partisanship had become a means of expressing and defending subcultural values, and through habituated partisan responses party itself had become a positive reference symbol."[24]

No doubt subcultural values as well as sectional and class linkages added to the intensity and persistence of party identification, but nothing is peculiarly American about such a process. On the contrary, in comparative perspective, the American attachment to party labels appears to be based less directly and fully on prior social and economic grouping than the European. In several nations, class divisions or religious and linguistic differences are thought to account for voting preferences to a greater degree than they do in the United States.[25] Consequently, political scientists have treated American party labels as more independently important determinants of voting behavior than European party labels. It is not that Europeans do less party voting than Americans; they presumably do more, because they usually choose only between legislative candidates closely linked to governmental parties. But their attachment to parties, until recently at least, has often been so plainly a derivative of class or other group membership that the attachment itself, however firm, was seldom used to explain actual voting behavior.

In the United States, however, identification with party labels is treated as an influence often distinguishable from that of class or other group associations with a party label. The belief in the distinctive influence of the American party label rests not only on the supposed weakness, relatively speaking, of

class or other social groupings as political cues. It is based also on the historical use of party labels to cope with the American long ballot, and on the subsequent institutionalization of two particular labels.

II

Measurement

Nothing is more familiar to scholars of the late-twentieth-century American
electorate, and now to more casual consumers of news reports, than the count
and analysis of party identifiers revealed by sample surveys. Partly because sample surveys provide national totals, their reports of party identifiers are given
wider attention than the nonuniform state tabulations of party registrants.
They are also more useful for academic analysts because their data ordinarily
include, along with party identification, the socioeconomic status, voting intentions or recollections, and other information about respondents. So well
established have survey findings become that party identification now derives
its meaning from those findings. To identify with a party is, in effect, to tell
or be willing to tell a pollster that one prefers that party.

It might be said that polling has thus itself institutionalized party labels,
although not in the legal sense of party registration or party-primary voting.
More evidently, however, the pollsters accepted the already established institutionalization of Republican and Democratic labels. From their start in the
1930s, survey questions about party identification almost always asked explicitly
whether voters considered themselves or thought of themselves as Republicans or Democrats. Although other party labels have occasionally been included in the wording of questions, the common form (Gallup's, for example)
now mentions by name only the two major parties and "Independent."[26] Or,
as in the 1982 exit poll, the option "something else" is added. In this respect,
most exit polls follow the pattern of the longer-established surveys whose interviews are conducted before and after election day. The difference lies not
so much in the nature of their questions as in their timing and especially in
the number of respondents; instead of 1,100 to 2,800 door-to-door or telephone interviews obtained in a typical national survey, an exit poll like the
one cited earlier includes about 24,000 voters inexpensively sampled as they
leave a carefully selected portion of election precincts. The larger number may
not provide a more reliable sample of the national electorate, but it produces
significantly larger subsamples of various demographic and regional groups.

Despite the advantages of exit polls for certain purposes, the academic community has drawn more heavily on the national data systematically gathered over three decades by the highly respected Center for Political Studies/Survey Research Center (CPS/SRC) at the University of Michigan. Its initial party-identification question, resembling that of other polling organizations, is: "Generally speaking, do you usually think of yourself as a Republican, a Democrat, an Independent, or what?" Following this question are two more, also much like those asked in many other surveys. One is put to those who answered Republican or Democrat: "Would you call yourself a strong Republican or Democrat or a not very strong Republican or Democrat?" The other question is put to those who answered Independent: "Do you think of yourself as closer to the Republican or Democratic Party?" Use of these questions during each biennial election campaign since 1952 allows for comparisons of at least medium-run historical significance. I am confident enough about the findings produced by the CPS/SRC questions to rely on them for most of my discussion of recent changes in numbers of party identifiers, but before that discussion I want to note three concerns about the significance of what is being measured by CPS/SRC and similar surveys.

The first concern arises from the wording of the usual party-identification questions. As in other surveys, the CPS/SRC questions specifically mention Republican and Democratic labels. They are thus name-choice questions, although not quite forced-choice questions as I was tempted to call them. A no-party option is provided along with the named major-party options, but the questions may prompt Republican or Democratic answers in larger numbers than would seem likely if respondents were merely asked whether they usually think of themselves as adherents of a party and if so what is its name. Studies elsewhere support that likelihood. In France, a name-choice question (like the American) led 76 percent of a sample to identify with a party, while in the same year an open-ended wording led only 50 percent of a comparable sample to volunteer a party label.[27] In Germany, a similar difference of 20 percent was found.[28]

Americans too, in 1980, displayed a parallel difference in answering the two forms of the question when the CPS/SRC included both in its national election questionnaire. Set well apart from its standard name-choice question, the CPS/SRC asked respondents first, "In your own mind, do you usually think of yourself as a supporter of one of the political parties or not?" and then followed by asking those who had responded positively, "Which political party do you support?" From this open-ended question, or pair of questions, only 45 percent of the whole sample identified themselves as Republican or Democratic supporters. In the same survey, 63 percent identified with the major-party labels in response to the standard initial question specifying those labels.[29] The words *support* and *supporter* in the new questions may, with the open-endedness, affect the comparison, but they seem if anything to ask for a less full party identification than does "thinking of yourself as a Republican or Democrat. . . ." In that case, the 18-point difference might understate the real difference between name-choice and open-ended choice.

Altogether, the American difference is close enough to the higher French and German differences to suggest the same phenomenon—a name-choice question that produces substantially more party identifiers than does the un-prompted opportunity to volunteer a party name. Or, to be more precise, the phenomenon was discerned in the United States in 1980 as it had been earlier elsewhere. I believe but cannot demonstrate that the name-choice question raised party identification in earlier years as well. If so, not many more than 55 percent of the American electorate would have been unprompted party identifiers even in the 1950s when polls showed about 75 percent answering Republican or Democrat to the name-choice question. Of course, 55 to 60 percent, and 45 percent too, represent impressive numbers. At any rate, the name-choice question is not flawed for comparisons over time as long as it regularly produces larger numbers of identifiers than a differently worded question. The overstatement merely resembles, though at a lower level, the over-statement of party preference already noted when discussing party registration.

The second measurement concern is with the degree to which party iden-tification is separable from current or short-term voting preferences. In the United States, this concern is not tied to the possibility, noted for European nations, that a voter's self-identification with a party label is so nearly synony-mous with voting intention as to be tautological when used as an explanatory device.[30] Even if the American-originated conception of party identification does not travel well, it is in this country analytically separable from particular voting preferences. We cannot even suspect that the two are synonymous when we know from surveys, over several decades, that American voters often say they cast ballots for one or more candidates whose party labels differ from those with which the same voters say they identify. It is partly because such deviations constitute substantial and varying minorities, even while most vot-ers cast most of their ballots in accord with their party identification, that the conception is meaningful rather than tautological in the United States. What remains at issue is just how, and how fully, party identification is sepa-rable from American voting preferences.

Presumably, party identification is more nearly stable than voting preference. For example, people are more likely to change their presidential votes from one party's nominee to the other party's, in successive elections, than they are to change their party identification. But since party identification itself involves responses to presidential nominees as well as to other leaders, a certain number of shifts in party could, over time, accompany presidential voting preferences. Insofar as those shifts then become fixed, they do not alter the view of party identification as a relatively stable condition but merely indicate an almost inevitable change of party as new leaders and issues arise in a dynamic society. On the other hand, something else would appear to be involved if there were many voters who identified with the party of their presidential choice, at or near a given election, and then soon afterward switched back to the other party. Instability of that kind did appear in the rise of Republican identifiers in late 1980,[31] with the first election of Ronald Reagan, and the subsequent decline of Republican identifiers over the next two years. It may have appeared again in the 1984 election, when the number of Republican identifiers (as revealed by an exit poll) rose to a much higher level than in 1980 — provided that the number again falls off sharply in subsequent years.[32] These instances may, of course, be consistent with a recent though noncontinuous trend toward increasing Republican identification in response to successive presidential candidacies, but they also suggest the possibility that at least some of those counted as party identifiers are merely expressing their current presidential preferences. Certain voters may even believe, when interviewed at or just after election time, that the party identification question should be answered in accord with their presidential choice. Others may simply like to associate with the party of the winning presidential candidate right after his victory.

Some of the possible inclusion of transient party identifiers is avoided by surveys taken before a presidential election, in the manner of the CPS/SRC studies. Their similar timing over the years permits reasonable comparisons. This is not to say that the preelection counts of party identifiers are unaffected by short-term campaign personalities and issues. Indeed, they have been shown to change during the course of a presidential campaign. In an impressive study based on successive CPS/SRC interviews of a panel of respondents in January, June, and October of 1980, Brody and Rothenberg observe that 21 percent shifted from party to party, from party to Independent, or from Independent to party. Another 31 percent changed only in strength of identification (that is, between the categories of strong, not-so-strong, or leaning toward).[33] Although fewer than half of the sample are thus completely stable in their identifying categories (the familiar ones of table 8.1), it is reasonable to add the 31 percent and thus say that over three-quarters retained their general party preferences throughout an election year in which defections might have been especially encouraged because of nominating results in both major parties and by the Independent candidacy of John Anderson. Hence, the relative stability of party identification is by no means destroyed.

More significantly, as Brody and Rothenberg seem to suggest, the results of their study challenge the view that party identification is an "unmoved mover" in explaining voting behavior.[34] It, too, moves substantially in response to short-term forces. I am uncertain that anyone ever denied that possibility, or that Brody and Rothenberg intend to say that anyone did. Surely we can believe that party identifications of a substantial minority of voters change during a campaign without rejecting the established belief of electoral analysts that precampaign party identifications account for most votes most of the time. All that is conceded is what seems implicit anyway in the conception of party identification: its origin in response to leaders and issues, and so its change in response to new leaders and issues. Only if change in identification became virtually equivalent to change in voting from election to election, or office to office, would its meaning be lost. And so far, at least, no evidence suggests that the American electorate approaches that condition.

The third concern about what is being measured is that the starting point in the CPS/SRC series is as late as 1952. The three decades since then are only a small portion of American electoral history, and it cannot be inferred from data for that period whether any decline in party identification is an extension of a longer-term trend or is a shorter-term drop from a cyclical high point. It is true that Gallup surveys, beginning in the 1930s, provide a little support for a longer-term trend. From what may be less than strictly similar surveys in earlier years, Gallup reports that between 1937 and 1948 about 80 to 85 percent of its samples were Republican and Democratic identifiers, and that in the 1950s the comparable figures were usually in the 75 to 80 percent range, though a few points lower in 1952. By the late 1960s, Gallup-counted identifiers declined still further. Then, as in the 1950s, the percentages ran a little higher than those reported by CPS/SRC, but the downward direction is parallel.[35] Hence, it is reasonable to cite Gallup data, though with caution, in behalf of a decline of identifiers from the late 1930s and 1940s. Note, however, that doing so adds only a decade and a half to the historical perspective.

Before the late 1930s, evidence concerning party identifiers is more circumstantial. Party-registration figures from closed-primary states are available from the second decade of the twentieth century, but their usefulness as measures of change in total party identification is limited, not only because similarly recorded figures are unavailable in all states but also because, as observed, voters may register by party for pragmatic reasons unrelated to their genuine preferences. In the absence of hard data on party identifiers before the middle years of this century, it is tempting to believe that many more voters must once have been loyal identifiers, since straight-ticket voting was more characteristic of earlier years. Of course, without interview data from the voters of those years, we can only assume when aggregate election results show similar totals for a party's candidates for several offices that those results were produced by straight-ticket voting rather than by a canceling-out of split-ticket patterns. The assumption is readily made, although we just as readily recognize that split-ticket voting may well be understated when calculated from gross election data. From such data, at any rate, substantial declines from nineteenth-century party-voting loyalty have been impressively tabulated in the well-known work of Walter Dean Burnham. His evidence includes increasing numbers of congressional districts recording split-party results in simultaneous House and presidential elections, greater variance from party loyalty in the same state elections, and greater amplitude of partisan swing between elections.[36]

Burnham's explanation for the late-nineteenth-century decline in party-line voting is disputed by scholars who attribute more of it to changes in ballot form than to the political and social characteristics of what Burnham calls the post-1896 electoral alignment.[37] But there is little dissent from his findings of lesser party voting in the first few decades of this century than in most of the preceding few decades, or from his showing that the 1900–1930 tendencies reappear after interruption and evidently temporary reversal in the New Deal years. Nevertheless, it must be noted that Burnham's data also indicate sharp variations between states at certain periods. The nature of each state's ballot form (office-group or party-column) is related to some of these variations, and so are unusual protest candidacies at particular elections.

Moreover, some of the early twentieth-century increase in split-ticket voting is more modest than it first appears. For example, Burnham shows that Michigan's "split-ticket-voting rate increased by a factor of approximately eight to twelve" from the post-Civil War decades to the 1920s.[38] But mean split-ticket voting, in Burnham's measurement, had been less than 1 percent in 1854–72 and less than 2 percent in 1878–92. Hence, their multiplication to near 10 percent in 1910–18 and 1920–30 still left intact most of the old straight-ticket pattern. A similar picture emerges from Burnham's use of more refined measurements of split-ticket voting in various states. Only occasionally, in apparently deviant elections, is split-ticket voting shown to be at spectacularly high levels in the early decades of the century. Split-ticket voting had not yet become massive although it had surely begun.

The question that remains is whether the early twentieth-century decline in party-voting loyalty, as measured by split-ticket ballots, meant a simultaneous decline in party identification of voters. Given the opportunity, voters presumably split their tickets for many reasons, some of which may be compatible with a large measure of continued party identification. Yet good impressionistic accounts of post-Civil War politics lead us to think that greater and more intense party identification, and not simply more straight-ticket voting, existed before the twentieth century. Election campaigns in the late nineteenth century were conducted more exclusively through party channels. Newspapers, before the era of modern mass media, were often party organs.[39] Party tickets were party documents rather than government-printed ballots. Party organizations, not primary voters, nominated candidates and dominated politics and government in other ways as well. In fact, America's nineteenth-century political circumstances seem so conducive to strong party loyalties that we might regard the presumably greater party identification and straight-ticket voting of a century ago as period pieces rather than as a norm of electoral behavior from which contemporary behavior has descended.

At any rate, the longer-range historical perspective is helpful in understanding the apparent decline of party identifiers during the last 30 years. Because the antecedents of the recent decline can be traced to the end of the last century, change in our own time must be expected. The remarkable feature, as I hope to show, is that change has been limited and held within the old and distinctively American institutionalized channels. The established Republican and Democratic labels are tenacious as habitual voting cues even while subject to erosion in response to new generations, issues, interests and leaders.

III
Recent Decline

In table 8.1 CPS/SRC data of the last three decades are arranged to indicate in three different ways the decline in party identifiers. The second set of rows, whose figures are for those who answered Republican or Democrat to the initial survey question, shows the decline in its most familiar form. Here party identifiers can be seen dropping from about three-quarters to two-thirds or less of the electorate—from 73–77 percent in 1952–64 to 60–68 percent in 1970–84. The figures themselves are not in dispute. Their downward move-

TABLE 8.1 Party Identification, 1952–84 (percent)

	1952	1954	1956	1958	1960	1962	1964	1966	1968	1970	1972	1974	1976	1978	1980	1982	1984
Strong Democrat	22	22	21	27	20	23	27	18	20	20	15	18	15	15	17	20	17
Weak Democrat	25	26	23	22	25	23	25	28	25	24	26	21	25	24	23	24	20
Independent Democrat	10	9	6	7	6	7	9	9	10	10	11	13	12	14	11	11	11
Independent Independent	6	7	9	7	10	8	8	12	11	13	13	15	15	14	13	11	11
Independent Republican	7	6	8	5	7	6	6	7	9	8	11	9	10	10	10	8	12
Weak Republican	14	14	14	17	14	16	14	15	15	15	13	14	14	13	14	14	15
Strong Republican	14	13	15	11	16	12	11	10	10	9	10	8	9	8	9	10	12
Apolitical, other	3	4	4	4	3	4	1	1	1	1	1	3	1	3	3	2	2
Total	100	100	100	100	100	100	100	100	100	100	100	100	100	100	100	100	100
Democrat (SD & WD)	47	48	44	49	45	46	52	46	45	44	41	39	40	39	40	44	37
Republican (SR & WR)	28	27	29	28	30	28	25	25	25	24	23	22	23	21	23	24	27
Total	75	75	73	77	75	74	77	71	70	68	64	61	63	60	63	68	64
Democrat (SD, WD, & ID)	57	57	50	56	51	53	61	55	55	54	52	52	52	53	51	55	48
Republican (SR, WR, & IR)	35	33	37	33	37	34	31	32	34	32	34	31	33	31	33	32	39
Total	92	90	87	89	88	87	92	87	89	86	86	83	85	84	84	87	87

Source: Center for Political Studies/Survey Research Center, data made available through Inter-university Consortium for Political and Social Research. Data derived from these questions: First, "Generally speaking, do you usually think of yourself as a Republican, a Democrat, an Independent, or what?" Second, to those responding Republican or Democrat to the first question, "Would you call yourself a strong Republican or Democrat or a not very strong Republican or Democrat?" Third, to those responding Independent to the first question, "Do you think of yourself as closer to the Republican or Democratic party?" The not-so-strong answers are classified as Weak Democrat or Weak Republican, and the answers indicating closer to one party or the other are called Independent Democrat or Independent Republican, leaving a pure category of Independent Independent above for those who say that they are not closer to either major party. (Samples vary from 1,130 to 2,850, and are generally closer to the larger number in presidential years.)

Note: Using a preelection survey in presidential years helps to explain why in 1984 the Republican percentages, especially, are lower than those appearing in exit polls and in certain postelection surveys. The CPS/SRC's own 1984 postelection survey shows slightly higher percentages for both Democrats and Republicans. Postelection surveys have been used in nonpresidential years. (Unlike exit polls, CPS/SRC data are from the whole electorate rather than from voters at a particular election.)

ment is like that reported by other polling organizations, including the finding by Gallup. The political significance, however, is unsettled, even apart from
the question whether the 30-year decline is a continuation or a resumption
of an earlier twentieth-century trend.

Immediately observable from the breakdowns of table 8.1 is the very large
advantage (around 20 points) of Democrats over Republicans from the 1950s
until the Republican revival of 1984 reduced, perhaps temporarily, the Democratic margin to 10 points. Both parties suffered declines during the 30-year
period, mainly in the strong identifier categories—that is, among those who
answer "strong" rather than "not so strong" when asked to choose between
those options after answering the first question " Democrat" or "Republican."
The loss is about the same for each party, and it is not compensated by an
increase in weak identifiers. Because the latter percentages changed very little
over the last three decades, we might suspect that any movement from strong
to weak identifiers was roughly balanced by a move of weak identifiers into
the independent categories. At any rate, the loss of strong Democratic and
strong Republican identifiers is obviously important. But it was not overwhelmingly large even in the 1970s, and it now appears to have been halted
or possibly reversed in the early 1980s—particularly if the Republican rise in
1984 is part of a long-term revival.

Less speculatively, the 30-year decline may be perceived as uncatastrophic
when it is realized that much of the loss of party identifiers, strong or weak,
was to those Independents who, in answering the relevant follow-up survey
question, said that they were closer to one party or the other. Such respondents, labeled Independent Democrat or Independent Republican in table 8.1,
are also appropriately called leaners. When they are added to the numbers of
initial party identifiers, as they are in the third set of rows of table 8.1, the
total of Republicans and Democrats in even most of the last decade is still
over 83 percent of the electorate and often only a few points lower than it
was in the 1950s. If so generous a definition of party identifiers is justified—
and I shall subsequently summarize the substantial though disputed evidence
in behalf of it—the rise of Independents is limited to the small numbers called
Independent-Independent in table 8.1.[40] To be sure, the percentage in that
category did increase between the 1950s and 1980s, when it reached the 11–15
percent range. Several million more citizens are thus represented as unwilling
to say that they were closer to one party or the other.

No one treats a change of that magnitude as inconsequential. But electorally, its impact is reduced by a turnout rate among pure Independents that
had so declined by the early 1980s that they are "no larger a proportion of

voters now than they were during the 1950s."[41] That finding may be related to the nature of contemporary pure Independents. A large share of the recent increase consists of respondents who do not use the word "Independent" in answering the survey question but instead say "no preference." They are not so much independent from parties as indifferent toward them. Yet they are not so indifferent to politics generally that they can be put in the apolitical category of table 8.1.[42] If their numbers were to continue to increase as they did in the 1970s, they would eventually modify the still-prevailing preponderance of party identifiers no matter how defined. But no such continuation can now be projected from the data of the early 1980s.

Because the preponderance of party identifiers is most impressive when it includes leaners, it is time to look at the justification for that inclusion. It rests on the finding, from CPS/SRC data of the mid-1970s, that leaners "are often more consistent in their support of the candidates of the party toward which they lean than are weak party identifiers,"[43] or that leaners are at least nearly as consistently partisan in their voting as are weak identifiers. From earlier surveys of reported presidential voting preferences and party identifications, Shively shows that between 1952 and 1972 the leaners adhered to their party's candidates in impressive numbers, 71 percent among Independent Democrats and 87 percent among Independent Republicans. In fact, the leaners voted for president in accord with their party preference more frequently—by 5 percentage points among Democrats and 3 percentage points among Republicans—than did weak party identifiers, and only less frequently—by 15 percentage points among Democrats and 9 points among Republicans—than did strong party identifiers. Nevertheless Shively is cautious about treating leaners as "partisans in disguise." Without rejecting that possibility, he believes that it is safer to think of them as Independents. It may be, he says, that these respondents leaned to the Democrats or the Republicans only as reflections of their voting choice—answering the question about which party they were closer to as though they had been asked how they had decided to vote in the election taking place during the period of the survey.[44] Insofar as that interpretation might be correct, the Independent Democrats and Independent Republicans would not have been responding to party cues as identifiers are ordinarily thought to respond. Their votes would not really be party votes.[45]

In any event, when casting votes for certain nonpresidential offices, leaners have been found less rather than more likely than party identifiers to behave in accord with expressed party preferences. From the 1950s into the 1970s, in choices for the U.S. Senate, the U.S. House, and governorships, both Independent Republicans and Independent Democrats departed more frequently from their party leaning than did weak identifiers from their preference.[46] Yet as in presidential voting, the leaners still showed a markedly greater partisan pattern than did pure (nonleaning) Independents. In other studies, too, with respect to nonpresidential as well as presidential office, the voting behavior of leaners is sufficiently partisan to look much more nearly like that of party identifiers than like that of pure Independents, even though it often falls somewhat short of the consistency of even the weak identifiers. Hence I believe that a persuasive case can be made, with only some qualification, for adding leaners to identifiers when calculating meaningful party preferences.

The case is most effectively made by Raymond Wolfinger and associates in a 1983 paper as well as in their earlier work. Besides citing the presidential data, which as in other studies show slightly higher partisan loyalty among leaners than among weak identifiers, they analyze voting for the U.S. House, in order to stress not the admittedly lower partisan loyalty of leaners than of weak identifiers but the still relatively high loyalty of the leaners. In the 12 House elections of 1962–82, the mean percentage of Independent Democrats who voted for Democratic House candidates was 72, compared with 77 percent among Weak Democrats and 90 percent among Strong Democrats but only 53 percent among pure Independents, 31 percent among Independent Republicans, 25 percent among Weak Republicans, and 12 percent among Strong Republicans.[47] Bolstering this impressive array of substantial though differing degrees of partisanship in leaners as well as identifiers, the same study provides considerable data on the relative stability of partisanship among Democrats and Republicans. Changes tend to be in degree of preference—leaning, weak, and strong—within each party, and less often between parties.[48]

Persuasive though Wolfinger and associates are in arguing that leaners approximate partisans and that therefore the total percentage of meaningful party identifiers is higher than the 60 to 65 percent displayed in many studies, nothing suggests the complete absence of significant change over the last three decades. On the contrary, the data just cited lend meaning to a change already observed. Note that 90 percent of Strong Democrats and almost that same high percentage of Strong Republicans (100 minus 12) voted for their party's House candidates, and that these figures are well above those for weak identifiers and leaners. Hence it is no small matter that strong identifiers appear in most recent years to have become less numerous. With fewer intense partisans and more leaners, we would surely expect and get less loyal partisan voting, even though a great deal of it remains.

From election results themselves, notably the now-usual difference between Republican presidential victories and Democratic House majorities, we readily infer extensive defection by many ostensible party identifiers and leaners.[49] But ticket-splitting during the last few decades can be more directly measured from answers to survey questions. So can the switching of parties from election to election. Summarizing the relevant CPS/SRC data for 1952–80, Wattenberg reports almost continuous increases in voting for different parties in presidential elections (from 29 to 57 percent), in ticket-splitting between presidential and House candidates (from 12 to 34 percent), in ticket-splitting between House and Senate candidates (from 9 to 31 percent), and in ticket-splitting for elections to other state and local offices (from 27 to 59 percent).[50] It is hardly surprising that Wattenberg finds in these changes support for the view that party identification has declined in importance and that the centrality of party labels may be less than the stability of those labels would lead us to believe.[51] Many more voters, though still at least loosely identifying with a party, now presumably respond to candidate appeal, either of personality, issue-orientation, or incumbency. The last of these was observed in chapter 3 as an advantage of House members standing for reelection, and it is worth noting that the 20 percent of partisan voters who defected to the House candidate of the other party in the late 1970s were about twice the number that did so in 1958.[52]

Whatever has caused less partisan loyalty in voting, the change coincides with other signs of disaffection discerned in the 1970s. For example, in analyzing CPS/SRC data from 1964 to 1972, Jack Dennis found a drop from over 40 percent to under 30 percent in respondents who said that parties helped a good deal in making government pay attention to what people want.[53] More telling, though based only on a Wisconsin sample, is Dennis's finding that between 1964 and 1976 the percentage wanting to keep party labels on the ballot decreased from nearly 70 percent to below 40 percent.[54] By other measures as well, Dennis perceived a delegitimation of partisanship in American political culture and a "partisan deinstitutionalization" as one of the major phenomena of our time.[55]

Illustrating the same tendency are the citizen evaluations of parties reported by Nie, Verba, and Petrocik in their well-known book describing the transformation in the 1960s and 1970s of the once relatively stable voter loyalties. They found, also from CPS/SRC data, that in the 1950s those who evaluated their own party positively and who had either negative or neutral views of the opposition party outnumbered those who supported neither party by more than two to one, but "by 1972 more Americans were either hostile or neutral toward the political parties than were supporters of one or the other parties."[56] Hence Nie, Verba, and Petrocik note in their general summary a decline in affection for parties along with the decline in psychological identification with parties and the decline in party as a guide to electoral choice and candidate evaluation. They conclude, "Party affiliation, once the central thread connecting the citizen and the political process, is a thread that has certainly been frayed."[57]

Frayed strikes me as an apt word for what has happened to party identification during the last three decades, particularly but not only between the mid-1960s and the mid-1970s. The word connotes a wearing that need not mean disintegration or abandonment. And it is consistent with the view that the American major-party labels are so old as to lose some of their force in a rapidly changing society, yet so institutionalized as to remain useful, if less regularly useful, cues for voters. After all, even now most voters are not merely party identifiers, by any measure, but still cast their votes most of the time for candidates carrying their party label. Furthermore, it is possible that new loyalties to the old labels will be built in response to new issues and new leaders associated with the Republican or Democratic labels. What is frayed may be mended or restored.

Now as in the past, American voters differ from voters in other nations where disenchantment with established major parties coincides with shifts to new parties or to previously minor parties. The aging in the twentieth century of our earlier electoral alignment, we have already observed, produces no new alignment. The familiar contrast is to the British electorate, whose declining attachments to the Conservative and Labour parties caused their midcentury electoral dominance to give way in the 1970s and early 1980s to a newly strengthened Liberal party, to sporadically revived Scottish and Welsh nationalists, and to an altogether new Social Democratic party.[58] Something similar though less far-reaching occurred in several continental European nations.[59] The difference between that process and the American is clear in a volume of essays on electoral change in democratic nations; explicitly, in comparison with *re*alignment discerned in other countries, the recent American experience is described as *de*alignment.[60] The occasionally popular third-party presidential candidacies, Wallace's in 1968 and Anderson's in 1980, produced nothing like the large-scale transfer of party loyalty from the old major parties that evidently occurred during the 1970s and early 1980s in other countries. Neither, it should be recalled, had any such American transfer followed from the earlier and proportionately larger votes cast for the third-party candidacies of Theodore Roosevelt in 1912 or of Robert La Follette in 1924.

The remarkable failure of new parties in the United States does not, I grant, testify to the positive attractions of the old parties. Instead, as I suggested earlier, it may well be the distinctively American institutionalization of the

Republican and Democratic labels that accounts for the continued identification of most voters with those labels. Even so, that identification has diminished in intensity and, more modestly, in frequency. The fraying is measurable and real. It is most sensitively and carefully addressed by Martin Wattenberg. Although his book's title refers to the decline of American parties, the text proclaims no inevitable process of dissolution or disintegration. By emphasizing that American feelings about party are neutral rather than negative, Wattenberg can concede that "the door remains open for party renewal."[61] At least it is open in the sense that voters may respond, as they have in the past, to the personalities and policies of leaders who themselves are strongly identified with party. In particular, one might infer that an ideologically motivated president elected for and serving two full terms could inspire that electoral response—as no one had in the decades just before the 1980s.

Wattenberg, however, is not sanguine about any such possibility, and it is fair to say that his doubts loom larger than his hopes for party renewal. The doubts are connected to his finding that party identification has become less central in voting behavior and that for voters, "the parties are losing their association with the candidates and the issues that the candidates claim to stand for."[62] Candidate-centered politics, in other words, sharply limit party loyalty. But acknowledging as much, as I surely do, is far from suggesting that our now well-established candidate-centered politics have destroyed, or will soon destroy, the significance of party identifications altogether.

IV

Interpreting the Change

Understanding the causes for the lessened attachment of American voters to party cues is more speculative than measuring the reduction in numbers of identifiers and straight-ticket voters. When the decline appears fairly modest, as it does in my presentation, it is no easier to explain. We must then try to account not only for the decline but also for its limits, in light of what might have been expected to happen to a party alignment as old as ours. Especially in a comparative perspective, what needs to be explained is why Republican and Democratic attachments have persisted so long and still serve as virtually the only, though now weakened, party attachments of American voters.

Here I hope that my earlier analysis provides the basis for an *institutional* explanation of the distinctive American phenomenon—specifically, that statutory recognition of the major parties and statutory control of their nominating practices, while organizationally disadvantageous, tend to maintain the electoral relevance of Republican and Democratic labels. Although serious candidates may now campaign and subsequently hold office with little regard for party organizations, they are as likely as ever to carry Republican or Democratic labels in general elections, often after having waged primary campaigns to secure one of the two labels that serve as cues for most voters most of the time. At the same time, the very age of these institutionalized labels helps to account for their now less commanding role.[63]

It is an important aspect of the last few decades that new youthful cohorts of voters have been less likely to identify with the old labels. Since the numbers of these voters are large, and augmented by the lowering of the voting age from 21 to 18, their behavior suggests a *generational* explanation for at least a portion of the decline in party identifiers. Whether such an explanation gives any comfort to believers in the continued significance of party identification depends a good deal on an understanding of the relevant findings. They cannot, however, be regarded as merely another instance of younger voters being less heavily identified than older voters whom they will eventually resemble as they become older themselves. For when voters are linked to the particular years of their entry in the age-eligible electorate, those able to vote for the first time in 1964 and especially in 1968, 1972, and 1976 were considerably less heavily identified with the major parties than were earlier new electoral cohorts.[64] First voters in 1980 continued in the same pattern, and in 1980, when certain pre-1972 cohorts showed a marked resurgence of party identification, only a modest strengthening of identification appeared in the 1972 and 1976 cohorts.[65] Thus in 1980, while voters over 40 became more like the party-identifying electorate of the 1950s, the generation of the 1970s remained in larger degree Independent than had earlier cohorts after two or three presidential elections.

Obviously, if the generation of the 1970s should continue to reflect its originally greater percentage of Independents and if it should be joined by succeeding generations also more heavily *and* durably Independent, the bulk of the electorate would soon have substantially fewer party identifiers. By no means, however, can such a forecast be confidently made.[66] We only know, from a sophisticated panel study of younger voters and their parents conducted through interviews in 1965, 1973, and 1982, that those entering the electorate in the late 1960s and early 1970s "have stabilized at a level of partisan loyalty notably below that of parents,"[67] but we cannot deduce from this persuasive finding that succeeding generations will behave similarly. Likely though a trend in that direction now seems, the generation of 1968–80 may turn out to be electorally untypical of the future as well as of the past. And even if later generations do resemble it, the end of Republican and Democratic identification is not inevitable. Party attachments may only be more changeable and more often compatible with deviations by way of ticket-splitting.

Insofar as a generational change suggests a long-run decline in party identification, it is often linked to an *educational* explanation. In other words, one might believe that the electoral cohorts of the late 1960s and 1970s identified less strongly with parties because they had more years of schooling rather than merely because they responded to special political circumstances in those turbulent decades. College education in particular is often thought to encourage independence and thus have produced fewer party identifiers by 1980, when 37 percent of the population had attended college in contrast to the 15 percent who had done so in 1952. Ladd and Lipset described the suspected impact over a decade ago: "Higher levels of information bearing on political issues and hence a higher measure of 'issue orientation,' along with a general feeling of confidence in one's ability to judge candidates and their programs apart from party links, are promoted by the experience of higher education."[68]

Coupled with some evidence that the Independent category has recently included more informed college-educated voters than in earlier decades, when it had been treated as a largely unconcerned-with-politics category,[69] the Ladd-Lipset emphasis seems plausible. It is, however, sharply challenged by the finding that the 1952–80 "decline in strength of party identification has been roughly parallel from one education bracket to another"—grade school, high school, and college.[70] And the challenge is bolstered by the further finding that increased split-ticket voting, like the decline in party identification, has also been approximately equal across educational categories.[71] The latter is especially important because increased ticket-splitting is a characteristic that also cuts across generational lines.[72] In other words, the young and the old, the less-educated and the college-educated, are less regularly loyal party voters than they used to be. That is consistent with the movement from strong party identification to weak and especially to leaning party identifying categories. But that movement, even if it were greater among the college-educated and among younger generations generally, would leave intact a surprisingly large portion of the old party-identifying order as long as leaners resemble, as they do, weak identifiers much more than they do the still-limited numbers of pure Independents.

Given the limited influence of generational and educational factors in accounting for the change in American electoral behavior, one turns to the widely accepted *ideological* explanation. I use the now-familiar term, although *program-*

matic or *issue-oriented* might be more appropriate when discussing American parties which have never been ideological in the doctrinaire sense of many European parties. *Left* and *right*, even *liberal* and *conservative*, are very loose terms when applied to Republicans and Democrats, now as in the past. Yet each major party has been associated with a bundle of policies, or at least a tendency toward such a bundle. Especially in the several decades beginning in the 1930s, the policies dividing the parties were those stemming from the New Deal of Franklin Roosevelt. The alignment was based heavily but not entirely on differences about business regulation, welfare expenditures, income taxes, labor legislation, and general governmental economic intervention that the Democratic national leadership supported more fully than did Republican national leadership. Roughly similar issues were significant in the politics of Truman's Fair Deal, Kennedy's New Frontier, and Johnson's Great Society. For some voters, these economic issues — all loosely called New Deal issues — only confirmed party attachments developed from earlier ideological preferences. For others, however, a party's pro- or anti–New Deal positions might have been newly attractive. For still others, such positions might have made it harder to continue maintaining traditional party attachments. In any case, party identifications during the New Deal era were not exclusively attributable to New Deal issues. Older party loyalties had endured, and they too were subject to erosion by the new issues of the 1960s and 1970s.

The new issues are familiar: civil rights (including integration and affirmative action), Vietnam and related anti-Communist military programs (now questioned as they had not been earlier), and the social issues of crime, drugs, abortion, and various aspects of the liberation of women and youth. Increasing public concern with these issues in the 1960s and 1970s is well documented.[73] A case is also made that beginning in 1964 a larger share of the public voted on the basis of issues generally, including the new issues, than had done so in the previous decade.[74] Issue voting is thus seen to have risen in importance relative to party voting in the presidential elections of 1964–72, and to have fallen back only in 1976, when party identification revived as an influence, although not to its 1956 and 1960 levels.[75]

Increased voter concern with issues need not always work against party voting. It might even reinforce party loyalties insofar as a party adopts issue positions congenial to its voters. Presumably the Democratic party did that successfully when it embraced New Deal positions in the 1930s. But it was much harder for the Democrats to take liberal positions on the new social issues, for instance, without alienating many of their economic-issue voters. And it was also harder for them to successfully champion the busing of school children or affirmative-action job opportunities for racial minorities when such policies were unfavorably perceived by many white working-class voters long identified as Democrats. Indeed, as the national Democratic party and particularly its presidential candidates were seen in the 1960s and 1970s to begin to champion such policies, they lost ground among two large groups of their old coalition, white Southerners and big-city white Catholics. In neither group, however, was there a similarly strong shift to Republican preferences in non-presidential voting.[76] Here, typically enough, the new issues appeared to weaken old party loyalties without in the 1970s producing new party loyalties in nearly as great a measure.[77] Black voters were exceptional in becoming more heavily Democratic during the last few decades. And because they were now able to vote in the South as well as the North, blacks constituted a larger share of Democratic electoral support than they had before.

Whether post-New Deal issues will produce a new party alignment and not simply the apparent dealignment of the 1960s and 1970s now depends on the capacity of the Republicans, under President Reagan and succeeding leadership, to attract more voters to their party and its candidates for other offices than president. And such attraction depends in turn on a continued coincidence, beyond 1984, of Reagan's ideologically oriented economic policies and considerable prosperity. The electoral alignment could then again be liberal versus conservative, principally although not wholly economic,[78] and yet distinct from the New Deal alignment in that the Republican party would have a more nearly equal number of identifiers. Exit polls in 1984 and surveys in the first few months after the 1984 election did show almost as many Republican as Democratic identifiers,[79] and even the figures gathered by the CPS/SRC just before that election and displayed in table 8.1 indicate a sharp Republican gain.

Much of any projected change is to be found in the South, where Republican presidential votes in almost all elections for over 20 years, not only in 1984, have run far ahead of Republican votes for other offices as well as of Republican party identification. Even an otherwise skeptical viewer of realignment concedes that the process is finally underway among white southerners.[80] *Process* is also a word used by the perceptive Republican pollster Richard Wirthlin when discussing realignment in the context of the 1984 election. In his eyes, a "rolling realignment" has been underway over a fairly long period, in contrast perhaps to the assumed shorter periods of realignment in 1894–96 and 1928–36.[81]

Reagan's conservatism extends beyond the economic sphere, where he stands for a curtailment of government regulation of business and of government spending for domestic programs. He also represents conservatism over a wide range of social issues and in foreign affairs and defense policy. Insofar as Reagan's leadership succeeds in making the Republican party appear generally conservative on noneconomic as well as economic issues while the Democratic party remains or becomes generally liberal, there would be a broader ideological basis for an electoral alignment than there was for the New Deal alignment. On the other hand, as in earlier decades, some economic-policy conservatives would not be conservative on social or foreign policy issues, and some economic-policy liberals would not be liberal on social or foreign policy issues. The cross-cutting cleavages that arose in the 1960s are also with us in the 1980s. Hence it may be more difficult than it was in the 1930s to build a party of regularly loyal identifiers. Even within a considerably realigned electorate, we seem likely to have a continuation of the recent tendency for a large minority of voters to prefer candidates whose issue positions as well as personalities are appealing regardless of party cues. So much seems inevitable, indeed natural, in a political culture where many voters believe that they have the capacity and the information to make candidate-centered choices.

One reason why more voters may now make such choices is that electronic communication brings the candidates and their personalities into American living rooms. This is a prominent element of a *technocratic* explanation for the change in voting behavior, and television does appear to be the most important of various other distinctly modern campaign methods: radio, telephone banks, computerized direct mail, professional public relations, commercial advertising, scientific polling, and specialized political management. Undoubtedly, the increased use of these methods enhances candidate-centered politics in the United States. Television and radio are conducive to the presentation of personalities, although they can also be used for party appeals. Most of the other new methods, however, appear no more suitable for candidate than for party exploitation. Yet until the last few years they were in fact used so much more fully by candidate organizations that they seemed substitutes for older party organizational means of campaigning. Thus Agranoff, writing over a decade ago, perceived that since the 1930s various technical specialists and systematic research have replaced professional party politicians and their impressionistic reports of voting behavior, and that various media, instead of organizations, are used to communicate with voters.[82]

In the 1980s, too, television is explicitly viewed, in Ranney's words, as having "preempted many of the parties' traditional functions."[83] Ranney emphasizes the preemption in the case of presidential nominations, where he sees the television news services providing the information that voters use to choose candidates in primaries that have superseded the old organizational screening of candidates.[84] But as Ranney would surely grant, television here is essentially facilitative rather than causal. It is because presidential nominating campaigns have become great participatory contests between national candidates that television plays so large a role. Television may help to maintain such contests, partly by its presentation of candidates in voters' living rooms, but it is far from being the creator of candidate-centered politics in the United States.[85]

The same point is readily made about the other modern campaign technologies. Not only have they not created candidate-centered politics, but unlike television, most of them do not seem any better suited to use by individual organizations than by party organizations. Why, then, have candidates rather than parties used the new methods so much more fully during most of the last few decades? To some degree, as the next chapter will indicate, campaign finance laws may have institutionalized fund raising by candidates and thus also their large-scale expenditures as required by the new technologies. But any such institutionalization in the 1970s was of an already well established practice of individual campaign financing.

Before the 1960s, in many places long before, most of the old state and local party organizations had ceased to dominate campaigns (insofar as they had ever done so), and they were seldom willing and able to adapt their fundraising and campaign activity to the demands of the new technologies. The modernized state party organization, described in chapter 5, was still unusual in the 1960s, and interestingly, one of them did attempt in 1968 to provide substantial technical service for its state legislative candidates.[86] For the most part, however, parties lagged well behind candidates. Their major effort began only in the late 1970s when Republican campaign committees pioneered in the expensive and massive national party services described at length in the preceding chapter. As suggested, such services turn out to have advantageous economies of scale when conducted from a central party headquarters, national as well as state, instead of separately by each legislative candidate.

While American parties are unlikely, despite the Republican national success, to replace candidates as the principal users of modern campaign technology, the experience of parties elsewhere supports the observation that the new technology itself does not produce candidate-centered politics. Available almost everywhere in the Western democratic world as in the United States, advanced technical means of campaigning have not generally diminished the dominance of parties. It is true that European parties have often employed modern advertising to promote the popularity of their individual leaders, and the leaders themselves have done so too. Television and certain other technological developments do lend themselves everywhere to direct personal appeals. But generally outside of the United States appeals for votes have remained party appeals even when advanced on the basis of the popularity of party leaders. Although television in particular often seems in Europe as in the United States to have replaced organized party workers as a means of communicating with voters, the communication, as before, is from the party. Campaigns are still party campaigns to which candidates are closely linked.[87] The United States is special in its association of modern technological communications with the decline of parties as electorally meaningful entities. But to conclude accordingly that technological developments cannot themselves explain contemporary American candidate-centered politics is not to put aside the facilitative contribution of such developments to such politics. Without modern technology, particularly that of electronic media, candidates might well have been less able to supply voters with individual cues that substitute for party cues.

On the other hand, the treatment of technological change as less than fully causal does mean that other explanations must help account for a decline in the efficacy of American party voting cues. In addition to those already offered, among which the aging of an institutionalized alignment and the rise of new issues look especially significant, an *organizational* explanation is implicitly suggested by the contrast between American and European parties in their use of the new campaign methods. Why did American parties differ not only from American candidates but also from European parties in their delayed exploitation of modern technology? To a large extent, I suspect that the answer lies in the customarily more candidate-centered nature of American politics that flows from the separate election of executive and legislative officers and, in this century, from the direct primary. Long before the last few decades, many American candidates were already accustomed to running their own campaigns and appealing for votes as individuals and not merely as partisans. Party organizations, along with party voting, were hardly pervasive, even if somewhat more consequential in the middle of this century than a little later. Most of the old machines had already disintegrated or become less effective in mobilizing voters by traditional means, and they were ill suited by structure and reputation for conversion to modern organizations capable of using the new campaign technology. Neither were the old machines being replaced, except sporadically, by mass-membership parties, nor were they being replaced, until very lately, by the professional bureaucratic headquarters exemplified by the new Republican National Committee. Whether party committees of that kind, now becoming active players in contemporary politics, can help arrest if not reverse the declining partisanship of the electorate is an open question that I shall explore in the next two chapters.

<hr />

V
Summary

Together, as well as separately, the several interpretations of the change in the frequency and behavior of party identifiers do not point toward an early massive revival of electoral partisanship. Nor, it should be emphasized, do they indicate an early demise of the heavily institutionalized Republican and Democratic alignment. Enhancing the significance of that alignment probably depends on fortuitous circumstances that no political scientist dares to project. Ideological and organizational possibilities exist, but their exploitation requires leaders, particularly presidential nominees, to associate their policies and personalities with their parties in ways that voters can find convincing at the same time that the leaders themselves find them expedient. No doubt a two-term president, preferably one whose party also controlled Congress, would be relevant for the purpose.[88] Even then, no one can be sure that voters would respond by becoming stronger and more durable partisans than they are now.

Here, however, is the place to reiterate that numerous loyal party identifiers are old and special artifacts of the American political system. They have survived a century of rapid social and economic change. The remarkable fact is that the measurable decline of party identifiers had been so modest that the overwhelming majority of American voters retain Republican and Democratic identifications. The identifications, it is true, are less strong than they used to be, and there is less straight-ticket voting. Parties have become, in Wattenberg's terms, less central in voting decisions. It appears that they provide cues for voters in the absence of countervailing candidate-centered appeals or in competition with such appeals. Party identifiers, in increased numbers, are more a group of potential supporters than the army of followers that they were thought to be in the past. But they remain significant, even if less automatically mobilized by the call to partisan electoral battle.

Chapter Nine

Private Funding
of Campaigns

Money is more than an afterthought. In this chapter and the next, it is the focus for an analysis of candidate-centered campaigns in relation to parties. Concern for that relation follows from the demonstrated decline in the centrality of party-voting cues. Without being certain about causation, we know that increasingly candidate-centered voting coincides with an increasingly candidate-centered campaigning that is funded by contributions gathered by candidates themselves. Campaigning and funding, though usually linked as candidate-centered activities, are separable analytically and even in practice. A candidate might run a campaign based mainly on personal rather than party appeals, yet be substantially financed by a party and perhaps also influenced by it. Thus parties can and do play roles even in candidate-centered campaigns.

How large a role parties will have in such campaigns, or in revived campaigns of their own, depends in part on national and state governmental legislation. Legislative regulation of private funding and legislative provision for public funding can be written to help or hinder parties. The impact of regulation is the subject of this chapter, and the impact of public funding is separately explored in the next chapter. In each area, opportunities to strengthen parties exist, but within formidable constraints imposed by the candidate-centered politics of the late twentieth century. I begin by reviewing the distinctive candidate-centered financing pattern, and then, with respect to private funding, I shall look at direct individual contributors, political action committees (PACs), the reaction to PACs, and how parties fare and might fare in the newly regulated environment.

I

The Candidate-Centered Pattern

It is worth stressing again that in other Western democratic nations, where voting cues remain more firmly party cues, campaigns are almost wholly party campaigns and their funding, whether private or public, is largely for party purposes. For example, even when British business groups financed political advertising against proposals to nationalize certain industries, they did so not in behalf of individual parliamentary candidates but to help the Conservative party, which opposed the nationalization. Similarly, British trade unions when financing particular parliamentary candidates, as they have done while also financing the Labour party's national campaign, effectively contribute to the Labour party's general cause. Under a major-party banner, a British parliamentary candidate's campaign expenditures in his constituency are his own only in a legal sense. Moreover, in Britain and other European nations, the national campaigns, often publicizing leaders and their programs by means of expensive advertising and modern technocratic methods, involve expenditures by parties and not candidates. Thus parties outside the United States dominate campaigns despite a political style that now requires roughly the same large sums of money that characterize American elections. Earlier, it is true, European parties, with their organized activists, had also, as Sorauf wrote of traditional American patronage parties, "dealt largely in nonfinancial resources." But it could not be said of European parties, as Sorauf said of American parties in 1980, that they "have never successfully made the transition to the cash economy of the new campaign politics."[1] When, like American parties, they lost certain nonfinancial resources, partly because many of their membership organizations declined in size or efficacy during recent decades, they did not yield campaign management to candidate-centered organizations.[2] Instead, parties outside the United States have ordinarily obtained the cash and used it as they have always used nonfinancial resources. Not only did they succeed in raising money from private sources, but they, more than individual candidates, secured the public funds and publicly provided communications that became available in many nations.[3]

In light of the comparison, the increased political role of financial resources cannot itself account for the American development of candidate-centered politics as a substitute for party politics. No more than the technocratic methods on which the money is spent does the cash economy of late-twentieth-century campaigns stand as a peculiarly American phenomenon. To be sure, American candidate-centered politics thrive on primarily financial resources, but the candidate-centered campaigning itself can hardly have been produced by the cash economy of modern politics when the same economy elsewhere has not led to similar campaigning. Other more distinctively American circumstances must help account for our candidate campaigns.

The relevant American circumstances are readily recalled. A constitution-ally inspired electoral separation of executive and legislative offices has led, throughout the country's history as well as recently, to more individualized campaigning than in a parliamentary system. American parties, while respond-ing with party tickets and other efforts to bridge the constitutional separa-tion, could not always suppress candidate-centered politics even in their glory days of the late nineteenth century. This is especially true of presidential and gubernatorial elections in which office-seekers often have strong incentives to ask the electorate to consider their personal capacities in addition to, if not instead of, their party labels. Significantly, when another Western democratic nation departs from the parliamentary norm and separately elects a powerful chief executive, as has France in the last few decades, a candidate-centered cam-paign develops to an extent not customarily found in parliamentary democ-racies.[4] But France, like most democratic nations apart from the United States, retains an otherwise largely uneroded party politics.

The even more uniquely American institution of the direct primary may also help explain the presence of candidate-centered politics in the United States and in particular the increase in such politics during the twentieth century. Not all candidates for American public offices, it is true, have needed to seek masses of votes in order to secure party labels. Even where no strong party organizations remain to dominate the selection process, many candidates, es-pecially incumbents, do not face serious competition for party nominations. Nevertheless, the primary can be seen to have encouraged candidate-centered campaigning often enough to be important. Traditional American party or-ganizations were simultaneously weakened by their loss of once-plentiful pat-ronage workers. Few developed the respectability and legitimacy of organized activist memberships in the European style.

Whether or not candidate-centered campaigning merely filled a gap created by already weakened parties, its development depended on private sources of campaign funds. The timing of the development is indicative. Individual can-didates and their committees, as well as parties, were already directly funded by substantial contributions from individuals and interest groups well before the granting in the 1970s of national and state governmental funds for par-ticular elections. Presidential candidate campaigns, entirely dependent on pri-vate contributions until federally funded in 1976, were the most conspicuous, but candidates in many state elections also raised their own campaign funds, and still do in most states. Strikingly, too, congressional elections, still unfunded by federal grants, became strongly candidate centered in their financing as in other respects. Changes in sources of the private contributions — numerous small rather than fewer large amounts, and notably more money from political action committees — are consequential, but they are consistent with the pattern in which private contributions from individuals and groups provided the main financial bases for the candidate-centered campaigns.

II
Individual Contributions, Large and Small

Among the private sources of campaign money, individual contributions given directly to candidates or parties are usefully distinguished from contributions by political action committees and other organized groups. Although such groups themselves collect money from individuals, they ordinarily give aggregate amounts to candidates or parties, or spend such amounts in behalf of candidates or parties as well as for their own political purposes. Separating and postponing the consideration of PACs leaves us with what is still the largest source of funds collected by candidates. For example, the largest share of all contributions to congressional candidates even in recent years has come from individuals.[5] These contributions vary considerably in size within the 1974 law's limit of $1,000 per federal candidate per election. Contributions in state elections vary within wider limits, because not all states impose effective maximums. The variation is also wide in federal elections, if one counts as contributions the legally unlimited sums that candidates themselves may supply from their own resources. I prefer such inclusion, despite the Supreme Court's ruling that candidate self-financing, as an "expenditure" rather than a "contribution," cannot be constitutionally restricted as can a contribution.[6] Practically, a candidate's own money is an alternative to contributions from others. It is no wonder that students, certainly all those I have taught, have difficulty understanding the legal distinction.

While this section treats individual contributions of all sizes, it is relevant to make a distinction between large and small amounts in an analysis of the fund-raising capacities of candidates and parties. "Large" and "small" contributions have no precise dollar equivalents in my usage. The suggested difference is between contributions so large that they ordinarily require candidates, their principal aides, or party leaders to establish personal contact with donors, and those that do not; the former are the sums suspected of purchasing political access and influence. In that light, $1,000 might not be large in a national or in a statewide campaign. Yet for most of us, a sum of several hundred dollars is a large contribution, and it is genuinely large in elections for state legislative positions and various other local offices. Personal solicitation might then be needed to secure much more than $100, or perhaps even that sum, from a single contributor. On the other hand, in national, statewide, and probably congressional elections, sums below $100 are small enough to be sought by mail, mass telephoning, and print or electronic advertising, and even sums of several hundred dollars can often be raised without cocktail parties or dinners to provide personal recognition. No one is likely to buy much access or influence in a national or statewide campaign by contributing only several hundred dollars, or for that matter $1,000, to a presidential candidate or a national party.

The elasticity of "small" contributions is marked. Relatively large amounts are raised not only because the sources are numerous but also because they include many who give more than, say, $25 at a time and often more than $100. Although I call these contributions small, in accord with a simple two-fold classification, the amounts suggest "medium-sized" giving. They are distinguishable from dues-level sums and from the modest sums collected by passing the hat at meetings. They constitute a typically middle-class pattern of political support rather than a working-class pattern associated with European socialist parties or with labor union collections in the United States. Yet the numbers who respond with medium-sized contributions, along with the still larger numbers responding more modestly to the same appeals, provide financial support on a scale only somewhat more limited than that of a party deriving its funds from many working-class members.

It should be recalled, however, that until very recently the middle-class pattern of small- to medium-sized contributions did not play nearly as important a part in twentieth-century American campaign finance as the less numerous large contributions. When our elections became expensive in cash rather than mainly in canvassing manpower, the most characteristic financial support came in large amounts, and often in very large amounts, especially for presidential and statewide campaigns. The pattern was evident in the last half of the nineteenth century and pervasive during all of this century. Almost from the start and certainly after the Civil War, the demands of the cash economy in modern American politics led to solicitation of large sums from limited numbers of wealthy persons and interests. Such solicitation was simply the most readily available means of obtaining the essential funds. The absence of dues-paying mass-membership party organizations in the United States meant that the task of gathering many small contributions was especially difficult at the national and even the state level until lately, when technologically advanced communication methods became available.

The outstanding exception was (and still is in some places) the collection of money from holders and prospective holders of government jobs that could be awarded as the spoils of election victory. Before civil service reform laws protected most federal employees from having to contribute, and similar laws did the same in most states, patronage jobholders were numerous enough to provide substantial sums. Unlike the public at large, patronage employees were easily reached. In fact, they were (and occasionally still are) assessed percentages of their government salaries. This grand old tradition of American politics goes back at least to the 1830s, although its heyday came a little later. In 1880, the victorious presidential candidate, James Garfield, appealed to his managers to assess government employees in order to finance his campaign. That presidential campaign, however, was the last in which the great bulk of federal employees could thus be legally solicited for political purposes.[7]

Few publicly mourn the passing of the large-scale assessment system in the national government or in the states where it has also been prohibited. Its remnants in certain states and cities remain the object of political reform, as does the very patronage principle of the non-policymaking jobs on which the assessment system rested.[8] Mourned or unmourned, the system, if it had survived, is unlikely to have produced the funds required in national or many statewide campaigns of the twentieth century. Even in the post-Civil War years, its use among federal employees had not sufficed. By 1868, large contributions from a relatively few sources had already begun to finance the major share of a winning presidential campaign.[9] They seem destined to be more important than the masses of patronage employees could have been either as canvassers or financial contributors. Although holders and seekers of certain government positions have continued to be important contributors, these individuals, interested in ambassadorships[10] and various policymaking positions outside of the career civil service, are themselves ordinarily prosperous enough and concerned enough to be among the limited numbers of large and fairly large givers. Their numbers, though not negligible, are too modest to supply a major share of the campaign funds now needed in a national or statewide contest.

Despite the practical limitations and the morally objectionable features of a mass-patronage basis for collecting campaign funds, it had a redeeming quality from one standpoint. The assessment system tended to support a party rather than individual candidates. No doubt candidates for president, governor, and other offices also benefited from mass employee assessments as employees received government positions from successful candidates for those offices, but the effectiveness of the system must always have depended on the continuity that a party could provide in much larger measure than a single elected official. Contributing patronage employees might count on holding their jobs as long as one or another of their party's candidates held the crucial appointing office, and the party could count on employee contributions over time, even though its candidates changed because of death, retirement, or other eventualities.

In contrast, the dominant twentieth-century pattern of large contributions from a fairly small number of contributors seems especially compatible with individual candidate campaigns. Certainly such campaigns readily adopted the pattern. So too, of course, did parties. In fact, they began to gather large contributions before candidate-centered politics became highly developed in the United States. The most famous early example is the presidential campaign of 1896, when Mark Hanna raised $3.5 million for the Republican National Committee to spend in the election of William McKinley. Operating before national laws prohibited direct contributions by corporations, Hanna collected large amounts from banks, insurance companies, and other business organizations.[11] Subsequently, in national campaigns and in some states, equivalent amounts were legally obtained from the officers and directors of such organizations and from other wealthy individuals. Before the 1970s, with virtually no laws effectively limiting the size of these contributions, they were a regular source of party as well as candidate campaigns for national, statewide, and other large-constituency offices.[12] It is true that individuals were not the only large contributors. Various organized interest groups, particularly labor unions after the 1930s, had political funds that allowed large sums to be given to parties and candidates.

Neither of the two parties as organizations remained the sole or even principal beneficiary of large contributions, despite their original exploitation of those sources. Large contributors, in twentieth-century United States, had reasons to invest in individual candidacies, and individual candidates had reasons to seek large contributions, especially when they could not count on party help in primaries and perhaps not much in general elections. For candidates, large contributors became more clearly essential to the conduct of competitive campaigns because tapping many small contributors looked even harder for them than for parties. This is not to say that the long-standing American pattern of large campaign contributions *sufficed* to produce the rise of candidate-centered politics. Large contributions (and large campaign expenditures) have existed in other nations where, as I noted earlier, parties have nevertheless continued to dominate election campaigns. Thus, I stress only the special suitability of large contributions for candidate-centered campaigns.

The usefulness of large contributions is demonstrable from their widespread collection by candidates during most of this century. Until limited in the mid-1970s, such contributions to candidate campaigns were a much more distinctively American pattern than the rising total campaign expenditures that critics so often deplored. American campaign expenditures have not been unusually high by foreign standards,[13] but as they increased in the 1950s and 1960s, partly because of expensive television time, they led to the solicitation of more large contributions. The most spectacular example was Nixon's presidential reelection campaign of 1972. His campaign war chest was filled mainly by limited numbers of very large contributors, and it was his own war chest or specifically his campaign committee's rather than the Republican party's.[14] Large if not always enormous contributions also characterized earlier mid-century presidential campaigns. For example, sums of $500 or more provided 69 percent of Truman's funds and 74 percent of Dewey's in 1948 when $500 was still a large amount of money. Givers of $10,000 or more numbered about 100 in 1952, 1956, and 1960, 130 in 1964, and 424 in 1968. Roughly similar patterns of very large contributions appeared in congressional races through 1972.[15] The sources included interest groups as well as wealthy individuals; significantly, their money by 1972 went much more heavily to candidates than to parties. As for individual contributors, the most dramatic figures are those for "centimillionaries." Of the 66 persons whom *Fortune* magazine so listed in 1968, 46 contributed $3.7 million to various Republican and Democratic candidates and committees in 1968, and 51 contributed $6.1 million in 1972.[16]

Nothing about the greater attention directed to national data, now more systematically available, should lead one to overlook the pervasiveness of the large-contribution pattern in state campaigns.[17] Allowing for state-by-state variations based on different customs as well as different laws, the importance of big-givers has been directly related to the size of the constituency. Thus statewide races for governor and for the U.S. Senate, especially in populous states, have been more heavily financed by large contributors (including rich candidates themselves)[18] than have most contests for the U.S. House of Representatives or state legislative offices.[19] State campaigns in general have also long benefited from large gifts. In 1952, for example, it is estimated that between 33 and 50 percent of state political funds came in amounts of $500 or more, and between 25 and 33 percent in amounts of $100 to $499.[20] Moreover, in at least one state in the 1960s, it was found that the larger contributions were more heavily relied on by statewide candidates than by party committees.[21] Generally, too, statewide candidate contribution totals have been impressive; many campaigns for governor and U.S. Senator were, and are, more expensive per vote than presidential campaigns.[22]

Although over a period of time large contributions in statewide as well as national elections became especially characteristic of candidate campaigns, party organizations at both the national and state levels surely continued to solicit, often with success, the same large donors. At the same time, candidates even in large constituencies frequently sought funds from small contributors as well as from their fewer and more important large contributors. Of course both parties and candidates sought money from large and small contributors alike, but at least until the 1960s, neither parties nor candidates had much success in raising large sums from numerous small and genuinely voluntary contributors.[23]

Parties, it might well be thought, would have special incentives to seek the large number of contributors that could give them sustained support for headquarters operations between elections as well as during campaigns. The need for continuity in such operations at national, state, and local levels suggests the usefulness of a large dues-paying membership to support organizational activities. Usually, however, American parties have not had regularized dues-payers to finance modern headquarters; the old patronage-based clubs, Tammany style, existed on a smaller scale and for another purpose. Most American parties thus differed not only from many twentieth-century parties elsewhere, and particularly from European labor or social democratic parties, but also from American labor unions that successfully collected political funds as well as standard dues from a mass membership.

Moreover, until lately most American parties differed from the many other American political groups substantially funded by large numbers of supporters serving as regular contributors if not dues-paying members. Despite earlier efforts to use direct-mail and other mass appeals,[24] only since the late 1970s have national party committees (notably Republican committees) succeeded in regularly collecting small sums from numerous givers in the manner of nonparty political groups. Now, as described in chapter 7, likely supporters are asked (usually by mail) to contribute to a party cause as they are asked to contribute to a nonparty political cause, like that of the environment, anti-abortion, liberalism, or conservatism, and also much as they are asked to contribute to a charity. Status as a "contributing" or "sustaining" member may be conferred, but the contact between organization and contributor tends to be exclusively by mail. The contributing pattern also differs from that of an ordinary dues-paying membership in that individual contributions vary considerably in accord with the elasticity of the "small" contribution category.

Although American parties now raise large sums from great numbers of small contributions, it is significant that in the 1960s and early 1970s certain presidential candidates were more dramatically successful than parties in exploiting the method. Barry Goldwater pioneered in 1964 when 300,000 persons contributed to his prenomination campaign after his televised appeal for funds. Following similar appeals during the general election campaign, still more contributors responded, so that altogether the committees working in behalf of his candidacy obtained 72 percent of their funds in individual contributions under $500 from about 650,000 persons (many of whom, of course, gave much less than $500). George Wallace reached even more small contributors to support his third-party presidential candidacy of 1968; 750,000 persons gave in amounts of less than $100, evidently in most instances much less than $100, and they provided 85 percent of the $6.7 million that Wallace raised from February to October, 1968. Wallace's scale of solicitation was followed by George McGovern's in 1972. Using, like Wallace, direct-mail and television appeals, McGovern stressed $25 contributions and received between $14 million and $15 million from 750,000 individuals for his primary and general election campaigns. Only a little more than a quarter of McGovern's total campaign fund came in gifts larger than $100.[25]

In addition to their great success in obtaining small contributions, the Goldwater, Wallace, and McGovern campaigns share other characteristics. All three went after such contributions *before* federal laws put effective limits on the size of individual contributions to campaigns for national office. It was not yet legally necessary for aspiring presidential candidates to broaden their financial support. In 1964–72 the only existing necessity was one that affected certain presidential candidates but not others, including the winning candidates. Goldwater, Wallace, and McGovern, while having access to some large contributors, could not raise enough money for serious campaigns unless they obtained it from contributors of modest amounts, who had until then seldom been directly tapped for national or other large-constituency campaigns.

Much has also been said about the ideological nature of each of the three innovative fund-raising efforts. In their different ways, Goldwater, Wallace, and McGovern did take more sharply defined positions on salient issues than have many other major-party presidential candidates. No doubt they were thus attractive to persons likelier to give to conservative or liberal causes than to consensual parties and their pragmatic, compromising candidates. By no means, however, is it clear that only ideological appeals, or only strongly ideological appeals, can raise money in this way. Beginning in 1976, under the stimulus of the new federal laws, less sharply ideological candidates (like Jimmy Carter) have obtained many gifts of less than $250 in order to qualify for federal matching funds in expensive presidential primary campaigns. The growing success in the 1980s of the Republican National Committee, too, and of related Republican Senate and House campaign committees, suggests (as noted in chapter 7) that direct-mail appeals are effective even though only broadly and loosely ideological. The general Republican conservatism of the early Reagan years was sufficient for fund raising even in competition with more stridently and more sharply focused conservative-cause organizations that were similarly successful in raising large sums from many small contributions.

More credible than ideological intensity as an explanation of recent national mass solicitation of small contributions is the technological development of the means by which parties and candidates can efficiently conduct their solicitation. After all, small contributions, often obtained personally, had long been important for campaigns in smaller than statewide constituencies.[26] Once computerized direct-mail lists and addressing devices became available, parties lagged only a decade or so behind nonparty groups in exploiting the means for reaching their contributors on a national scale. The time lag was just long enough to indicate the unmodern character of midcentury American parties.

Perhaps the lag would have been longer if it had not been for the campaign finance legislation of the 1970s. Now parties as well as candidates, a few of whom had already conducted successful national mass solicitation by television if not by direct mail, had another reason to broaden their fund raising. Regulations by the states, about half of which have limited the size of individual contributions, were of some consequence in this respect,[27] but new national laws had the most marked impact. Like state-imposed limits, the national laws of the 1970s rest on a moral distinction between large and small contributions. Those so large as to suggest that givers might be buying influence are prohibited; specifically, in the decade after the mid-1970s, with no provision for inflation-linked increases, a contributor could give in presidential and congressional elections no more than $1,000 per candidate per election (that is, $1,000 in a primary and another $1,000 in a general election), no more than $5,000 a year to a PAC, no more than $20,000 a year to a national party committee, and no more than $25,000 a year altogether.[28] These upper limits allow only "fairly large" contributions—in practice, a few times more than the specified amounts because of separately listed contributions from members of the same family.

Nevertheless, the totals that even the most extended family might contribute within the legal limits are modest by comparison with past experience. Given these limits, candidates and parties would find it difficult to mount expensive campaigns if they depended mainly on small numbers of individual contributors. Apart from PAC contributions, two significant exceptions appear: first, wealthy candidates can use unlimited amounts of their own family resources; and second, other wealthy individuals, as well as groups, can spend on their own, independently of candidates and parties, even though such expenditures are designed to help particular candidates or parties. Both exceptions were created by the U.S. Supreme Court when it invalidated portions of the relevant congressional legislation while upholding what it regarded as valid limits on the size of contributions, as the Court and Congress defined that term.[29] Expenditures by candidates of their own money and "independent" expenditures by others were not all that the Court put outside the bounds of legislative regulation. Ceilings on candidate *expenditures* generally, whether from the candidate's own funds or from the contributions of others, were declared unconstitutional (unless a candidate voluntarily accepted a ceiling along with public funds). But in upholding *contribution* limits, the Court, like the Congress and probably much of the American public, accepts the invidious distinction between large and small contributions, or at least between very large contributions and all others. One consequence is to encourage parties and candidates to raise more money in small contributions although continuing to collect contributions that are large according to the criteria that most of us use.

Legal encouragement of small contributions also came in a more positive form in the 1970s. Providing at first a choice between a small tax credit and a somewhat larger deduction for political contributions, Congress in 1978 settled on the tax credit of 50 percent, fixing the maximum credit at $50 on a single return or $100 on a joint return.[30] For example, a couple giving $200 in a year could claim a tax credit of $100 and, as a result, a net cost of only $100 when contributing the $200. It is uncertain, however, that the tax saving has caused many citizens to contribute who would not otherwise have done so.[31] Possibly more effective as a stimulus for modest political giving is legislation inducing presidential primary candidates to obtain amounts of $250 or less in order to qualify for federal funds available to match individual contributions only in those limited amounts. The incentive for candidates is substantial. Simply put, four or more contributions, each no greater than $250 but which total $1,000, will bring $1,000 of federal money, and that is a good deal more than a single $1,000 contribution brings. As will be observed in chapter 10, not only have candidates responded, but so have givers in turn responded to the candidates.

The legally provided encouragements are still so recent, however, that their durable impact is hard to estimate. Large contributions might revive with an expansion of already evident legislative loopholes. Or fund raising by direct mail, despite its continuing success in the early 1980s, might eventually burden the public with so many appeals that all become less productive. Even if small political contributions remain popular, as seems more likely, will they be particularly useful to parties? Undoubtedly, national and state party organizations have special incentives to broaden their financial support; their more or less permanent bureaucratic existence makes it possible for them to collect small contributions in large numbers, as the solicitation by the national Republican committees in the late 1970s and early 1980s has impressively demonstrated. Among candidates, those seeking the presidency and some seeking statewide offices have shown a similar capacity. But fund raising through direct mail has been difficult for the less well known individuals who seek seats in the U.S. House of Representatives. Several House members soliciting money for reelection campaigns in the early 1980s found that the return was not worth the effort.[32] At their level as well as in still smaller constituencies, candidates appear to be at a disadvantage in direct-mail solicitation. The disadvantage is in relation to presidential and perhaps statewide candidates, and also to parties and PACs, whose solicitation is often in larger constituencies than theirs and in any case is regularly bureaucratized.

III
Political Action Committees

During the first years of legally induced dependence on small individual contributions, political action committees more than parties became known as collectors and dispensers of campaign funds. Indeed, they became so prominent that they appeared to be *the* organizational financiers of an increasingly candidate-centered politics. Whether PACs are thus actually displacing parties is a possibility that I shall skeptically explore.

PACs, at the least, are now the highly publicized and evidently effective means by which interest groups of all kinds pursue their long-standing political purposes in election campaigns. Special-interest money is hardly new in

American politics. Before the mid-1970s, it came in large sums from individuals and groups of individuals often acting in behalf of corporations that were themselves prohibited, by the federal law of 1907 and by some state laws, from contributing their own funds. Not only was the size of each contribution unlimited, but many large contributions from suspicious sources undoubtedly escaped disclosure.[33] Businesses, agricultural producers, professional associations, and many other economic interests found ways to finance campaigns long before the 1970s. Noneconomic groups also played important political roles in campaigns as well as in lobbying. For example, the Anti-Saloon League and its allies were spectacularly successful single-issue groups when, early in the century, they secured congressional and state legislative approval of the constitutional amendment prohibiting the manufacture and sale of alcoholic beverages. Such groups were more conspicuous in lobbying legislators than in electing them, but the two activities were linked even as they are today.

The PAC itself, under that name or a variation, can be traced back to the 1930s when labor unions established affiliated political education committees, and more plainly from the next decade when, first in 1943 and then definitively in 1947, federal law prohibited unions, like corporations, from contributing their own funds to political campaigns. To comply with federal law and similar laws in certain states, union committees became separate organizations. They collected money from union members, subsequently distributing aggregated sums to candidates or parties, and they also spent in behalf of candidates or parties. The best-known midcentury example was the Committee on Political Education (COPE) of the AFL-CIO.[34]

By the 1960s, similar committees were organized by several general and particularized business associations, by specialized professional societies (medical practitioners most prominently), and by individuals dedicated to ideological causes.[35] Among the ideological groups, both the conservative Americans for Constitutional Action and the liberal National Committee for an Effective Congress collected funds from a fair number of contributors for distribution to candidates in constituencies often well removed from the states in which most contributors lived.

A general pattern of the PAC type of activity thus existed before it became more pervasive and threateningly dominant after the mid-1970s. The early PACs, while in many instances collecting large contributions from wealthy donors, also collected small or modest contributions from many others. Obviously, union PACs did so through their ready access to dues-paying members who could persuasively be asked for additional sums for political purposes. Certain other PACs, notably ideological ones and various other nonbusiness groups, began, however, to gather small contributions through the mail. Whether the contributions were large or small or a combination of the two, the collecting PAC could serve candidates as parties also sought to do—by giving a substantial aggregate amount that a candidate would have had trouble raising alone (especially in small donations), or by buying services or advertising in behalf of a candidate or slate of candidates.

PAC is now the generic though not the statutory term for any nonparty committee raising and spending money in election campaigns. In 1984, over 4,000 PACs registered with the Federal Election Commission (FEC), and about 3,000 made contributions to federal candidates. Many PACs operate in the states. They have been established by labor unions, business corporations, trade associations, professional societies, and various other economic and noneconomic interest groups. Familiar examples are the UAW-V-CAP of the United Auto Workers, the Amoco PAC, the Realtors PAC, the American Medical Association's AMPAC, and the National Rifle Association's NRA Political Victory Fund. Notable also are the nonconnected PACs created by no union, business, or association but separately by groups devoted to a particular issue, set of issues, or broad ideological cause. Examples are the National Conservative Political Action Committee (NCPAC) and the older National Committee for an Effective Congress (NCEC). Nonconnected PACs ordinarily solicit from a less well defined constituency than do labor, business, and association PACs, which solicit within their own ranks, and they often dispense most of their funds themselves rather than contributing to candidates in the manner of most connected PACs. Still other kinds of PACs are created by prospective candidates themselves, or by groups acting for them. Nevertheless a PAC is distinguished, under the law, from a candidate's official campaign committee and from a party committee. Most of the important PACs are "multicandidate" committees and thus qualified under the 1974 federal law to give $5,000 to a candidate for a primary and $5,000 for a general election.[36]

Although PACs are not defined by name under federal law, they are, like party and candidate committees, regulated by the Federal Election Commission (and by various state agencies for state elections). Besides being subject to regulation and disclosure, federal PACs differ from the old interest-group pattern of funding in that they have been prohibited by law from collecting more than $5,000 a year from any one person and from contributing more than $5,000 to a federal candidate per election or more than $15,000 a year to committees of a national party. Like individuals, they can spend unlimited amounts independently of particular candidates, but the contribution-to-candidate limit, while five times as high as that allowed individuals, is restrictive compared with the easy giving of the past. And, most significantly, the limit of $5,000 on an individual contribution to a PAC, while again substantially higher than the individual-to-candidate limit, precludes the acquisition by PACs of huge sums from only a few very large contributors. Contemporary PACs thrive financially because of the numerous small and medium-sized contributions they secure by direct mail, personal contact, and payroll deductions.

Partly because PACs gather their funds from a multitude of givers, their champions proclaim not only the legitimacy of interest-group representation but also the democratic virtues of participation by large numbers of modest contributors. The participation is even viewed as now somehow more appropriate than traditional party involvement. For example, Lee Ann Elliott, formerly the associate executive director of AMPAC and subsequently a member of the Federal Election Commission, has called PACs the "Precincts of the '80's."[37] Their "precincts" are not small geographic units, like wards and districts that provided building blocks for our old parties, but rather economic or other issue-oriented concerns shared by individuals on a national or statewide basis.

Although interest groups have always transcended neighborhoods in mobilizing their members, PACs now do so openly, on a large scale, and in ways especially well suited to candidate-centered politics. They developed rapidly after the mid-1970s, and not only because interest-group politics were filling a gap created by the absence of strong party organizations. The growth of PACs, and most specifically the growth of business PACs to match or outmatch the already existing labor union PACs, is in large part attributable to the campaign finance legislation of the 1970s. By allowing a PAC to obtain $5,000 from an individual and in turn to contribute $5,000 to a candidate, while an individual could give a candidate only $1,000, the new federal limits plainly made PACs more useful than they would have been when persons could contribute unlimited amounts to candidates. They were well situated to raise large sums from their many contributors. Nor was that legislated advantage the only statutory change favorable to PACs in the 1970s.

Most directly helpful to PACs was a legitimation of their structure that occurred in the early 1970s.[38] Although business PACs turned out to be its chief beneficiaries, the legitimation was prompted by the concern of labor unions to maintain their already large-scale PACs, whose operations were being challenged in the courts. In seeking congressional action in 1972 to establish clearly the legality of their sponsorship of PACs, the unions drafted a crucial amendment to the Federal Election Campaign Act of 1971. To enhance its political acceptability, the amendment specified that corporations could communicate on any subject (including politics) with their stockholders as unions could with their members; that corporations as well as unions could conduct nonpartisan registration and get-out-the-vote drives in their respective constituencies; and, most significantly for the future of PACs, that company money, like union money, could be spent to establish and administer a separate segregated fund for political purposes. Thus a corporation, like a union, could finance a PAC that would collect contributions for subsequent expenditure or distribution to candidates and parties. In 1974 these provisions became still more useful, when further legislation provided that corporations and labor unions with government contracts were not prohibited from establishing PACs. Again, labor unions led the effort to broaden the opportunities for PACs. They certainly succeeded.

Business corporations soon began to use the new legal opportunities on a scale that labor unions must not have envisioned. A precipitating cause was a very liberal interpretation of the legislation by the Federal Election Commission (FEC) in its 1975 ruling on the Sun Oil Company's PAC. That interpretation was modified by a 1976 statute, but the statute's modest limits on solicitation by corporate PACs were less important than its provision authorizing payroll deductions for union PACs when corporate PACs also made use of such deductions to collect their contributions.[39] Most of the stimulus to corporate PACs remained.[40] They could still solicit all employees and their families twice a year, and their executive or administrative personnel and their families, as well as stockholders, as often as they liked.[41]

In a general sense, another pro-PAC impact can be traced to campaign finance legislation. Before the 1970s, with hardly any effective legal limits on individual and party fund raising and expenditures, only corporations and unions, it has been pointed out, "faced significant constraints on their political activity; after the amendments, all political activity was heavily regulated."[42] In other words, PACs were beneficiaries of legal equalization. Some of that equalization stemmed from constitutional doctrines developing at about the same time as the statutory reforms. PACs, like individuals, could not be subject to the expenditure ceilings invalidated by *Buckley v. Valeo* in 1976. Nor, it later became clear, could they be subject to a ceiling even when their "independent" spending was to help a candidate who had accepted a ceiling as a condition for the receipt of public funds.[43] Here PACs were freer than parties, whose expenditures to help particular candidates were not, apparently by definition, "independent," but were, like contributions, legally limited.

The conspicuous users of that constitutionally provided opportunity were nonconnected, ideological PACs, chiefly those supporting Ronald Reagan in

1980 and 1984. But unlimited independent expenditures are options also available to the connected PACs. The point is important because such PACs, while now concentrating on contributions to candidates, might well turn to constitutionally protected independent expenditures if their contributions were more stringently limited by law. Indeed, under recent judicial interpretations of the First Amendment, corporations themselves, not merely their PACs, enjoy constitutional protection when spending money to influence public policy in referendum campaigns.[44] It is less certain that such protection extends to corporation expenditure in behalf of candidates.[45] If it did, corporations could spend for (but not contribute to) candidates from their own funds. Such expenditures might well be larger than those that corporate-created PACs now make.

The rapid growth of PACs after legal legitimation in the early 1970s is readily apparent from data on committees required to register with the Federal Election Commission (FEC) because of their participation in federal elections. Similar growth occurred in states reporting registration of PACs operating in their elections, but the national figures to be cited here are impressive enough. Most dramatic though not most telling is the increase in the number of PACs. From only 113 in 1972, when the new legislation went into effect, the number rose to 608 by the end of 1974, to 2,000 by the end of 1979, to 3,371 by the end of 1982, and to 4,009 by the end of 1984.[46] The totals reflect increases in all types of PACs, but most notably in corporate PACs, numbering 1,682 in 1984 (compared to 89 in 1974) and nonconnected PACs (1,053 in 1984 compared to 110 in 1977). Trade, membership, and health association PACs, 698 of which existed in 1984, had roughly doubled in number over ten years, and so had labor union PACs in reaching 394 in 1984. Overall, the increase in numbers slowed somewhat in the early 1980s, after the spectacular growth of the 1970s, but not enough to suggest that the number of PACs had reached its conceivable maximum. At any rate, because many PACs (especially corporate PACs) are small and inactive, their number is a less important indicator of their political role than the dollars that all of them collect and distribute. Here too the growth has been large and rapid—from expenditures of $19.1 million in 1972 to over $190 million in 1982 and to almost $267 million in 1984—and in all types of PACs, although the increases by labor PACs were less spectacular than those by nonlabor PACs.[47]

Of the $190 million spent by PACs in 1981–82, over $83 million was in contributions to House and Senate candidates. Of the nearly $267 million they spent in 1984, over $105.3 million went to those candidates.[48] Contributions, the major form of disbursement by connected but not by nonconnected PACs, became the object of critical attention because they appear to make congressional candidates increasingly dependent on financing by the economic interests that the PACs represent. "Increasingly dependent" refers especially to House candidates, for whom PAC money constituted 31 percent of all their receipts in 1982 and 34 percent in 1984, compared to 17 percent in 1974. The Senate figures were 18 percent in 1982 and 17 percent in 1984, compared to 11 percent in 1974.[49] Over the whole decade, the larger contributing role of PACs coincided with generally rising campaign costs, even beyond the rate of inflation, and thus with increased fund raising from all sources. But PAC contributions to House and Senate candidates were well over ten times as great as party contributions in 1982 and 1984. The difference is much less sharp though still large when the parties' coordinated expenditures in behalf of candidates are taken into account.

By one measure, however, parties in the 1980s were not financially overshadowed by PACs. In total 1981–82 disbursements under federal election laws, the two major parties spent over $254 million, compared to the $190 million spent by all PACs. The $254 million includes money spent by Republican and Democratic national committees, Senate and House campaign committees, and state and local party committees participating in federal elections. The bulk of it—$215 million—was Republican money. Then in 1984, when Democratic party expenditures sharply increased to $97 million and the Republican party total rose to over $300 million, the two-party total of nearly $400 million was still farther ahead of the total PAC expenditures of about $267 million.[50] The now very large party expenditures indicate a capacity both to raise money and to spend it in order to foster the cause of Republican or Democratic candidates in less direct ways than by contributions to candidates or by coordinated expenditures in behalf of candidates. General party expenditures, legally unlimited much as are independent expenditures by PACs, may be less useful to particular candidates than contributions or coordinated help, but their very size suggests as much significance as the often noticed large independent expenditures of ideological, nonconnected PACs (over $3 million, for example, by NCPAC in 1982).

However much party expenditures as well as the still dominant individual contributions provide a balancing perspective, the role of PACs remains impressive. In some respects it is even more impressive than the gross figures have indicated. Some PACs provide in-kind services to candidates that rival those of parties and that can be calculated so as to be reported at much less than cost.[51] In particular, labor unions and their PACs engage in a great deal of political activity—voter registration, for instance—that is useful to candidates whom they support but that is not subject to legal spending limits.

The importance of contributions to candidates by connected PACs is further enhanced by a concentration that is possible despite the legal limit on per-candidate contributions and the regulatory rule against separate contributions by affiliates or spin-offs of a given PAC. It is legal for a PAC to transfer funds to another PAC, and for a PAC to persuade another PAC to contribute. Nor can PACs with closely related economic or other interests — say, each of several different oil and gas company PACs or union PACs — be prevented from giving up to the maximum contribution. Thus a set of interests may provide certain candidates with a very large sum of money. Another kind of concentration exists when a given PAC contributes near the maximum to each of many congressional candidates. Prime examples are the total contributions in 1982 and 1984 of $2.1 million and $2.4 million by the Realtors PAC, of $1.7 million and $1.8 million by the American Medical Association's PAC, of $1.6 million and $1.4 million by the UAW-V-CAP, of $1.4 million and $1.3 million by the Machinists Non-Partisan Political League, and of $1.2 million and $1.6 million by the National Education Association PAC.[52] Still more pointedly concentrated is the distribution of these and other PAC contributions so as to favor most incumbents. An evidently incidental result of proincumbent giving is that Democrats, predominant in the House, have received more PAC money than Republicans. For instance, in 1984 when PAC contributions to House and Senate incumbents were over 70 percent of PAC contributions to all federal candidates, incumbent Democrats received so much that they, together with nonincumbent Democratic candidates, had nearly 57 percent of all PAC contributions.[53]

In giving disproportionately to incumbents, whether Democrats or Republicans, PACs add to the advantage that sitting members, as power-holders, established dispensers of favors, and likely winners, have in raising money from individual contributors too. When 67 percent of all PAC money in 1982 House races went to incumbents, about 55 percent of all other money also went to incumbents, so that they had about 59 percent of total receipts in House contests. Only in open-seat races and occasionally when challengers are unusually promising do nonincumbents have fund-raising opportunities among PACs or individuals that match those of incumbents.[54]

Granting that PAC resources are somewhat more heavily concentrated than contributions generally does not mean that all PACs give heavily to incumbents. Nor are all PACs large contributors. A vast majority of PACs have not given the $5,000 maximum to any candidate and in 1982 the median PAC contribution to a House candidate was about $500 and to a Senate candidate

about $1,000.[55] Similarly modest figures appear with respect to the sources
of PAC money. Average contributions *to* PACs have been put at less than $100.
Even average contributions to corporate PACs are not much above that level,
and average contributions to union PACs are lower.[56] Plainly, then, PACs are
tapping a great number of contributors for modest amounts, much as are the
national party committees. That is hardly surprising with respect to the nonconnected, ideological PACs, several of which had reached direct-mail contributors in large numbers before parties did so, or with respect to labor PACs
that had earlier succeeded in collecting money, though not by direct mail,
from masses of union members. Corporate as well as trade association PACs
(themselves not so new) have joined the process, and on a scale that adds many
additional givers of campaign dollars.

How many Americans altogether contribute to PACs can only be estimated.
Figures of eight to ten million in 1980 might be inferred from the positive
responses of 7 percent of the sampled electorate to a survey question asking
whether respondents had contributed to PACs. Also, seven percent said that
they had contributed to a candidate, and 4 percent to a party.[57] The rates are
suspiciously high, since many interviewed citizens are believed to overstate
their political involvement. On the other hand, underreporting is possible among
those whose contributions to PACs are through payroll deductions.[58] Nevertheless, for federal PACs, Frank Sorauf made a more conservative estimate.
Dividing total PAC receipts by an average contribution and then discounting
by 20 percent to allow for repeat contributors, he arrived at 2.9 to 4.8 million
PAC contributors in 1980.[59] Less spectacular than higher figures inferred from
survey results, the numbers are still strikingly large. They are larger, though
not overwhelmingly larger, than the now substantial numbers of those who
contribute to the several national party committees.

The nearly simultaneous growth of party and PAC contributions in the
last decade should itself raise doubts about projected replacement of parties
by PACs. Competitive solicitation obviously occurs between a party and certain nonconnected ideological PACs, for example between the Republican National Committee and NCPAC, and both parties and ideological PACs spend
most of their money for general political purposes. But it is not the ideological
PACs that are supposed to constitute the "Precincts of the '80s"; it is the vast
array of interest-group PACs whose solicitations take place within their organizations. Such fund raising can be viewed as complementary to that of
parties and candidates; the money is mainly for contributions rather than for
expenditures in a PAC's own political cause. Most connected PACs do not

have the size, breadth, or inclination to rival parties. Labor PACs are exceptional, but their long-standing performance of party-like functions has been
in collaboration with the Democratic party.

PACs, especially connected PACs, do appear to substitute for parties in that
their share of congressional campaign receipts rose during a decade when the
party share declined. For House candidates between 1972 and 1978, the PAC
percentage of all receipts rose from 14 to 25, while the party percentage dropped
from 17 to 4. By 1984, when the PAC percentage was 34, the party percentage
was about 3.[60] The lowered party shares conceal recent increases in absolute
amounts by way of contributions, and they omit the growing coordinated
party expenditures in behalf of candidates. Note, too, that individual contributions, still providing the largest share of all receipts in congressional elections, would presumably have grown more vastly without the $1,000 limit.
Indeed, insofar as PAC dollars substitute for any older source, it may well be
the heavy contributors whose place PACs have taken in campaign finance. That
process may be nearly completed as the rising curve of PAC contributions as-
cended a little less sharply in the 1980s than in the 1970s. Still, the increased
number of PACs makes it likely that total PAC contributions will continue
to be much greater than total party contributions. The 1974 law itself works
in that direction. Each of a few thousand PACs can contribute up to the same
$5,000 limit imposed on the much more limited number of party committees
in House elections. Even when those committees, notably the Republican,
have very large funds to spend, their contributions are legally limited and they
spend far larger amounts for general purposes than for contributions.

PACs, it should be recalled, contribute to parties as well as to candidates.
Under the law allowing up to $15,000 a year from a PAC to a national party's
committees, about one-third of the PACs gave at least something to parties
in 1981–82. Their total contributions to parties then came to $6 million, and
the figure rose to over $10 million in 1983–84. Although the amounts are
well below those that PACs give to House and Senate candidates and are only
about 2.5 percent of all party funds, the contributions are hardly negligible.
Not only might they increase in response to still more diligent party fund
raising, but the direct monetary contribution to parties is only one of the ways
in which PACs may serve party interests. Labor union PACs do so in well-
established channels, and more recently, corporate and other PACs have been
exposed to considerable party influence with respect to supporting candidates.
Except for certain nonconnected ideological PACs that may be hostile to parties, the opportunity is at least open for a party to persuade a PAC, or a given

set of similarly interested PACs, to support candidates identified with a common program. The relationship is aptly described as a "mating dance."[61] The dance has by no means ended.

IV
Reacting to Political Action Committees

My presentation of PACs reflects a neutral—I am tempted to say an objective—view of their role that is uncharacteristic of public discussion of the subject. Far from accepting PACs as open and relatively respectable means for interest groups to help finance campaigns, many commentators treat them as corrupters of politics. PACs, much more than parties, now embody the menacing special interests which the heirs of the progressive tradition would restrict. Reform-minded critics are not, however, so much interested in strengthening parties at the expense of PACs as they are in limiting large-scale private funding generally, by PACs or parties. Reformers are possible allies when pro-party advocates turn to public funding, but with respect to private funding, they are unlikely to share the pro-party advocacy of massive party organizational resources. They share only the reaction to PACs as representatives of special interests—for which parties would substitute their proclaimed broader coalitional interests, and general reformers the still broader "public interest."

At any rate, the general anti-PAC reaction of reformers is potentially of enough indirect benefit to parties, if only by curtailing the relative importance of PACs, to make it worth considering here before we turn to the regulatory measures designed to help parties directly. How extensive is the anti-PAC reaction? More explicitly, are the well-known views of reformers held by a large portion of the public? A negative answer would be surprising in light of the bad press inherent in periodic reports of large aggregate contributions by PACs (or a set of related PACs) to powerful incumbent members of Congress, and of the large expenditures by nonconnected ideological PACs to defeat or elect certain candidates. Relentlessly, the news is of the size, growth, and concentration of PAC money. FEC releases themselves pinpoint such items, and the news media understandably add emphasis even when they do not sensationalize the stories. Occasionally, too, news reports are based on alarmist press releases from critics of PACs like Common Cause. Rarely if ever do the media find it newsworthy to tell us about how many small and modest contributions PACs receive and distribute or about how small and various are the PACs that now exist. Predictably, then, the public has a fairly adverse view of PACs in general, and especially of corporate PACs, when asked survey questions about them or about the desirability of limiting them.[62] The significance of the adverse opinion, however, is reduced somewhat by the favorable views that majorities have of certain PACs and by the absence of knowledge of PACs by many respondents. Popular support for curbing PACs is not overwhelming, but it is widespread.

A good deal of public anti-PAC sentiment can be inferred from the behavior of politicians. Not only have many legislators supported proposals to curb PACs, but they have attacked their opponents for accepting PAC money, particularly the money of out-of-state PACs or of large PACs perceived to be buying influence for private interests. Some candidates have refused to accept PAC money, or particular PAC money, in their own campaigns. Conspicuously indicative of the ill repute of PACs was the pledge of Walter Mondale and Gary Hart to reject PAC contributions in their presidential nominating campaigns of 1984, and the subsequent commitment by Mondale, under criticism from Hart, to return PAC money that had been collected by his delegate committees (though not by Mondale's own committee). The original pledge was itself disingenuous; PAC contributions are not very relevant for a presidential candidate's committee as long as that committee's nominating campaign is financed partially by federal funds matching only *individual* contributions up to $250. Moreover Mondale, while not collecting financial contributions from unions, hardly shunned the AFL-CIO's endorsement or the expensive and active support of its member unions, and Hart had obtained large union PAC contributions for his Senate reelection campaign of 1980. But any hypocrisy in the renunciations would make them no less important as signs of the felt political need to appease anti-PAC sentiment.

That money from labor PACs should have become the controversial issue for Democratic presidential candidates is ironic, because labor PACs were by no means the chief source of anti-PAC reaction among Democrats or among most reformers. Democrats had been accustomed to receiving labor PAC contributions on a large scale ever since unions pioneered in developing PACs in the 1940s and 1950s, and they received the overwhelming share of those contributions in the 1970s and early 1980s. But union PAC contributions to congressional candidates, while rising from $6.3 million in 1974 to $20.2 million in 1982 and almost $26 million in 1984, constituted a little less than a quarter of all PAC contributions in 1982 and 1984, compared with 50 percent in 1974. Accordingly, what troubled Democrats were the much more rapidly growing contributions to corporate and trade/membership/health association PACs, which together provided almost 60 percent of all PAC contributions (to congressional candidates) in 1982 and 1984, and whose money went more heavily to Republican than to Democratic candidates.[63] The source as well as the size of the contributions was especially troubling to liberal Democrats suspicious of business interests. Labor PACs did, however, share the opprobrium of special interests that all PACs carried by 1984.

For liberal Democrats, many nonconnected PACs were also troublesome. Although not entirely synonymous with ideological PACs, since some connected PACs are also ideological and some nonconnected ones are not, the large ideological PACs are sufficiently dominant among the nonconnecteds, and not in other categories, so that the rapid growth in the nonconnected category is ordinarily treated as that of ideological PACs. That growth has been much more pronounced on the right than on the left. Only a little of the concern here is with contributions to candidates. In 1984, nonconnected PACs contributed $15.3 million to federal candidates, but that was not a large portion of their total disbursements of over $97 million or of the $113 million in contributions by all PACs.[64] Spending by conservative PACs independently of candidates had attracted attention in 1980 because of the defeat of several Democratic senators who had been the targets of negative advertising. Most conspicuous then and in 1982 was the National Conservative PAC (NCPAC); its independent expenditures were over $3 million in each year.[65] Whether there should be much concern about such amounts or generally about ideological nonconnected PACs is open to question. Objectionable though negative advertising may be, it is sometimes thought to be counterproductive from the standpoint of the candidate whom it is meant to help. Nor are the massive receipts of ideological PACs from direct-mail solicitation as significant as they seem; very large portions of the receipts are used to pay for the high costs of solicitation. Yet as long as conservative PACs remain more impressive than old or new liberal PACs, they are likely to be seen as part of the menace that many Democrats want to curb.

At the same time, ideological PACs are of special concern to Republican as well as Democratic pro-party advocates because they perform, more than most connected PACs apart from unions, certain traditional party tasks. They encourage candidates to run, provide services to candidate campaigns, develop campaign issues, and try to increase voting turnouts.[66] A PAC of this type may appear to be developing the kind of political organization that Sorauf suggested would be "midway between the party and the PAC," "neither limited to a single issue nor fully comprehensive in its program," and with an electoral role combining "the activities and strategies of voter mobilization with those of legislative influence."[67] But such a development, as Sorauf subsequently pointed out, does not mean that an individual PAC approaches anything like "the totality of the party role."[68] He adds that the more narrowly defined PACs have most plainly prospered and that only in an aggregated and uncoordinated way do PACs perform as parties might have done in the past.

However much they compete with parties, for contributions no less than for political influence, ideological PACs do not pose for reformers the corrupting menace of the connected PACs sponsored by economic interests and occasionally by other special-interest groups. Their menace is thought to flow from the lobbying activities of PAC-sponsoring corporations, associations, and unions, most of which are represented in Washington. It is true that many PACs do not themselves have headquarters in Washington, and their leaders or contributors may disagree with preferences of their organizational lobbyists, especially for supporting incumbents.[69] Nevertheless, a relationship between an organization's lobby and its PAC certainly exists, and a PAC appears to serve the purposes of lobbyists when an elected member to whose campaign a PAC has generously contributed votes in accord with the preferences of the PAC's supporting organization. This is especially true when a legislator has received near the maximum of $5,000 or $10,000 from each of several closely related PACs sponsored by organizations with a common interest in a particular legislative measure. So too is there a strong suspicion of the purchase of access, if not of votes, when PACs representing organizations interested, for example, in tax legislation give most generously to senior members of the House Ways and Means Committee. Hence it is easy to understand the source of the cynical remark that Congress (or a state legislature) is the best that money can buy. No doubt influence buying is thus overstated. It is at least as likely, as the House Democratic Whip has said, that "money follows votes and not the other way around."[70]

Recognizing an exaggeration in the charge against connected PACs should not lead us to disregard the seriousness of the attack by reformers. It is led by Common Cause, itself a lobbying organization supported by direct-mail contributions in its effort to reform campaign finance. Its response to PACs, ever since their development, has been to treat them as a major threat to the legislative process. Members of Congress, a leader of Common Cause has said, become unduly subject to special-interest influence when their campaign funds come heavily from PACs.[71] PAC money is as suspect as the old and very large individual contributions that Common Cause and other reform groups in the post-Watergate years fought to limit both directly and by substituting public money for private money in presidential campaigns. Failure to achieve further reform after the mid-1970s and the continuing growth of PAC money in congressional campaigns only spurred Common Cause to renew its effort. A fair sample is a fund-raising letter in early 1985. Headed "People Against PAC\$," it includes a petition telling Congress that the influence of PACs threatens our representative form of government and disproportionately serves special interest groups. An accompanying leaflet announces: "There's always been some corruption in American politics. What has happened with political action committees is we've institutionalized that corruption. . . ."[72]

The closest that anti-PAC forces came to curbing PACs, between 1974 and 1985, was in 1979–80 when the Obey-Railsback bill, applying only to U.S. House races, actually passed the House but was kept from the Senate floor by a threatened filibuster. In the form of its House passage, the bill would have restricted each PAC to a \$3,000 contribution per House candidate per election (that is, \$6,000 for a primary and a general election instead of the existing limit of \$5,000 or \$10,000 for both elections), and, more important, it would have limited each House candidate's receipts from all PACs to a total of \$70,000. Subsequently, in 1983, Representative Obey and others proposed a ceiling of \$90,000, along with various other anti-PAC measures, including public funding.[73] The ceiling itself, even if detached from public funding, would presumably be constitutional because it applies to contributions, though to an aggregate received by a candidate rather than to expenditures. And it would affect an increasingly large number of candidates receiving large sums of PAC money. For example in 1984, even before reporting was completed, 284 House candidates had each received more than \$90,000 from PACs; 46 of these had received over \$200,000 and one over half a million dollars.[74] Yet pro-ceiling advocates seldom propose a much higher limit than \$90,000. Thus in 1984, the Twentieth Century Fund's prestigious Task Force, studying PACs under the chairmanship of Edmund Muskie, endorsed a \$100,000 limit while one of its 13 members preferred a lower limit and only two members opposed ceilings altogether.[75] Even a somewhat realistically higher ceiling might cause the most generous PACs to distribute their contributions among more candidates, or more probably, as critics of ceilings argue, to spend much larger sums independently of candidates and yet in ways to help them. The potential of the latter is plain from the scale of independent expenditures of PACs in 1983–84: \$22.2 million for and against federal candidates, of which \$17.3 million was in the presidential contest where PAC *contributions* were effectively restricted by the conditions attached to public funding.[76]

The existence of the independent expenditure option provides a weighty argument against aggregate ceilings or other new limits on the size of PAC contributions. The now-established unconstitutionality of regulatory barriers to independent expenditures is a hard rock in the path of those who would curb PACs or any big spenders. Limiting contributions may still be justified because it deprives PACs of the most direct means of purchasing access or influence. After all, candidates tend to be most appreciative of cash contributions whose subsequent use they themselves control. But they could well come more fully to appreciate independent expenditures in their behalf if they were unable, by law, to obtain large contributions from PACs. That would seem especially likely when a particular PAC or set of PACs spent very large sums to publicize a candidate or to attack an opponent. No one should underestimate that eventuality, since massive independent expenditures are feasible, as large, wealthy PACs have already demonstrated. These are mainly but not solely nonconnected ideological PACs; the biggest trade and professional association PACs are in the same league. They too have substantial professional staffs who provide a continuity that ensures the maintenance of PAC activity in one form or another.

Only small PACs, now contributing modestly and probably inoffensively even in the minds of reformers, would find it difficult to switch to independent expenditures. They could, however, join a consortium of like-minded PACs, perhaps led by a larger PAC. That would hardly serve the purpose of reformers. Those who would curb PAC contributions recognize the possibilities for greater PAC activity through independent spending, but their responses are necessarily limited. For example, the Twentieth Century Fund's Task Force accompanied its endorsement of a $100,000 contribution ceiling with a recommendation that "Congress strengthen its safeguards to prevent collusion between candidates and those making independent expenditures."[77] Although an effort of that kind might well be made, it is hard to see how terms like *collusion* and *independence* could be so defined as to preclude many expenditures without interfering with the First Amendment freedom that the Supreme Court accords campaign expenditures in general.

Limiting PAC contributions, in order to reduce total PAC activity, is probably not aimed at the separate activities of the smaller but more typical PACs. For instance, in 1979–80, of 1,349 essentially active PACs, 65 percent contributed less than $50,000 to federal candidates and 92 percent less than $100,000.[78] Only in aggregate are their contributions enormous. Furthermore, the many smaller PACs are less often based in Washington than the larger PACs, and they are less vulnerable to the charge that PACs have so centralized their money raising and contributing that they are able to flood constituencies with funds from a few major urban centers. Also, because small PACs tend to be sponsored by organizations, their leadership is more clearly accountable to something like a membership than is a headquarters staff of a nonconnected PAC.

Curbing mainly large, Washington-based PACs may be feasible, but it should be recognized that their central funding parallels that of national party committees and that both reflect an increased nationalization of American politics. Collecting money from New York or California for distribution to candidates in Alabama or Wyoming is surely understandable in light of congressional policymaking that affects economic interests and various other preferences of the whole country. The voters in a particular constituency have the opportunity to learn about the money, now that disclosure of contributions and their sources is required by federal law, and they may even elect an opponent of a candidate who receives so many outside contributions that his capacity to represent his constituency is threatened. That possibility is far from enough to reassure reformers, who are much more impressed by the numerous big-PAC supported candidates, chiefly incumbents, who win elections. For them, PACs exemplify the evil of massive special-interest money, even though the money is now plainly reported and aboveboard. Moreover, many members of Congress have become increasingly troubled about the rising tide of PAC money. Their concern was expressed in a Senate bill in 1985 to lower to $3,000 the maximum PAC contribution to a candidate, to impose a ceiling on the total amount of PAC money that a candidate could receive, and to raise to $1,500 the legal maximum that an *individual* could give to a candidate.[79] Though enactment was not predicted (as this was being written), the bill had considerable support. Similar congressional efforts are likely to continue.

The relative share of PAC contributions might also be reduced without imposing new direct limits. A simple way is to increase the amount that an individual can contribute to a federal candidate from $1,000 to a figure much closer to the $5,000 that an individual can contribute to a PAC. The limit of $1,000 seemed low in 1974, and it was certainly so by 1985 after the amount lost about half of its original real value during an inflationary decade. To be sure, individual contributions of a few thousand dollars are as likely to be from "interested" persons as are PAC contributions, but at least they further diversify the sources of fairly substantial sums without restoring anything near the overwhelmingly large amounts that a few were once able to contribute. Also, a higher individual contribution limit would tend to maintain the still predominant share of campaign receipts that come from individual contributors as opposed to the growing proportion from PACs. Such purposes, however, do not relate directly to parties. The proposals that do are my chief concern, and I turn to them in the next section.

V
Helping Parties

Anti-PAC support for helping parties is diffuse as well as limited. Not only are reform-minded foes of corruption almost as hostile to heavily and privately funded parties as they are to similarly funded PACs, but others, including some members of Congress, react to PACs with legislative proposals that would allow candidates, not parties, to receive larger individual contributions or public funds for their campaigns. They would thus bolster a candidate-centered pattern antedating the rise of PACs in the 1970s. Nonetheless it is also important that parties lately have been viewed as relatively benign, while PACs have become much more threatening in the eyes of guardians of the public good. From the 1970s until the mid-1980s, anti-partyism played virtually no part in campaign finance legislation. And as will be evident, pro-party efforts can be detected in the legislation and in certain proposals for further legislation. That successes for these efforts are modest testifies to the strength of the candidate-centered pattern. But that they occur at all suggests that American reform-minded attitudes toward parties no longer reflect only the active hostility to the old machines. Fear that party organizations might be too strong has plainly receded when they are thought to be almost down and out.

In one consequential way, however, a highly specific fear stands in the way of helping parties through liberalizing their opportunities to raise and spend private contributions. Democrats worry that Republican party committees are so much better money raisers that only they would gain from more permissive legislation. While Democratic candidates (for Congress, for example) do at least as well as Republican candidates in total fund raising, especially from PACs and individuals, they receive much less from party organizations in the way of contributions, expenditures, and services. Also, as described in chapter 7, the three Republican national committees had a very large advantage in total spending over the three Democratic counterparts even in 1984 after striking Democratic gains.[80]

Before considering the mainly Republican liberalization proposals, it is well to review the ways in which existing legislation of the 1970s affects the private funding and spending by parties. Federal legislation commands attention despite important parallel legislation by several states. It is novel for parties to have as much federal statutory recognition as they have received since the 1970s. Until then, national party committees, like other political committees, had been subject to a series of ineffectual limits on expenditures and contributions, but neither they nor any other party agencies were regulated as were parties in the several states. Using the terms of my earlier discussion of such regulations, parties had no *national* status as public utilities. Only in the 1970s did Congress begin to treat parties, national and to some extent state and local units too, in anything like the manner that states had done in the twentieth century. And, it must be stressed, the context for the congressional measures was campaign finance and not general regulation of organizational and electoral activities. The latter was still left to the states.

How much Congress originally intended to favor parties in its campaign finance reforms of the 1970s is open to question. Certain regulatory provisions are consistent with a pro-party purpose. Nevertheless these provisions seem minor in light of the general legislative tendency to confirm the candidate-centered nature of campaign financing. That tendency is most familiarly a consequence of the much more bountiful public funding of candidates than of parties in presidential elections, but it is also a result, intended or unintended, of the regulatory treatment of PACs on a basis very like that of parties and, in effect, more favorably with respect to independent expenditures.[81]

Only in limited ways were there pro-party provisions in the congressional legislation of the 1970s. First is the opportunity for an individual to contribute $20,000 annually to a national party committee, but only $5,000 to a PAC and $1,000 per election to a federal candidate. It is improbable, however, that an individual will give $20,000 to a party when also subject to the overall legal limit of $25,000 annually in contributions to candidates, PACs, and parties. Anyone rich enough to give $20,000 will almost certainly want to give more to PACs and candidates than the total of $5,000 that would be permitted after a maximum gift to a party. Thus in practice, parties are less advantaged by the higher contribution limit than one might infer from the figures themselves. Moreover, certain of their activities traditionally required access to large contributors. Thus the Democratic National Committee found it hard to finance its telethons when it was unable, under the legislation of the early 1970s, to obtain its once-customary large sums to guarantee bank loans for advance payments of network production costs. Ironically, as a scholarly study of the telethons suggests, the Democratic party was thus legally handicapped in its effort to raise money from the numerous small contributors that the laws sought to encourage.[82]

A second advantage, some of which is also more apparent than real, is conferred on national party committees by the legislative provision permitting each of them to spend an inflation-adjusted two cents per eligible voter in conjunction with its presidential nominee's campaign. The significance of this provision, which allowed each national committee to spend $4.6 million in

1980 and about \$6.9 million in 1984, is substantial, since the Republican committee, but not the Democratic committee, actually raised and spent near the maximum in each year.[83] The amounts are welcome additions to the greater but limited public funds granted to each major-party presidential candidate (near \$30 million in 1980 and \$40 million in 1984). They would have been even more welcome if they were the only substantial additions to spending for presidential candidates. That is what Congress intended when it severely restricted any other expenditures in behalf of presidential nominees who accepted public funds, as the Republican and Democratic nominees did in 1976, 1980, and 1984. But the Supreme Court's invalidation of that restriction (explained in note 43) created a giant loophole for independent expenditures by individuals and PACs, several of which have taken advantage of it on a large scale in presidential as well as congressional campaigns. The result is to reduce the significance of the special permission for parties directly and openly to spend in conjunction with their presidential nominees. At the same time parties, unlike PACs and individuals, are assumed unable to spend "independently" in behalf of a candidate, although they are not subject to legal limitation in spending for more general party purposes.

A third legislated advantage for party spending is of greater import. It permits in congressional campaigns the kind of expenditures authorized in presidential campaigns. Apart from its contributions to candidates, a national committee (one for each party) can make coordinated expenditures, *adjusted for post-1974 inflation*, of \$10,000 on behalf of a House candidate in a state with more than one district, and of two cents per eligible voter (or \$20,000 if higher) on behalf of a Senate candidate or a House candidate in a single-district state. The allowable amounts are substantial: in 1982 nearly \$666,000 for a Senate candidate in the largest state (California), and \$18,400 for a House candidate in most districts.[84] And, as the Republicans have demonstrated in recent elections, these figures are only half of the totals that national committees can and do spend in conjunction with Senate and House candidates. The law's authorization of *state* party expenditures in the same amounts has been interpreted first by the Republicans and then by the Supreme Court to allow "agency agreements" under which a national party committee picks up an often impecunious state party's share and spends it as the state party's designated agent.[85]

The resulting large national party expenditure, especially by the Republicans, was emphasized in the description of the developing national organizations, but it deserves to be noted again. In 1984 the mainly national Republican committees spent \$13.1 million in behalf of Senate and House candidates, in addition to their contributions of $4.8 million. The Democratic figures for 1984 were $6 million in behalf of Senate and House candidates, plus $1.8 million in contributions. Or to express the magnitude in a different way, in 1982 the coordinated Republican party expenditures averaged over $260,000 per *Senate* candidate. More than half a million dollars was spent for each of four Senate candidates, including $1.3 million in California.[86]

The amounts are certainly large in relation to contributions from any individual PAC, and they do not suffer much by comparison with total contributions by a set of PACs to particular candidates. The picture differs if independent expenditures of PACs are taken into account, but their value to candidates is less clear than is a party's coordinated party expenditures in behalf of candidates. Plainly, with respect to such expenditures, the law provides a fairly ample opportunity for a successful fund-raising party to spend as no nonparty group is allowed to do—that is, above contribution limits and openly in coordination with a candidate's campaign. The agency agreement with state parties enhances that opportunity, consistent incidentally with a previously accepted understanding that Senate and House campaign committees can act as agents for the RNC or DNC, and with the law's provisions for transfer of funds between party committees.

In addition to the three already described provisions included in the major legislation of 1974, Congress subsequently enacted two other measures specifically to help parties. One in 1978 was merely an extension to parties of the same low postage rate available to groups qualifying as nonprofit or educational organizations. Then in 1979 Congress amended earlier legislation so as to provide an apparently marginal spending opportunity that parties have exploited and may yet more significantly exploit. The opportunity is for state and local parties to engage in activities supporting federal candidates. Generally available before the legislation of the 1970s, the opportunity was effectively denied in the 1976 contest for the presidency because state and local party spending in presidential campaigns would have been counted as part of the limited expenditure allowed a national party whose nominee had accepted public funds. In response, the 1979 amendment authorized state and local parties to conduct, without financial limit, voter-registration and get-out-the-vote drives on behalf of presidential candidates and at the same time allowed these parties to buy, also without limit, buttons, bumper stickers, handbills, brochures, posters, and yard signs for any federal candidate. Although mass media advertising (but not phone banks) remained restricted, the enhancement of party activities is much more substantial than was implied when the 1979 legislation was called the bumper-sticker amendment. As early as 1980, before the opportunity was fully appreciated, Republican party committees spent an *estimated* $15 million on the volunteer activity and material now authorized by law.[87] The *actual* expenditure is unknown for 1980 or for later elections, because the federal law exempts a state or local party committee from reporting its contributions and expenditures if within specified and likely limits.

Reportable or not, state and local party spending in behalf of federal candidates, perhaps in conjunction with spending for state and local candidates, is obviously expansible. If state and local parties have trouble raising money, a national party can help not only through joint money-raising efforts but also through the legally sanctioned transfer of its funds for certain kinds of expenditures by state and local parties. Accordingly, Republican national party committees in particular, because of their demonstrated fund-raising capacity, have in effect added state and local party activities to their own extensive, coordinated activities in behalf of federal candidates.[88] It is the element of coordination that distinguishes the opportunity allowed parties from the opportunity available to PACs and individuals for independent expenditures on behalf of federal candidates. The allowed coordinated expenditures are almost certainly more helpful, dollar for dollar, than the now legally unlimited independent expenditures of nonparty groups and individuals. Coordination is likely to appeal to candidates because of their own involvement.

Considered together, the several pro-party provisions of federal campaign finance legislation are meaningfully linked to the recent and current development of national party organizations. It is harder to say whether any similar link exists between new regulatory state legislation and state party organizations. Here and there state laws give parties opportunities denied to PACs, but arrangements vary greatly and their impact is not well understood.[89] In many states, laws remain less strict generally than the federal legislation, and parties may share with candidates and nonparty groups many money-raising advantages. For example, not all states limit the size of contributions in state elections, and several allow unions and corporations to contribute their own funds directly to campaigns for state offices. In certain states, parties have also been helped by national committee funds raised outside the restrictions on contributions solicited for federal candidates. Misleadingly called "soft money," the funds obtained from these and other sources may be larger than we suspect.[90] They are likely to be indirectly useful in campaigns; a more fully equipped headquarters or a general voter-registration drive, conducted by nationally financed local organizations, could enhance a party's effort in behalf of its candidates.

Neither the intended nor the unintended legal advantages of parties come close to the desires of successful party practitioners. As early as 1979, the executive director of the National Republican Congressional Committee declared that "the law really only throws us a few small crumbs. If Congress and the commission are serious about wanting to help to rebuild the parties, then they will have to look at us as something more than just super-PACs, and grant us major new authority and maneuvering room."[91] From that standpoint, the 1979 amendments added another crumb, but both it and certain earlier provisions came to look more substantial in the early 1980s. A good deal more is advocated. Raising the amounts that can be contributed to parties is the most obvious possibility. It might be favored by Democrats as well as Republicans. The Democratic national party organization, so far able to raise less from small contributions than the Republican organization, has a special need for larger individual contributions. The idea is to increase the effective differential now allowed between contributions to parties and contributions to candidates and PACs. Doing so is not primarily a matter of raising the present $20,000 limit on individual contributions to parties. That would be useful, but it is more relevant to change the overall limit of $25,000 on an individual's federal contributions in a given year so that a rich person can give generously to a party without legal curtailment of his other contributions. The simplest step is to abolish the $25,000 ceiling altogether, but it is probably politically more feasible to exempt contributions to parties of $20,000 (or more) from the ceiling. Still another proposal to help parties raise money is to give a special income-tax credit for contributions to parties; it might replace the present tax credit for any political contribution, or it might be an addition but only for contributions to parties.[92]

More divisive along partisan lines than liberalizing the limits on money raising are proposals for more generous disbursements by parties. They are bound to be favored by more Republicans than Democrats as long as they benefit only or principally the much more successful money-raising organization. So far, the Democratic national committees have lacked the financial capacity to go beyond most existing legal limits. Even they, however, may now be restrained in particular congressional races, as Republican committees certainly are, by the legal limits on their contributions to candidates. Putting aside temporarily the larger coordinated expenditures in behalf of candidates, maximum national party *contributions* are $17,500 (in total) per election year for a U.S. Senate candidate and $5,000 per election for a House candidate (or $10,000 for primary and general elections). The latter, we know, is no more than the 1974 law's limit on a contribution by a single PAC, and it is only moderately enhanced by a provision that allows the congressional campaign committee as well as the national party committee and a state party committee each to give $5,000 per election.

A measure to raise these limits, to $30,000 for a Senate candidate and $15,000 for a House candidate, was introduced in 1983 by Senator Paul Laxalt, the general chairman of the Republican party, and Representative Bill Frenzel, a Minnesota Republican long active with political scientists and others in the Committee for Party Renewal.[93] The proposed increases are not so great as to raise significantly the now-small party share of total contributions received by candidates, but the larger amounts could be materially helpful in selected constituencies. Particularly for promising challengers of incumbent House members, whose success demonstrably requires large-scale funding, a party's $15,000 would be useful at the start of a campaign when other funds are scarce.[94] Understandably, raising the contribution limit is attractive to its Republican party sponsors. They need to fund more challengers than do Democrats in order to win control of the House. The Democratic party, however, might at least occasionally want to give $15,000 rather than $5,000 to a challenger or to an underdog open-seat candidate. Moreover the increased amount, though reaching several million dollars when aggregated over the many races, is not beyond the new capacity of Democratic fund-raising committees.

Less attractive to Democrats is any Republican proposal to raise significantly the already substantial amount allowed for coordinated party expenditures in behalf of candidates. The Laxalt-Frenzel bill would have abolished altogether the inflation-adjusted limits for Senate and House campaigns, and so freed the Republican national committees to pour massive funds, well beyond anything yet conceivable for Democratic committees, into selected congressional campaigns. Ominously threatening though it is for Democrats, the pro-party argument for such freedom is impressive. More than party contributions that are spent by candidates themselves, coordinated party expenditures are subject to management by a party organization. So, of course, are the now unlimited general party expenditures, but they are less directly related to electing candidates. Coordinated party expenditures are useful in candidate-centered elections and yet they involve substantial organizational activity.

Still another party-building proposal in the Laxalt-Frenzel bill would raise the limit a national party is allowed to spend in behalf of its presidential nominee. That limit, now an inflation-adjusted two cents a voter, would rise, under the bill, to three cents. Here the Republican bill is modest when compared to a suggestion made by Herbert Alexander, the long-time scholarly specialist in the field of campaign finance. Alexander would consider abolition of the

presidential party-expenditure ceiling altogether, and also the extension of unlimited spending in presidential campaigns to state and local parties that now
enjoy that privilege only with respect to certain activities.[95] In thus contemplating greater opportunity for party spending even with public funding,
Alexander lends support to the general argument that public funding should
be a floor and not a ceiling on campaign expenditures, especially on expenditures that a party makes in behalf of its nominee.

VI
Another Perspective

Proposals so far discussed for helping parties have been in the form of amendments to national legislation, but similar changes are also advanced at the state
level. Statutes regulating state and local elections might be modified so that
contributions to parties, party contributions to candidates, and party expenditures for candidates would be subject to less stringent limits than they now
are. In these respects, state party advantages, if any, could be increased relative
to those of PACs and individuals. As in feasible federal proposals, the advantages would alter only marginally the prevailing candidate-centered pattern
of American politics. Giving parties special roles within that pattern, however, has an even clearer historical basis in state than in national legislation,
since during most of this century it has been the states that have given parties
a special statutory status.

Those who cherish decentralization within our federal system are likely to
perceive the usefulness of providing further legal opportunities for state parties
to match any allowed national parties. It is true that a practical money-raising
advantage probably exists for national parties, and at least in the Republican
case that has already led to a kind of patron-client financial relationship between national and state party organizations. That development, however, is
all the more reason for believers in strong state parties to urge that regulatory
state statutes be as helpful as possible to state organizations. Campaign finance
laws can surely affect the balance between parties at various levels in any political system. In Great Britain, for example, where national statutes control
at national and constituency levels, an expenditure ceiling is imposed on each
parliamentary candidate and thus on what can be spent in a given constituency
campaign, but no ceiling is imposed on national party expenditures as long
as they are not devoted to a particular parliamentary candidate's campaign.[96]
Consequently, national party spending is encouraged legally, as it is also, one

suspects, by other forces. Those other forces, having to do with economies of scale in fund-raising and services, now operate powerfully in the United States as well. Legal changes by the several states are unlikely to arrest those forces, but they might lessen their impact.

In any event, further statutory help for American parties, national if not state, is conceivable within the private regulatory framework that I have presented. I stress the practical limits of that help. The limits are not only those of the heavily candidate-centered pattern long flourishing in American politics, but also those associated with an acceptance of PACs within that pattern. PACs are not going to disappear. Nor are their activities likely to be seriously diminished by new legal limits when they can switch to a kind of campaigning that is constitutionally protected from legislative restrictions. Moreover, weakening PACs, even if achievable, is hardly essential for the maintenance of parties. Rather than being replaced by PACs, parties themselves have developed as campaign organizations, even during the years of the most rapid growth of PACs. Although PACs do in certain respects compete with parties, they also work with them. Therefore, rather than trying to help parties by curbing PACs, a better pro-party agenda is to legislate relative regulatory advantages for parties. Such advantages, as currently modest provisions already indicate, are meaningful though not overwhelming. I have more hope for them than for public funding as the means to assist parties.

Chapter Ten

Public Funding
of Campaigns

Crucial to an understanding of American public funding is that it has not been developed primarily to help parties. Lately, it is true, organizational Democrats have detected advantages in public funding and so have scholarly champions of parties. Mainly, however, the argument for taxpayer-provided subsidies comes from reformers seeking to reduce the importance of private money. For them, public funding is a means to accomplish what they have also pursued through regulatory limits on large private contributions. Government money, even more than small private contributions, looks clean and uncorrupting while also virtuous in its tendency to equalize election contests between major competitors. These characteristics became especially attractive to campaign finance reformers in the late 1970s and early 1980s, as limits on private financing were frustrated by PACs and by constitutional obstacles in the way of their regulation.

Helping parties, though not itself a principal objective for reform-minded advocates of public funding, might nonetheless be included in actual or proposed legislation for government subsidies. Parties, now generally less threatening than PACs, might readily be saved from temptation by public funds. Yet even with reformers as potential allies, advocates of party funding with government dollars confront the now-established American expectation that public, like private, funds are mainly if not entirely for candidates. That expectation, fortified by political self-interest, can be observed most tellingly among legislators contemplating proposals for funding their own elections. Furthermore, not all pro-party champions favor public funding. Just as Democrats are chary about liberalizing the regulatory limits on private funding of

310

parties, many Republicans are reluctant to extend public funding. For example, no less a champion of party organization than the successful Republican National Committee chairman, William Brock, opposed public funding generally and went only so far, in 1979, as to agree with the Democratic National Committee chairman that if there were to be public financing of congressional campaigns some of the money should go to parties.[1] Republicans, it should be added, argue against public funding on grounds of principle and not merely partisanship. Conservatives, in particular, are ideologically resistant to the substitution of government support for private support of activities generally and of political activities specifically. In their perspective, *taxpayer money* or *governmental subsidies* are better descriptive terms for what is more usually called public funding. I adopt the latter term because it is familiar, but without judging whether it is any more appropriate than the alternatives.

In analyzing the actual and potential impact of public funding on the party-candidate relationship, I begin by summarizing the constitutional doctrines that allow and even encourage the development of such funding as the means for accomplishing reform. Subsequently, I discuss the actual provision of federal dollars in presidential campaigns, the use by several states of tax dollars for their campaigns, and finally, the prospects for extending public funding. Along the way, especially in the last section, foreign comparisons are introduced in order to stress how American parties are treated distinctively in public funding as they are in so many other ways.

I

The Constitutional Situation

No one doubts that judicial interpretations of the U.S. Constitution impose substantial constraints on the development of national and state legislation for campaign finance. Unlike courts in most other nations, the U.S. Supreme Court has always had the authority to nullify legislative reforms in this field as in many others, and its use of that authority was apparent in its effective rewriting of congressional regulations of private funding. Plainly, the Court's exercise of its authority in the campaign finance field has not receded as it has in large areas of economic and social legislation. On the contrary, the Supreme Court has become even more critical in scrutinizing campaign finance legislation because of its possible threat to the political freedom that the Court has increasingly put in a preferred position relative to other values.[2] Primarily, this reflects the Court's liberal interpretation of the First Amendment's protection of freedom of expression against national government action (and, through the Fourteenth Amendment's due process clause, against state government action). Also, however, the Court is concerned with the way in which campaign finance legislation might infringe on the guarantees of equal protection of the laws as provided in the Fourteenth Amendment and inferentially in the Fifth Amendment.

Altogether, as we have seen, the constitutional hurdles are so high that the Court has invalidated expenditure limits in most circumstances and, in effect, provided loopholes for lavish private financing that Congress had wanted to restrict. Necessarily, then, the remaining legislative provisions have become *the* relevant ones for reformers. Along with the contribution limits already discussed, public funding is the most important element of the congressional campaign finance legislation to emerge as constitutionally valid from *Buckley v. Valeo*.[3] The nature and extent of its validity require examination in order to appreciate the potential use of public funding to help parties as well as to accomplish other purposes.

The clearest and most certain conclusion from *Buckley v. Valeo* is that public funds can constitutionally be provided to candidates and parties for primary and general election campaigns. On that principle the Court was nearly unanimous. Of the eight justices participating in the 1976 decision, only Chief Justice Burger dissented root and branch from the portion of the Court's per curiam opinion upholding the power of Congress to appropriate money for political campaigns. One other justice, Rehnquist, dissented with respect to public funding, accepting the principle but objecting to what he regarded as the discriminatory method of the particular legislation. Thus, however divided or indefinite the Court was on other aspects of its review of the campaign finance legislation, it left no question where it stood generally on public funding. Congress, the Court held, had the constitutional authority to spend money to subsidize election campaigns; in the familiar language of implied powers, Congress had chosen means "'necessary and proper' to promote the general welfare. . . ."[4] These means included the special way in which the campaign money was handled—not by a straightforward appropriation from general revenue but through a campaign fund to which a taxpayer could (without increasing tax liability) contribute one dollar (two dollars for taxpayers filing jointly) by checking a box on the tax return. Except for the first year of the fund, the law did not give a taxpayer the opportunity to earmark contributions for candidates of a particular party. By the mid-1970s, over 30 million taxpayers used the checkoff, putting enough money into the campaign fund to support the quadrennial presidential contest as Congress had specified.[5] The voluntary nonpartisan giving by taxpayers for eventually partisan distribution was accepted without implying that another arrangement, allowing taxpayer choice of party or party candidate, would have been unconstitutional.[6]

The import of the Court's acceptance of public funding becomes most apparent when contrasted with Chief Justice Burger's dissent. Unlike his judicial colleagues, Burger did not regard "this novel public financing of political activity as simply another congressional appropriation whose validity is 'necessary and proper' to Congress' power to regulate and reform elections and primaries. . . ." Correctly enough, he notes that "no federal scheme allocating public funds in a comparable manner has ever been before us." Burger quotes approvingly from Senator Howard Baker's opposition during debate on the legislation: ". . . there is something politically incestuous about the Government financing and, I believe, inevitably then regulating the day to day procedures by which the Government is selected. . . ."[7] However likely as a practical argument, Burger's opinion was unpersuasive constitutionally.

More significantly controversial as a contemporary judicial issue than the Court's acceptance of well-established breadth of congressional spending powers was the holding that the particular public funding arrangement was compatible with rights guaranteed by the key constitutional amendments. Although the funding here in question was federal financing of *presidential* nominations and elections, the Court's opinion was broad enough to uphold a similar federal financing of congressional campaigns as well as similar state financing of state campaigns (unless, of course, a state constitution imposed unusual restrictions). *Similar* in the preceding sentence is necessarily inexact. No doubt, future public-funding legislation could be different enough to be seriously challenged in the courts. But the judicial latitude is fairly wide, since several kinds of federal funding pertaining to presidential politics were upheld in *Buckley v. Valeo*. Money was provided for each major party's nominating convention, for its nominee's general election campaign, and, on a matching basis, for the primary campaigns of candidates seeking nominations. Upholding these provisions required judicial acceptance of the special standing of a "major party"—defined, in the legislation, as a party whose presidential candidate received at least 25 percent of the popular vote in the last general election. Also involved was judicial acceptance of lesser though proportionate funding for a "minor party"—defined as a party whose presidential nominee received between 5 and 25 percent of the vote—and of no funding for a party below the 5 percent figure.

In upholding the constitutionality of provisions favoring major parties, the Court was a little less definitive than it was in accepting the general principle of public funding. This was not mainly because Justice Rehnquist dissented from the Court's validation of the particular funding provisions; his dissent, plus Chief Justice Burger's, still meant that six of eight participating justices accepted the distribution. Greater uncertainty flows from the Court opinion itself. The holding was merely that the statutory arrangements were not invalid on their face—that is, simply because they provided funds for major parties and not similarly, if at all, for other parties. Writing early in 1976, before the public-financing provisions were in operation, the Court noted the absence of "factual proof that the scheme is discriminatory in its effect." The Court added, in the same well-loaded footnote, that its present rejection of the arguments concerning discrimination did "not rule out the possibility of concluding in some future case, upon an appropriate factual demonstration, that the public financing system invidiously discriminates against nonmajor parties."[8] That possibility may yet develop, but it now looms less large after three publicly funded presidential elections produced no successful challenge from a nonmajor party.

Nor did a challenge to the funding arrangement reach the Court as a result of John Anderson's independent candidacy of 1980. It was averted by the FEC's treatment of Anderson's claim for federal funds as that of a minor party nominee rather than of a nonparty independent. Accordingly, no need arose for judicial resolution of the issue suggested by another footnote in *Buckley v. Valeo*: "Serious questions might arise as to the constitutionality of excluding from free annual assistance candidates not affiliated with a 'political party' solely because they lack such affiliation."[9]

Apart from the funding of Anderson, on a disadvantaged *post*-election basis that I shall describe, and the small-scale funding of one candidate for a 1984 third-party nomination, which I shall also note again, federal money for candidates in the three presidential elections of 1976, 1980, and 1984 went entirely to Republicans and Democrats. And, more significantly in my perspective, federal money for parties, to run their conventions, went only to the RNC and DNC.[10] Being able to achieve that result constitutionally may be essential if parties are to be funded at all. It is hard to believe that Congress would pay the price of having to fund minor-party *organizations* on any regularly generous basis comparable to that of major parties. Doing so seems less tolerable politically than having to finance a few individual nonmajor-party candidates.[11]

The legal basis for funding principally Republicans and Democrats is so important that it deserves closer examination. It follows from the law's definition of a major party as one whose candidate for president in the most recent election received 25 percent or more of the popular vote. Apart from the extraordinary election of 1912, when the Republican candidate received only 23 percent of the vote and the third-party candidate (ex-President Theodore Roosevelt) received 27 percent, both the Republican and Democratic proportions were above the 25 percent standard for over a century and comfortably above that figure since 1924. Moreover, after 1912 no third-party candidate came close to 25 percent; the high points were La Follette's 17 percent in 1924 and George Wallace's 13.5 percent in 1968. Otherwise, from 1916 into the 1970s no third-party or independent candidate polled more than 3.5 percent. Clearly, therefore, Congress meant only Republicans and Democrats in its definition of a major party and in its funding of a nominee of such a party both more certainly and at a higher level than the nominee of a minor party.

Further, the congressional definition of a minor party made it unlikely that even lesser amounts would go to small or new parties. Not often in the previous half-century had any nonmajor-party presidential nominee won the requisite 5 percent of the popular vote so that it could have qualified for funding in the next presidential election, or (as the law would also allow) for funding of the already completed campaign in which the 5 percent had been won. Not only did no party qualify as "minor" in 1976, when the law went into effect, but only two could have qualified in the preceding 50 years: La Follette's Progressive party after its 1924 performance and George Wallace's American Independent party (AIP) after its 1968 performance. For the obviously more desirable preelection funding, La Follette's Progressive party did not exist in 1928. The AIP, however, did remain in 1972 and thus would have been entitled to the same substantial share of public funds for a campaign in that year as it could have secured after the 1968 election (when it had won nearly a third of each major party's presidential vote). But by the time Congress actually provided campaign money in the mid-1970s, the AIP was ineligible, because its 1972 presidential candidate, John G. Schmitz, had polled much less than 5 percent of the popular vote. Congress, it seems reasonable to assume, was well aware of that ineligibility as well as of the ineligibility of all other small parties for minor-party funding in 1976.

When the law's provision for a minor party did come into effect in 1980, John Anderson's candidacy, while that of an independent rather than of a party in the usual organizational sense, received public funds after winning 6.6 percent of the popular vote. Anderson thus qualified for roughly the same proportion of a major party's funding that a minor party could have claimed during the campaign if it had received 6.6 percent of the vote in the prior presidential election.[12] The disadvantage of postelection payment was apparent in Anderson's case. Federal funds would have been much more useful during the campaign than afterward. Unlike his major-party opponents, Anderson had to finance his campaign by borrowing and by otherwise raising money that he could only hope to repay from federal funds if he reached the 5 percent vote level. Almost certainly, he would have spent more and have spent it more planfully if he had been able at the start to secure his eventual share of federal funds. Only in 1984, when Anderson's time had so obviously passed that he did not run, would he and his legally defined party have been eligible for preelection funding. Even the likelihood of almost $6 million in general election campaign money, plus money for a nominating convention and perhaps for a primary campaign, did not persuade Anderson to enter the 1984 race.[13] His decision is significant because it reduces the force of the argument that the constitutionally necessary provision for a minor party leads to the untoward funding of a candidate who has no hope, in a second election, of receiving 5 percent of the vote.

The net result of the Anderson experience is to bolster, at a modest price paid only in 1980, the constitutionality of presidential funding. Now that a nonmajor-party nominee, even one running without being a party choice in the usual sense, has actually qualified for funds, it looks even harder than it was in 1976 to persuade a Court majority that the public-financing legislation is so discriminatory as to be unconstitutional. It is not suggested, however, that funding the Anderson candidacy would have changed Justice Rehnquist's (or Chief Justice Burger's) dissenting views. Rehnquist, while (unlike Burger) accepting the power of Congress to provide public campaign funds, was unequivocal in asserting that Congress had unconstitutionally discriminated by establishing requirements for nonmajor parties to which the major parties are not subject. Congress, he said, "has enshrined the Republican and Democratic parties in a permanently preferred position. . . ."[14] Nothing about the Anderson case or any other experience under the campaign finance legislation substantially alters that preferred position. But the major-party advantages have not become newly objectionable since the 1976 opinion. Hence the 1976 Court majority, five of whom remained as justices in 1985, have no more cause to find those advantages unconstitutionally discriminatory than they had in *Buckley v. Valeo*. One should be less confident about a future Court with a sharply different membership.

In noting judicial acceptance of major-party advantages under the law, I recognize what I shall later spell out: most of the advantages are not organizational. The bulk of the federal funds go to individual candidates. Yet it is consequential that these candidates are Republicans and Democrats. Not only does the law favor major-party nominees in funding general elections, but its provision of matching federal funds for nominating campaigns is plainly meant for candidates seeking to win the publicly contested Republican and Democratic nominations. Technically, in nominating campaigns, a candidate in any party, even one less than minor under the law, can qualify for matching funds, and one nonmajor-party candidate actually did so in 1984. The candidate—so far the only one—was Sonia Johnson, seeking the nomination of the Citizens party and of several other small parties in various states. She received almost $200,000, a substantial sum, but small compared with the amount, between two and ten million dollars, given to each of six candidates for major-party nomination.[15] Her funding, like Anderson's general election funding four years earlier, is significant in the present context less because of its practical use than because its provision reduces the chance for successful constitutional challenge to the major-party advantages virtually ensured by the law. The Johnson case is another useful exception. It enhances the likelihood that the successful Republican and Democratic candidates can continue to be twice blessed by millions of federal funds—once in the spring when seeking a major-party label, and again in the summer when carrying that label in the general election.

Although even presidential candidate funding can be said to provide a kind of party advantage for Republicans and Democrats, the funding of nominating conventions, whose constitutionality was also upheld in *Buckley v. Valeo*, is a much more direct organizational benefit. In no way, however, did the Court opinion encourage the funding of parties more than it did the funding of candidates. For reformers, the importance of *Buckley v. Valeo* was that it left public funding in general as the sole means for limiting private campaign expenditures. While holding that Congress could not flatly impose ceilings on expenditures, the Court allowed such ceilings to be enforced as conditions that candidates and parties would accept if they took public funds.[16] In fact, limits on total expenditures have been accepted by candidates for major-party nominations when taking matching funds, by major-party nominees taking general election funds, by major parties taking funds for their conventions, and by major-party committees whose presidential nominees have taken general election funds. By contrast, as noted in the previous chapter, *Buckley v. Valeo* explicitly invalidated the several other congressional provisions for limiting campaign expenditures. These included overall dollar limits on presidential nominating and general election campaigns (for candidates not obtaining federal funds), on Senate and House campaigns (where no federal funds were provided), and on expenditures by candidates from their personal and family funds. If these expenditures were to be limited, it could now be done only as an accompaniment of public funding. The fact that it was actually done in the presidential campaigns of 1976, 1980, and 1984 might help to make the case for public funding of Senate and House campaigns.

Much less encouraging to public-funding reformers was the invalidation of another expenditure ceiling — the $1,000 limit on what an individual or group could spend independently to help a candidate.[17] We have already observed how the Court, by finding this ceiling in violation of the First Amendment, created a loophole for PACs in particular to spend freely in congressional elections beyond their legally limited contributions. That the same loophole existed in publicly funded presidential campaigns seemed to be suggested by the generality of the Court's language in *Buckley v. Valeo* when it freed independent expenditures even for "express advocacy of candidates" from any dollar limitation. The Court distinguished expenditures "made totally independently of the candidate and his campaign" from those "controlled by or coordinated with the candidate and his campaign" and thus subject to treatment as contributions. Unlike the latter, the independent expenditures, in the Court's view, "may well provide little assistance to the candidate's campaign and indeed may prove counterproductive." Accordingly, the independent expenditure ceiling failed "to serve any substantial governmental interest" while limiting First Amendment expression.[18]

Despite its evidently broad exemption of independent expenditures from dollar limitations, *Buckley v. Valeo* did not specifically rule on the constitutionality of the $1,000 ceiling on the amount that any unauthorized political committee could spend in behalf of *a presidential candidate who accepted public financing*. That particular statutory provision was not itself at issue in *Buckley v. Valeo*, and its invalidity was not yet taken for granted by everyone. Indeed, the FEC and others sought to enforce the $1,000 ceiling against PACs that independently spent large sums to help Ronald Reagan in both 1980 and 1984.[19] But the PACs, challenging the constitutionality of such enforcement, first won an inconclusive victory in 1982 and then a definitive ruling in 1985 when the Supreme Court, by a seven to two vote, held that the ceiling on independent expenditures in public-funded presidential campaigns, like ceilings on independent expenditures generally, was unconstitutional.[20] It is hard to see how any other result would have been consistent with *Buckley v. Valeo*.[21] Why should the previously recognized First Amendment rights to spend independently be any less valid when a candidate accepts public funds? The rights of independent spenders are not surrendered when a candidate, even their favored candidate, agrees to an expenditure ceiling for himself and his committee. For this reason, the case at issue, *FEC v. NCPAC*, looks like one in which the Court reaffirmed its earlier opinion rather than extending it.

At any rate, *FEC v. NCPAC* means that public funding cannot be used to limit one large and potentially much larger source of private spending in election campaigns. Nevertheless, public funding remains the means by which reformers can constitutionally limit *candidate* expenditures. And, as I have emphasized, public funding is also a constitutionally valid way by which pro-party advocates can seek to help parties. Most specifically, the help can be given almost entirely to major parties without violating the rights of smaller parties and independents.

II
Federal Dollars

However inviting the constitutional opportunity to help parties by public funding, its use at the federal level has been almost as slight as might have been expected. It would have been as difficult in the 1970s to develop federal financing without a candidate-centered orientation as it would have been to develop such financing without regard to the special status of the two major-party labels. The point was appreciated even by public finance advocates who would have liked to strengthen parties. For example, Adamany and Agree, writing at the time the public finance provisions were being enacted, took into account "the realities of American politics" and granted that support "must go mainly to candidates, although some aid to parties may be appropriate for certain activities. . . ."[22]

Curiously, Congress had ignored or overridden those realities in a slightly earlier and abortive effort to provide federal funds for presidential campaigns. It actually enacted legislation in 1966 that, while in many other respects resembling the later operative legislation of the 1970s, would have paid out money not to candidates themselves but to the national party committees. Senator Russell Long was chiefly responsible for developing these 1966 provisions and for adding them as an amendment to an unrelated tax bill that Congress passed and President Johnson signed. Despite its enactment, the Long plan did not take effect. Congress repealed it in 1967, partly in response to arguments that it gave too much power to national committees and particularly to their chairpersons. Subsequently Senator Long as well as other proponents of public funding concentrated on direct help to candidates.[23]

The time for treating parties as the principal presidential campaign agencies

was evidently gone. So it was, I suspect, even in 1966 when the Long plan
was enacted. Only earlier in the century, before public funding was widely
considered, would American party organizations have been the likely recipients. In 1907, for example, President Theodore Roosevelt had proposed, though
to an unresponsive Congress, that "each of the great national parties" receive
"an appropriation ample enough to meet the necessity for thorough organization and machinery. . . ."[24]

In light of the now-ascendant American candidate-centered campaign management, especially in presidential contests, the provision of any federal funds for
national party committees is remarkable. The amounts are limited, being only
for nominating conventions and not for campaigns, but they are hardly negligible. Moreover, they have increased substantially. Congress first funded each
major party at $2 million plus a post-1974 cost-of-living adjustment (COLA),
but in 1979 it raised the sum to $3 million plus COLA, so that $4.4 million
was available in 1980. After 1980 it again raised the base, to $4 million plus
COLA, so that each party was entitled to $8.1 million in 1984. No matching
funds are required, and the principal conditions are that the national committee spend none of the accepted money to benefit a particular candidate or delegate and that the committee spend no more than the federal allotment on
its convention. In raising its payment for major-party conventions beyond levels that COLAs alone would have justified, Congress responded more generously than it did for candidates, whose allowable funds increased only in line
with COLAs. Accordingly, each party convention's available subsidy almost
quadrupled (from $2.2 million in 1976 to $8.1 million in 1984), while each
major-party nominee's maximum subsidy approximately doubled (from $21.8
million in 1976 to $40.4 million in 1984).[25]

Generosity in funding conventions can even look like payment for party
campaign activities. Each party's convention is itself a campaign event, now
mainly consequential as a kind of political coronation occurring after primaries
have already determined the nomination. Freeing a party from having to use
privately raised funds to pay for this ceremonial occasion allows more of such
funds to be spent for other campaign purposes. The hard-pressed Democratic
National Committee might thus be helped.

No one is likely, however, to regard convention funding as a great detrac-
tion from the candidate-centered thrust of the other provisions for federal financing of presidential campaigns. The thrust is clearest for nominating contests, which by their nature are conducted not between parties but among
party voters in primaries and, less publicly, among smaller numbers of regulars
and activists in caucuses and state conventions. Granting federal money to in-

dividual candidates in these contests is an important recognition of the established character of intraparty electoral competition. The word *recognition* avoids any implication that federal financing of presidential nominating campaigns created the intraparty competition especially of the dominant presidential primaries. Those primaries had become more numerous and consequential independently of public funding. The shift of states to primaries between 1968 and 1972 occurred before public funding was available, and neither the continued adoption of primaries in 1976 and 1980 nor the modest decline in primaries in 1984 is attributable to the public funding available to presidential candidates in all three election years. It is possible, however, that public funding bolstered the new and emerging pattern by encouraging the use of primaries, perhaps by more or different kinds of candidates, and thus contributed to the ascendancy of candidate-centered politics and to the further weakening of party organizational influence in presidential nominating contests. To explore that possibility, it is useful first to recall the federal provisions for financing candidates seeking their party nominations.

Unlike other federal campaign funds, those for presidential primary contestants are matching funds. To qualify, a candidate must raise $5,000 in individual contributions of $250 or less in each of 20 states. As observed in chapter 9, the federal government then also matches, dollar for dollar, subsequent individual contributions of $250 or less (meaning, for instance, that it would match only the first $250 of a $1,000 contribution), but it does so only within a total expenditure ceiling that primary candidates must observe in order to obtain the federal funds. Apart from a sum allowed for fund-raising, that ceiling was $10.9 million in 1976, $14.7 million in 1980, and $20.2 million in 1984. Candidates seeking nominations could receive half of those amounts, provided of course that they raised enough of the remainder in individual contributions of no more than $250 each. They would also have to accept ceilings on their state-by-state expenditures within the overall national expenditure limit.[26]

Judged by its use, federal funding of nominating campaigns appears to have succeeded. In each of the three presidential election years, 1976, 1980, and 1984, all but one serious candidate sought to qualify and did qualify for federal funds. The lone exception, John Connally in his campaign for the 1980 Republican nomination, showed that large sums could still be raised without federal funds, but his lack of success in winning delegates, whatever the reasons, has not led other candidates to follow his course, even though it avoids the expenditure ceilings. Unless candidates are willing and able to spend freely from their own family fortunes, they must now, given the legal contribution limits, reach many individuals who can give no more than $1,000 (or PACs that can give $5,000). No longer can a presidential nominating campaign, or any other federal campaign, be financed by a relatively limited number of large contributors. Even Connally, who raised $12.7 million and 93 percent of it from individuals, had to reach many fairly modest contributors, because the $1,000 contribution limit itself induces such solicitation. In fact, 43 percent of Connally's individual contributors gave less than $500 each.[27] The matching provision surely makes broad solicitation of contributions still more useful, when every private dollar in a gift up to $250 adds another federal dollar.

In this perspective, the law extends special advantages to candidates most willing and able to raise their funds from as many as 50,000 to 250,000 individual contributors. For example, Reagan raised in 1980 the right qualifying sums to secure over $6 million in federal matching money, and in 1984, without a Republican nominating contest, $10.1 million to qualify for the maximum federal grant (the other half of the $20.2 million expenditure limit).[28] Taken alone, Reagan's success might support the view that apparently ideological candidates most readily benefit from the matching system because their activist supporters respond heavily to mass solicitation. But, as was noted in the earlier discussion of private contributions, less ideological candidates than Reagan have also succeeded in reaching numerous modest givers. Thus Jimmy Carter in 1976 qualified for almost $3.5 million in federal matching money, and in 1980 for $5 million. Also in 1980 George Bush qualified for $5.7 million. In 1984, Walter Mondale qualified for $9.5 million and Gary Hart for $5.3 million.[29] Although none of these more moderate or centrist candidates did as well as Reagan in gathering matching funds, or for that matter in any other campaigning respect, each raised enough money to indicate that sharp ideological salience is not essential for success.

The matching-fund arrangement itself was hardly responsible for the development of mass fund-raising by ideological or nonideological candidates. That had begun in campaigns preceding the legislation for public funding, most specifically in the relatively ideological campaigns of Barry Goldwater in 1964, George Wallace in 1968, and George McGovern in 1972. Further, as noticed in chapter 7, mass solicitation of small contributions became the hallmark of the Republican party's successful appeal for funds on an only partly ideological basis. The common factor has been the availability not of federal matching funds but of computerized mass mailing, combined, in the case of candidates, with national media exposure. At most, the matching funds, as well as the legal limits on individual contributions, encourage broad solicitation by candidates who would not otherwise have the incentive. At the same time, a certain kind of ideological candidate — one without enough initial national recognition for successful early mass solicitation or without the resources for that solicitation — might find it harder to raise money under the legislation of the mid-1970s than before. That possibility is suggested by Herbert Alexander. In his view, the large loans that George McGovern initially obtained from wealthy supporters, in order to finance his successful direct-mail solicitation in 1972, would later have been barred as contributions over the legal limit.[30]

That the matching-fund arrangement is not entirely or only to the advantage of ideological candidates is of consequence in considering the effect that public funding of nominating campaigns has on parties. It bears on the view that the new legal provisions for financing presidential nominating campaigns add to the impact of other post-1968 reforms in producing the plebiscitary system in which ideological candidates, or perhaps party outsiders in general, are more likely to become party nominees. The holders of that view, preferring that American parties perform their former brokerage and coalitional roles at nominating conventions, understandably deplore whatever has made such roles unlikely if not virtually impossible. Because their argument puts the most weight on the effect of new nominating rules and practices, I dealt with it at length when discussing presidential nominations in chapter 4. Here it is only useful to say that federal matching funds, even more clearly than Democratic party reform and the growth of presidential primaries, represent mainly an accommodation to the way in which the public now expects major-party nominees to be selected. The plebiscitary system, essentially established by 1972, antedated the use of public funding, and it is reasonable to regard the matching arrangement as a recognition of the existence of large and expensive campaigns now conducted in numerous primaries. Nor can the matching funds, any more than the nominating rules themselves, be shown to have produced more ideological nominees than might have succeeded in the absence of those funds.

Another specific party-oriented objection to the public funding of presidential nominating contests is that the availability of federal money prolongs those intraparty contests and thus delays party consensus. Once qualified, a candidate remains eligible for additional grants matching continued individual contributions up to $250 each, unless the candidate fails to win at least 10 percent of the vote in two successive primaries. Even that failure can be compensated and eligibility then restored by the subsequent winning of at least 20 percent of a primary vote.[31] Hence no major contender is likely to lose the opportunity to obtain matching funds. Granting as much, however, is far from conceding that the federal funds cause candidates to continue hopeless or nearly hopeless campaigns longer than they would otherwise do or than candidates have done in the past.

The record since public funding shows no new pattern of persistence. In 1976, Reagan's candidacy against President Ford remained alive into the convention because he was in fact close to winning; and Jimmy Carter's 1976 opponents lasted only through the last primaries when they lost their last chance and then responded to produce a consensual nomination. In 1980 George Bush, following other Republican candidates, left the race soon enough after he had plainly lost so that party ranks could close well before the convention. Only Edward Kennedy in 1980, on the Democratic side, actually persisted in a losing candidacy throughout the whole primary season and into the convention itself, but he had some slight reason to think that the candidacy was not entirely hopeless and also other longer-term reasons to continue. The same can be said for Gary Hart and Jesse Jackson in 1984. Their persistence, like Kennedy's in 1980, probably did disturb Walter Mondale's pursuit of Democratic unity, but Hart and Jackson each saw advantages in remaining contestants. At most, the matching funds made it a little easier to pursue those perceived advantages.

Without attributing to public funding either the prolongation of nominating contests or the special fostering of ideological candidacies, it is evident that governmental financing of presidential nominating campaigns means large-scale support for candidate-centered politics. Specifically, $23.7 million went to 13 Democratic and two Republican candidates in 1976, $30.8 million to four Democratic and six Republican candidates in 1980, and about $36.5 million to nine Democratic, one Republican, and one nonmajor-party candidate in 1984.[32]

The support of fairly numerous candidates in nominating campaigns contrasts with the general election funding of only the two major-party nominees plus the less than full funding of Anderson. Each major-party nominee was eligible to receive $21.8 million in 1976, $29.4 million in 1980, and $40.4 million in 1984.[33] The $40.4 million was more than the total of $36.5 million received by *all* candidates for the 1984 party nominations. Yet the larger amounts for general elections are, like those for nominating contests, granted to individuals, and neither the Republican nor Democratic nominees have turned over their government grants to their party organizations. It is uncertain that they could do so and also readily comply with accounting requirements under the law. At any rate, all major-party nominees in 1976, 1980, and 1984 spent the public funds through their own campaign committees. These committees, in varying ways, coordinated their efforts with those of the national party committees, each of which could legally spend a more modest amount ($3.2 million in 1976, $4.6 million in 1980, and $6.9 million in 1984) of privately raised funds in behalf of its presidential nominee.[34] In other words, each candidate-centered committee was assured by the federal government of six to seven times the amount that the national party committee was allowed to spend *directly* on the presidential race.[35]

Candidate-controlled financing, it is worth reiterating, is nothing new in presidential campaigns. Precedents existed before public funding, and the pattern looks as though it became almost inevitable once nominating efforts required candidates to build and finance their own electoral organizations for primary competition. A nominee who must first use a committee of his own to raise funds in order to win a party label tends to retain that committee as his principal campaign agency whether it is funded by private or public funds. In other words, public funds for presidential general elections are handled in accord with the previously established expectations of candidate-centered campaign management. No new antiparty import can be discerned, even though there is nothing like the direct help for parties in the distribution of federal funds for campaigns that there is in the funding of conventions.

Perhaps, however, public funding of campaigns has indirectly helped national party organizations to develop the many nonpresidential activities described in chapter 7. The suggested connection is that full federal funding of the presidential general election frees a national committee from the campaign task of raising large sums of money as well as from the responsibility, after the campaign, of paying off the debts that candidates, especially Democrats, often accumulate.[36] The connection is credible in the sense that organizational developments have coincided with the decade of public funding, but the notably successful Republican party effort surely thrived mainly for reasons unrelated to any lesser responsibility for funding presidential campaigns. At most, the RNC might have devoted fewer of its expanding resources to nonpresidential elections and to general party building if it had also financed presidential campaigns more fully. Even that is doubtful, since the RNC seems able to raise so much money that it would not have to curtail other activities in order to spend more for its presidential candidate. Certainly the RNC has not had to stint when it did spend for its presidential candidate the limited though substantial amount ($6.9 million in 1984) that a party was allowed to spend as a coordinated expenditure for a publicly funded nominee. Nor, as also observed in the last chapter, has the RNC been unable to take advantage of the legal opportunities for less direct financing of a presidential campaign, particularly by transferring funds for voter-registration and other programs of state and local Republican parties.

A party's presidential campaign expenditures, though limited, are enhanced by the conditions attached to public funding. No *non*party group is permitted to spend in coordination with the nominee's campaign, and the nominee is limited by the expenditure ceiling accepted along with full public funding. Hence, the dollars that the RNC or DNC can spend are made more valuable. They would be still more valuable if independent expenditures by PACs and individuals could be constitutionally curbed in accord with the original congressional legislation. Yet a residual pro-party effect remains in that coordinated expenditures are probably more useful than the more generous independent expenditures. Thus public funding of nominees, while intended mainly as a substitute for private funding, may in a curious way have allowed national parties to become more important, relative to other private sources, in financing presidential campaigns than they were in 1972. No doubt such indirect help is less substantial, especially for the Democratic party, than the provision of public funds for a party-conducted campaign, but it is not meaningless.

III
State Dollars

Both the direct and indirect consequences of public funding for party-candidate relations may be observed in state legislation as in the national law's provisions for presidential campaigns. Public funding by the states was also developed in the 1970s, and like the national legislation, it has not grown much since that reform-minded decade. A high-water mark was reached in 1980 when 17 states had public-finance legislation. In the early 1980s, one of the 17 (Oregon) allowed its legislation to expire, and the laws of two of the others (Maryland and Oklahoma) remained at least temporarily inoperative. As of 1982, two additional states (California and Alaska) enacted legislation for public funding, but they did so in limited ways and provided no substantial operating experience for analysis in the early 1980s.[37] My account, therefore, is based on the 17 states whose laws were the subject of scholarly analysis before 1984.

Legislative provisions among the 17 states vary sufficiently to allow useful comparisons with respect to their impact on parties. In passing, many other variations may be observed. For example, state public-funding laws differ on how much must be raised privately (and in what sums) for a candidate to

be eligible for public funds, on expenditure ceilings accompanying the acceptance of public funds, on which campaigns (for executive, legislative, or judicial office) can be funded, on the funding of primaries as well as general elections, and on the means of collecting and distributing the public funds. In
these and other respects, the states are "laboratories of reform"[38] as they traditionally have been in other policy areas.

Two other preliminary notes are in order. One is that public funding by
the states, like public funding by the national government, is not readily dis-
entangled from legislative regulation of private financing of campaigns. The
usefulness of public funds, from the standpoint of possible recipients, is affected by the varying limits that the several states impose on private contributions by individuals, PACs, and parties and by the varying effectiveness of the
enforcement of such limits. Second, the states, again like the national government, function under the constitutional constraints of *Buckley v. Valeo*; the
states too can only impose *expenditure* ceilings as conditions accompanying the
acceptance of public funds. Hence states that want expenditure ceilings are
encouraged to adopt public funding partly to establish those ceilings. But states,
no more than the national government, can impose ceilings on individuals
or groups spending "independently" of those accepting the ceilings along with
the public funds.

The modest scope of state public funding is partly related to the fact that
none of the six largest states was among the 17 that adopted such funding
in the 1970s. Michigan, number seven in population, was the largest state
to do so. Furthermore, not all of the 17 states provided much money. Several
were slow to accumulate attractive amounts in their campaign accounts. Others fixed their maximum funding at a level that became less attractive as campaign costs mounted. Four states made it virtually certain that their campaign
accounts would have little money to distribute by asking taxpayers to *add* a
dollar or two to their income-tax liability instead of following the federal practice that enabled taxpayers to check off from their liability a dollar or two
for a political fund. Only in the checkoff states were useful amounts of money
produced.[39]

Mainly because of four medium-sized checkoff states — Michigan, Minnesota, New Jersey, and Wisconsin — the total of state campaign funds distributed in the early 1980s looks fairly impressive. Though less than $3 million
in 1980, when few states held statewide elections, it was over $20 million for
elections in 1981 and 1982. Of that total, however, more than $18 million
went to individual candidates and only a little more than $2 million to parties.
All four of the big-funding states gave money only for candidates, and the

two biggest (by far) gave money to primary as well as general election candidates for governor—almost $8.8 million in New Jersey's 1981 election and $5.7 million in Michigan's 1982 election.[40] In this light, state public funding resembles the federal in confirming candidate-centered campaigns. It does so not only in New Jersey, Michigan, Minnesota, and Wisconsin, but also in four other states where money, in lesser amounts, has similarly been distributed only to candidates.[41] Thus in eight of the 17 states, any pro-party result would be merely in the dubious form of indirect benefits that Republican and Democratic organizations could derive from having their general election nominees financed by state funds. And in five of those eight states, including New Jersey and Michigan, one must take into account the strictly candidate-centered effect of funding primary campaigns.[42] New Jersey's experience in 1981 is striking; $6.4 million, or over 70 percent of the total that the state provided for gubernatorial campaigns, went to primary candidates—ten Democrats and six Republicans.[43] More than any other experience with public funding, this large-scale support for primary campaigns in New Jersey attracted attention to candidate-centered effects and to an accompanying decline of party organizational influence over nominating and election campaigns.[44] New Jersey continued to fund primary as well as general election candidates for governor in 1985.

The large aggregate amounts that states have given exclusively to candidates may, however, be a less significant innovation in late-twentieth-century American politics than the smaller-scale funding of parties by eight states (and the planned funding by Oklahoma).[45] Six of the eight allowed parties to use substantial portions for their own administrative expenses as well as for financing campaigns;[46] another of the eight, Iowa, has given parties considerable flexibility with respect to organizational spending.[47] The eight states include a few that are fairly populous; all but one gave over $100,000 to parties in at least one of the two years, 1981 or 1982, four gave over $200,000 in at least one of those years, and North Carolina gave over $350,000 in 1980.[48] That these amounts are not as large as those for candidates in several other states is but partially explained by differences in population. Providing only small amounts may be the only way to fund parties at all. Candidates, it has been suggested, could more likely exert pressure to obtain funds for their own campaigns if more were to be distributed.[49]

Nevertheless, for parties, the public money obtained in seven of the eight states has been useful.[50] In North Carolina, public funds provided both of the state's major parties with about a quarter of their revenue over a two-year period, plus a like amount to be disbursed among their candidates; the funds enabled the Democratic party to purchase a computer that it used to increase

direct-mail solicitation and to target potential voters (helped by additional public funding in the early 1980s).[51] The Kentucky Democratic party developed
a sizable campaign headquarters for use in congressional and statewide races.
Generally, state parties have been helped to provide in-kind services of the sort
that they, like national party committees, have increasingly sought to offer.
State tax dollars thus sustain the bureaucratic expansion of the traditional cadre
party much as do private direct-mail contributions.

Two party-funding states (Iowa and Idaho), without specifically providing
for headquarters activities, nevertheless help party organizations by designat-
ing them as the agencies for distributing the state funds to party nominees.[52]
Such designation, made also in the several states that allow party organizations
to keep some but not all of their public funds, ordinarily means that a state
party central committee or its leadership equivalent has discretionary decision-
making power in distributing tax dollars to candidates.[53] Both the Democratic
and Republican state chairpersons from Iowa testified enthusiastically in behalf of the merits of their arrangements, organizationally and otherwise, when
a congressional public-funding bill was considered in 1979 by a committee
of the House of Representatives. Iowa had provided $187,000 for the 1976
campaign and $191,000 for 1978.[54] In 1980 the amount was $230,000, in 1981
$240,000, and in 1982 $243,000.[55] Although these totals may not account
for a very large share of all campaign expenditures, they are enough to give
party leaders potentially influential roles, especially because of the early and
regular availability of the public dollars.

Among the states that allocate funds to or through parties or both, it is
common to ask taxpayers, as the federal government does not, to check the
name of the party to which they want their dollars to go. The same option
is also provided even in a few states that distribute public funds directly to
candidates; that is, taxpayers may note which party's nominees should receive
their money. The results in the mid-1970s often heavily favored the Democratic party or its nominees, but the Republican party and its nominees tended
to come closer to equal status by the end of the decade. Yet a Democratic
advantage remained, apparently because Democratic identifiers more often outnumbered Republican identifiers.[56] Party designation thus favors the majority
party, although not always by as large a margin as its share of the electorate
might justify. On the other hand, a minority party clearly does better in states
where at least some of the money is put in a general fund and then distributed
in equal amounts to each major party.[57] The result is consistent with a policy
of encouraging interparty competition even if it is not most desirable from
the standpoint of the majority party's organization.

For those who want public funding to help parties, a more intriguing subject than that of party designation by taxpayers is the attempt to account for the nearly even division of public-funding states between those allocating something to parties and those allocating only to candidates. How are the eight party-funding states distinguishable from the candidate-helping states? The latter might well be expected to include the traditionally progressive antiparty organizational states. Accordingly, it is no surprise to find that Minnesota, Wisconsin, and Michigan provide money only for candidates. The other five candidate-funding states are not so readily classified. Massachusetts might conceivably qualify as antiorganizational, though not exactly in the progressive sense, but Maryland and New Jersey appear well outside the tradition.

On the party-funding side, it is similarly hard to generalize about the predominant political culture. Oregon had a progressive background resembling that of Minnesota and Wisconsin; yet it funded parties until it ceased public funding altogether. Several other party-funders—Iowa, Idaho, Kentucky, North Carolina, and Utah, for example—do not fit the strong party organization pattern associated with certain northeastern states. Understandably, then, one cannot support the view that party organizational strength is positively correlated with state provisions for public funding of parties. Strong parties do not appear to get state funds more often than do somewhat weaker parties. The point is troubling because it seems at odds with a broader comparative perspective in which European national parties, unlike American national parties, have been publicly funded as a natural consequence of their greater strength in dominating campaigns and elections. At the least, that perspective does not fit the American interstate comparison.

One of the most knowledgeable observers of state funding has even suggested an apparent reverse of the explanation that I would have drawn from the cross-national comparison. "The candidate states," Ruth Jones has written, "tend to be the states with traditionally strong party systems, and many of the party states are generally considered to have weak party systems."[58] Her "party systems" refer to the degree of a state's interparty competition, and it is true that in the standard classification of states by their competitiveness four of the candidate-funding states—Massachusetts, Wisconsin, Michigan, and Minnesota—are identified as competitive two-party. And three of the party-funding states—North Carolina, Kentucky, and Rhode Island—are identified as "Democratic majority" (though not as "Democratic dominant" or one-party states). On the other hand, five of the party-funding states—Oregon, Utah, Maine, Iowa, and Idaho—are two-party competitive, and two of the candidate-funding states—Maryland and Hawaii—are Democratic majority states.[59] Hence, from strong or weak party systems no safe generalization emerges to account for party as opposed to candidate funding.

Perhaps, however, Jones's suggested hypothesis could be sustained by a more direct measure of party organizational strength than that which is merely inferred from the presence of party competition. One such measure is provided by Jewell and Olson when they classify state parties according to whether they are organizationally cohesive or factional (determined partly by effectiveness of party endorsements in primary races). It does turn out that only in Iowa and Utah, among the party-funding states, is there a cohesive party that matters (apart, that is, from any cohesive minority party that does not seriously contend for power); most of the candidate-funding states also lack cohesive parties.[60] Consequently, one cannot conclude that the absence of such parties is a sufficient cause for states to support parties when they decide on public funding of any kind. The most that might be said is that states are somewhat more likely to support parties that are not strongly cohesive.

Why should even that likelihood exist? It can be explained, according to an experienced state party chairperson, "if one thinks about the threat an elected official may perceive in giving money to the Oregon Democratic Party as compared with the threat in giving the same kind of money to the Cook County Democratic Party. Where elected officials have been exposed to the limits that strong parties can impose upon the official's independent decision making, they are naturally reluctant to impose additional restrictions upon their ability to make policy."[61] In other words, state legislators would be more willing to help party organizations that lacked the capacity, actually or potentially, to determine their nomination and their policies. That capacity might not be expressed wholly or even satisfactorily by quantitative measures of organizational cohesion with respect to statewide success, nor by the more remote index of interparty competition.

Instead, party "strength" could be subjectively yet realistically perceived in terms of experience with a particular organization, like the Cook County Democratic party, that long dominated elected officials from a large section of a state. Thus one might account for New Jersey's especially generous candidate-funding arrangement as a rejection of the state's historically strong big-city machines. Obviously, however, these machines were not strong enough, at least in the 1970s, to control legislative decision-making with respect to public funding. Unlike European parties, New Jersey's organizations did not, and presumably could not, arrange for taxpayers' money to be appropriated for their purposes. Nor did parties in other states with relatively recent histories of big-city machines, like New Jersey's, receive public funds, but it must be noted that in such states—New York, Illinois, and Pennsylvania are the leading examples—no public funding exists for candidates *or* parties.

My uncertain belief is that the old party organizations of the Cook County Democratic type are not now strong enough, partly because they are not respectable enough, to obtain state funding, but that they remain sufficiently threatening in certain states to lead legislators (if and when they enact any public funding laws) to give money to candidates rather than to parties. That belief is consistent with the fact that none of the notorious old machine states appropriate money to parties, and with the fact that none of the eight party-funding states recently experienced anything like the Cook County kind of politics. Party organizations in the party-funding states may not appear entirely benign, but they have not earned reputations for either wickedness or domination. Iowa's party organizations, for example, look respectable and moderately but hardly oppressively effective. Nor are they or their counterparts in the other party-funding states as reputedly ideological as several of the party organizations in Wisconsin, Minnesota, and Michigan. Because these last-named are all candidate-funding states, it is tempting to think that their parties are threatening enough, not as old-fashioned machines but as militantly liberal or conservative issue-activists, to cause legislators to resist the idea of funding their organizations or of giving them discretion in allocating state funds among candidates.

The threat may be mainly incipient, rather than retrospective as it is in the case of the old machines, but nonetheless significant enough so that ideological parties would be as unlikely prospects for funding as the old machines. Again, however, it must be stressed that party strength, in this instance of the ideological organizations, would be only great enough, and then only potentially, to cause legislators to avoid helping them. As I remarked earlier about the old machines, if ideological parties were really strong, they would presumably be able, like European parties, to determine legislative decision-making in this area. We are left, then, with the hypothesis that states tend to support parties whose organizations are relatively bland, nonthreatening, and yet able to provide useful services for candidates.

Reluctant as legislators apparently are to provide funds for parties perceived as possibly powerful in any respect, they may tolerate the use of their financing laws to assist parties more indirectly. Wisconsin, a determinedly candidate-funding state, is illustrative. A statewide or legislative candidate receiving Wisconsin's public funds must agree not only to an overall expenditure ceiling that effectively restricts the use of private funds to an amount only slightly more than the maximum allotment of public funds, but also to a ceiling—

specifically, 45 percent of the overall expenditure ceiling — on the amount that can be received from the state and PACs together. For example, a gubernatorial candidate receiving $450,000 in state funds for a campaign whose total expenditure ceiling was $1 million would not be able to accept any PAC money. The other $550,000 could be sought from individuals and parties, but since the law also specifies that no more than 65 percent can come from state funds, PACs, and parties (altogether), the candidate with $450,000 of state money could receive no more than $200,000 (20 percent) from parties. The remaining $350,000 (35 percent) could be sought from individuals. The intent is anti-PAC more than pro-party, and the legal limit on the party share is lower than pro-party advocates, especially on the Republican side, would prefer. Yet it is generous, given the likelihood that PAC contributions would be almost entirely eliminated for candidates accepting public funding. That likelihood exists in part because of the special encouragement that Wisconsin offers a candidate to accept public funds; a candidate need not observe the accompanying ceiling if an opponent rejects the funds and so the ceiling.[62] In that event, the candidate first accepting the public funds can spend them and also as much private money as is raised.

Experience with the Wisconsin law is limited, since until 1980 public funds were inadequate. By 1982, however, sufficient public funds were available to attract statewide candidates and over half of the major-party legislative candidates qualifying as general election nominees.[63] The result, as intended, was at least a modest reduction in the percentage of legislative candidate funding that came from PACs, but the increase from 1980 in party contributions to candidates was so slight as to leave the party percentage well below figures from the mid-1970s.[64] Of course, increasing the party share had been less an intention than a hoped-for incidental result. It may have been achieved marginally in one curiously indirect way, for the campaign committees of the legislative party caucuses. Under an amended version of the campaign finance law, they were eligible, along with extragovernmental party organizations, to contribute to a candidate as a party committee but not as a PAC could do when public funds were accepted. The caucus campaign committees made good use of the opportunity in 1982 by collecting substantial PAC money and then distributing it in legally laundered form to candidates as party contributions.[65] The potential thus opened for party influence is considerable, but it is not the kind of party influence that pro-party champions often have in mind. The only organization strengthened by the special operation of the Wisconsin arrangement is that of a party-in-government — which happened as of 1982 to be especially well organized to collect money. Nevertheless, the strengthening of that kind of party, it can surely be argued, is consequential as a means of countering the effects of candidate-centered politics in legislative elections.

In one way or another, parties can thus be helped at least a little by public funding laws that provide no state dollars for parties. When parties themselves are less suspect than they have traditionally been in Wisconsin, a state might well provide more liberal contribution limits for parties, while restricting PAC contributions within an expenditure ceiling accompanying public funding of candidates. But an obvious difficulty in the way of even indirect party help is that public funding itself is not being adopted by states as it was in the 1970s. And where it remains, its popularity is occasionally in doubt.[66]

IV
Prospects

Resistance to public funding, after its initial development in the 1970s, is tenacious at the national as well as the state level. In the mid-1980s, it became part of a strong conservative opposition to many governmental domestic programs. As President Reagan said in explaining why he had included in his 1985 tax reform a proposal to eliminate the checkoff for presidential campaigns, "I've never believed in government funding of campaigns" because "the government decides who gets it." Candidates, he believed, should be able to raise funds from their supporters. "If they can't get that kind of support," he added, "they shouldn't be seeking public office."[67] With or without such ideological underpinning, Republican party organizational interests would, as we have seen, be much better served by liberalizing the private contribution and spending limits for parties than by funding parties publicly. On the other side, public funding remains popular among liberal Democrats and reformers more generally as a solution for both the iniquity of politics dominated by special interests and the inequality of privately financed campaigns. Their preference is strengthened, as we have noticed, by constitutional rulings that allow a ceiling on candidate expenditures (though not on independent expenditures) only when a candidate accepts such a ceiling along with public funds. Existing arrangements for presidential campaign funding are vigorously defended, probably enough to preclude their abolition, and the extension of public funding to other campaigns is conceivable if reformism and liberalism were to revive.

Even in a future political environment more favorable for public funding, the American precedents are mainly for funding candidates and not parties. Accordingly, the most seriously considered bills for funding congressional campaigns have been wholly candidate centered. Proposals for those campaigns continued to appear in the 1980s, but the ones presented in 1979 are worth special attention because chances for enactment were not as remote as they became in the 1980s. Democrats still had majorities in both houses of Congress, and President Jimmy Carter was sympathetic to reform.

Public funding solely for House of Representatives campaigns was the subject of five days of hearings before the Committee on House Administration in 1979. Although the committee did not in the end report favorably on any of several funding proposals, the hearings reveal a good deal about congressional perspectives on the distribution of any public funds that might be appropriated for House campaigns. The revelation is bad news for pro-party advocates. Of the five bills that the committee considered, all gave funds only to candidates and their designated committees.[68] The differences between the bills were occasionally material in other respects (funding primaries in one instance), but none gave anything to parties. The principal proposal, H.R. 1, had 130 House sponsors, including some Republicans, chiefly liberal or moderate Republicans, and many Democrats. Several of the 130 representatives were House members in high standing—Abner Mikva, John Anderson, Richard Bolling, Thomas Foley, Barber Conable, Morris Udall, and Henry Reuss —and their names, along with a fairly broad bipartisan sponsorship, lent weight to the bill.

H.R. 1 would have funded only general election candidates, and it would have done so by matching individual (not PAC) contributions of $100 or less. Among its other provisions were expenditure limitations of $150,000 total and of $25,000 from personal and family funds, such limitations to be imposed as conditions for candidates accepting public funds.[69] Innovatively at the federal level, H.R. 1 stipulated that a candidate accepting public funds and the accompanying conditions would not be bound by those conditions if a non-public-funded opponent spent more than $75,000 total or more than $25,000 from personal and family funds. This suspension of the ceilings struck the FEC as so difficult to enforce that its chairperson objected to the bill.[70] A politically more salient objection to the provision was that it made H.R. 1 look like a measure to protect incumbents, because a candidate could accept public funds and still raise as large a sum as ever from private sources if the money were needed in a race against a rich or privately well-financed opponent. Although challengers would have had the same legal opportunity as incumbents to use the waiver provision, incumbents were especially likely to regard it as a helpful safeguard. Thus the bill could perhaps attract House members worried about big-spending opponents. That kind of attraction was enhanced in a 1983 bill that allowed a candidate choosing the public-financing option, while an opponent rejected it, not only to spend above the ceiling with private funds but also to become eligible for a two-to-one match in public funds instead of the one-to-one match.[71] But like the more modest 1979 waiver, the 1983 provision did not win majority support for the bill. Members might well have been more worried in both years by the public funding of challengers who in most instances would be neither rich themselves nor able to match the private money-raising of incumbents.

Suggestions for giving money to parties were made at the 1979 hearings, but from outside the ranks of congressional sponsors of legislation. This is not to say that the sponsors regarded their proposals as antiparty. On the contrary, one of the chief sponsors of H.R. 1, Representative Mikva, argued that the expenditure ceilings in his bill would enhance the influence of parties—presumably because the role of PACs would be reduced when publicly funded candidates had less or no use for PAC contributions.[72] The point was explicit in written testimony from the chairperson of the Democratic National Committee, John White. In endorsing public financing of congressional elections, White said: ". . . public financing will, in my opinion, come to the assistance of our two party system. Let's be honest! If the single or special interest groups are restricted in the amount of money they can spend in House and Senate races—and with the Presidential campaign already foreclosed—much of that money will go to the parties."[73] It would be hard to substantiate the last clause, and the statement generally was far from the view of the Republican National Committee. Its representative stated at the hearings: "The effect on parties of H.R. 1 surely has to be devastating. The system of matching grants emphasizes the personal fund raising appeal of individuals rather than any kind of affiliation with organizations in the political process."[74] A similar point was made by a Republican member of the Committee on House Administration in an exchange with Representative Mikva.[75]

To some extent, different issues were addressed by each side. Proponents of H.R. 1 argued that their bill could help parties indirectly although it funded only candidates; opponents stressed that the plainly candidate-centered funding was necessarily so antiparty that it rendered any projected indirect party benefits most inadequately compensatory. Perhaps also the two sides represented contrasting party perspectives. The Democratic organization might collect more money from PACs, notably union PACs, if PACs were unable to contribute much to candidates; certainly the Democratic organization needed

PAC money more than did the Republican party with its highly successful direct-mail solicitation of individual givers. The Republican national organization was already thus well-enough financed so that it could do without public funds as well as without additional PAC funds. At the hearings, the RNC representative urged, instead of H.R. 1 or any other public-funding bill, that Congress simply allow parties to spend more privately raised money to help candidates than the regulatory law now allowed.[76]

Not all pro-party supporters of the principle of public funding were willing to accept H.R. 1's fully candidate-centered financing, and some, while going along with H.R. 1, would have liked it much better if it had provided at least some money for parties and not merely for candidates. So it was that Iowa's party chairpersons, pleased with their own state's distribution of public funds through their organizations, urged that Congress follow a similar pattern in funding House campaigns. Specifically, they suggested that federal money, like Iowa's state money, should be given to *state* party organizations.[77] Iowa itself provided a precedent for such treatment of state parties; the state's public funding, unlike that in most other states, could be used for congressional as well as state-office campaigns. But it goes a little farther to argue that the national government's money should also be given to state party organizations. The argument represents a significant reassertion of the confederative party tradition in American politics.

Iowans were not alone in making the case for state parties. It was more fully developed by Morley Winograd, Michigan's Democratic state chairperson. Testifying as president of the Association of State Democratic Chairpersons, Winograd presented that association's public-funding proposal as an alternative to H.R. 1. Specifically, he proposed that dollars checked off for congressional campaigns by federal income tax payers be returned to the taxpayers' states, directed to parties of the taxpayers' choice, and then so distributed by state parties that 50 percent would go to U.S. House candidates and 25 percent to U.S. Senate candidates. The remaining 25 percent, to be kept by state parties to finance their federal election activities, was the direct party-strengthening provision. There appeared to be little organizational discretion in distributing the other 75 percent to winners of party nominations for the House and Senate.[78] Nevertheless, the manner of distribution was fairly presented as a means of raising party consciousness among candidates as well as among taxpayers who designated their dollars for Republicans or Democrats. Altogether, Winograd's proposal was certainly pro-party in a sense that H.R. 1 was not, and he offered it on that basis. In helping state as opposed to national party organizations, he seemed to assume their appropriateness as the traditionally consequential extragovernmental party units. So they also seemed several years later in the scholarly work of another Democratic state party chairperson, David Price, whose advocacy of partial public financing of congressional campaigns similarly specified that funds be channeled through state parties.[79]

The fact is that in many states during much of this century neither national nor state party organizations have regularly been major participants in congressional campaigns. The large-scale efforts of the Republican National Committee, in conjunction with congressional campaign committees, are recent and novel. State party roles have been less conspicuous. Thus a Connecticut representative at the 1979 committee hearings asserted that even in his traditionally strong party state it would be a radical departure for state party organizations to have as much of a role in a congressional campaign as Winograd's proposed public funding gave them. Winograd's response was that he and the other state Democratic chairpersons would welcome the departure in Connecticut and in other states where parties had not been active in congressional races.[80] But one suspects that congressional members from those states would not similarly welcome the change and that they would be most reluctant to vote public funds for the purpose of effecting it. Why should they make themselves more dependent on a state party organization within which they could not be sure of exerting much influence? It is hard to believe that many members of Congress would be so worried about PAC domination as to accept greater party roles as a substitute.

If members of Congress were willing to strengthen any party organizations for congressional campaigning, it is more likely that they would favor Washington-based committees that they themselves controlled. The obvious ones are not the Republican and Democratic national committees but the congressional and senatorial campaign committees whose officers and staffs are chosen, in each party, by the representatives and senators themselves. Yet the possibility received almost no attention in the 1979 hearings. It was not even clearly advocated in the testimony of the 14 political scientists who belonged to the Committee for Party Renewal. In urging Congress to appropriate funds to parties and not merely to candidates, they said that "the appropriate bodies would be the national and state committees of the parties as recognized by state law."[81] The national committees thus recognized appear to be the RNC and DNC. Only later did one of the 14 political scientists add that party organizations receiving public funds "should be, perhaps, National, State, or congressional campaign committees."[82]

Any reference to congressional committees was untypical not only of the

hearings but of subsequent public-funding proposals from sources other than
the political scientists' Committee for Party Renewal. For example, a reform-
minded panel of President Carter's Commission for a National Agenda for
the Eighties specified "the national committees of the parties"[83]—evidently
the RNC and DNC—as the organizations to receive a portion of the federal
funds that the panel wanted appropriated for congressional general election
campaigns. In this proposal, the remainder of the appropriated funds would
go directly to congressional candidates, and even the portion going to the national committees was meant for redistribution to the candidates rather than
for organizational expenses. The committees, however, were apparently to have
some discretion in redistributing their public funds among candidates. As the
panel said, "Such funding also would allow the parties to penalize incumbents if they have been flagrantly disloyal, and to warn other incumbents of
the consequences of disloyalty to the party."[84] The avowed purpose may itself
explain the choice of national party committees rather than congressional
campaign committees; the latter, controlled as they are by incumbents, would
rarely want to penalize their own members.

Issues of this kind, as they affect congressional campaigns, are seldom discussed in much detail as long as proposals with the greatest support are for
funding candidates only. For example, the 1984 recommendation of the Twentieth Century Fund's Task Force, like H.R. 1 in 1979 and the 1983 congressional bill, specifies that Congress partially fund candidates, and thus does not
raise the question of which parties should be funded.[85] No doubt many pro-
party advocates would be happy to have public funds for any party organization rather than for none. Nevertheless they would surely recognize that the
choice of party organization is a meaningful one. If the objective is to strengthen
ideological, programmatic, or issue-oriented cohesion in a congressional party,
national party organizations seem more relevant than sets of 50 separate state
party organizations. And, as suggested already, the RNC and DNC seem likelier, or at least less unlikely, to serve the purpose than the congressional campaign committees.

On the other hand, public funding of the RNC and DNC for congressional
campaigning would foster organizational forces readily perceived as threats to
individual members of Congress accustomed to candidate-centered financing
bolstered by funds from the congressional campaign committees that the members collectively control. The RNC or DNC in particular would be threatening when dominated, as is often the case, by an incumbent president interested in having members of Congress loyal to his leadership. In this perspective,
for Congress to appropriate congressional campaign funds for an extracon-

gressional though national party organization is as improbable as an appropriation for state party organizations. Apart from that hard political reality, it should also be appreciated that the strengthening of national party organizations at the expense of the working autonomy of individual members of Congress and their own congressional parties would constitute a profound change in the American political system. For better or worse, such a change should not be expected to come solely or principally from public-funding legislation.

The same question about which parties to fund does not arise in nations whose parliamentary systems preclude separate legislative and executive party organizations. In those nations, however, a choice may exist between a parliamentary party and an extraparliamentary organization bearing the same label but influenced by different leaders. Thus elsewhere, too, the distribution of public funds, varying from nation to nation, has consequences for intraparty relations even at a strictly national level. And public funding may also affect the national-regional-local relationships of party organizations. In federal arrangements like Canada's or West Germany's, funding from both national and provincial, or state, governments tends to preserve party organizations at both national and regional levels. A similar tendency shows up in Sweden, a nonfederal nation that nevertheless provides public funds for both national and local party organizations.[86] Yet even in Canada and West Germany, as well as in Finland, Italy, and Austria, it is believed that government controls and subsidies "strengthen the central party organizations vis-à-vis local parties and reinforce the position of the dominant groups within the leadership against minority factions and their leaders."[87] The latter point flows not merely from funding at the national level but from funding of organizations controlled by parliamentary party leaders. Moreover, because these organizations are often funded between elections as well as during campaign periods, their professional and bureaucratic staffs are substantially strengthened.

The relevance of foreign experience for American concerns is no doubt limited by the assumption in other nations that parties of some kind should be the principal recipients of any public funding. Apart from a few limited exceptions — Canada, Japan, and France — government money has gone only to parties so that they could continue their dominant campaign roles.[88] In the United States, however, the question is whether parties, not now dominant in campaigns, should be helped by public subsidy to become more significant. To be sure, the American parties to be helped are the already established ones. As in Europe, where subsidies are ordinarily allocated on the basis of past party performance as measured by votes or parliamentary seats, so in the United States the major parties are intended to be the prime beneficiaries.

Indeed, they already are, where any American parties have been subsidized — for their national conventions and certain state organizational purposes. Such treatment is consistent with the traditional status of the Republican and Democratic parties as regulated and privileged public utilities. But it may be inconsistent with the now established candidate-centered campaigns and with a broader American ideological perspective. The institutionalization of parties in the United States has, after all, been strongly antiorganizational, and thus different from the corporatism of European-style public funding. Helping to maintain bureaucratic party organizations is hardly what progressive-inspired regulations were meant to accomplish.

Whatever the reasons, American parties do not emerge in my account of public funding as likely recipients of much if any additional direct help. The outlook is somewhat brighter for more public funding of candidates and thus probably for further reinforcement of candidate-centered campaigns. Indirectly, it is true, such funding could help parties if they were able to spend more in coordination with and in behalf of candidates who themselves accepted expenditure ceilings along with government money. But such help requires the liberalization of limits now imposed on the privately funded efforts of parties, and that would be useful even in the absence of public funding. Unhappily, liberalization may not be much more feasible politically, given Democratic opposition, than is an expansion of public funding in light of Republican opposition.[89]

A pro-party proposal on which Republicans and Democrats might have less disagreement is for legislation requiring that free radio and television time be provided for political parties. Although the legislation need not involve taxpayer money,[90] I note it here rather than among regulations of private funding. It is a kind of government-instigated subsidy at the expense of the owners of radio and television facilities. Legislation would have to be congressional for application both to networks in national elections and to stations in state elections. A practical limitation is that in some states, many congressional districts, and most smaller constituencies the media market, especially television's, does not coincide with the relevant electorate. Yet the usefulness of free media time has been amply demonstrated by the telecasting of presidential debates and debates between candidates for governor and U.S. Senator in certain states. The debates have been carried as news events, not in response to legal stipulations, and they have been candidate rather than party oriented. The television networks have, however, provided something similar for parties by covering their national conventions and by giving opposition party representatives equal time to respond to a president's televised speech. It would

not seem a big step to provide campaign time for parties to use as they like—
perhaps to present their nominees as well as their policies. Constitutionally,
legislating free air time should be no more difficult than legislating public
funds; independents and minor parties must be taken into account, but as our
public funding laws already demonstrate, the problems are not beyond the
capacity of legal minds to solve in ways nonetheless favorable to major parties.

An evidently greater departure from past American practice would be involved, it may be granted, in specifying allotments of time, by law, for particular organizations rather than merely for public-service programming in
general. Such a requirement, however, is so prevalent in other nations that
its absence in the United States astounds many foreign observers of American
election campaigns. The difference cannot be explained by government ownership of radio and television, because elsewhere free political time is required
even for privately owned services.[91] True, other nations (like Britain) couple
the free time with a prohibition on the purchase of any additional time for
political advertising. Such prohibition would probably be unconstitutional in
the United States. Therefore we lack one incentive for adopting the requirement of free time; reformers could not use it to curb total expenditures by
cutting off campaign advertisements of "independent" individuals and groups
unbound by limits accepted by the recipients of the free air time. They could
only frame the legislation in a way that would keep parties, as the recipients,
from buying additional time. Doing so would make the proposal more un-
appealing to Republicans for the same reason that expenditure ceilings make
public funding proposals more unattractive to them. Therefore, proponents
of free air time for parties would have reason to resist accompanying limits
on the purchase of such time.

However appealing free air time for parties might become for Republican
as well as Democratic organizations, does it not go against the candidate-
centered grain of American campaigns as does public funding of parties? A
largely affirmative answer cannot be avoided, but the difficulty might be lessened if little or no tax money were required and if only a few time slots were
provided principally or entirely at the national level.

Chapter Eleven
An Unbreakable Mold?

The modesty of my suggestions for helping parties through campaign finance legislation reiterates a theme of the book: parties can be maintained and strengthened but only within a well-established political culture that is hostile to both the revival of older American party organizational forms and the emergence of European-style parties. In that perspective, our parties change in limited though important ways. Recently, for example, the congressional party has enlarged its apparatus in order to cope with the results of increasingly candidate-centered elections, a new kind of presidential following has emerged, extragovernmental party organizations have become more regularly funded professional bureaucracies, and parties have developed a greater national presence. At the same time, any general nationalization is countered by an evidently increased capacity of a party's officeholders, in state governments and in Congress, to win elections while distancing themselves from national party leaders. As voters have become less regularly responsive to party cues, candidates, without shedding party labels, depend increasingly on their own appeals.

In analyzing these and other changes, I have emphasized their compatibility with the porousness of American parties. I have devoted many pages to describing how that porousness has been institutionalized, thereby contributing to the persistence of the Republican and Democratic parties even while limiting their organizational effectiveness. An important instrument for this has been the direct primary, in which voters have at least the opportunity to choose party nominees, and in which organizational leaders and activists often can do no more than exert influence over nominations. Extending the primary to presidential nominations fits the pattern, and it is not, therefore, viewed as a recent and readily reversible aberration.

When and where the primary is used, it bolsters individual representation of a kind always encouraged by the electoral separation of legislative and executive branches. Elected officials are expected to respond to their constituencies and not merely to parties whose labels they carry. Having less than cohesive policymaking parties is, after all, part of the American system of government. Popular expectations of party loyalty do exist, but they seldom go so far as to bind elected representatives to organizationally determined policy positions.

Accepting the constraints of our system makes for a skeptical approach to highly ambitious party-strengthening measures. Like some of the pro-party campaign finance proposals, ideas for greater use of caucuses and conventions to nominate candidates appear politically unrealistic. I am even doubtful about fostering effectively closed primaries in states whose established practices permit easy ballot access for voters regardless of prior party preference. Indeed, opening several of the primaries that are now closed is a more likely political response to the increasing numbers of voters who only lean toward a party rather than fully identifying with it. Parties are not thereby destroyed or rendered meaningless. They continue to be useful in the United States, even though their roles are different and in certain respects more limited than those of parties elsewhere.

No doubt my perspective is deeply conservative in its belief that American parties will persist, with merely incremental changes, in a now-settled mold. Cannot that mold, itself the institutionalized product of our political culture, be broken? Its continuity over many decades may not mean that a radical transformation is inconceivable. The possibilities are of two kinds. One is a disintegration or decomposition of parties that leaves only interest groups as mediating agencies in the conduct of elections and government. But the prospect of politics without parties is so novel in the universe of democratic nations that it is ordinarily rejected as the undesirable outcome of a continuing decline of parties. The second kind of transformation, however, has more champions. It would establish responsible party government of a sort long advocated by those scholars whose commitment has always been to parties stronger than the indigenous American variety. In that advocacy, measures to strengthen party organizations are coupled with the encouragement of sharper ideological distinctions between parties. The Republican and Democratic parties, somewhat realigned, are most often assumed to be the vessels of transformation, but the development of new parties is occasionally contemplated. Either course requires breaking the institutional mold in which our major parties are now set.

Breaking the mold may have recently become less remote because of the constitutional challenge to long-standing state laws that foster party duopoly while also limiting the exercise of organizational power within that duopoly. If, as I have argued, those laws deter third-party development by providing protest movements with ready access through primaries to advantageous major-party nominations, would not a judicial destruction of state-run party primaries effectively encourage multipartyism, since Republican and Democratic organizations would then control their own nominations and make entry by outsiders much more difficult? The result might well be the election of enough third-party candidates so that the virtually automatic Republican or Democratic majorities in Congress and state legislatures would cease to exist.[1] In that event, interparty coalitions would presumably substitute for what is called the "adversary" two-party system. Institutionally, that would amount to a radical change, especially in the organization of legislative bodies, but in policymaking the need for interparty coalitions would not be so dramatically different from the cross-party coalitions now often made possible by the looseness of Republican and Democratic party loyalties. The major American parties do not practice the kind of adversary politics often thought to mark Britain's Labour and Conservative parties.

Third-party champions, however, are not the most salient challengers of the legally institutionalized treatment of the major parties as public utilities. In the forefront of the attack are the proponents of responsible party government who are committed to two-partyism as most compatible with their majoritarian principles. Understandably, they welcome recent decisions freeing party organizations from a few especially onerous restrictions and marginally increasing the capacity of those organizations to determine rules for entry in the nominating contests run by state governments. But would responsible party government really be advanced by a surprisingly sweeping deregulation of parties that prevented states from managing elections in which *party* candidates are nominated? Despite that kind of deregulation, states could find other means to meet the well-established American custom of voter participation in the selection process preceding a general election. An available option is to establish nonpartisan primaries for state and congressional offices, like those now often used for municipal and judicial offices, and thus afford voters the opportunity to choose among several candidates and thereby determine the top two vote-getters to run against each other in the next round. Or states could adopt the modified nonpartisan system pioneered by Louisiana in the

1970s and allow candidates to put party labels beside their ballot listings while competing individually for election rather than for state-sanctioned party nominations.[2] Like a completely nonpartisan election, the Louisiana system appears more heavily candidate-centered than a party primary followed by a contest between party nominees. Of course, party organizations could endorse and support candidates competing in nonparty primaries, but the circumstances would be less advantageous than those of party primaries in which endorsement and support are also possible.

With or without endorsements by Republican, Democratic, and perhaps third-party organizations, the maintenance of some kind of primary strikes me as more probable in most states than a return to legally recognized nomination by caucuses and conventions if state-run primaries should unexpectedly be ruled unconstitutional.[3] Except in Virginia, where state law permits parties to nominate in conventions, primaries are widely used, although states could even now obviously abolish them despite their constitutionality. During the last few decades primaries have spread rather than diminished. They fit American expectations, and their present form turns out to be compatible with the persistence of the Republican and Democratic parties, if not with their ideological realignment or with the development of strong third parties. In any case, direct primaries are far from being solely responsible for our candidate-centered politics. They are best understood as a means for practicing the American preference for that style of politics.

Deinstitutionalization of the major parties might well destroy their duopoly along with their porousness, but it is hardly clear whether more effective parties would then exist. The circumstances conducive to candidate-centered politics will surely remain to make it difficult for a new kind of party to respond more successfully than have our established parties. For as should be apparent from the record of the last decade, today's institutionalized Republican and Democratic parties have developed significant organizational roles within the candidate-centered pattern. Thus they survive and even moderately prosper in a society evidently unreceptive to much stronger parties and yet unready, and probably unable, to abandon parties altogether.

Appendices
Notes
Index

Appendix A

Republicans and Democrats in Congress and the Presidency, 1939–85

(D = Democratic, R = Republican. Data for beginning of first session of each Congress, except as noted; exclude vacancies at beginning of session.)

Year	Party and President	Congress	House Majority Party	House Minority Party	House Other	Senate Majority Party	Senate Minority Party	Senate Other
1939	D (F. Roosevelt)	76th	D-261	R-169	4	D-69	R-23	4
1941	D (F. Roosevelt)	77th	D-268	R-162	5	D-66	R-28	2
1943	D (F. Roosevelt)	78th	D-218	R-208	4	D-58	R-37	1
1945	D (F. Roosevelt)	79th	D-242	R-190	2	D-56	R-38	1
1947	D (Truman)	80th	R-245	D-188	1	R-51	D-45	0
1949	D (Truman)	81st	D-263	R-171	1	D-54	R-42	0
1951	D (Truman)	82d	D-234	R-199	1	D-49	R-47	0
1953	R (Eisenhower)	83d	R-221	D-211	1	R-48	D-47	1
1955	R (Eisenhower)	84th	D-232	R-203	0	D-48	R-47	1
1957	R (Eisenhower)	85th	D-233	R-200	0	D-49	R-47	0
1959[a]	R (Eisenhower)	86th	D-284	R-153	0	D-65	R-35	0
1961	D (Kennedy)	87th	D-263	R-174	0	D-65	R-35	0
1963	D (Kennedy)	88th	D-258	R-177	0	D-67	R-33	0
1965	D (Johnson)	89th	D-295	R-140	0	D-68	R-32	0
1967	D (Johnson)	90th	D-247	R-187	0	D-64	R-36	0
1969	R (Nixon)	91st	D-243	R-192	0	D-57	R-43	0
1971[b]	R (Nixon)	92d	D-255	R-180	0	D-54	R-44	2
1973[b,c]	R (Nixon)	93d	D-242	R-192	1	D-56	R-42	2
1975[d]	R (Ford)	94th	D-291	R-144	0	D-60	R-37	2
1977[e]	D (Carter)	95th	D-292	R-143	0	D-61	R-38	1
1979[e]	D (Carter)	96th	D-276	R-157	0	D-58	R-41	1
1981[e]	R (Reagan)	97th	D-243	R-192	0	R-53	D-46	1
1983	R (Reagan)	98th	D-269	R-165	0	R-54	D-46	0
1985	R (Reagan)	99th	D-253	R-182	0	R-53	D-47	0

Source: Except for minor changes and the addition of 1985 data from newspaper sources, table is a reprint of table 408 from Statistical Abstract of the United States, 1985 (Washington, D.C.: U.S. Department of Commerce, 1985), p. 245. The Abstract's table was compiled from successive editions of the Congressional Directory.

[a]Includes Hawaii; members seated August 1959.
[b]Senate had 1 Independent and 1 Conservative Republican.
[c]House had 1 Independent-Democrat.
[d]Senate had 1 Independent, 1 Conservative-Republican, and 1 undecided (New Hampshire).
[e]Senate had 1 Independent.

National Election Results by Party
in the Eleven States of the Old Confederacy,[a]
1940–84

Year	Presidential Electoral Votes[b]			U.S. Senators[c]		U.S. Representatives	
	Democrat	Republican	Other	Democrat	Republican	Democrat	Republican
1940	124	0	0	22	0	100	2
1942				22	0	103	2
1944	127	0	0	22	0	103	2
1946				22	0	103	2
1948	88	0	39	22	0	103	2
1950				22	0	103	2
1952	71	57	0	22	0	100	6
1954				22	0	99	7
1956	60	67	1	22	0	99	7
1958				22	0	99	7
1960	81	33	14	22	0	99	7
1962				21	1	95	11
1964	81	47	0	20	2	90	16
1966				19	3	83	23
1968	25	57	46	18	4	80	26
1970				16	5	79	27
1972	0	129	1	14	7	74	34
1974				15	6	81	27
1976	118	12	0	16	5	81	27
1978				15	6	77	31
1980	12	118	0	11	10	69	39
1982				11	11	82	34
1984	0	138	0	12	10	73	43

Sources: Statistical Abstract of the United States, 1985 (Washington, D.C.: U.S. Department of Commerce, 1985), p. 239; *Congressional Directory* (Washington, D.C.: G.P.O., various editions, 1941–83); *Guide to U.S. Elections* (Washington, D.C.: Congressional Quarterly, 1975); and news accounts for 1984 data.

[a]The eleven states are Alabama, Arkansas, Florida, Georgia, Louisiana, Mississippi, North Carolina, South Carolina, Tennessee, Texas, and Virginia.

[b]Electoral votes cast for nonmajor party candidates: 39 for States' Rights candidate in 1948, 1 for Walter B. Jones in 1956, 14 for Harry F. Byrd in 1960, 46 for George C. Wallace in 1968, and 1 for John Hospers in 1972.

[c]Count of U.S. Senators includes holdovers as well as Senators newly elected in each election year. The total of Democrats and Republicans is one short of 22 from 1970 through 1980, because Senator Harry F. Byrd, Jr., of Virginia held office as an Independent during those years although obtaining committee assignments as a Democrat. John Tower of Texas was first elected as a Republican Senator in 1961.

Appendix C
Party Funds[a] in Federal Elections, 1977–84
(millions)

	Republicans				Democrats			
	1983–84	1981–82	1979–80	1977–78	1983–84	1981–82	1979–80	1977–78
Raised	$297.9	$215.0	$169.5	$84.5	$98.5	$39.3	$37.2	$26.4
Spent	300.8	214.0	161.8	85.9	97.4	40.1	35.0	26.9
Contributed	4.9	5.6	4.5	4.5	2.6	1.7	1.7	1.8
Coordinated expenditures[b]	20.1	14.3	12.4	4.3	9.0	3.3	4.9	.4

Source: Federal Election Commission, press release, December 5, 1985, pp. 2, 4. Here and in FEC press releases of December 1 and 8, 1985, cited in subsequent tables and in the text, data are from the FEC's final reports on the 1984 elections.

[a]Party funds include those raised by the several national committees and also those from state and local parties when relevant to federal elections.

[b]Coordinated expenditures on behalf of candidates are neither contributions to candidates nor general party expenditures, but are made by parties within legal limits established for both presidential and congressional general elections. In 1983–84, the Republican total of $20.1 million (shown above) includes $7 million for the presidential campaign, and the Democratic total of $9 million includes $2.8 million for the presidential campaign.

Appendix D
Federal Contribution Limits

	To			
By	Candidate per Election	National Party per Year	Any Other Committee per Year	Total per Year
Individual	$1,000	$20,000	$5,000	$25,000
Political committee	1,000	20,000	5,000	No limit
Multicandidate committee[a]	5,000	15,000	5,000	No limit

Source: Federal Election Commission, *The First 10 Years* (Washington, D.C.: FEC, 1985), p. 12. Limits are those in effect as of 1984.

[a] "Multicandidate committee" is the category to which most PACs belong. The $5,000 limit on such a committee's contribution to a candidate also applies to a national party committee, but a party, through its national committee or its Senate campaign committee, can contribute a total of $17,500 per election year to a Senate candidate. Legally, a multicandidate committee is any committee with more than 50 contributors which has been registered for at least six months and, with the exception of state party committees, has made contributions to five or more federal candidates.

Appendix E

Financial Activity of PACs in Federal Elections, 1983–84

Type of PAC	Net Disbursements (millions)	Contributions to Candidates[a] (millions)
Corporation	$ 59.2	$ 39.0
Labor organization	47.5	26.2
Trade/Member/Health	54.0	28.3
Cooperative	4.5	2.6
Corporation w/o stock	4.2	1.5
Nonconnected organization	97.4	15.3
Total	$266.8	$113.0

Source: Federal Election Commission, press release, December 1, 1985, p. 3.

[a]Contributions include those given to presidential candidates ($1.5 million) and also those given to some candidates who did not run in 1983–84. Thus the total is higher than the $105 million often cited as PAC contributions to Senate and House candidates in 1983–84. Because of rounding, the several contribution figures do not add to the total of $113 million.

Appendix F

Disbursements by Parties and PACs
in Federal Elections,[a]
1981–84

(millions)

	1983–84	1981–82
Total spent		
Major parties	$398.2	$254.1
PACs	266.8	190.2
Contributed to candidates		
Major parties	7.5	7.3
PACs	113.0	87.6
Coordinated expenditures		
Major parties	29.1	17.6
Independent expenditures on behalf of or against candidates		
PACs	22.2[b]	5.7

Source: Federal Election Commission, press releases, November 29, 1983, pp. 1–2; December 1, 1985, pp. 1–2; and December 5, 1985, pp. 1–3.

[a]Party funds include those spent by the several national committees and also those spent by state and local parties in federal elections, presidential as well as congressional. PAC totals, too, are for all federal elections, and they include (as do party figures) contributions to candidates who did not actually run for office in the given election cycle.

[b]$17.3 million of the $22.2 million was for or against presidential candidates.

Appendix G

Funds in U.S. House and Senate Campaigns, 1983–84

(millions)

Net receipts[a]	$397.2
Democratic candidates	205.7
Republican candidates	190.8
Others	0.8
Total PAC contributions[b]	105.3
To Democrats	60.4
To Republicans	44.9
Total major-party contributions[b]	6.6
Democrats	1.8
Republicans	4.8
Total major-party expenditures on behalf of candidates[b]	19.0
Democrats	6.0
Republicans	13.1

Source: Federal Election Commission, press release, December 8, 1985, pp. 1–5. Rounding of figures means that they do not always add to totals shown.

[a]The largest source of candidate receipts consists of individual contributions, totaling $218.2 million, which together with candidates' own loans and contributions are included in total net receipts of $397.2 million.

[b]PAC and major-party contributions, as well as major-party expenditures on behalf of candidates, are somewhat lower here than are the figures for 1983–84 in Appendix F, because in this table the figures pertain only to House and Senate campaigns and only to candidates actually running for office in 1983–84 elections.

Appendix H

Federal Matching Funds
for Presidential Primary Candidates, 1984

(millions)

Ronald Reagan (R)	$10.1
Walter F. Mondale (D)	9.5
Gary Hart (D)	5.3
John Glenn (D)	3.3
Jesse Jackson (D)	3.1
Alan Cranston (D)	2.1
Reubin Askew (D)	1.0
Ernest F. Hollings (D)	0.8
George McGovern (D)	0.6
Lyndon H. LaRouche (D)	0.5
Sonia Johnson (Citizens)	0.2
Total	$36.5

Source: Federal Election Commission, press release, March 21, 1985. The FEC's exact dollar figures have here been rounded.

Notes

Chapter 1: Introduction

1. A sample of titles: David S. Broder, *The Party's Over: The Failure of Politics in America* (New York: Harper & Row, 1971); Gerald M. Pomper, ed., *Party Renewal in America: Theory and Practice* (New York: Praeger, 1980); Joel L. Fleishman, ed., *The Future of American Political Parties: The Challenge of Governance* (Englewood Cliffs, N.J.: Prentice-Hall, 1982); Walter Dean Burnham, *The Current Crisis in American Politics* (New York: Oxford University Press, 1982); William Crotty, *American Parties in Decline* (Boston: Little, Brown, 1984); Martin P. Wattenberg, *The Decline of American Political Parties, 1952–1980* (Cambridge, Mass.: Harvard University Press, 1984); David E. Price, *Bringing Back the Parties* (Washington, D.C.: Congressional Quarterly, 1984); and, published after the completion of my manuscript, Xandra Kayden and Eddie Mahe, Jr., *The Party Goes On: The Persistence of the Two-Party System in the United States* (New York: Basic Books, 1985). In addition to these and other interpretive works, several excellent textbooks include arguments about the prospects for party development.

2. I am even more impressed by the limits than are Robert Harmel and Kenneth Janda in *The Parties and Their Environments: Limits to Reform?* (New York: Longman, 1982).

3. Leon D. Epstein, *Political Parties in Western Democracies* (New York: Praeger, 1967; republished with postscript, New Brunswick, N.J.: Transaction, 1980).

4. Philip M. Williams, "Power and the Parties: The United States," in *Parties and Democracy in Britain and America*, ed. Vernon Bogdanor (New York: Praeger, 1984), pp. 7–37, at pp. 7–11.

5. Sixty years ago, Arthur N. Holcombe found that the view of American parties as "empty bottles" was an old one and that authors even in the nineteenth century thought that any golden age of parties had passed. *Political Parties of To-day* (New York: Harper & Bros., 1924), chap. 1.

6. Arthur Schlesinger, Jr., "The Crisis in the American Party System," in *Political Parties and the Modern State*, ed. Richard L. McCormick (New Brunswick, N.J.: Rutgers University Press, 1984), pp. 71–85, at p. 77.

Chapter 2: The Scholarly Commitment

1. Not every subject important enough for political scientists to study has led to a similar commitment. Interest groups, for example, are studied by specialists who seldom believe that they should be stronger and more effective policymakers, even when they treat them as useful and legitimate.

2. E. E. Schattschneider, *Party Government* (New York: Holt, Rinehart and Winston, 1942), pp. 4–6, 15.

3. Barry D. Karl, *Charles E. Merriam and the Study of Politics* (Chicago: University of Chicago Press, 1974), p. 33, describes the reaction to Burgess by graduate students when Merriam, later a leading party specialist, attended Columbia in the late 1890s. The nature of Burgess's formalism is apparent in his *Reminiscence of an American Scholar* (New York: Columbia University Press, 1934).

4. Francis Lieber, *Manual of Political Ethics* (Boston: Little and Brown, 1838; 2d ed. Philadelphia: Lippincott, 1876), vol. 2, bk. 5, chap. 2.

5. Austin Ranney and Willmoore Kendall, *Democracy and the American Party System* (New York: Harcourt, Brace, and World, 1956), discuss Lieber and Tocqueville along with other early commentators in their chapter 6, "An Intellectual History of Political Parties."

6. Austin Ranney, "The Reception of Political Parties into American Political Science," *Southwestern Social Science Quarterly* 32 (December 1951): 183–91.

7. Washington spoke of "the baneful effects of the spirit of party generally" and of the inseparability of that spirit "from our nature, having its root in the strongest passions of the human mind." Farewell Address of September 17, 1796, in Henry Steele Commager, ed., *Documents of American History* (Englewood, Cliffs, N.J.: Prentice-Hall, 1973), pp. 169–75, at p. 172.

8. Richard Hofstadter, *The Idea of a Party System* (Berkeley: University of California Press, 1969), chaps. 1–2.

9. Madison's exposition of this pluralist view is in the famous and familiar Number 10 of *The Federalist*. Thomas Jefferson, though with Madison the organizer of a party that won control of the national government, regarded it as only a temporary means of establishing a true republican government in which party opposition would cease to be needed. And James Monroe, third in Virginia's presidential line begun by Jefferson, proclaimed the virtues of nonpartisanship that he thought achieved in 1822: "Surely our government may go on and prosper without the existence of parties. I have always considered their existence as the curse of the country. . . ." Hofstadter, *The Idea of a Party System*, p. 200.

10. Martin Van Buren, *Inquiry into the Origin and Course of Political Parties in the United States* (New York: Hurd and Houghton, 1867).

11. James Bryce, *The American Commonwealth* (Chicago: Sergel, 1891), vol. 2, p. 4.

12. Ibid., p. 5. Henry Jones Ford, an influential American scholar discussed later in this chapter, reflected a similar view of the importance of American parties in *The Rise and Growth of American Politics* (New York: Macmillan, 1898).

13. Bryce, *The American Commonwealth*, vol. 2, pt. 3, "The Party System," especially chapters on party organizations, machines, bosses, and spoils.

14. These sentiments appear even more explicitly in Bryce's later work, *Modern Democracies* (New York: Macmillan, 1921), vol. 2, chaps. 40, 45.

15. Antiparty preferences of many progressive reformers are described by Martin

Shefter, "Party, Bureaucracy, and Political Change in the United States," in *Political Parties: Development and Decay*, ed. Louis Maisel and Joseph Cooper (Beverly Hills, Calif.: Sage Publications, 1978), pp. 211–65, at pp. 229–37.

16. Reformers of municipal administration seem to have been the most antagonistic to parties, but the proponents of an improved national civil service also wanted to reduce the influence of parties (and of members of Congress) on administrative appointments — occasionally to enhance presidential discretion. See Herbert Kaufman, "Emerging Conflicts in the Doctrines of Public Administration," *American Political Science Review* 50 (December 1956): 1057–73.

17. Samuel P. Hays, "The Politics of Reform in Municipal Government in the Progressive Era," *Pacific Northwest Quarterly* 55 (October 1964): pp. 157–69.

18. Charles R. Adrian, "Some General Characteristics of Nonpartisan Elections," *American Political Science Review* 46 (September 1952): 766–76; and "Nonpartisanship," *International Encyclopedia of the Social Sciences* (New York: Crowell, Collier and Macmillan, 1968), vol. 11, pp. 201–3. See also Willis D. Hawley, *Nonpartisan Elections and the Case for Party Politics* (New York: Wiley, 1973).

19. Charles A. Beard, "Politics and City Government," *National Municipal Review* 6 (March 1917): 201–6.

20. So it was particularly for Frank J. Goodnow, a leading early student of municipal government. His belief that the direct primary would make bosses responsible is described by Austin Ranney, *The Doctrine of Responsible Party Government* (Urbana: University of Illinois Press, 1954), p. 106. Although Goodnow seems exceptional even among early political scientists in sharing so fully the progressive faith in the direct primary, considerable support for the still new institution could be found in the early 1920s. Thus *The Annals of the American Academy of Political and Social Science* 106 (March 1923), a special issue on the direct primary, included a report (pp. 55–62) of more proprimary than antiprimary preferences among political scientists, along with articles in varying degrees openly skeptical or favorable. Interestingly, however, the only article making the case for the direct primary as a means of helping to destroy party influence was by Senator George Norris (pp. 22–30).

21. Ford's dislike of the direct primary is analyzed by Ranney, *Doctrine of Responsible Party Government*, pp. 85–87. It also appears in Ford's response to a canvass of scholarly opinion. Karl, *Charles E. Merriam*, p. 57.

22. *Annals* 106 (March 1923): 40–54, at p. 54.

23. Merriam's fullest consideration of the reform is in the second edition of *Primary Elections* (Chicago: University of Chicago Press, 1928), written jointly with Louise Overacker but including chapters from Merriam's own first edition of 1908.

24. Ranney, *Doctrine of Responsible Party Government*, pp. 134–47.

25. An exception is James Ceaser, who treats Wilson's preference for strong parties as only a means for achieving his end of executive leadership. *Presidential Selection: Theory and Development* (Princeton: Princeton University Press, 1979), p. 197.

26. Seymour Martin Lipset praises these qualities, while conceding the naiveté

of Ostrogorski's solutions, in his introduction to an abridged paperback edition of M. Ostrogorski, *Democracy and the Organization of Political Parties* (Garden City, N.Y.: Doubleday, 1964), vol. 1, p. lxiv. The two volumes were first published in English by Macmillan in 1902. See also Ostrogorski's *Democracy and the Party System in the United States* (New York: Macmillan, 1910).

27. Ostrogorski, *Democracy and the Party System*, pp. 441–42.

28. Preface to *Democracy and the Organization of Political Parties*, vol. 1, p. lxxii in the 1964 edition.

29. Ibid., p. lxxiii.

30. A. Lawrence Lowell, *The Government of England* (New York: Macmillan, 1909), vol. 1, pp. 467–68, n. 1.

31. Arthur W. Macmahon, "Ostrogorsky, Moisey Yakovlevich (1854–1919)," *Encyclopedia of the Social Sciences* (New York: Macmillan, 1933), vol. 11, pp. 503–4.

32. Charles E. Merriam specifically rejected Ostrogorski's views despite respect for his work. *The American Party System* (New York: Macmillan, 1922), pp. 380–81.

33. Robert Michels, *Political Parties*, trans. Eden and Cedar Paul (Glencoe, Ill.: The Free Press, 1949), pp. 377–92 (on "Democracy and the Iron Law of Oligarchy").

34. Ibid., p. 400.

35. All four of these writers, along with Ostrogorski and Croly, are treated by Ranney, *Doctrine of Responsible Party Government*.

36. Jesse Macy, *Political Parties in the United States 1846–1861* (New York: Macmillan, 1900), p. 162. Although he denies that he is an advocate of "our party system," Macy adds that he does "advocate the use of our parties until some better agency is discovered" (p. vi).

37. Jesse Macy, *Party Organization and Machinery* (New York: Century, 1912), p. xv. See also James Albert Woodburn, another early textbook author, *Political Parties and Party Problems in the United States*, 3d ed. (New York: G. P. Putnam's Sons, 1924). Earlier editions date back to 1903 and 1914. The 1924 edition includes the introductory statement, "In a democracy, government leadership and control depend largely upon party leadership and control. The people will not be better governed than their parties are governed" (p. iv).

38. Bryce, *Modern Democracies*, vol. I, p. 119.

39. Merriam, *The American Party System*, p. 391.

40. Joseph Schumpeter, *Capitalism, Socialism, and Democracy* (New York: Harper & Brothers, 1950), p. 283, is the most frequently cited source of this revisionist, or realist, approach.

41. Herman Finer, *Theory and Practice of Modern Government* (New York: Henry Holt, 1949), pp. 274–82.

42. Ibid., pp. 353–61.

43. Ibid., p. 362.

44. Carl J. Friedrich, *Constitutional Government and Democracy* (Boston: Ginn and Company, 1946), p. 257.

45. Ibid., p. 294.

46. Ibid., p. 347.

47. R. M. MacIver, *The Modern State* (1926; London: Oxford University Press, 1964), p. 398.

48. R. M. MacIver, *The Web of Government* (1947; New York: Macmillan, 1965), p. 157.

49. Maurice Duverger, *Political Parties*, trans. Barbara and Robert North (New York: Wiley & Sons, 1954), p. 427.

50. Giovanni Sartori, *Parties and Party Systems* (New York: Cambridge University Press, 1976), vol. 1, p. 25.

51. Ibid., p. 28.

52. Sigmund Neumann, *Modern Political Parties* (Chicago: University of Chicago Press, 1956), p. 397.

53. Ibid., p. 421.

54. Robert Dahl, *Pluralist Democracy in the United States* (Chicago: Rand McNally, 1967), p. 203. A later version of this text appears as *Democracy in the United States*, 3d ed. (Chicago: Rand McNally, 1976). My references are all to the 1967 edition, but they are not at odds with the presentation in the 1976 edition.

55. Dahl, *Pluralist Democracy*, p. 210.

56. Ibid., p. 243.

57. Ibid., p. 250.

58. For example, Judson L. James, *American Political Parties in Transition* (New York: Harper & Row, 1974), pp. 6, 260–62.

59. Samuel J. Eldersveld, *Political Parties* (Chicago: Rand McNally, 1964), pp. 20–21.

60. Ranney, *Doctrine of Responsible Party Government*, pp. 48–69.

61. Ibid., pp. 70–91, for references to Ford's work after *The Rise and Growth of American Politics*.

62. Edward M. Sait, *American Parties and Elections* (New York: Century Co., 1927), pp. 159–64.

63. Ibid., chaps. 10, 16.

64. Ibid., p. 373.

65. Arthur N. Holcombe, *The Political Parties of To-day* (New York: Harper & Bros., 1924), p. 384.

66. Herbert Agar, *The Price of Union* (Boston: Houghton Mifflin, 1950), pp. xv–xvi.

67. Ibid., p. 689.

68. Edward C. Banfield, "In Defense of the American Party System," and Morton Grodzins, "Party and Government in the United States," in *Political Parties, U.S.A.*, ed. Robert A. Goldwin (Chicago: Rand McNally, 1964), pp. 21–39, 102–36.

69. Ranney and Kendall, *Democracy and the American Party Systems*, p. 500.

70. Ibid., p. 523.

71. Ibid., p. 533.
72. William J. Keefe, *Parties, Politics, and Public Policy in America* (New York: Holt, Rinehart and Winston, 1972), p. 50.
73. Pendleton Herring, *The Politics of Democracy* (New York: W. W. Norton, 1940), pp. 112–13.
74. Ibid., pp. 103–4.
75. Ibid., p. 102.
76. Ibid., p. 111.
77. Ibid., p. 113.
78. Ibid., p. 421.
79. Ibid., p. 245.
80. Ibid., p. 248.
81. Ibid., p. 241.
82. Ibid., p. 423.
83. Don K. Price, "The Parliamentary and Presidential Systems," *Public Administration Review* 3 (Autumn 1943): 317–34; and Pendleton Herring, *Presidential Leadership* (New York: Rinehart, 1940), p. 142.
84. Accordingly, Judson James treats Key as a proponent of a "responsible party" model rather than of a "party government" model in a classification that emphasizes Key's desire to strengthen existing parties, and especially the minority party, in order to have effective two-party competition. James contrasts both these party schools with status quo defenders as well as with progressives and nonpartisan advocates. *American Political Parties*, pp. 9–28. I recognize that Key can thus be distinguished from status quo defenders, and I have tried to do so, even though in my twofold classification he seems close enough to the defenders of indigenous institutions to belong in their general category. I prefer to think of responsible party advocates as wanting more drastic changes than Key suggests and consequently as belonging to the responsible-party-government school, not to a third school of their own.
85. V. O. Key, Jr., *Southern Politics in State and Nation* (New York: Knopf, 1950), chap. 14.
86. V. O. Key, Jr., *American State Politics: An Introduction* (New York: Knopf, 1956), chap. 6.
87. To some extent, the dissatisfaction appears in his text *Politics, Parties, & Pressure Groups* (New York: Crowell, 1964). Nevertheless, Key believes that at least in presidential politics the American parties offer voters a meaningful choice. *The Responsible Electorate* (Cambridge, Mass.: Belknap Press, 1966).
88. Key is critical of the loose "confederative" organization of American national parties. *Politics, Parties, & Pressure Groups*, p. 334. Certainly he does not prize this confederative feature as do some of the defenders of traditional American parties. Neither, however, does he insist that it can and should be changed, as responsible-party-government advocates do with considerable fervor.
89. Ranney, *Doctrine of Responsible Party Government*, pp. 25–47.

90. In *The Wesleyan Argus*, March 5, 1971, p. 2, as quoted by David Adamany, "The Political Science of E. E. Schattschneider: A Review Essay," *American Political Science Review* 66 (December 1972): 1321–35, at p. 1321. I have used Adamany's essay and also another insightful review by Richard W. Boyd. "Schattschneider, E. E.," *International Encyclopedia of the Social Sciences*, vol. 18, Biographical Supplement (New York: Macmillan and The Free Press, 1979), pp. 697–701.

91. Schattschneider, *Party Government*, p. 208.

92. E. E. Schattschneider, *The Semi-Sovereign People* (New York: Holt, Rinehart and Winston, 1960), p. 35.

93. He sounded this theme in his first book, originally published in 1935, *Politics, Pressures and the Tariff* (Hamden, Conn.: Archon Books, 1963), when he wrote, "To manage pressures is to govern; to let pressures run wild is to abdicate" (p. 293), and he maintained it in all of his subsequent work.

94. Schattschneider, *Party Government*, p. 60.

95. Schattschneider, *The Struggle for Party Government* (College Park: University of Maryland, 1948), pp. 29–30.

96. Schattschneider, *Party Government*, p. 128.

97. Ibid., pp. 132–33. Chapter 6 describes the disadvantages of decentralization, and chapter 7 the antipublic purposes of local bosses.

98. Ibid., p. 137.

99. Ibid., p. 207. "The assumption made here is that party government (party centralization) is the most practicable and feasible solution to the problem of organizing American democracy."

100. Committee on Political Parties, American Political Science Association, "Toward a More Responsible Two-Party System," *American Political Science Review* 44, Supplement (September 1950): 35–36.

101. Evron M. Kirkpatrick, "'Toward a More Responsible Two-Party System': Political Science, Policy Science, or Psuedo-Science?" *American Political Science Review* 65 (December 1971): 965–90.

102. The report was ably defended in the 1970s by Gerald M. Pomper, "Toward a More Responsible Two-Party System? What, Again?" *Journal of Politics* 33 (November 1971): 916–40. Moreover, its recommendations were drawn upon by the influential journalist David S. Broder in *The Party's Over* (New York: Harper & Row, 1972), pp. 182, 244–46. Broder's extended argument for stronger parties was widely read by political scientists as well as by a broader public. His reputation among academic students of American politics is such that he may well be counted as a de facto member of the political science profession.

103. APSA, "Toward a More Responsible Two-Party System," pp. 5–10.

104. Ibid., pp. 71–72.

105. John S. Saloma III and Frederick H. Sontag, *Parties: The Real Opportunity for Effective Citizen Politics* (New York: Vintage Books, 1973).

106. As he was by Ceaser, *Presidential Selection*, p. 197.

107. James MacGregor Burns, *Leadership* (New York: Harper & Row, 1978), chap. 12, "Party Leadership."

108. James MacGregor Burns, *The Deadlock of Democracy* (Englewood Cliffs, N.J.: Prentice-Hall, 1963), p. 326.

109. James MacGregor Burns, *Presidential Government* (Boston: Houghton Mifflin, 1965), p. 111; *Uncommon Sense* (New York: Harper & Row, 1972), chap. 8, "A Party Fit to Govern."

110. Kirkpatrick, "Toward a More Responsible Two-Party System," p. 974, n. 29.

111. I have discussed these favorable references to Britain in "What Happened to the British Party Model," *American Political Science Review* 74 (March 1980): 9–22.

112. Charles E. Hardin, *Presidential Power and Accountability: Toward a New Constitution* (Chicago: University of Chicago Press, 1974), pp. 2–5.

113. Most committee members appear to have greater expectations for party renewal than mine, but I should note that I too have joined.

114. Hearings of the Committee on House Administration of the House of Representatives, *Public Financing of Congressional Elections*, 96th Congress, 1st Session (Washington, D.C.: Government Printing Office, 1979), pp. 392–93.

115. Gerald M. Pomper, ed., *Party Renewal in America* (New York: Praeger, 1980), p. 5.

116. Walter Dean Burnham, *Critical Elections and the Mainsprings of American Politics* (New York: Norton, 1970). Burnham has also written extensively since 1970 on the continued decline of party efficacy in the United States.

117. Benjamin R. Barber is an exception. Specializing in political philosophy, he has adopted Rousseau's view of representation and specifically regards parties, either traditional or reformed, as obstructing rather than facilitating real citizen participation. Accepting Michels's view of the inevitability of oligarchy in political parties, Barber would in effect follow Ostrogorski in seeking to avoid that result by eliminating parties altogether. "The Undemocratic Party System: Citizenship in an Elite/Mass Society," in *Political Parties in the Eighties*, ed. Robert A. Goldwin (Washington, D.C.: American Enterprise Institute, 1980), pp. 34–49.

118. Frank J. Sorauf, *Party Politics in America* (Boston: Little, Brown, 1984), p. 5.

119. Anthony King, "Political Parties in Western Democracies," *Polity* 2 (Winter 1969): 111–41.

Chapter 3: The Congressional Presence

1. William J. Crotty and Gary C. Jacobson, *American Parties in Decline* (Boston: Little, Brown, 1980), p. 245.

2. Randall B. Ripley, *Majority Party Leadership in Congress* (Boston: Little, Brown, 1969), p. 1.

3. Rather than diminishing in recent years, the preponderance of Republicans and Democrats in Congress has since 1950 become so great that no more than one or two members, and sometimes no members, of either house have been elected with-

out one of the two major-party labels. The few thus elected have ordinarily been Independents, and only temporarily so in certain instances. Third-party elections to Congress were more common earlier, although never numerous enough after 1867 to preclude majority-party control. House high points were 40 in 1897, 17 in 1913, and 13 in 1937. Senators without Republican or Democratic labels numbered as many as eight in the late nineteenth century and as many as four from 1937 through 1940. U.S. Department of Commerce, Bureau of the Census, *Historical Statistics of the United States: Colonial Times to 1970*, pt. 2 (Series Y 204–10), p. 1083.

4. Richard E. Neustadt, *Presidential Power* (New York: Wiley & Sons, 1980), p. 26.

5. Nelson W. Polsby, *Congress and the Presidency* (Englewood Cliffs, N.J.: Prentice-Hall, 1976), p. 74.

6. David Truman, "The Prospects for Change," in *The Congress and America's Future*, ed. David Truman (Englewood Cliffs, N.J.: Prentice-Hall, 1973), pp. 202–11, at p. 203.

7. David M. Olson, *The Legislative Process: A Comparative Approach* (New York: Harper & Row, 1980), p. 21.

8. Ibid., p. 23.

9. Charles M. Hardin, *Presidential Power and Accountability* (Chicago: University of Chicago Press, 1974), pp. 183–84.

10. Olson, *The Legislative Process*, pp. 270–77. In the 1980s, the British House of Commons established "select committees" which, unlike its standing committees, are specialized by subject matter. But the select committees do not deal with legislative bills. They conduct inquiries into the administration of policies.

11. John E. Schwarz and L. Earl Shaw, *The United States Congress in Comparative Perspective* (Hillsdale, Ill.: Dryden Press, 1976), pp. 77–82.

12. Congressional Quarterly, *Origins and Development of Congress* (Washington, D.C.: Congressional Quarterly, 1976), pp. 90–91, 187.

13. Samuel C. Patterson, "The Semi-Sovereign Congress," in *The New American Political System*, ed. Anthony King (Washington, D.C.: American Enterprise Institute, 1978), pp. 127–77, at p. 132.

14. Woodrow Wilson, *Congressional Government* (New York: Meridian, 1956), pp. 24, 82.

15. Congressional Quarterly, *Origins and Development*, p. 103. Here and elsewhere, I follow the established and continuing usage *in Congress* of the term *chairman* although I regard *chairperson* as now more appropriate. I do substitute *chair* or *chairperson* in certain contexts.

16. Ibid., p. 136.

17. Charles O. Jones, *The United States Congress: People, Place, and Policy* (Homewood, Ill.: Dorsey Press, 1982), pp. 202, 273.

18. Congressional Quarterly, *Origins and Development*, pp. 153–69.

19. Norman J. Ornstein, Thomas E. Mann, Michael J. Malbin, Allen Schick, and John F. Bibby, *Vital Statistics on Congress, 1984–1985 Edition* (Washington, D.C.: American Enterprise Institute, 1984), pp. 109–10. Each house also has subcommittees

of its select, special, and joint committees. The figures I cite relate only to subcommittees of standing committees.

20. Jones, *The U.S. Congress*, p. 203, specifies that in the 1979–80 Congress 151 of the 276 House Democrats held committee or subcommittee chairs.

21. Nelson Polsby, "The Institutionalization of the House of Representatives," *American Political Science Review* 62 (March 1968): 144–68.

22. Ibid., pp. 146–47.

23. Randall B. Ripley, *Congress: Process and Policy* (New York: Norton, 1983), p. 107; Ornstein et al., *Vital Statistics*, pp. 3–4, 18–19. Forty representatives retired voluntarily in 1982, a redistricting year, and only 27 in 1984; many of them ran for other offices. *Congressional Quarterly Weekly Report* 40 (Oct. 30, 1982): 2756, and 42 (Nov. 10, 1984): 2900.

24. Polsby, "Institutionalization," p. 168.

25. Nelson W. Polsby, Miriam Gallaher, and Barry S. Rundquist, "The Growth of the Seniority System in the U.S. House of Representatives," *American Political Science Review* 63 (September 1969): 787–807, at pp. 803–4.

26. Barbara Hinckley, *Stability and Change in Congress* (New York: Harper & Row, 1983), p. 123. House Republicans also changed their rules, in the same period, so that their party conference was given the power to choose ranking minority members of standing committees.

27. Barbara Hinckley, "Seniority 1975: Old Theories Confront New Facts," *British Journal of Political Science* 6 (October 1976): 383–99.

28. *Congressional Quarterly Weekly Report* 43 (Jan. 5, 1985): 7–9. The deposed chairman was Melvin Price, who had himself succeeded to his position after the deposition of F. Edward Hebert in 1975. Price's successor was Les Aspin. In 1975, the Democrats had deposed W. R. Poage of Agriculture and Wright Patman of Banking along with Hebert of Armed Services. Each of the three was elderly and each was objectionable especially to junior members on grounds apart from, or in addition to, ideological positions. Moreover, each was succeeded by a relatively senior committee Democrat. On that score, Aspin's elevation in 1985 was a sharper break with precedent.

29. Polsby, "Institutionalization," p. 168.

30. Hinckley, *Stability and Change*, p. 162.

31. Jones, *The U.S. Congress*, p. 204. In 1977, the caucus did reject one subcommittee chairman.

32. Burdett A. Loomis, "The Congressional Office as a Small (?) Business: New Members Set Up Shop," *Publius* 9 (Summer 1979): 35–55, at p. 39. By 1983, a representative was allowed 22 staff employees and a payroll of over $350,000. Ornstein et al., *Vital Statistics*, p. 132.

33. Ornstein et al., *Vital Statistics*, pp. 116, 120.

34. Ibid., p. 124.

35. Ibid., pp. 128–29, 131.

36. By the 1970s even British backbench M.P.s, while still voting much more frequently with their parties than American members vote with theirs, were found to deviate in significantly larger numbers than in previous decades. Philip Norton, *Dissension in the House of Commons 1974–1979* (Oxford: Clarendon Press, 1981).

37. Congressional Quarterly, *Origins and Development*, pp. 81–99, 182–83. See also John F. Hoadley, "The Emergence of Political Parties in Congress, 1789–1803," *American Political Science Review* 74 (September 1980): 757–79.

38. Ripley, *Congress*, pp. 67–73. Garrison Nelson, "Partisan Patterns of House Leadership Change," *American Political Science Review* 71 (September 1977): 918–39, at pp. 938–39.

39. The 1985 figures are from *Congressional Quarterly Weekly Report* 43 (Feb. 9, 1985): 283, which notes that House Democrats had just increased the number of deputy whips from four to seven and the number of at-large whips from 21 to 31. Also recorded in the same account is the decision of House Democrats to elect the majority whip in the future instead of having him appointed by the Speaker and majority leader. As in the past, however, the Speaker, majority leader, and majority whip would appoint the chief deputy whip, the deputy whips, and the at-large whips (although at least three of the at-large whips were really selected by special-interest caucuses — blacks, women, and freshmen — within the larger Democratic caucus). The size and elaborateness of the whip system are relatively recent developments, as Barbara Sinclair indicates in her *Majority Leadership in the U.S. House* (Baltimore: Johns Hopkins University Press, 1982), pp. 55–67. I have used her book along with other standard works on Congress, but I have also, in discussing the nature and activity of the whip's office in 1983, relied heavily on information supplied by Dr. George Kundanis, a member of the whip's staff in the early 1980s.

40. Hinckley, *Stability and Change*, pp. 183–88.

41. Ralph K. Huitt, "Democratic Party Leadership in the Senate," in *Congress: Two Decades of Analysis*, ed. Ralph K. Huitt and Robert L. Peabody (New York: Harper & Row, 1969), pp. 136–58, at p. 141.

42. *Congressional Quarterly Weekly Report* 41, supplement (Jan. 8, 1983): 5. Gramm subsequently resigned from the House and from the Democratic party, but secured reelection as a Republican in early 1983 and also a Republican place on the Budget Committee. Gramm won election to the U.S. Senate as a Republican in 1984.

43. The means is the House Democratic Steering and Policy Committee, serving as the party's committee on committees. Its 1977–78 membership is specified by Olson, *Legislative Process*, p. 240.

44. *Congressional Quarterly Weekly Report* 39 (Jan. 31, 1981): 223–28.

45. *Congressional Quarterly Weekly Report* 41 (Feb. 5 and March 12, 1983): 313, 503. The Democratic overloading of committees in 1983 produced so sharp a Republican reaction that in 1985 the Democratic leadership modified the distribution of committee seats slightly more substantially than the increased number (14) of Republicans in the House would have itself have supported. Nevertheless Democrats,

with 58 percent of total House membership, retained more than 58 percent of the seats on each of the subject-matter standing committees and substantially more on the Rules Committee (69.2 percent), Ways and Means (63.9 percent), and Appropriations (61.4 percent). *Congressional Quarterly Weekly Report* 43 (Jan. 26, 1985): 142.

46. Ripley, *Congress*, p. 190.

47. Hinckley, *Stability and Change*, p. 136.

48. Ripley, *Congress*, p. 208.

49. Joseph Cooper and David W. Brady, "Institutional Context and Leadership Style: The House from Cannon to Rayburn," *American Political Science Review* 75 (June 1981): 411–25.

50. Marjorie Randon Hershey, *Running for Office* (Chatham, N.J.: Chatham House, 1984), pp. 139–43.

51. The lineage of this kind of party committee can be traced to 1866, when members of Congress organized to win House seats in an election at which the Republican majority was at odds with its national executive leadership (President Andrew Johnson). Although thus created in a special situation, the congressional campaign committee and eventually the Senate campaign committee too became Washington fixtures. Particular committees were sometimes inactive and sometimes dominated by limited interests, but they were also occasionally revived, even before the present period. Jesse Macy, *Party Organization and Machinery* (New York: Century, 1912), pp. 87–88; and John S. Saloma III and Frederick H. Sontag, *Parties: The Real Opportunity for Effective Citizen Politics* (New York: Random House Vintage Books, 1973), pp. 132–33. Recently increased activities of the campaign committees are discussed in my chapters 7 and 9.

52. The Anglo-American comparison was made as early as the turn of the century in the pioneering quantitative roll-call study by A. Lawrence Lowell, "The Influence of Party upon Legislation in England and America," *Annual Report of the American Historical Association for the Year 1901* (Washington, D.C.: Government Printing Office, 1902), vol. 1, pp. 321–542.

53. Walter Dean Burnham, "Insulation and Responsiveness in Congressional Elections," *Political Science Quarterly* 90 (Fall 1975): 411–35, at pp. 426–27.

54. Historical data resembling Burnham's in their import are also presented by David W. Brady, Joseph Cooper, and Patricia A. Hurley, "The Decline of Party in the U.S. House of Representatives, 1887–1968," *Legislative Studies Quarterly 4* (August 1979): 381–407.

55. William J. Keefe, *Parties, Politics, and Public Policy in America* (Hinsdale, Ill.: Dryden Press, 1976), pp. 139–40.

56. Hinckley, *Stability and Change*, pp. 204, 207.

57. Frank B. Feigert, "On the 'Decline' in Congressional Party Voting," paper for annual meeting of the Southern Political Science Association, Savannah, Ga., November 1984.

58. Ripley, *Congress*, pp. 211–12; Ornstein et al., *Vital Statistics*, p. 183. In *Con-*

gressional Quarterly Weekly Report 39 (Sept. 12, 1981): 1743, it is noted that Republican senators during the first seven months of the Reagan presidency voted unanimously on 30 percent of 248 recorded votes and that on 67 percent of those votes the Republican majority was deserted by five or fewer Republican senators. Variations in the preceding two decades are evident in a graph of congressional party voting, 1955–77, in Patterson, "The Semi-Sovereign Congress," p. 170. A good example of how different measures produce different results is to be found in a recent statistical analysis that displays a very sharp decline as measured by an index of "party unlikeness" in roll-call voting but no similar change as measured by "cohesion" scores. Jerome M. Clubb, William H. Flanigan, and Nancy H. Zingale, *Partisan Realignment: Voters, Parties, and Government in American History* (Beverly Hills, Calif.: Sage, 1980), pp. 232–46.

59. John W. Kingdon, *Congressmen's Voting Decisions* (New York: Harper & Row, 1973), chap. 4.

60. Ibid., p. 113.

61. David Mayhew, *Party Loyalty among Congressmen: The Difference between Democrats and Republicans 1947–1962* (Cambridge, Mass.: Harvard University Press, 1966), chap. 5.

62. Aage R. Clausen, *How Congressmen Decide: A Policy Focus* (New York: St. Martin's, 1973); and Clausen and Carl E. Van Horn, "The Congressional Response to a Decade of Change: 1963–1972," *Journal of Politics* 39 (August 1977): 624–66.

63. Barbara Deckard Sinclair, "Party Realignment and the Transformation of the Political Agenda: The House of Representatives, 1925–1938," *American Political Science Review* 71 (September 1977): 940–53. See also her *Congressional Realignment 1925–1978* (Austin: University of Texas Press, 1982), chap. 2.

64. Ripley, *Majority Party Leadership*, chaps. 3 and 6.

65. David W. Brady, "Critical Elections, Congressional Parties and Clusters of Policy Changes," *British Journal of Political Science* 8 (January 1978): 79–100, at p. 98. Increases in congressional party voting in Civil War years as well as after 1896 and 1932 are reported by Brady in "Congressional Party Realignment and Transformations of Public Policy in Three Realignment Eras," *American Journal of Political Science* 26 (May 1982): 333–60.

66. *Congressional Quarterly Weekly Report* 42 (Oct. 27, 1984): 2802.

67. Ibid.

68. David H. Everson, *American Political Parties* (New York: Watts, 1980), pp. 205–14.

69. *Congressional Quarterly Weekly Report* 42 (Oct. 27, 1984): 2802.

70. Ornstein et al., *Vital Statistics*, p. 183. To be sure, the measure here is the gross one whose usefulness is dubious, for reasons already noted.

71. Ibid.

72. David W. Brady and Charles S. Bullock III, "Is There a Conservative Coalition in the House?" *Journal of Politics* 42 (May 1980): 549–59.

73. Ornstein et al., *Vital Statistics*, p. 185.

74. Republicans held 36 percent of the House seats from the 11 southern states after the 1980 election, 29 percent after the 1982 election, and 37 percent after the 1984 election.

75. Possible long-run diminution of the southern Democratic base for the conservative coalition is discussed by Jack Bass and Walter DeVries, *The Transformation of Southern Politics* (New York: Basic Books, 1976), pp. 371–83. A considerable ideological difference between Republicans and Democrats, despite still-numerous southern conservative Democrats, is emphasized for 1965–76 by William R. Shaffer, *Party and Ideology in the United States Congress* (Washington, D.C.: University Press of America, 1980).

76. On the frequency and importance of congressional primaries, see Harvey L. Schantz, "Contested and Uncontested Primaries for the U.S. House," *Legislative Studies Quarterly* 4 (November 1980): 545–62.

77. Donald E. Stokes, "Parties and the Nationalization of Electoral Forces," in *The American Party Systems*, ed. William N. Chambers and Walter D. Burnham (New York: Oxford University Press, 1975), pp. 182–202, at pp. 188–89, 195–96. Stokes's study suggested an increased nationalization of the vote, but that suggestion is sharply challenged by the findings of William Claggett, William Flanigan, and Nancy Zingale, "Nationalization of the Electorate," *American Political Science Review* 78 (March 1984): 77–91.

78. Pendleton Herring, *Presidential Leadership* (New York: Rinehart, 1940), p. 27.

79. Ripley, *Congress*, p. 76. Italics in Ripley text.

80. E. E. Schattschneider, *Party Government* (New York: Rinehart, 1942), pp. 134–58. In my chapter 2, I have discussed the significance of his critical view of the relative strength of conventional local party organizations.

81. Democrats gained 37 House seats in 1964. Republicans gained 34 seats in 1980 and 14 in 1984 (after losing 26 in 1982). In 1984 Republican House candidates won 47 percent of the popular vote while winning only 42 percent of the seats. The disparity is partly explicable as a result of the greater Democratic gerrymandering made possible (notably in California) by Democratic control of post-1980 redistricting in state legislatures. Popular vote totals are in *Congressional Quarterly Weekly Report* 43 (April 13, 1985): 687. The 47 percent Republican total, relative to 52 percent Democratic, is based on 419 districts (excluding from the House's 435 districts only 16 where no contest occurred and no votes were recorded). A different result, showing a larger popular-vote percentage for Republicans, is reached by excluding not only the 16 unrecorded districts but also other districts where there was no Republican-versus-Democratic contest (but sometimes a nonmajor-party opponent for either a Republican or a Democrat). More Democrats than Republicans ran without major-party opponents.

82. Evidence of a recently sharp decline, as well as a long-term decline, in the behavioral connection between presidential and congressional voting is convincingly presented by John A. Ferejohn and Randall L. Calvert, "Presidential Coattails in

Historical Perspective," *American Journal of Political Science* 28 (February 1984): 127–46.

83. The same party lacked control of all three branches in ten of the 16 Congresses 1955–86, in only two of the 15 Congresses 1925–54, and in only three of the 15 Congresses 1895–1924, but in seven of the 15 Congresses 1865–94. Accordingly, the most recent three decades resemble no earlier period except that of the post-Civil War decades. And that resemblance is superficial, because divided government in those early decades, unlike that of 1955–84, was most often the result of the loss of only one house by the party holding the other house and the presidency. Also, that loss was a consequence of much closer party competition for control of Congress than that characterizing recent decades. Moreover, in 1865–94 only twice was there divided control in the two years following a presidential election, whereas it developed five times in 1955–86.

84. David W. Brady and Naomi B. Lynn, "Switched-Seat Congressional Districts: Their Effect on Party Voting and Public Policy," *American Journal of Political Science* 17 (August 1973): 528–43.

85. Congressional Quarterly, *Guide to U.S. Elections* (Washington, D.C.: Congressional Quarterly, 1975), p. 928; and Ornstein et al., *Vital Statistics*, p. 45.

86. In the 1972–80 elections, 67 percent of the 361 unredistricted House seats did not change parties. Hinckley, *Congressional Elections*, p. 128.

87. Ibid., p. 39, except for 1982 and 1984, for which I relied on news accounts.

88. The assumption may be questioned, because occasionally an open seat is harder for an opposition-party candidate to win against a new and vigorous campaigner who succeeds an old and tired incumbent as the nominee of the incumbent's party.

89. Hinckley, *Congressional Elections*, p. 39.

90. David Mayhew, "The Congressional Elections: The Case of the Vanishing Marginals," *Polity* 6 (Spring 1974): 295–317; Morris P. Fiorina, *Congress: Keystone of the Washington Establishment* (New Haven: Yale University Press, 1977).

91. Ornstein et al., *Vital Statistics*, p. 53.

92. Thomas E. Mann, *Unsafe at Any Margin* (Washington, D.C.: American Enterprise Institute, 1978), pp. 106–7. See also David R. Mayhew, *Congress: The Electoral Connection* (New Haven: Yale University Press, 1974), p. 34.

93. Thomas E. Mann and Raymond E. Wolfinger, "Candidates and Parties in Congressional Elections," *American Political Science Review* 74 (September 1980): 617–32, at p. 621. See also Candice J. Nelson, "The Effect of Incumbency in Congressional Elections, 1964–1974," *Political Science Quarterly* 93 (Winter 1978–79): 665–78.

94. Hinckley, *Congressional Elections*, pp. 67–68.

95. See Mayhew, *The Electoral Connection*, and Fiorina, *Congress*.

96. Alan I. Abramowitz, "A Comparison of Voting for U.S. Senator and Representative in 1978," *American Political Science Review* 74 (September 1980): 633–40.

97. Mann and Wolfinger, "Candidates and Parties," p. 626.

98. David Jessup, "Can Political Influence Be Democratized? A Labor Perspec-

tive," in *Parties, Interest Groups, and Campaign Finance Laws*, ed. Michael J. Malbin (Washington, D.C.: American Enterprise Institute, 1980), pp. 26–55, at p. 34.

99. Richard Fenno, *Home Style: House Members in Their Districts* (Boston: Little, Brown, 1978), p. 114.

100. Joseph Cooper and William West, "Voluntary Retirement, Incumbency, and the Modern House," *Political Science Quarterly* 96 (Summer 1981): 279–300; Richard Born, "Generational Replacement and the Growth of Incumbent Reelection Margins," *American Political Science Review* 73 (September 1979): 811–17. In chapter 9, I emphasize the import of the sources of campaign funds, particularly for congressional candidates.

101. Ripley, *Congress*, pp. xvi, 208.

Chapter 4: Presidential Focus

1. Thomas Jefferson's characterization in 1787 of the presidency as an "elective monarchy" is cited by Samuel Huntington in his critical analysis of the eighteenth-century nature of the U.S. Constitution. *Political Order in Changing Societies* (New Haven: Yale University Press, 1968), p. 114.

2. James W. Ceaser summarizes the scholarly controversy over the founders' intentions in *Presidential Selection: Theory and Development* (Princeton: Princeton University Press, 1979), pp. 42–46.

3. In Ceaser's words, "The president might earn the people's respect, but he was not to solicit their favor." Ibid., p. 51. Unquestionably, then, the now evidently necessary modern presidential campaigns seeking such favor are antithetical to the founders' intentions.

4. The troubling possibility that the electoral college, by failing to produce a majority winner, would become merely a screening device to reduce the number of candidates to those from whom the House of Representatives would have to choose a president seemed real enough in 1800 because of an electoral college tie (of a sort soon precluded by constitutional amendment), and again in 1824 when the House chose from among the top three candidates because none had an electoral college majority. After 1824, despite a few close calls, the only uncertain electoral college result, in 1876, involved a dispute over which of two candidates had actually won in certain states.

5. Richard P. McCormick, *The Second American Party System: Party Formation in the Jacksonian Era* (Chapel Hill: University of North Carolina Press, 1966), p. 343.

6. Richard P. McCormick, *The Presidential Game: The Origins of American Presidential Politics* (New York: Oxford University Press, 1982), pp. 4–5, distinguishes a period of factional politics between the early 1820s, when the "Virginia game" ceased to prevail through the congressional caucus, and the years 1832–44, when the new party game developed.

7. McCormick, *The Second American Party System*, p. 342.

8. Ibid., p. 13. For the importance of the Whigs in this period, see Daniel Walker

Howe, *The Political Culture of the American Whigs* (Chicago: University of Chicago Press, 1979).

9. Ibid., p. 335.

10. The phenomenon is not so entirely recent as my post-1945 dates might indicate. James M. Burns writes of Theodore Roosevelt's "personal party, headed by the former presidential politicians that he had gathered around himself in his Administration, that summoned him back to political combat in 1912." *Presidential Government* (Boston: Houghton Mifflin, 1965), p. 160.

11. John H. Kessel, *Presidential Parties* (Homewood, Ill.: Dorsey Press, 1984), p. 322. The quoted passage is in boldface type in Kessel's work.

12. Ibid., pp. 323–26, where he discusses "advocacy parties."

13. The services of the national party committees have lately become much more substantial and generously funded for *non*presidential campaigns and certain general party purposes. In fact, they appear to be more regularly significant organizations in ways that they never before were. As such, they will receive a good deal of attention in chapter 7. Here it is enough to note that their recent development is entirely compatible with, and perhaps partly a result of, their currently more limited role in conducting presidential campaigns.

14. Richard E. Neustadt, *Presidential Power: The Politics of Leadership from FDR to Carter* (New York: Wiley & Sons, 1980), p. 26.

15. Austin Ranney, *Curing the Mischiefs of Faction: Party Reform in America* (Berkeley: University of California Press, 1975) pp. 64–69.

16. Theodore J. Lowi, "Party, Policy, and Constitution in America," in *The American Party Systems: Stages of Political Development*, ed. William Nisbet Chambers and Walter Dean Burnham (New York: Oxford University Press, 1975), pp. 238–76, at p. 248.

17. Thomas E. Cronin puts the point well when he refers to a major paradox in the expectation that a president will be "a pure and neutral public servant, avoiding political and party considerations" when he is also supposed to lead his party. "The Presidency and the Parties," in *Party Renewal in America*, ed. Gerald M. Pomper (New York: Praeger, 1980), pp. 176–94, at p. 180.

18. Nelson W. Polsby presents so fully developed a critique in *Consequences of Party Reform* (New York: Oxford University Press, 1983) that I shall most often refer to it for both information and well-argued positions.

19. Something comparable to congressional-caucus nomination of presidents prevails in other systems whose parliamentary party members alone are able to choose their leader and potential or actual prime minister. Until the 1980s, both major British parties retained such exclusive peer review, and the Conservative party still does. The contrast to contemporary American practice is lucidly made by Anthony King, "How Not to Select Presidential Candidates: A View from Europe," in *The American Elections of 1980*, ed. Austin Ranney (Washington, D.C.: American Enterprise Institute, 1981), pp. 303–28. My own different comparison of British practices, notably

the Labour party's, may be found in "Redistributing Power in British Parties," in *Parties and Democracy in Britain and America*, ed. Vernon Bogdanor (New York: Praeger, 1984), pp. 39–69.

20. Ceaser, *Presidential Selection*, pp. 217–27, distinguishes 1912–20 from the next several decades because of the greater popularity of presidential primaries in their first years.

21. Certain states, however, had regulated delegate-selection practices in various ways, and Florida authorized a party to use a presidential primary in 1904. Austin Ranney, *Participation in American Presidential Nominations, 1976* (Washington, D.C.: American Enterprise Institute, 1977), pp. 3–4.

22. That certainly is the view of at least one historian of late-nineteenth-century politics. Allan Peskin, "Who Were the Stalwarts? Who Were Their Rivals? Republican Factions in the Gilded Age," *Political Science Quarterly* 99 (Winter 1984–85): 703–16, at p. 707.

23. Some such dominance of each national party by its "regulars," despite occasional exceptions, is often viewed as characteristic of the whole era from Andrew Jackson until the most recent decades of this century. For example: "Barons strongly based in interest groups, regions, or machines, collectively had power to decide, or at least veto, and their number at a given time was never very large. Perhaps fifty or a hundred men—buttressed, of course, by aides, friends, and clients—were crucial to each party's nomination and campaign, crucial in convention, canvassing, and funding. And they were a known circle, shifting over time but usually quite easy to identify at any time." Richard Neustadt, "The Constraining of the President," in *Perspectives on the Presidency*, ed. Aaron Wildavsky (Boston: Little, Brown, 1975), pp. 431–46, at p. 434. That view is by no means incompatible with the belief that the old convention was a reasonably representative body. After all, party leaders could have had a good sense of the preference of their party's voters.

24. Ceaser, *Presidential Selection*, pp. 222–23. Note that over half of the delegates at the Democratic convention were not then sufficient to nominate. A two-thirds majority was required until 1936.

25. Saying that he hoped the subject could "be handled promptly and without serious controversy of any kind," Wilson urged the "enactment of legislation which will provide for primary elections throughout the country at which the voters of the several parties may choose their nominees for the Presidency without the intervention of nominating conventions." President Woodrow Wilson's First Annual Message of December 2, 1913, in Fred L. Israel, ed., *The State of the Union Messages of the Presidents 1790–1960* (New York: Chelsea House, 1966), vol. 3, p. 2548.

26. Ceaser, *Presidential Selection*, pp. 227–28.

27. Ranney, *Participation*, pp. 5–6.

28. Polsby, *Consequences*, p. 11, tabulates primary-election winners between 1912 and 1980. His table is my source.

29. Nelson W. Polsby and Aaron Wildavsky, *Presidential Elections: Strategies of American Electoral Politics* (New York: Scribner's, 1980), p. 225.

30. The then still required two-thirds majority at Democratic conventions was directly responsible for the deadlock, but it might well have been regarded as an ordinarily useful device to ensure a consensual choice so dear to the defenders of brokered coalitional conventions.

31. Harding's nomination cannot be dismissed as merely the product of a peculiarly manipulated convention. He was more than a "dark-horse" choice in a "smoke-filled room." A U.S. Senator since 1914, from the president-producing state of Ohio, and the Republican convention's keynote speaker in 1916, Harding arrived at the convention as the second choice of many delegates whose first choices could not win the nomination. Although he had not been the first choice of many delegates outside Ohio, he was a national figure within the party and thus the kind of consensual choice that the convention system had often made. The story is well told by Randolph C. Downes, *The Rise of Warren Gamaliel Harding 1865–1920* (Columbus: Ohio State University Press, 1970), chaps. 16–18.

32. Ceaser, *Presidential Selection*, p. 5.

33. Jeane Jordan Kirkpatrick, *Dismantling the Parties* (Washington, D.C.: American Enterprise Institute, 1978), p. 2.

34. Ranney, *Curing the Mischiefs*, p. 206.

35. William J. Crotty, *Political Reform and the American Experiment* (New York: Crowell, 1977), pp. 243–45. See also *Mandate for Reform: A Report of the Commission on Party Structure and Delegate Selection to the Democratic National Committee* (Washington, D.C.: DNC, 1970). The fullest account of how the commission (formally the Commission on Party Structure and Delegate Selection) won party approval of its far-reaching proposals is Byron E. Shafer's *Quiet Revolution: The Struggle for the Democratic Party and the Shaping of Post-Reform Politics* (New York: Sage Foundation, 1983). I have drawn on it in chapter 7 when discussing the commission's proposals in more detail under the rubric of national party organizational development.

36. Everett Carll Ladd, "The Proper Role of Parties in Presidential Nominee Selection," *Commonsense* 4 (1981): 33–39, at p. 34. His italics.

37. Barbara G. Farah, "Convention Delegates: Party Reform and the Representativeness of Party Elites, 1972–1980," paper prepared for 1981 annual meeting of the American Political Science Association, New York City, September 1981.

38. Steven E. Schier, *The Rules and the Game: Democratic National Convention Delegate Selection in Iowa and Wisconsin* (Washington, D.C.: University Press of America, 1980), pp. 309–12.

39. Data on 1984 primaries are from *Congressional Quarterly Weekly Report* 42 (June 16, June 23, and July 7, 1984): 1441–44; 1504–6; and 1618–20. For earlier years, see Polsby, *Consequences*, p. 64; Ceaser, *Presidential Selection*, pp. 237–38. Both Polsby and Ceaser provide data not only on the increased number of delegates chosen as a result of primaries after 1968, but also on the larger percentages of those delegates —and of all convention delegates—who came to the convention committed to national candidates.

40. Jonathan Moore, *The Campaign for President: 1980 in Retrospect* (Cambridge, Mass.: Ballinger, 1981), p. 278.

41. *Congressional Quarterly Weekly Report* 42 (July 7, 1984): 1629.

42. *Congressional Quarterly Weekly Report* 42 (March 24, 1984): 653–55.

43. Illustrative of the intent is the McGovern-Fraser Commission's successful effort to move all delegate selection into the election year itself, and so eliminate the naming of leaders or anyone else to be delegates before the presidential candidates themselves were known. Something was inherently wrong, in the eyes of reformers, with the selection of delegates who could not be committed to popular preferences. James W. Ceaser, *Reforming the Reforms: A Critical Analysis of the Presidential Selection Process* (Cambridge, Mass.: Ballinger, 1982), pp. 42, 150.

44. Polsby, *Consequences*, p. 58.

45. Between 1980 and 1984, caucuses replaced primaries as first steps in Democratic delegate selection in Arkansas, Kansas, Kentucky, Montana, Nevada, Texas, and Wisconsin. Montana and Wisconsin shifted because of the newly enforced national party rule against the use of their primaries. Michigan, whose open primary had still been used by Republicans but not Democrats in 1980, abolished it for both parties in 1984.

46. Ceaser, *Presidential Selection*, p. 263, has an interesting note about several possible explanations for the post-1968 change to primaries by state legislatures. My own inquiries at the Democratic National Committee, whose staff had informally surveyed state party officers to ask why presidential primaries had been adopted, lead to no more definitive a conclusion than Ceaser's, although I found that in at least a few states party officers preferred primaries in order to avoid the flooding of caucuses by candidate enthusiasts.

47. Neustadt, "The Constraining of the President," pp. 431–46, at p. 434.

48. David S. Broder, *Washington Post*, December 23, 1979, p. E7.

49. F. Christopher Arterton, "Campaign Organizations Confront the Media-Political Environment," in *Race for the Presidency: The Media and the Nominating Process*, ed. James David Barber (Englewood Cliffs, N.J.: Prentice-Hall, 1978), pp. 3–25, at p. 9.

50. Michael J. Robinson, "The Media in 1980: Was the Message the Message?" in *The American Elections of 1980*, ed. Ranney, pp. 177–211, at pp. 190–92.

51. Polsby, *Consequences*, pp. 70–71, has a table drawn from Robinson's work showing CBS and UPI coverage state by state.

52. Democratic National Committee, *Delegate Selection Rules for the 1984 Democratic National Convention* (Washington, D.C.: DNC, 1983), pp. 11–12. The rule was not fully enforced in 1984; New Hampshire's primary was 14 days before and Iowa's caucuses 22 days before the 13-week season.

53. Figures for 1984 are tabulated in *Congressional Quarterly Weekly Report* 42 (June 16 and July 7, 1984): 1444 and 1620. For 1980, see *The American Elections of 1980*, ed. Ranney, pp. 361–65. Note there that percentages tend to be higher for earlier

and still meaningful primary contests, and lower especially in the late Republican primaries when the contest had effectively ended as a result of Reagan's successes.

54. For example, Duke University in conjunction with the Woodrow Wilson Center conducted a Forum on Presidential Nominations and published *A Statement of Purpose for Political Parties* (Chapel Hill: Duke University Institute of Policy Sciences and Public Affairs, 1981).

55. Polsby, *Consequences*, p. 3.

56. Ibid., p. 77.

57. Nixon is excluded because the nomination that brought him the presidency was made before the flowering of the new system, and Ford is excluded because he became president without benefit of nomination or election and was then, like Nixon, renominated under the new system.

58. The point is convincingly made by Charles O. Jones, "Nominating 'Carter's Favorite Opponent': The Republicans in 1980," in *The American Elections of 1980*, ed. Ranney, pp. 61–98. He describes Reagan's campaign as "trifocal" (p. 98) to emphasize that he simultaneously looked to winning the nomination and election and to uniting his party in the process.

59. Jones, ibid., and Kessel, *Presidential Parties*. See also John F. Bibby, "The Role of Political Parties in the Nomination Process," *Commonsense* 4 (1981): 21–32.

60. *The American Elections of 1980*, ed. Ranney, pp. 361–65, provides the turnout percentages for the primaries. I have made my own rough calculation of the turnout percentage for the Iowa caucuses. Only one very late primary (Rhode Island's) had a smaller turnout percentage than Iowa's caucuses.

61. Paul T. David and James W. Ceaser, *Proportional Representation in Presidential Nominating Politics* (Charlottesville: University Press of Virginia, 1980), pp. 84, 237–38, indicate a capacity of regulars in 1976 to control caucuses in certain places, particularly within Virginia.

62. James M. Burns, "Party Renewal: The Need for Intellectual Leadership," in *Party Renewal*, ed. Pomper, pp. 194–99, at p. 198, declares his preference for caucuses over primaries evidently for all offices as well as for the presidency.

63. Democratic National Committee, *Delegate Selection Rules*, pp. 8–10. The 14 percent requirement, like the shorter nominating season, was adopted on the recommendation of the Hunt Commission that the Democratic party had established after 1980, just as there had been commissions after 1968 (McGovern-Fraser), 1972 (Mikulski), and 1976 (Winograd). In addition to the 14 percent ex officio *and* uncommitted, the 1984 Democratic convention, like that of 1980, had another 10 percent from leadership and officeholding ranks who were committed to presidential candidates.

64. Presumably, Democratic officeholders had been discouraged from attending the Democratic national convention by the need, from 1972 through 1980, to commit themselves to presidential candidates, and perhaps also by the need to compete for delegate positions against nonregular activists. At any rate, the numbers of Democratic representatives and senators at conventions dropped sharply after the 1960s and

by 1980 only 14 to 15 percent of them attended as voting delegates or alternates. No comparable drop among Republican members of Congress occurred. Polsby, *Consequences*, p. 114.

65. Both of Mondale's principal opponents, Gary Hart and Jesse Jackson, believed that they would have done better if proportional representation had been more strictly observed, rather than diluted by the 1984 counterreforms. And, of course, they would have done better without the pro-Mondale 14 percent. *Congressional Quarterly Weekly Report* 42 (June 30, 1984): 1568–69. For the Fairness Commission's limited response, ibid. 43 (Oct. 26, 1985): 2158–59.

66. Richard Jensen, *How the Midwest Was Won* (Chicago: University of Chicago Press, 1971), p. 273.

67. Louis W. Koenig, *The Chief Executive* (New York: Harcourt, Brace, 1964), p. 95.

68. Ibid., p. 118.

69. Funding provisions are summarized by Herbert E. Alexander, *Financing Politics* (Washington, D.C.: Congressional Quarterly, 1980), pp. 163–76. Because the public-funding provision allows for inflation, the $40 million in 1984 was well above roughly $30 million in 1980 and roughly $22 million in 1976. My chapter 10 includes more detail on public funding generally.

70. Again, see Jones, "Nominating," pp. 61–98, for a full presentation of Reagan's success under the new system.

71. Kessel, *Presidential Parties*, p. 312.

72. I stress the importance of party nationalization in chapter 7.

73. Kay Lawson, "Constitutional Change and Party Development in France, Nigeria, and the United States," in *Political Parties: Development and Decay*, ed. Louis Maisel and Joseph Cooper (Beverly Hills, Calif.: Sage Publications, 1978), pp. 145–78, at pp. 172–73.

74. Jean Blondel, "The Rise of a New Style President," in *France at the Polls*, ed. Howard R. Penniman (Washington, D.C.: American Enterprise Institute, 1975), pp. 41–69. The Fifth Republic's first president, Charles de Gaulle, was undoubtedly elected mainly because of his personal appeal; the party supporting him, while electorally the largest, owed more of its success to de Gaulle than he owed to it. His immediate successor, Georges Pompidou, represents a less decisive case, because his Gaullist party support may have outweighed his considerable independent personal appeal. More clearly significant is the election of Giscard d'Estaing in 1974; he headed what was then a fairly small party and yet in the first round of voting ran ahead of the Gaullist party candidate, partly as a result of a division among Gaullists, and so emerged in the runoff election as the candidate of the right against the Socialist candidate whom the Communists also supported. French parties do not dominate the presidential election as they do parliamentary elections. In fact, the main parties have not even held nominating conventions to institutionalize their choices (Blondel, p. 64). Socialist party support for Francois Mitterand's successful presi-

dential campaign in 1981 may, however, represent a somewhat more familiar partisan effort.

75. In the presidential general elections of 1960, 1976, 1980, and 1984, television played a special role as the medium through which the debates were staged. Unquestionably the thrust of the televised debates was to provide voters with opportunities to make judgments of personal qualities of the nominees. Although most viewers might have their partisan predispositions merely confirmed by the debates, possibly crucial numbers appear to have been influenced. See especially Steven H. Chaffee and Jack Dennis, "Presidential Debates: an Empirical Assessment," in *The Past and Future of Presidential Debates,* ed. Austin Ranney (Washington, D.C.: American Enterprise Institute, 1979), pp. 1–50, at p. 39.

76. Polsby, *Consequences,* pp. 102–5. See also Nelson W. Polsby, "Presidential Cabinet Making: Lessons for the Political System," *Political Science Quarterly* 93 (Spring 1978): 15–25.

77. The coupling of the position of postmaster general with the national committee chairmanship was a long-established custom, broken only in recent decades. It recognized the large-scale patronage, notably in postmasterships throughout the country, available to an incoming president and his party. No doubt the end of massive post office patronage marked the end not only of the postmaster general's status as the major dispenser of jobs but also of a large patronage-based organization of campaign workers.

78. Polsby, *Consequences,* pp. 104–5.

79. Ibid., pp. 103–4.

80. David Stockman (director of the Office of Management and Budget), Drew Lewis (secretary of transportation), Raymond Donovan (secretary of labor), and, in a different way, Jeane Kirkpatrick (ambassador to the U.N.) had all had links to Reagan's presidential campaign.

81. For Reagan, choosing cabinet members from his own presidential adherents was not incompatible with the filling of certain cabinet positions with interest-group representatives of importance to a Republican Administration. Thus both the Treasury and Commerce secretaries (Donald Regan and Malcolm Baldrige) came from the business community, the Agriculture secretary (John Block) from a farm background, and the Interior secretary (James Watt) from a western constituency interested in a less-than-strict conservationist use of Interior's natural resource domain.

82. John H. Kessel, *The Domestic Presidency: Decision-Making in the White House* (North Scituate, Mass.: Duxbury Press, 1975), p. 72.

83. Roger G. Brown, "Party and Bureaucracy: From Kennedy to Reagan," *Political Science Quarterly* 97 (Summer 1982): 279–94.

84. Stephen Hess, *Organizing the Presidency* (Washington, D.C.: Brookings Institution, 1976), pp. 180–82. Hess treats White House management as largely impractical, and he prefers departments run by officers responsible to Congress as well as to the president.

85. Ibid., p. 9; Kessel, *The Domestic Presidency*, p. 17; Neustadt, *Presidential Power*, pp. 194, 213.

86. Hess, *Organizing the Presidency*, p. 9.

87. Richard P. Nathan, *The Plot that Failed: Nixon and the Administrative Presidency* (New York: Wiley, 1975).

88. Hugh Heclo, *A Government of Strangers: Executive Politics in Washington* (Washington, D.C.: Brookings Institution, 1977), pp. 49, 67.

89. Lester G. Seligman, "The Presidential Office and the President as Party Leader (with a Postscript on the Kennedy-Nixon Era)," in *Parties and Elections in an Anti-Party Age*, ed. Jeff Fishel (Bloomington: Indiana University Press, 1978), pp. 295–302.

90. *New York Times*, February 3, 1985, sec. 4, p. 2.

91. John F. Manley, "Presidential Power and White House Lobbying," *Political Science Quarterly* 93 (Summer 1978): 255–75, at p. 266.

92. Hugh Heclo and Rudolph G. Penner, "Fiscal and Political Strategy in the Reagan Administration," in *The Reagan Presidency: An Early Assessment*, ed. Fred I. Greenstein (Baltimore: Johns Hopkins University Press, 1983), pp. 21–47.

93. The difficulties posed by the new decentralized Congress are stressed by Eric L. Davis, "Legislative Reform and the Decline of Presidential Influence on Capitol Hill," *British Journal of Political Science* 9 (October 1979): 465–79. Polsby's emphasis when discussing Carter's relations with Congress is on the president's shortcomings (*Consequences*, pp. 113–14). The question remains, however, whether the shortcomings were peculiar to Carter or could be found in any president nominated and elected under the new plebiscitary system.

94. Seligman, "The Presidential Office," p. 300.

95. Neustadt, *Presidential Power*, p. 238.

96. Fred I. Greenstein, *The Hidden-Hand Presidency* (New York: Basic Books, 1982), pp. 5, 57, 151.

97. Cornelius P. Cotter persuasively argues, with substantial documentary support, that "as president, Eisenhower exerted considerable influence over the Republican party and pursued a well-informed and sustained program to strengthen it." Moreover, he treats his findings as consistent with Greenstein's. "Eisenhower as Party Leader," *Political Science Quarterly* 98 (Summer 1983): 255–83, at p. 256.

Chapter 5: State and Local Structures

1. The durability of American states is a principal theme of my "The Old States in a New System," in *The New American Political System*, ed. Anthony King (Washington, D.C.: American Enterprise Institute, 1978), pp. 325–69.

2. In the early 1980s, parties other than the two major Canadian national parties held governing majorities in three of ten provinces and were also the principal opposition in one of those three and in two other provinces.

3. James Buckley, elected to the U.S. Senate in 1970, was a conspicuous exception in that he won under the Conservative label against a Republican and a Demo-

crat. Significantly, however, he became a Republican in the Senate and subsequently added that label in his unsuccessful campaign for reelection in 1976.

4. The relevant legal opportunities and their use are carefully explained by Howard A. Scarrow, *Parties, Elections, and Representation in the State of New York* (New York: New York University Press, 1983), pp. 23–25, 55–75.

5. Maine elected an Independent governor in 1974.

6. *The Book of the States 1984–85* (Lexington, Ky.: Council of State Governments, 1984), p. 85. My count of third-party legislators excludes New York's Conservatives and Liberals, who also served as Republicans or Democrats. In other recent years there has been only a scattering of third-party state legislators; for example, in 1979 there was one Libertarian in Alaska and two independent Republicans in Mississippi (plus eight Independents in various states). *Book of the States 1980–81*, p. 85.

7. Malcolm E. Jewell and David M. Olson, *American State Political Parties and Elections* (Homewood, Ill.: Dorsey Press, 1982), pp. 37–38.

8. Fuller amplification may be found in my *Politics in Wisconsin* (Madison: University of Wisconsin Press, 1958), pp. 33–56.

9. Charles R. Adrian, "Nonpartisanship," *International Encyclopedia of the Social Sciences*, ed. David L. Sills (New York: Macmillan Co. and Free Press, 1968), vol. 11, pp. 201–3, at p. 202. The 1976 figure is from *The Municipal Yearbook 1976* (Washington, D.C.: International City Management Association, 1976), p. 69.

10. Milwaukee elected its first Socialist mayor in 1910, when he obtained a plurality but no majority against Democratic and Republican opponents. The nonpartisan ballot, with a runoff election, appeared to make it easier for an anti-Socialist coalition to win the mayoralty in 1914, but another Socialist won the position in 1916 and held it until 1940, always on the nonpartisan ballot. Bayrd Still, *Milwaukee: The History of a City* (Madison: State Historical Society of Wisconsin, 1948), pp. 318, 520–22. The Milwaukee Socialists were themselves devoted to efficiency-minded good government as well as to moderate versions of their ideology. Except for party organizational commitments, they had little in common with traditional big-city machines.

11. Jewell and Olson, *American State Political Parties*, p. 13.

12. Ibid., pp. 24–29. Thus measured, "two-party competitive" states were somewhat more numerous in the 1961–82 period than they were between 1932 and 1958. From the same source, it should also be noted that there were now more "Democratic majority" states then "Republican majority" states and that between 1961 and 1982 Democrats more often than Republicans won control in "two-party competitive" states.

13. V. O. Key, Jr., *American State Politics: An Introduction* (New York: Knopf, 1956), pp. 88–97.

14. Ibid., pp. 99–100.

15. Ibid., p. 117.

16. Howard R. Penniman, "The State of the Two-Party System," *The Wilson Quarterly* 2 (Winter 1978): 83–89.

17. John H. M. Laslett and Seymour Martin Lipset, eds, *Failure of a Dream? Essays in the History of American Socialism* (Garden City, N.Y.: Anchor Press/Doubleday, 1974).

18. Although short lived, these third-party presidential candidacies received impressive percentages of the popular vote: 27 percent for Theodore Roosevelt (in a year when the Socialist candidate, Eugene Debs, received 6 percent), just under 17 percent for La Follette, a little over 2 percent for Henry Wallace and also for Thurmond in the same election, over 13 percent for George Wallace, and just under 7 percent for Anderson.

19. An attempt to go national by Wisconsin Progressives, notably by their leader and then-governor Philip La Follette, quickly failed in 1938. La Follette describes his abortive National Progressives of America in *Adventures in Politics: The Memoirs of Philip LaFollette*, ed. Donald Young (New York: Holt, Rinehart and Winston, 1970), pp. 246–56.

20. The survey is reported in *Comparative State Politics Newsletter* (Lexington: Department of Political Science of the University of Kentucky) 1 (May 1980): 7–21. See also the same *Newsletter* 2 (August 1981): 9–16.

21. Samuel C. Patterson, "American State Legislatures and Public Policy," in *Politics in the American States*, ed. Herbert Jacob and Kenneth Vines (Boston: Little, Brown, 1976), chap. 4, at p. 143.

22. Scarrow, *Parties, Elections*, pp. 18–19; Malcolm E. Jewell and Samuel C. Patterson, *The Legislative Process in the United States* (New York: Random House, 1977), pp. 383–88.

23. Not only is the control of executive and legislative branches often divided between the two parties but so is the control of two-house legislatures. Recent experience is tabulated by John F. Bibby, "State House Elections at Midterm," in *The American Elections of 1982*, ed. Thomas E. Mann and Norman J. Ornstein (Washington, D.C.: American Enterprise Institute, 1983), pp. 111–32, at p. 123.

24. Milton Rakove, *Don't Make No Waves — Don't Back No Losers* (Bloomington: Indiana University Press, 1975), p. 112.

25. Dennis R. Judd, *The Politics of American Cities: Private Power and Public Policy* (Boston: Little, Brown, 1979), p. 59. See also John M. Allswang, *Bosses, Machines, and Urban Voters: An American Symbiosis* (Port Washington, N.Y.: Kennikat Press, 1977).

26. Ari Hoogenboom, *Outlawing the Spoils: A History of the Civil Service Reform Movement, 1865–1883* (Urbana: University of Illinois Press, 1961), pp. 200, 224–25, describes the use of financial assessments of federal employees.

27. Samuel J. Eldersveld lists ten characteristics of the "classic type" of machine, in *Political Parties in American Society* (New York: Basic Books, 1982), p. 149.

28. Edward C. Banfield and James Q. Wilson, *City Politics* (New York: Random House, 1963), p. 116.

29. Frank J. Sorauf, "State Patronage in a Rural County," *American Political Science Review* 50 (December 1956): 1046–56.

30. A good Republican example is Thomas C. Platt's New York state organization. Richard L. McCormick, *From Realignment to Reform: Political Change in New York State, 1893–1910* (Ithaca: Cornell University Press, 1981), chap. 3.

31. Richard Hofstadter, *The Idea of a Party System* (Berkeley: University of California Press, 1970), p. 210.

32. Jesse Macy, a pioneering scholarly writer on parties, regarded the Jacksonian spoils system as originally in line with American desires for popular government, but its late-nineteenth-century development as offensive. *Political Parties in the United States, 1846–1861* (New York: Macmillan, 1900), p. 81.

33. James Bryce, *The American Commonwealth* (Chicago: Charles Sergel, 1891), vol. 2, pp. 3–236, 491–92.

34. David H. Rosenbloom, *Federal Service and the Constitution* (Ithaca: Cornell University Press, 1971), pp. 58–59, 95, provides a sharp description of the spoils system against which the reformers launched their campaign.

35. Leonard D. White, *The Republican Era: A Study in Administrative History, 1869–1901* (New York: Macmillan, 1958), p. 291.

36. Ibid., p. 293.

37. Ibid., p. 310.

38. Rakove, *Don't Make No Waves*, p. 123; Allswang, *Bosses*, p. 59.

39. Rakove, *Don't Make No Waves*, p. 127.

40. Banfield and Wilson, *City Politics*, p. 126.

41. Robert K. Merton, *Social Theory and Social Structure* (Glencoe, Ill.: Free Press, 1957), pp. 77–81.

42. Judd, *The Politics of American Cities*, pp. 71, 74.

43. McCormick, *From Realignment to Reform*, p. 80, describes Platt's method of influencing New York state legislative nominations.

44. Rakove, *Don't Make No Waves*, pp. 95–96.

45. Writing about New York City in a work originally published in 1899, Matthew P. Breen made the now-familiar point: "These Machine Bosses, great and small, have no idea of being in politics except for the purpose of obtaining office either for themselves or their immediate followers, and getting money directly or indirectly out of the City Treasury." *Thirty Years of New York Politics* (New York: Arno Press, 1974), p. 826.

46. James Q. Wilson, *Political Organizations* (New York: Basic Books, 1973), pp. 97–101. Wilson carefully notes, however, our limited knowledge of patronage, even of the number of jobs in a given city.

47. John D. Buenker, *Urban Liberalism and Progressive Reform* (New York: Scribner's, 1973), emphasizes the extent to which the urban machines responded to urban liberalism in the twentieth century.

48. Judd, *The Politics of American Cities*, pp. 124–25.

49. Rakove, *Don't Make No Waves*, p. 71.

50. White, *The Republican Era*, pp. 26, 278, 384. See also Herbert Kaufman, "The

Growth of the Federal Personnel System," in *The Federal Government Service* (New York: American Assembly, 1954), pp. 15–51, at pp. 28–30.

51. Eldersveld, *Political Parties*, p. 150. Even in 1985, however, the Nassau County (New York) Republican party displayed the marks of an old-style machine.

52. Raymond E. Wolfinger, "Why Political Machines Have Not Withered Away and Other Revisionist Thoughts," *Journal of Politics* 34 (May 1972): 365–98, cites New Haven as well as New York City and Chicago; Martin and Susan Tolchin, in *To the Victor . . . Political Patronage from the Clubhouse to the White House* (New York: Random House, 1971), stress the importance of the remaining federal as well as state and local patronage.

53. Bruce M. Stave, *The New Deal and the Last Hurrah: Pittsburgh Machine Politics* (Pittsburgh, University of Pittsburgh Press, 1970), p. 162.

54. Lyle W. Dorsett, *Franklin D. Roosevelt and the City Bosses* (Port Washington, N.Y.: Kennikat Press, 1977).

55. Frank J. Sorauf, "Patronage and Party," *Midwest Journal of Political Science* 3 (May 1959): 115–26; and W. Robert Gump, "The Functions of Patronage in American Party Politics: An Empirical Reappraisal," *Midwest Journal of Political Science* 15 (February 1971): 87–107.

56. Allswang, *Bosses*, pp. 118, 143.

57. *Elrod v. Burns*, 427 U.S. 347 (1976), at 372.

58. *Branti v. Finkel*, 445 U.S. 507 (1980).

59. *Shakman v. Democratic Organization of Cook County*, 481 F. Supp. 1315 (N.D. Ill. E. D. 1979).

60. New programs, however, may still provide many if temporary patronage jobs much as did earlier New Deal programs. The opportunity is illustrated by a study of the way in which, in 1974, the New Haven Democratic organization distributed 675 jobs created by the U.S. Comprehensive Employment and Training Act (CETA) to give work experience to the hard-core unemployed. The distribution strongly suggested that jobs were used to reward areas, especially Italian-American wards, that cast heavy votes for the organization's candidates. Significantly, the study also shows that the patronage was not an effective means of organizational maintenance. It leads its author to question not only the organizational usefulness of that kind of patronage job but also the usefulness of patronage jobs in general. Michael Johnson, "Patrons and Clients, Jobs and Machines: A Case Study of the Uses of Patronage," *American Political Science Review* 73 (June 1979): 385–98.

61. Important differences in party organizational strength existed between western and eastern sections of the country. Martin Shefter, "Regional Receptivity to Reform," *Political Science Quarterly* 98 (Fall 1983): 459–83. The characteristic American cadre party structure is described by Frank J. Sorauf, *Party Politics in America* (Boston: Little, Brown, 1984), pp. 59–86.

62. Distinguishing the old machines from cadre parties is a modification of Maurice Duverger's evident inclusion of traditional American party organizations among the

cadre parties that he contrasts with European-style mass-membership parties. *Political Parties*, trans. Barbara and Robert North (New York: Wiley, 1954), pp. 61–79.

63. Samuel J. Eldersveld's description of Detroit's parties in the 1950s indicates considerable participation. *Political Parties: A Behavioral Analysis* (Chicago: Rand McNally, 1964).

64. William E. Wright, ed., *A Comparative Study of Party Organization* (Columbus, Ohio: Charles E. Merrill, 1971), pp. 17–54.

65. Eldersveld, *Political Parties: A Behavioral Analysis,* pp. 341–56.

66. Wilson, *Political Organizations*, p. 95.

67. In addition to Eldersveld's description of Detroit's nonclub parties, there is a more recent account of participation in Minnesota's statutory and cadre structure. Thomas R. Marshall, "Minnesota: The Party Caucus-Convention System," in *Party Renewal in America*, ed. Gerald M. Pomper (New York: Praeger, 1980), pp. 139–58.

68. James Q. Wilson, *The Amateur Democrat* (Chicago: University of Chicago Press, 1966), pp. 96–125; Epstein, *Politics in Wisconsin*, pp. 77–97.

69. On the other hand, middle-class activist associations now existed in New York City, where by the early 1970s many old patronage clubs had been converted. Norman M. Adler and Blanche Davis Blank, *Political Clubs in New York* (New York: Praeger, 1975), pp. 28, 65.

70. Leon D. Epstein, *Political Parties in Western Democracies* (New Brunswick, N.J.: Transaction, 1980), pp. 98–129, 233–60, 369–77.

71. John H. Kessel, *Presidential Campaign Politics* (Homewood, Ill.: Dorsey Press, 1984), pp. 75–91, 321.

72. Key, *State Politics*, p. 169.

73. Ibid., p. 120.

74. Scarrow, *Parties, Elections*, pp. 29–54.

75. Jewell and Olson, *American State Political Parties*, p. 113.

76. Scarrow, *Parties, Elections*, pp. 29–54.

77. Some southern states even now allow each party to decide whether it wants a primary or a convention to nominate its candidates. In the past, the option accommodated minority Republicans who would have had few primary voters in state elections, but lately in Virginia both Republicans and Democrats have nominated by convention. Jewell and Olson, *American State Political Parties*, p. 107.

78. Ibid., pp. 107–10, for more detail on the variety of primaries. I have also drawn on the tabulation of states by Steven E. Finkel and Howard A. Scarrow, "Party Identification and Party Enrollment: The Difference and the Consequence," *Journal of Politics* 47 (May 1985): 620–42. Of the states that do not in any degree close their primaries, nine are open in the sense of merely allowing voters to decide in secret which party's primary to participate in on a given day; two (Washington and Alaska) are more generously open in that they allow voters in their "blanket primary" to cast a ballot for a candidate of one party for one office and for a candidate of another party for a different office. To these 11 open and blanket primary states Louisiana

should be added, because it has moved farther away from the management of an internal party contest than any other state despite its maintenance of party registrations. Louisiana specifies that all candidates, though bearing different party labels, should run against each other at an initial election in which a candidate who wins at least 50 percent of the votes for a particular office is elected. Only without a 50 percent winner is there a runoff election between the two leading candidates (whether or not they bear different party labels). Thomas H. Kazee, "The Impact of Electoral Reform: 'Open Election' and the Louisiana Party System," *Publius* 13 (Winter 1983): 131–39; Charles D. Hadley, "The Louisiana Open Elections System Reform: Elite Perceptions and Political Realities," paper for the 1983 meeting of the Southern Political Science Association, Birmingham, Ala.

79. Craig Carr and Gary L. Scott, "The Logic of State Primary Classification Schemes," *American Politics Quarterly* 12 (October 1984): 465–76, at p. 472. It would not now be constitutional to impose a waiting period of more than about a year for voters wanting to change party affiliation. The relevant judicial decisions, discussed in my next chapter, are *Rosario v. Rockefeller*, 410 U.S. 752 (1973) and *Kusper v. Pontikes*, 414 U.S. 51 (1973).

80. Charles E. Merriam and Louise Overacker, *Primary Elections* (Chicago: University of Chicago Press, 1928), pp. 211, 214.

81. Jewell and Olson, *American State Political Parties*, pp. 112–13. Utah (among the six states) is a little different, in that convention endorsement is the only way to get on the ballot; yet a primary contest remains likely because *two* convention choices for each office go on the ballot unless the top choice has 70 percent of the convention vote.

82. This is to say that all six states providing a legal advantage to an endorsed convention choice differ from Virginia, whose party conventions (as indicated in note 77) have lately been the nominating authorities as such conventions once were in the other states.

83. Sarah McCally Morehouse, "The Effect of Preprimary Endorsements on State Party Strength," paper for the 1980 meeting of the American Political Science Association, Washington, D.C.

84. Andrew D. McNutt, "The Effect of Preprimary Endorsement on Competition for Nominations: An Examination of Different Nominating Systems," *Journal of Politics* 42 (February 1980): 257–66.

85. Malcolm E. Jewell, "The State Party Convention as a Device for Influencing Primary Elections: A Study of Five States in 1982," paper for the 1983 meeting of the American Political Science Association, Chicago.

86. Ibid., pp. 26–27.

87. Ibid., p. 28. See also E. Lester Levine. "Is Minnesota a Two-Party State Again?" *Publius* 9 (Winter 1979), at 197–204, 199–201, on DFL endorsement in 1978. It may be added that in 1984 the DFL did succeed in nominating, though not electing, its endorsed choice for the U.S. Senate.

88. Marshall, "Minnesota," p. 141. Minnesota statutes require that caucuses be open to all of a party's declared supporters.

89. Jewell, "The State Party Convention," p. 3.

90. Ibid., p. 25.

91. Peter F. Gladerisi, "Primary Reform as Participatory Incentive: Party Renewal in a Changing American Political Universe," paper for the 1982 meeting of the American Political Science Association, Denver, Colo.

92. Kay Lawson, "California: The Uncertainties of Reform," in *Party Renewal*, ed. Pomper, pp. 116–38. In 1984, pro-party forces in California won a U.S. District Court judgment against the constitutionality of state restrictions on the activities of the statutory parties. The legal issues are discussed in the next chapter.

93. Article VIII of the constitution of the Democratic Party of Wisconsin states: "Neither in convention nor in any other manner shall the state organization endorse or support any candidate for elective office in any primary election. No county unit nor subdivision thereof shall endorse or support any candidate for any elective office in any primary election." Section 2 of Article VIII of the constitution of the Republican Party of Wisconsin now reads: "In the years in which there is a statewide election the Convention may endorse by majority vote one candidate for each of the five state constitutional offices and the United States Senate. Any endorsement ballot must be preceded by a majority vote of the assembled delegates to make an endorsement for that office."

94. See chapter 7 for national party organizational developments. The institutional modernization of state governments is briefly summarized in my "The Old States in a New System," in *The New American Political System*, ed. King, pp. 325–69, at pp. 348–54.

95. Robert J. Huckshorn, *Party Leadership in the States* (Amherst: University of Massachusetts Press, 1976), pp. 54–57, 254, 263–66.

96. James L. Gibson, Cornelius P. Cotter, John F. Bibby, and Robert J. Huckshorn, "Assessing Party Organizational Strength," *American Journal of Political Science* 27 (May 1983): 193–222. The same authors report their findings more fully in Cornelius P. Cotter, James L. Gibson, John F. Bibby, and Robert J. Huckshorn, *Party Organizations in American Politics* (New York: Praeger, 1984), especially chap. 2.

97. Cotter et al., *Party Organizations*, p. 30.

98. Ibid., pp. 157–58.

99. Pamela J. Edwards, "State Party Organization Revitalization: A Critical Assessment," paper for the 1984 meeting of the Southern Political Science Association, Savannah, Ga., pp. 7, 10–11.

100. Timothy Conlan, Ann Martino, and Robert Dilger, "State Parties in the 1980s," *Intergovernmental Perspective* 10 (Fall 1984): 6–11, 23, at pp. 7–9.

101. Samuel J. Eldersveld, "The Condition of Party Organization at the Local Level," paper for the 1984 meeting of the Southern Political Science Association, Savannah, Ga.

102. Cotter et al., *Party Organizations*, chap. 3.

103. The extragovernmental party organization is not the only party agency to provide help, especially financial help, to legislative candidates. Legislative party caucuses, like congressional party caucuses, collect and distribute large sums in some states. Their role will be discussed in chapter 9.

104. Conlan, Martino, and Dilger, "State Parties in the 1980s," pp. 9, 11.

Chapter 6: Parties as Public Utilities

1. Despite a few exceptions and numerous variations, party labels are almost everywhere standard fixtures on ballots in national and state elections. As observed in chapter 5, nonpartisan ballots are widely used in judicial, school board, and other local elections, as well as in certain statewide elections of educational authorities, but not to elect state legislators (except in Nebraska) or most major state executive officers. Virginia's ballots, however, omit party labels.

2. Leon D. Epstein, "A Comparative Study of Australian Parties," *British Journal of Political Science* 7 (January 1977): 1–21, at p. 9.

3. See, for example, the ballot reproduced in Howard R. Penniman, ed., *Britain at the Polls, 1979* (Washington, D.C.: American Enterprise Institute, 1981), p. 331. By putting their party labels on the ballot, British candidates make it even easier for voters to know their party's choice than it was when they depended, as Australian voters had also depended, on campaign advertising of a candidate's party identification. By no means does the absence of a government-conferred party label convert either a British or an Australian election into a nonpartisan contest. Neither nation has any such intention, and elections in Britain and Australia are more fully party contests than are the contemporary American elections in which candidate-centered politics have become prominent.

4. Austin Ranney, "Candidate Selection," in *Democracy at the Polls*, ed. David Butler, Howard R. Penniman, and Austin Ranney (Washington, D.C.: American Enterprise Institute, 1981), pp. 75–106, at pp. 76–82.

5. Clair Wilcox, "Regulation of Industry," *International Encyclopedia of the Social Sciences* (New York: Crowell, Collier and Macmillan, 1968), vol. 13, pp. 390–96, at p. 390. The phrase "affected with a public interest" comes from the similar language of the U.S. Supreme Court in *Munn v. Illinois*, 94 U.S. 113 (1877).

6. The formality of American governmental regulation is stressed in an Anglo-American comparison by David Vogel, "Cooperative Regulation: Environmental Protection in Great Britain," *The Public Interest*, no. 72 (Summer 1983), pp. 88–106, at p. 101. Vogel regards Britain's more flexible, informal, and voluntary method of controlling industrial emissions as an example of a general regulatory tradition different from the more heavily legal American practice.

7. Wilcox, "Regulation of Industry," p. 396.

8. "A perusal of state codes in the mid-nineteenth century indicates a rather complete disinterest on the part of lawmakers with the organization and activities

of parties." James S. Fay, "The Legal Regulation of Political Parties," *Journal of Legislation* 9 (Summer 1982): 263–81, at p. 263.

9. Austin Ranney, *Curing the Mischiefs of Faction: Party Reform in America* (Berkeley: University of California Press, 1975), p. 60.

10. Frederick W. Whitridge, "Caucus System," 1883 work republished in *The Caucus System in American Politics* (New York: Arno Press, 1974), pp. 3–27, at p. 13. Also Frederick W. Dallinger, *Nominations for Elective Office in the United States* (1897; New York: Arno Press, 1974), pp. 46–47.

11. Ari Hoogenboom, *Outlawing the Spoils: A History of the Civil Service Reform Movement, 1865–1883* (Urbana: University of Illinois Press, 1961), p. 26.

12. Ibid., p. 25.

13. Whitridge, "Caucus System," pp. 16–22.

14. Charles Edward Merriam and Louise Overacker, *Primary Elections* (Chicago: University of Chicago Press, 1928), p. 6. I cite the second edition of this standard study of the development of the direct primary; the first edition, written by Merriam alone almost 20 years earlier, reflected progressive reform commitments. These remain present in the second edition, but along with an empirical examination of the first two decades of experience with the primary.

15. Ibid., pp. 6–7.

16. Ibid., p. 7.

17. Dallinger, *Nominations*, p. 173.

18. Merriam and Overacker, *Primary Elections*, pp. 12–14.

19. Arthur Chester Millspaugh, *Party Organization and Machinery in Michigan Since 1890* (Baltimore: Johns Hopkins Press, 1917), pp. 19–20.

20. In addition to the absence of secrecy, the old party ballots were thought to be defective in the accuracy with which they listed nominees, in the burdens of printing and distribution that they imposed on poor parties, in the uncertainty that they would provide advance notice of those nominated and running, and in the noise, violence, and confusion accompanying their distribution at the polls. Eldon Cobb Evans, *A History of the Australian Ballot System in the United States* (Chicago: University of Chicago Press, 1917), pp. 10–16.

21. Ibid., pp. 29–30. The importance of the Australian ballot to a state's official recognition of major parties is stressed by Howard A. Scarrow, *Parties, Elections, and Representation in New York* (New York: New York University Press, 1983), pp. 1–3.

22. Merriam and Overacker, *Primary Elections*, p. 24.

23. Charles R. Adrian, "Nonpartisanship," *International Encyclopedia of the Social Sciences* (New York: Crowell, Collier and Macmillan, 1968), vol. 11, pp. 201–3. See chapter 5 for my brief discussion of nonpartisan elections.

24. Jerrold G. Rusk, "The Effect of the Australian Ballot Reform on Split Ticket Voting: 1876–1908," *American Political Science Review* 64 (December 1970): 1220–38.

25. L. E. Fredman, *The Australian Ballot: The Story of an American Reform* (East Lansing: Michigan State University Press, 1968), p. 47. In New York, after voting

machines were adopted, the office-column ballot was so arranged that one could vote a straight ticket merely by sticking to the same horizontal row of a party's candidates for various offices. Scarrow, *Parties*, p. 16.

26. Fredman, *The Australian Ballot*, pp. 67–68.

27. Ibid., pp. 50–51, 54, 65.

28. Accordingly, the Australian ballot appealed not only to more or less independent reformers but also in New York to some Republicans, because the need for English literacy to use the new ballot could disenfranchise urban Democratic voters. Richard L. McCormick, *From Realignment to Reform: Political Change in New York State, 1893–1910* (Ithaca: Cornell University Press, 1981), pp. 115–18.

29. Merriam and Overacker, *Primary Elections*, p. 25.

30. Ibid., p. 140, from *Commonwealth v. Rogers*, 63 N.E. 421 (Mass. 1902), at 423.

31. Dallinger, *Nominations*, pp. 173, 185.

32. Millspaugh, *Party Organization*, pp. 25–55.

33. Scarrow, *Parties*, pp. 30–33.

34. Epstein, "A Comparative Study of Australian Parties," pp. 16–18.

35. Ranney, *Curing the Mischiefs*, p. 121.

36. Jesse Macy, *Party Organization and Machinery* (New York: Century, 1912), p. 207; Merriam and Overacker, *Primary Elections*, p. 61.

37. A comprehensive list of state nominating procedures, recent enough to be nearly up to date, can be found in "Developments in the Law—Elections," *Harvard Law Review* 88 (April 1975): 1111–1339, at pp. 1151–1217.

38. Richard Hofstadter, *The Age of Reform: From Bryan to F.D.R.* (New York: Knopf, 1955), p. 5.

39. Ibid., p. 257.

40. J. Morgan Kousser, *The Shaping of Southern Politics: Suffrage Restriction and the Establishment of the One-Party South 1880–1910* (New Haven: Yale University Press, 1974), p. 82.

41. V. O. Key, Jr., *Politics, Parties, & Pressure Groups* (New York: Crowell, 1964), pp. 344–45.

42. "Developments in the Law." Later tabulations of state laws regulating parties and of state laws governing party roles in the electoral process are provided by Timothy Conlan, Ann Martino, and Robert Dilger, "State Parties in the 1980s," *Intergovernmental Perspective* 10 (Fall 1984): 6–11, 23, at pp. 12–13.

43. Douglas D. Anderson, "State Regulation of Public Utilities," *The Politics of Deregulation*, ed. James Q. Wilson (New York: Basic Books, 1980), pp. 3–41 at pp. 13–16.

44. Clarence A. Berdahl, "Party Membership in the United States," *American Political Science Review* 36 (February and April 1942): 16–50, 241–62, at p. 241.

45. Joseph R. Starr, "The Legal Status of American Political Parties," *American Political Science Review* 34 (June and August 1940): 439–55, 685–99, at pp. 452–55.

46. Robert J. Huckshorn, *Party Leadership in the States* (Amherst: University of Massachusetts Press, 1976), p. 14.

47. John G. Kester, "Constitutional Restrictions on Political Parties," *Virginia Law Review* 60 (May 1974): 735–84, at pp. 748–60. Even 20 years earlier, soon after the white-primary decisions, there had been a similar scholarly appreciation of the special status of party electoral activities. G. Theodore Mitau, while not drawing so sharp a line as Kester's between electoral and other activities, concluded his analysis, "Judicial Determination of Political Party Organizational Autonomy," by saying: "The more remote the locus of party organizational dispute was from the actual nominating process, the less acute seemed to be the likelihood of judicial intervention." *Minnesota Law Review* 42 (December 1957): 245–68, at p. 268.

48. Kester, "Constitutional Restrictions," p. 760.

49. *Newberry v. United States*, 256 U.S. 232 (1921).

50. *Nixon v. Herndon*, 273 U.S. 536 (1927).

51. *Nixon v. Condon*, 286 U.S. 73 (1932).

52. *Grovey v. Townsend*, 295 U.S. 45 (1935).

53. *United States v. Classic*, 313 U.S. 299 (1941).

54. *Smith v. Allwright*, 321 U.S. 649 (1944), at 663.

55. Ibid., pp. 664–65.

56. *Chapman v. King*, 154 F. 2d 460 (5th Cir. 1946).

57. *Rice v. Elmore*, 165 F. 2d 387 (4th Cir. 1947), at 391, 389. South Carolina tried once more; its Democratic party turned over operation of its primary to private clubs that excluded blacks, and opened its primary to black voters meeting certain onerous requirements. The circuit court again found state involvement and so enjoined the practices of the private clubs. *Baskin v. Brown*, 174 F. 2d 391 (4th Cir. 1949).

58. 345 U.S. 461 (1953).

59. Ibid., p. 463.

60. Ibid., p. 469.

61. Ibid., p. 482.

62. Ibid., pp. 470–77.

63. Ibid., pp. 484–94.

64. Kester, "Constitutional Restrictions," p. 755.

65. John G. Francis and Paul K. Warr, "American Court-Party Reactions," paper for the 1984 meeting of the Midwest Political Science Association, Chicago, pp. 12–18.

66. David Fellman, *The Constitutional Right of Association* (Chicago: University of Chicago Press, 1963), p. 40.

67. *State v. Pierce*, 163 Wis. 615 (1916).

68. See chapter 5's discussion of *Elrod v. Burns*, 427 U.S. 347 (1976), and *Branti v. Finkel*, 445 U.S. 507 (1980).

69. "Developments in the Law—Elections," pp. 1121–51.

70. 393 U.S. 23 (1968).

71. *Jenness v. Fortson*, 403 U.S. 431 (1971).

72. Laurence H. Tribe, *American Constitutional Law* (Mineola, N.Y.: Foundation Press, 1978), p. 783.

73. *Moore v. Ogilvie*, 394 U.S. 814 (1969).

74. *Illinois v. Socialist Workers Party*, 440 U.S. 173 (1979).

75. Tribe believes that petition requirements as high as 5 percent are not unconstitutional per se but that requirements substantially higher "probably are." *American Constitutional Law*, p. 784. In 1980, a federal court seemed to regard a North Dakota requirement of 15,000 signatures as high, although it was the equivalent of only a 3.3 percent requirement. But in this instance the court invalidated the North Dakota statute principally because it set a filing deadline of January 1, more than 90 days before the primary and more than 150 days before the general election. *McLain v. Meier*, 637 F. 2d 1159 (8th Cir., 1980).

76. 415 U.S. 724 (1974).

77. *American Party of Texas v. White*, 415 U.S. 767 (1974).

78. Ibid., p. 785. The Court did, however, invalidate a statutory provision that excluded all but major-party candidates from absentee ballots.

79. 75 L. Ed. 2d 547 (1983).

80. Ibid., pp. 560, 561.

81. Ibid., p. 566.

82. 410 U.S. 752 (1973).

83. 414 U.S. 51 (1973).

84. Ibid., p. 61.

85. 417 F. Supp. 837 (D. Conn., 1976); affirmed on appeal, 429 U.S. 989 (1976). Technically, the affirmance is a holding of the Supreme Court and thus has precedential effect even though it may not customarily carry the same weight as an opinion.

86. Jurisdictional Statement by counsel for Nader and Snyder, on appeal from the U.S. District Court for the District of Connecticut to the U.S. Supreme Court, No. 76–20, October Term, 1976, p. 14.

87. Ibid., p. 3.

88. Ibid., pp. 14–15.

89. Tribe suggests that when the Court next looks at voting-affiliation requirements it should regard them with "a most critical eye." He adds: "Contemporaneous affiliation requirements are far less troubling" (less troubling, evidently, than requirements of prior declaration or enrollment, as upheld in *Rosario*). *American Constitutional Law*, p. 793.

90. *Republican Party of Connecticut v. Tashjian*, 599 F. Supp. 1228 (D. Conn., 1984); upheld by the U.S. Court of Appeals for the Second Circuit, No. 1165, August 8, 1985, 5531–81.

91. *Sweezy v. New Hampshire*, 354 U.S. 234 (1957), and *N.A.A.C.P. v. Alabama*, 357 U.S. 449 (1958). A much later nonparty case that extends private associational rights is *Consolidated Edison Company v. Public Service Commission*, 447 U.S. 530 (1980).

92. *Lynch v. Torquato*, 343 F. 2d 370 (3d Cir. 1965).

93. *Maxey v. Washington State Democratic Committee*, 319 F. Supp. 673 (W.D. Washington 1970) and *Dahl v. Republican State Committee*, 319 F. Supp. 682 (W.D. Washington 1970).

94. 419 U.S. 477 (1975).

95. 450 U.S. 107 (1981).

96. A more cautious note about the breadth of *Cousins* and *La Follette* is sounded by Antonin Scalia, "The Legal Framework for Reform," *Commonsense* 4 (1981): 40–49, at p. 45.

97. *Fahey v. Darigan*, 405 F. Supp. 1386 (D. R.I. 1975).

98. 442 U.S. 191 (1979).

99. Ibid., p. 197.

100. 611 P. 2d 1256 (Wash. 1980).

101. A blanket primary is simply more open than an open primary, in that it allows voters to choose, say, a Republican candidate for one office and a Democratic candidate for another instead of requiring voters to choose only Democrats or only Republicans at a given primary election. In neither the blanket nor the open primary do voters have to declare or register by party in order to obtain ballots.

102. Not long before *Heavey*, an Oregon attorney general had advised his state's legislature that a bill was unconstitutional because, by allowing independents to vote in what was Oregon's closed primary, it would infringe First Amendment associational rights of party members. Arnie R. Braafladt, "The Constitutionality of Non-Member Voting in Political Party Primary Elections," *Willamette Law Journal* 14 (Spring 1978): 259–93, at pp. 259–60.

103. 599 F. Supp. 1228 (1984).

104. Ibid., p. 1230.

105. Ibid., pp. 1230–31. The judge described the action of Republican convention delegates in amending their party rules to permit unaffiliated voters to join with enrolled Republicans in voting for candidates for the offices of U.S. senator, U.S. representative, governor, and the gubernatorial "underticket" in primary elections.

106. Ibid., p. 1237.

107. Ibid., p. 1231. The appellate court, cited in n. 90, took just as strong a position in asserting the right of a party to determine its primary electorate.

108. *Abrams v. Reno*, 452 F. Supp. 1166 (S.D. Fla. 1978). Affirmed 649 F. 2d 342 (5th Cir. 1981). Certiorari denied 455 U.S. 1016 (1982).

109. Kay Lawson, "California: The Uncertainties of Reform," *Party Renewal in America*, ed. Gerald M. Pomper (New York: Praeger, 1980), pp. 116–38.

110. *San Francisco County Democratic Central Committee v. March Fong Eu*, unpublished opinion, May 3, 1984, of U.S. District Judge, N.D. Cal. The judge refrained from deciding the constitutionality of the provision prohibiting parties from taking part in nonpartisan elections because that issue was before a California state court.

111. 446 N.E. 2d 43 (Mass. 1983).

112. *Comparative State Politics Newsletter* 3 (June 1982): 2–3.

113. 434 N.E. 2d 960 (Mass. 1982).

114. 446 N.E. 2d 43 (Mass. 1983), at 46–47.

115. *Bellotti v. Commonwealth* and *Langone v. Commonwealth*, 460 U.S. 1057 (1983).

116. *Buckley v. Valeo* 424 U.S. 1 (1976).

117. The point was not so evident about a half-century ago when a learned American parties scholar expected European parties, as their organizations were becoming more elaborate than they had been in the nineteenth century, to be subject to the greater governmental regulation typical of the United States. Edward M. Sait, *American Parties and Elections* (New York: Century, 1927), pp. 174–75, n. 2. Although correctly observing the twentieth-century growth of European parties, notably socialist parties, Sait was wrong in thinking that such growth itself would lead to American-style regulation of candidate selection and related practices. European parties, as they developed, did not generally offend public moral standards as had the old American parties; the parties themselves were often less offensive because less corrupt and less dependent on masses of government jobs. Moreover, their dues-paying membership provided a sufficiently legitimate basis for selecting candidates in societies without the American popular participatory tradition.

Chapter 7: National Organization

1. V. O. Key, Jr., *Politics, Parties, & Pressure Groups* (New York: Crowell, 1964), p. 334.

2. David B. Truman analyzes the relationship in "Federalism and the Party System," in *Federalism: Mature and Emergent* (New York: Russell and Russell, 1962), ed. Arthur W. MacMahon, pp. 115–36. See also Theodore J. Lowi, "Party, Policy, and Constitution in America," in *The American Party Systems*, ed. William N. Chambers and Walter D. Burnham (New York: Oxford University Press, 1975), pp. 238–76; and Leon D. Epstein, "A Comparative Study of Australian Parties," *British Journal of Political Science* 7 (January 1977): 1–21, at p. 13. In neither Canada nor Australia does a decentralized party structure preclude nationally cohesive legislative parties that appear to be the product of British-style parliamentary government.

3. John C. Courtney, *The Selection of National Party Leaders in Canada* (Toronto: Macmillan of Canada, 1973), p. 227. On Australian practice, see Epstein, "A Comparative Study," p. 19.

4. Kenneth Janda, "A Comparative Analysis of Party Organizations: The United States, Europe, and the World," in *The Party Symbol*, ed. William Crotty (San Francisco: Freeman, 1980), pp. 339–58, at p. 355.

5. Morton Grodzins, "American Political Parties and the American System," *Western Political Quarterly* 13 (December 1960): 974–98; William H. Riker, *Federalism: Origin, Operation, Significance* (Boston: Little, Brown, 1964), pp. 100–101, 136.

6. The terms *federalize* and *nationalize* in this context come from Gary D. Wekkin, "National-State Party Relations: The Democrats' New Federal Structure," *Po-

litical Science Quarterly 99 (Spring 1984): 45–72; and *Democrat versus Democrat: The National Party's Campaign to Close the Wisconsin Primary* (Columbia: University of Missouri Press, 1984).

7. William N. Chambers, *Political Parties in a New Nation* (New York: Oxford University Press, 1963), pp. 49, 66, 85–86. See also Manning J. Dauer, *The Adams Federalists* (Baltimore: Johns Hopkins Press, 1953); and Richard P. McCormick, "Political Development and the Second Party System," in *The American Party Systems*, ed. Chambers and Burnham, pp. 90–116, at pp. 94, 104.

8. Austin Ranney, *Curing the Mischiefs of Faction* (Berkeley: University of California Press, 1975), p. 16.

9. William N. Chambers, *The Democrats in American Politics* (New York: Van Nostrand, 1972), pp. 21, 45.

10. Franklin L. Burdette, *The Republican Party* (New York: Van Nostrand, 1972), pp. 9–22.

11. Key believed that the two-thirds rule was a kind of counter to the possible minority nomination resulting from votes cast under the unit rule by a few large states whose delegates were almost evenly divided between candidates. *Politics, Parties, & Pressure Groups*, pp. 427–28.

12. Ranney, *Curing the Mischiefs*, p. 17.

13. Cornelius P. Cotter and Bernard C. Hennessy, *Politics Without Power: The National Party Committees* (New York: Atherton, 1964), pp. 21–22. The Republicans soon returned to confederative equality by providing places for every state party's chairperson, as well as for a national committee man and woman — thus three rather than two members from each state. The inclusion of state party chairpersons, however, remained significant because of the link it established between national and state parties. The Democrats established a similar link in the 1970s when they put both the state party chairperson and the highest-ranking state party officer of the opposite sex on the DNC. Cornelius P. Cotter, James L. Gibson, John F. Bibby, and Robert J. Huckshorn, *Party Organizations in American Politics* (New York: Praeger, 1984), p. 62.

14. Robert D. Marcus, *Grand Old Party* (New York: Oxford University Press, 1971), p. 264. On Republican origins, see Marcus at pp. 22–23, 136–38, 252; and Malcolm Moos, *The Republicans: A History of Their Party* (New York: Random House, 1956), pp. 36–37.

15. Cotter and Hennessy, *Politics Without Power*, p. 11. Also pp. 3, 40.

16. Ibid., pp. 177–82.

17. Ibid., p. 189.

18. Harry M. Scoble, *Ideology and Electoral Action* (San Francisco: Chandler, 1967).

19. Cornelius P. Cotter and John F. Bibby, "Institutional Development of Parties and the Thesis of Party Decline," *Political Science Quarterly* 95 (Spring 1980): 1–27, at pp. 6–12.

20. APSA Committee on Political Parties, "Toward a More Responsible Two-Party System," *American Political Science Review* 44, supplement (September 1950): 49, n. 8.

21. Cotter and Bibby, "Institutional Development," p. 5; and Hugh A. Bone, *Political Party Management* (Morristown, N.J.: General Learning Press, 1973), p. 18.

22. The twentieth-century growth of national two-party competitiveness is clearly shown in Frank J. Sorauf's table of the standard deviations of presidential popular vote in the states. The table displays an unmistakable trend toward a smaller dispersal of states from the average. *Party Politics in America* (Boston: Little, Brown, 1984), p. 56.

23. Truman, "Federalism," pp. 119–20.

24. John H. Kessel, *Presidential Parties* (Homewood, Ill.: Dorsey Press, 1984), pp. 578–81.

25. Ranney, *Curing the Mischiefs*, pp. 20, 180–83.

26. Byron E. Shafer, *Quiet Revolution: The Struggle for the Democratic Party and the Shaping of Post-Reform Politics* (New York: Sage Foundation, 1983), pp. 13–132.

27. Ibid., pp. 367–95.

28. The new official guidelines are summarized, ibid., pp. 541–45.

29. William J. Crotty, *Decision for the Democrats* (Baltimore: Johns Hopkins University Press, 1978), p. 134.

30. In addition, one can see, from Steven E. Schier's study of the changed practices in Iowa, how the new rules reduced state organizational control in delegate selection and so in delegation leadership. "National Party Guidelines and Democratic National Convention Delegate Selection in Iowa and Wisconsin, 1968–1976," *Publius* 10 (Summer 1980): 101–27; and *The Rules and the Game* (Washington, D.C.: University Press of America, 1980), pp. 518–20.

31. Crotty, *Decision for the Democrats*, pp. 257–58. Shafer, *Quiet Revolution*, has details on implementation at the state level, pp. 269–340.

32. Crotty, *Decision for the Democrats*, p. 257.

33. Ibid., p. 260.

34. Austin Ranney, "The Political Parties: Reform and Decline," in *The New American Political System*, ed. Anthony King (Washington, D.C.: American Enterprise Institute, 1978), pp. 213–47, at p. 226.

35. Ibid., p. 230.

36. Ibid., pp. 237, 239.

37. Rule 10, *Delegate Selection Rules for the 1984 Democratic National Convention* (Washington, D.C.: DNC, 1982). Iowa and New Hampshire effectively secured the extra week, beyond the specific exemptions under the rule, when they insisted, partly in response to certain nonbinding processes scheduled in other states, that their state laws required earlier scheduling, and when presidential candidates found it expedient to observe the dates chosen by Iowa and New Hampshire.

38. Wekkin, "National-State Party Relations." Here and in his *Democrat versus Democrat* Wekkin provides full accounts of the open-primary controversy. I discuss it again in the third section of this chapter because of its important legal consequences.

39. *The Charter and the By-Laws of the Democratic Party of the United States* (Washington, D.C.: DNC, n.d.), p. 2.

40. The 1982 conference was planned so as to be considerably smaller than its 1978 predecessor and to more heavily represent party and public officials. *Congressional Quarterly Weekly Report* 39 (Sept. 26, 1981): 1857. The decision to scrap the midterm convention in 1986 is reported in the *New York Times*, June 26, 1985, p. 18.

41. *The Charter*, pp. 3–4.

42. *Congressional Quarterly Weekly Report* 39 (Feb. 28, 1981): 394.

43. John F. Bibby, "Party Renewal in the National Republican Party," in *Party Renewal in America*, ed. Gerald M. Pomper (New York: Praeger, 1980), pp. 102–15, at p. 106.

44. That is what I was told, with emphasis, by an aide to Chairman Brock, in 1979.

45. Charles H. Longley, "National Party Renewal," in *Party Renewal*, ed. Pomper, pp. 69–86, at pp. 83–84.

46. Larry Sabato, "New Campaign Techniques and the American Party System," in *Parties and Democracy in Britain and America*, ed. Vernon Bogdanor (New York: Praeger, 1984), pp. 185–212, at p. 205.

47. The situation of parties under federal law is described by David Adamany, "Financing Political Parties in the United States," in *Parties and Democracy*, ed. Bogdanor, pp. 153–84, at p. 157. I take up the subject in detail in chapters 9 and 10.

48. The 1983–84 dollar amounts are from the Federal Election Commission, press release, December 5, 1985, p. 3. Earlier data on contributors, along with dollar totals, are in Bibby, "Party Renewal," p. 113; Adamany, "Financing Political Parties," pp. 166–67; Larry Sabato, "Parties, PACs, and Independent Groups," in *The American Elections of 1982*, ed. Thomas E. Mann and Norman J. Ornstein (Washington, D.C.: American Enterprise Institute, 1983), pp. 72–110, at p. 75; and appendix O, in Mann and Ornstein, eds., *The American Elections of 1982*, pp. 189–91.

49. The quotation is from David Adamany, "Political Parties in the 1980s," in *Money and Politics in the United States*, ed. Michael J. Malbin (Chatham, N.J.: Chatham House, 1984), pp. 70–121, at p. 75. Adamany is amending Frank Sorauf's historical view that parties had not successfully made "the transition to the cash economy of the new campaign politics." His point is that in 1980 one of the two national parties was making this transition. Sorauf's view is from his "Political Parties and Political Action Committees: Two Life Cycles," *Arizona Law Review* 22 (1980): 445–63, at p. 451.

50. Cotter and Bibby, "Institutional Development," p. 5; Adamany, "Financing Political Parties," p. 173.

51. Adamany, "Political Parties in the 1980s," p. 108.

52. Ibid., p. 113.

53. *Congressional Quarterly Weekly Report* 41 (Feb. 5, 1983): 316.

54. Sabato, "Parties, PACs, and Independent Groups," pp. 105–6 (n. 17).

55. Adamany, "Financing Political Parties," p. 172; Adamany, "Political Parties in the 1980s," pp. 83–84; Sabato, "Parties, PACs, and Independent Groups," pp. 77–79.

56. FEC, press release, December 5, 1985, pp. 2, 4. The expenditure and contri-

bution figures include state and local party expenditures in national elections along with the larger amounts from the three national party committees.

57. Sabato, "Parties, PACs, and Independent Groups," pp. 74–75; appendix B, Mann and Ornstein, eds., *The American Elections of 1982,* p. 156.

58. The $145 million is calculated from figures in Mann and Ornstein, eds., *The American Elections of 1982*, appendices K and L, pp. 180, 182. Comparable calculations for 1980 are in Adamany, "Political Parties in the 1980s," pp. 81–82.

59. Mann and Ornstein, eds. *The American Elections of 1982*, appendix O, p. 191.

60. Sabato, "New Campaign Techniques," pp. 202–4; Sabato, "Parties, PACs, and Independent Groups," pp. 76–77; Adamany, "Financing Political Parties," p. 171; Adamany, "Political Parties in the 1980s," p. 80. Funds were also contributed through GOPAC, "a state-oriented, national, Republican-affiliated political action committee. . . ." Ruth S. Jones, "Financing State Elections," in *Money and Politics in the United States*, ed. Malbin, pp. 172–213, at pp. 193–94.

61. Cotter and Bibby, "Institutional Development," p. 19; Bibby, "Party Renewal," pp. 107–12; and John F. Bibby, "Political Parties and Federalism: The Republican National Committee's Involvement in Gubernatorial and Legislative Elections," *Publius* 9 (Winter 1979): 229–36.

62. Bibby, "Party Renewal," p. 110.

63. Rule No. 26 (f), in *Republican Party Rules* (Washington, D.C.: RNC, 1980), pp. 11–12. For calling my attention to the adoption of this rule, I am indebted to John Bibby—as I am also for his original work on the RNC. The rule itself, as distinguished from self-restraint, does not apply to the party's Senate and House campaign committees.

64. Bibby, "Political Parties and Federalism," p. 235.

65. Timothy Conlan, Ann Martino, and Robert Dilger, "State Parties in the 1980s," *Intergovernmental Perspective* 10 (Fall 1984): 6–11, 23, at p. 9.

66. M. Margaret Conway, "Republican Political Party Nationalization, Campaign Activities, and Their Implications for the Party System," *Publius* 13 (Winter 1983): 1–17.

67. Data for 1983–84 are from the FEC, press release, December 5, 1985, pp. 1–4. As cited here, they do not include the state and local party receipts reported to the FEC ($43.1 million by Republican committees and $18.5 million by Democratic committees). Earlier data on contributors and party totals are in Mann and Ornstein, eds., *The American Elections of 1982*, appendix O, pp. 190–91; Adamany, "Financing Political Parties," pp. 169, 173; and Adamany, "Political Parties in the 1980s," pp. 79–81.

68. Sabato, "Parties, PACs, and Independent Groups," pp. 82–86.

69. Nor have political parties, until very recent campaign finance legislation, even appeared significantly in federal statute law.

70. *Georgia v. National Democratic Party*, 447 F. 2d 1271 (D.C. Cir. 1971), at 1275.

71. *Bode v. National Democratic Party*, 452 F. 2d 1302 (D.C. Cir. 1971), at 1304.

72. The same court, however, reflected doubts about the validity of its state ac-

tion doctrine in 1975 *after* the U.S. Supreme Court had upheld national party rights in the first of the two leading cases that I later discuss. The doubts of the Court of Appeals may be observed in *Ripon Society v. National Republican Party*, 525 F. 2d 567 (D.C. Cir. 1975), at 576.

73. *O'Brien v. Brown*, 409 U.S. 1 (1972), at 4.

74. 419 U.S. 477 (1975).

75. The other 1972 dispute had concerned California delegates. It did not return to the Court as did the Illinois matter.

76. 419 U.S. 477 (1975), at 487. Justice Brennan spoke for himself and four colleagues in giving the Court's opinion. Three other justices concurred, differing only in thinking the Court's language unnecessarily broad (at 491–96). Justice Powell concurred in part, agreeing that the national convention could not be compelled to seat the Wigoda delegation but disagreeing with the conclusion that the Illinois courts were without power to enjoin the Cousins group from sitting as delegates (at 496–97).

77. Ibid., p. 489.

78. Ibid., p. 490.

79. Ronald D. Rotunda, "Constitutional and Statutory Restrictions on Political Parties in the Wake of *Cousins v. Wigoda*," *Texas Law Review* 53 (June 1975): 935–63, at p. 950.

80. Peter Kobrak, "Michigan," in *The Political Life of the American States,* ed. Alan Rosenthal and Maureen Moakley (New York: Praeger, 1984), pp. 99–128, at p. 114. See also Wekkin, "National-State Party Relations." Before 1984, with its governorship as well as its legislature in Democratic hands, as had not been true for 1980, Michigan repealed its presidential primary law so that Republicans as well as Democrats chose delegates through the caucus method. The Michigan experience in 1980 gave rise to an interesting federal court decision in which the state was precluded from requiring Michigan Democrats to use the primary to elect national convention delegates and from treating the caucuses as though they were state elections subject to state rules. *Ferency v. Austin*, 493 F. Supp. 683 (W.D. Michigan, 1980) affd. 666 F. 2d 1023 (6th Cir. 1981).

81. In a last effort before 1984 to provide a sufficiently closed primary to satisfy the DNC and yet be as inoffensive as possible to Wisconsin voters, a few Democrats proposed legislation that retained the presidential open primary for those who wanted to vote in it (for either Republican or Democratic candidates), and *added* a special primary to be conducted on the same day and at the same polling places for those willing to identify themselves as Democrats. Thus the state would simultaneously run two different kinds of presidential primary and voters could, if they liked, vote in both — in one without publicly revealing party preference and in the other only by expressing a Democratic preference (which would be recorded but destroyed soon after the primary). Although seriously discussed at a legislative hearing in 1983, the proposal was not acted upon. It posed problems of administrative expense and confusion while still violating Wisconsin tradition sufficiently to be politically unattrac-

tive to most legislators. Of course, the caucuses actually used in 1984 for expressing presidential preferences, in the process of choosing Wisconsin's delegates to the national Democratic convention, were also unattractive in the state. Therefore, Wisconsin Democrats sought again in 1985, now with considerable expectation of success, to obtain the DNC's approval to use the open primary in 1988.

82. Wisconsin provides a rich example of the moralistic political culture that Daniel J. Elazar describes as one of the three political cultural patterns found among American states. *American Federalism: A View from the States* (New York: Crowell, 1966), pp. 89–92, 96–111.

83. *La Follette v. Democratic Party of the United States*, 93 Wis. 2d 473 (1980); 287 N.W. 2d 519 (1980).

84. 93 Wis. 2d 473 (1980), at 521.

85. The Wisconsin court believed, contrary to the DNP's position, that the national party had not shown, as the court thought it needed to show, that it was unconstitutionally burdened by the statute.

86. 450 U.S. 107 (1981). The full title of the case is *Democratic Party of the United States v. Wisconsin ex rel La Follette*.

87. Ibid., p. 121.

88. It is true that a state might prevail by showing a "compelling interest" sufficient to overcome the First Amendment claims of the national party. But, as *La Follette* indicates, the Court is reluctant to find a state's interest compelling enough to justify its imposition on a national party.

89. The resolution is quoted approvingly by the Commission on Presidential Nomination and Party Structure (Winograd Commission), *Openness, Participation and Party Building: Reforms for a Stronger Democratic Party* (Washington, D.C.: DNC, 1978), pp. 31–32.

90. *La Follette*, 450 U.S. 107 (1981), at 122, 126.

91. Ibid., p. 131. Justice Powell had dissented in part in *Cousins*. Justice Rehnquist, in concurring in that opinion, had wanted to narrow its language, but Justice Blackmun, the third dissenter in *La Follette*, had been one of the Court majority in *Cousins*. Because these three justices might now be assumed to be unwilling in subsequent cases to draw the broadest inferences from the Court opinion in *La Follette* and because Justice Stewart has left the Court, only five remaining justices can be counted in 1985 as apparently committed to a judicial interpretation of the First Amendment that might encourage challenges even to conventional state regulation of state parties.

92. Ibid., p. 131. The other opinion was from *Rosario v. Rockefeller*, 410 U.S. 752 (1973), at 769, where Justice Powell also dissented.

93. *La Follette*, 450 U.S. 107 (1981), at 137.

94. *New York Times*, October 19, 1985, p. 9.

95. Xandra Kayden, "The Nationalizing of the Party System," in *Parties, Interest Groups, and Campaign Finance Laws*, ed. Michael J. Malbin (Washington, D.C.: Ameri-

can Enterprise Institute, 1980), pp. 257–82, at p. 263. For a later analysis by Kayden, see "The New Professionalism of the Oldest Party," *Public Opinion* 8: (June/July 1985): 229–36.

96. Kayden, "The Nationalizing," p. 258.

97. Sabato, "Parties, PACs, and Independent Groups," p. 104.

Chapter 8: Party Identifiers

1. V. O. Key, Jr., *Politics, Parties, & Pressure Groups* (New York: Crowell, 1964), p. 164. Similar language can be found in his third edition of 1953, p. 181.

2. Frank J. Sorauf, *Party Politics in America* (Boston: Little, Brown, 1984), p. 133.

3. Ibid., p. 162. The most familiar definition is from the University of Michigan's Survey Research Center: "Generally this tie is a psychological identification, which can persist without legal recognition or evidence of formal membership and even without a consistent record of party support. Most Americans have this sense of attachment with one party or the other. And for the individual who does, the strength and direction of party identification are facts of central importance in accounting for attitude and behavior." Angus Campbell, Philip E. Converse, Warren E. Miller, and Donald E. Stokes, *The American Voter* (New York: Wiley, 1960), p. 121.

4. The best-known comparison is with French data. Philip E. Converse and Georges Dupeux, "Politicization of the Electorate in France and the United States," *Public Opinion Quarterly* 26 (Spring 1962): 1–23.

5. Daniel J. Boorstin, *The Americans: The National Experience* (New York, Random House, 1965), pp. 428–29.

6. Seymour Martin Lipset emphasizes this possibility in *Emerging Coalitions in American Politics* (San Francisco: Institute for Contemporary Studies, 1978), p. 440.

7. For a fuller exposition of the timing and the varied forms of state-provided ballots, see Jerrold G. Rusk, "The Effect of the Australian Ballot Reform on Split Ticket Voting, 1876–1908," *American Political Science Review* 64 (December 1970): 1220–38.

8. The relevant cases are discussed in chapter 6.

9. In chapter 5, the more extended discussion of the impact of the direct primary on the number of parties pays special attention to V. O. Key, Jr., *American State Politics: An Introduction* (New York: Knopf, 1956), chaps. 4–5. See also Arthur N. Holcombe, *The Political Parties of To-Day* (New York: Harper, 1924), pp. 317–18; and Howard R. Penniman, "The State of the Two-Party System," *The Wilson Quarterly* 2 (Winter 1978): 83–89.

10. Charles Hauss and David Rayside, "The Development of New Parties in Western Democracies Since 1945," in *Political Parties: Development and Decay,* ed. Louis Maisel and Joseph Cooper (Beverly Hills, Calif.: Sage Publications, 1978), pp. 31–57, at p. 47.

11. Sources for the classification of states with respect to their registration requirements include those cited in chapter 5's discussion of closed and open primaries.

Biennial issues of *The Book of the States* (Lexington, Ky.: Council of State Governments) also provide useful compilations.

12. Steven E. Finkel and Howard A. Scarrow, "Party Identification and Party Enrollment: The Difference and the Consequence," *Journal of Politics* 47 (May 1985):
620–42, at pp. 622–23; and Howard A. Scarrow, *Parties, Elections, and Representation
in the State of New York* (New York: New York University Press, 1983), pp. 10–14.

13. Finkel and Scarrow, "Party Identification and Party Enrollment," pp. 622–23.
Of the 19 states that they include, I omit Kansas because it differs from the other
18 by counting as independents (unaffiliateds) any registrants who have never voted
in a party primary, as indicated by Finkel and Scarrow at p. 641. If Kansas were included, it would appear as an aberrant case. Its percentage of surveyed party identifiers
was 8 points *higher* than its recorded party primary voters. The two states of the 18
that have only 1 or 2 percentage points more registered party voters than surveyed
identifiers are Iowa and Colorado, and their results may also be explained by relatively permissive procedures. Both Iowa and Colorado are, like Kansas, among the
party-registration states that allow unaffiliated voters to declare affiliation at the primary for the purpose of voting in the particular primary.

14. The exact wording of the exit-poll question (ABC's) is given by Finkel and
Scarrow, "Party Identification and Party Enrollment," p. 623; "Regardless of how
you voted, in politics today do you consider yourself a Democrat, Republican, Independent, Something Else."

15. Kentucky practices are briefly but strikingly illustrated by Malcolm E. Jewell
in *Comparative State Politics News Letter* 5 (October 1984): 7.

16. Again the reference is to Finkel and Scarrow, "Party Identification and Party
Enrollment," whose findings I cited above. Relevant data may also be noted in Malcolm E. Jewell and David M. Olson, *American State Political Parties and Elections* (Homewood, Ill.: Dorsey Press, 1982), pp. 40–42.

17. Scarrow, *Parties, Elections*, pp. 10–14.

18. The percentages are calculated from data reported in editions of the *Legislative Manual* published by New York's Department of State, Albany, N.Y. The 1960
figures are in the 1961–62 edition, pp. 1065–66; the 1975 and 1976 figures are in
the *Supplement Manual*, 1977–79, pp. 1423–26; and the 1979 figures are in the 1980–81
edition, pp. 1114–15. Each *Manual* lists what I call nonparty registrants as "blank,
void, and missing," in contrast to actual party enrollments. About 2 to 3 percent
of each year's party enrollments are in third parties.

19. As in New York, these increases were greater than the very modest figures
recorded for third parties. Data are from successive issues of the *Report of Registration
State of California* (Sacramento, Calif.: Secretary of State), specifically January 1965,
p. 3; October 1974, p. 5; October 1976, p. 5; October 1978, p. 5; and from *Statement
of Vote: General Election 1982* (Sacramento, Calif.: Secretary of State), p. vi.

20. *Pennsylvania Statistical Abstract* (Harrisburg: Pennsylvania Department of Commerce, 1983), p. 144.

21. *Connecticut Register and Manual* (Hartford, Conn.: Secretary of State), successive editions, but particularly 1958, p. 611, and 1982, p. 729.

22. From its inception in the 1950s, Connecticut's primary law has stipulated that a challenger of the convention's choice could qualify for the primary only if he or she obtained at least 20 percent of the convention's delegate votes. The 20 percent requirement has been difficult to meet, and proponents of primaries have sought to reduce it to 10 percent. To date, however, they have failed to change the law.

23. The likelihood of a partially open primary in Connecticut arises from judicial rulings discussed near the end of chapter 6.

24. Paul Kleppner, *The Third Electoral System, 1853–1892: Parties, Voters, and Political Cultures* (Chapel Hill: University of North Carolina Press, 1979), p. 367.

25. Warren E. Miller, "The Cross-National Use of Party Identification as a Stimulus to Political Inquiry," in *Party Identification and Beyond*, ed. Ian Budge, Ivor Crewe, and Dennis Fairlie (London: Wiley, 1976), pp. 21–31, at p. 27; W. Phillips Shively, "The Development of Party Identification among Adults: Exploration of a Functional Model," *American Political Science Review* 73 (December 1979): 1039–54, at pp. 1049–50.

26. In 1940 Gallup included Socialist as an option along with Republican, Democrat, and Independent. Cited by James L. Sundquist, *Dynamics of the Party System* (Washington, D.C.: Brookings Institution, 1983), p. 218.

27. Greg A. Caldeira and Fred I. Greenstein, "Partisan Orientation and Political Socialization," *Political Science Quarterly* 93 (Spring 1978): 35–49, at pp. 39–40.

28. William H. Flanigan and Nancy H. Zingale, "Partisanship: A Summary Evaluation and Bases for Further Disagreement," paper for Workshop on Electoral Instability and Decay in Western Europe, University of Minnesota (May 1980), p. 12.

29. Jack Dennis, "On Being an Independent Partisan Supporter," paper for annual meeting of the Midwest Political Science Association (April 1981), pp. 2–3, table 2. Significant for other purposes are Dennis's findings that some respondents described themselves as both Independents and Republican or Democratic supporters, and that others (fully 28 percent) were best classified as unattached because, in answering the new questions, they did not describe themselves as either party supporters or Independents.

30. The possibility is raised but not disposed of by Ian Budge and Dennis Fairlie in "A Comparative Analysis of Factors Correlated with Turnout and Voting Choice," in *Party Identification*, ed. Budge, Crewe, and Fairlie, pp. 103–26.

31. To some extent, such a rise may have appeared because the question's wording solicited relatively transient preferences. For example, late in 1980 Gallup asked, "In politics, as of today, do you consider yourself a Republican, a Democrat, or Independent?" It has been observed that "as of today," following Reagan's 1980 election, probably produced the sharp rise in Republican identification that Gallup then recorded. James L. Sundquist and Richard M. Scammon, "The 1980 Election: Profile

and Historical Perspective," in *A Tide of Discontent*, ed. Ellis Sandoz and Cecil V. Crabb, Jr. (Washington, D.C.: Congressional Quarterly, 1981), pp. 19–44, at p. 42.

32. NBC News exit-poll data for both 1980 and 1984 are cited by Laurily K. Epstein, "The Changing Structure of Party Identification," *PS* 18 (Winter 1985): 48–52, at p. 48.

33. Richard A. Brody and Lawrence S. Rothenberg, "Dynamics of Partisanship During the 1980 Election," paper for the 1983 meeting of the American Political Science Association, Chicago, p. 5.

34. Ibid., p. 1.

35. Gallup data and CPS/SRC data can be compared in Jack Dennis, "Trends in Public Support for the American Party System," *British Journal of Political Science* 5 (April 1975): 187–230, at pp. 192–93. The full Gallup time series, 1937–84, is in *Public Opinion* 7 (April/May 1984): 32. See also the discussion by David H. Everson, *American Political Parties* (New York: Watts New Viewpoints, 1980), p. 50.

36. Walter Dean Burnham, "The Changing Shape of the American Political Universe," *American Political Science Review* 59 (March 1965): 7–28, and *Critical Elections and the Mainsprings of American Politics* (New York: Norton, 1970), pp. 109, 111–15. I have drawn mainly on these two works to summarize Burnham's findings for my purpose, but he has presented additional findings and analysis in other works, notably "Party Systems and the Political Process," in *The American Party Systems*, ed. William N. Chambers and Walter Dean Burnham (New York: Oxford University Press, 1975), pp. 277–307, and his own *The Current Crisis in American Politics* (New York: Oxford University Press, 1982).

37. Jerrold G. Rusk, "The Effect of the Australian Ballot Reform," began a controversy in which Burnham responded to Rusk and Rusk to Burnham in "Communications," *American Political Science Review* 65 (December 1971): 1149–57. A more extended exchange appeared later in the same journal when Burnham wrote "Theory and Voting Research: Some Reflections on Converse's 'Change in the American Electorate,'" Philip E. Converse and Rusk commented, and Burnham wrote a rejoinder, *American Political Science Review* 68 (September 1974): 1002–57. Burnham acknowledged that the Australian ballot facilitated split-ticket voting and that important effects also followed from stiff personal registration requirements, the direct primary, and various other progressive antiparty reforms. But he adhered to his emphasis on the influence of the 1896 realignment process and its accompanying general change in the nature of American politics.

38. Burnham, "The Changing Shape," p. 13. It must be noted that the measurement cited here is one that Burnham later put aside in favor of a more refined index ("Communications," p. 1150) that he employed in *Critical Elections*, pp. 195–203. He had described the earlier index in these terms: "Split-ticket voting has been measured rather crudely here as the difference between the highest and lowest percentages of the two-party vote cast for either party among the array of statewide offices in any given election" ("The Changing Universe," p. 9). Although I recognize the advan-

tages for most purposes of the sophisticated statistical index that Burnham subsequently preferred, I find the original measurement device, because of its simplicity, useful for my limited purpose. Data derived from it do not appear to be at odds with data from Burnham's more sophisticated measurements. In neither instance do I challenge his findings.

39. Richard Jensen vividly describes the intensity of party politics in the late nineteenth century in *The Winning of the Midwest* (Chicago: University of Chicago Press, 1971), pp. 1–33. He cites Indiana and Illinois interviews in the mid-1870s, disclosing only 2 percent without party attachments (p. 7). At least through 1888, Jensen finds an "army" style of campaigning to have been dominant; each party organization concentrated on bringing its loyal troops to the polls. Beginning in the 1890s, he perceives a new "merchandising" style for less fully partisan voters (pp. 164–67, 170–75, 208, 306–8).

40. In contrast to the numbers recorded as Independents in response to the standard CPS/SRC questions, 43 percent of the CPS/SRC's 1980 sample answered yes to a new and additional question, "Do you ever think of yourself as a political independent, or not?" Dennis, "On Being an Independent Partisan Supporter," tables 1 and 2.

41. Raymond E. Wolfinger, "Dealignment, Realignment, and Mandates in the 1984 Election," paper for American Enterprise Institute's Public Policy Week, December 1984, p. 5.

42. Martin P. Wattenberg, *The Decline of American Political Parties 1952–1980* (Cambridge, Mass.: Harvard University Press, 1984), pp. 36–49.

43. Warren E. Miller and Teresa E. Levitin, *Leadership and Change* (Cambridge, Mass.: Winthrop, 1976), p. 225. Drawing on other polls, Andrew M. Greeley also stresses the tendency of many nominal Independents to behave like party identifiers. "Catholics and Coalition: Where Should They Go?," in *Emerging Coalitions*, ed. Lipset, pp. 271–95, at pp. 275–76.

44. W. Phillips Shively, "The Nature of Party Identification: A Review of Recent Developments," in *The Electorate Reconsidered*, ed. John C. Pierce and John L. Sullivan (Beverly Hills, Calif.: Sage, 1980), pp. 219–36, at pp. 233–35.

45. With only a little less plausibility, the same interpretation might apply to the behavior of certain usually defined party identifiers. Conceivably, some Weak Republicans and Weak Democrats could merely reflect their current voting choices when they admit to thinking of themselves as Republicans or Democrats.

46. John R. Petrocik, "Continued Sources of Voting Behavior: The Changeable American Voter," in *The Electorate Reconsidered*, ed. Pierce and Sullivan, pp. 257–77, at p. 266.

47. Bruce E. Keith, David B. Magleby, Candice J. Nelson, Elizabeth Orr, Mark C. Westlye, and Raymond E. Wolfinger, "Further Evidence on the Partisan Affinities of Independent 'Leaners,'" paper for the 1983 meeting of the American Political Science Association, Chicago, p. 9. (Paper to be published by *British Journal of Political*

Science.) Their figures for Republican identifiers, because they show their votes for Democratic House candidates, reflect an expected progressively lower percentage from Independent Republican through Weak Republican to Strong Republican. That is, relatively few Strong Republicans have defected.

48. Ibid., p. 14.

49. The same ticket-splitting inference is made from the now-common state election results that divide party control of gubernatorial and legislative offices. So, too, is ticket-splitting apparent in elections for a state's several executive offices. In Illinois, for example, where the major parties shared control of the state's top four executive offices throughout the 1960s and 1970s, the difference between the highest and lowest percentages of votes cast for a given party's candidates in the four contests quadrupled from 1960 to 1978. David H. Everson and Joan A. Parker, "Ticket Splitting: An Ominous Sign of Party Weakness," *Illinois Issues* 5 (August 1979): 9–12.

50. Wattenberg, *The Decline*, p. 20. See also Jerome M. Clubb, William H. Flanigan, and Nancy H. Zingale, *Partisan Realignment: Voters, Parties, and Government in American History* (Beverly Hills, Calif.: Sage, 1980), pp. 128–30.

51. Wattenberg, *The Decline*, p. 27.

52. The landmark study of the 1958 congressional election is by Donald E. Stokes and Warren E. Miller, "Party Government and the Saliency of Congress," *Public Opinion Quarterly* 26 (Winter 1962): 531–46. Comparable data for subsequent years are in Barbara Hinckley, *Congressional Elections* (Washington, D.C.: Congressional Quarterly, 1981), p. 66.

53. Dennis, "Trends in Public Support," p. 204.

54. Jack Dennis, "Changing Public Support for the American Party System," in *Paths to Political Reform*, ed. William J. Crotty (Lexington, Mass.: D. C. Heath, 1980), pp. 35–66, at pp. 38–39.

55. Ibid., p. 61.

56. Norman H. Nie, Sidney Verba, and John R. Petrocik, *The Changing American Voter* (Cambridge, Mass.: Harvard University Press, 1979), p. 57.

57. Ibid., p. 73.

58. Differences as well as similarities in British and American electoral developments before the rise of the British SDP are analyzed by Ivor Crewe in "Prospects for Party Realignment: An Anglo-American Comparison," *Comparative Politics* 12 (July 1980): 379–400. Australia and Canada are also included in a comparison by Martin P. Wattenberg, "Party Identification and Party Images," *Comparative Politics* 15 (October 1982): 23–40.

59. Flanigan and Zingale, "Partisanship," p. 18.

60. The volume includes separate studies of individual countries and general comparative chapters. Russell J. Dalton, Scott C. Flanigan, and Paul Allen Beck, eds., *Electoral Change in Advanced Industrial Democracies: Realignment or Dealignment?* (Princeton: Princeton University Press, 1984). Beck's chapter on recent American experience (pp. 240–66) stresses its dealigning character. An even more pointed comparison ap-

pears in another work where C. Neal Tate shows that voters in Britain and the Netherlands tend to express their disenchantment with old established parties by accepting other party labels, while similarly disenchanted American voters become Independents. "The Centrality of Party in Voting Choice," in *Western European Party Systems*, ed. Peter H. Merkl (New York: Free Press, 1980), pp. 367–401, p. 398.

61. Wattenberg, *The Decline*, p. 51.

62. Ibid., p. 89.

63. For a different emphasis on the labelling role of contemporary American parties, see Ruth K. Scott and Ronald J. Hrebenar, *Parties in Crisis* (New York: Wiley, 1979), p. 87.

64. Nie, Verba, and Petrocik, *The Changing American Voter*, pp. 62–64, 363–65.

65. Warren E. Miller and J. Merrill Shanks, "Policy Directions and Presidential Leadership: Alternative Interpretations of the 1980 Presidential Election," *British Journal of Political Science* 12 (July 1982): 299–356, at pp. 308–9.

66. To some extent a belief in a continuously descending percentage of party identifiers rests on the existence of an evidently lessened family influence in transmitting political preferences from generation to generation. The point is discussed in an interesting way by Jeane Jordan Kirkpatrick, *Dismantling the Parties* (Washington, D.C.: American Enterprise Institute, 1978), p. 17.

67. M. Kent Jennings and Gregory B. Markus, "Partisan Orientations over the Long Haul: Results from the Three-Wave Political Socialization Panel Study," *American Political Science Review* 78 (December 1984): 1000–18, at p. 1016.

68. Everett Carll Ladd, Jr., and Seymour Martin Lipset, *Academics, Politics, and the 1972 Election* (Washington, D.C.: American Enterprise Institute, 1973), p. 46.

69. Early in mid-twentieth-century survey research, Independents appeared less involved in politics than party identifiers, less well informed about issues, and less interested in campaigns. Campbell et al., *The American Voter*, pp. 143–45.

70. Wattenberg, *The Decline*, p. 118.

71. Ibid., p. 119. See also Shively, "The Development of Party Identification," pp. 1044, 1050–51.

72. Nie, Verba, and Petrocik, *The Changing American Voter*, pp. 67–68.

73. Ibid., chap. 6.

74. Ibid., p. 300. The case has been challenged on the ground that the apparent rise in issue voting may have been a product of a change in the way CPS/SRC questions were asked, beginning in 1964. John L. Sullivan, James E. Piereson, and George E. Marcus, "Ideological Constraint in the Mass Public: A Methodological Critique and Some New Findings," *American Journal of Political Science* 22 (May 1978): 233–49.

75. Nie, Verba, and Petrocik, *The Changing American Voter*, pp. 374–75.

76. Everett Carll Ladd, Jr., *Where Have All the Voters Gone?* (New York: Norton, 1982), pp. 42–43.

77. At least before the Reagan era of the early 1980s, it seemed doubtful that

many white southerners were identifying as Republicans even when (especially in presidential voting) they broke their old Democratic ties. For various views, see Edward G. Carmines and James A. Stimson, "The Racial Reorientation of American Politics," in *The Electorate Reconsidered*, ed. Pierce and Sullivan, pp. 199–218; and Gerald B. Finch, "Physical Change and Partisan Change: The Emergence of a New American Electorate, 1952–1972," in *The Future of Political Parties*, ed. Louis Maisel and Paul M. Sacks (Beverly Hills, Calif.: Sage, 1975), pp. 13–62, at pp. 43–44, 46, 53–54.

78. James L. Sundquist, *Dynamics of the Party System*, p. 438.

79. For example, a poll in late February 1985 showed Republican identifiers and leaners at 44 percent and Democratic at 50 percent, compared to 36 percent Republican and 57 percent Democratic in 1980. *Washington Post National Weekly Edition*, March 18, 1985, p. 37. Some other polls between the 1984 election and mid-1985 showed the two parties virtually even.

80. Wolfinger, "Dealignment, Realignment," p. 18. Significantly, he emphasizes other than racial factors in explaining the shift of white southerners.

81. *Party Line* (newsletter of the Committee for Party Renewal), Winter 1985, no. 19, p. 15.

82. Robert Agranoff, *The New Style in Election Campaigns* (Boston: Holbrook Press, 1972), pp. 4–5, 15.

83. Austin Ranney, *Channels of Power* (New York: Basic Books, 1983), p. 110.

84. Ibid., p. 111.

85. Discussions of the political role of mass communication and particularly of television are numerous. See, for example, William J. Crotty, *American Parties in Decline* (Boston: Little, Brown, 1984), pp. 73–116; F. Christopher Arterton, "Campaign Organizations Confront the Media-Political Environment" and "The Media Politics of Presidential Campaigns," in *Race for the Presidency*, ed. James David Barber (Englewood Cliffs, N.J.: Prentice-Hall, 1978), pp. 3–54; Michael J. Robinson, "The Media in 1980: Was the Message the Message?" in *The American Elections of 1980*, ed. Austin Ranney (Washington, D.C.: American Enterprise Institute, 1981), pp. 177–211; Thomas E. Patterson and Robert D. McClure, *The Unseeing Eye* (New York: Putnam, 1976); Austin Ranney, ed., *The Past and Future of Presidential Debates* (Washington, D.C.: American Enterprise Institute, 1979).

86. The effort was by the Democratic-Farmer-Labor party of Minnesota. Agranoff, *The New Style*, pp. 96–116.

87. For a fuller exposition of the point, see my comparative essay "Political Parties: Organization," in *Democracy at the Polls*, ed. David Butler, Howard R. Penniman, and Austin Ranney (Washington, D.C.: American Enterprise Institute, 1981), pp. 52–74.

88. Clubb, Flanigan, and Zingale emphasize the usefulness of a unified party control of government over an extended period in achieving a substantial electoral realignment. *Partisan Realignment*, p. 166.

Chapter 9: Private Funding of Campaigns

1. Frank J. Sorauf, "Political Parties and Political Action Committees: Two Life Cycles," *Arizona Law Review* 22 (1980): 445–63, at p. 451.

2. Howard R. Penniman, "Campaign Styles and Methods," in *Democracy at the Polls*, ed. David Butler, Howard R. Penniman, and Austin Ranney (Washington, D.C.: American Enterprise Institute, 1981), pp. 107–37; and Leon D. Epstein, *Political Parties in Western Democracies* (New Brunswick, N.J.: Transaction, 1980), pp. 369–76.

3. Different national patterns are described by Khayyam Zev Paltiel, "Campaign Finance: Contrasting Practices and Reforms," in *Democracy at the Polls*, ed. Butler, Penniman, and Ranney, pp. 138–72.

4. See chapter 4, n. 74.

5. For 1984, 63 percent of Senate candidate receipts came from individual contributions (plus 2 percent from the candidates' own contributions and 12 percent from candidate loans); 48 percent of House candidate receipts came from individual contributions (plus 2 percent from the candidates' own contributions and 8 percent from candidate loans). Federal Election Commission, press release, December 8, 1985, p. 8.

6. The U.S. Supreme Court upheld contribution limits but not expenditure limits, except when the limits were accepted by candidates who sought and received public funds. *Buckley v. Valeo*, 424 U.S. 1 (1976).

7. Herbert E. Alexander, *Financing Politics* (Washington, D.C.: Congressional Quarterly, 1980), pp. 45–46.

8. How antipatronage reform reached even Chicago in the 1970s is described in chapter 5.

9. Alexander, *Financing Politics*, pp. 46–48.

10. William J. Crotty reproduces a table showing the contributions made by ambassadors appointed by President Nixon; altogether they gave $1.8 million. *Political Reform and the American Experiment* (New York: Crowell, 1977), pp. 158–59.

11. Alexander, *Financing Politics*, p. 47.

12. The federal Corrupt Practices Act of 1925 and the Hatch Act of 1940 provided, as President Lyndon Johnson is supposed to have said, more loophole than law. The Hatch Act limited individual contributions to $5,000 and the federal gift tax imposed progressive tax rates on annual contributions of more than $3,000 to a single committee, but both provisions were readily and legally evaded by giving to each of several committees working for the same candidate. Ibid., pp. 26–27. Similar state laws could be similarly evaded.

13. David W. Adamany summarized a comparative 1963 study showing that campaign expenditures, as a ratio between expenditure per vote and the average hourly wage of a manufacturing worker, were lower in the United States than in five of the nine nations in the study. *Campaign Finance in America* (North Scituate, Mass.: Duxbury Press, 1972), p. 33. A more recent review of expenditures per eligible voter in several nations makes the same point. Howard R. Penniman, "U.S. Elections: Really a Bargain?" *Public Opinion* 7 (June/July 1984): 51–53. Some nations (but not

Britain) record expenditures in about the same range as the American, and occasionally higher, even though their publicly owned radio and television networks provide free advertising time.

14. The Nixon campaign of 1972 raised $63.2 million, of which almost 28 percent came from 37 contributors of $50,000 or more. Most of the rest came from large, if not so overwhelmingly large, contributions. Little was raised in amounts under $100. David W. Adamany and George E. Agree, *Political Money* (Baltimore: Johns Hopkins University Press, 1975), pp. 31–32.

15. Adamany and Agree, *Political Money*, pp. 31–33.

16. Alexander, *Financing Politics*, pp. 52–53.

17. Contemporary regulations in each of the 50 states are now conveniently compiled by the Federal Election Commission, *Campaign Finance Law 84* (Washington, D.C.: FEC, 1984).

18. Before the most recent wave of rich candidates still more generously funding their own campaigns for governor or U.S. Senator, Nelson Rockefeller's 1970 gubernatorial reelection campaign budget of $7.7 million included family contributions of $4.5 million. Crotty, *Political Reform*, pp. 126–27.

19. For a comparison of contribution amounts in different-level races in Connecticut in the 1960s, see Adamany, *Campaign Finance in America*, pp. 152–55.

20. Alexander Heard, *The Costs of Democracy* (Chapel Hill: University of North Carolina Press, 1960), pp. 49–50.

21. Adamany, *Campaign Finance in America*, p. 154.

22. Ibid., pp. 35–38. Since the 1960s and early 1970s, these races have become still more expensive. The prohibition of very large contributions in federal elections did not preclude the record expenditure of $22 million by the two major-party candidates for a U.S. Senate seat in North Carolina in 1984. *Congressional Quarterly Weekly Report* 42 (Nov. 10, 1984): 2901. For a discussion of 1980 and 1982 expenditures and contributions in several selected states, see Ruth S. Jones, "Financing State Elections," in *Money and Politics in the United States,* ed. Michael J. Malbin (Chatham, N.J.: Chatham House, 1984) pp. 172–213.

23. Crotty, *Political Reform*, pp. 120–21.

24. Cornelius P. Cotter and Bernard C. Hennessy, *Politics Without Power: The National Party Committees* (New York: Atherton, 1964), pp. 184–87. The Republicans began national direct-mail solicitation in the early 1960s, and the Democrats soon followed. Small contributions have also been sought through advertising especially on television. For example, the Democratic National Committee, which had tried a "Dollars for Democrats" solicitation with only limited success in 1959, did somewhat better with its televised appeals in 1972–75. In each of those four years, between 200,000 and 400,000 contributors responded in amounts averaging 11 to 15 dollars. Costs of the telethons were high; about one dollar was needed to collect two dollars. Net profits, however, were nearly $2 million in 1972 and 1973, nearly $3 million in 1974, and nearly $1 million in 1975. John W. Ellwood and Robert J.

Spitzer, "The Democratic National Telethons: Their Successes and Failures," *Journal of Politics* 41 (August 1979): 828–64, at pp. 830, 835.

25. Crotty, *Political Reform*, p. 121; David W. Adamany, "The Sources of Money: An Overview," *Annals of the American Academy of Political and Social Science* 425 (May 1976): 17–32, at pp. 22–23.

26. Adamany, "The Sources of Money," p. 22.

27. Alexander, *Financing Politics*, pp. 128–29.

28. Here and at later pages the statutory limits and other specifications are those in effect from 1980. They are the product of the Federal Election Campaign Act of 1971 as amended significantly in 1974, again in 1976, and less substantially in 1979. These statutes, along with relevant provisions of the Revenue Act of 1971 (allowing tax credits for small political contributions and establishing the presidential election campaign fund from taxpayer checkoffs) are conveniently summarized by Alexander, ibid., pp. 28–43, 163–76, and presented in more detail by the Federal Election Commission, *Federal Election Campaign Laws* (Washington, D.C.: FEC, 1980).

29. *Buckley v. Valeo*, 424 U.S. 1 (1976).

30. Alexander, *Financing Politics*, p. 30.

31. Adamany and Agree, *Political Money*, pp. 123–28. In May 1985, President Reagan proposed the abolition of the tax credit as part of his tax reform measure.

32. *Congressional Quarterly Weekly Report* 40 (Oct. 23, 1982): 2714.

33. Larry J. Sabato, *PAC Power: Inside the World of Political Action Committees* (New York: Norton, 1984), p. 4.

34. Edwin M. Epstein, "The PAC Phenomenon: An Overview," *Arizona Law Review* 22 (1980): 355–72, at p. 357.

35. Sabato, *PAC Power*, pp. 5–7.

36. Frank J. Sorauf, "Background Paper," in Twentieth Century Fund, *What Price PACs?* (New York: Twentieth Century Fund, 1984), p. 31. The publication includes a Report of the Fund's Task Force on PACs.

37. Lee Ann Elliott, "Political Action Committees—Precincts of the '80s," *Arizona Law Review* 22 (1980): 539–54.

38. Bernadette A. Budde, "Business Political Action Committees," in *Parties, Interest Groups, and Campaign Finance Laws*, ed. Michael J. Malbin (Washington, D.C.: American Enterprise Institute, 1980), pp. 9–25, at p. 10.

39. Sabato, *PAC Power*, pp. 9–10.

40. Edwin M. Epstein, "Business and Labor under the Federal Election Campaign Act of 1971," in *Parties, Interest Groups*, ed. Malbin, pp. 107–51, at pp. 112–14.

41. John R. Bolton, "Constitutional Limitations on Restricting Corporate and Union Political Speech," *Arizona Law Review*: 22 (1980): 373–426, at p. 409.

42. Ibid., p. 405.

43. Although independent expenditures generally appeared to have been constitutionally exempted from restrictions by *Buckley v. Valeo*, the U.S. Supreme Court did not then specifically exempt such expenditures in behalf of a presidential nominee

who had accepted public funds. It did so in *Federal Election Commission v. National Conservative PAC*, 84 L. Ed. 2d 455 (1985). NCPAC had spent generously in behalf of Ronald Reagan in both 1980 and 1984. Its subsequent judicial success established the legitimacy of the independent-expenditure loophole where, even after 1976, the FEC and public funding advocates had hoped to be able to close it. *FEC v. NCPAC* should, therefore, be read along with *Buckley v. Valeo* if one is to appreciate the full significance of the constitutional constraints, which are discussed in the next chapter.

44. In *First National Bank of Boston v. Bellotti*, 435 U.S. 765 (1978), the Court invalidated a Massachusetts law prohibiting corporations from spending to influence the outcome of ballot initiatives. Bolton, "Constitutional Limitations," pp. 411–13.

45. In Justice Rehnquist's opinion for the Supreme Court in *FEC v. NCPAC*, 84 L. Ed. 2d 455 (1985), at 469, he made the point that neither here nor in *Bellotti* was there any need to reach the question whether "a corporation can constitutionally be restricted in making independent expenditures to influence elections for public office." Accordingly, as of this writing, a grey area exists for corporations between constitutionally protected independent expenditures for many political purposes and unprotected—now prohibited—contributions to candidates.

46. Numbers are from the Federal Election Commission, press release, January 28, 1985. See also Sabato, *PAC Power*, pp. 10–16, 117–21 (on state and local PACs); Jones, "Financing State Elections," pp. 180–93; Charles D. Hadley and Rainer Nick, "State PACs through the National Looking Glass," paper for the 1985 meeting of the Midwest Political Science Association, Chicago.

47. Sabato, *PAC Power*, p. 14; Federal Election Commission, press release, December 1, 1985, pp. 1–2.

48. FEC, press release, December 1, 1985, pp. 1–2.

49. Sabato, *PAC Power*, p. 16; FEC, press release, December 8, 1985, p. 8.

50. The 1984 figures are from FEC press releases, December 1 and 5, 1985. The 1982 figures are calculated from data in Thomas E. Mann and Norman J. Ornstein, eds., *The American Elections of 1982* (Washington, D.C.: American Enterprise Institute, 1983), pp. 189–91.

51. Sabato, *PAC Power*, pp. 94–95.

52. Ibid., p. 17; FEC, press release, December 1, 1985, p. 8.

53. FEC, press release, December 1, 1985, p. 1. Earlier data on PAC contributions are in *What Price PACs?*, pp. 45–48.

54. Calculations are based on data in Federal Election Commission, press releases, November 29 and December 2, 1983. On the appeal of incumbents to individual contributors as well as to PACs, see Gary C. Jacobson, *Money in Congressional Elections* (New Haven: Yale University Press, 1980), pp. 101–4.

55. Sabato, *PAC Power*, pp. 84–85.

56. Sorauf, in *What Price PACs?*, pp. 70–71. From a sample of PACs, Sabato, *PAC Power*, p. 59, shows the average 1981–82 donation to a PAC at $100, but the corporate PAC figure was $160 and the labor PAC figure was $14.

57. Ruth S. Jones and Warren E. Miller, "Financing Campaigns: Modes of Individual Contribution," paper for the 1983 meeting of the Midwest Political Science Association, Chicago, pp. 10–12.

58. In *PAC Power*, p. 62, Sabato reports that 81 percent of corporate PACs, and 50 percent of labor PACs used payroll deductions in 1983.

59. Sorauf, in *What Price PACs?*, pp. 81–82.

60. The 1972–78 figures are from Gary C. Jacobson, "The Pattern of Campaign Contributions to Candidates for the U.S. House of Representatives 1972–78," in *An Analysis of the Impact of the Federal Election Campaign Act, 1972–78* (Washington, D.C.: U.S. House of Representatives, Committee on House Administration, 1979), pp. 20–42. The 1984 figures are from the FEC, press release, December 8, 1985, p. 8; they may not be strictly comparable with the earlier data, but the basis for calculation is unlikely to be very different. The same press release shows that of 1984 Senate candidate receipts, the PAC share was 17 percent and the party's share 1 percent.

61. Sabato, *PAC Power*, pp. 144–49, for both the phrase and the 1981–82 data on party contributions to PACs. See also David W. Adamany, "Political Parties in the 1980s," in *Money and Politics*, ed. Malbin, pp. 70–121, at pp. 84–85, 91–92. The 1983–84 data are from Federal Election Commission, *Record* 11 (August 1985): 6.

62. Sorauf, in *What Price PACs?*, pp. 101–3.

63. Figures for 1984 are from the FEC, press release, December 8, 1985, p. 8. Earlier figures are from Gary C. Jacobson, "Money in the 1980 and 1982 Congressional Elections," in *Money and Politics*, ed. Malbin, pp. 38–69, at p. 42. Jacobson's figures, at p. 43, show that in 1982, 34 percent of corporate PAC money, 43 percent of trade/membership/health association money, and 95 percent of labor PAC money went to Democrats.

64. FEC, press release December 1, 1985, p. 3.

65. Margaret Ann Latus, "Assessing Ideological PACs: From Outrage to Understanding," in *Money and Politics*, ed. Malbin, pp. 142–71, at p. 156.

66. Ibid., pp. 157–63.

67. Sorauf, "Political Parties and PACs," p. 458.

68 Sorauf, in *What Price PACs?*, p. 80.

69. Theodore J. Eismeier and Philip H. Pollock III, "Political Action Committees: Varieties of Organization and Strategy," in *Money and Politics*, ed. Malbin, pp. 122–41, at pp. 125–26.

70. Michael J. Malbin, "Looking Back at the Future of Campaign Finance Reform: Interest Groups and American Elections," in *Money and Politics*, ed. Malbin, pp. 232–76, at p. 247.

71. Fred Wertheimer, "The PAC Phenomenon in American Politics," *Arizona Law Review* 22 (1980): 603–26, at pp. 604–5.

72. Undated literature from Common Cause, Washington, D.C.

73. Sorauf, in *What Price PACs?*, pp. 104–5; Malbin, "Looking Back," p. 237.

74. My count of 284 is from a tabulation by Michael J. Malbin and Thomas W.

Skladony, *Campaign Finance, 1984: A Preliminary Analysis of House and Senate Campaign Receipts* (Washington, D.C.: American Enterprise Institute, 1984). Their tabulation is of receipts from January 1, 1983, through October 17, 1984, and thus excludes receipts just before and after the election date.

75. In *What Price PACs?*, pp. 6, 20, 21–22.

76. FEC, press release, December 1, 1985, p. 2. All independent spending in 1983–84 was $23.4 million, rather than $22.2 million, because it included individual as well as the much larger PAC amounts. FEC, *Record* 11 (October 1985): 5.

77. In *What Price PACs?*, p. 7. Some members of the task force also suggested free media time for candidates to respond to hostile allegations.

78. Eismeier and Pollock, "PACs: Varieties," p. 129.

79. *Congressional Quarterly Weekly Report* 43 (Nov. 23, 1985): 2445–46. The bill proposed a ceiling on a candidate's receipts from PACs of $100,000 for a House general election (plus another $25,000 if a candidate had a primary as well as a general election contest), and a ceiling of $175,000 to $750,000 for a Senate candidate (the amount depending on the size of the candidate's state).

80. The 1984 Republican advantage is close to three-to-one even when state and local party expenditures in federal elections are included. FEC, press release, December 5, 1985, p. 3.

81. PACs, like individuals, are advantaged relative to parties in that the latter's expenditures in behalf of candidates are apparently assumed to be coordinated rather than independent and are accordingly subject to the statutory limits Congress imposed on party expenditures in behalf of candidates. On the other hand, PACs and individuals, though without the authority to spend anything in coordination with candidates (beyond contribution limits), can spend constitutionally unlimited amounts independently and yet in behalf of candidates. This particular disparity is more the consequence of judicial interpretation than of congressional intent. Indeed, it could be argued that the coordinated expenditure allowance was meant to give parties a substantial advantage when Congress believed that it could constitutionally restrict all expenditures in behalf of candidates.

82. Ellwood and Spitzer, "Telethons," p. 864.

83. Herbert E. Alexander, "Making Sense About Dollars in the 1980 Presidential Campaigns," in *Money and Politics*, ed. Malbin, pp. 11–37, at p. 20; Federal Election Commission, press release, May 7, 1985.

84. Jacobson, "Money," pp. 46–47. Even party *contributions* may not be so small as $5,000 per election suggests. A national and a congressional committee can each contribute $5,000 to a candidate. Since the amount is per election (primary and general), the maximum for each party committee is really $10,000. Hence a party's national and state units altogether can contribute as much as $30,000. That appears to be a substantial minority share of the $200,000 that Jacobson considered necessary to run a minimally competitive House campaign in 1980 and 1982, but it is hardly a big piece of the total expenditures of the top 50 spenders in 1984 House

races. Each of the 50 spent over $578,000, and four spent over $1 million. FEC, press release, December 8, 1985, p. 13. The failure to raise contribution limits since they were first established in the mid-1970s means that their value has greatly eroded because of inflation in general and campaign costs in particular.

85. Jacobson, "Money," pp. 46–47. The relevant Supreme Court opinion is *Federal Election Commission v. Democratic Senatorial Campaign Committee*, 454 U.S. 27 (1981). Democrats were objecting to the FEC's ruling in favor of the agency agreements of the National Republican Senatorial Committee, itself acting as the agent of the Republican National Committee, specifically authorized along with the Democratic National Committee to make the coordinated expenditures in behalf of candidates.

86. Jacobson, "Money," pp. 48–49. The 1984 figures, as before, are from the FEC, press release, December 8, 1985, and they include state party expenditures along with national committee expenditures.

87. Alexander, "Making Sense," p. 21.

88. David Adamany, "Financing Political Parties in the United States," in *Parties and Democracy in Britain and America*, ed. Vernon Bogdanor (New York: Praeger, 1984), pp. 153–84, at pp. 158–59.

89. In Wisconsin, for example, parties were advantaged by an anti-PAC provision more severely restricting candidate receipts from PACs than from parties and individuals when candidates accept public funds and accompanying expenditure ceilings. Legislative party committees have used the opportunity to distribute money, which they collect from PACs and individuals, to candidates. See FEC, *Campaign Finance Law 84*, for state-by-state provisions, and p. WI-15 for the relevant Wisconsin regulation. See also Jones's discussion of party roles in financing state elections, in *Money and Politics*, ed. Malbin, pp. 193–97.

90. Alarming estimates of "soft money" appear in Elizabeth Drew, *Politics and Money: The New Road to Corruption* (New York: Macmillan, 1983).

91. Steven F. Stockmeyer, "Commentaries," in *Parties, Interest Groups*, ed. Malbin, pp. 309–14, at p. 313.

92. For discussion of the various suggestions, see "Report of the Task Force" and Herbert Alexander's "Comment" in *What Price PACs?*, pp. 10–11, 24; Malbin, "Looking Back," pp. 240–41; and David E. Price, *Bringing Back the Parties* (Washington, D.C.: Congressional Quarterly, 1984), p. 257.

93. The Laxalt-Frenzel proposal is summarized in *Commonsense* 6 (December 1983): 77–78, along with other campaign finance bills current in 1983.

94. Jacobson, *Money in Congressional Elections*, shows most persuasively the value of money for congressional challengers. Incumbents are always able to raise large sums, but only some challengers, including successful ones, can do so.

95. Alexander, "Making Sense," pp. 33–34.

96. A full exposition of British practices can be found in Michael Pinto-Duschinsky, *British Political Finance 1830–1980* (Washington, D.C.: American Enterprise Institute, 1981), pp. 268–76.

Chapter 10: Public Funding of Campaigns

1. Brock's agreement was reported by John White, the DNC Chairman, without disputing Brock's continued opposition to public funding of congressional campaigns. *Washington Post*, September 21, 1979, p. A16.

2. The same judicial emphasis on political freedom accounts for recent rulings, observed in chapters 6 and 7, against previously established state legislation regulating parties.

3. 424 U.S. 1 (1976).

4. Ibid., p. 91.

5. In the late 1970s the number of contributing taxpayers rose to nearly 40 million. See Kim Quaile Hill, "Taxpayer Support for the Presidential Election Campaign Fund," *Social Science Quarterly* 62 (March 1981): pp. 767–71, at p. 769; and Federal Election Commission, *The First 10 Years* (Washington, D.C.: FEC, 1985), p. 5.

6. *Buckley v. Valeo*, 424 U.S. 1 (1976), at 91–92.

7. Ibid., pp. 247–48. Burger illustrated ill effects by pointing to the possibility of governmental regulation of nominating conventions following from the governmental subsidy of those conventions. Given the history of state legislation, however, regulation of nominating conventions is evidently both constitutionally and politically feasible without any government subsidy of the conventions.

8. Ibid., p. 97 (n. 131). The chance for subsequent invalidation was almost immediately discussed by Albert J. Rosenthal, "The Constitution and Campaign Finance Regulation after *Buckley v. Valeo*," *Annals of the American Academy* 425 (May 1976): 124–33, at pp. 132–33.

9. 424 U.S. 1 (1976), at 87 (n. 118). The "serious questions" had not been dealt with in the 1976 case because Eugene McCarthy, the independent presidential candidate who joined in the legal complaint against the constitutionality of the statute, was not seeking federal funds.

10. Money would have been available for Anderson's "party" to finance a nominating convention in 1984.

11. Providing constitutionally for minor-party *candidates* without much likelihood of having to fund them can also be managed a little differently from the federal arrangement. For example, Wisconsin's exclusively candidate-funding plan provides money for any general election candidate, regardless of party, who has polled 6 percent of all primary election votes for the given office (and who raised a given amount privately). Thus major- and minor-party candidates are treated alike, but only major-party nominees are expected to win enough primary votes to qualify for public funds. Herbert E. Alexander and Jennifer W. Frutig, *Public Financing of State Elections* (Los Angeles: Citizens' Research Foundation, 1982), p. 256.

12. Anderson's popular vote (6.6 percent) entitled him to $4.2 million in federal funds, compared to $29.4 million for each major-party candidate. Getting one-seventh of a major party's funds was in accord with the fact that Anderson's popular vote was about one-seventh of the average vote polled by the major-party candidates. The

not ungenerous legal formula provides dollars for a minor party in proportion to dollars for a fully funded major party according to the ratio of a minor party's popular vote to the average major-party popular vote. Federal Election Commission, *Federal Election Campaign Laws* (Washington, D.C.: FEC, 1980), pp. 61–62 (reproducing relevant sections from Chapter 95, Title 26 of the Internal Revenue Code). Here and elsewhere my references to statutes are drawn from the FEC publication.

13. The $6 million figure is the inflation-adjusted portion determined by Anderson's share of the total vote in 1980.

14. 424 U.S. 1 (1976), at 293.

15. Federal Election Commission, *Record* 10 (October 1984): 8; and press release, March 21, 1985.

16. 424 U.S. 1 (1976), at 57–59 (nn. 65, 66).

17. Ibid., p. 48.

18. Ibid., pp. 47–48.

19. In 1984 total independent spending (mainly by PACs but also by individuals) was $15.8 million for Reagan and only $.8 million for Mondale, apart from smaller sums spent against each of the candidates. FEC, *Record* 11 (October 1985): 7.

20. The inconclusiveness of the 1982 decision, *Common Cause v. Schmitt*, 455 U.S. 129 (1982), was that the Supreme Court, without explanation, merely affirmed a lower court ruling in favor of the PACs, and did so in a four-to-four vote (with the then newly appointed Justice O'Connor abstaining). The definitive ruling was in *Federal Election Commision v. National Conservative PAC*, 84 L. Ed. 2d 455 (1985), whose importance for the freedom of PACs was stressed in n. 43 of chapter 9.

21. Justice White, dissenting in *FEC v. NCPAC*, did argue for the validity of the particular provision despite *Buckley*, but he also adhered to his belief, expressed when *Buckley* had been decided, that expenditure ceilings more generally were valid. *FEC v. NCPAC*, 84 L. Ed. 2d 455 (1985), at 476–83.

22. David W. Adamany and George E. Agree, *Political Money: A Strategy for Campaign Financing in America* (Baltimore: Johns Hopkins University Press, 1975), p. 182.

23. Ibid., pp. 131–35.

24. Seventh Annual Message (Dec. 3, 1907), in *The Works of Theodore Roosevelt* (New York: Scribner's 1926), vol. 15, p. 461. President Roosevelt's proposal consisted of a few sentences in the context of a brief discussion "Campaign Expenses," one of 45 sections in his message to Congress. He himself called the proposal "a very radical measure" whose early adoption he did not expect (pp. 460–61).

25. Data are from FEC, *The First 10 Years*, p. 12.

26. The state limit, subject to COLA, is the greater of $200,000 or 16 cents multiplied by the state's voting age population. FEC, *The First 10 Years*, p. 12. The state ceilings are inconvenient for presidential candidates, but at least in 1976 and 1980 they appeared to hamper candidates only in small states that elected delegates early and were therefore places where candidates would have preferred to concentrate their

resources more heavily than the federally imposed state ceilings allowed. Gary R. Orren, "Presidential Campaign Finance," *Commonsense* 4 (no. 2): 50–66, at p. 58.

27. F. Christopher Arterton, "Finances in Presidential Prenomination Campaigns," paper for the 1982 meeting of the Midwest Political Science Association, Milwaukee, Wis., p. 39.

28. Herbert E. Alexander, "Making Sense about Dollars in the 1980 Presidential Campaigns," in *Money and Politics in the United States,* ed. Michael J. Malbin (Chatham, N.J.: Chatham House, 1984), pp. 11–37, at p. 13; FEC, press release, March 21, 1985.

29. Ibid., for 1980 and 1984 figures. Carter's 1976 amount is calculated from data in John H. Aldrich, *Before the Convention* (Chicago: University of Chicago Press, 1980), p. 72.

30. Herbert E. Alexander, *Financing Politics* (Washington, D.C.: Congressional Quarterly, 1980), p. 60.

31. In 1984, Jesse Jackson first lost his eligibility by receiving less than 10 percent of the popular votes cast in consecutive May primaries and then regained it by receiving over 20 percent in New Jersey's primary on June 5. FEC, *Record* 10 (July 1984): 2.

32. Alexander, "Making Sense," pp. 12–14; and FEC, press release, March 21, 1985.

33. FEC, *The First 10 Years*, p. 12.

34. Ibid.

35. Legally unlimited expenditures of national committees for general party-building might also be said to provide indirect help for a presidential nominee, and so might the state and local party presidential campaign activities that are exempt from expenditure ceilings but serve national party purposes and receive national party help, as described in chapter 9.

36. John F. Bibby and Cornelius P. Cotter, "Presidential Campaigning, Federalism, and the Federal Election Campaign Act," *Publius* 10 (Winter 1980): 119–36, p. 134.

37. In addition to Oregon, Maryland, and Oklahoma, the other 14 of the 17 states with public funding laws are Hawaii, Idaho, Iowa, Kentucky, Maine, Massachusetts, Michigan, Minnesota, Montana, New Jersey, North Carolina, Rhode Island, Utah, and Wisconsin. Alexander and Frutig, *Public Financing of State Elections* (cited in n. 11) have useful summaries of each state's statutory provisions. They add Alaska and California as special cases, and note that California's legislation was only for a tax add-on rather than for the more productive checkoff.

38. Ruth S. Jones, "State Public Financing and the State Parties," in *Parties, Interest Groups, and Campaign Finance Laws*, ed. Michael J. Malbin (Washington, D.C.: American Enterprise Institute, 1980), pp. 283–303, at p. 285.

39. Jack L. Noragon, "Political Finance and Political Reform: The Experience with State Income Tax Checkoffs," *American Political Science Review* 75 (September 1981): 667–87, at 667–75. In the four add-on states—Maine, Maryland, Massachusetts, and Montana after 1979—the percentage of participating taxpayers ranged from only .5 to 2.8 percent. Alexander and Frutig, *Public Financing*, p. 7.

40. Ruth S. Jones, "Financing State Elections," in *Money and Politics*, ed. Malbin, pp. 172–213, at pp. 198–200. For 1981 and 1982, I have calculated from Jones's data in order to present summary figures. Party receipts for 1981 and 1982 are counted together, and the New Jersey candidate receipts are for the state's election of 1981.

41. Noragon, "Political Finance," p. 681. The four additional candidate-funding states are Hawaii, Maryland, Massachusetts, and Montana. Oklahoma's law was also originally only for candidate funding.

42. The three primary-funding states besides New Jersey and Michigan are Hawaii, Massachusetts, and Maryland. Ibid., p. 682.

43. Ruth S. Jones, "Patterns of Campaign Finance in the Public Funding States," paper for the 1982 meeting of the Midwest Political Science Association, Milwaukee, Wis., p. 15.

44. *New York Times*, March 8, 1981, p. 6E. The temptation to attribute party decline in New Jersey to the public funding of candidates is resistible in light of evidence that the decline had mainly preceded the funding. David Adamany, "Political Finance in Transition," *Polity* 14 (Winter 1981): 314–31, at p. 324. (n. 28).

45. The eight party-funding states are Idaho, Iowa, Kentucky, Maine, North Carolina, Oregon, Rhode Island, and Utah. Oregon's law lapsed and Maine's add-on provision means that little money has become available. Alexander and Frutig, *Public Financing of State Elections*, pp. 6–7.

46. Noragon, "Political Finance," pp. 680–81, 683.

47. Alexander and Frutig, *Public Financing of State Elections*, pp. 49–58.

48. Jones, "Financing State Elections," p. 199.

49. Noragon, "Political Finance," p. 680.

50. Only in Maine has the amount been negligible.

51. David E. Price, *Bringing Back the Parties* (Washington, D.C.: Congressional Quarterly, 1984), p. 254.

52. Minnesota also distributes candidate funding through parties, but only according to an allocation so fixed by statute that the parties exercise no discretion. Noragon, "Political Finance," p. 671, n. d.

53. Jones, "State Public Financing," p. 292.

54. Hearings before the Committee on House Administration, House of Representatives, 96th Congress, 1st Session, *Public Financing of Congressional Elections* (Washington, D.C.: Government Printing Office, 1979), pp. 412–17, 455–58.

55. Jones, "Financing State Elections," p. 199.

56. Ibid., p. 198; Noragon, "Political Finance," pp. 667, 677.

57. Ruth S. Jones, "State Public Campaign Finance: Implications for Partisan Politics," *American Journal of Political Science* 25 (May 1981): 342–61, at pp. 352, 358–59. Note that states conform to constitutional necessity by allowing minor parties to become eligible for funds, and that in 1982 minor parties did receive small amounts —from $2,000 to $4,500—in three of the party-funding states. In no instance was the minor-party grant greater than 7 percent of the grant received by the less-well-

funded of the two major parties. My calculations, from Jones, "Financing State Elections," p. 199.

58. Jones, "State Public Financing," p. 302.

59. The classification of party competitiveness comes from the second edition of Malcolm E. Jewell and David M. Olson, *American State Political Parties and Elections* (Homewood, Ill.: Dorsey Press, 1982), which has later but similar data to those in the first edition (1978), chap. 2, cited by Jones, "State Public Financing."

60. Jewell and Olson, *American State Political Parties*, p. 58 (2d ed.).

61. Morley Winograd (Michigan State Democratic Party), in Malbin, ed., *Parties, Interest Groups*, p. 306, commenting on Jones's analysis in the same volume.

62. The anti-PAC aspect of the Wisconsin law is described in n. 89 of chapter 9. For a fuller explanation of the public-funding connection, and of primary votes and minimum private fund-raising needed to qualify, see Alexander and Frutig, *Public Financing of State Elections*, pp. 255–62.

63. Elizabeth G. King and David G. Wegge, "The Rules are Never Neutral: Public Funds in Minnesota and Wisconsin Legislative Elections," paper for the 1984 meeting of the Midwest Political Science Association, Chicago, p. 6. The actual number of legislative candidates accepting public funds in 1982 was 129, (and 147 in 1984), compared with only 51 in 1978 and 89 in 1980. In each year, 99 Assembly seats and 16 or 17 Senate seats were filled, but some were uncontested. It is important to qualify the apparent numerical success of Wisconsin's public funding by noting that the accompanying expenditure ceilings discourage candidates in hotly contested races from accepting state money, and that the number of taxpayers participating in the one-dollar checkoff declined in the early 1980s.

64. Ibid., table 5.

65. The fund raising by caucus committees was depicted in detail and as scandalous by the *Wisconsin State Journal*, April 24, 1983, sec. 1, pp. 1, 4–5.

66. In Kentucky, participation in the tax checkoff ($1.75 for a party of one's choice) declined for seven straight years to only 9.5 percent in 1983. *Comparative State Politics Newsletter* 6 (April 1985): 25.

67. Quoted by James J. Kilpatrick, *Wisconsin State Journal*, June 9, 1985, sec. 1, p. 19.

68. Hearings, *Public Financing*, pp. 2–122.

69. The $150,000 ceiling was low, and so was the $200,000 ceiling included in the most prominent proposal in 1983. *Congressional Quarterly Weekly Report* 41 (July 16, 1983): 1451–54.

70. Hearings, *Public Financing*, pp. 127–28.

71. *Congressional Quarterly Weekly Report* 41 (July 16, 1983): 1452.

72. Hearings, *Public Financing*, p. 227.

73. Ibid., p. 357.

74. Ibid., p. 378. Professor Ralph Winter was the spokesperson for the RNC. The then chairperson of the RNC, William Brock, wrote to the same effect in "Add-

ing Insult to Incumbency: Taxpayer Financing of Congressional Campaigns," *Commonsense* 2 (Winter 1979): 11–22, at p. 20.

75. Hearings, *Public Financing*, p. 227.

76. Ibid., p. 387.

77. Ibid., pp. 412–17. The Iowa Republican chairperson, while defending his state's method of public financing, did not so clearly support public financing in general.

78. Ibid., pp. 363–64.

79. Price, *Bringing Back the Parties*, pp. 255–56. He also advocated increased public funding of national parties.

80. Hearings, *Public Financing*, p. 366.

81. Ibid., p. 393.

82. Ibid., p. 395.

83. The President's Commission for a National Agenda for the Eighties, *The Electoral and Democratic Process in the Eighties* (Washington, D.C.: Government Printing Office 1980), p. 31.

84. Ibid., p. 34.

85. Twentieth Century Fund, *What Price PACs?* (New York: Twentieth Century Fund, 1984), p. 8. At the same time that the Task Force recommended candidate funding, it also suggested (p. 10) the strengthening of parties, though not apparently with public funds, in order to counter the effects of candidate-centered campaigning.

86. K. Z. Paltiel, "Public Financing Abroad: Contrasts and Effects," in *Parties, Interest Groups*, ed. Malbin, pp. 354–70, at pp. 356–65.

87. K. Z. Paltiel, "Campaign Finance: Contrasting Practices and Reforms," in *Democracy at the Polls*, ed. David Butler, Howard R. Penniman, and Austin Ranney (Washington, D.C.: American Enterprise Institute, 1981), pp. 138–72, at pp. 169–70.

88. Ibid., pp. 164–66, where public subsidies in selected democratic nations are tabulated as of 1979. Canada has a place for parties along with candidates in its public funding, and France funds only presidential candidates. Paltiel's entire chapter is especially helpful as an analytical review of campaign financing in general. The German emphasis on party in campaign finance can be found in Arthur B. Gunlicks, "Campaign and Party Finance at the State Level in Germany," *Comparative Politics* 12 (January 1980): 211–23. A useful study of still another country is Leon Boim's "The Financing of Elections," in *Israel at the Polls: The Knesset Elections of 1977*, ed. Howard R. Penniman (Washington, D.C.: American Enterprise Institute, 1979), pp. 199–225.

89. Party organizational interests are not always the same as the interests of party candidates. Some Republicans favor public funding of candidates, and some Democrats are opposed. With respect to liberalizing private-funding limits for parties, Republicans generally—not only Republican organizations—may discern advantages, while Democrats generally, given the lesser capacity of their organizations, are unlikely to see many advantages for themselves. In congressional campaigns, as noted earlier, Democratic *candidates* are about as well funded as Republican candidates.

90. Price, *Bringing Back the Parties*, p. 256, includes in his proposal for giving parties free television time the possibility of public funds to cover network or station costs.

91. Britain, for example, imposes its requirement of free air time on privately owned facilities as well as on the nationally owned British Broadcasting Corporation. The arrangement is described by Martin Harrison, "Broadcasting," in *The British General Election of 1983*, ed. David Butler and Dennis Kavanagh (London: Macmillan, 1984), pp. 147–74, at pp. 147–56. Incidentally Britain, unlike most continental nations, has so far provided no public funds for campaigns, but only annual subsidies for parliamentary parties.

Chapter 11: An Unbreakable Mold?

1. Theodore J. Lowi is unusual among contemporary American political scientists in vigorously arguing for the advantages of third-party representation. "Presidential Power: Restoring the Balance," *Political Science Quarterly* 100 (Summer 1985): 185–213.

2. Louisiana's open-election law is briefly described, with appropriate references to fuller explanations, in n. 78 of chapter 5.

3. The constitutionality of primaries as such does not seem at issue even in the significant challenge by Connecticut Republicans, discussed near the end of chapter 6. The question is whether the state must yield to certain party rules in running party primaries. Nevertheless, the U.S. Supreme Court, which is likely to decide the case in 1986, may substantially modify the regulatory status of political parties if it affirms the lower federal court decisions against the state. A state could then find it more difficult to run party primaries.

Index

Abramowitz, Alan I., 371

Abrams v. Reno, 393

Activists, party, 36, 112, 205; in cadre party, 144, 145, 146, 148, 151; at caucuses, 149, 153; dues-paying, 153; ideological, 85, 173; as nationalizing force, 146; nominating role of, 34–35; policymaking by, 34; in responsible-party government, 36

Adamany, David W., 319, 363, 397, 398, 409, 410, 411, 413, 415, 417, 419

Adler, Norman M., 385

Adrian, Charles R., 359, 381, 389

Advertising, 220, 224, 296

Advisory Commission on Intergovernmental Relations, 152

Affirmative action, 215, 229, 231

AFL-CIO PAC, 285

Agar, Herbert, 26, 361

Agranoff, Robert, 268, 408

Agree, George E., 319, 410, 411, 417

Alaska, 326

Aldrich, John H., 418

Alexander, Herbert E., 307–8, 323, 378, 409, 410, 411, 414, 415, 416, 418, 420

Alignment, party, 8–9; aging, 262; class-based, 136; congressional, 54, 57, 60, 61, 64–65; ideological, 266–67, 268; institutionalized, 271; party identification as basis of, 241; presidency as focus of, 241; registration recognizes, 248; state party continues national, 6, 84, 124–26, 127, 128, 130, 131, 132–33, 153; two-party, 243 (*see also* Two-partyism); 19th century, 83–84; after 1896, 255

Allswang, John M., 382, 383, 384

American Independent party, 181, 315

American Medical Association PAC, 286, 291

American Party of Texas v. White, 392

American Political Science Association's Committee on Political Parties, 33–35, 36, 395

Americans for Constitutional Action, 285

Amoco PAC, 286

AMPAC, 286, 291

Anderson, Douglas D., 390

Anderson, John, 335; as minor-party candidate, 132, 183–84, 244, 254, 262, 314, 315; public funding for, 314, 315–16, 317, 324, 416

Anderson v. Celebrezze, 183–84

Andrus, Cecil, 116

Anti-Masonic party, 203

Antipartyism, 12, 261; and campaign finance legislation, 301, 330–31, 336–37; of constitutional founders, 11, 135–36, 158–59; direct primary as, 155–56; and machines, 135–36; in municipal elections, 13–14; nonpartisan ballot as, 164; of progressives, 13, 170, 171; and reform, 5, 163–64, 301; and state regulations, 180

Anti-Saloon League, 285

Antitrust legislation, 170

Appropriations Committee, 49, 51, 58

Armed Services Committee, 51

Arterton, F. Christopher, 376, 408, 418

Aspin, Les, 366

Assessments, 135, 277–78

Association of State Democratic Chairpersons, 337

Associations, parties as, 7, 155, 157, 158–59, 160, 161, 162, 163, 166, 167, 174, 179, 188, 189–91, 192, 193–97, 225, 227. *See also* Freedom of association

Australia, 45–46, 168, 201. *See also* Ballot, Australian

Austria, 340

Baker, Howard, 313

Ballot: access, 165, 173, 174, 180–84, 196–97, 198, 244; Australian, 156, 159, 162–67, 169, 172, 173, 199, 404; -box stuffing, 163; British, 156; government-provided, 156, 158, 162, 163, 164, 165, 166, 243–44; institutionalizes parties, 162, 164, 173; labels on, 162, 163, 164, 165, 172, 173, 181, 243–44, 250; and legal status of parties, 162, 163, 165–66; literacy required by, 164–65; long, 164, 242, 243, 250; nonpartisan, 14, 126–27, 156, 164, 388; office-column, 164; party-column, 164, 243; party-provided, 156, 159–60, 162–63, 164, 242, 256; reform of, 14, 127, 162, 163, 164, 165, 168, 255; regulation of, 126–27, 162, 165–66, 180–81, 199; secrecy of, 163; straw, 177; and split-ticket voting, 164, 243, 404; and straight-ticket voting, 255

Banfield, Edward C., 361, 382, 383
Barber, Benjamin R., 364
Bass, Jack, 370
Beard, Charles, 14, 359
Beck, Paul Allen, 406
Bell, Griffin, 116
Bellotti v. Commonwealth, 394
Berdahl, Clarence A., 172, 390
Bergland, Bob, 116
Bibby, John F., 365, 377, 382; on national Republican party, 215, 222, 223, 395, 396, 397, 398, 418; on state party organizations, 151–52, 387
Bicameralism, 45, 47
Black, Justice Hugo, 177–78
Blackmun, Justice Harry A., 234, 400
Blank, Blanche Davis, 385
Bliss, Ray, 216
Blondel, Jean, 378
Bode v. National Democratic Party, 398
Bogdanor, Vernon, 357, 374, 397, 415
Boim, Leon, 421
Bolling, Richard, 335
Bolton, John R., 411, 412
Bone, Hugh A., 396
Boorstin, Daniel J., 401
Born, Richard, 372
Boyd, Richard W., 363
Braafladt, Arnie R., 393
Brady, David W., 368, 369, 371
Branti v. Finkel, 384, 391
Breen, Matthew, 383
Brennan, Justice William J., 228, 233, 234, 399
Brock, William, 216, 219, 222, 225, 311, 397, 416, 420
Broder, David S., 100, 357, 363, 376
Brody, Richard A., 253, 254, 404
Brown, Roger G., 117, 379
Bryan, William Jennings, 94, 109
Bryce, James, 12–13, 15, 16, 17, 18, 25, 26, 137, 358, 360, 383
Buckley, James, 380–81
Buckley v. Valeo, 288, 312, 313, 314, 316, 317, 318, 327, 394, 409, 411, 416
Budde, Bernadette A., 411
Budge, Ian, 403
Budget Committee (House), 57–58
Buenker, John D., 383
Bullock, Charles S., III, 369
Burdette, Franklin L., 395
Burger, Justice Warren E., 312, 313, 314, 316, 416
Burgess, John W., 11, 358
Burnham, Walter Dean, 38, 62, 255–56, 357, 364, 368, 404
Burns, James M., 35–36, 37, 38, 106, 364, 373, 377

Bush, George, 322, 324
Businesses: contributions by, 224, 279, 280, 285; and machines, 134, 137, 138–39. *See also* Political action committees

Cabinet: candidate's staff provides, 116–17; Carter's, 115–17; as collective decision-maker, 114; ideological appointments to, 117; interest groups in, 116; parliamentary, 48, 114; party influences, 114–18, 119; Reagan's, 117; F. D. Roosevelt's, 115; symbolic representation in, 116; technocrats in, 115–16, 117
Cadre parties, 146–48, 149, 152; activists in, 144, 145, 146, 148, 151; as dues-paying, 145, 146; financing role of, 150–51; machines compared to, 144, 145; as national, 146; nominating role of, 150–51; Republicans as, 216; as skeletal, 144–45; voter mobilization by, 145
Caldeira, Greg A., 403
California: on ballot access, 182, 183; dues-paying parties in, 145, 150; endorsement regulations in, 150, 195–96; nominating process in, 162; nonparty registration in, 246, 247–48; public funding in, 326; Senate race in, 221
California Democratic Council, 150
California Republican Assembly, 150
Calvert, Randall L., 370
Campaign: cost of, 279, 280, 290, 325; debts, 224, 325; committees (*see* Congressional parties, campaign committees of; Democratic National Committee; Republican National Committee); European, 270, 273; financing (*see* Campaign financing, fundraising in; Campaign financing, private spending as; Campaign financing, via public funding); media in, 100, 279; party role in, 86, 109, 113, 205, 208, 215, 216–25, 269, 273, 292; regulated, 173 (*see also* Campaign finance legislation); services, 220, 224, 235, 236, 238, 269. *See also* Candidate-centered organizations; Election campaigns, congressional; Election campaigns, local; Election campaigns, presidential; Election campaigns, state
Campaign finance legislation, 95, 219–20, 272; as antiparty, 301, 330–31, 336–37; and candidate-centered organizations, 8, 110, 217, 302, 331; Congress on, 155, 302, 303, 312–13, 319–20; on congressional races, 303, 306–7; contribution limits as, 217, 224, 275, 276, 278, 281, 282, 283–84, 285, 286, 287, 300, 302, 306, 318, 335, 352; expenditure ceilings as, 100, 110, 282, 283, 286–87, 298, 299, 303, 306–7, 312, 317–18, 327, 332–33, 334, 352; fundraising affected by, 269, 282; in Great Britain, 308–9; matching-fund restric-

tions as, 100, 110, 282, 283–84, 288, 295,
298, 303, 317, 318, 321, 324, 326–27, 335;
national, 276; nominating process affected by,
323–24; on PACs, 282, 286–87, 288–89, 298–
99, 352; parties affected by, 155, 217, 225–26,
301–8, 309, 344; as reform, 111, 317, 327 (see
also Campaign financing, via public funding);
state, 275, 282, 303, 305, 308, 321, 326–27,
329; Supreme Court on, 283, 288, 299, 303,
311–12, 317–18
Campaign financing, fundraising in, 272; by assessments, 135, 277–78; from businesses, 224,
279, 280, 285 (see also Political action committees); by caucus campaigns, 333–34; by
congressional campaign committees, 123, 284;
for congressional races, 275, 279, 355; by
DNC, 216, 224, 236, 302; by direct mail (see
Direct-mail solicitation); by family contributions, 283; finance legislation affects, 269,
282; ideological issues and, 237, 281–82; by
individual contributions, 110, 217, 224, 275,
276, 279–81, 282, 283–84, 285, 286, 287,
292, 355; institutionalized, 269; by large contributions, 275–76, 277, 278, 279–80, 282–83,
284, 285, 306; as nationalization mechanism,
218; by PACs, 206, 217, 285–86, 287, 292,
352; Republican success in, 110, 206, 215–16,
218, 224, 278, 284, 301, 305, 325; self-financ-
ing as, 275, 279, 283; by small contributions,
217, 224, 275–76, 280, 281, 282–84, 285–86,
287, 295, 321–23, 335; for state races,
279–80; as tax credit, 283, 286, 306;
technology aids, 282; by television appeals,
281, 282, 302
Campaign financing, private spending as, 8, 60,
61, 76, 272–309; between elections, 280, 340;
by cadre parties, 150–51; by candidates, 275,
279, 283; as candidate-centered, 220, 272,
274–75, 284, 287, 289–90, 293, 295, 298,
325–26; for congressional races, 221, 222,
223, 280, 289–90, 293, 295, 298, 303–4, 307,
338; in Great Britain, 273; independent expenditures as, 219–20, 283, 286, 288–89, 290,
298–99, 302, 303, 304, 318, 325–26; "in behalf of" expenditures as, 219, 220–21, 238,
290, 293, 298, 299, 303, 304–5, 307, 341; as
nationalizing mechanism, 222–23, 236; by national parties, 153, 206, 217, 218, 219, 220–
21, 222, 223, 235, 237–38, 273, 290, 293,
301, 303–4, 307, 325–26, 338, 341, 351, 354;
nominating process affected by, 150–51; by
PACs, 206, 275, 284–94, 295, 296, 298, 299,
302, 303, 304, 326, 354; for party causes,
217, 219–20, 238, 290; for state races, 218,
219, 221–22, 280; by state/local parties, 152,
154, 304–5, 308

Campaign financing, via public funding, 8, 272,
310–42; acceptance-restrictions on, 100, 110,
282, 283, 288, 298, 317, 318–19, 326, 327,
332–33, 334; as candidate-centered, 111, 217,
310, 319–21, 324–25, 327–28, 330, 331, 332–
33, 335, 336, 337, 339, 341; candidate-party
relationship affected by, 311, 324–25, 326,
338, 340; Congress on, 319–20; for congressional races, 38, 335–37, 338, 339–40; for
conventions, 198, 217, 226, 314, 317, 320;
DNC on, 336; as equalizing, 310; European,
198–99, 273, 330, 332, 340; FEC on, 335; as
floor not ceiling, 308; for ideological candidates, 322–23, 332; incumbents favored by,
335–36; matching, 110, 111, 282, 283–84,
295, 317, 318, 321–24, 326–27, 335, 336, 356;
for minor parties, 314–16, 317, 324; as national regulation, 198; nominating process affected by, 328; parties affected by, 38, 198,
308, 310–11, 313–17, 319, 320, 321, 323–25,
328–31, 332, 333–34, 336, 337–38, 339, 340–
41; for presidential campaigns, 198, 226, 313–
14, 316, 319–21, 322, 324–25, 356; for primaries, 321, 328, 356; as reform, 310, 311,
317, 319, 327, 331–32, 333, 334; Republicans
on, 311, 320, 334, 336, 337; state, 326–34,
337, 416; Supreme Court on, 312–14, 416; by
taxpayer checkoff, 312–13, 337
Campbell, Angus, 401, 407
Canada, 45–46, 124, 201, 340
Candidate: compromise, 93; congressional (see
Election campaigns, congressional); consensual, 93, 94; dark-horse, 93; -enthusiasts, 96,
97, 99, 106; electability of, 92, 93; ideological, 94, 99, 106, 281–82, 322, 323; independent, 132, 183–84, 244, 254, 262, 314, 315;
minor-party, 124, 132, 183–84, 244, 254,
262, 314, 315; own committee of (see
Candidate-centered organizations); PACs
created by, 286; and party, 71, 103, 110, 112,
208, 238, 263, 264, 269, 270, 278–79, 311,
324–25, 326, 338, 340; protest, 255; selection
(see Nominating process)
Candidate-centered organizations, 4, 60, 99–100,
212, 238, 261, 301; as American, 270; Bryan's, 109; Carter's, 111; congressional, 70, 73,
74, 77, 78, 275; 343; and constituent activity,
76; direct primary affects, 46–47, 70, 72, 155,
156, 274, 346; disadvantages of, 111; campaign finance legislation affects, 8, 110, 217,
302, 331; in France, 113, 274; in general election, 71, 108–13; governing role of, 110, 116–
17; increase in, 121–22; J. F. Kennedy's, 109–
10; McGovern's, 111; media enhances, 6, 113,
268–69; Nixon's, 110, 111, 279; and PACs,
284, 287; in parliamentary systems, 113, 274;

Candidate-centered organizations (*continued*)
and party alignment, 9; and party identification, 263, 268; party role in, 112, 272, 273,
308, 346; party threatened by, 37, 38, 235;
president v. Congress in, 119–20; as presidential party, 42, 204; presidential primaries foster, 99; private spending for, 272, 274–75,
284, 287, 325–26; public funding for, 111,
198, 217, 310, 319–21, 324–25, 327–28, 330,
331, 332–33, 335, 336, 337, 339, 341; Reagan's, 111; separation of powers as basis of,
270, 274; in state/local elections, 128, 133,
154; and White House staff, 119
Carmines, Edward G., 408
Carr, Craig, 386
Carter, Jimmy, 87, 93, 99, 100, 101, 104, 105,
114, 324; cabinet of, 115–17; candidate-
centered organization of, 111; congressional
relations of, 67–68, 119, 380; energy bill of,
67; matching funds for, 322; nomination of,
102–3; party government under, 67; as party
leader, 121; small contributions to, 282
Casey, William, 117
Cash economy politics, 218, 273–74, 276
Caucus, 215, 321; activists in, 149, 153; called
"primaries," 160, 161–62; congressional, 43,
50–51, 54, 86, 87, 89, 136, 202, 203, 211,
212; closed, 96, 161, 170; delegate-selection
by, 90, 91, 97, 105, 160–61, 212–23, 226,
229, 230; Democratic, 98. 100, 229; Democrats on, 102, 229, 230; ideological candidates
in, 106; interest groups in, 97, 106; Iowa, 96,
97, 100, 101, 102, 106, 212–13; machine controls, 139; manipulated, 161; in Michigan,
229; in Minnesota, 149; nominating role of,
43, 86, 87, 89, 90, 91, 105, 139, 202, 203;
open, 96–97, 99, 106, 149, 170; packed, 106,
161; as party-builder, 106; in Pennsylvania,
168; presidential primary compared to, 170;
regulated, 161–62, 165–66, 167; Republican,
98; as restrictive primary, 96–97; return to,
98, 105, 106; secret ballot in, 168; in Texas,
98; voter turnout in, 106. *See also* Convention, national
Ceaser, James W., 359, 363, 372, 374, 375, 376,
377
Center for Political Studies/Survey Research
Center (CPS/SRC), 250, 251, 253, 254, 257,
259, 261, 267
Chaffee, Steven H., 379
Chambers, WIlliam N., 395
Chapman v. King, 391
Chicago, 135, 139, 140–41, 142–43, 331, 332.
See also Illinois
Citizens for Eisenhower, 109
Citizens party, 317

Civil service: in Cook County, 143; in Great
Britain, 136, 159; as reform, 13, 137, 159;
state/local, 134–35, 137, 142–43; Supreme
Court on, 143
Civil Service Commission, 137
Claggett, William, 370
Clark, Justice Tom C., 178
Clark, William, 117
Class parties, 21, 136, 249, 276
Clausen, Aage R., 64–65, 369
Clay, Henry, 48–49
Clubb, Jerome M., 369, 406, 408
Colorado, 402
Commission for a National Agenda for the
Eighties, 339
Commission on Party Structure and Delegate
Selection. *See* McGovern-Fraser Commission
Committee on House Administration, 335, 336
Committee for Party Renewal, 38, 195, 307,
338, 339
Committee on Political Education, 285
Committee to Re-elect the President (CREEP),
110, 111
Common Cause, 294, 297–98
Common Cause v. Schmitt, 417
Commonwealth v. Rogers, 390
Communist party, 190
Conable, Barber, 335
Congress: cabinet appointments from, 115, 116;
on campaign finance legislation, 155, 302,
303, 312–13, 319–20; committee system in,
45, 48, 49, 50–51, 52, 53, 54, 56, 57–58, 59,
67, 70, 78; conference committees of, 45, 67;
conservative coalition in, 68–69; constituency
relations of, 76; as decentralized, 48–53, 54,
70, 77, 78, 120; electoral/resource base of, 43,
52, 70, 71, 74, 77, 81; impeachment power
of, 44, 87; implied powers of, 312–13; joint
committees in, 49; leadership in, 49–50, 51,
54, 55, 56, 57, 59, 64; minor parties in, 42;
nominating role of, 43, 44, 86, 87, 89, 107,
202, 203, 234; on PACs, 300; parliamentary
system compared to, 43–44, 45–46, 48, 53;
on parties, 225, 302, 304, 313, 315, 316; parties in (*see* Congressional parties); and president, 44, 67–68, 69, 81, 86–87, 119–20, 121,
122, 349; on primaries, 169; roll-call votes in,
55, 57, 60, 62–63, 64, 66, 67; select committees of, 49; seniority in, 50–51, 52, 55, 56,
59; single-member districts of, 45–46, 243;
special committees of, 49; staff of, 52–53;
standing committees of, 48, 49, 50, 51, 53,
56, 57–58, 59; subcommittees of, 48–49, 51,
70, 78; as two-party, 42. *See also* Election
campaigns, congressional; House of Representatives; Senate

Congressional parties, 33, 34, 40–78, 83, 200; alignment of, 54, 57, 60, 61; and bicameralism, 45; campaign committees of, 55, 60–61, 70, 78, 123, 224, 282, 304, 333–34, 338–39; candidate-centered organizations affect, 70, 343; caucuses of, 43, 50–51, 54, 86, 87, 89, 136, 202, 203, 211, 212; as centripetal, 54; cohesion in, 42, 57, 60, 62, 64–65, 67–68, 70, 71; committee assignments affected by, 48–50, 51, 56, 57–58, 78; constituent-oriented, 45–46, 47; Constitution affects, 42–43, 48; and decentralization, 43, 48–53, 54; durability of, 42, 77; as essential, 41; institutionalized, 43–47, 48–50, 51, 54–55, 57; leadership of, 54–57, 58, 59, 61, 64, 65, 87–88; limits on, 42–43, 47; as national, 41, 85; nominating role of, 86, 87, 107; organization of, 54–61; as party-in-government, 6; parliamentary parties compared to, 41, 62, 79; party votes in, 62–63, 64, 66, 70; policymaking role of, 42, 54, 59–60, 62–69, 78; as porous, 78; and presidential parties, 35, 84, 86–87; realignment of, 65–66, 68–69; and responsible-party government, 36–37, 40; separation of powers affects, 43–45, 46, 47; staff of, 55
Conlan, Timothy, 387, 388, 390, 398
Connally, John, 321, 322
Connecticut: direct primary in, 146–47, 185–87, 188, 189, 193, 194–95, 197, 198, 248, 403, 422; endorsements in, 149–50; party registration in, 248; unaffiliated voters in, 248
Conservatism, Republican, 68, 267–68, 282
Conservative coalition, 68–69
Conservative party (Great Britain), 207, 241, 262, 273
Conservative party (New York), 124, 132, 381
Consolidated Edison Company v. Public Service Commission, 392
Constitution of the United States, 34, 36; as antiparty, 11, 135–36, 158–59; congressional parties limited by, 42–43, 47; on electoral college, 81; parliamentary system compared to, 28, 37; and party function, 24–25, 33, 47, 48; and party regulation, 156, 174–97; on presidency, 79, 81–82; and public funding, 311–19; 1st Amendment to, 143, 156, 179, 180, 185, 189, 191, 192, 233, 289, 299, 311–12; 14th Amendment to, 175, 176, 178, 179, 180, 181, 182, 185, 186, 187, 189, 192, 233, 312; 15th Amendment to, 174, 175, 176, 178, 187; 17th Amendment to, 186; 19th Amendment to, 175. *See also* Separation of powers doctrine
Convention: district, 89, 90; midterm (mini), 213–14; state, 89, 90, 146–47, 149, 150, 192, 346, 385, 386; for state office, 146–47

Convention, national (nominating), 34, 191, 214; affirmative action in, 215; brokered, 93, 95; compromise candidate in, 93; as confederative, 226; consensual candidate in, 93, 94; courts on, 226; credentials dispute in, 209, 227–28 (*see also* Delegate selection); dark-horse candidate in, 93; defended, 93; delegates to (*see* Delegates; Delegate selection); Democratic, 97–98, 107–8, 193, 204; factionalism in, 93; as federative, 207–8; national party role in, 217; nominating role of, 43–44, 86–87, 88, 89–95, 105, 139, 202–3, 204, 209; proportional representation in, 108; public funding for, 198, 217, 226, 314, 317, 320; Republican, 204, 215, 222; state/local party role in, 202–3, 222; two-thirds rule in, 204, 209; unit rule in, 204, 209; 1984, 97–98, 107. *See also* Caucus
Converse, Philip E., 401, 404
Conway, M. Margaret, 223, 398
Cook County Democratic party, 135, 331, 332
Cooper, Joseph, 368, 372
Corrupt Practices Act of 1925, 409
Cotter, Cornelius P., 151, 152, 206, 380, 387, 388, 395, 396, 397, 398, 410, 418
Courtney, John C., 394
Cousins v. Wigoda, 190, 195, 198, 229, 232, 233, 234; associational rights in, 191, 228; national party over state regulations in, 227–28, 231
Crewe, Ivor, 406
Croly, Herbert, 15, 360
Cronin, Thomas E., 373
Crotty, William J., 41, 210–11, 357, 364, 375, 396, 408, 409, 410, 411
Cuomo, Mario, 149

Dahl, Robert, 22, 23, 361
Dahl v. Republican State Committee, 393
Daley, Richard, 139, 140–41, 142–43, 227, 231
Dallinger, Frederick W., 161–62, 389, 390
Dauer, Manning J., 395
David, Paul T., 377
Davis, Eric L., 380
Dealignment, 262, 266–67, 270. *See also* Identification with party, decline in
Debates, presidential, 379
Decentralization: of Congress, 48–53, 54, 70, 77, 78, 120; of parties, 23, 26, 27, 33, 43, 48–53, 54, 201, 203, 205
de Gaulle, Charles, 378–79
Deinstitutionalization, 189–90, 346
Delegates: committed, 91, 97, 98, 170, 231; ex officio, 107, 108, 212; favorite-son, 91, 97; uncommitted, 91, 97–98, 106–7, 108
Delegate selection, 89, 96, 204; affirmative action in, 215, 229, 231; by caucus-convention,

Delegate selection (*continued*)
90, 91, 97, 105, 160–61, 212–13, 226, 229, 230; credentials in, 209, 227–28; Democratic rules for, 107–8, 209–11, 212, 213, 223, 227, 229, 231–32, 235–36; as nationalizing mechanism, 210–11, 212, 223; national party role in, 91, 191, 193, 205, 209–14, 215, 226, 227–28, 229–35, 236; national regulation of, 227; by primaries, 89, 91, 97, 98–99, 105, 170, 215, 226, 231–31; Republican rules for, 209, 215; state party role in, 90, 203; state regulations for, 191, 193, 205, 209–14, 226, 227–28; Supreme Court on, 227–28, 232–33; in Wisconsin, 230–33

Democratic Congressional Campaign Committee, 61

Democratic-Farmer-Labor party, 149. *See also* Farmer-Labor party

Democratic National Committee (DNC), 85, 115, 195, 200; ads by, 224; campaign services of, 224; chairman's role on, 214, 225; Compliance Review Commission of, 213; composition of, 214; as confederative, 123; fundraising by, 216, 224, 236, 302; headquarters of, 212, 214; midterm convention of, 213–14; on open primaries, 229, 236; on party reform, 210, 377; public funding for, 314, 338, 339; on public funding, 336; voter-registration drive by, 224; v. Wisconsin state party, 229–30, 231, 236. *See also* Democrats

Democratic Party of the United States v. Wisconsin ex rel La Follette, 191, 193, 194, 195, 197, 198, 232, 233, 234, 400

Democratic Republicans, 203

Democratic Senatorial Campaign Committee, 61

Democrats: black voters as, 267; on caucuses, 98, 100, 229–30; charter of, 213–14, 235; coalition, 267; cohesion of, 69; as confederative, 209, 211, 213–14, 225, 235, 236; in Congress, 41, 42, 50–51, 54, 55, 56, 57–58, 61, 68–69, 72, 78, 224, 291, 304, 349 (*see also* Congressional parties); counterreform by, 104, 212; delegate-selection rules of, 107–8, 209–11, 212, 213, 223, 227, 229, 231–32, 235–36; direct-mail solicitation by, 223, 236; funding and, 237–38, 301, 334; label of, 242–45, 250, 251, 329; as liberal, 126; local, 135, 142, 331, 332; as mass participation party, 237, 258; minor parties merge with, 125, 131; national conventions of, 97–98, 107–8, 193, 204; national, 102, 207, 208, 209–16, 223–25, 231–32, 235, 236, 237–38, 306 (*see also* Democratic National Committee); on nominating process, 96, 103–4; on nonparty identifiers, 229; and PACs, 238, 293, 295–96; porousness of, 78; in South, 129, 171; state, 125–26, 150,

152, 190, 192, 229–30, 231–32, 236; states' rights background of, 204, 209; Whigs v., 83, 84, 124

Dennis, Jack, 261, 379, 403, 404, 405, 406

Deregulation of parties, 157, 197–99, 345

DeVries, Walter, 370

Dewey, Thomas E., 279

Dilger, Robert, 387, 388, 390, 398

Direct-mail solicitation, 110, 276–77, 280; congressional parties use, 61, 284; Democrats use, 223, 236; disadvantages of, 284; as ideological, 237, 281–82; PACs use, 237, 292, 296; Republicans use, 61, 206, 217–18, 237, 282; of small contributions, 322–33; by state parties, 218

Dixiecrats, 209

Dorsett, Lyle W., 384

Downes, Randolph C., 375

Drew, Elizabeth, 415

Dues-paying party memberships, 168, 280, 281; activitist, 153; in cadre parties, 145, 146; in California and Wisconsin, 145, 150; in Europe, 4, 144, 145, 160

Duopoly. *See* Two-partyism

Dupeux, Georges, 401

Duverger, Maurice, 21, 22, 361, 384

Edwards, Pamela J., 387

Eisenhower, Dwight D., 67, 92, 93, 115; candidate-centered organization of, 109; elected monarch role of, 121; nonpartisan role of, 94, 120–21; as party leader, 121; presidential party of, 85; relations with Congress of, 119

Eisenhower Center, 218

Eismeier, Theodore J., 413, 414

Elazar, Daniel J., 400

Eldersveld, Samuel J., 23, 152, 361, 382, 384, 385, 387

Election campaigns, congressional, 284; as candidate-centered, 70, 73, 74, 77, 78, 275, 343; Democratic spending on, 304; direct primaries for, 70, 72; electoral base for, 70, 71, 74, 77; campaign finance legislation on, 303, 306–7; individual contributions to, 275, 279, 355; leaners in, 260; as local, 71–72; machines on, 141; PACs fund, 289–90, 293, 295, 298; party role in, 141, 293, 303, 306–7, 338; public funding for, 38, 335–37, 338, 339–40, 355; Republican spending on, 221, 222, 223, 303–4, 307, 338

Election campaigns, local: as antiparty, 13–14; candidate-centered, 128; congressional elections as, 71–72; minor parties in, 127, 128, 132; as nonpartisan, 13, 126–28, 162; as one-party, 128–30; states regulate, 126–28

Election campaigns, presidential, 72, 79, 83–84, 108–13, 242; candidate in, 87, 92, 93, 95, 103, 112, 202 (*see also* President; Presidential party); as candidate-centered, 71, 108–13; direct popular, 81, 82; by primaries (*see* Primaries, presidential (preferential)); public funding for, 198, 226, 313–14, 316, 319–21, 322, 324–25, 326. *See also* Nominating process

Election campaigns, state, 30, 152, 308; candidate-centered, 128, 133, 154; conventions in, 146–47, 169; for governor, 222, 280, 328; labels in, 124, 133, 243–44; large contributions in, 279–80; nonpartisan, 84, 126, 345–46; one-party, 128–30, 153; primaries in, 155, 163, 166, 167, 169, 174, 176, 184–85, 188, 189, 198, 222; private spending on, 218, 219, 221–22, 280

Electoral college, 81–82, 202–3, 372
Electoral party. *See* Identification with party
Electorate. *See* Voters
Elliott, Lee Ann, 287, 411
Ellwood, John W., 410–11, 414
Elrod v. Burns, 384, 391
Endorsements, 154, 346; preprimary, 148–49, 195–96; state regulates, 150, 195–96
Enrollment. *See* Registration, party
Epstein, Edwin M., 411
Epstein, Laurily K., 404
European parties/politics, 12, 156, 394; campaign methods in, 270, 273, 274; centralized, 27; class-based, 136, 249; dues-paying, 4, 144, 145, 160; ideological, 136; mass, 4, 136, 144, 145, 146; media used by, 269–70, 342; as multiparty, 131, 241; publicly funded, 198–99, 273, 330, 332, 340
Evans, Eldon Cobb, 389
Everson, David H., 67, 369, 404, 406
Executive Office staff, 118
Exit polls, 250, 253, 267
Extragovernmental party organizations, 12, 16, 134, 333, 343. *See also* Cadre parties; Democratic National Committee; Machines; Republican National Committee
Extralegal parties, 145, 150

Fahey v. Darigan, 393
Fahrenkopf, Frank, 219
Fairlie, Dennis, 403
Farah, Barbara G., 375
Farley, James A., 115
Farmer-Labor party, 125, 132, 149
Fay, James S., 389
Federal Election Campaign Act of 1971, 287–88
Federal Election Commission (FEC), 226, 286, 294, 318; on Anderson, 314; on PACs, 286, 288, 289, 319; on public funding, 335

Federal Election Commission v. Democratic Senatorial Campaign Committee, 415
Federal Election Commission v. National Conservative PAC, 319, 412, 417
Federalists, 11, 83
Feigert, Frank B., 368
Fellman, David, 391
Fenno, Richard, 76, 372
Ferejohn, John A., 370
Ferency v. Austin, 399
Finch, Gerald B., 408
Finer, Herman, 20, 360
Finkel, Steven E., 385, 402
Finland, 79, 340
Fiorina, Morris P., 371
First National Bank of Boston v. Bellotti, 412
Flanigan, William H., 369, 370, 403, 406, 408
Fleishman, Joel L., 357
Florida, 195
Foley, Thomas, 335
Ford, Gerald, 66, 67, 104, 105, 119, 324
Ford, Henry Jones, 14, 18, 24–25, 358, 359, 361
France, 79, 113, 251, 274, 340
Francis, John G., 391
Frankfurter, Justice Felix, 178
Fredman, L. E., 389, 390
Freedom of association, 155, 157, 158–59, 160, 161, 162, 166, 167, 174, 179, 186, 188, 193–97, 225, 231; as constitutional right, 185, 189, 192, 233; Supreme Court on, 143, 190–91, 192, 197, 227, 228, 233, 234
Frenzel, Bill, 307
Friedrich, Carl J., 20, 360
Frutig, Jennifer W., 416, 418, 419, 420

Gallaher, Miriam, 366
Gallup polls, 250, 254, 258
Garfield, James, 277
George, Henry, 164
Georgia, 176–77, 181–82, 183
Georgia v. National Democratic Party, 398
Gerrymandering, 370
Gibson, James L., 151, 152, 387, 395
Giscard d'Estaing, Valéry, 378–79
Gladerisi, Peter F., 387
Goldman, Ralph M., 239
Goldwater, Barry, 94, 99; as ideological candidate, 281–82, 322
Goodnow, Frank J., 18, 359
Governors: campaign for, 222, 280, 328; minor-party, 124, 125; as party leaders, 134, 151; parties formed by, 133
Gramm, Phil, 57–58, 367
Grant, U. S., 92, 94, 112
Great Britain: cabinet in, 48, 114; campaign financing in, 273; candidate-centered politics in,

Great Britain (*continued*)
113, 274; civil service in, 136, 159; cohesion in, 36, 37; Conservative party in, 207, 241, 262, 273; constituency impact in, 71; extraparliamentary parties in, 83; finance legislation in, 308–9; free air time in, 342; House of Commons in, 36, 43–44, 45–46, 48, 53, 365; Labour party in, 36, 241, 262, 273; Liberal party in, 262; mass parties in, 136; minor party significance in, 241; as multiparty, 131; parliamentary system in (*see* Parliamentary system); partisan ballots in, 156; parties in, 5, 12, 15–16, 24, 25, 29, 40, 41, 46, 79, 136, 159, 200; party-centered campaigns in, 273; party leaders in, 36, 37, 114; party loyalty in, 36, 262; prime minister in, 37; responsible-party government in, 29, 36
Greeley, Andrew M., 405
Greenstein, Fred I., 120–21, 380, 403
Grodzins, Morton, 361, 394
Grovey v. Townsend, 391
Gump, W. Robert, 384
Gunlicks, Arthur B., 421

Hadley, Charles D., 386, 412
Hall, Arnold Bennett, 14, 15
Hamilton, Alexander, 40
Hamilton, John D. M., 207
Hanna, Mark, 205, 278
Hardin, Charles M., 37, 47, 364, 365
Harding, Warren, G., 93–94, 375
Harmel, Robert, 357
Harris, Fred, 210
Harrison, Martin, 422
Hart, Gary, 295, 322, 324, 378
Hatch Act, 409
Hauss, Charles, 401
Hawaii, 330
Hawley, Willis D., 359
Hays, Samuel P., 359
Hays, Will, 207
Heard, Alexander, 410
Heavey v. Chapman, 193, 197
Hebert, F. Edward, 366
Heclo, Hugh, 118–19, 380
Hennessy, Bernard C., 206, 395, 410
Herring, Pendleton, 27–29, 71, 362, 370
Hershey, Marjorie Randon, 368
Hess, Stephen, 118, 379, 380
Hill, Kim Quaile, 416
Hinckley, Barbara, 62–63, 75, 366, 367, 368, 371, 406
Hoadley, John F., 367
Hofstadter, Richard, 170, 358, 383, 390
Holcombe, Arthur N., 25–26, 357, 361, 401
Holmes, Justice Oliver W., 165, 166, 197
Hoogenboom, Ari, 382, 389

Hoover, Herbert, 94, 104, 105
House Democratic Caucus, 50–51, 54, 69. *See also* Congressional parties
House of Representatives: campaign committees in, 236; campaigns for (*see* Election campaigns, congressional); decentralized, 77, 78; Democrats in, 50–51, 54, 55, 57–58, 61, 63, 69, 72, 78, 224, 291, 304; incumbents in, 73–74, 75–76; institutionalized, 50, 51; legislative caldendar of, 59; legislative power of, 45, 47; PACs and, 290, 298; partisan turnover in, 72–73; party caucus in (*see* Congressional parties, caucuses of); party leadership in, 54, 56, 59, 64; party voting in, 62–63; president chosen by, 86; Republicans in, 56, 63, 66, 78; seniority in, 50–51, 52; standing committees of, 48–49, 50, 51, 58, 59, 60; subcommittees of, 48, 49, 51, 78. *See also* Congress; Congressional parties; Election campaigns, congressional
House Republican Conference, 54
Howe, Daniel Walker, 372–73
Hrebenar, Ronald J., 407
Huckshorn, Robert J., 151–52, 387, 391, 395
Huitt, Ralph K., 367
Hull, Cordell, 115
Humphrey, Hubert, 95, 210
Hunt Commission, 212
Huntington, Samuel, 372
Hurley, Patricia A., 368

Ickes, Harold, 115
Idaho, 229, 329, 330
Identification with party, 239–71; age as factor in, 264–65; candidate-centered organizations affect, 263, 268; decline in, 4, 7, 74, 75, 240, 254–55, 256–63, 264–65, 271; defined, 401; Democratic, 250, 329; economic level as factor in, 267; education level as factor in, 265; family influences, 407; ideology as factor in, 265–66; as Independent, 246, 250; influence of, 241; labels and, 239, 240, 241; leaders mobilize, 240–41, 253, 254, 263; measured, 250–56; not required, 229–30; polls on, 250, 251–52, 254, 258, 267; as public, 245–46; and registration, 246–48, 254–55, 402; Republican, 250, 253, 329; as self-identified, 240; stability of, 240, 241, 252–54; strong, 5, 251, 258, 260; technology affects, 268–70; transient, 253; and unaffiliated voters, 229, 246; and voting behavior, 252–53, 254, 259–60; weak, 258, 259, 260, 265
Ideology, 111, 126; of activists, 85, 173; alignment based on, 266–67, 268; in cabinet appointments, 117; of candidates, 94, 99, 106, 281–82, 322–23; in fundraising, 237, 281–82;

in party identification, 265–68; public funding and, 322–23, 332. *See also* Political action committees, ideological
Illinois, 127, 143, 182, 183, 185, 186, 187–88, 227–28, 332. *See also* Chicago
Illinois v. Socialist Workers Party, 392
Impeachment powers, 44, 87
Incumbents, 61, 104–5, 238, 261, 291, 300, 307; congressional, 73–74, 75–76; and public funding, 335–36
Independent: candidates, 42, 173, 183–84, 254, 314, 315–16, 317, 324 (*see also* Minor parties); and party identification, 246, 250; voters, 75, 125, 126, 184, 185–87, 188–89, 194–95, 197, 198, 246, 250, 258–60, 264, 265
Independent Republican party, 149
Indiana, 146–47
Institutionalization, 341; of alignment, 271; by ballot, 162, 164, 173; of congressional parties, 43–47, 48–50, 51, 54–55, 57; of fundraising, 269; of labels, 244–45, 248–50, 262–63, 264; of progressive reform, 5; of state parties, 7, 151–53, 154; of two-partyism, 131
Interest groups, 16, 32, 97, 106, 116, 279; parties differ from, 21–22. *See also* Political action committees
Iowa: caucuses, 96, 97, 100, 101, 102, 106, 212–13; party identification in, 402; state funding in, 329, 330, 331, 332, 337; state parties in, 332, 337
Issue-orientation. *See* Ideology
Italy, 340

Jackson, Andrew, 86, 136; political era of, 11, 89, 374
Jackson, Jesse, 324, 378, 418
Jacobson, Gary C., 41, 364, 412, 413, 414, 415
James, Judson, 361, 362
Janda, Kenneth, 201, 357, 394
Japan, 340
Jaybird Democratic Association, 177–78, 179
Jefferson, Thomas, 358, 372
Jeffersonians, 83
Jenness v. Fortson, 392
Jennings, M. Kent, 407
Jensen, Richard, 109, 378, 405
Jessup, David, 371
Jewell, Malcolm E., 148–49, 331, 381, 382, 385, 386, 387, 402, 420
Johnson, Andrew, 44
Johnson, Lyndon B., 56, 65, 66, 67, 87, 119, 266, 319
Johnson, Michael, 384
Johnson, Sonia, 317
Jones, Charles O., 365, 366, 377, 378

Jones, Ruth S., 330–31, 398, 410, 412, 413, 415, 418, 419, 420
Judd, Dennis R., 382, 383

Kansas, 402
Karl, Barry D., 358, 359
Kaufman, Herbert, 359, 383
Kayden, Xandra, 237, 357, 400, 401
Kazee, Thomas H., 386
Keefe, William J., 27, 62, 362, 368
Kefauver, Estes, 92, 93
Keith, Bruce E., 405
Kendall, Willmoore, 26–27, 358, 361
Kennedy, Edward, 324
Kennedy, John F., 67, 85, 92, 109–10, 115, 119, 266
Kentucky, 163, 329, 330
Kessel, John H., 85, 112, 117, 373, 377, 378, 379, 380, 385, 396
Kester, John, 174–75, 178, 391
Key, V. O., Jr., 24, 29–30, 390; on national parties, 200, 394, 395; on party identification, 239–40, 401; on primaries, 130, 146, 381, 385; and responsible party government, 31, 362
King, Anthony, 364, 373
King, Elizabeth G., 420
Kingdon, John W., 64, 369
Kirkpatrick, Evron M., 363, 364
Kirkpatrick, Jeane J., 95, 375, 407
Kleppner, Paul, 403
Koch, Edward, 149
Kobrak, Peter, 399
Koenig, Louis W., 109, 110, 378
Kousser, J. Morgan, 390
Kundanis, George, 367
Kusper v. Pontikes, 185, 386

Labels, party, 5–6, 8, 61, 70, 134, 241–50, 343, 344; attachment to, 249; on ballots, 162, 163, 164, 165, 172, 173, 181, 243–44, 250; as class-representative, 249; continuity/durability of, 241–42, 249; as cues, 242, 243, 250, 262, 263, 264, 271; cultural values expressed by, 249; eliminated, 126, 127 (*see also* Nonpartisanship); historical emphasis on, 242; and identification with party, 239, 240, 241; institutionalized, 244–45, 248–50, 262–63, 264; and legal status of parties, 156; as nationalizing mechanism, 243; polls on, 250; and registration, 245–46; relevance of, 245, 249, 264; stability of, 260, 261; in state elections, 124, 133; and two-partyism, 124, 241, 242–45, 250, 251, 262–63; voting behavior determined by, 133, 249
Labor unions. *See* Political action committees, union; Unions

Labour party (British), 36, 241, 262, 273
Ladd, Everett C., 96, 265, 375, 407
La Follette, Bronson C., 231, 232. See also
    Democratic Party of the United States v. Wiscon-
    sin ex rel La Follette
La Follette, Philip F., 125, 382
La Follette, Robert M. Jr., 125
La Follette, Robert M. Sr., 125, 170–71, 230; as
    minor-party candidate, 132, 243, 262, 315
La Follette v. Democratic Party of the United States,
    400
Lance, Bert, 116, 117
Langone v. Commonwealth, 196, 197, 394
Laslett, John H. M., 382
Latus, Margaret Ann, 413
Lawson, Kay, 378, 387, 393
Laxalt, Paul, 219, 307
Laxalt-Frenzel bill, 307, 415
Leadership, party, 29–30; in Canada, 201;
    Carter's, 121; congressional, 49–50, 51, 54–
    57, 58, 59, 60, 61, 64, 65, 87–88; guberna-
    torial, 134, 151; as nationalizing mechanism,
    33; party identification as response to, 240–
    41, 253, 254, 263; by president, 15, 28,
    35–36, 37, 38, 87–88, 103, 114, 121, 267;
    Reagan's, 66, 68, 85, 103, 111, 121, 253,
    267
Leaners, 258, 259–260, 261, 265, 344
Legislative parties, 40–41, 79, 133, 394
Lehrman, Lewis, 149
Levine, E. Lester, 386
Levitin, Teresa E., 405
Liberal party (British), 262
Liberal party (New York), 124, 132, 381
Libertarian party, 132
Lieber, Francis, 11, 358
Lincoln, Abraham, 82, 94, 114
Lipset, Seymour M., 265, 359, 382, 401, 407
Lobbying, 206, 285, 297. See also Political action
    committees
Local parties, 28, 31, 123–54, 200, 331, 332;
    campaign role of, 269, 304–5; and candidate-
    centered organizations, 112, 235; candidate in-
    dependence from, 208; and congressional poli-
    tics, 141; constituent-oriented, 72; delegate se-
    lection by, 90, 91, 203, 215, 227–28, 229–35,
    236; and national parties, 141; nominating
    role of, 202–3, 235; as weak, 95; voter drives
    by, 304–5. See also Machines
Long, Russell, 319, 320
Longley, Charles H., 216, 237, 397
Loomis, Burdett A., 366
Louisiana, 176; nonpartisan system in, 147, 345–
    46, 385–86, 422
Lowell, A. Lawrence, 16, 18, 24, 360, 368
Lowi, Theodore J., 87, 373, 394, 422

Loyalty, party, 4–5, 7, 8, 12, 28, 239, 240, 255,
    256, 263; British, 36, 262. See also Identifica-
    tion with party; Machine; Voting,
    straight-ticket
Lynch v. Torquato, 393
Lynn, Naomi B., 371

McCarthy, Eugene, 92, 100, 416
McClure, Robert D., 408
McCormick, Richard L., 383, 390
McCormick, Richard P., 83–84, 372, 395
McGovern, George, 85, 93, 100, 101, 103, 106,
    111, 323; as ideological candidate, 99, 281–82,
    322
McGovern-Fraser Commission, 96, 97, 210–11,
    227, 231, 376
Machines, 4, 12, 33, 134–44, 199, 270; busi-
    nesses and, 134, 137, 138–39; cadre parties
    compared to, 144, 145; city, 13–14, 139, 140–
    41, 142–43; and congressional elections, 141;
    as corrupt, 139, 159; Daley's, 139, 140–41,
    142–43, 227, 231; decline of, 141–43; and
    direct primary, 7, 139–40; as extragovernmen-
    tal, 25, 159; goals of, 140; governing by,
    138–39, 159; hostility to, 13–14, 135–36, 159,
    163, 170–71; and immigrants, 138; are local,
    72, 140–41, 153; loyalty to, 138; mass fran-
    chise as basis of, 136; New Deal affects, 140,
    141–42; nominating role of, 139, 147, 148,
    154, 159, 170; as nonideological, 140; patron-
    age as basis of, 13, 136–37, 141, 142, 153,
    159, 384; reform of, 13, 17, 127, 135, 137,
    139–40, 159, 170–71; Republican, 139; ser-
    vices of, 137–39, 140; state, 135; and state
    funding, 331–32; as vote-getting organiza-
    tions, 135, 136, 139
Machinists Non-Partisan Political League, 291
MacIver, Robert M., 20–21, 361
McKinley, William, 278
McLain v. Meier, 392
Macmahon, Arthur W., 16, 360
McNutt, Andrew D., 148, 149, 386
Macy, Jesse, 18, 360, 368, 383, 390
Madison, James, 11, 159, 358
Magleby, David B., 405
Mahe, Eddie, Jr., 357
Maine, 330
Major parties, 181–82; ballot access for, 180,
    198, 243–44; defined, 313, 315, 316; minor
    parties merge with, 125, 131, 132; public
    funding for, 198, 313–17, 319, 324–25, 340–
    41; states protect, 184. See also Democratic
    National Committee; Democrats; Republican
    National Committee; Republicans
Malbin, Michael J., 365, 372, 397, 398, 400,
    410, 411, 413–14, 415, 418, 419, 421

Manatt, Charles, 214, 225
Manley, John F., 380
Mann, Thomas E., 75, 365, 371, 397, 398, 412
Marchioro v. Chaney, 191–92, 193
Marcus, George E., 407
Marcus, Robert D., 395
Markus, Gregory B., 407
Marshall, Thomas R., 385, 387
Martino, Ann, 387, 388, 390, 398
Maryland, 326, 330
Massachusetts, 149, 164, 165, 166, 167, 196–97, 330
Mass parties, 4, 21, 23, 29, 136, 144, 145, 146, 236; Democrats as, 237, 258
Maxey v. Washington State Democratic Committee, 393
Mayhew, David, 369, 371
Media: candidate-centered organizations enhanced by, 6, 113, 268–69; cost of, 279; free, 341–42; in Europe, 269–70, 342; impact of, 100–102, 268–69, 279; nationalization effect of, 207; parties affected by, 95, 268–69, 270–71; president uses, 120; on primaries, 95, 101, 105; voting behavior affected by, 268. *See also* Television
Membership, party, 5, 200–201; dues-paying, 4, 144, 145, 146, 150, 153, 160, 168, 280, 281; mass, 4, 21, 23, 29, 136, 144, 145, 146, 236; national, 234–35; Republican, 236; self-defined, 160–61; Supreme Court on, 234–35; voters counted as, 167. *See also* Identification with party; Registration, party
Merriam, Charles E., 15, 18, 148, 161, 165, 359, 360, 386, 389, 390
Merton, Robert K., 138, 383
Michels, Robert, 17, 22, 360, 364
Michigan, 162, 166; caucus, 229; state funding in, 327, 328, 330, 332
Mikva, Abner, 335, 336
Miller, Warren E., 401, 403, 405, 406, 407, 413
Millspaugh, Arthur Chester, 389, 390
Minnesota, 126, 150; caucus, 149; Farmer-Labor party in, 125, 132, 149; state funding in, 327, 328, 330, 332
Minor parties, 40; ballot access for, 165, 173, 180–84, 198, 244; in Congress, 42; disadvantaged/discouraged, 131, 183, 243, 244, 262; gubernatorial candidates of, 124, 125; in local elections, 127, 128, 132; merge with major parties, 125, 131, 132; in other countries, 124, 241, 245; percentage of votes for, 315; presidential candidates of, 99, 124, 132, 183–84, 243, 244, 254, 262, 314, 315, 380–81; primaries deter, 131–32, 173; public funding for, 314–16, 317, 324; regional, 124; short-lived, 132; single-state, 132; at state level, 124–25,

126, 128, 132, 153, 182, 183, 243, 381; state regulations on, 173, 180–81, 345
Minton, Justice Sherman, 178
Missouri, 162
Mitau, G. Theodore, 391
Mitterand, François, 378–79
Mondale, Walter, 93, 98, 100, 107, 108, 112, 322, 324, 378, 417; on PACs, 295; unions help, 97, 106
Monroe, James, 358
Montana, 229
Moore, Jonathan, 376
Moore v. Ogilvie, 392
Moos, Malcolm, 395
Morehouse, Sarah McCally, 386
Morgenthau, Henry, 115
Multipartyism, 131, 241, 242, 345
Munn v. Illinois, 388
Muskie, Edmund, 298

NAACP, 190, 191
NAACP v. Alabama, 191
Nader, Nathra, 185–87, 188
Nader, Ralph, 185
Nader v. Schaffer, 185, 193, 194
Nathan, Richard P., 380
National Committee for an Effective Congress, 206, 285, 286
National Conservative Political Action Committee (NCPAC), 286, 290, 292, 296
National conventions. *See* Convention, national (nominating)
National Education Association PAC, 291
Nationalization mechanisms, 202, 205–6, 343; activists as, 146; campaigning as, 216, 223; delegate selection as, 210–11, 212, 223; funding as, 218, 222–23, 236; labels as, 243; leadership as, 33; media as, 207; nominating process as, 207–8; PACs as, 300
National parties, 31, 200–38, 290, 326, 338, 341, 351, 354; as associations, 225; between-election roles of, 86, 204; cadre parties as, 146; campaign role of, 83–84, 112, 173, 205, 292; as confederative, 7, 200, 201, 202, 204, 205, 206, 209, 211, 213–14, 225, 235; congressional parties as, 41, 85; in convention (*see* Convention, national (nominating)); decentralized, 203, 205; delegate selection by, 209, 210, 211, 212, 215, 227–28, 229–35, 236; development of, 83, 84, 202–8, 235; campaign finance legislation on, 226, 282, 293, 301–3, 306–7; functions of, 204, 205; fund state parties, 153, 218, 221–22, 235, 305; headquarters of, 206, 207 (*see also* Democratic National Committee; Republican National Committee); institutionalized, 207, 225; legal status of,

National parties (*continued*)
  225–35; national committees of, 85–86, 112,
  204–5, 206, 217, 219, 225, 282, 293–94, 301–
  3, 306–7, 319, 320 (*see also* Democratic National Committee; Republican National Committee); national regulation of, 225–26; nominating role of, 102, 217; nonpresidential activities of, 325; PACs fund, 293–94; in parliamentary systems, 83; as presidential in focus,
  35, 84, 85, 219 (*see also* Presidential parties);
  professionalized, 237; public funding for, 319,
  320; and state parties, 6, 128, 141, 153, 155,
  191, 201, 202, 205, 209, 211, 212–13, 221–22,
  229–30, 231, 235, 236, 242–43, 303, 304,
  305, 308; and state regulations, 191, 193, 205,
  209–14, 226, 227–28, 229–35; strength of,
  201, 208. *See also* Democrats; Republicans
National Republican Congressional Committee
  (NRCC), 61, 76, 218, 219, 220, 223, 236, 303
National Republicans, 203
National Republican Senatorial Committee
  (NRSC), 60–61, 218, 219, 220, 223, 236
National Rifle Association PAC, 286
Nebraska, 125, 126, 133
Nelson, Candice J., 371, 405
Nelson, Garrison, 367
Neumann, Sigmund, 22, 361
Neustadt, Richard E., 43, 86, 99, 120, 365,
  373, 374, 376, 380
New Deal, 27, 28, 29, 140, 141–42, 266
New Hampshire primary, 100, 101, 102, 212–
  13
New Jersey, state funding in, 327, 328, 330, 331
New York, 332; direct primary in, 146, 147,
  168, 185; endorsements in, 149; indirect pri-
  mary in, 166–67; minor parties in, 124, 132,
  381; nominating process in, 161–62; party
  registration in, 167, 185, 186, 246, 247
Newberry v. United States, 391
Nick, Rainer, 412
Nie, Norman H., 261–62, 406, 407
Nixon, Richard M., 44, 66, 67, 85, 94, 105,
  112, 115, 118, 119; candidate-centered organization of, 110, 111, 279
Nixon v. Condon, 391
Nixon v. Herndon, 391
Nominating process, 80, 88–108, 132; abuses in,
  161; activists in, 34–35; cadre parties in, 150–
  51; caucus role in, 43, 86, 87, 89, 90, 202,
  203; Congress in, 43, 44, 86, 87, 89, 107,
  202, 203, 234; counterreform of, 102–8; democratized, 81–82, 83, 87, 88–89, 90–91, 99,
  102, 105, 160, 169, 210; deregulation of, 197–
  99; funding role in, 150–51, 323–24, 328; incumbent in, 104–5; machines' role in, 139,
  147, 148, 154, 159, 170; media influences,

100–101; nationalization of, 7, 207–8; national
  party's role in, 34–35, 43–44, 86–87, 88, 89–
  96, 98, 102, 103–4, 105, 106–7, 146, 147–48,
  165, 168, 174, 202–3, 204, 209, 212, 217,
  321, 323, 328, 333, 343; for nonincumbent,
  103; in other countries, 156, 168; peer review
  in, 89, 93, 94, 103; plebiscitary (post-1968),
  7, 94, 95–102, 103, 104, 108, 114, 121–22,
  208, 210, 215, 235, 323; by primary (*see* Primary, direct; Primary, presidential (preferential)); reform of, 95–96, 102–3, 111, 207, 210;
  state/local parties' role in, 70, 86, 146–47,
  153–54, 202–3, 235; states regulate, 147, 155,
  161–62, 163, 165–66, 169–70, 174, 182–83,
  226, 346; by state convention, 89, 90, 169;
  Supreme Court on, 190; timing of events in,
  101–2; voters control, 95. *See also* Ballot;
  Candidate; Convention, national; Delegate selection; Primary, direct; Primary, presidential
  (preferential)
Nonpartisanship, 358; of ballot, 14, 126–27, 156,
  164, 388; of local elections, 13, 126–28, 162;
  in Louisiana, 147, 345–46, 385–86; of presidency, 80, 82, 87, 94, 108, 114, 120–21, 122;
  in primaries, 345–46; in state elections, 84,
  345–46
Noragon, Jack L., 418, 419
Norris, George, 359
North Carolina, 328–29, 330
Norton, Philip, 367
Norway, 156
NRA Political Victory Fund, 286

Obey-Railsback bill, 298
O'Brien v. Brown, 399
O'Connor, Justice Sandra Day, 417
Office of Congressional Relations, 119–20
Ohio, 162; minor-party candidates in, 181, 183–
  84
Oklahoma, 326, 328
Oligarchy, iron law of, 17, 364
Olson, David M., 44, 331, 365, 367, 381, 385,
  386, 402, 420
O'Neill, Thomas P., 56, 67
One-partyism, 133, 243; in Chicago, 139; direct
  primary and, 129–30, 132, 146, 173; in local
  elections, 128–30; in North, 130–31; social
  basis of, 130; in South, 30, 129, 130, 171; in
  state elections, 128–30, 153
Oregon, 326, 330
Ornstein, Norman J., 365, 366, 368, 369, 370,
  371, 397, 398, 412
Orr, Elizabeth, 405
Orren, Gary R., 418
Ostrogorski, Moisey Y., 15–16, 17, 19, 22, 25,
  360, 364

Overacker, Louise, 148, 161, 165, 359, 386, 389, 390

PACs. *See* Political action committees
Paltiel, Khayyam Zev, 409, 421
Parker, Joan A., 406
Parliamentary system, 28, 33, 136, 340; cabinet in, 48, 114; candidate-centered organizations in, 113, 274; Congress compared to, 36, 41, 43–44, 45–46, 48, 53, 62, 79; executive in, 79, 84, 373–74; leadership in, 36, 114; parties in, 40–41, 62, 79, 83
Parties: accomplishments of, 22–23, 25; activists in (*see* Activists); as agents of representation, 20–21; alignment (*see* Alignment; party); broad appeal of, 25–26; cadre (*see* Cadre parties); class-based, 14, 21, 136, 249, 276; coalitional, 27, 32; competing-teams concept of, 20, 30, 32–33, 329 (*see also* Two-partyism); dealignment of (*see* Dealignment); decentralized, 23, 26, 27, 33, 43, 48–53, 54, 201, 203, 205; decline, 3, 4, 13; defended, 22–23, 24–30; defined, 19–20, 21–22; deinstitutionalized, 189–90, 346; deregulated, 157, 197–99, 345; in-the-electorate (*see* Identification with party); as extragovernmental, 16, 134; functions of, 6, 11, 13, 17–19, 20, 21, 22, 24–25, 33, 268–71; future of, 344–45; historical role of, 24; hostility to (*see* Antipartyism); ideological, 136, 265–68, 332 (*see also* Candidates, ideological); as inevitable, 18, 19; institutionalized (*see* Institutionalization); interest groups differ from, 21–22; Jacksonian, 11, 89; labels (*see* Labels); legal status of, 156, 162, 163, 165–66, 225–35; as majoritarian, 32; as monopolies, 158 (*see also* One-partyism); movements become, 40–41, 131; as necessary evil, 11; organs of, 256; origin of, 40–41; patronage as basis of, 4, 134–35, 136–37, 159, 174; porousness of, 5, 6, 23, 78, 245, 343–44, 346; as private associations, 7, 155, 157, 158–59, 160, 161, 162, 163, 166, 167, 174, 179, 188, 189–91, 193–97, 225, 227; as public utilities, 7, 156–58, 162, 163, 166, 167, 168, 172, 189–90, 341, 345, 346; as quasi-governmental, 155; realignment of (*see* Realignment); regulation of (*see* Campaign finance legislation; Regulation; Regulation, state); renewal, 3, 38, 263 (*see also* Committee for Party Renewal); self-reform of, 161; separation of powers bridged by, 6, 24–25, 33; strengthened, 32, 39, 344; 19th-century, 4, 5, 11, 89, 137
Patman, Wright, 366
Patronage, 16, 18, 23, 33; assessment under, 135, 277–78; civil service reforms, 13; federal, 141, 142, 379, 384; machines based on, 13, 136–37, 141, 142, 153, 159, 384; parties based on, 4, 134–35, 136–37, 159, 174; Supreme Court on, 143; vote-getting and, 134–35
Patterson, Samuel C., 48–49, 365, 369, 382
Patterson, Thomas E., 408
Peabody, Robert L., 367
Pendleton Act, 137
Penner, Rudolph G., 380
Penniman, Howard R., 381, 388, 401, 409
Pennsylvania, 142, 162, 168, 190, 248, 332
Perkins, Frances, 115
Peskin, Allan, 374
Petrocik, John R., 261–62, 405, 406, 407
Pierson, James E., 407
Pinto-Duschinsky, Michael, 415
Plebiscitary system. *See* Primary, presidential (preferential), plebiscitary
Poage, W. R., 366
Policymaking: by activists, 34; by congressional parties, 42, 54, 59–60, 62–69, 78
Political action committees (PACs), 4, 8, 272, 283, 353; associational, 285, 286, 287, 292, 295–96, 299; association rights of, 289; business/corporate, 286, 287–88, 289, 292, 293, 295; candidate-created, 286; Congress on, 300; conservative, 237, 288–89, 290, 292, 296; consortium of, 291, 299; as corrupt, 294, 297, 300; challenge ceilings, 289, 318; defined, 286; Democrats and, 238, 293, 295–96; development of, 285, 289; direct-mail solicitation by, 237, 286, 292, 296; FEC on, 286, 288, 289, 319; campaign finance legislation on, 217, 282, 286–87, 288–89, 291, 293, 298–99, 300, 318, 319, 352; functions of, 296–97; fund candidate-centered organizations, 284, 287; fund congressional candidates, 289–90, 291, 293, 295, 298; funding by, 206, 284–94, 296, 299, 354; fund parties, 275, 293–94, 336–37; fundraising by, 206, 217, 282, 285–86, 287, 292, 352; ideological (nonconnected), 285, 286, 288–89, 290, 292, 296–97, 299; incumbents favored by, 238, 291, 300; independent spending by, 286, 288–89, 298–99, 302, 303, 304, 326; influence of, 291; in-kind services by, 290–91; legitimated, 287–88; and lobbies, 206, 297; multicandidate, 286; as national, 206, 300; negative ads by, 296; number of, 286; as participatory, 287; and parties, 284, 287, 292–93, 294, 296–97, 309, 336–37; payroll deduction used by, 287, 288, 292; politicians on, 295; polls on, 292; reaction to, 294–300; reformers on, 294, 297–98, 300; small, 299–300; states regulate, 286, 333, 334; union, 285, 286, 287–88, 289,

436

Index

Political action committees (PACs) (*continued*) 290, 292, 293, 295, 296; vote-getting drives by, 290, 296

Political scientists, 9–39; as pro-party, 17–18, 19–21, 23–29; and reform, 12–15; on responsible-party government, 30–37, 38

Pollock, Philip H., III, 413, 414

Polls, 95, 100; exit, 250, 253, 267; Gallup, 250, 254, 258; on labels, 250, 258; name-choice questions in, 251, 252; open-ended questions in, 251–52; on PACs, 292; on party identification, 240, 250, 251–52, 254, 258, 267

Polsby, Nelson W., 374, 375, 376, 377; on Congress, 44, 50, 51, 365, 366; on presidency, 114–16, 379, 380; on presidential nominations, 93, 103, 121, 373, 378

Pomper, Gerald M., 38, 357, 363, 364

Pompidou, Georges, 378–79

Populists, 131, 164

Postmaster general, 115, 379

Powell, Justice Lewis F., 234–35, 399, 400

Precinct captains, 137–38, 139, 142. *See also* Machines

President: as alignment basis, 241; ambiguity in, 80–88; and bureaucracy, 118–19; coattails of, 67, 72; and Congress, 44, 65–66, 67–68, 69, 81, 86–87, 119–20, 121, 122, 349; Constitution on, 79, 81–82; direct popular election of, 81, 82; elected monarch role of, 79, 81–82, 116, 120, 121, 122; electoral base of, 81, 87, 88, 120, 122, 202; as leader of party, 15, 28, 35–36, 37, 38, 84–85, 87–88, 103, 114, 121, 219, 267; mandate of, 35; media used by, 120; nominated (*see* Nominating process; Primary, presidential (preferential)); nonpartisan role of, 80, 82, 87, 94, 108, 114, 120–21, 122; in other countries, 79, 80; and party, 68, 82–83, 104–5, 111, 115, 123, 200, 241, 243; personal following of (*see* Presidential party); as realignment focus, 253; staff of, 118–20. *See also* Election campaigns, presidential

Presidential party, 6–7, 88, 200, 343; cabinet appointments from, 117; as candidate-centered, 42, 204; and congressional parties, 35, 84, 86–87; development of, 83–84; governmental role of, 113–21, 122; as ideological, 117; as national, 35, 84, 85, 112, 207, 219; and party, 85, 86, 114; and White House staff, 118; after 1968, 235

Price, David E., 338, 357, 415, 419, 421, 422

Price, Don K., 362

Price, Melvin, 366

Primary: caucus called, 160, 161–62; indirect, 166–67

Primary, direct, 4, 160, 167–74; abuse in, 175, 176; as antiparty, 155–56; APSA report on, 34; blanket, 193, 385–86, 393; and candidate-centered organizations, 46–47, 70, 72, 155, 156, 274, 346; closed, 34, 147–48, 172–73, 180, 184–89, 193, 194, 198, 246, 247, 248, 344; competition in, 129–30; in congressional races, 70, 72; in Connecticut, 146–47, 185–87, 188–89, 193, 194–95, 197, 198, 248, 403; constitutional challenges to, 174–75, 180, 185, 186, 187, 188, 189, 193, 194; criticized, 14–15; crossover, 188; as democratic, 169, 198; Independents vote in, 184, 185–87, 188–89, 194–95, 197, 198; in Indiana, 146–47; institutionalizes labels, 244–45; as local, 72; in Louisiana, 147, 385–86; machines affected by, 7, 139–40; matching funds for, 328; minor parties in, 131–32, 173; in New York, 146, 147, 166–67, 168, 185; nominating role of, 139, 146–48; nonpartisan, 345–46; for nonpresidential offices, 70, 72, 91, 99, 105, 169, 222; and one-partyism, 129–30, 132, 146, 173; open, 34, 126, 129, 147, 188, 193, 197, 385–86, 403; opening, 198, 344; optional, 168; partially open, 188–89, 194, 198, 403; parties and, 14– 15, 25, 146–48, 153–54, 168, 172–73, 184, 186, 244–45, 247, 343–44; political scientists on, 14–15; as progressive reform, 5, 14, 15, 25, 32, 139–40, 170; in South, 171, 174–79, 187; state-established/state-run, 155, 163, 166, 167, 169, 176, 187, 188, 189, 198, 222; state parties and, 146–47; states regulate, 7, 147; as state elections, 174, 176, 184–85, 187; Supreme Court on, 174, 175, 176, 180, 185, 186; two-partyism in, 30, 130–31; voter eligibility in, 171, 174–75, 176, 177–78, 184, 186, 187; whites-only, 171, 174–79, 187; in Wisconsin, 126, 130, 168. *See also* Primary, presidential

Primary, presidential (preferential), 89, 91, 95–102, 156; abandoned, 97, 98, 105, 106; caucus-convention system compared to, 96, 106; candidate-centered organizations in, 99; Congress on, 169; effectiveness of, 90–93; ideological candidates in, 99; media on, 95, 101, 105; in Michigan, 229; national party rules on, 98, 99; national (single), 88, 91, 108, 234; New Hampshire, 100, 101, 102, 212–13; nominating role of, 4, 90–91; open, 96, 215, 229–30, 231; plebiscitary (post-1968), 7, 88, 94, 95–102, 103, 104, 107, 108, 114, 121–22, 170, 208, 210, 215, 235, 323; progressivism and, 235; as reform, 99; regional, 108; states prefer, 170; timing of, 102; voter turnout in, 102, 106; winner-take-all, 215; in Wisconsin, 106, 229–30, 231, 232, 236

Progressive party, 315; in Wisconsin, 125–26, 132

Progressives, 24, 157–58; as antibusiness, 170–71; as antiparty, 5, 13, 170, 171, 235; reform by, 5, 14, 25, 32, 139–40, 170, 235; in Republican party, 115, 125–26

Protest: candidates, 255; movements, 129–30

Public Citizen Litigation Group, 185

Public utilities, 156, 157, 158; parties as, 7, 156–58, 162, 163, 166, 167, 168, 189–90, 341, 345, 346

Rakove, Milton, 141, 382, 383

Ranney, Austin, 38, 358, 359, 360, 362, 373, 374, 375, 390; on national parties, 211, 395, 396; on party reform, 159, 388, 389; on television, 268–69, 408; on traditional American parties, 26–27, 361

Rayside, David, 401

Reagan, Ronald, 67, 100, 101, 105, 112, 219, 324; cabinet of, 117; candidate-centered organization of, 111; and Congress, 119, 121; conservatism of, 267–68, 282; funding of, 288–89, 318, 322, 334, 417; as ideological candidate, 99; media used by, 120; as party leader, 66, 68, 85, 103, 111, 121, 253, 267; public support for, 121

Realignment, 74, 254, 261, 262, 267, 268, 344–45, 346; of congressional parties, 65–66, 68–69; president as focus of, 253. See also Identification with party, decline in

Realtors PAC, 286, 291

Redistricting, 74

Reform, 161; as antiparty, 5, 163–64, 301; of ballot, 14, 127, 162, 163, 164, 165, 168, 255; campaign finance legislation as, 111, 317, 327; civil service as, 13, 137, 159; by McGovern-Fraser Commission, 96, 97, 376; of machines, 13, 17, 127, 135, 137, 139–40, 159, 170–71; of nominating process, 95–96, 102–3, 111, 207, 210; of PACs, 294, 297–98, 300; political scientists on, 12–15; primary as, 99; progressive, 13–14, 170–71; public funding as, 310, 311, 317, 319, 327, 331–32, 333, 334

Registration (enrollment) party, 147, 166, 172; alignment recognized by, 248; labels and, 245–46; in New York, 167, 185, 186, 246, 247; and party identification, 245–48, 254–55, 402; switching, 185, 186

Regulation, local, 162

Regulation, national, 198, 225–26. See also Campaign finance legislation

Regulation, state, 7, 171–72, 387; as anti-machine, 159; as antiparty, 180; of ballot, 126–27, 162, 165–66, 180–81, 199; of campaign activity, 173; of caucuses, 161–62; constitutional challenges to, 174–97; of delegate selection, 191, 193, 205, 209–14, 215, 226,

227–28, 232–33, 234; of endorsements, 150, 195–96; on campaign financing, 275, 282, 303, 305, 307, 321, 326–27, 329; of local elections, 126–28; of minor parties, 173, 180–81, 345; of national parties, 173, 174, 191, 193, 205, 209–14, 226, 227–28, 229–35; of nominating process, 147, 155, 161–62, 163, 165–66, 169–70, 174, 182–83, 226, 346; of PACs, 286, 333, 334; of primary, 7, 147 (see also Primary, direct, state-established/state-run); as progressive reform, 157–58; of state parties, 189–96, 197, 226, 302; two-partyism favored by, 171–72, 180, 181–82, 183, 345; of voter eligibility, 171

Rehnquist, Justice William H., 234, 312, 314, 316, 400, 412

Reorganization Act of 1946, 49

Republican Governors Association, 222

Republican National Committee (RNC), 85, 109, 110, 195, 200; ad campaign by, 220; campaign role of, 221, 222, 235, 236, 238, 338; chairman of, 216, 219; as confederative, 123, 214, 215, 216, 221, 235; on delegate selection, 215; direct-mail solicitation by, 217–18, 237, 282; funding by, 206, 218, 219, 220–22, 223, 238, 325–26; fundraising by, 206, 215–16, 218, 224, 278, 284, 301, 325; headquarters of, 216, 218–19, 236–37, 270; literature of, 220; Local Elections Campaign Division of, 222; as nationalizing mechanism, 222–23; partybuilding by, 325; public funding for, 314, 338, 339; and state parties, 215, 216, 222, 235. See also Republicans

Republican Party of Connecticut v. Tashjian, 194, 392

Republicans, 83, 99; as cadre party, 216; caucus of, 98; as confederative, 203, 222, 223; in Congress, 41, 42, 56, 63, 66, 68, 69, 78, 221 (see also Congressional parties); conservatism of, 68, 267–68, 282; conventions of, 203–4, 215, 222; delegate selection by, 209; as elite, 216, 237; funding by, 153, 208, 215, 216–21, 222, 223, 237–38, 269, 290, 301, 303–4, 307, 308; fundraising by, 61, 110, 206, 305, 325; labels for, 242–45, 250, 251; machines of, 139; minor parties merge with, 125; national party structure of, 78, 207, 214–16 (see also Republican National Committee); number of, 103–4, 258; on party cause, 217, 219–20, 230; party identification of, 250, 253, 329; porousness of, 78; progressive wing of, 115, 125–26; on public funding, 311, 320, 334, 336, 337; southern, 69, 267; state organizations of, 130, 150, 152, 153, 190, 229

Responsible-party government, 6, 10, 23, 24, 25, 30–37, 40, 65–67, 72–73, 344, 345; activ-

438 Index

Responsible-party government (*continued*)
ists in, 36; APSA on, 34; British model of,
29, 36; decentralization in, 33; majoritarian
premise of, 32–33; as national, 31; political
scientists on, 30–37, 38; presidential leadership
in, 35–36, 38; at state level, 31, 133–34
Reuss, Henry, 335
Rhode Island, 191, 330
Rice v. Elmore, 391
Riker, William H., 394
Ripley, Randall B., 71–72, 77, 364, 366, 367,
368, 369, 370, 372
Ripon Society v. National Republican Party, 399
Robinson, Michael J., 376, 408
Roosevelt, Franklin D., 65, 85, 87, 94, 115, 119,
125, 126, 266
Roosevelt, Theodore, 132, 243, 262, 315, 320,
373, 417
Rosario v. Rockefeller, 185, 186, 386, 400
Rosenbloom, David H., 383
Rosenthal, Albert J., 416
Rothenberg, Lawrence S., 253, 254, 404
Rotunda, Ronald D., 399
Rousseau, Jean Jacques, 19, 20, 38, 364
Rundquist, Barry S., 366
Rusk, Jerrold G., 389, 401, 404

Sabato, Larry, 397, 398, 401, 411, 412, 413
Sait, E. M., 25, 361, 394
Saloma, John S., III, 363, 368
*San Francisco County Democratic Central Commit-
tee v. March Fong Eu,* 393
Sartori, Giovanni, 21, 361
Scalia, Antonin, 393
Scammon, Richard M., 403
Scarrow, Howard A., 381, 382, 385, 389, 390,
402
Schantz, Harvey L., 370
Schattschneider, E. E., 11, 32–34, 35, 36, 358,
363, 370
Schick, Allen, 365
Schier, Steven E., 375, 396
Schlesinger, Arthur, Jr., 5, 357
Schmitz, John G., 315
Schumpeter, Joseph, 360
Schwarz, John E., 365
Scoble, Harry M., 395
Scott, Gary L., 386
Scott, Ruth K., 407
Seligman, Lester G., 380
Senate: campaigns for (*see* Election campaigns,
congressional); conservative coalition in, 69;
Democrats in, 56; incumbents in, 75; leader-
ship of, 56; legislative calendar in, 59; parties
in (*see* Congressional parties); power in, 45,
47; seniority in, 51; staff of, 52; standing

committees in, 48, 49, 51, 53; subcommittees
in, 48, 49. *See also* Congress
Senate Democratic Conference, 54
Senate Republican Conference, 54
Seniority. *See* Congress, seniority in
Separation of powers doctrine, 6, 36, 79, 89;
candidate-centered politics based on, 270, 274;
congressional parties affected by, 43–45, 46,
47; parties bridge, 6, 24–25, 33, 86, 120; be-
tween presidency and Congress, 81, 86–87,
119–20; at state level, 134
Shafer, Byron E., 210, 375, 396
Shaffer, William R., 370
*Shakman v. Democratic Organization of Cook
County,* 384
Shanks, J. Merrill, 407
Shaw, L. Earl, 365
Shefter, Martin, 358–9, 384
Shively, W. Phillips, 259, 403, 405, 407
Sinclair, Barbara D., 367, 369
Skladony, Thomas W., 413–14
Smith, William French, 117
Smith v. Allwright, 176, 177, 178, 391
Snyder, Albert, 185–87, 188
Social Democratic party (British), 262
Socialist Labor party, 181
Socialist party (U. S.), 40, 125, 127, 131–32,
381, 382
Sontag, Frederick H., 363, 368
Sorauf, Frank J., 364; on campaign financing by
parties, 273, 397; on party competition, 396;
on party identification, 239–40, 401; on pa-
tronage, 384; on political action committees,
292, 296–97, 409, 411, 412, 413
South, 350; blacks disfranchised in, 171, 174–79;
Democrats in, 129, 171; one-partyism in, 30,
129, 130, 171; Republicans in, 69, 267; white
primaries in, 171, 174–79, 187
South Carolina, 177
Speaker of the House, 50, 54, 55–56, 57, 59, 60
Spitzer, Robert J., 410–11, 413
Spoils system. *See* Patronage
Starr, Joseph R., 390
Stassen, Harold, 92
State/state government, 31; civil service in, 134–
35, 137, 142–43; ballots provided by, 243–44;
conventions, 89, 90, 146–47, 149, 150, 192,
346, 385, 386; durability of, 123; election to
(*see* Election campaigns, state); legislatures,
42, 124–25, 133, 188; machines, 135; minor
parties in, 124–25, 126, 128, 132, 153, 182,
183, 243, 381; PACs in, 286; parties as agent
of, 171, 174, 175, 176–79, 190; public funding, 326–34, 337, 416; separation of powers
in, 134; regulates parties (*see* Regulation,
state); -run primaries, 89, 91, 155, 163, 166,

167, 169, 176, 187, 188, 189, 198, 222. *See also* State parties

State parties, 28, 83, 123–54, 200, 337; campaign role of, 112, 205, 208, 235, 269, 304–5, 338; delegate selection role of, 90, 91, 203, 215, 227–28, 229–35, 236; Democratic, 125–26, 152, 190, 192, 229–30, 231–32, 236; direct-mail solicitation by, 218; durability of, 134; endorsements by, 154; and federal patronage, 134; financing role of, 152, 154, 304–5, 308, 329; headquarters of, 151, 152, 153, 154; institutionalized, 7, 151–53, 154, 205; legal status of, 150; national convention role of, 202–3, 222; and national parties, 141, 191, 201, 209, 211, 212–13, 215, 216, 219, 229–30, 231, 236, 242–43, 308; national party as agent for, 155, 205, 303, 304; national party alignment continued by, 6, 84, 124–26, 127, 128, 130, 131, 132–33, 153; national party funds, 153, 218, 221–22, 235, 305; nominating role of, 70, 86, 146–47, 153–54, 202–3, 235; in other countries, 46; post-machine, 144–53; regulated, 154, 189–96, 197, 226, 302, 303, 305; Republican, 130, 150, 152, 153, 190, 218, 219, 221–22, 223, 229; state funding for, 328–31, 332, 333–34; strength of, 5, 134, 152, 330, 331

State v. Pierce, 391

Stave, Bruce M., 384

Stevenson, Adlai, 85, 93

Stewart, Justice Potter, 232, 233, 234, 400

Still, Bayrd, 381

Stimson, James A., 408

Stockmeyer, Steven F., 415

Stokes, Donald E., 370, 401, 406

Storer v. Brown, 182, 183, 184

Sullivan, John L., 407

Sun Oil Company PAC, 288

Sundquist, James L., 403, 408

Surveys. *See* Polls

Sweden, 340

Sweezy v. New Hampshire, 392

Taft, Robert, 92

Taft, William Howard, 104

Tate, C. Neal, 407

Tax: checkoff system, 312–13, 327, 337; credit, 283, 286, 306

Technocrats, 115–16, 117

Television, 4; candidate-centered organizations enhanced by, 6, 113, 268–69; cost of, 279; in European politics, 269–70, 342; free, 341–42; fundraising via, 281, 282, 302, 410–11; impact of, 100–102, 268–69; as nationalizing mechanism, 207; on plebiscitary system, 101; president uses, 120

Terry v. Adams, 177–78

Texas, 98, 175–76, 177–78, 179, 182–83

Third parties. *See* Minor parties

Thurmond, J. Strom, 132

Ticket: party (*see* Ballot, party-provided); split-, 8, 164, 243, 255–56, 261, 265, 404; straight-, 4, 5, 7, 8, 74, 164, 255, 256, 271

Tocqueville, Alexis de, 11

Tolchin, Martin, 384

Tolchin, Susan, 384

Tories (British), 40

Tribe, Laurence H., 392

Truman, David B., 44, 207–8, 365, 394, 396

Truman, Harry S., 126, 266, 279

Turkey, 156

Twentieth Century Fund's Task Force, 298, 299, 339, 421

Two-partyism, 22, 28, 330–31; as American, 241, 242–43; competitiveness in, 29–30, 128, 129, 133, 146, 207, 242; in Congress, 42; development of, 131; favored status of, 171–72, 180, 181–82, 183, 345; institutionalized, 131, 173; labels and, 124, 241, 242–45, 250, 251, 262–63; primary and, 30, 130–31; in responsible-party government, 31, 33–34; at state level, 42, 128–29, 130, 132–33, 153, 242–43

Two-thirds vote to nominate, 204, 209

UAW-V-CAP, 286, 291

Udall, Morris, 335

Unicameralism, 125

Unions: funding by, 224, 280, 305; Mondale helped by, 97, 106; PACs of, 285, 286, 287–88, 289, 290, 291, 292, 293, 295, 296

United States Supreme Court: on ballot access, 180–84, 244; on campaign finance legislation, 275, 283, 288, 299, 303, 311–12, 317–18; on civil service, 143; on delegate selection, 227–28, 232–33; on freedom of association, 143, 190–91, 192, 197, 227, 228, 233, 234; on independent candidates, 183–84; on nominating process, 190; on parties, 7, 226–35; on party membership, 234–35; on party as state agent, 174, 175, 176–79; on primaries, 174, 175, 176, 180, 185, 186, 422; on public funding, 312–14, 316; on state regulations of parties, 179, 180, 191–92, 228, 232–33, 234; on voter rights, 174, 179

United States v. Classic, 391

Unit rule, 204, 209, 215

Utah, 330, 331

Van Buren, Martin, 12, 136, 358

Van Horn, Carl E. 369

Verba, Sidney, 261–62, 406, 407

Virginia, 346, 385, 386
Vogel, David, 388
Voters: counted as party members, 167; disen-
    chanted, 261–62; eligibility of, 165, 171, 172,
    174–79, 184, 186, 187; independent, 75, 125,
    126, 184, 185–87, 188–89, 194–95, 197, 198,
    246, 250, 258–60, 264, 265; mobilization of,
    106, 134–35, 136, 139, 145, 166, 296, 304–5;
    nominating role of, 95; stability of, 241;
    turnout of, 102, 106, 296. See also Identifica-
    tion with party; Registration
Voting: behavior, 249, 252–53, 254, 259–60,
    268; party identification affects, 252–53, 254,
    259–60; intimidation in, 163; issue, 266; by
    leaners, 259–60; media affects, 268; oral, 163;
    party, 36, 62–65, 66, 70, 255; roll-call (con-
    gressional), 55, 57, 60, 62–63, 64, 66, 68;
    split-ticket, 8, 164, 243, 255–56, 261, 265,
    404; straight-ticket, 4, 5, 7, 8, 74, 164, 255,
    256, 271

Wallace, George, 99, 124, 132, 181, 243, 262,
    281–82, 315, 322
Wallace, Henry, 115, 132
Wallas, Graham, 28
Warr, Paul K., 391
Washington, George, 11, 40, 82, 159, 358
Washington (state), 190, 191–92, 193
Wattenberg, Martin P., 261, 263, 271, 357, 405,
    406, 407
Ways and Means Committee, 58
Wegge, David G., 420
Weicker, Lowell, 187, 188
Weinberger, Caspar, 117
Wekkin, Gary D., 213, 394, 396, 399
Wertheimer, Fred, 413
West Germany, 17, 48, 156, 251, 340
West, William, 372
Westlye, Mark C., 405
Whigs (British), 40
Whigs (U.S.), 83, 84, 124, 203
Whip system, 55, 56, 64. See also Congress,
    leadership in

White, Justice Byron R., 417
White, John, 336, 416
White, Leonard D., 137, 383
White House staff, 118–20
Whitridge, Frederick W., 389
Wilcox, Clair, 388
Wildavsky, Aaron, 93, 374
Williams, Philip M., 5, 357
Williams, v. Rhodes, 181
Willkie, Wendell, 94
Wilson, James Q., 382, 383, 385
Wilson, Pete, 221
Wilson, Woodrow, 18, 37, 65, 92; on British
    politics, 24, 33; on Congress, 40, 49, 365;
    leadership by, 87; on national primary, 91,
    374; on president's mandate, 35; on responsible-
    party government, 15, 31
Winograd, Morley, 337–38, 420
Winter, Ralph, 420
Wirthlin, Richard, 267
Wisconsin: affirmative action in, 231; caucus
    campaign committees in, 333–34; delegate se-
    lection in, 230–33; Democrats in, 125–26,
    150, 229–30, 231–32; dues-paying organiza-
    tions in, 145, 150; endorsements in, 387;
    moralistic politics in, 229–34; national party
    v. state of, 229–30, 231–33, 234, 236; non-
    partisan elections in, 127; PACs in, 290, 296,
    333, 334; party identification in, 229–30; pri-
    maries in, 106, 126, 130, 168, 197, 213, 229–
    31, 232, 236, 399–400; Progressive party in,
    125–26, 132; Republicans in, 125–26, 130,
    150; state funding in, 327, 328, 330, 332–34,
    415, 416
Wolfinger, Raymond E., 75, 260, 371, 384, 405,
    408
Woodburn, James A., 360
Wright, William E., 385

Young, Andrew, 116

Zingale, Nancy H., 369, 370, 403, 406, 408